FreeCAD 1.0

Basics Tutorial

Tutorial Books

Send us an email to freecadtuts@gmail.com to get resource files

Contents

INTRODUCTION

FreeCAD, as a topic of learning, is very vast and has a broad scope. It is a package of many workbenches delivering exceptional value to enterprises. It offers a set of tools, which are easy-to-use to design, document, and simulate 3D models. Using this software, you can design your products free of cost.

This book provides a step-by-step approach for users to learn FreeCAD. It is aimed at those with no previous experience with FreeCAD. The user is guided by starting a FreeCAD session to creating parts, assemblies, and drawings. Each chapter has components explained with the help of real-world models.

Scope of this book

This book is written for students and engineers who are interested to learn FreeCAD for designing mechanical components and assemblies, and then create drawings.

This book provides a step-by-step approach to learning FreeCAD. The topics include Getting Started with FreeCAD, Basic Part Modeling, Creating Assemblies, Additional Modeling Tools, Creating Drawings, Sheet Metal parts, and CAM overview.

Chapter 1 introduces FreeCAD. The user interface and terminology are discussed in this chapter.

Chapter 2 takes you through the creation of your first FreeCAD model. You create simple parts.

Chapter 3 teaches you to create assemblies. It explains the Top-down and Bottom-up approaches for designing an assembly. You create an assembly using the Bottom-up approach.

Chapter 4: In this chapter, you learn the sketching tools.

Chapter 5: In this chapter, you learn additional modeling tools to create complex models.

Chapter 6 teaches you to create drawings of the models created in the earlier chapters.

Chapter 7 teaches you to create a sheet metal model.

Chapter 8 teaches you simulate manufacturing operations and generate toolpaths.

Chapter 1: Getting Started with FreeCAD

This tutorial book brings in the most commonly used features of FreeCAD.

In this chapter, you will:

- Understand the FreeCAD terminology
- Start a new file
- Understand the User Interface
- Understand different workbenches in FreeCAD

In FreeCAD, you create 3D parts and use them to create 2D drawings and 3D assemblies.

FreeCAD is Feature Based. Features are shapes that are combined to build a part. You can modify these shapes individually.

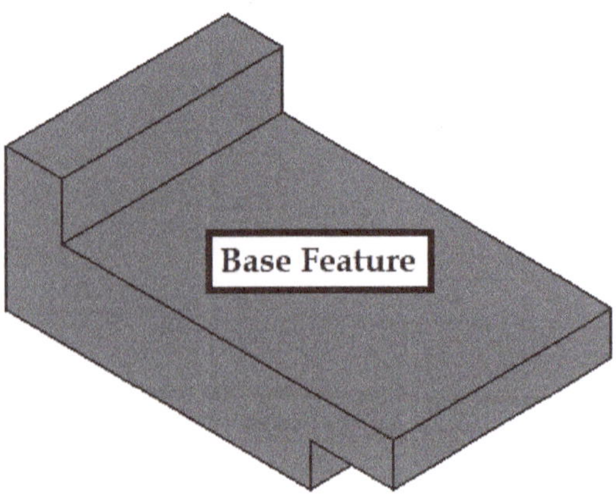

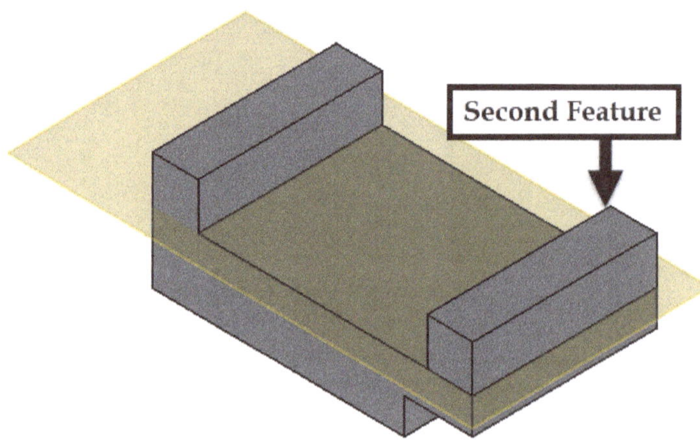

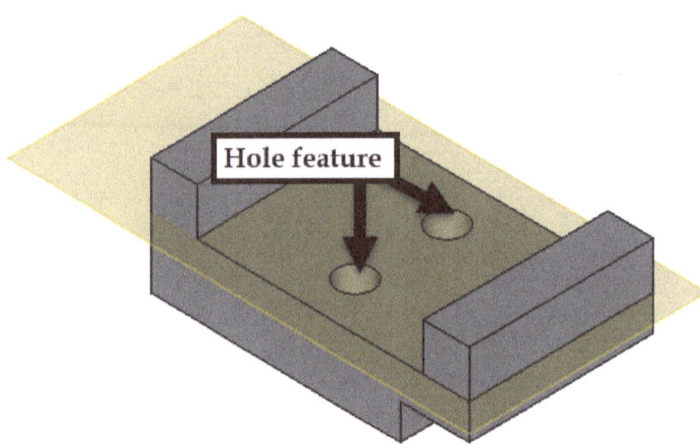

Most of the features are sketch-based. A sketch is a 2D profile and can be extruded, revolved, or swept along a path to create features.

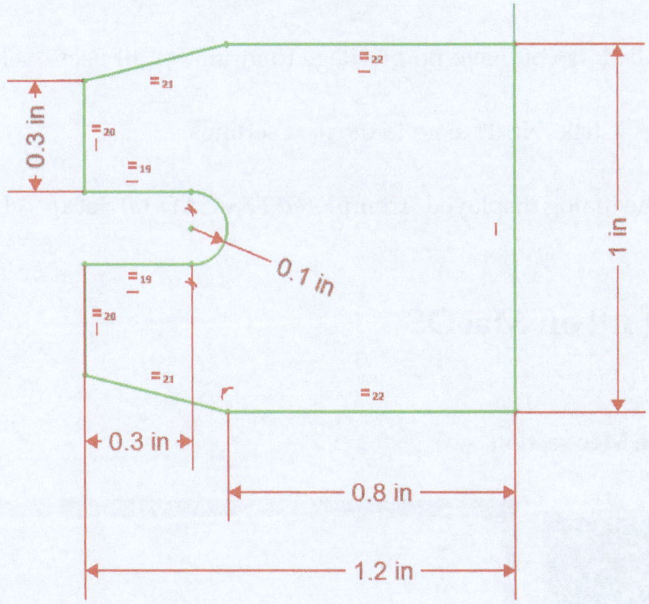

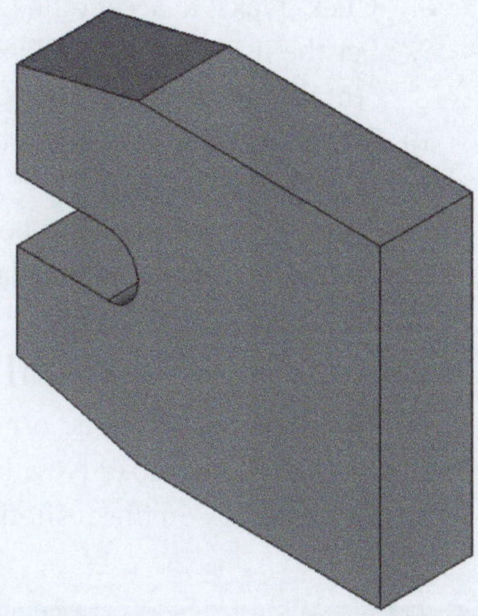

FreeCAD is parametric. You can specify standard parameters between the elements. Changing these parameters changes the size and shape of the part. For example, see the design of the body of a flange before and after modifying the parameters of its features.

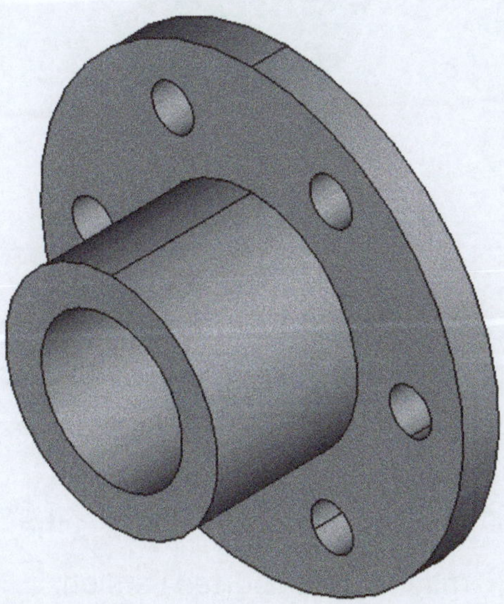

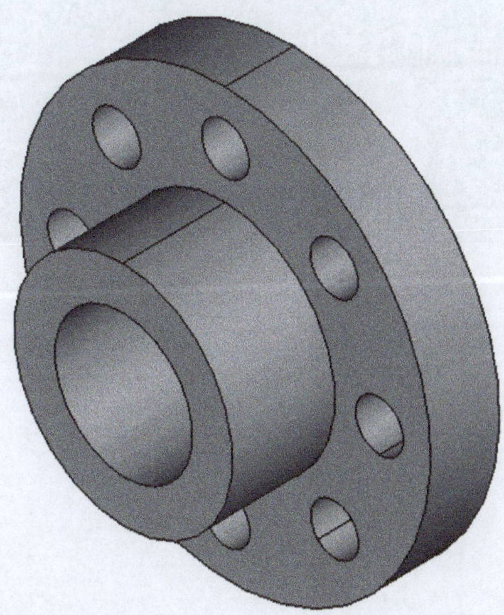

Downloading and Installing FreeCAD 1.0 on Windows

1. Go to the www.freecad.org
2. Click the **Download Now** button.
3. Double-click on the **x86_64 installer** button in the **Windows** section.
4. Specify the location of the downloaded file and click **Save** on the **Save As** dialog.
5. Double-click on the FreeCAD_1.0.0-conda-Windows-x86_64-installer-1.exe file.
6. Click **Yes** on the **User Control** dialog.
7. Click Next on the FreeCAD 1.0.1 Setup dialog.

8. Click "Next" to accept the License agreement
9. Set the users for whom FreeCAD is to be installed. If you have no privilege to install for all users, select "**Intall Just for me.**"
10. Normally there is no need to change the settings. Click "Next" to go to the next settings
11. Click **Install.**
12. After the installation has been completed and the dialog displayed "**Completed FreeCAD 1.0 Setup**", click "**Finish**" to finish all installation process.

Downloading and Installing FreeCAD 1.0 on MacOS

1. Go to the www.freecad.org
2. Click the **Download Now** button.
3. Double-click on the desired disk image from the **Mac** section.

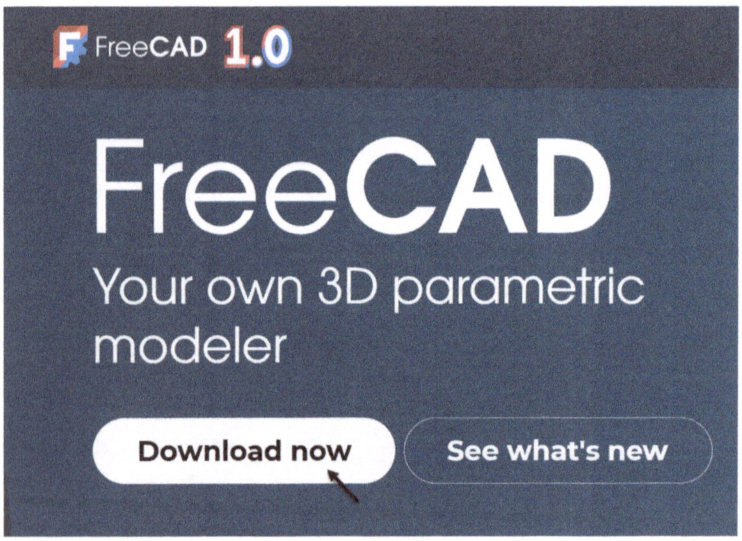

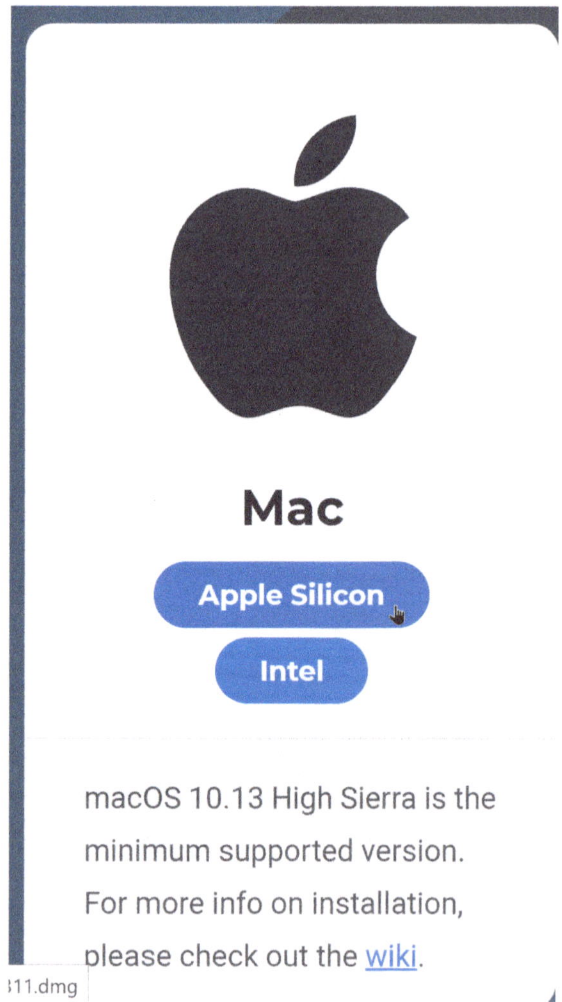

4. Once the download is complete, open the .dmg file.
5. Drag and drop the FreeCAD icon into the **Applications** folder.

6. FreeCAD is now installed and ready to use.

Starting FreeCAD

- Click the Windows icon on the taskbar.
- Click F > **FreeCAD 1.0 > FreeCAD**.
- On the ribbon, click **File > New** to start a new part file.

If you are working in MacOS, click the **Lauchpad** button on the **Dock**. Next, click on the **FreeCAD** icon.

Notice these essential features of the FreeCAD window.

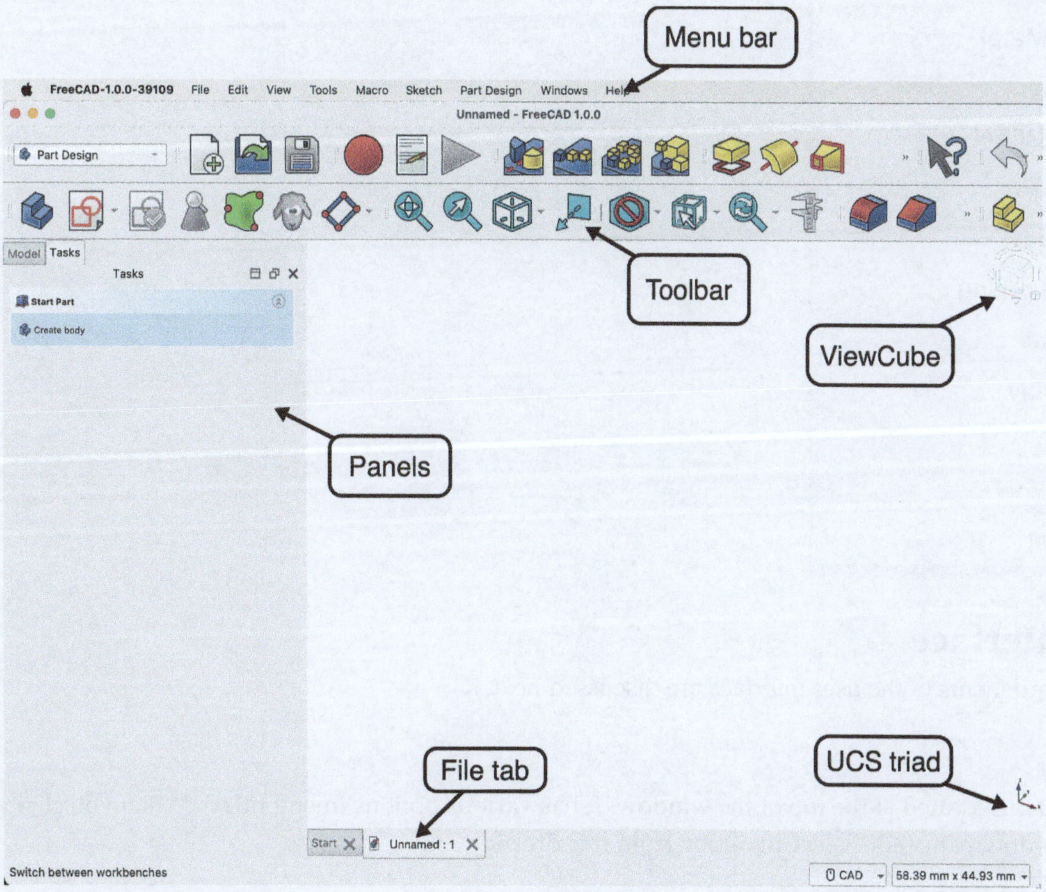

Workbenches in FreeCAD

A workbench is a set of tools and environments that can be used to create parts, assemblies, drawings, and so on. There are many workbenches available in FreeCAD. You can activate different workbenches by using the **Workbenches** drop-down located on the top-left corner.

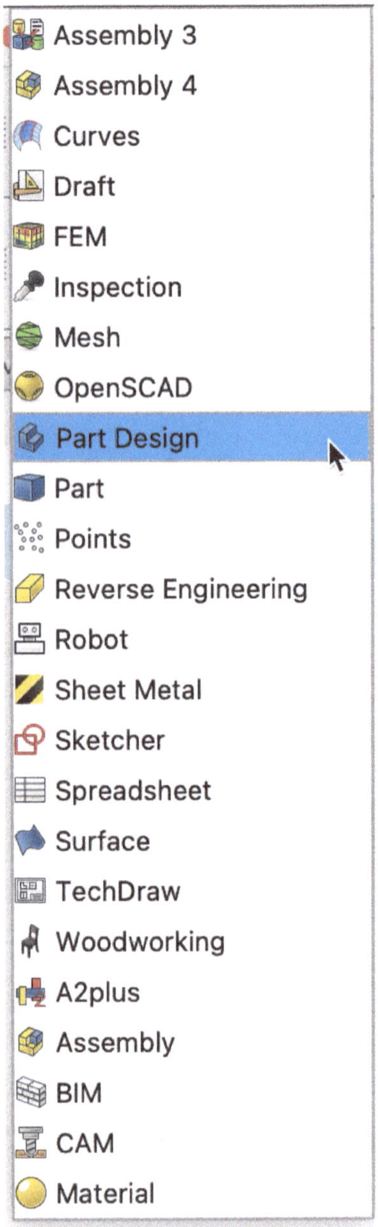

User Interface

Various components of the user interface are discussed next.

Menu bar

The menu bar is located at the top of the window. It has various options (menu titles). When you click on a menu title, a drop-down appears. Select an option from this drop-down.

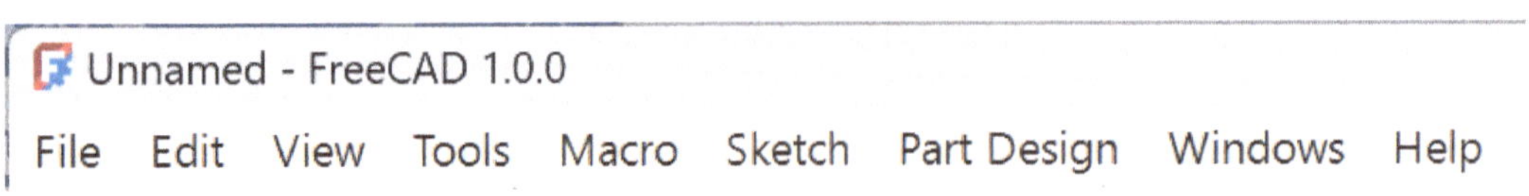

File Menu

The **File Menu** appears when you click on the **File** option located at the top left corner of the window. This menu contains the options to open, print, export, save, and close a file.

Toolbar

A toolbar is a set of tools, which help you to perform various operations. Various toolbars available in different workbenches are given next.

Start Toolbars
Workbench 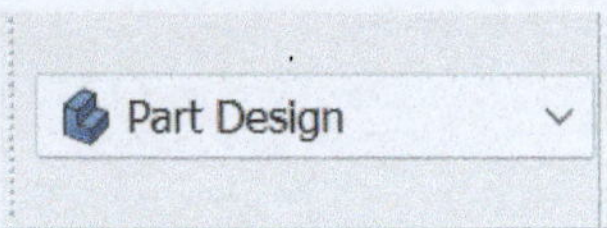 This toolbar has a drop-down to change the workbench.
Macro  This toolbar has tools to create and execute macros.
File  This toolbar has tools to create, open, and save files.
View  This toolbar has tools to manipulate the view of the model.
Structure

It has tools to create or open part files.

Sketcher Toolbars

Sketcher edit mode

This toolbar has tools to start or exit a sketch.

Sketcher geometries

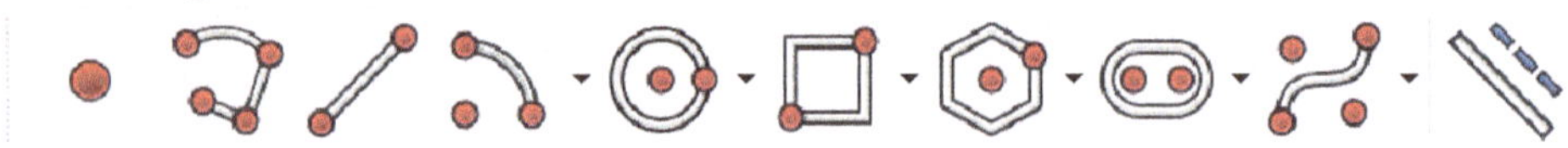

This toolbar has tools to create sketch elements.

Sketcher constraints

This toolbar has tools to apply constraints between sketch elements.

Sketcher B-spline tools

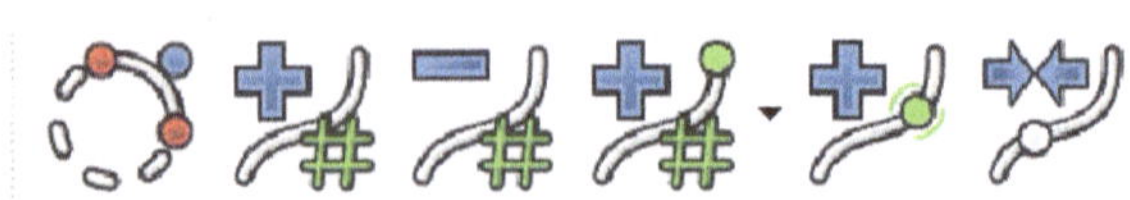

This toolbar has tools to create and edit B-splines.

Sketcher Virtual Space

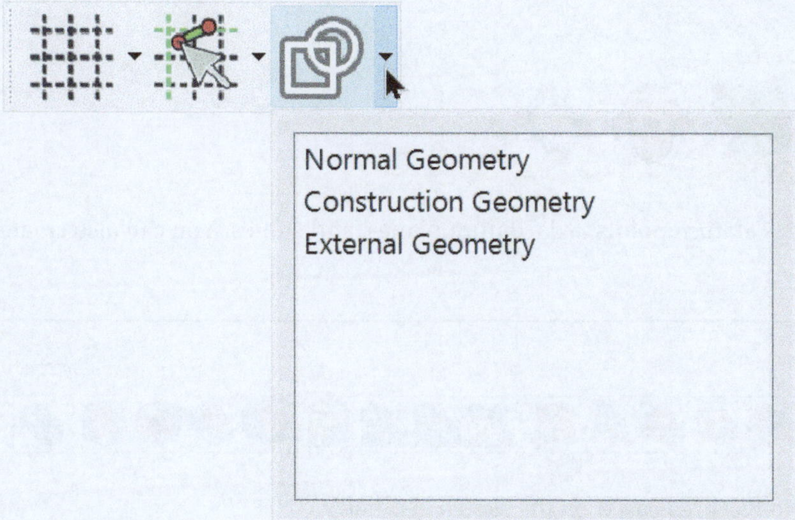

This toolbar controls the order of sketch geometry types (Normal, Construction, External) and grid display settings (Grid Snap, Grid Visibility, Grid Spacing).

Sketcher Visual

This toolbar has various selection tools and options that aid you in creating sketch elements very fast. It also has tool to hide or show constraints.

Sketcher edit tools

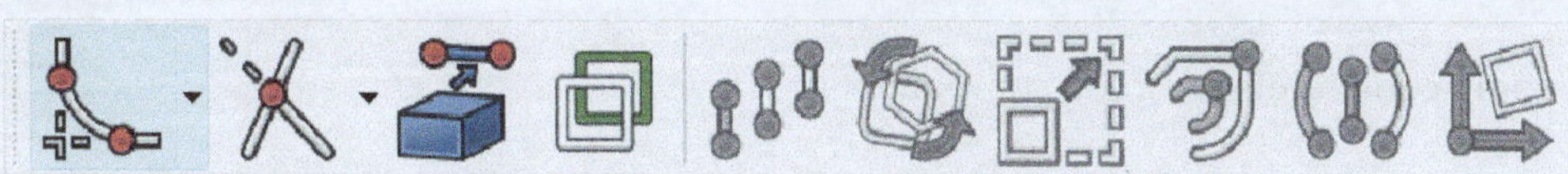

This toolbar has sketch editing tools

Part Design Toolbars

Part Design Helper

This toolbar has tools to create new bodies, datum points, axis, datum planes, and clones. You can also create a new sketch.

Part Design Modeling

This toolbar has commands to create solid features based on the sketch geometry.

Assembly Toolbars

Assembly

This toolbar has tools to create components or insert existing components into an assembly.

Assembly Joints

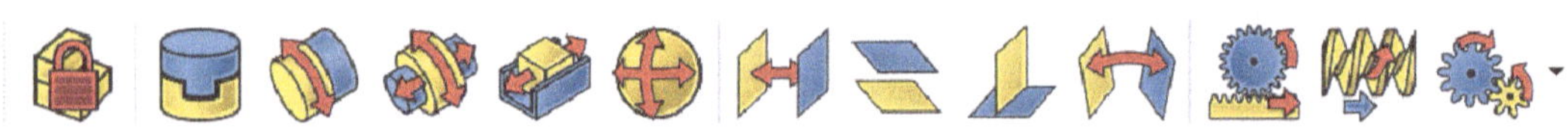

This toolbar also has tools to apply constraints between components.

TechDraw Toolbars

TechDraw Views

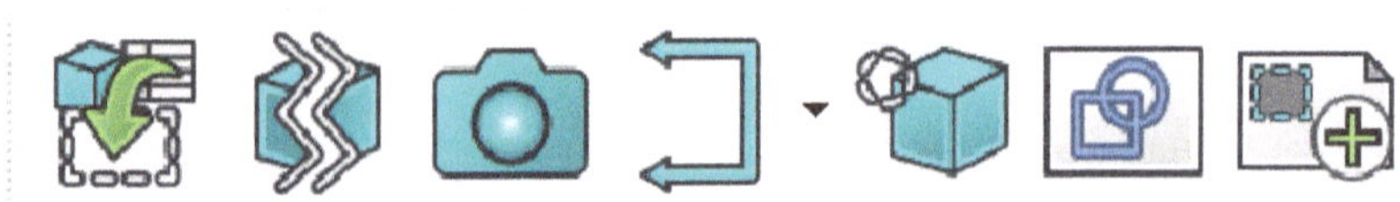

This toolbar has tools to generate standard views of a 3D geometry.

TechDraw Pages

The tools on this toolbar help you to add a new page.

TechDraw Dimensions

The tools on this toolbar help you to add dimensions to the drawing views.

TechDraw File Access

This toolbar helps you to export the drawing page to the SVG or DXF format.

TechDraw Decoration

The tools on this toolbar help you to change the hatch patterns and insert images.

TechDraw Attributes

The tools on this toolbar help you to modify the attributes of the dimensions.

TechDraw Centerlines

The tools on this toolbar help you to add centerlines and centermarks to the drawing views.

TechDraw Annotations

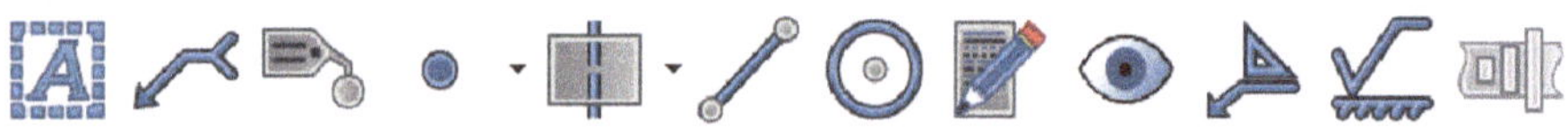

The tools on this toolbar help you to add annotations such as text, leaders, surface symbols, and so on.

TechDraw Extend Dimensions

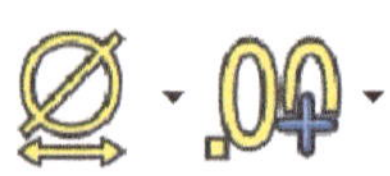

The tools on this toolbar help you to additional types of dimensions to the drawing view such as chain dimensions, coordinate dimensions, chamfer dimensions, and so on.

Sheet Metal Toolbars

Sheet Metal

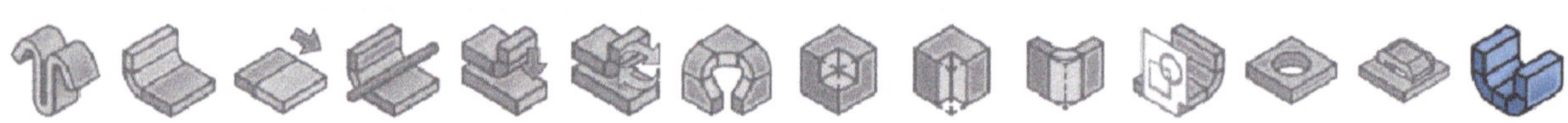

The tools on this toolbar help you to create a sheetmetal model.

FEM Toolbars

Model

It has tools to define materials and element geometry of the model.

Mechanical boundary conditions and loads

It has tools to define mechanical constriants.

Thermal boundary conditions and loads

It has tools to add thermal constraints.

Mesh

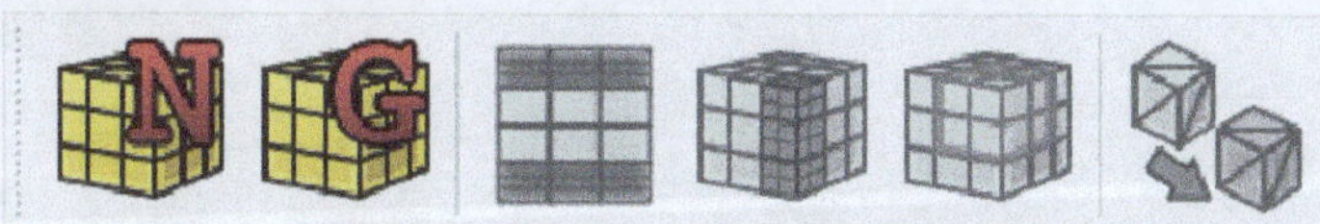

It has tools to mesh the model.

Fluid boundary conditions

It has tools to add fluid constraints.

Electronstatic Constraints

It has tools to add electrostatic constraints.

Solve

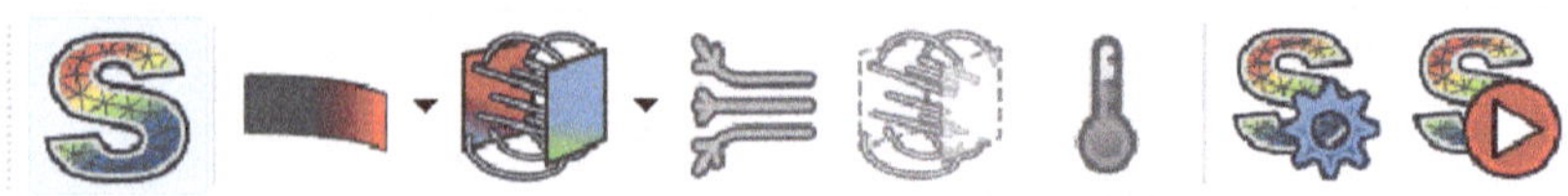

It has tools to perform the finite element analysis.

Results

It has tools display the results of finite element analysis.

Utilities

It has tools to clip and unclip faces.

CAM Toolbars

Project Setup

It has tools to create a job and export G-Code.

Tool Commands

It has tools to create and manage tools.

New Operations  It has tools to create machining operations.
Path Modification  It has tools to modify tool paths.

You can hide or show toolbars in the application window. To do this, click **View > Toolbars**, and then select the toolbar name from the list displayed.

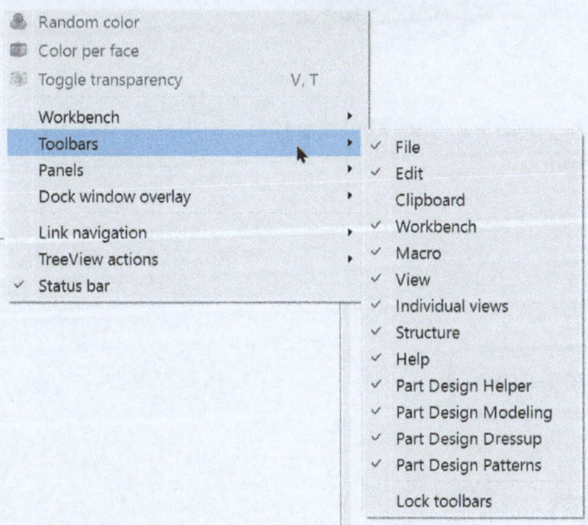

Status bar

The Status bar is available below the graphics window. It shows the action taken while using the commands.

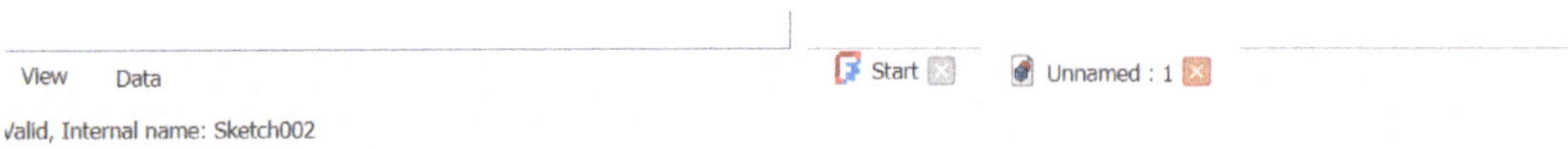

Model panel

It contains the list of operations carried while constructing a part.

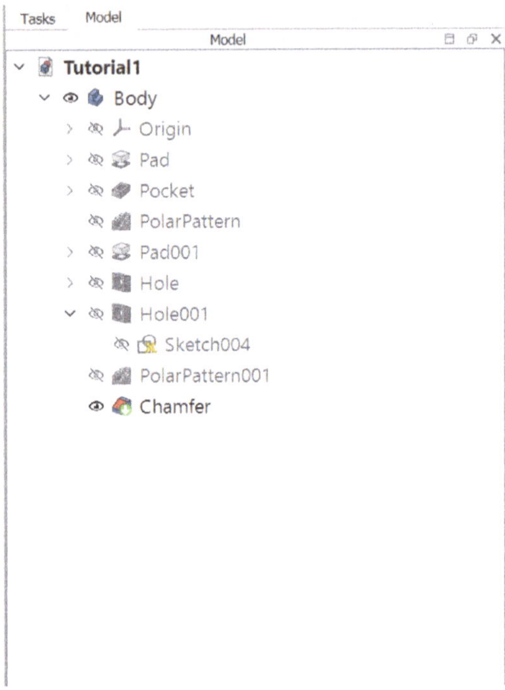

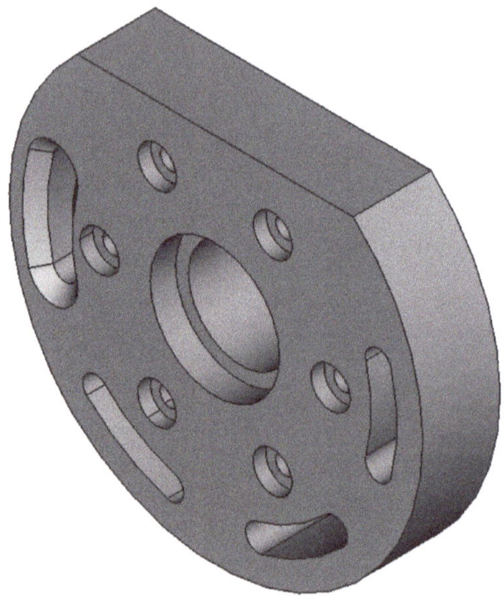

Dialog

When you click any tool in FreeCAD, the dialog related to it appears in the **Tasks** panel. A dialog has various options. The following figure shows various components of a dialog.

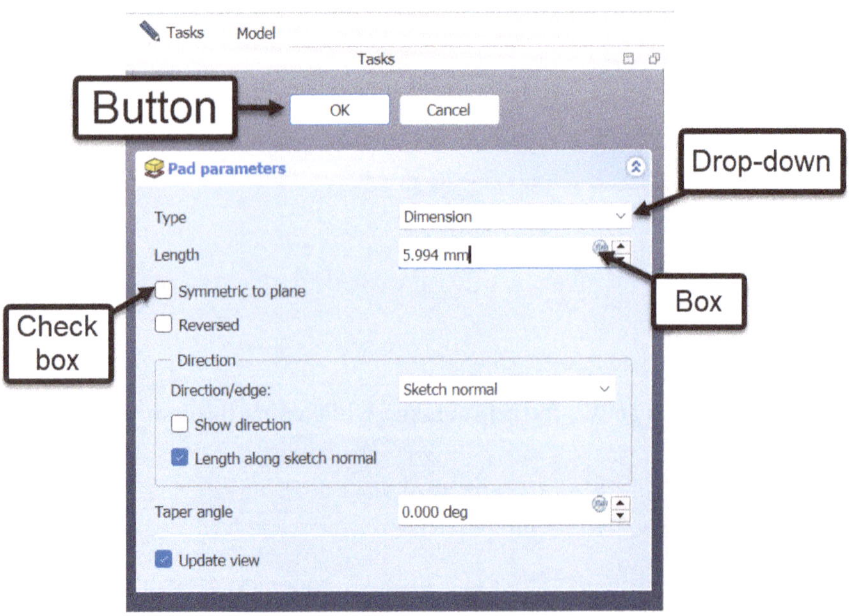

This book uses the default options on the dialog.

Navigation Styles

FreeCAD provides you with different types of mouse navigation styles: **OpenInventor**, **CAD**, **Revit**, **Blender**, **MayaGesture**, **TinkerCAD**, **Touchpad**, **Gesture**, and **OpenCascade**. You can select the desired navigation style from the drop-down located at the bottom right corner.

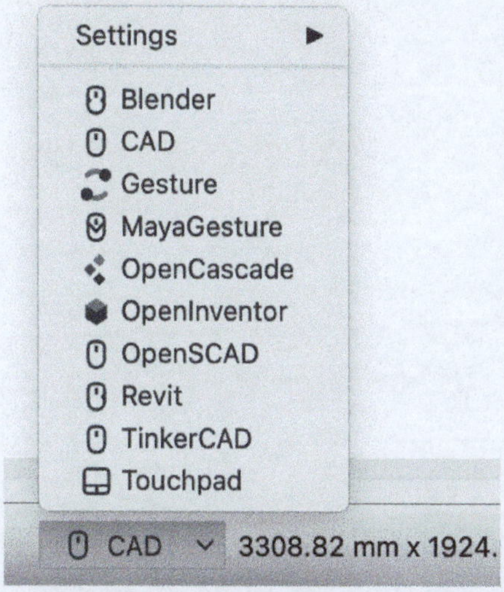

This book uses the CAD Navigation Style for your mouse. Select the **CAD** option from the **Navigation Styles** drop-down. Next, place the mouse cursor on the drop-down; the various mouse functions are displayed.

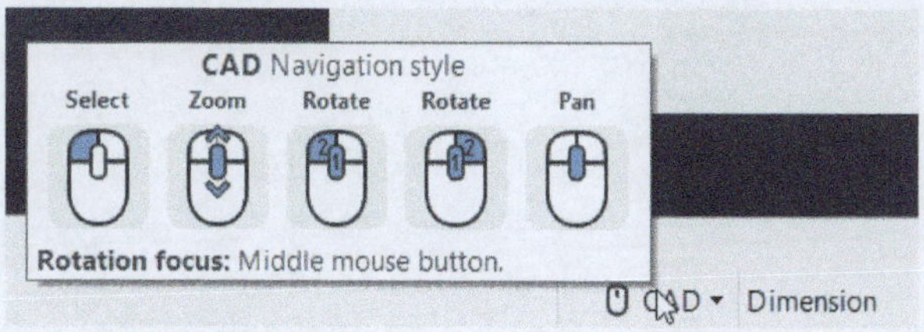

Background

To change the background color of the window, click **Edit > Preferences** on the Menu bar. On the **Preferences** dialog, click **Display > Colors** on the left side. Next, set the colors for various element types.

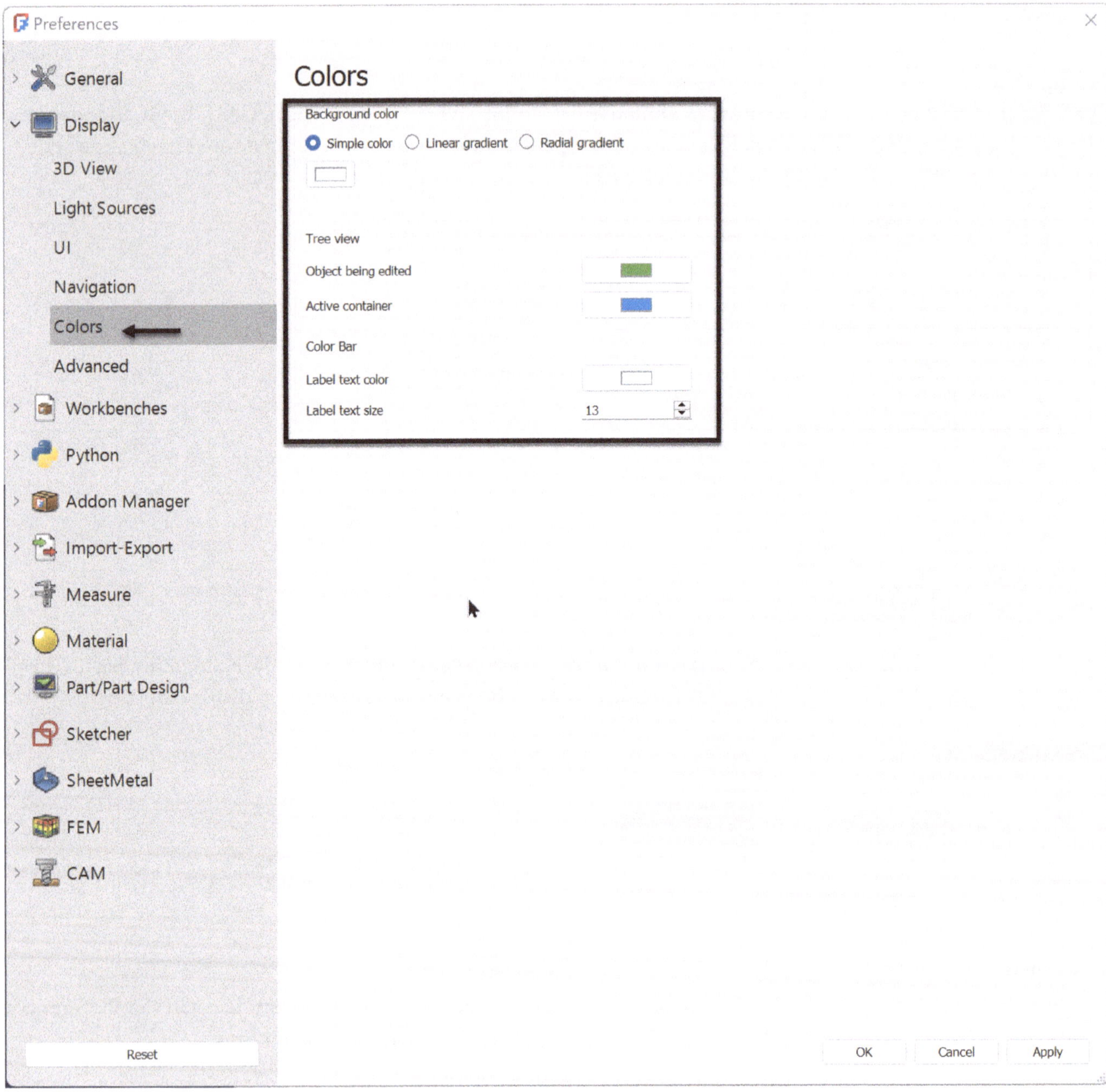

To change the color of sketch elements, click **Sketcher** > Appearance on the left side. Next, change the **Sketch colors**. Click **OK** to apply the changes.

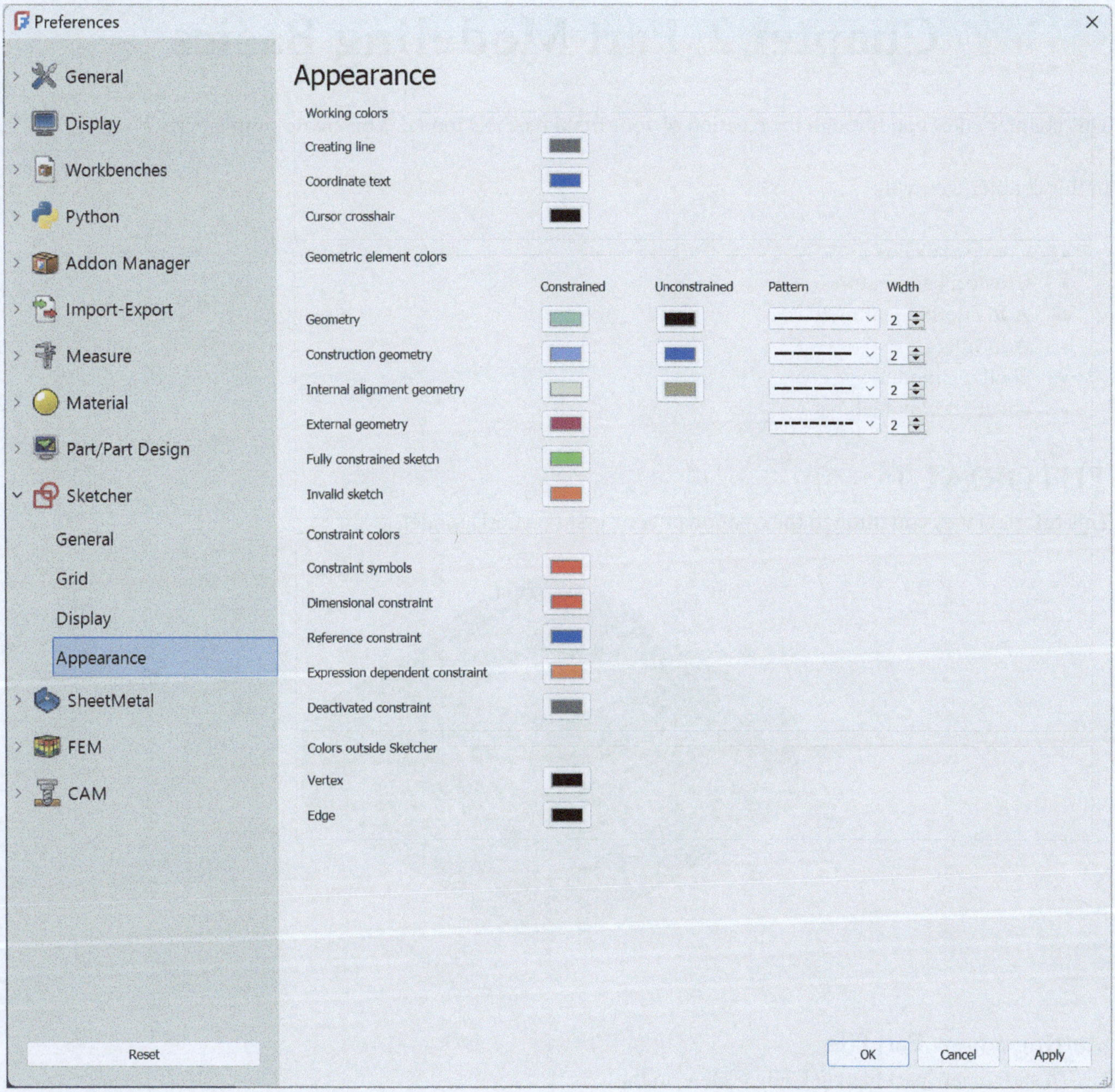
Preferences
General
Display
Workbenches
Python
Addon Manager
Import-Export
Measure
Material
Part/Part Design
Sketcher
General
Grid
Display
Appearance
SheetMetal
FEM
CAM
Reset
Appearance
Working colors
Creating line
Coordinate text
Cursor crosshair
Geometric element colors
Constrained
Unconstrained
Pattern
Width
Geometry
Construction geometry
Internal alignment geometry
External geometry
Fully constrained sketch
Invalid sketch
Constraint colors
Constraint symbols
Dimensional constraint
Reference constraint
Expression dependent constraint
Deactivated constraint
Colors outside Sketcher
Vertex
Edge
OK
Cancel
Apply

Chapter 2: Part Modeling Basics

This chapter takes you through the creation of your first FreeCAD model. You create simple parts:

In this chapter, you will:

- Create Sketches
- Create a base feature
- Add another feature to it
- Add fillets
- Shell the model
- Create Pocket features

TUTORIAL 1

This tutorial takes you through the creation of your first FreeCAD model.

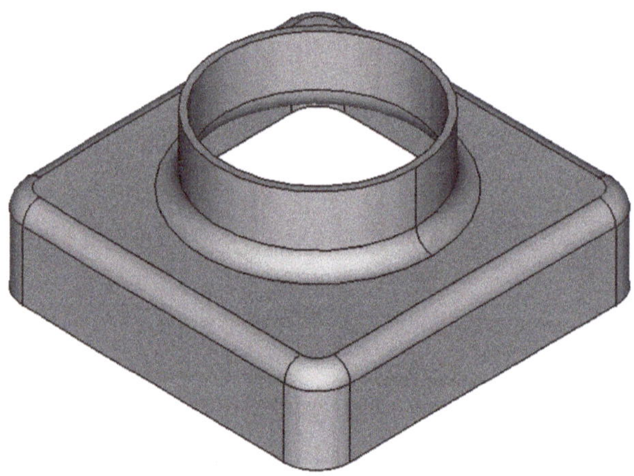

Starting a New Part File

1. To start a new part file, click **File > New** on the Menu Bar (or) click the **New** icon on the **File** toolbar.

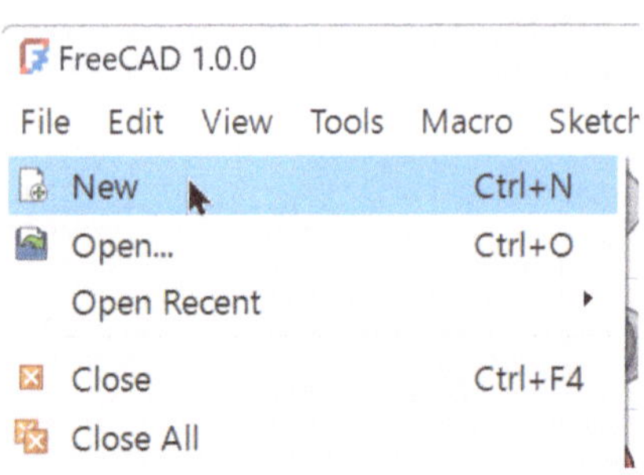

(or)

A new model window appears.

2. On the **Workbench** toolbar, select **Workbench** drop-down > **Part Design** (or) select **View > Workbench > Part Design** on the Menu bar.

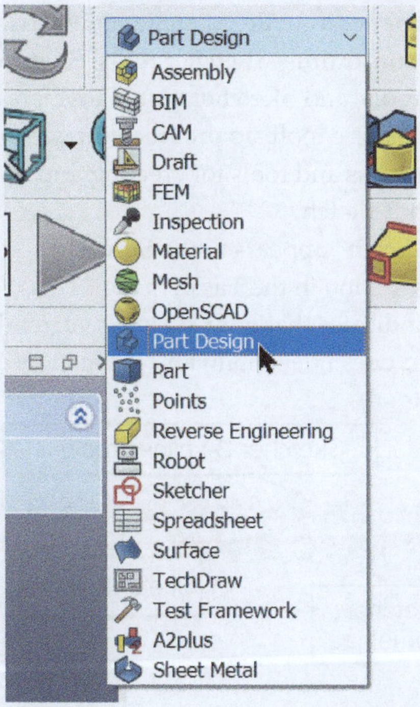

(or)

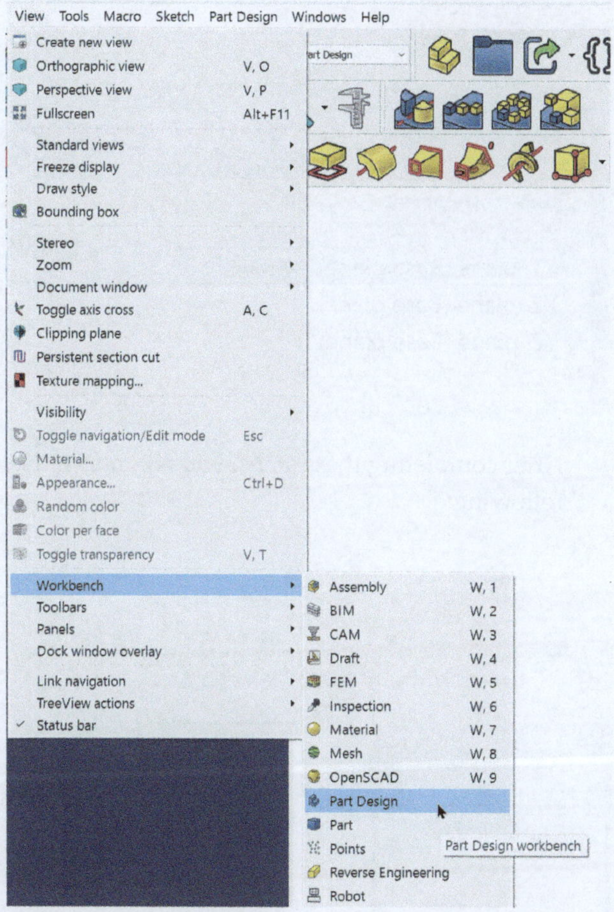

Starting a Sketch

1. To start a new sketch, click **Part Design Helper** toolbar **> Create New Sketch**  (or) click **Sketch > Create Sketch** on the Menu bar. This step is done to initiate the sketching process and create a new workspace for your design.

2. Select the **XY-Plane**, and then click **OK**. The sketch starts. This step is necessary to define the plane on which you will be sketching your design.

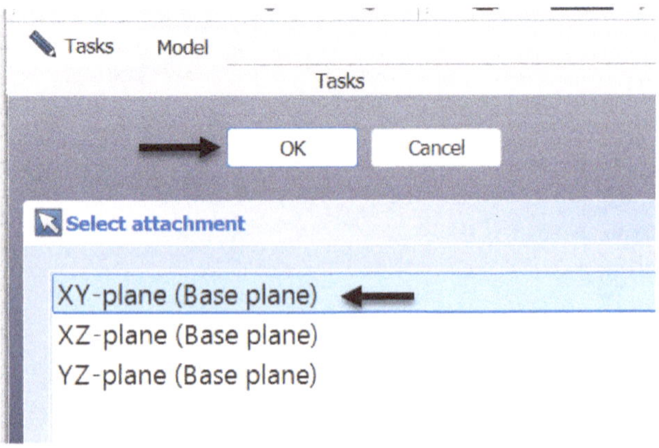

After completing these steps, you will notice the following:

- The sketch origin appears at the center. This indicates the reference point for your sketch and helps in positioning and aligning your design elements
- The **Sketcher edit mode**, **Sketcher geometries**, **Sketcher constraints**, **Sketcher tools**, **Sketcher B-spline tools**, and **Sketcher visual** toolbars are displayed. These toolbars provide you with various options and tools for creating and editing your sketch.
- "**Empty Sketch**" appears in the **Solver Messages** section in the **Tasks** panel. This message indicates that your sketch is currently empty and does not contain any geometries or constraints.

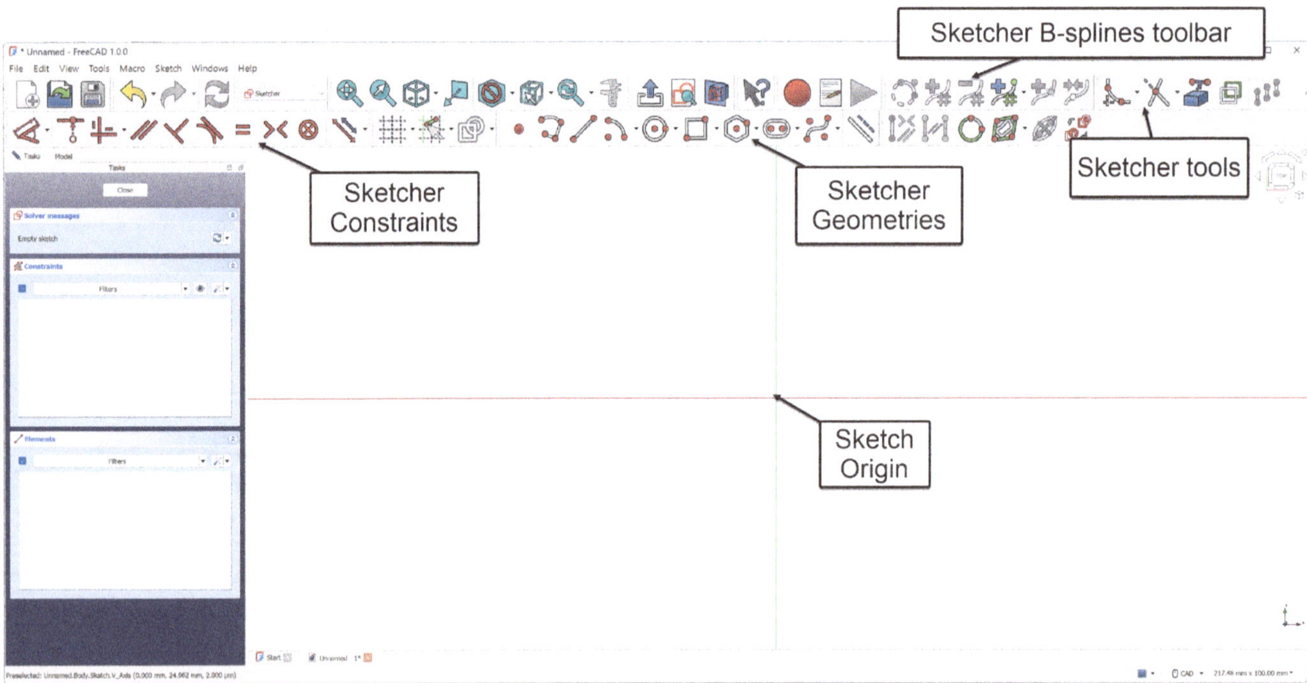

Before you begin sketching, it is recommended to ensure that your FreeCAD settings match the settings used in this tutorial. Follow the next steps to adjust the settings.

3. Click **Edit > Preferences** on the Menu bar. If you are working on MacOS, then click **FreeCAD > Preferences** on the title bar. This will open the **Preferences** dialog box, where you can customize various settings for your FreeCAD workspace.
4. On the **Preferences** dialog box, click the **General** option at the left side and then click the **General** tab. This step is done to access the general settings for your FreeCAD workspace.
5. Select **Default unit system > Standard (mm/kg/s/degree)**. This setting ensures that your FreeCAD workspace uses the standard units of measurement (millimeters, kilograms, seconds, and degrees).
6. Type **2** in the **Number of decimals** box. This setting determines the number of decimal places displayed for measurements and dimensions in your FreeCAD workspace.

7. Click **OK** to save the changes and close the **Preferences** dialog box. These settings will help you work with accurate measurements and dimensions in your sketch.
8. Click the **Toggle grid** 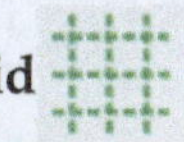 icon on the **Sketcher edit tools** toolbar. This step is done to enable the grid display in your sketch, which can help you align and position your sketch elements.
9. Click the down-arrow next to the **Toggle grid** icon and select the **Grid auto spacing** option; the grid spacing adjusts automatically according to the view's size, ensuring a consistent grid display.
10. Type **10** in the **Spacing** box; it indicates the distance between two consecutive grid lines. It serves as the default value when the **Grid auto spacing** option is selected.

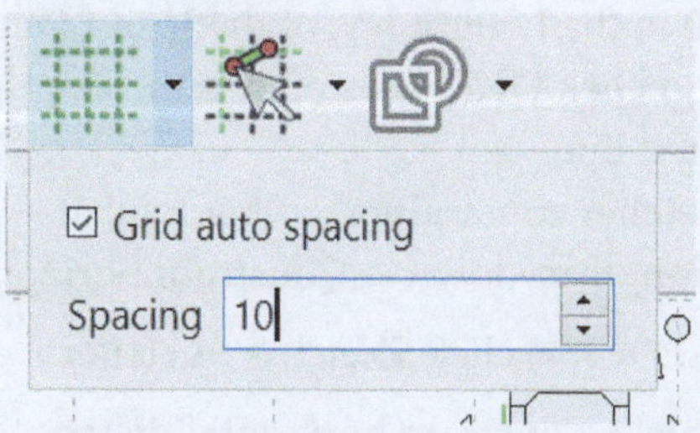

In this tutorial, the first feature is an extruded feature from a sketched rectangular profile. You begin by sketching the rectangle.

11. On the **Sketcher geometries** toolbar, click the **Rectangle** icon (or) click **Sketch > Sketcher geometries > Create Rectangle.**

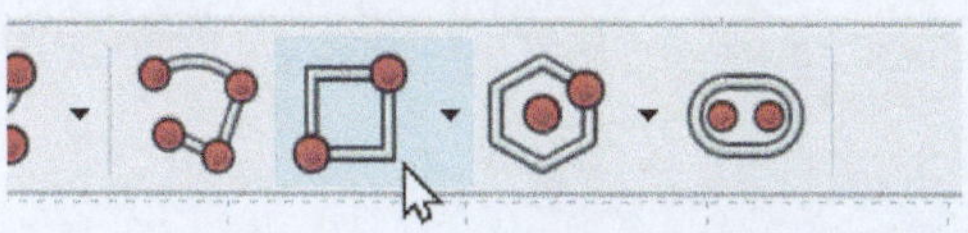

12. Move the cursor to the sketch origin located at the center of the graphics window, and then click on it.
13. Drag the cursor towards the top right corner, and then click to create a rectangle. This step creates a rectangle by dragging the cursor from the origin towards the top right corner and clicking to set the size of the rectangle.

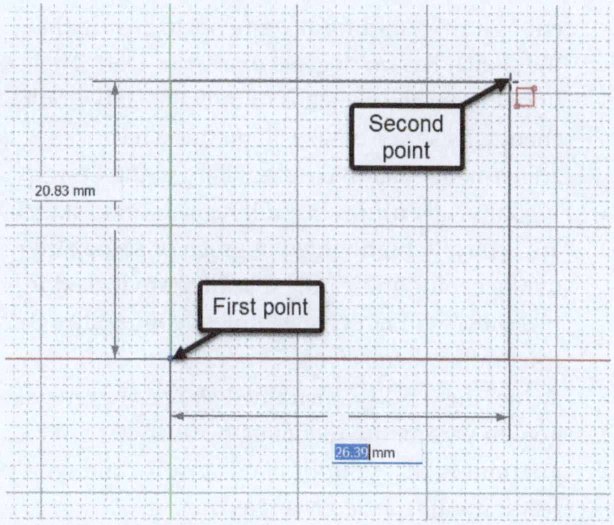

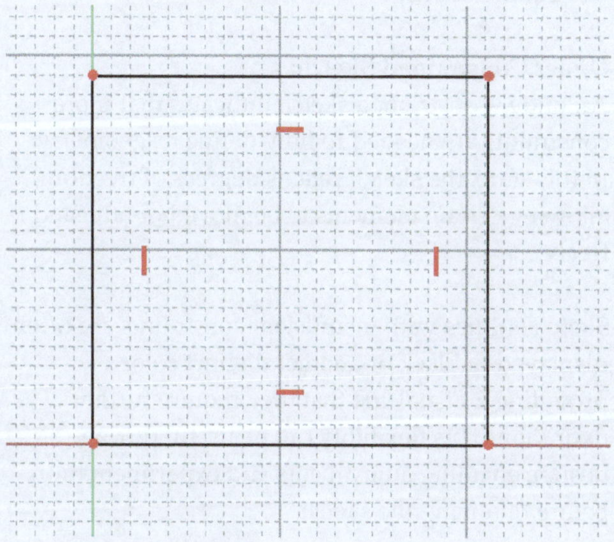

Adding Constraints

In this section, you specify the size of the sketched rectangle by adding constraints. As you add constraints, the sketch can attain any one of the following states:

Fully Constrained Sketch:

- When you're working on a fully constrained sketch, it means that every element within the sketch is precisely defined by constraints. These constraints can include dimensions, angles, distances, and relationships between sketch entities.

- In a fully constrained sketch, you've applied enough rules and measurements to ensure that the sketch has no degrees of freedom left. This implies that the sketch is immovable and won't change its shape or size no matter what adjustments you make elsewhere in the design.
- Visually, all entities in a fully constrained sketch are typically highlighted in green or some other distinct color, indicating that they are locked in place and will not change unless you modify the constraints themselves.
- Achieving a fully constrained sketch is a crucial goal in parametric modeling because it guarantees that your design is precise and won't result in unexpected changes during modifications.

Under Constrained Sketch:
An under-constrained sketch indicates that more constraints are needed to fully define its geometry. In this state, the sketch retains degrees of freedom, allowing certain elements to be moved or adjusted freely.

Sketch entities with insufficient constraints are often displayed in black or another distinct color, providing a visual cue that they require further definition. This flexibility can be useful during design, enabling adjustments and experimentation before finalizing the sketch.

However, leaving a sketch under-constrained can lead to unintended issues. Changes made elsewhere in the model may cause unconstrained elements to shift unexpectedly, altering the intended design.

Redundant Constraints:
Redundant constraints are unwanted constraints that you add to an already fully defined sketch. FreeCAD has a special option called **Auto remove redundants** to delete the unwanted constraints. You can select this option from the **Settings** drop-down available on the **Constraints** section of the Tasks panel. On doing so, the redundant constraints are deleted automatically when you try to add them to a fully constrained sketch.

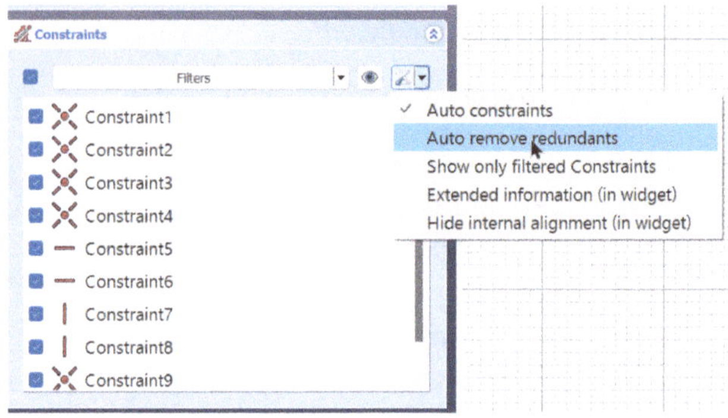

1. Click **Sketcher constraints** toolbar > **Dimension** drop-down **> Constrain vertical distance** (or) click **Sketch > Sketcher constraints > Constrain vertical distance** on the menu bar.
2. Select the right vertical line of the rectangle.
3. Enter **100** in the **Length** box of the **Insert Length** dialog and click **OK**. This step sets the length of the selected line.
4. Click **Sketcher constraints** toolbar toolbar > **Dimension** drop-down > **Constrain horizontal distance** (or) click **Sketch > Sketcher constraints > Constrain horizontal distance** on the menu bar.
5. Select the bottom horizontal line of the rectangle.
6. Enter **100** in the **Length** box of the **Insert Length** dialog and click the **OK** button. This step sets the length of the selected line.

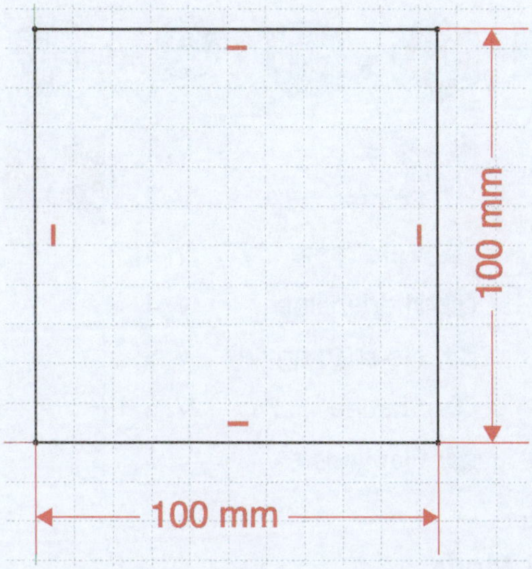

7. Press **Esc** to deactivate the **Constrain horizontal distance** tool.
8. To display the entire rectangle at full size and to center it in the graphics area, use one of the following methods:

   - Click **Fit All**  on the **View** toolbar.
   - Click **View > Standard Views > Fit All** on the Menu bar.

9. Click **Close** on the **Tasks** panel.

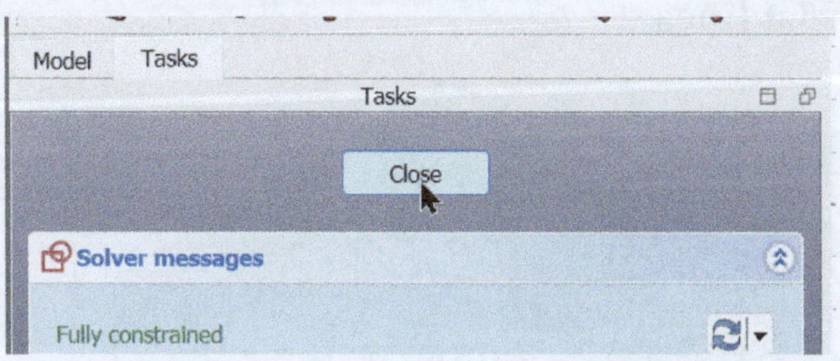

10. Again, click **Fit All**  on the **View** toolbar.

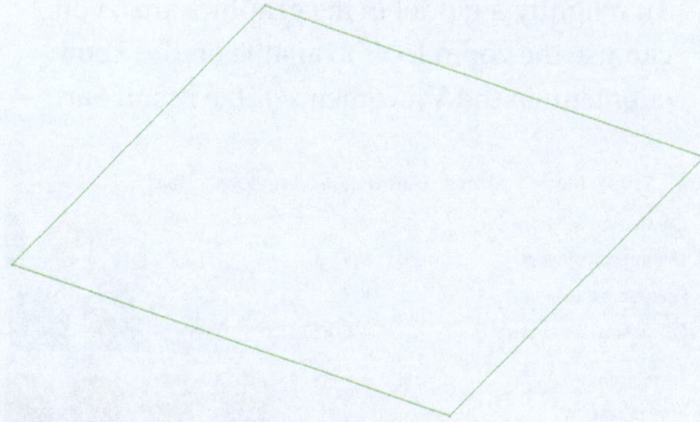

Creating the Base Feature

The first feature in any part is called a base feature. You now create this feature by extruding the sketched rectangle.

1. Click **Part Design Modeling** toolbar **> Pad**  (or) click **Part Design > Pad** on the Menu bar.
2. Type-in 25 in the **Length** box available on the **Pad parameters** dialog on the **Tasks** panel.
3. Click **OK** on the **Tasks** panel to create the pad feature.

Notice the new feature, **Pad**, in the **Model** panel.

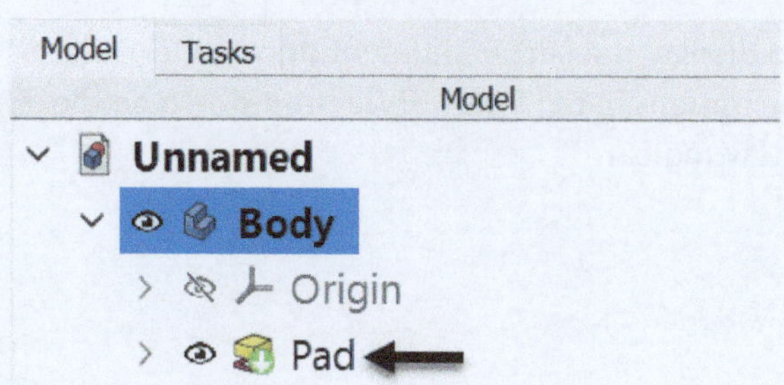

To magnify a model in the graphics area, you can use the zoom tools available on the **Zoom** submenu in the **View** menu of the Menu bar.

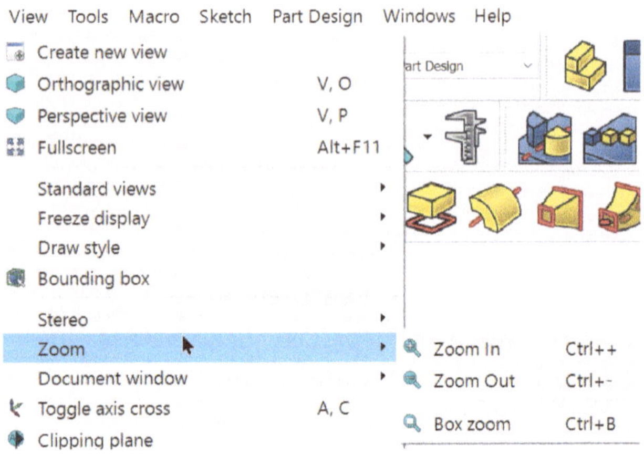

Click **Zoom In** to zoom into the model.

Click **Zoom Out** to zoom out of the model.

Click **Box Zoom**, and then drag the pointer to create a rectangle; the area in the rectangle zooms to fill the window.

The **View** toolbar has two more zoom tools: **Fit All** and **Fit Selection**.

Click **Fit All**  to display the full part size in the current window.

Click on a vertex, an edge, or a feature, and then click **Fit Selection** 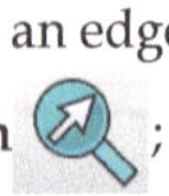; the selected item zooms to fill the window.

To display the part in different draw styles, select the options in the **Draw Style** drop-down on the **View** toolbar.

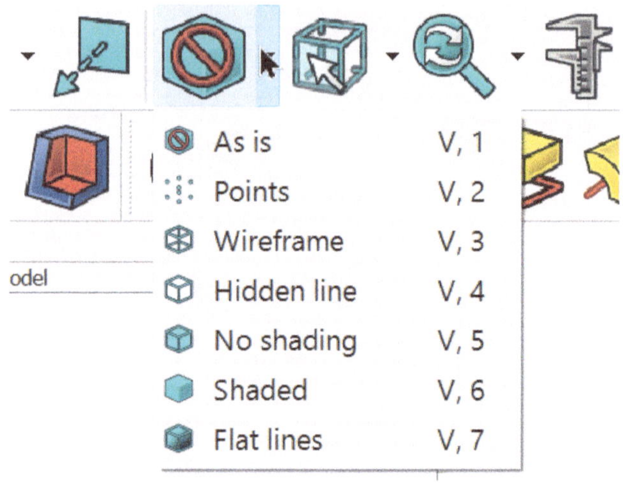

Normal Mode

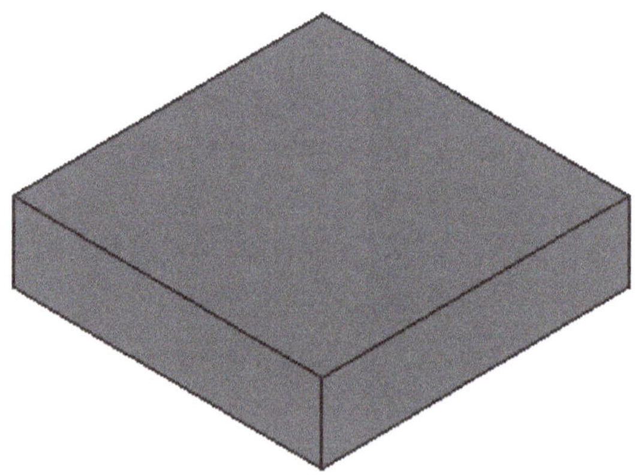

Flat lines

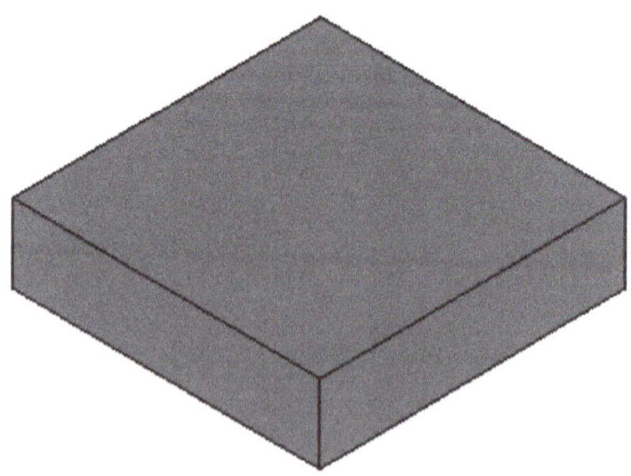

Shaded

Wireframe

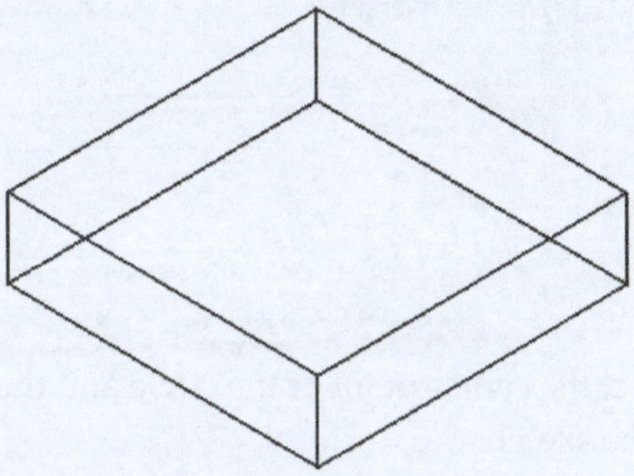

Points

Hidden Line

No Shading

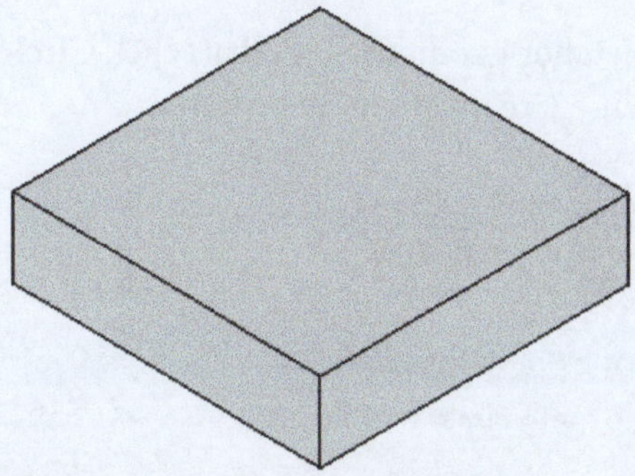

The default draw style for parts and assemblies is **Normal Mode**. You may change the draw style whenever you want.

Adding a Pad Feature

To create additional features on the part, you need to draw sketches on the model faces or planes, and then extrude them.

1. Click on the top face of the first feature.

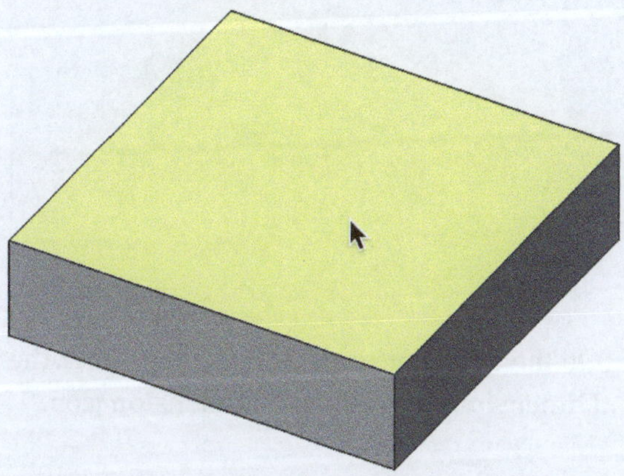

2. Click **Create Sketch** on the **Face tools** section of the **Tasks** panel. A new sketch is started.

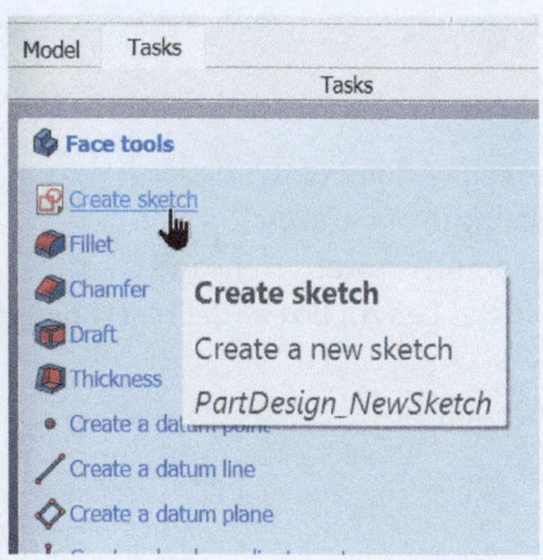

3. On the **Sketcher geometries** toolbar, click **Circle** drop-down > **Create circle by center.**

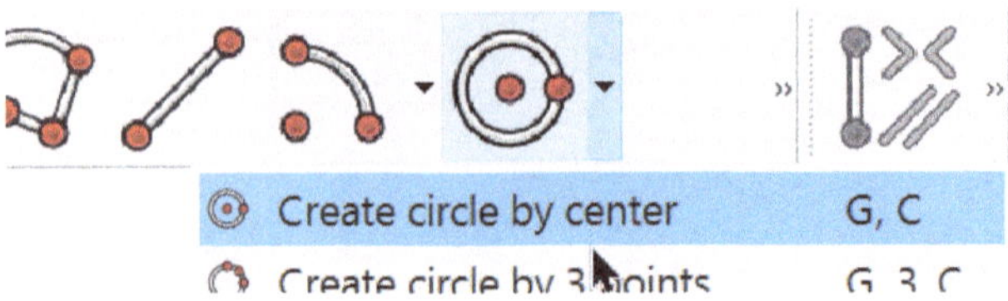

4. Click to specify the center point of the circle.
5. Move the pointer outward and click to create the circle.

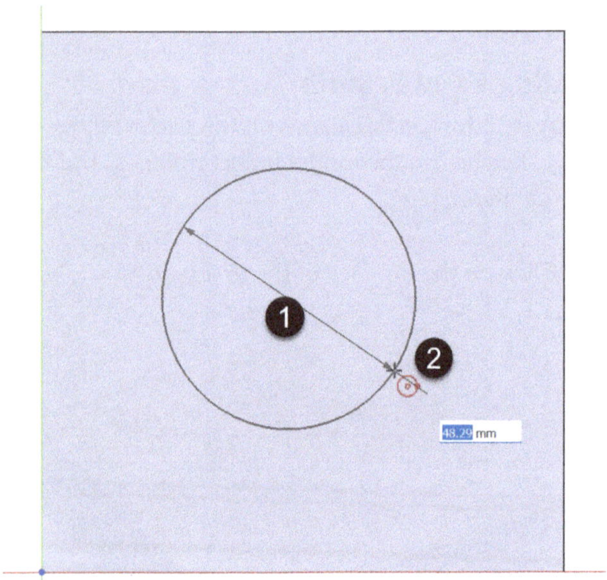

6. On the **Sketcher constraints** toolbar, click the **Dimension** drop-down > **Dimension** icon.

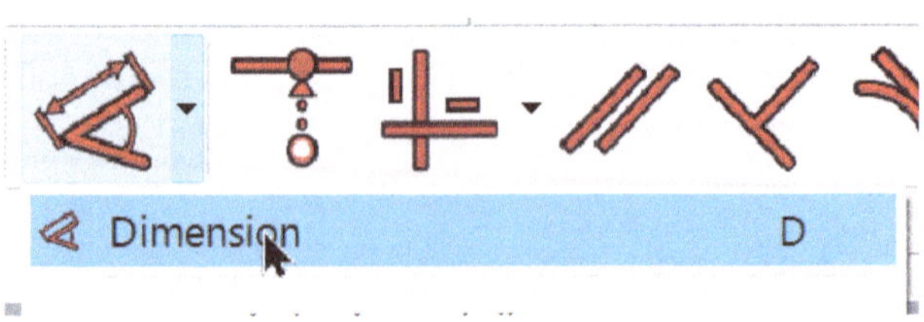

7. Select the center point of the circle.
8. Select the origin of the sketch.
9. Move the pointer toward right and click.
10. Type **50** in the **Length** box of the **Insert Length** dialog.
11. Click **OK**.

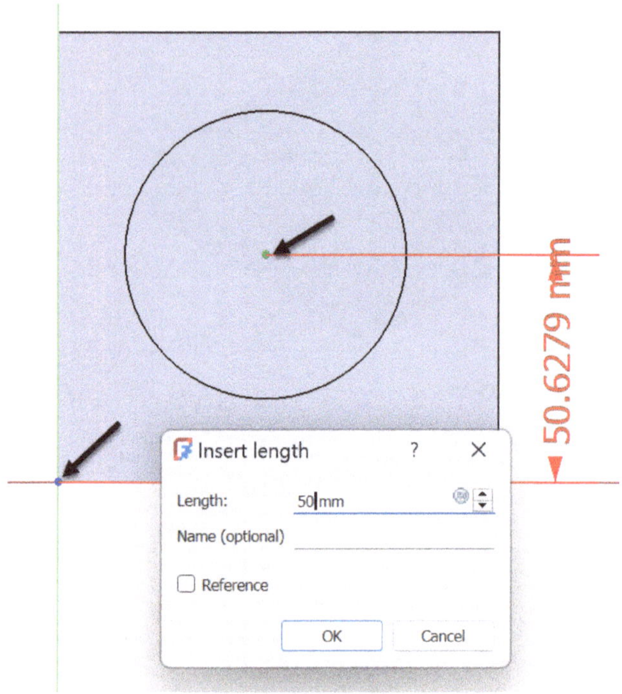

12. Select the center point of the circle and the origin of the sketch.
13. Move the pointer toward up and click.
14. Type **50** in the **Length** box and click **OK**.

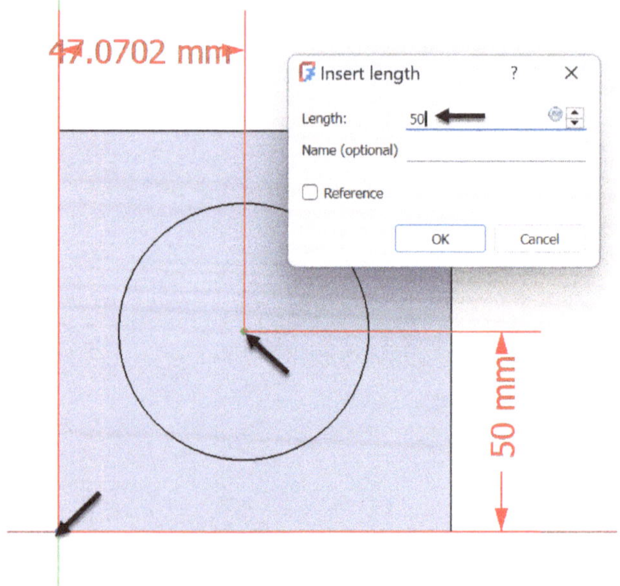

15. On the **Sketcher constraints** toolbar, click the **Dimension** drop-down **> Constrain diameter**.

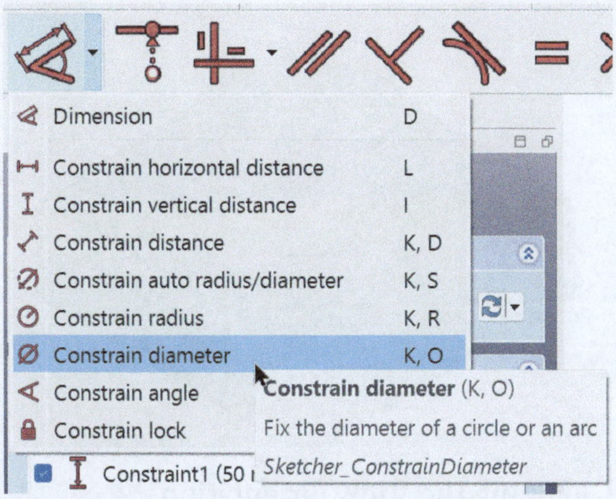

16. Select the circle and type **60** in the **Diameter** box of the **Insert diameter** dialog.

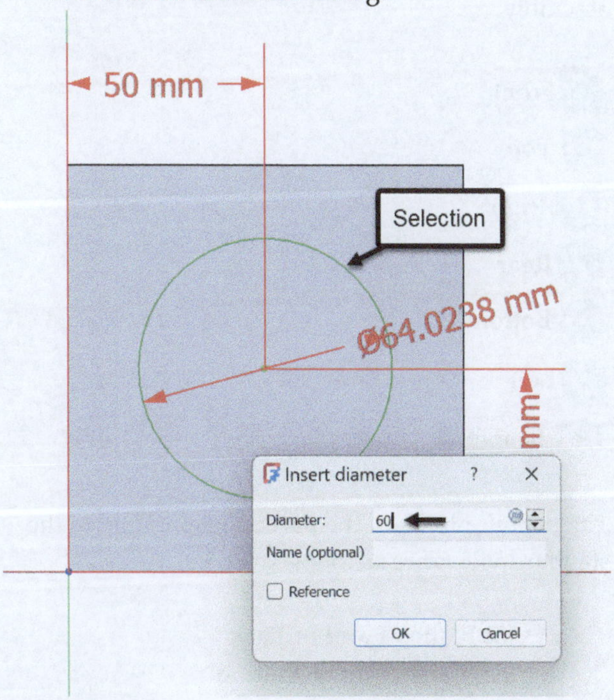

17. Click **OK**.
18. On the **Sketcher edit mode** toolbar, click the **Leave Sketch**  icon.
19. On the **Part Design Modeling** toolbar, click the **Pad**  icon.
20. Type **20** in the **Length** box of the **Pad Parameters** dialog.
21. Click **OK**.

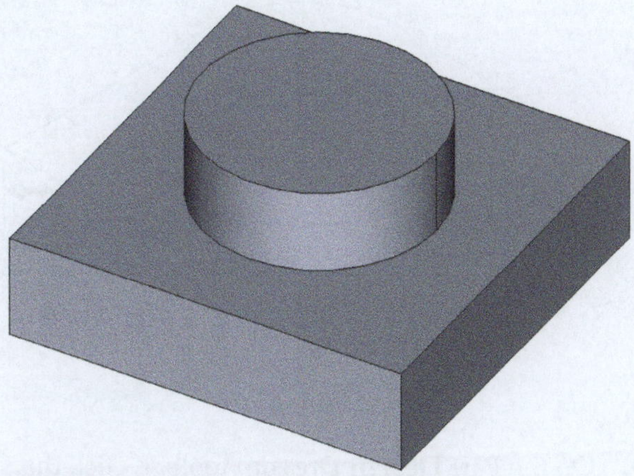

Filleting the Corners

The **Fillet** tool allows you to fillet the corners of the model.

1. On the **View** toolbar, select **Draw style > Wireframe**.

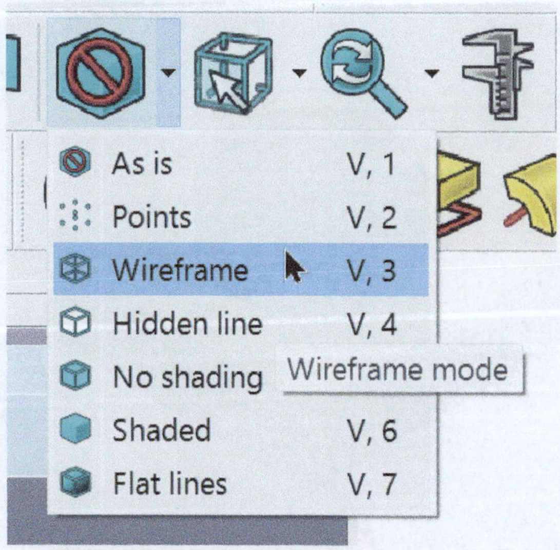

2. Press and hold the Ctrl key (Command key for MacOS users) and select the vertical edges of the model, as shown.

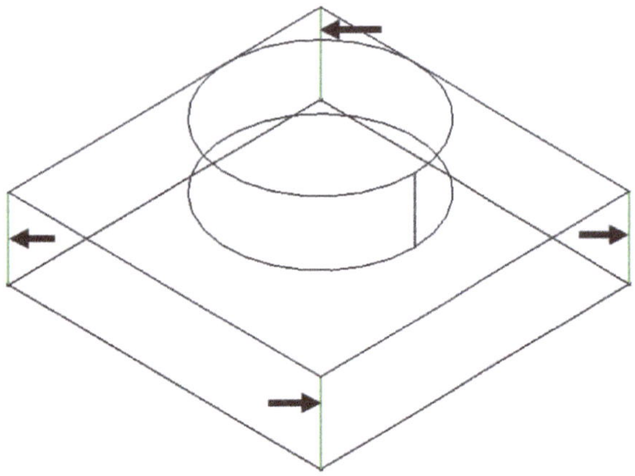

3. On the **Part Design Dressup** toolbar, click the **Fillet** icon.
4. Type **10** in the **Radius** box.
5. Click **OK**.
6. On the **View** toolbar, select **Draw style > Flat lines**.
7. Click on the horizontal face of the model, as shown.

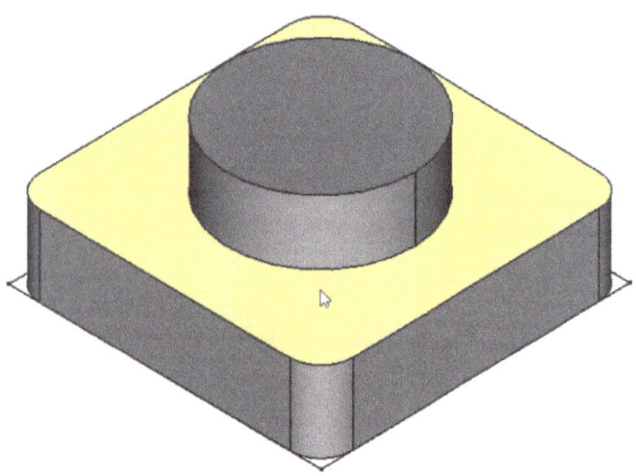

8. Click the **Fillet** icon on the **Part Design Dressup** toolbar.
9. Type **5** in the **Radius** box and click **OK**.

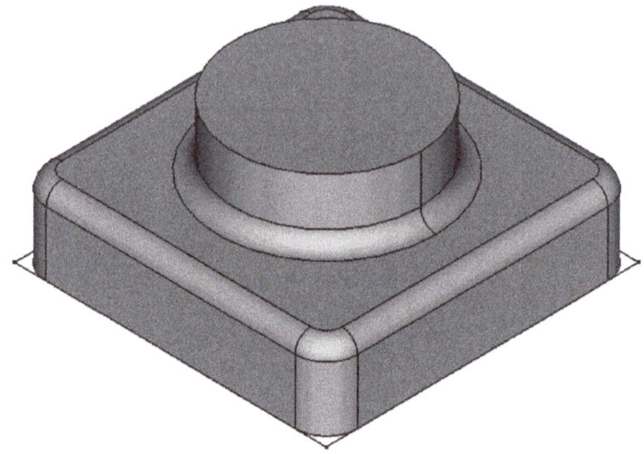

Changing the View Orientation

You can use the icons available on the **View** toolbar to change the view orientation of the sketch, part, or assembly.

Front

Top

Right

Rear

Bottom

Left

Isometric

The default planes of the part corresponding to the standard views are as follows:

- **XZ Plane - Front** or **Back**
- **YZ Plane - Top** or **Bottom**
- **XY Plane - Right** or **Left**

Rotating and Moving the Part

In addition to standard views, you can view the model from different angles by rotating them. By doing so, you can select the hidden faces and edges easily.

To rotate the part, use one of the following methods:

- On the Menu bar, click **View > Standard Views > Rotate Left** to rotate the model towards left.

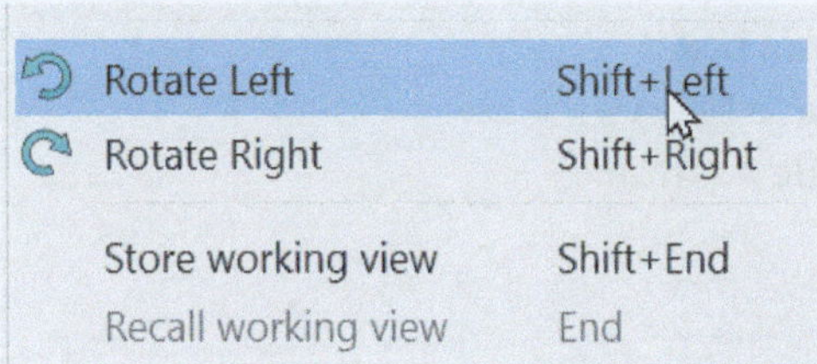

- On the Menu bar, click **Views > Standard Views > Rotate Right** to rotate the model towards the right.
- Press and hold the middle and the right mouse buttons. Next, drag the cursor to rotate the model.
- To rotate the part in 90° increments, press and hold the **Shift** key and use the arrow keys.

To move the part view, use one of the following methods:

- Press and hold the middle mouse button and drag the cursor.
- Press and hold the **Alt** or **Ctrl** key (**Command** key for Mac users) and use the arrow keys to move the view up, down, left, or right.

Shelling the model

The **Thickness** tool allows you to shell the model.

1. Press and hold the middle and right mouse buttons.
2. Drag the cursor upward to display the bottom face.
3. Click on the bottom face.

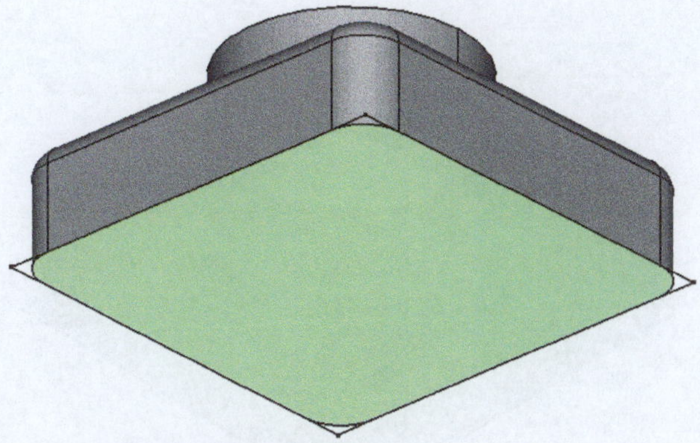

4. On the **Part Design Modeling** toolbar, click the **Thickness** icon.
5. In the **Thickness Parameters** dialog, select **Mode > Skin**.
6. Select **Join Type > Intersection**.
7. Type **2** in the **Thickness** box.
8. Check the **Make thickness inwards** option.
9. On the **View** toolbar, click the **Isometric** icon.
10. On the **Thickness parameters** dialog, click the **Select** button.
11. Select the top face of the second feature.

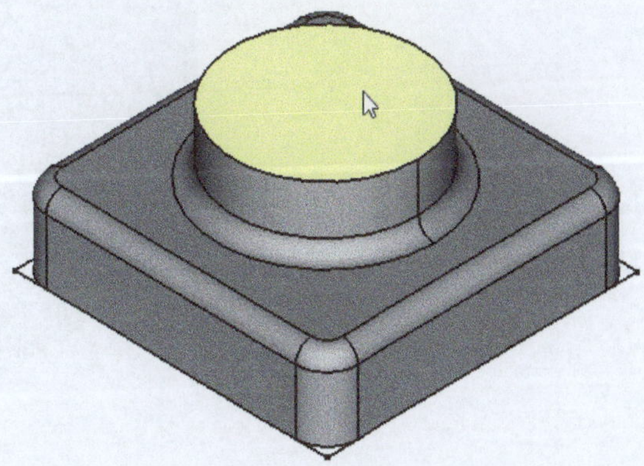

12. Click **OK**.

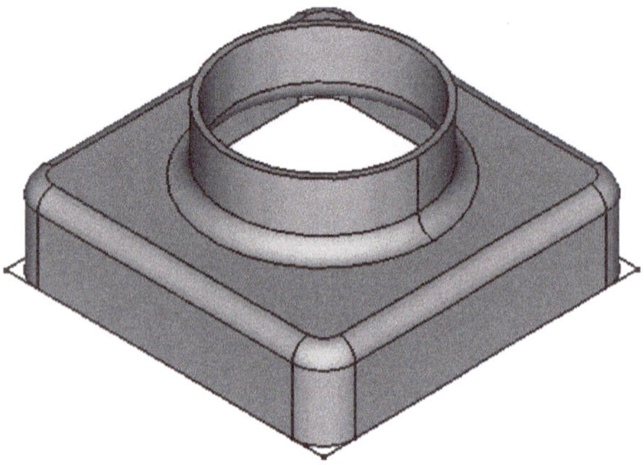

Saving the Part

1. Click **File > Save** on the Menu bar.
2. On the **Save As** dialog, type-in **Tutorial1** in the **File name** box.
3. Click **Save** to save the file.
4. Click **File > Close**.

Note:
*.FCStd is the file extension for all the files that you create in FreeCAD.

TUTORIAL 2

In this tutorial, you create the part shown below.

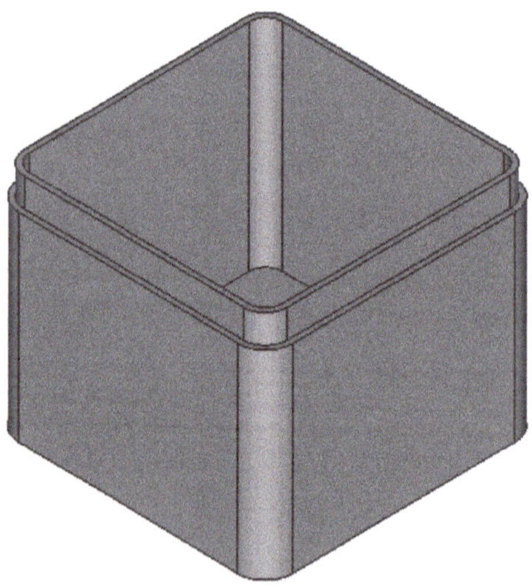

Starting a New File

1. On the Menu bar, click **File > New**.
2. Select **Part Design** from the **Workbench** drop-down.

Sketching for the Pad Feature

1. Click **Create Sketch**  icon on the **Part Design Helper** toolbar.
2. Select the XY-Plane from the **Tasks** panel and click **OK**.
3. Click **OK**.

4. Click **Rectangle** 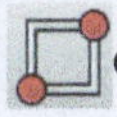 on the **Sketcher geometries** toolbar.
5. Create a rectangle, shown in the figure.

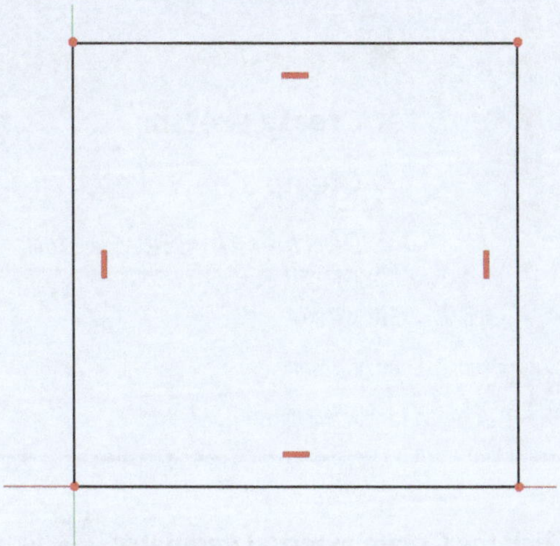

6. Add vertical and horizontal distance constraints to the rectangle, as shown.

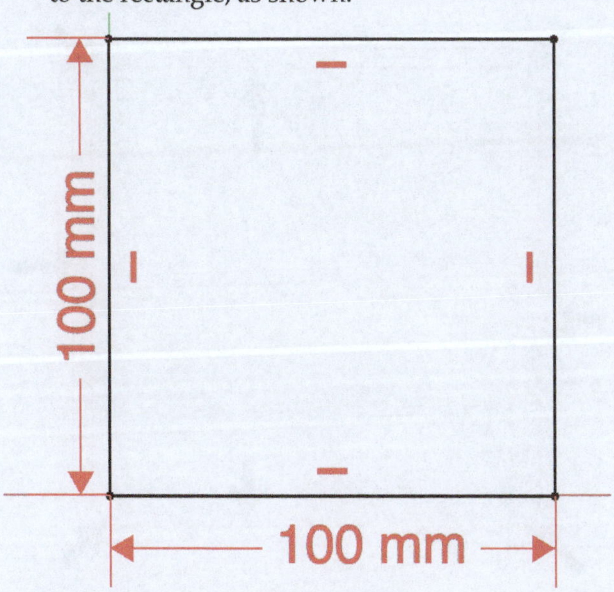

7. Click the **Leave Sketch**  icon on the **Sketcher edit mode** toolbar.
8. Click **Pad**  on the **Create** panel.
9. Type **80** in the **Length** box and click **OK**.

10. Select **Draw Style > Wireframe** on the **View** toolbar.
11. Press and hold the Ctrl key (**Command** key for Mac users) and select the vertical edges.

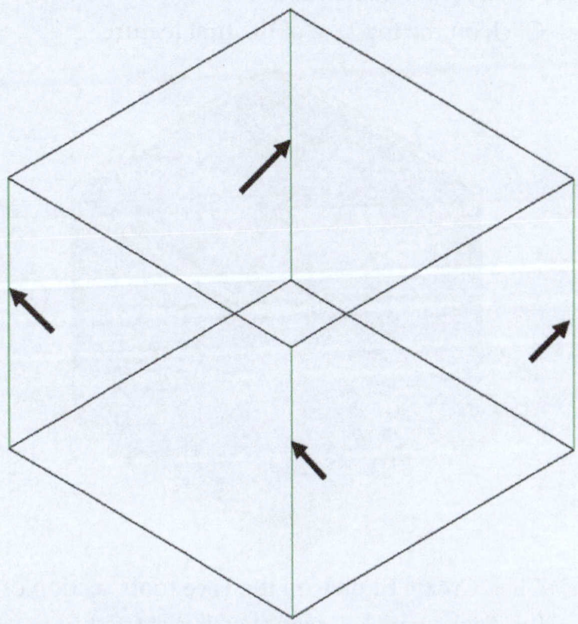

12. On the **Part Design Dressup** toolbar, click the **Fillet**  icon.
13. Type 10 in the **Radius** box.
14. Click **OK**.
15. On the **View** toolbar, select **Draw Style > Flat lines** 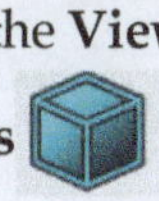.

16. Click on the top face of the model.
17. Click the **Thickness** icon on the **Part Design Dressup** toolbar.
18. Type 4 in the **Thickness** box.
19. Select **Join Type > Intersection**.
20. Check the **Make thickness inwards** option.
21. Click **OK**.

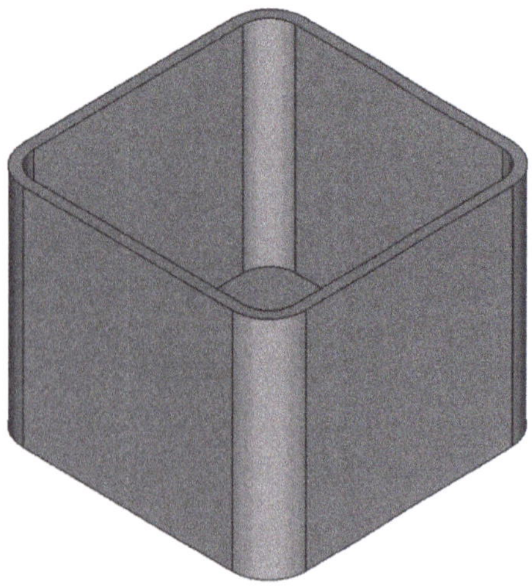

Creating the Cut Feature

1. Click on the top face of the first feature.

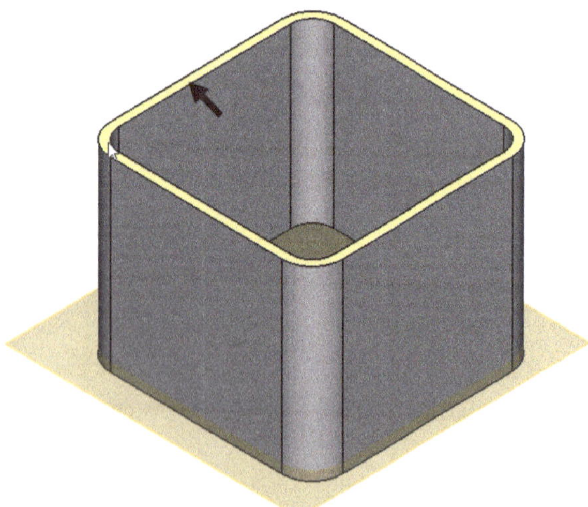

2. Click **Create Sketch** on the **Face tools** section of the **Tasks** panel. A new sketch is started.

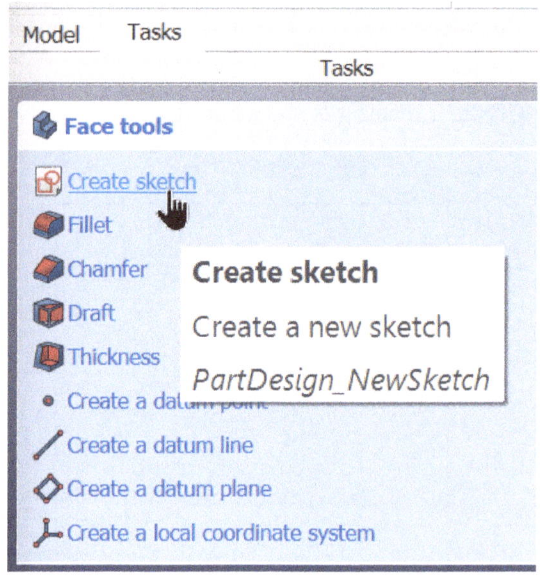

3. Click the **Create external geometry** icon on the **Sketcher tools** toolbar.
4. Click on the inner edges of the model.

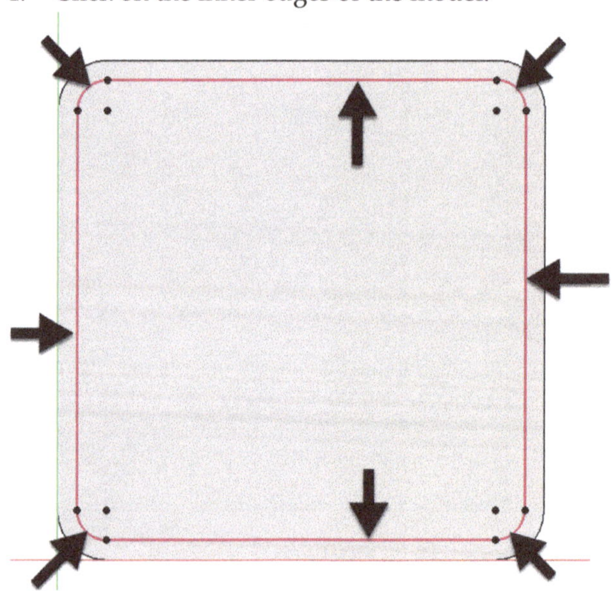

5. Click the **Rectangle** icon on the **Sketcher geometries** toolbar.
6. Create a rectangle, as shown.

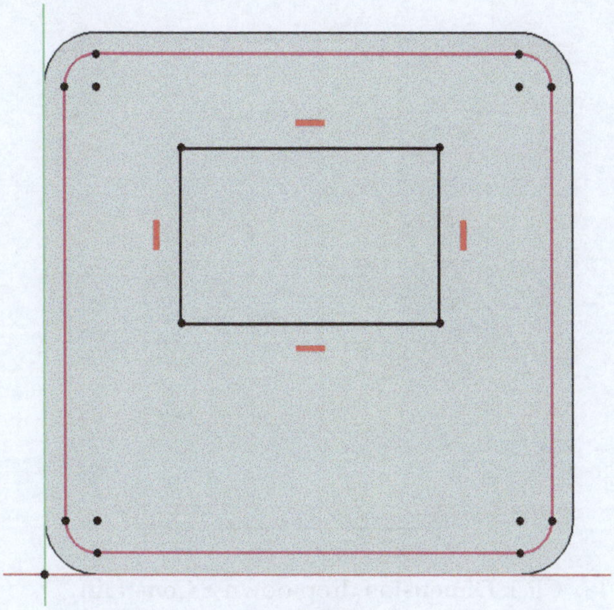

7. Click the **Create fillet** 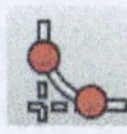 icon on the **Sketcher tools** toolbar.
8. Click on the left vertical and the top horizontal line.

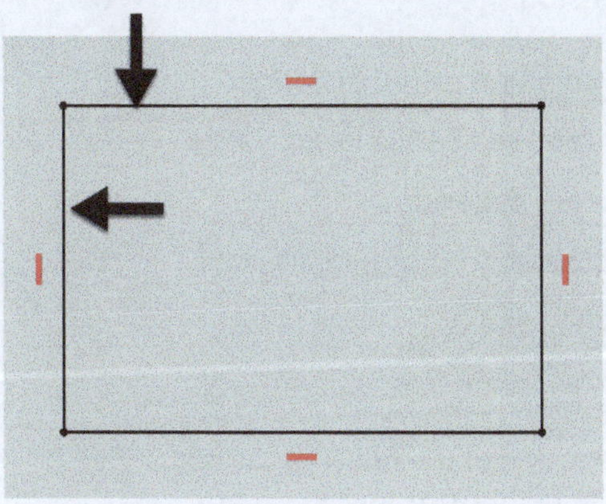

A fillet is created at the corner.

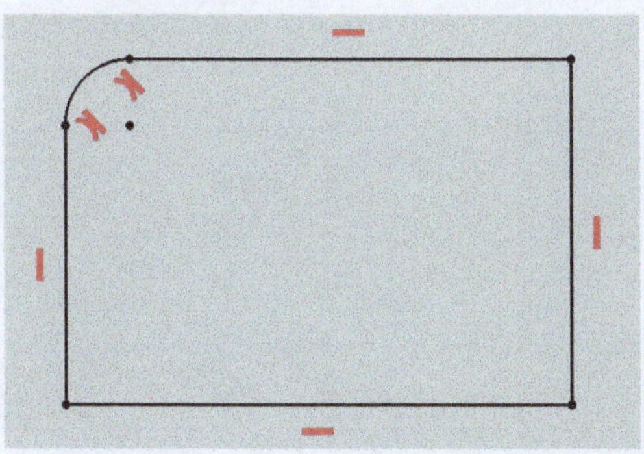

9. Likewise, create fillets at the remaining corners, as shown.

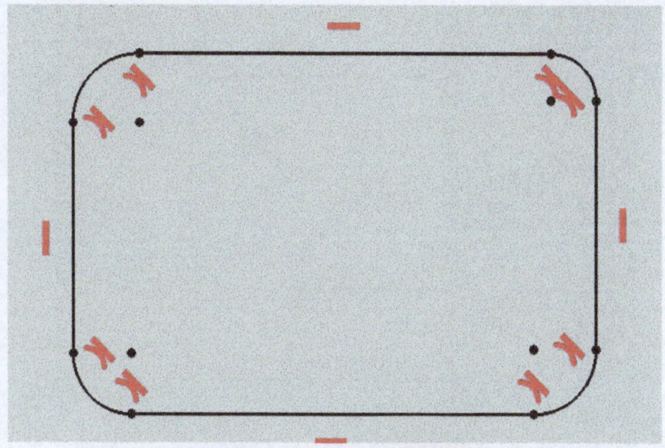

10. Click the **Constrain equal** 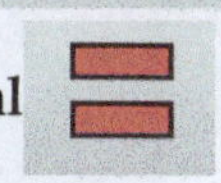 icon on the **Sketcher constraints** toolbar.
11. Select the top-right and top-left fillets of the rectangle; the fillets are made equal.
12. Select the top-left and bottom-left fillets of the rectangle.
13. Select the bottom-left and the bottom-right fillets of the rectangle.

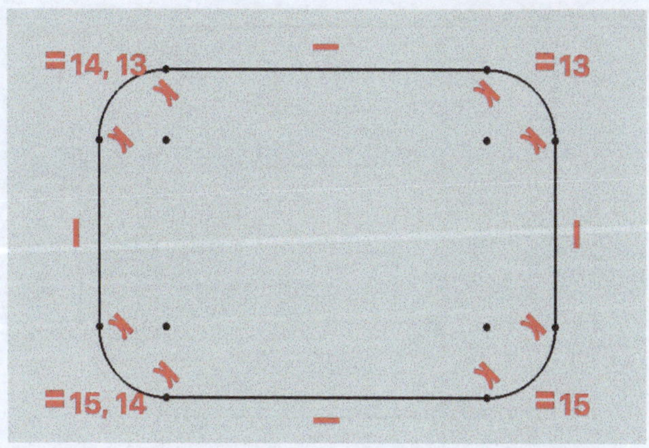

14. Click the **Constrain Coincident** 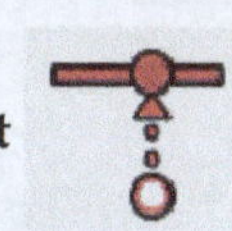 icon on the **Sketcher constraints** toolbar.
15. Select the center point of the top right fillet of the rectangle.
16. Select the center point of the top right fillet of the external geometry.

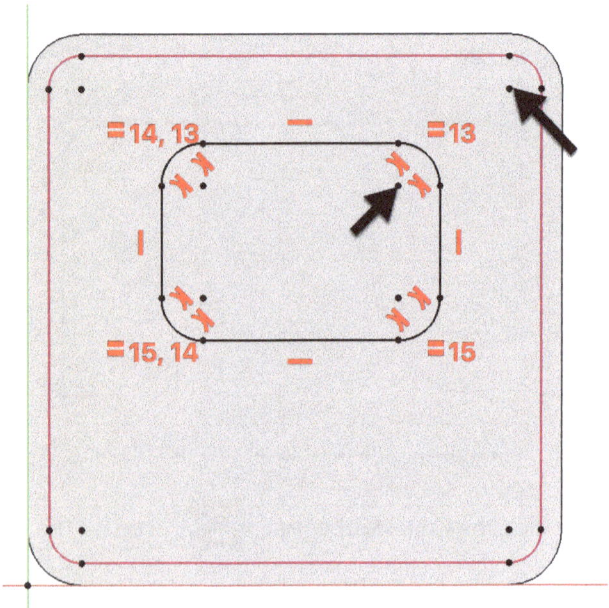

17. Select the center point of the bottom-left fillet of the rectangle.
18. Select the center point of the bottom-left fillet of the external geometry.

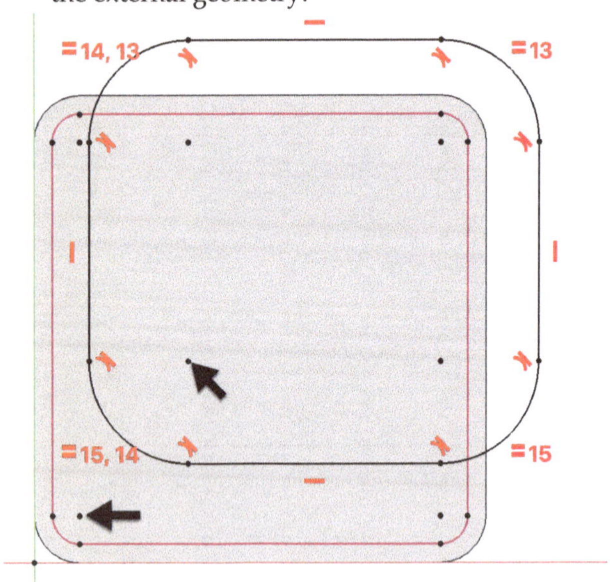

The centerpoints of the fillets are coincident with each other.

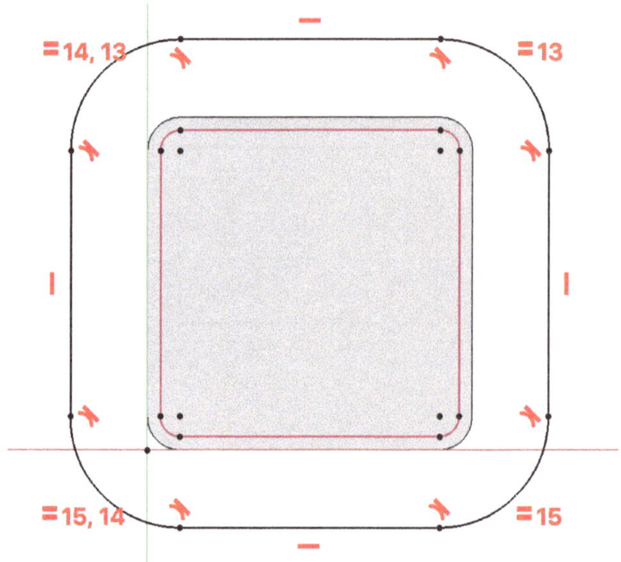

19. Click **Dimension** drop-down > **Constrain radius** on the **Sketcher constraints** toolbar.

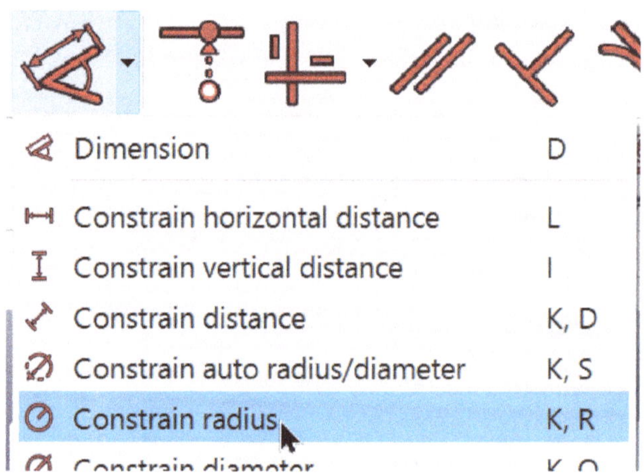

20. Select any one of the fillets of the rectangle.
21. Type 8 in the **Radius** box.
22. Click **OK**.

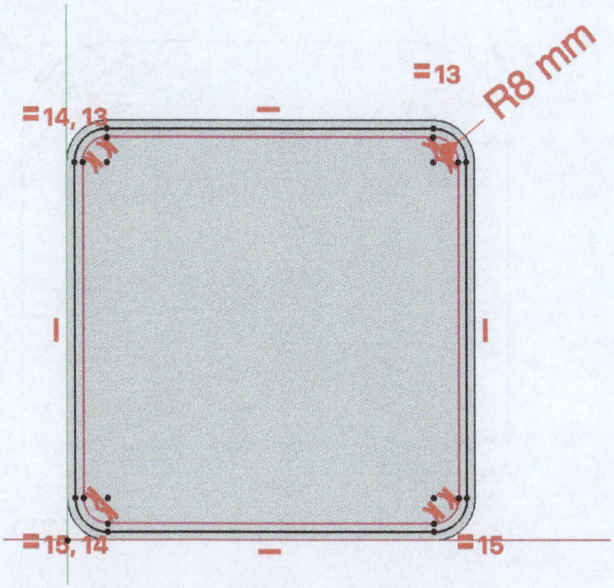

23. Likewise, create another rectangle with fillets.
    - Click the **Rectangle** 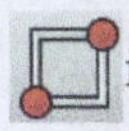 icon on the **Sketcher geometries** toolbar.
    - Create a rectangle, as shown.

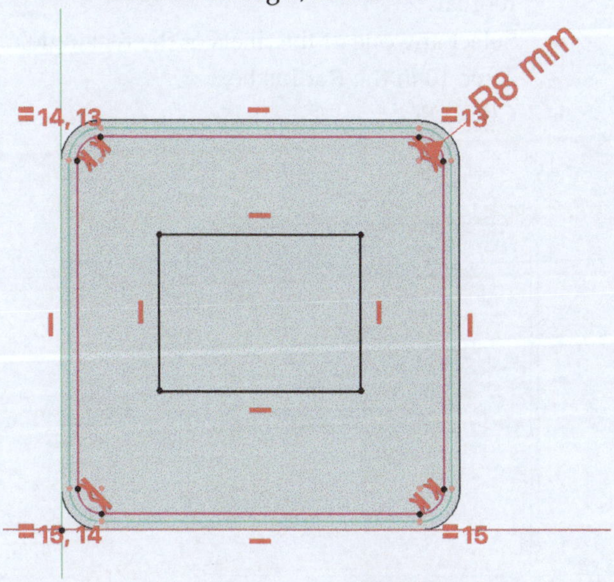

- Click the **Create fillet** 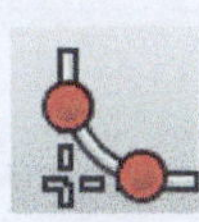 icon on the **Sketcher tools** toolbar.
- Create fillets at the corners of the rectangle, as shown.

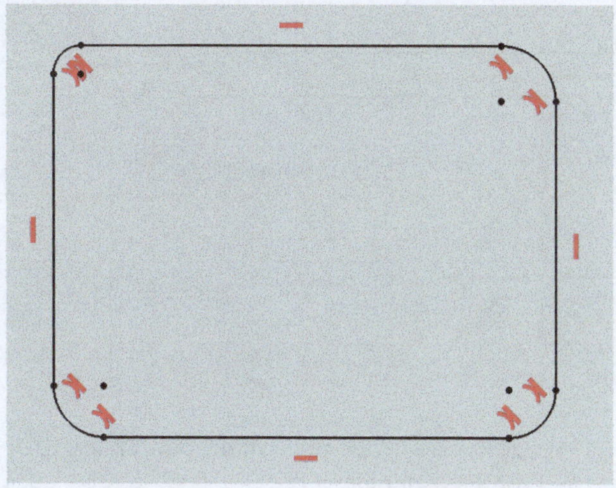

- Click the **Constrain equal** 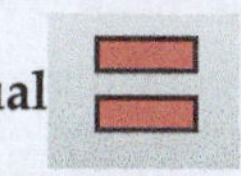 icon on the **Sketcher constraints** toolbar.
- Select the top-right and top-left fillets of the rectangle; the fillets are made equal.
- Select the top-left and bottom-left fillets of the rectangle.
- Select the bottom-left and the bottom-right fillets of the rectangle.

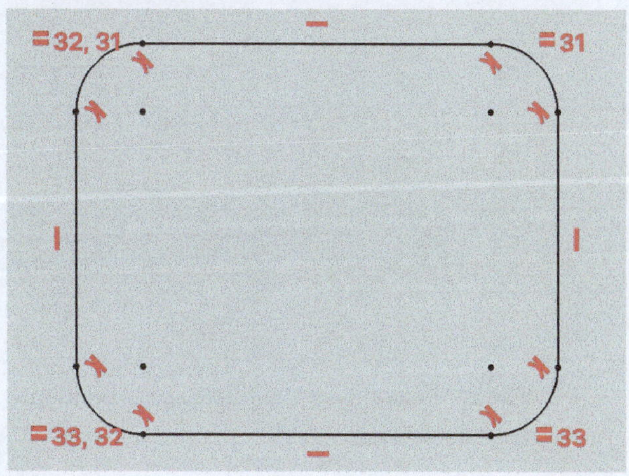

- Click the **Constrain Coincident** 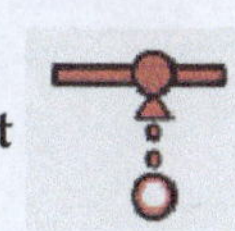 icon on the **Sketcher constraints** toolbar.
- Select the center point of the top right fillet of the rectangle.
- Select the center point of the top right fillet of the external geometry.

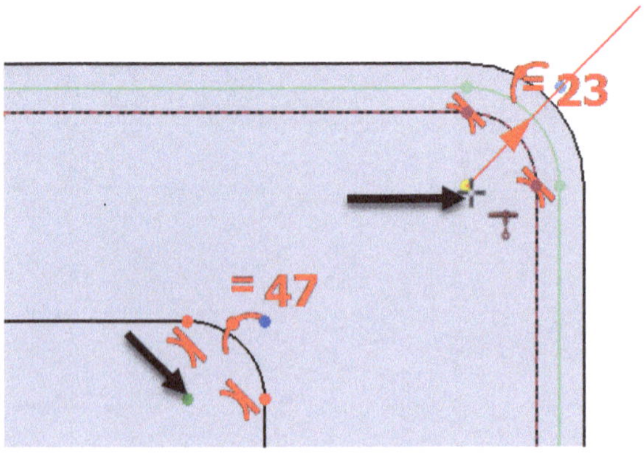

- Select the center point of the bottom-left fillet of the rectangle.
- Select the center point of the bottom-left fillet of the external geometry.

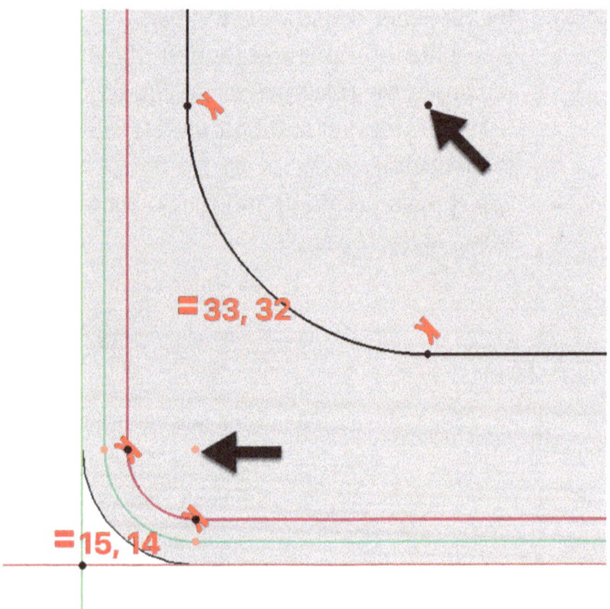

- The centerpoints of the fillets are coincident with each other.

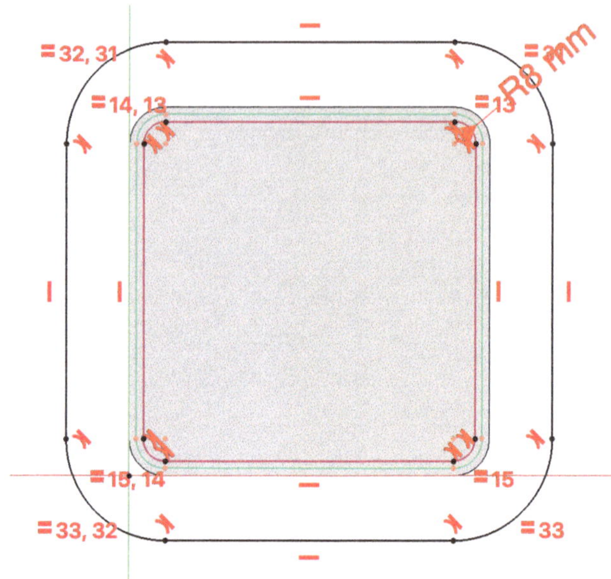

- Click **Dimension** drop-down > **Constrain radius**  on the **Sketcher constraints** toolbar.
- Select any one of the fillets of the rectangle.
- Type 10 in the **Radius** box.
- Click **OK**.

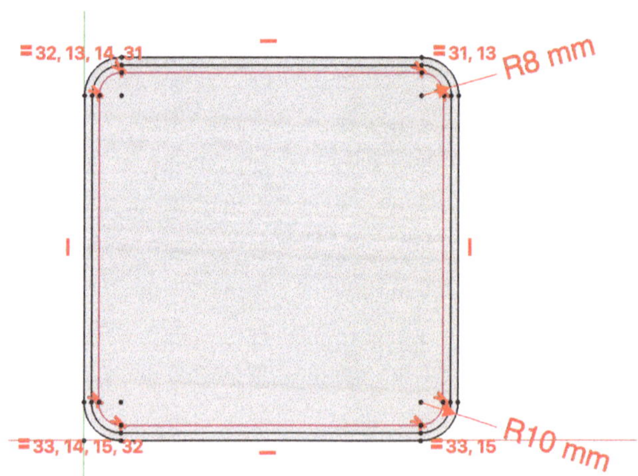

24. Click **Leave Sketch**  on the **Sketcher edit mode** toolbar.
25. Click the **Pocket**  icon on the **Part Design Modeling** toolbar.
26. Type **10** in the **Length** box in the **Pocket parameters** dialog.
27. Click **OK**.

28. Save and close the file.

Chapter 3: Assembly Basics

In this chapter, you will:

- Add Components to assembly
- Apply constraints between components

TUTORIAL 1

This tutorial takes you through the creation of your first assembly.

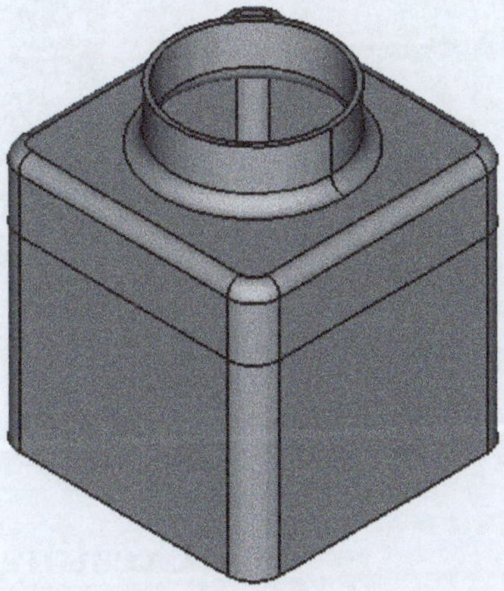

Starting a New Assembly File

1. Open the **FreeCAD** application.
2. On the **File** toolbar, click the **Save** icon.
3. Type **Assembly_tutorial** in the **File Name** box on the **Save** dialog.
4. Click **Save**.
5. Click **Workbenches** drop-down menu and select the **Assembly** Workbench from the list.
6. Click the **Create Assembly** icon on the **Assembly** toolbar.

Inserting the Base Component

1. Click the **Insert Component** icon on the **Assembly** toolbar (or) click **Assembly > Insert Component** on the menu bar.
2. On the **Insert Component** section of the **Tasks** panel, click the **Open file** button.
3. Browse to the location of the **Tutorial 2** file of Chapter 1, and then double-click on it. The selected part is listed in the **Insert Component** section.
4. Select the **Body** under the Tutorial2 file from the **Insert Component** section; the selected body is inserted into the assembly.

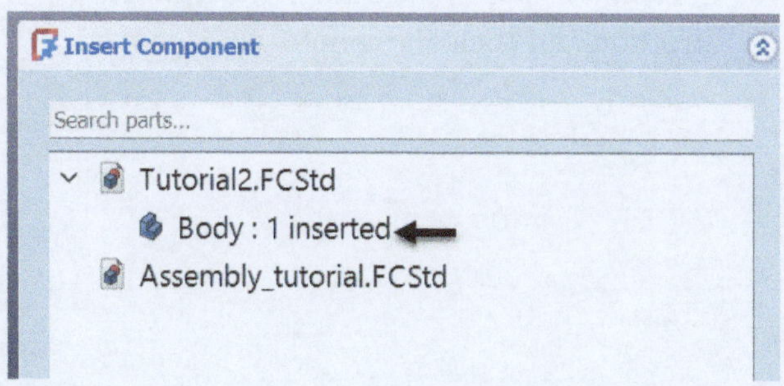

5. Click **Yes** on the **Ground Part** message box.

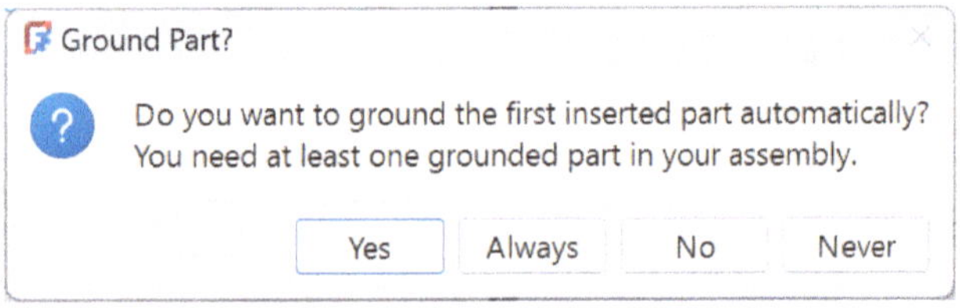

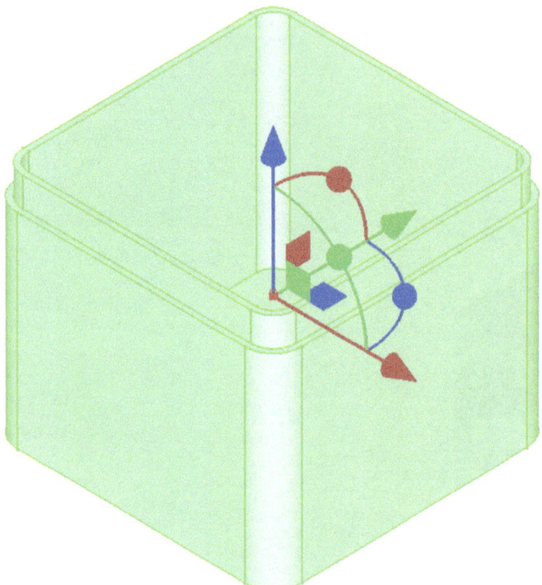

Adding the second component

1. On the **Insert Component** section of the **Tasks** panel, click the **Open file** button.
2. Browse to the location of the **Tutorial** 1 file of Chapter 1, and then double click on it.
3. Select the **Body** under the Tutorial1 file from the **Insert Component** section; the selected body is inserted into the assembly.
4. Click and Z-axis of the triad in the upward direction and click; the component is moved.

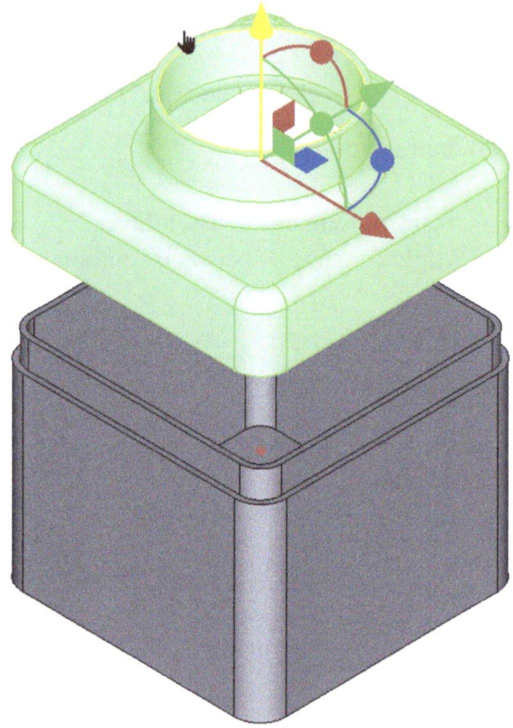

5. Click **OK** on the **Tasks** panel.

Creating Joints

After adding the components to the assembly environment, you need to create joints between them. By creating joints, you establish relationships between components.

The **Assembly Joints** toolbar has various tools to apply constraints between the components.

Different assembly joints that can be applied are given next.

Rigid Joint: A Rigid Joint fully constrains components, leaving zero degrees of freedom, effectively binding them into a single rigid body. You need select faces, edges, or points from the components to define this joint.

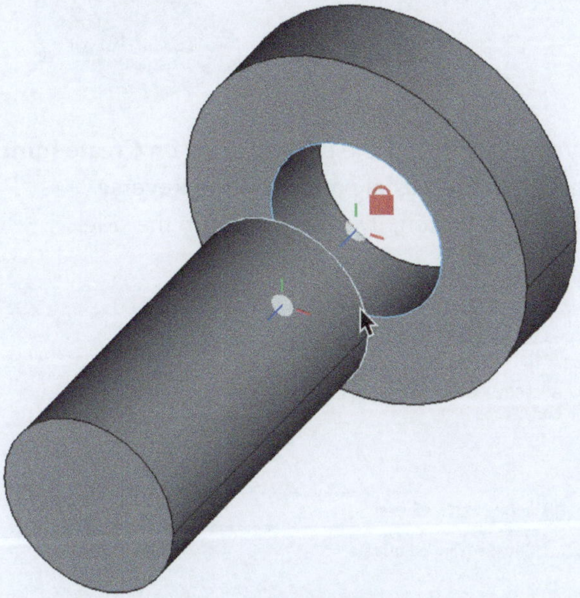

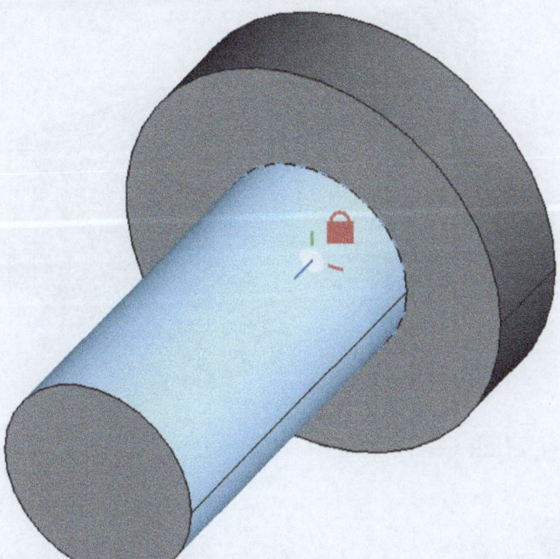

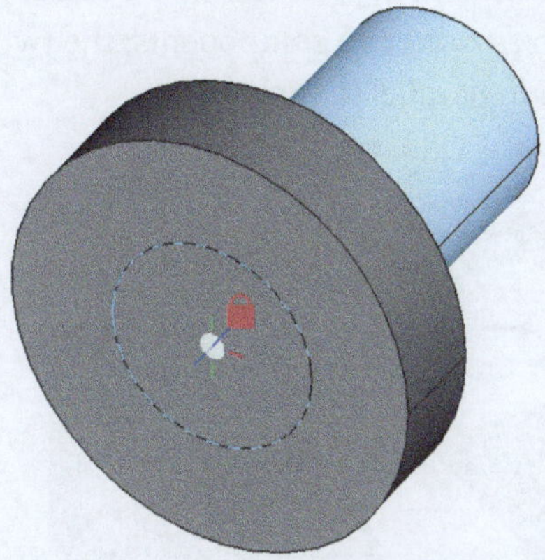

Addtionally, you can enter values in the **Offset** or **Rotation** boxes if components need precise positioning.

Click the **Reverse direction** button on the **Create Joint** dialog to reverse the direction.

Parallel Joint: The **Parallel Joint** constrains two components to maintain parallel alignment along a specified direction. It allows controlled movement while ensuring selected edges, axes, or planar faces remain parallel.

Activate the **Parallel Joint** command select faces, edges, or axes from two components; the two selections are made parallel to each other.

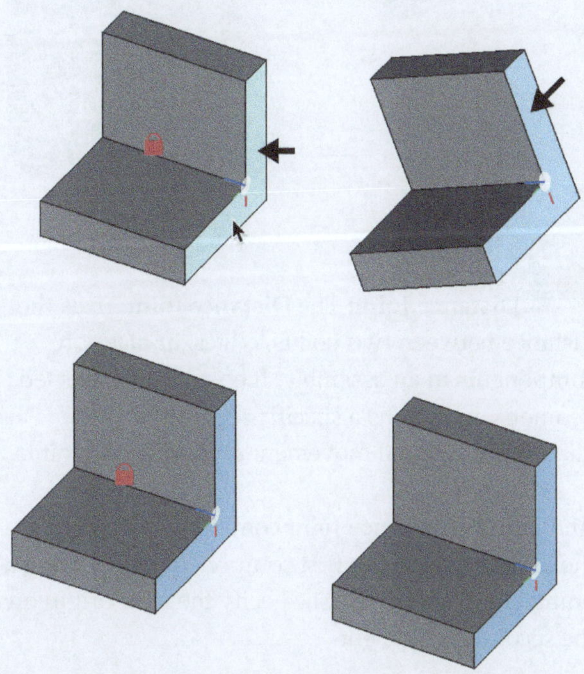

Parallel Joint: This joint forces the two components to stay at a 90-degree angle relative to each other.

Activate the **Perpendicular Joint** command select faces, edges, or axes from two components; the two selections are made parallel to each other.

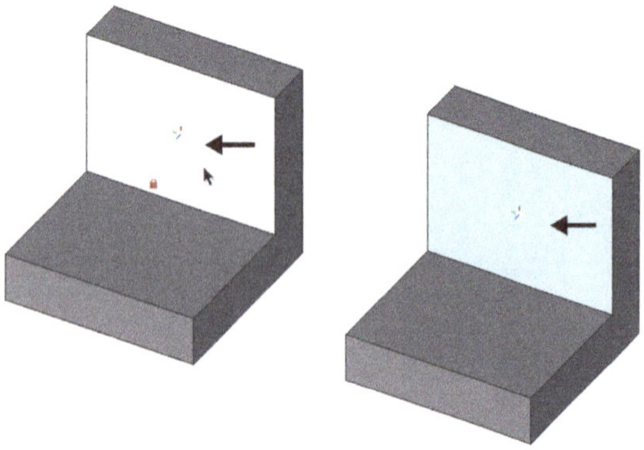

Distance Joint: The **Distance Joint** fixes the distance between two points, edges, or faces on components in an assembly. It ensures the selected geometry maintains a specific separation while allowing rotational movement around those points.

Activate the **Distance Joint** command and specify the joint origin on the first component by selecting a point, edge, or face. Next, specify the joint origin on the second component.

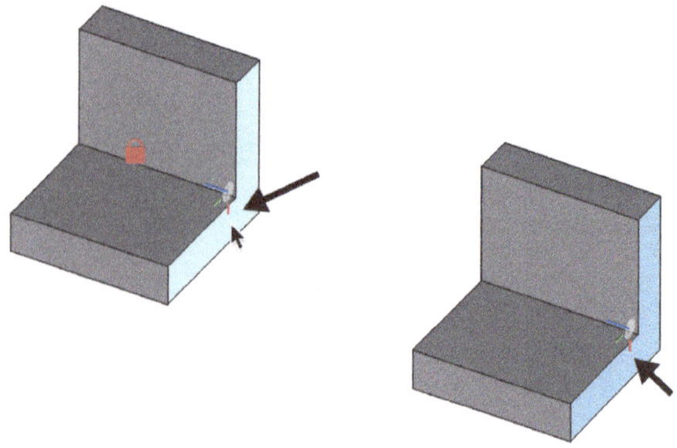

Type-in a value in the **Distance** box on **Create Joint** section of the **Tasks** panel. Use the **Reverse Direction** button, if you want to flip the side.

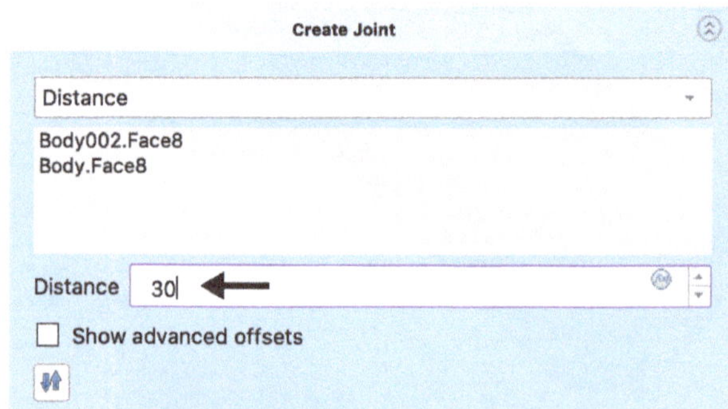

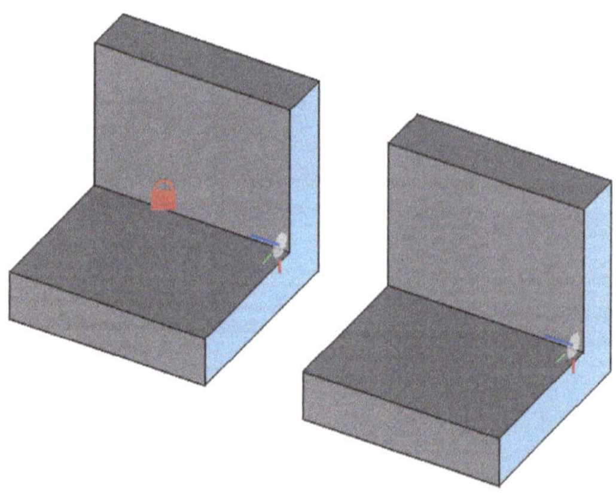

Next, click **OK.**

Cylindrical Joint: This joint allows two components to rotate and translate along a common axis. By integrating the rotational capability of a Revolute Joint and the translational capability of a Slider Joint, this constraint enables simultaneous rotational and linear motion along a single axis.

Activate the **Cylindrical Joint** command and specify the joint origin by selecting a cylindrical edge on the first component. Next, specify the joint origin by selecting a cylindrical edge on the second component.

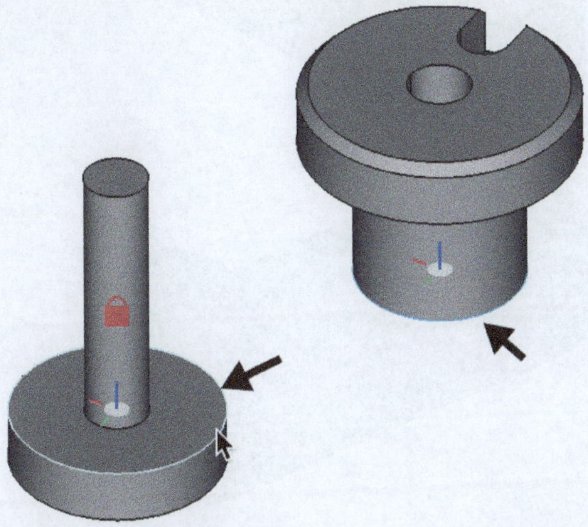

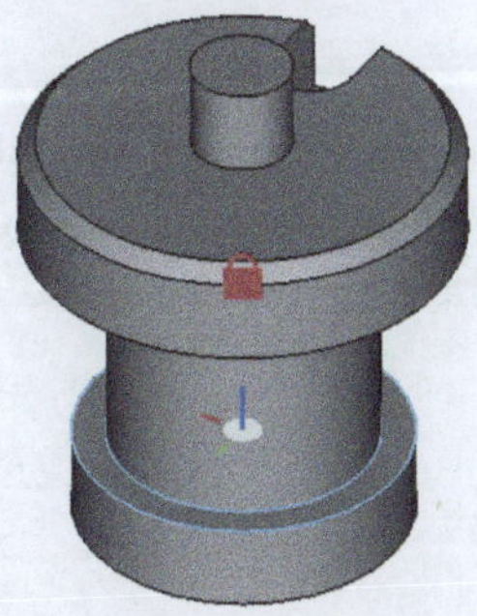

In the **Limits** section, check the **Min Length** and **Max Length** boxes and enter values in the respective boxes. This limits sliding distance.

Check the **Min angle** and **Max angle** boxes and enter values in the respective value box. This restrict rotational range.

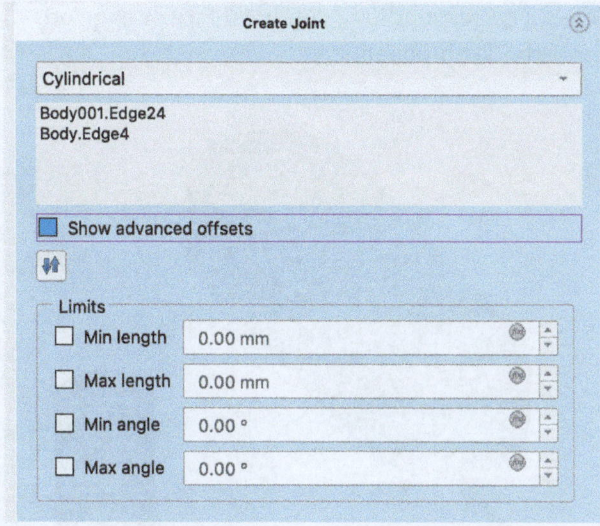

Note: Leaving values at 0 allows unrestricted motion.

Click **OK** to create the cylindrical joint. Click and drag anyone of the component and notice that it can rotate and slide along the shared axis.

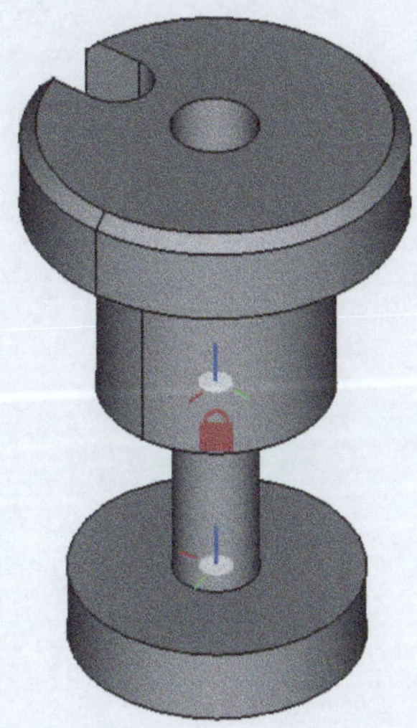

 **Revolute Joint:** A **Revolute Joint** restricts two components to rotate around a shared axis, mimicking hinge-like motion. It allows 1 rotational degree of freedom (DOF) while preventing translation along or perpendicular to the axis.

Activate the Revolute Joint command and select a cylindrical face or edge on the first component to define the joint origin.

Select a corresponding cylindrical face or edge on the second component.

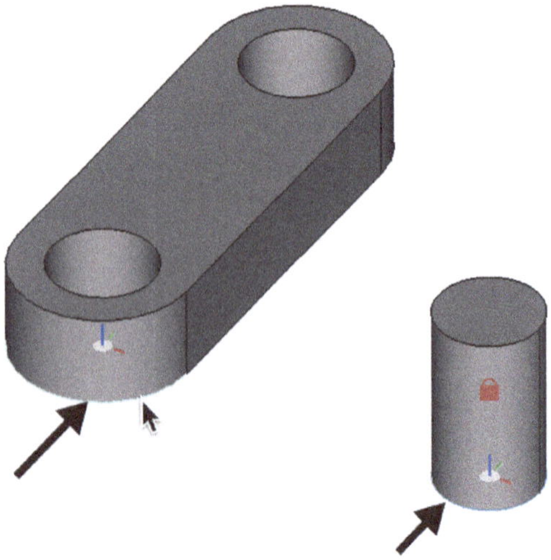

In the Limits section, enter values in the Min angle and Max angle boxes, to restrict rotational range.

Note that leaving both fields at 0.00° allows unrestricted 360° rotation.

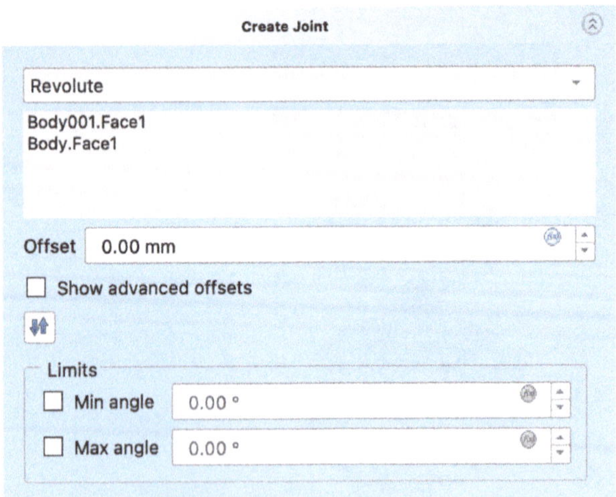

Click **OK** to apply the Revolute Joint.

The component can now rotate freely around the defined axis.

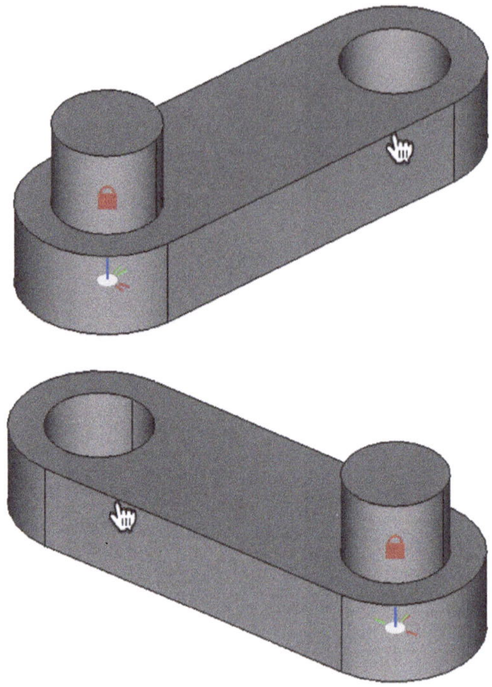

Angle Joint: Applies the angle constraint between two components. Activate the Create Angle Joint command and specify the angle value in the Angle box.

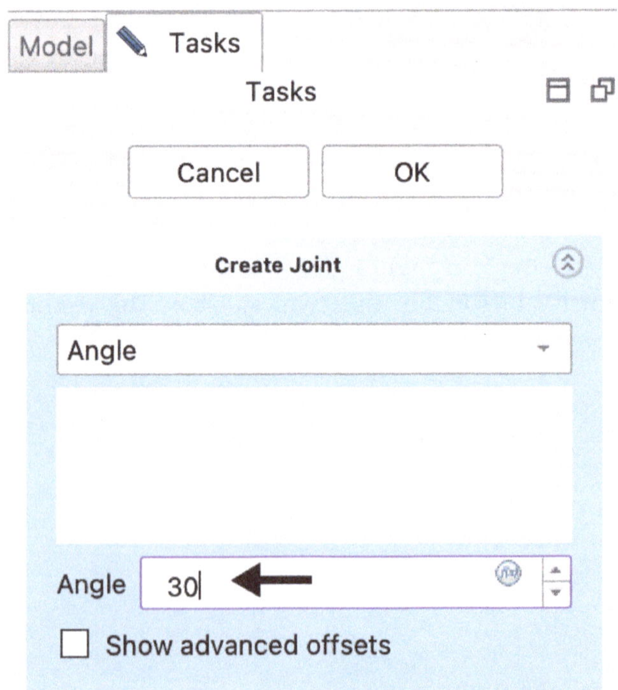

Select faces or edges on each component to define the joint origins (one selection per component).

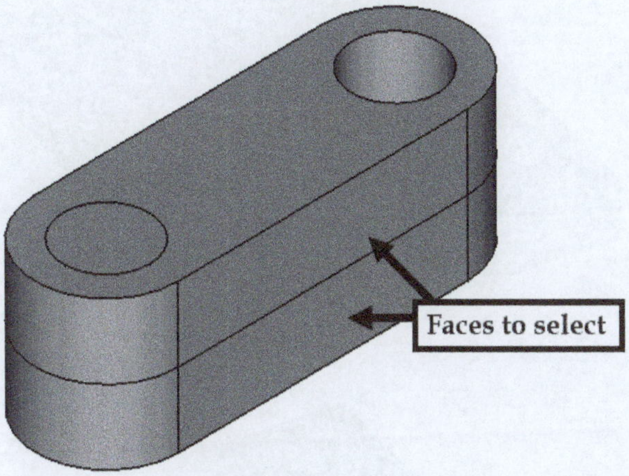

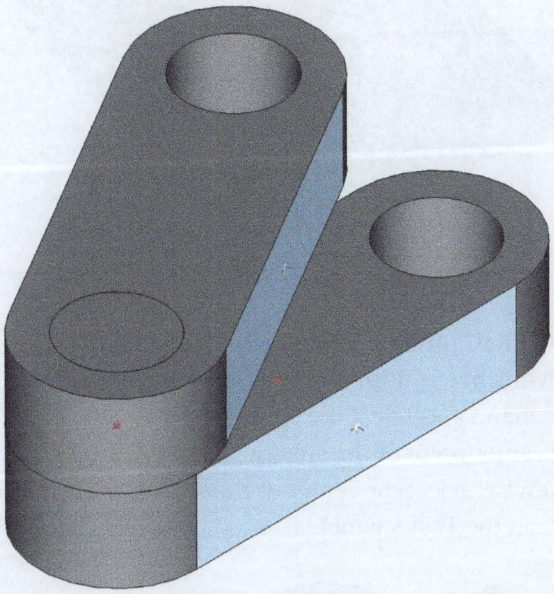

Click **OK** to create the angle joint.

Slider Joint: The slider joint allows the second component to move in a straight line along the direction defined by the selected faces/edges. It restricts rotation or sideways movement. Ensure the selected geometry aligns with the desired sliding path.

Activate the **Create Slider Joint** command. Next, specify the joint origin by selecting a face or edge on the first component (fixed part). For example, click on the middle portion of the edge, as shown to define the joint origin.

Likewise, click on the middle portion of the horizontal edge of the second component, as shown.

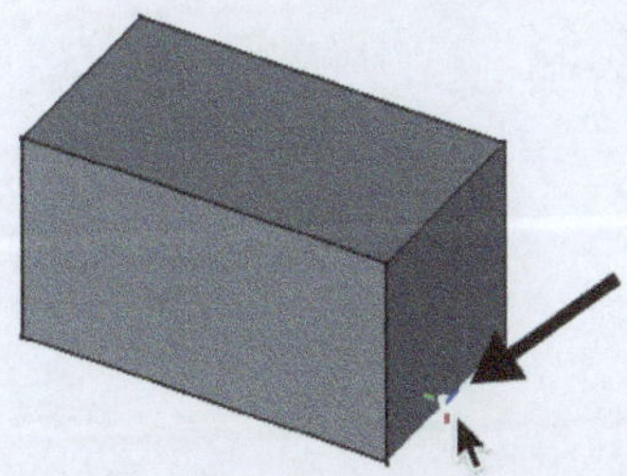

The selected edges are aligned together.

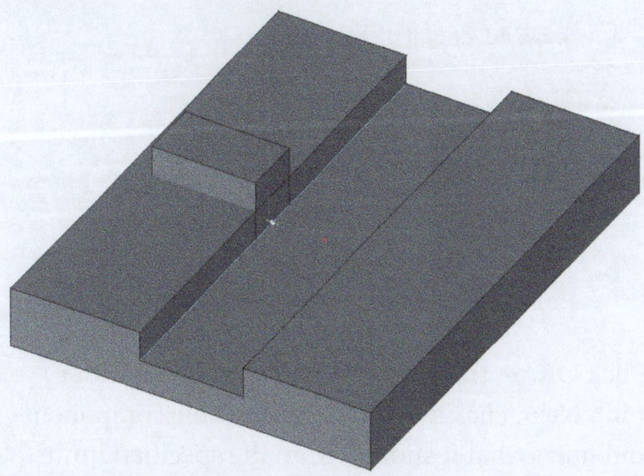

Click the **Reverse direction** icon to flip the movable part, if needed.

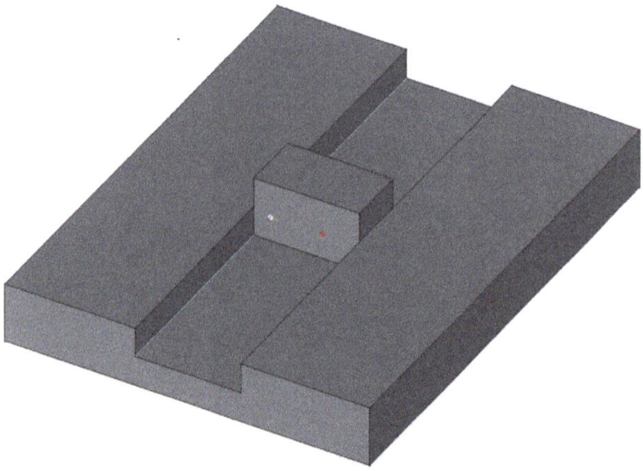

Check the **Min Length** and **Max Length** options and specify values in the respective value boxes. This restricts the sliding motion to the specified range. For example, with -30 to 30, the joint can move **30** units forward and **30** units backward from its starting position.

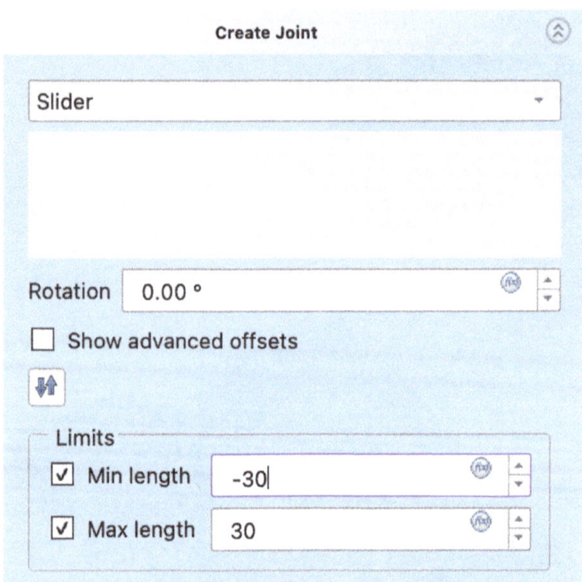

Click **OK** on the **Tasks** panel to create the slider joint. Next, click and drag the movable component and notice that it slides within the specified limits.

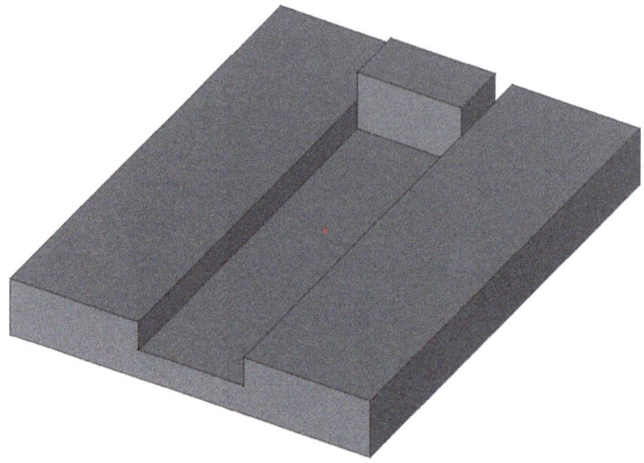

 **Ball Joint:** This Joint allows rotational movement in multiple axes. Activate the Ball Joint command and select the spherical face of the ball; the center point of the spherical face is snapped. Likewise, select the center of the socket cavity. Click **OK** on the **Tasks** panel.

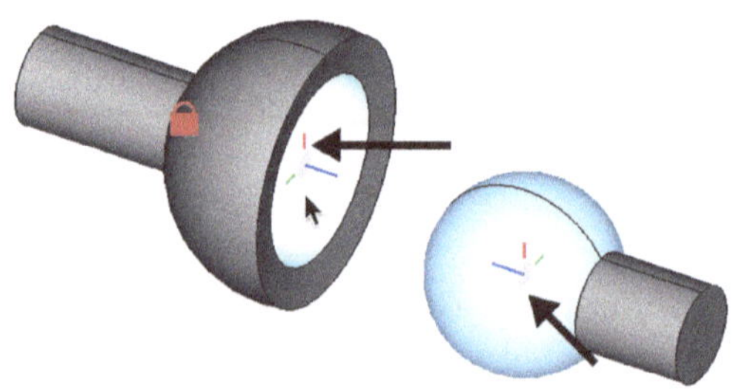

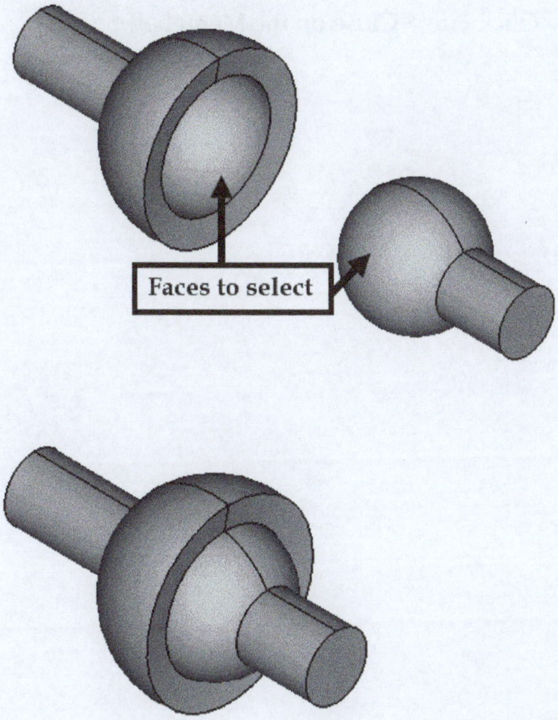

1. Click **Create Fixed Joint** icon on the **Assembly** toolbar.
2. Place the pointer on the midpoint of the lower horizontal edge of the Tutorial 1 component.
3. Make sure that the axes of the joint origin are oriented in the direction, as shown.

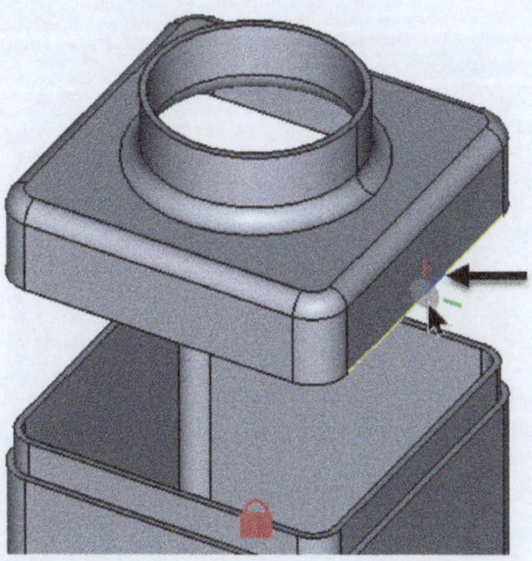

4. Click to define the joint origin.
5. Place the pointer on the midpoint of the horizontal edge of the Tutorial 2 component.
6. Make sure that the axes on the joint origin are oriented in the direction, as shown.

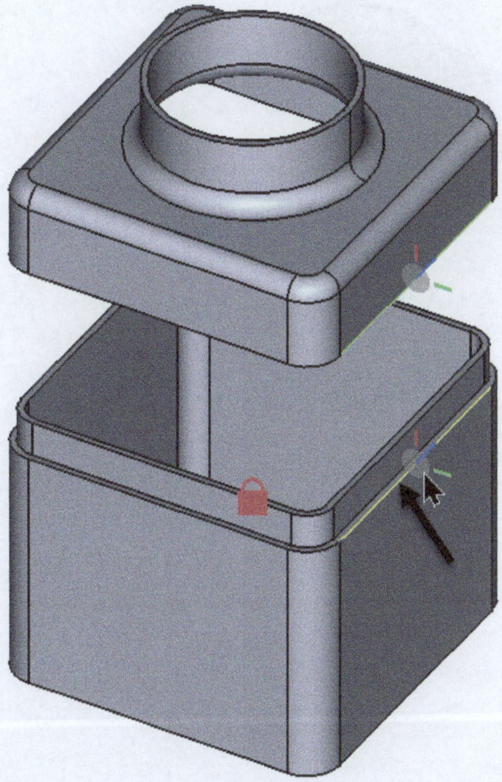

7. Click to define the joint origin.
8. Click **OK** on the **Tasks** panel to create the fixed joint.

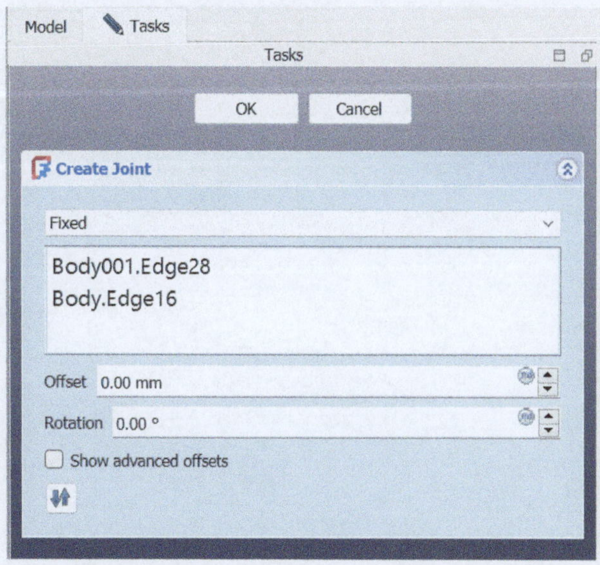

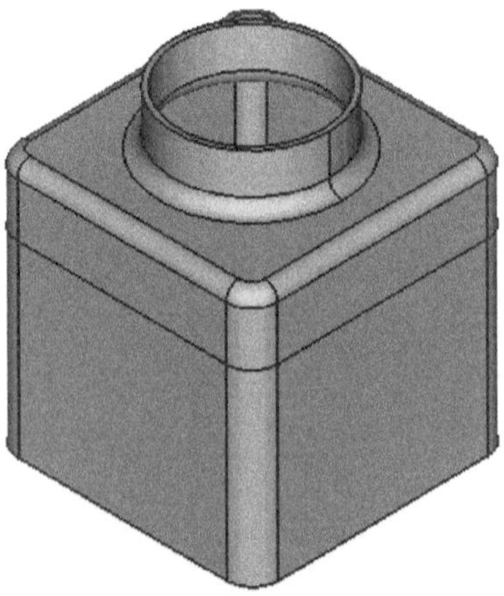

9. Click **File > Save** on the Menu bar.
10. Click **File > Close** on the Menu bar.

Chapter 4: Sketching

In this chapter, you learn the sketching tools. You learn to create:

- Polylines
- Polygons
- Slots
- Constraints
- B-Splines
- Ellipses
- Circles
- Trim
- Extend
- Toggle Construction geometry

Creating Polylines

The **Create Polyline** tool is the most commonly used while creating a sketch.

1. To start a new part file, click **File > New** on the Menu Bar.
2. On the **Workbench** toolbar, select **Workbench** drop-down > **Part Design**.
3. Click **Sketch > Create Sketch** on the Menu bar.
4. Select the **XY_Plane**. The sketch starts.
5. To activate this tool, you need to click the **Create Polyline** 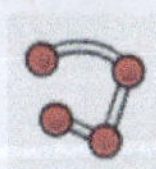 icon on the **Sketcher geometries** toolbar.
6. Click in the graphics window and move the pointer.
7. Click to create a line. Notice that another line is attached to the cursor.

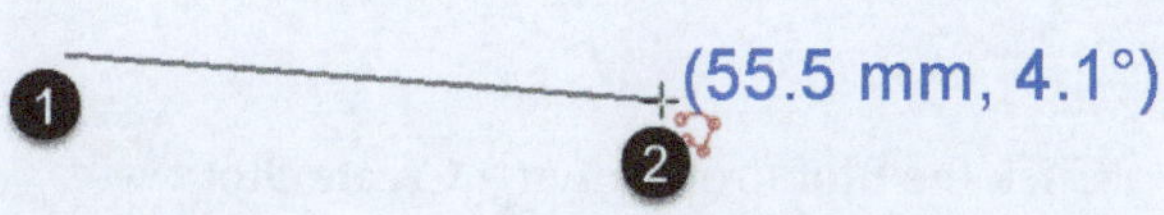

8. Move the pointer and click to create another line.

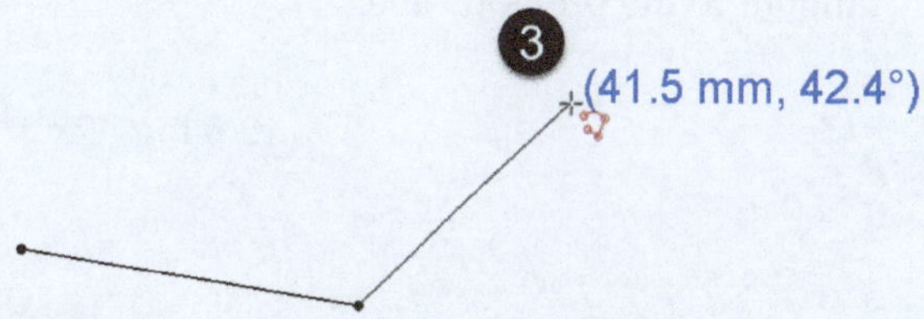

9. Press the **M** key on your keyboard.
10. Move the pointer and click to create a line perpendicular to the previous line.

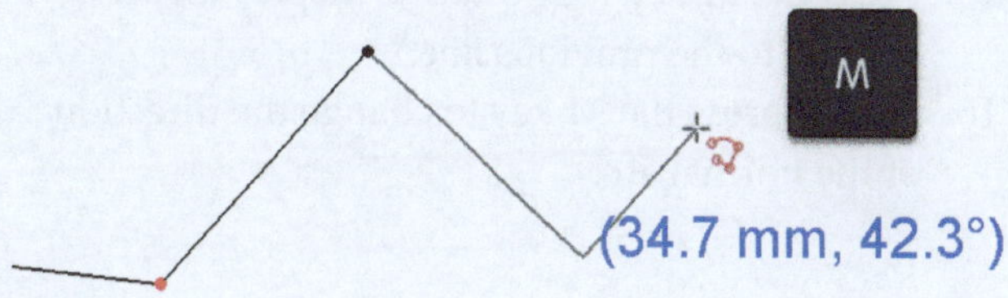

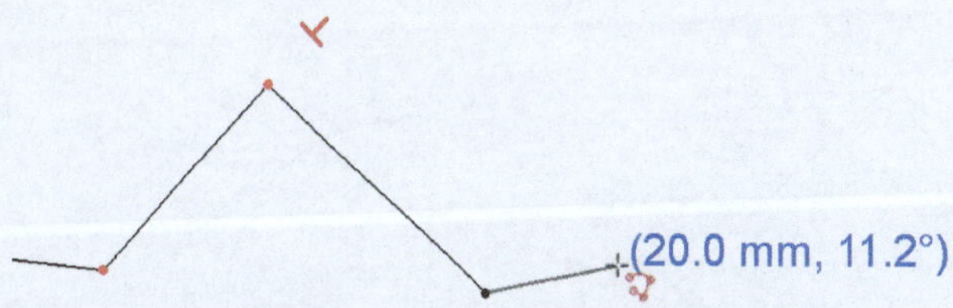

11. Press the **M** key twice on your keyboard.
12. Move the pointer and click to create a line colinear to the previous line.

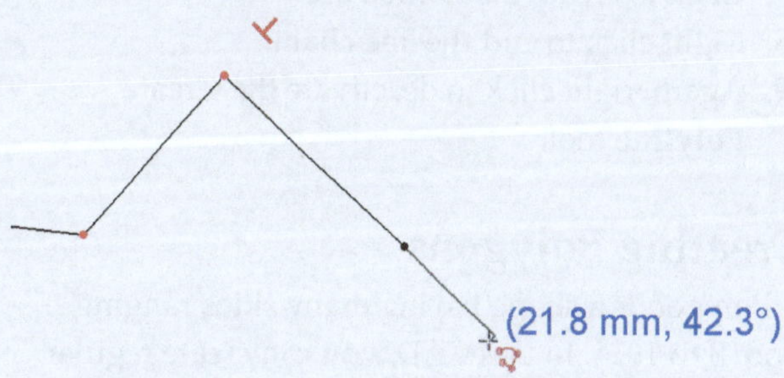

13. Press the **M** key thrice on your keyboard; a grey arc tangent to the previous line appears.

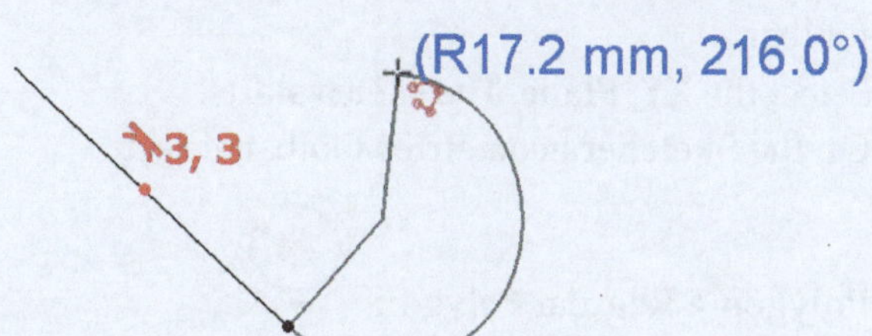

14. Move the pointer and click to create an arc

tangent to the previous line.

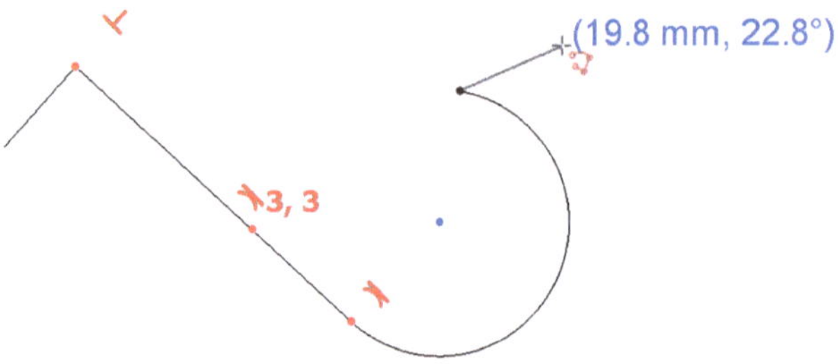

15. Press the **M** key four times to display an arc normal to the previous line.
16. Again, press the **M** key to change the direction of the normal arc.

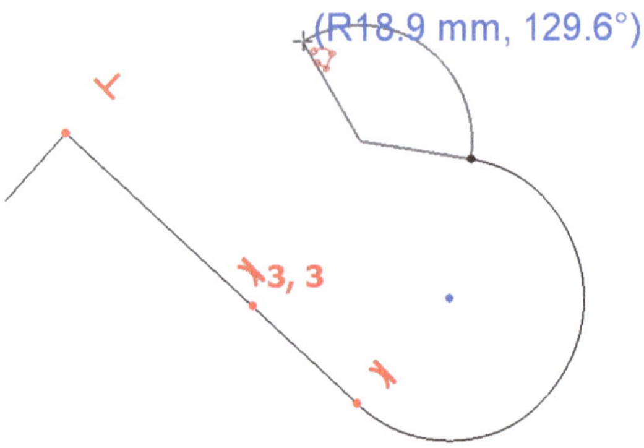

17. Click to create the normal arc.
18. Right click to end the line chain.
19. Again, right click to deactivate the **Create Polyline** tool.

Creating Polygons

A Polygon is a shape having many sides ranging from 3 to 1024. In FreeCAD, you can create regular polygons having sides with equal length. Follow the steps given next to create a polygon.

1. Click the **Create Sketch** icon on the **Sketcher** toolbar.
2. Select the **XY_Plane**. The sketch starts.
3. On the **Sketcher geometries** toolbar, select **Polygon > Regular Polygon** .
4. On the **Create regular polygon** dialog, type **8** in the **Number of Sides** box.
5. Click **OK**.
6. Click to define the center of the polygon.
7. Move the pointer and click to define the size and angle of the polygon.

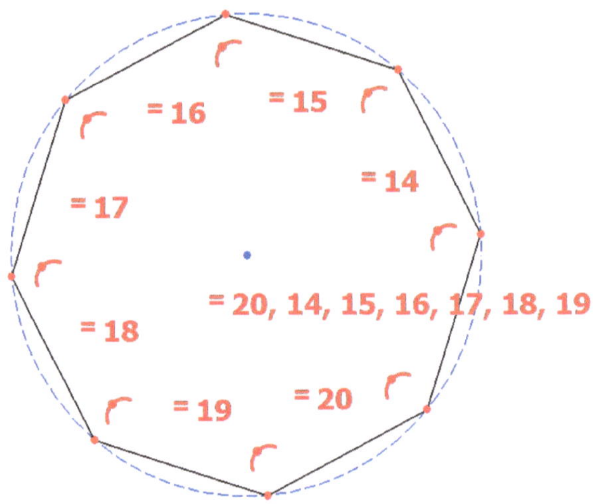

Creating a Slot

The **Create Slot** tool is used to create slots.

1. Click the **Slot** drop-down > **Create Slot**  icon on the **Sketcher geometries** toolbar.
2. Click to specify the centerpoint of the first semicircle.
3. Move the pointer and click to specify the centerpoint of the second semicircle.

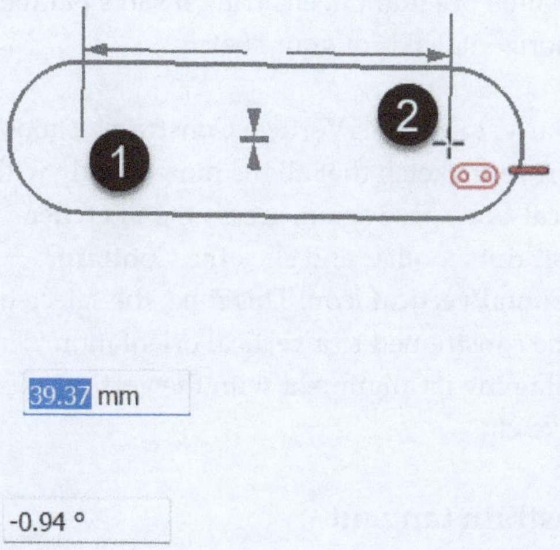

4. Move the pointer outward and click to specify the radius of the arc.

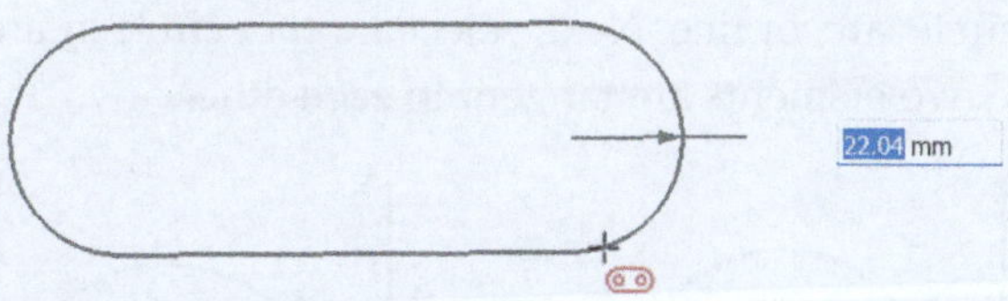

Creating an arc Slot

The **Create arc Slot** tool is used to create slots.

1. Click the **Slot** drop-down > **Create arc Slot** icon on the **Sketcher geometries** toolbar.
2. Click to specify the centerpoint of the arc slot.
3. Move the pointer and click to specify the start point of the arc slot.

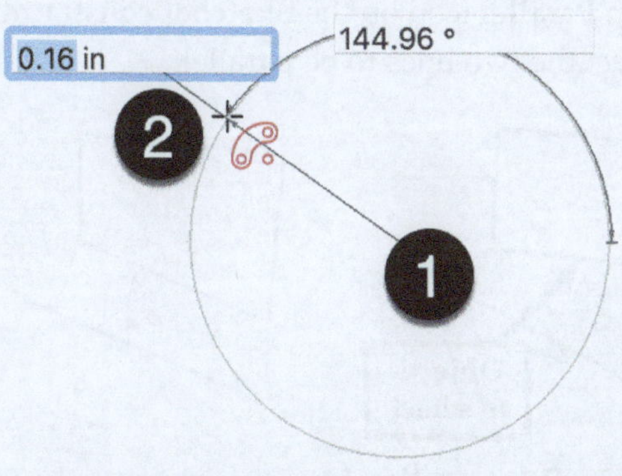

4. Move the pointer and click to specify the endpoint of the arc slot.

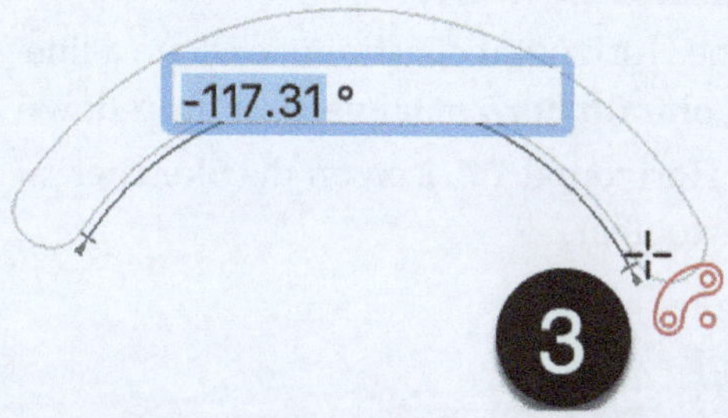

5. Move the pointer and click to specify the width of the arc slot

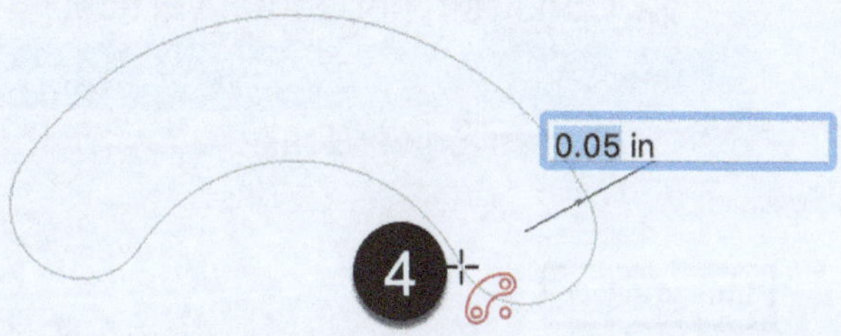

Constraints

Constraints are used to control the shape of a sketch by establishing relationships between the sketch elements. You can add constraints using the tools available on the **Sketcher constraints** toolbar.

Constrain Coincident

This constraint connects a point to another point.

1. On the **Sketcher constraints** toolbar, click  **Constrain Coincident**.
2. Select two points. The selected points are connected.

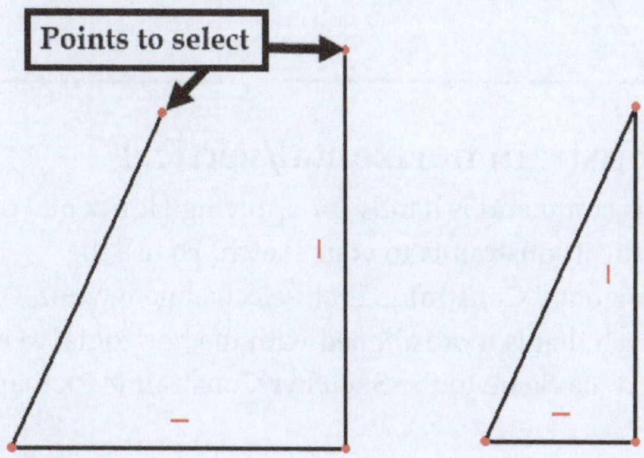

Constrain horizontally

To apply the **Horizontal** constraint, click on a line and click **Contrain horizontal/vertical** drop-down > **Constrain Horizontal** icon on the **Sketcher constraints** toolbar.

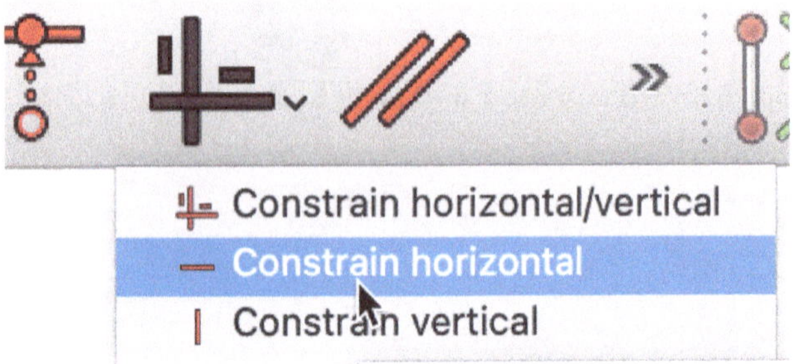

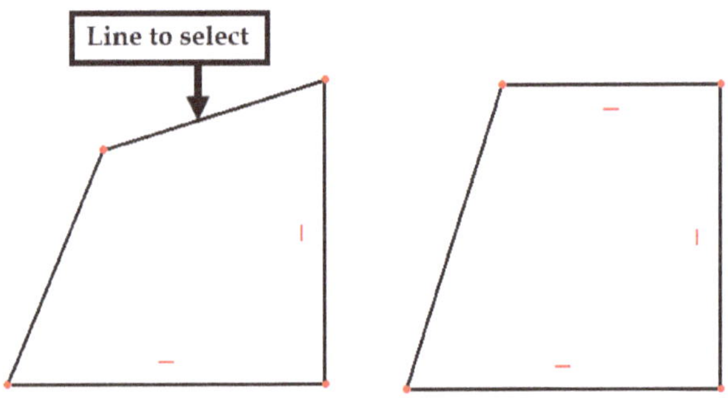

Constrain Vertically

Use the **Constrain Vertical** icon to make a line vertical.

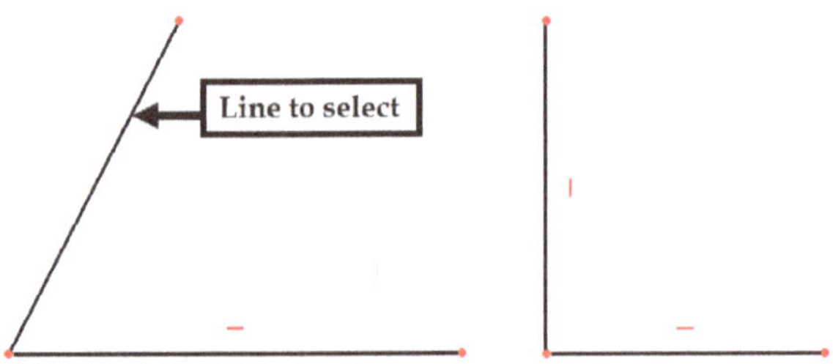

Constrain horizontal/vertical

This command is handy for applying Horizontal or Vertical constraints to your sketch. To use the Horizontal Constraint, first, select a line in your sketch that is more aligned with the horizontal axis. Next, navigate to the **Sketcher Constraints** toolbar and click the **Constrain horizontal/vertical** icon. This action locks the selected line into a horizontal orientation, ensuring it stays parallel to the horizontal axis of your sketch.

Similarly, to apply a Vertical Constraint, choose a line in your sketch that aligns more closely with the vertical axis. Once again, access the **Sketcher Constraints** toolbar and click the **Contrain horizontal/vertical** icon. This time, the selected line will be constrained to a vertical orientation, maintaining its alignment with the vertical axis of the sketch.

Constrain tangent

This constraint makes an arc, circle, or line tangent to another arc or circle. Click the **Constrain Tangent** icon on the **Sketcher constraints** toolbar. Select a circle, arc, or line. Next, select another circle or arc; the two elements are tangent to each other.

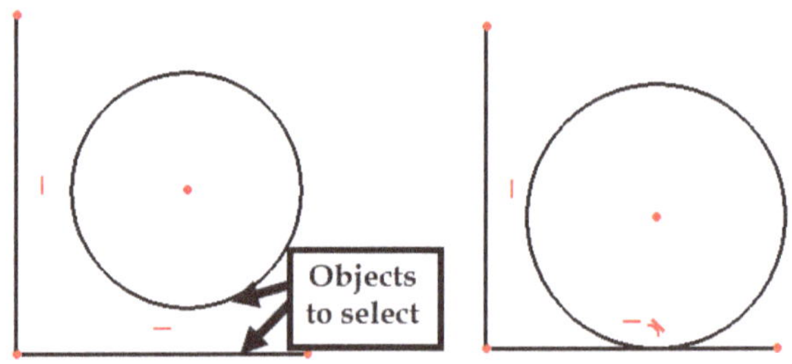

Constrain Parallel

Use the **Constrain Parallel** icon to make two lines parallel to each other. To do this, click the **Constrain Parallel** icon on the **Sketcher constraints**. Next, select the two lines to be parallel.

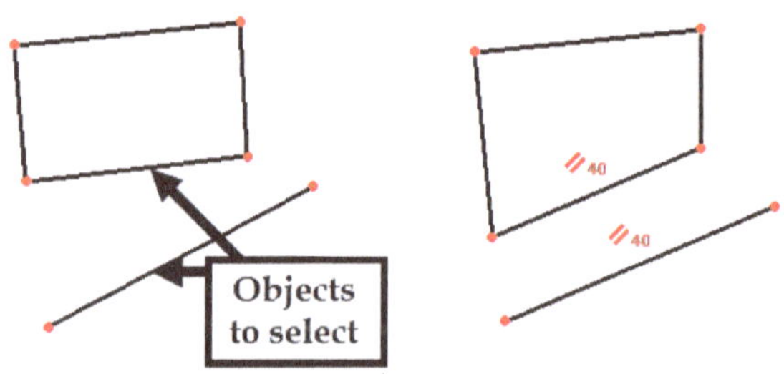

Constrain Perpendicular

Use the **Constrain Perpendicular** icon to make two entities perpendicular to each other.

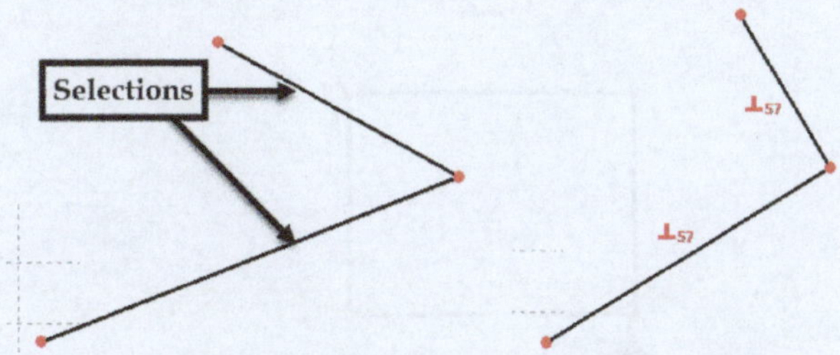

Auto Constraints

FreeCAD automatically adds constraints when you create sketch elements.

1. Start a new sketch and activate the **Create** 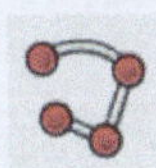 **Polyline** tool from the **Sketcher geometries** toolbar.
2. Click to specify the start point of the line.
3. Move the pointer in the horizontal direction.
4. Click to create a line with the **Horizontal** constraint.

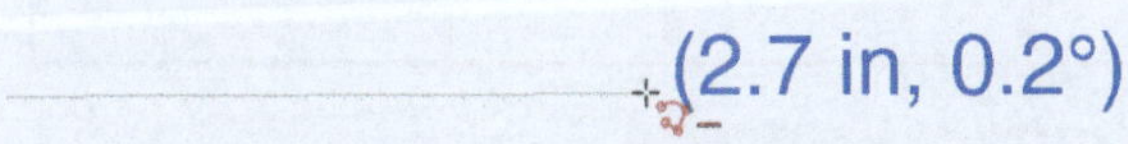

5. Move the pointer vertically in the upward direction .
6. Click to create a line with the **Vertical** constraint.

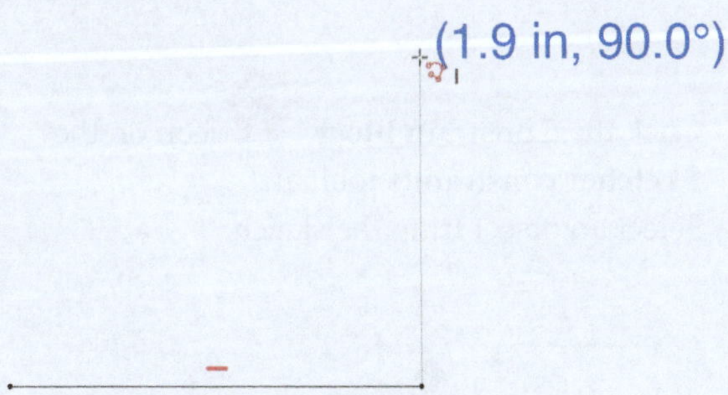

7. Create an inclined line, as shown.

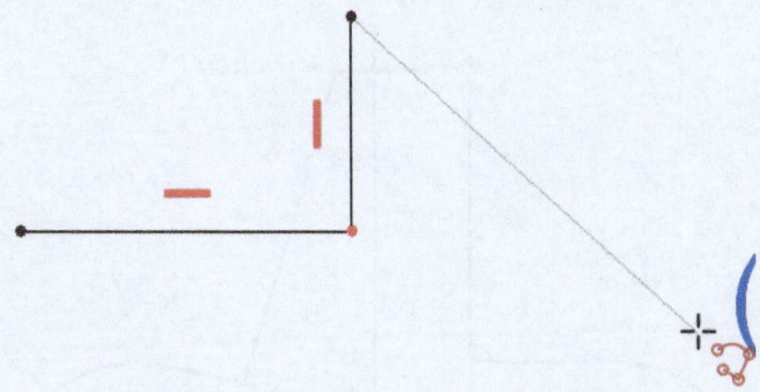

8. Right-click twice to deactivate the tool.

Deleting Constraints

Select the constraint and press **Delete** on your keyboard.

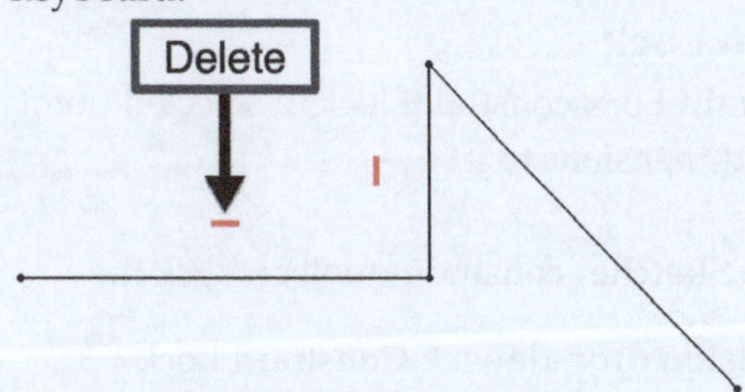

Constrain symmetrical

Use the **Constrain symmetrical** tool to make two sketch elements symmetric about a centerline.

1. Click on the elements to make symmetric.
2. Click on the symmetry line.
3. Click the **Constrain symmetrical** icon on the **Sketcher constraints** toolbar.

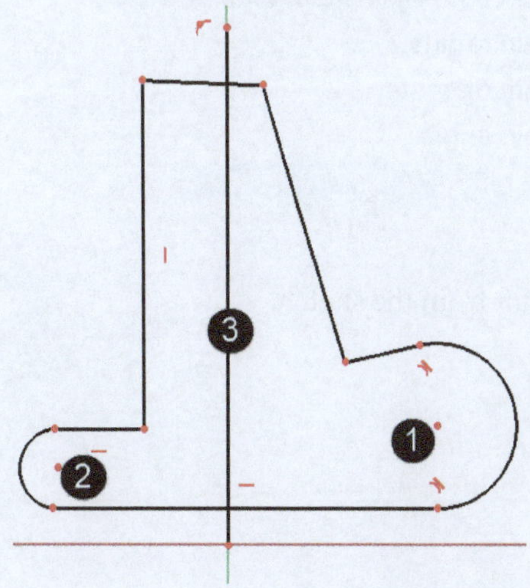

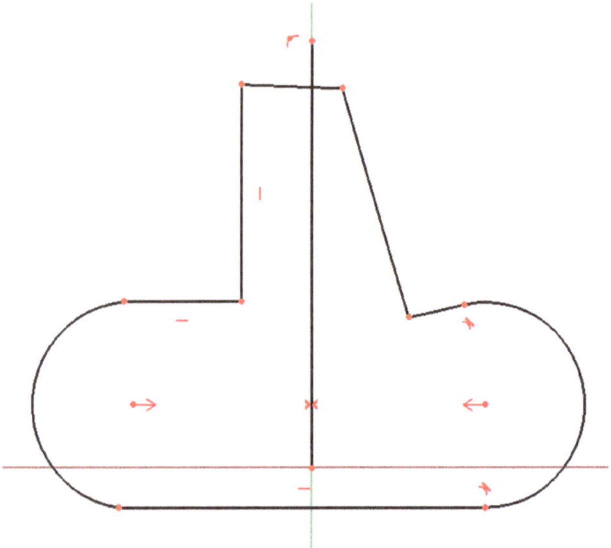

Constrain Lock

The **Constrain Lock** constraint locks a selected point by adding dimensions to it.

1. On the **Sketcher constraint** toolbar, click the **Dimension** drop-down > **Constrain Lock** icon.

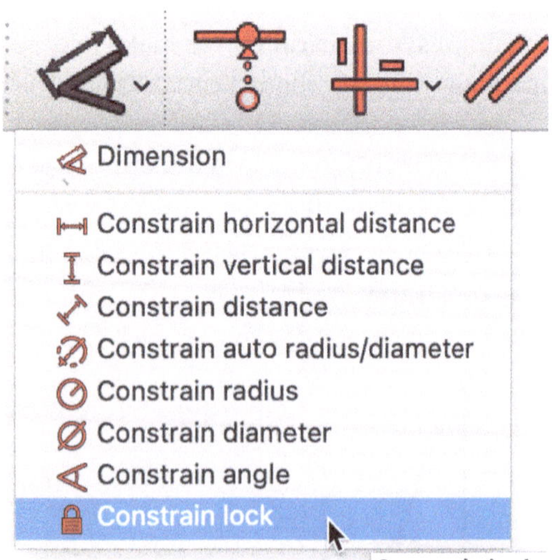

2. Select a point from the sketch.

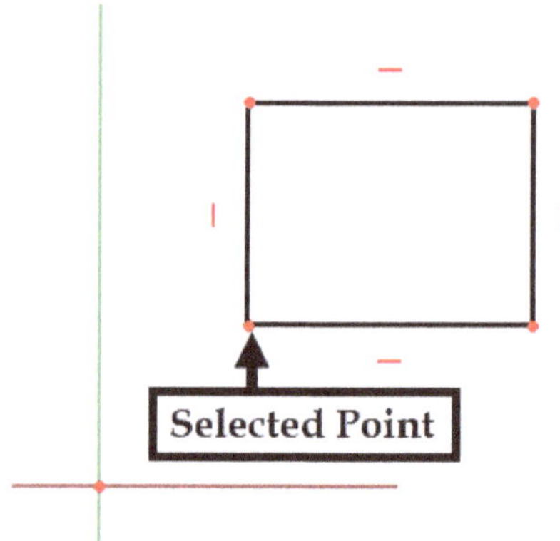

Dimensions are created between the selected point and the origin.

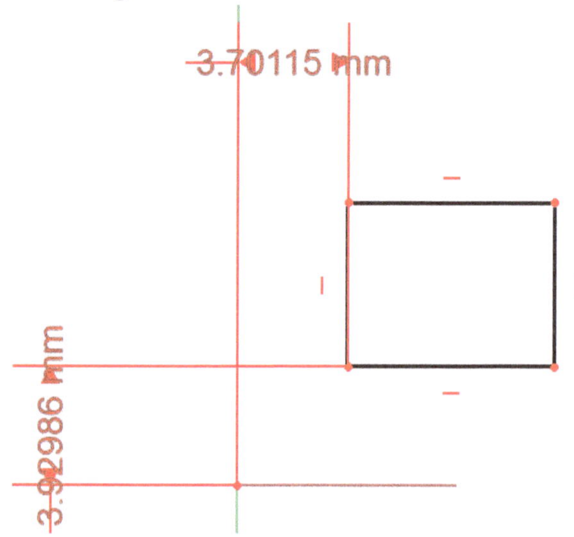

Constrain Block

This constraint fixes the sketch object at its location.

1. Click the **Constrain Block** icon on the **Sketcher constraints** toolbar.
2. Select an object from the sketch.

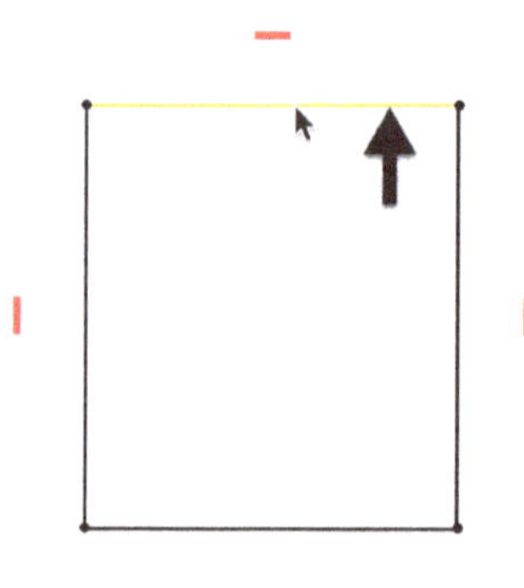

3. Click the object and drag; notice that it is fixed at its location.

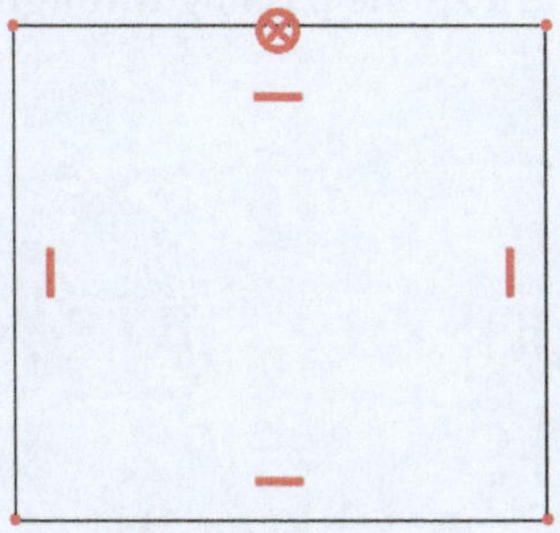

Hiding Constraints

To hide sketch constraints, uncheck the checkbox next to it in the **Constraints** section located in the **Taska** panel.

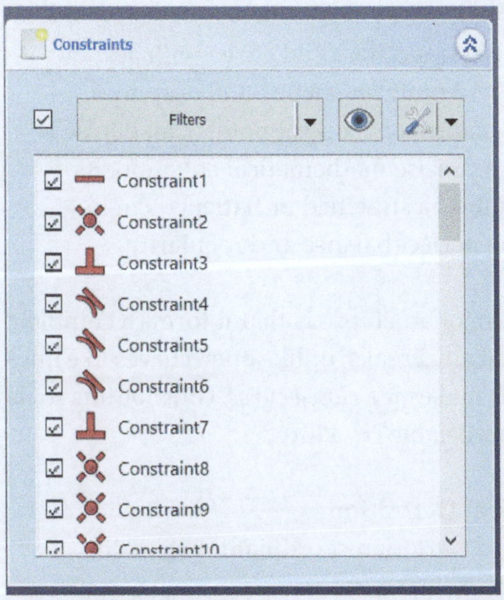

Create B-Spline

A B-spline curve is a smooth curve defined by a set of control points. These control points guide the shape of the curve, acting like reference points that influence its direction. The key advantage of B-splines is their flexibility – they produce smooth curves while allowing precise adjustments by moving the control points. The curve does not necessarily pass through all control points but smoothly follows their general arrangement. This makes B-splines useful for modeling complex shapes with smooth transitions.

1. On the **Sketcher geometries** toolbar, click **B-Spline** drop-down > **B-Spline by control points** 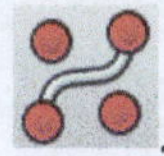.
2. Click to define points in the graphics window.

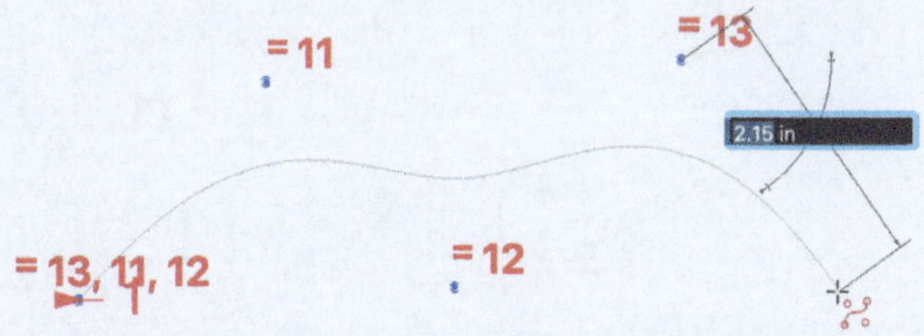

3. Right click to create a spline controlled by the selected points.
4. Press Esc to deactivate this command.

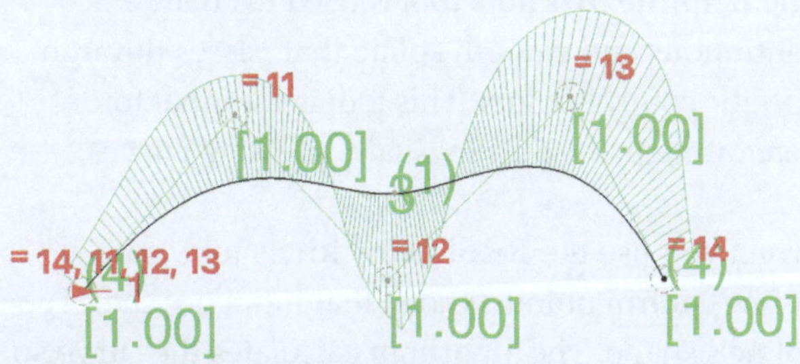

Create periodic B-spline

If you want to create a closed B-spline, then click the **B-spline** drop-down > **Create periodic B-spline** 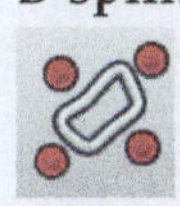 on the **Sketcher geometries** toolbar. Next, specify the control points. Right click to create a closed B-spline.

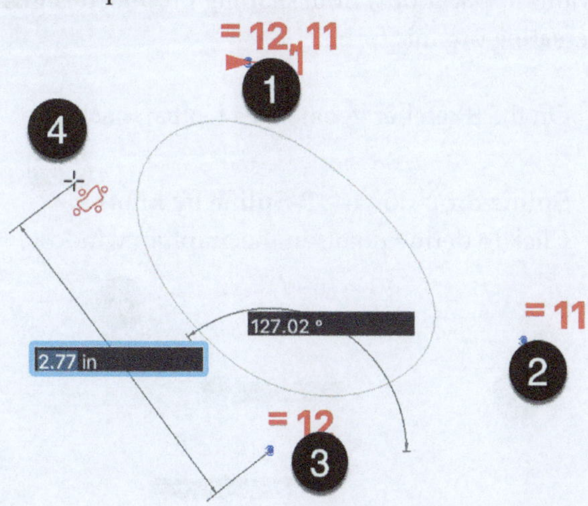

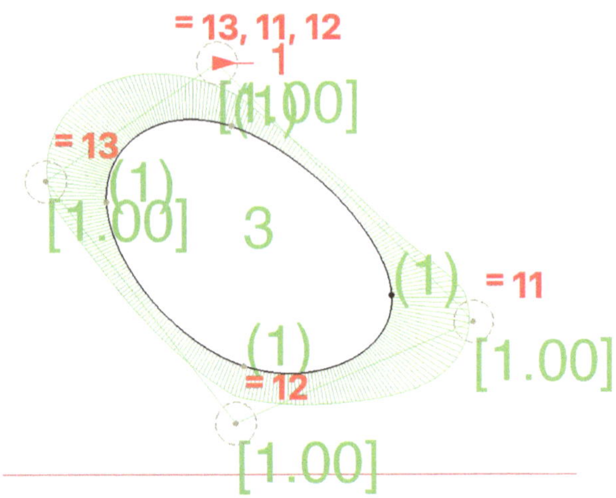

Create B-Spline by knots

The **B-spline by knots** tool is used to create a continuous and smooth spline that passes through specific control points. This tool is essential for generating precise and visually pleasing curves.

When you use the **B-spline by knots** tool, you define control points (knots) that influence the spline's shape. The algorithm calculates the curve so that it smoothly traverses these control points while maintaining smooth transitions between segments.

One key advantage of the B-spline is its flexibility. You can add or adjust control points to fine-tune the curve's shape to meet design requirements accurately. This adaptability makes it useful for various applications, from shaping product designs to creating organic forms.

1. On the **Sketcher geometries** toolbar, click **B-Spline** drop-down > **B-Spline by knots** .
2. Click to define points in the graphics window.

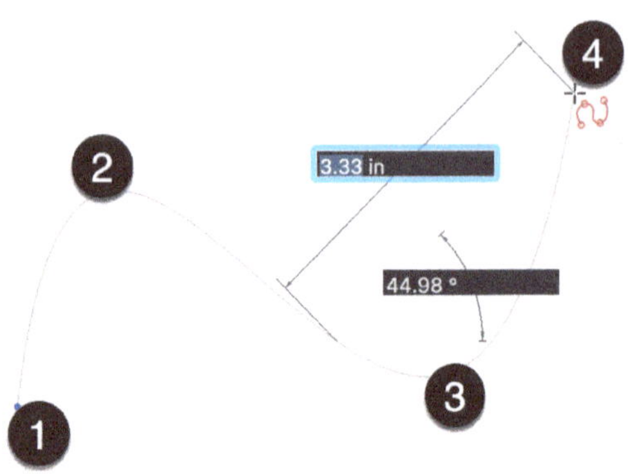

3. Right click to create a spline passing through the selected points.

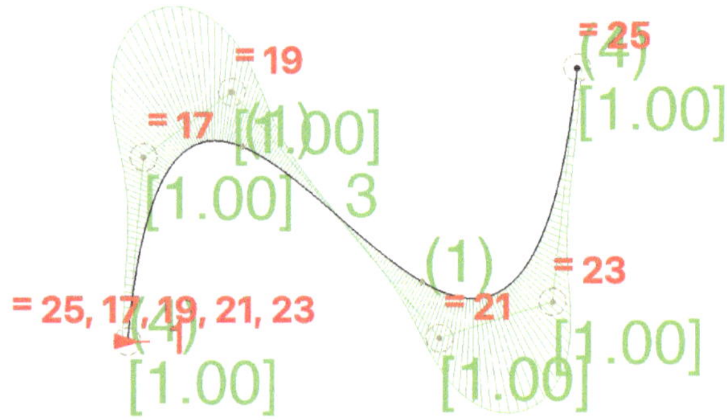

4. Press Esc to deactivate this command.

Ellipses

An ellipse is a smooth, closed curve with a symmetric and uniform shape. Unlike splines (which are made from control points), an ellipse is defined by a precise mathematical equation. Its shape resembles a stretched or flattened circle, maintaining perfect balance and regularity.

A key feature of an ellipse is that it forms a complete loop without any breaks, unlike open curves like lines or arcs. This makes it a *closed curve*, contributing to its neat and predictable structure.

Mathematical Definition

In a standard Cartesian coordinate system, the equation of an ellipse is:

$$\frac{x2}{a2}+\frac{y2}{b2}=1$$

Here:

- **a** = semi-major axis (half of the longest diameter)
- **b** = semi-minor axis (half of the shortest diameter)

These axes determine the ellipse's size and shape, ensuring its symmetry.

1. Click the **Create Sketch** icon on the **Sketcher** toolbar.
2. Select any one of the datum planes from the **Tasks** panel.

3. Click **OK**.
4. On the **Sketcher geometries** toolbar, click **Circle** drop-down > **Create ellipse by center** .

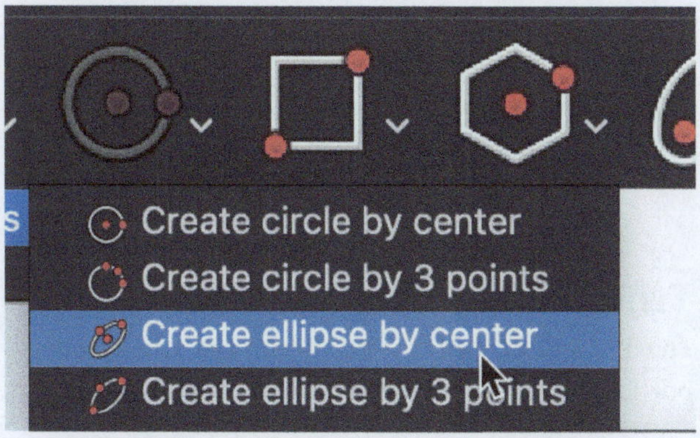

5. Pick a point in the graphics window to define the center of the ellipse.
6. Move the pointer and click to define the radius and orientation of the first axis.

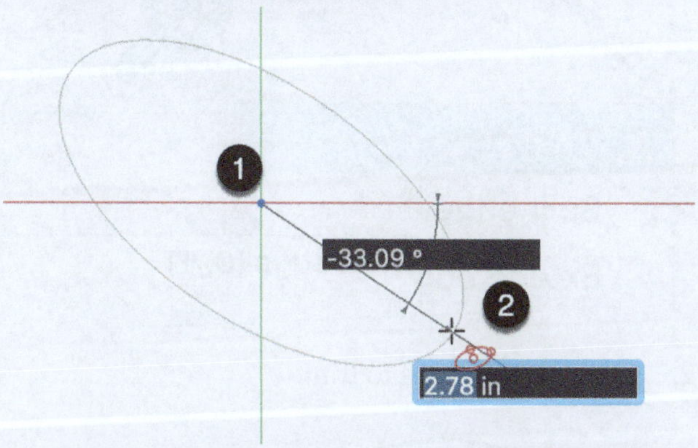

7. Move the pointer and click to define the radius of the second axis.

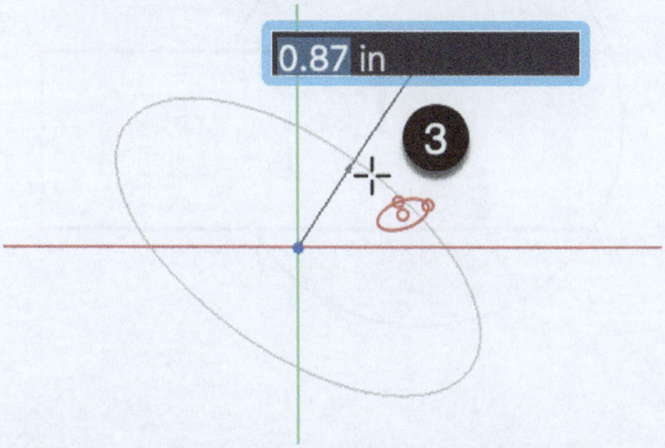

Click and drag the ellipse to notice that it is under-defined. You need to add dimensions and constraints to fully define the ellipse.

8. On the **Sketcher constraints** toolbar, click **Dimension** drop-down > **Constrain angle** 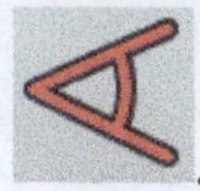.
9. Select the lines, as shown.

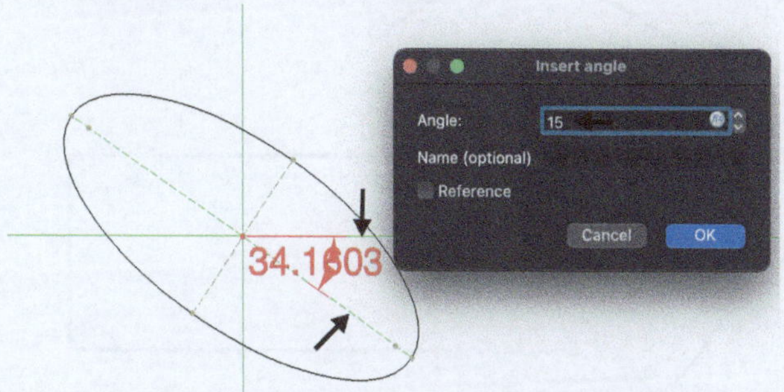

10. Type 15 in the **Angle** box and click **OK**.
11. Click **Dimension** drop-down > **Constrain distance** icon on the **Sketcher constraints** toolbar.
12. Select the major axis line.
13. Type 25 in the **Length** box and click the **OK** button.

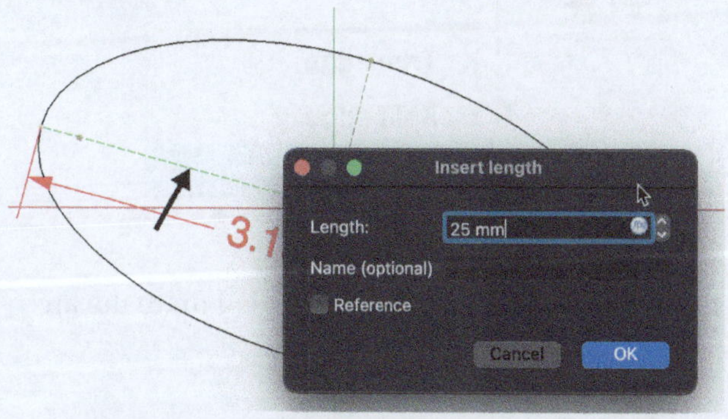

14. Likewise, add the distance constrain to the minor axis. The sketch is fully defined.

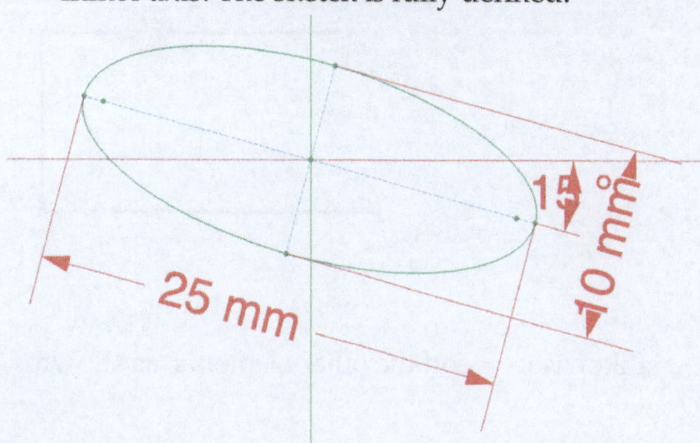

Extend Edge

The **Extend Edge** tool is used to extend lines, arcs, and other open entities to connect to other objects.

1. Create a sketch, as shown below.

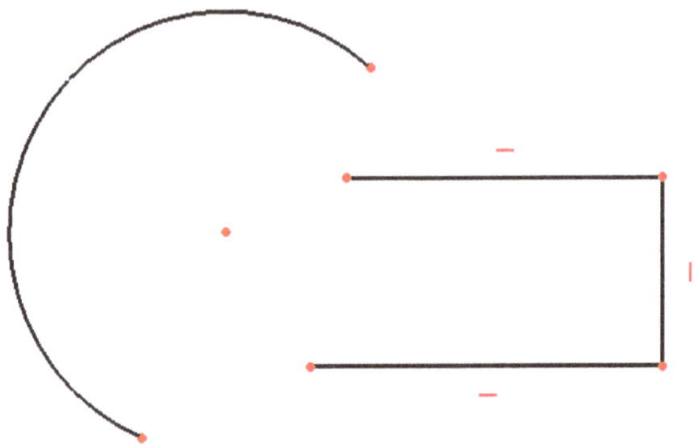

2. Click the **Trim** drop-down > **Extend edge** icon on the **Sketcher geometries** toolbar.

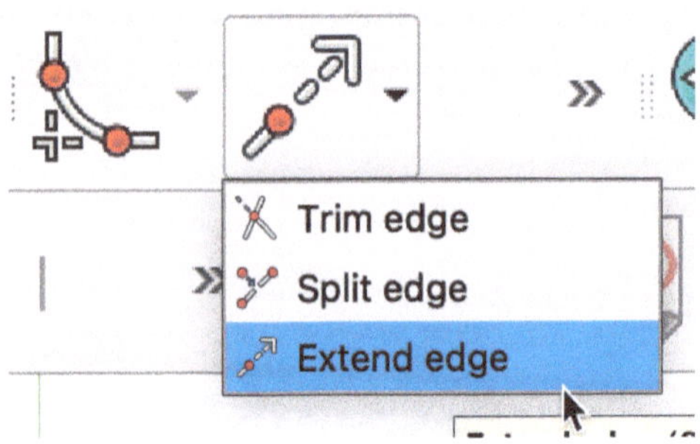

3. Select the horizontal open line.
4. Select the arc; the line is extended up to the arc.

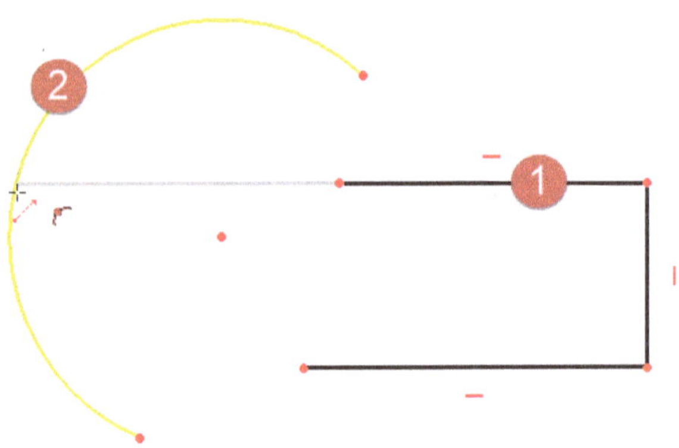

Likewise, extend the other elements, as shown.

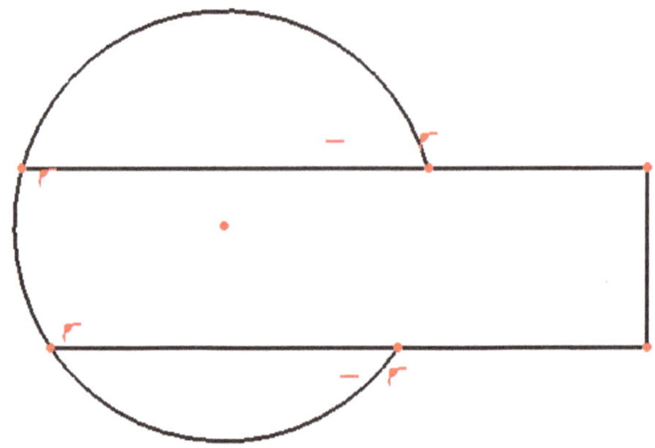

Trim Edge

The **Trim Edge** tool is used to trim the unwanted portions of the sketch using an intersecting edge.

1. Click the **Trim** drop-down > **Trim edge** icon on the **Sketcher tools** toolbar.

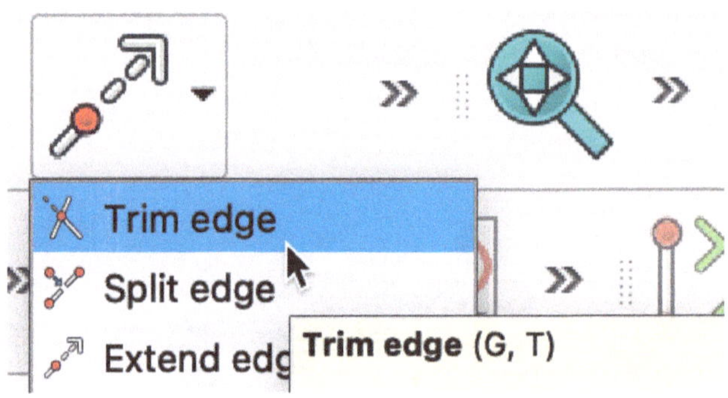

2. Click on the edges to trim.

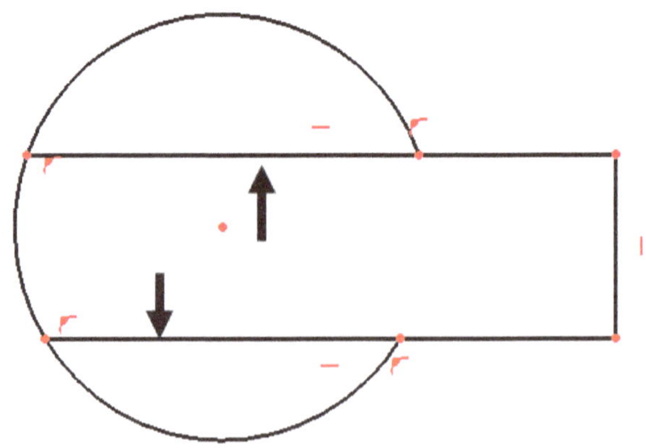

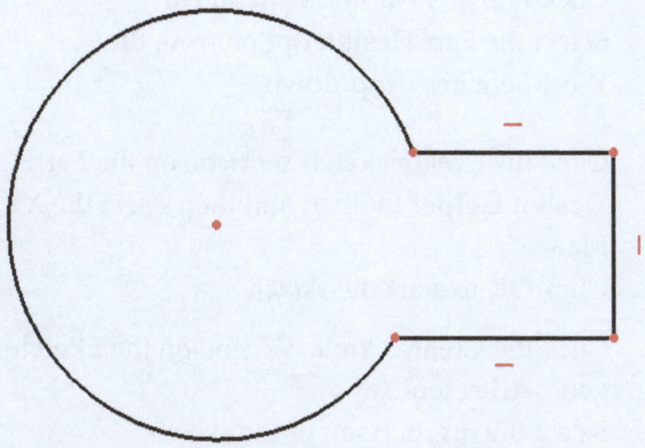

Constrain coincident

This constraint makes a point coincident with a sketch element.

1. Click the **Constrain coincident**  icon on the **Sketcher constraints** toolbar.
2. Select the point and object, as shown.

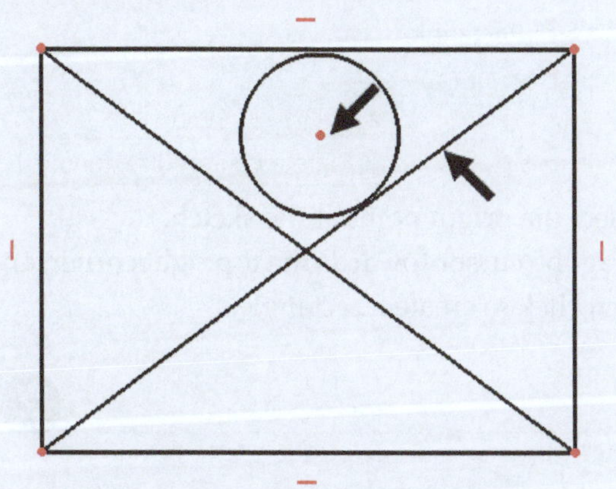

The point is made coincident with the object. Likewise, make the point coincident with another object, as shown.

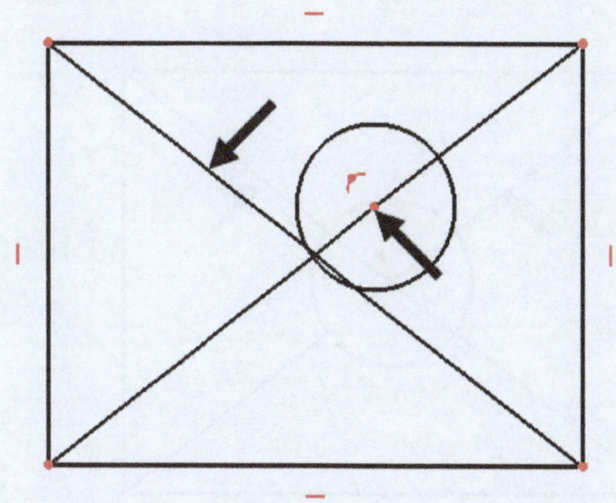

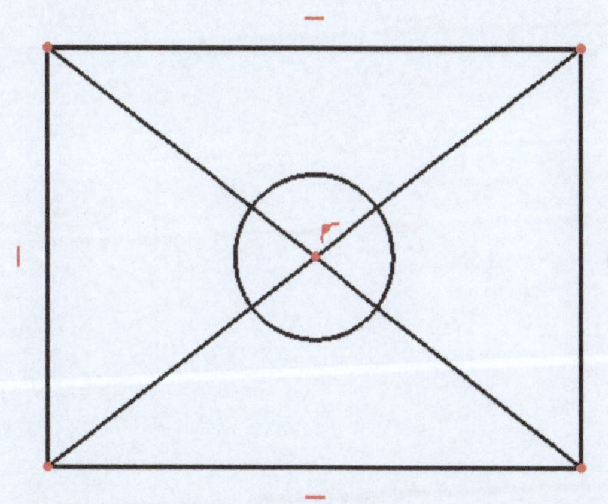

Toggle Construction geometry

This command converts a standard sketch element into a construction element. Construction elements support you to create a sketch of a desired shape and size. To convert a standard sketch element to construction element, click on it and select **Toggle Construction geometry** 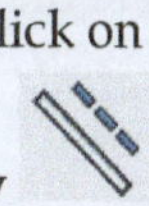 on the **Sketcher geometries** toolbar.

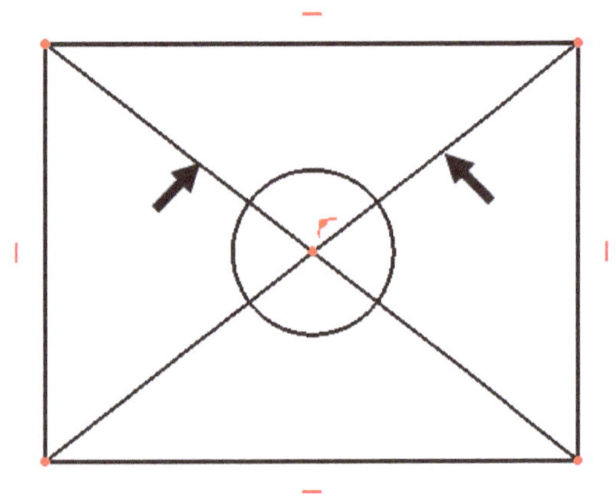

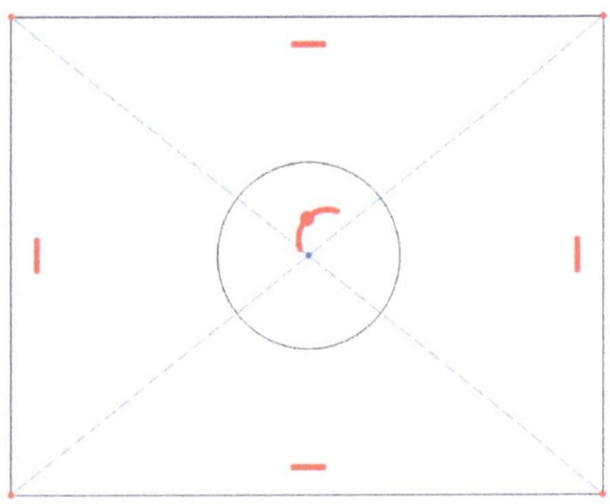

You can also convert it back to a standard sketch element by clicking on it and selecting the **Toggle Construction geometry** icon on the **Sketcher geometries** toolbar.

TUTORIAL 1

In this tutorial, you create the sketch shown in the figure.

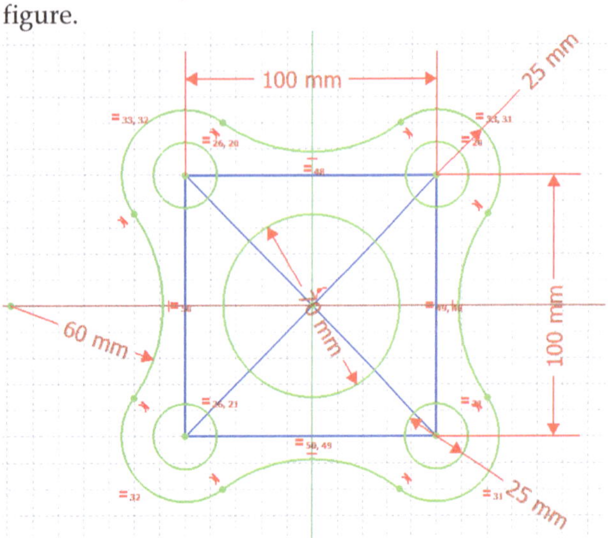

1. Open the FreeCAD application.
2. Click **File > New** on the Menu bar.
3. Select the **Part Design** option from the **Workbenches** drop-down.
4. Click the **Create sketch** icon on the **Part Design Helper** toolbar, and then select the XY Plane.
5. Click **OK** to start the sketch.
6. Click the **Create Circle** icon on the **Sketcher geometries** toolbar.
7. Select the origin point of the sketch.
8. Move the pointer outward and click to create a circle.
9. On the **Sketcher geometries** toolbar, click the **Rectangle** drop-down > **Centered Rectangle** (or) click **Sketch > Sketcher geometries > Create centered rectangle**.

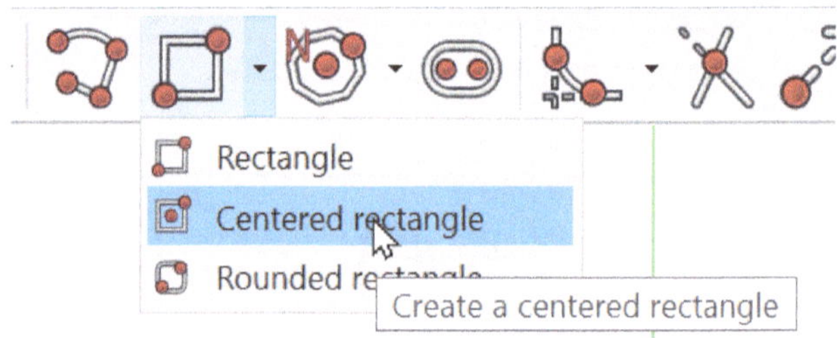

10. Select the origin point of the sketch.
11. Drag the cursor towards the top right corner, and then click to create a rectangle.

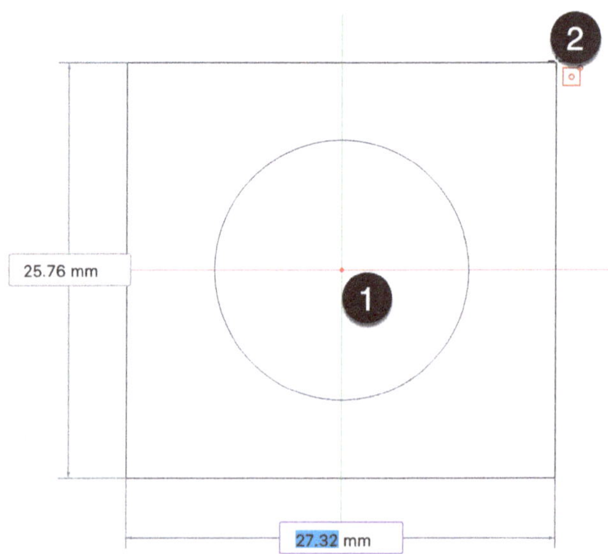

12. Click the **Create Circle** icon on the **Sketcher**

geometries toolbar.

13. Select the top-left corner point of the rectangle.
14. Move the pointer outward and click to create a circle.

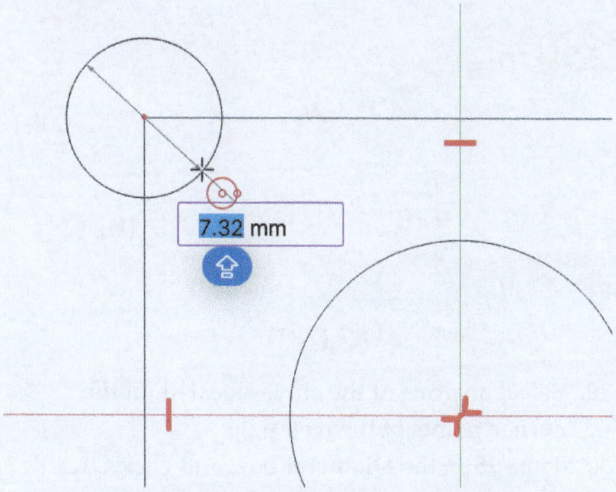

15. Likewise, create three more circles on the remaining corners. Next, press ESC.

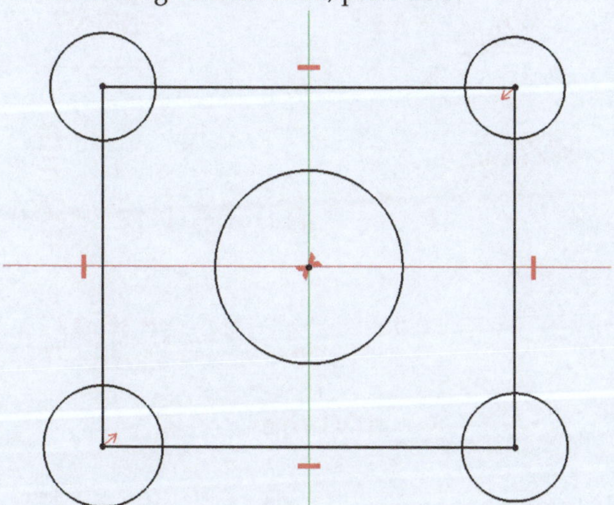

16. Select the edges of the rectangle.
17. Click **Toggle Construction geometry** 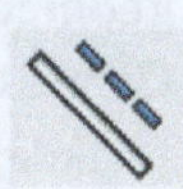 on the **Sketcher geometries** toolbar.

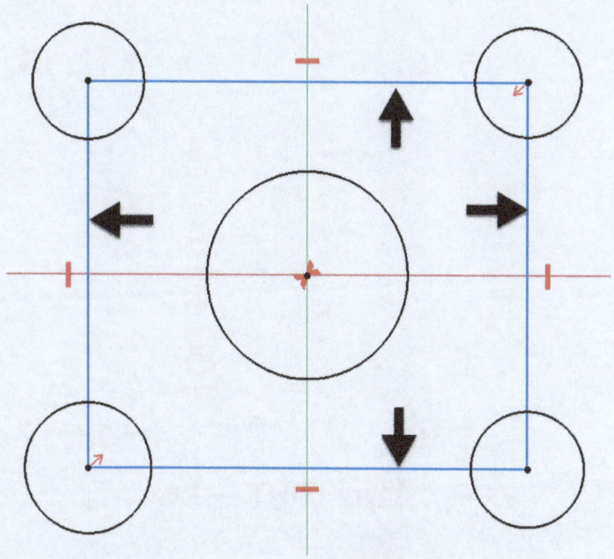

18. Click the **Constrain equal** 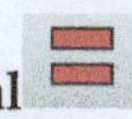 icon on the **Sketcher constraints** toolbar.
19. Select the circles located on the corner points of the rectangle (start from the top-left corner circle).
20. Select the bottom-left and top-left circles; the diameters of the circles are made equal.

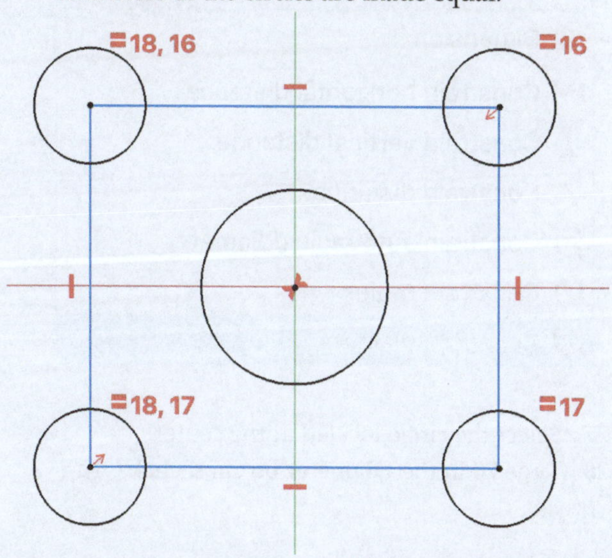

21. Click **Constrain distance** 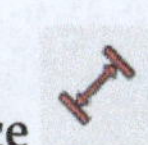 on the **Sketcher constraints** toolbar.
22. Select the vertical line of the rectangle.
23. Type 100 in the **Length** box, and then click **OK**.
24. Select the horizontal line of the rectangle.
25. Type 100 in the **Length** box, and then click **OK**.

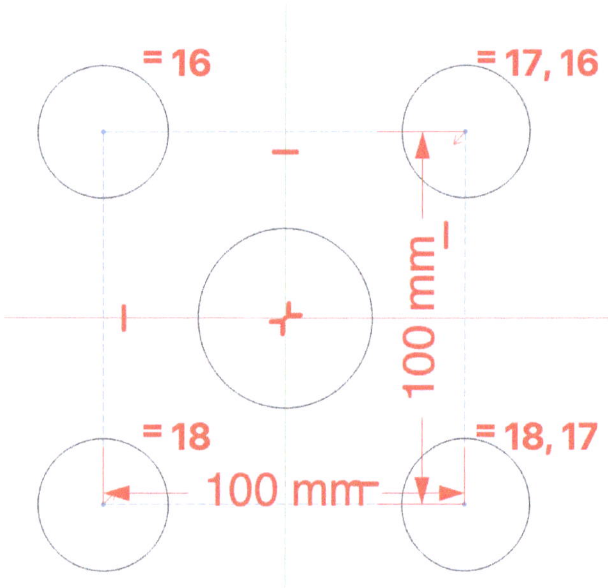

26. Click the **Dimension** drop-down **> Constrain diameter** on the **Sketcher constraints** toolbar.

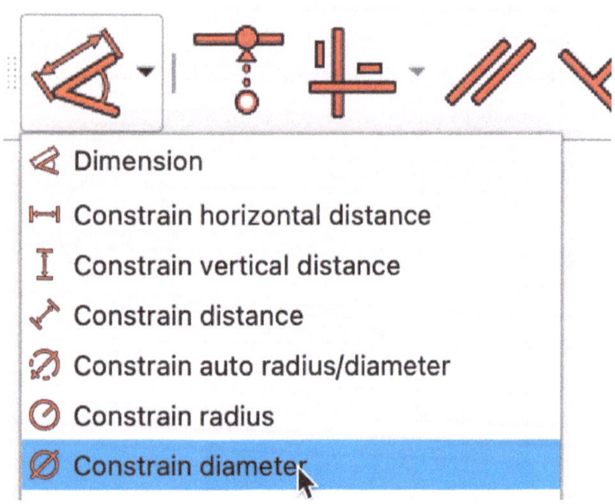

27. Select the circle located at the center.
28. Type **70** in the **Diameter** box and click **OK**.

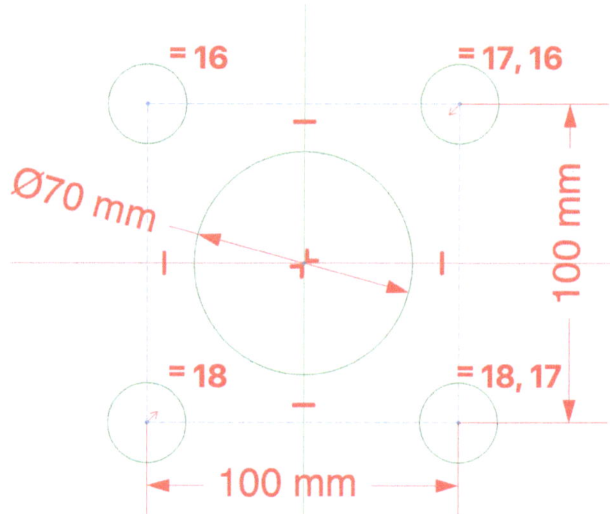

29. Select any one of the circles located on the corner points of the rectangle.
30. Type **25** in the **Diameter** box, and click **OK**.

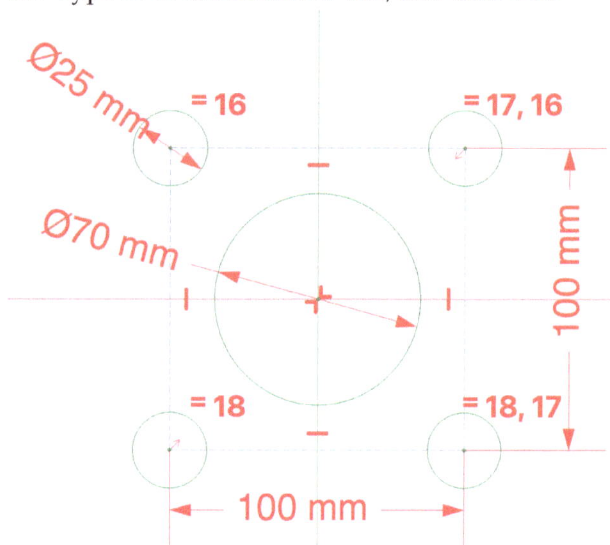

31. Click the **Create Circle** icon on the **Sketcher geometries** toolbar.
32. Create circles on the corner points of the rectangle, as shown.

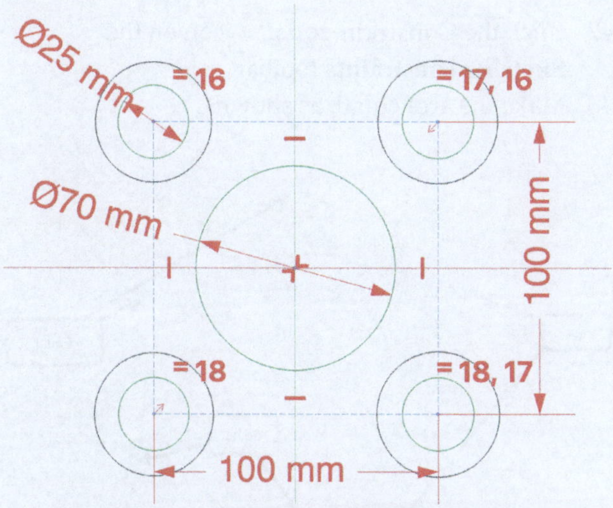

33. Click the **Constrain equal** icon on the **Sketcher constraints** toolbar.
34. Select the bottom-left and top-left circles; the diameters of the circles are made equal.
35. Select the bottom-left and bottom-right circles.
36. Select the bottom-right and top-right circles.

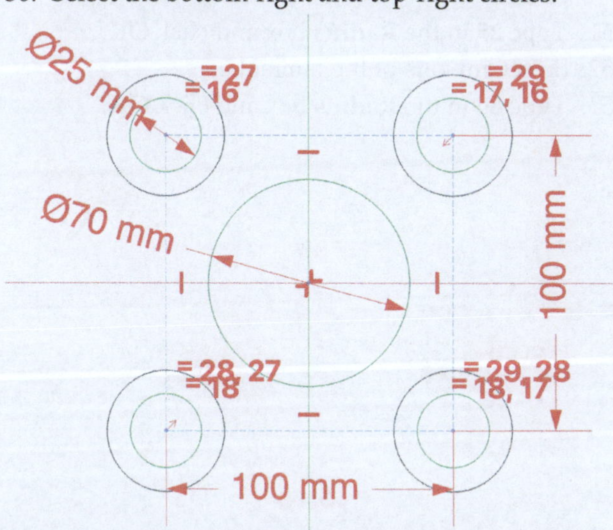

37. Click **Arc** drop-down **> Create arc by 3 points** on the **Sketcher geometries** toolbar.

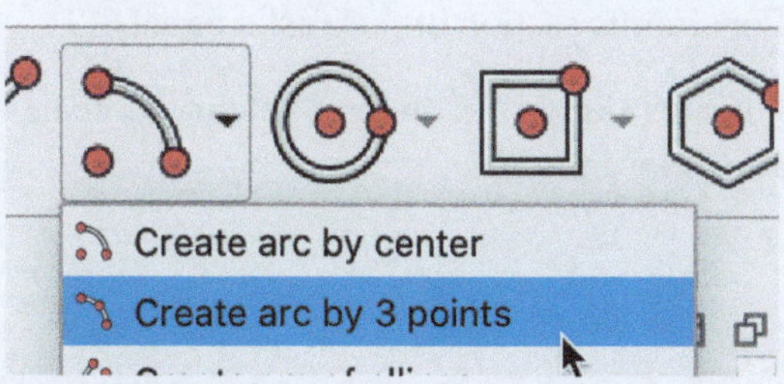

38. Select the outer circle located on the top-left corner.
39. Select the outer circle located on the bottom-left corner.

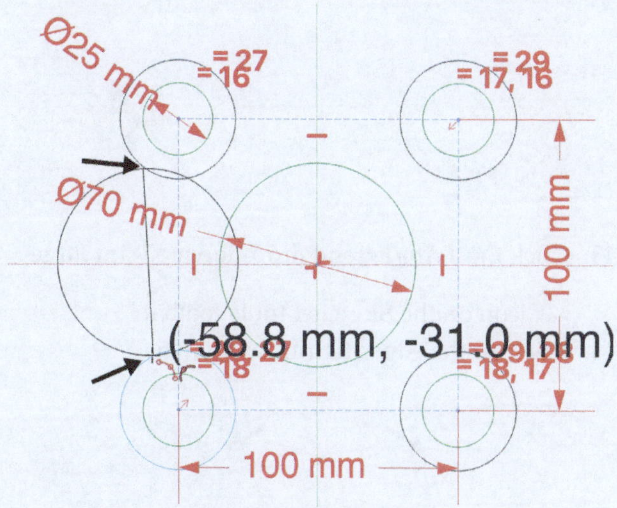

40. Move the pointer toward the right and click to create an arc.

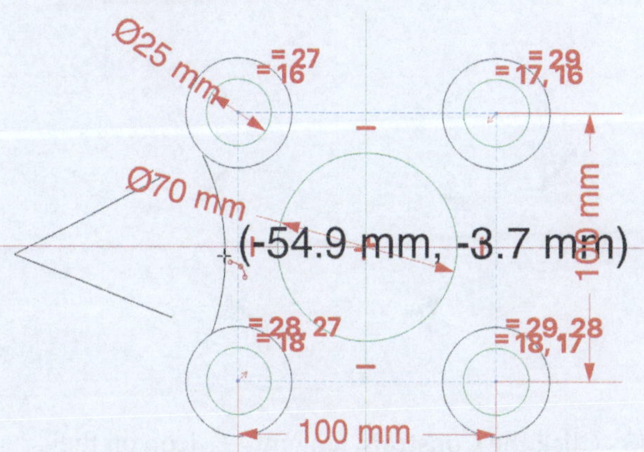

41. Likewise, create three more arcs, as shown.

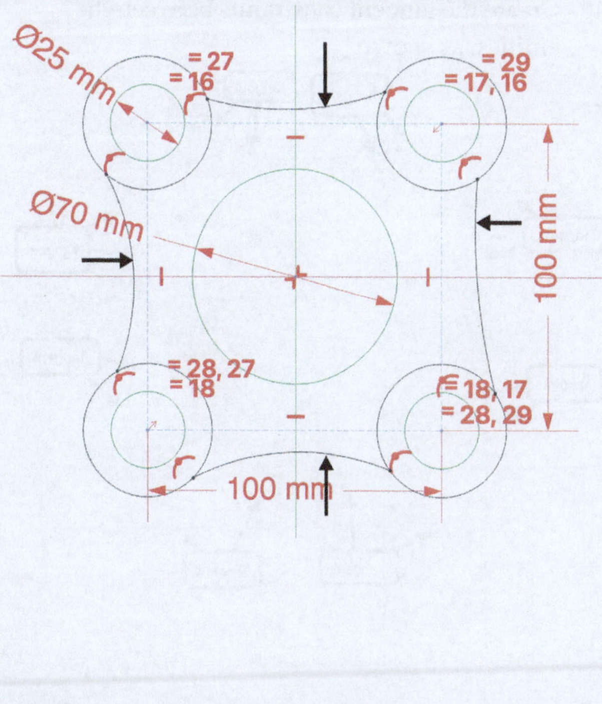

42. Click the **Show/hide all constraints** button on the Constraints section of the **Tasks** panel.

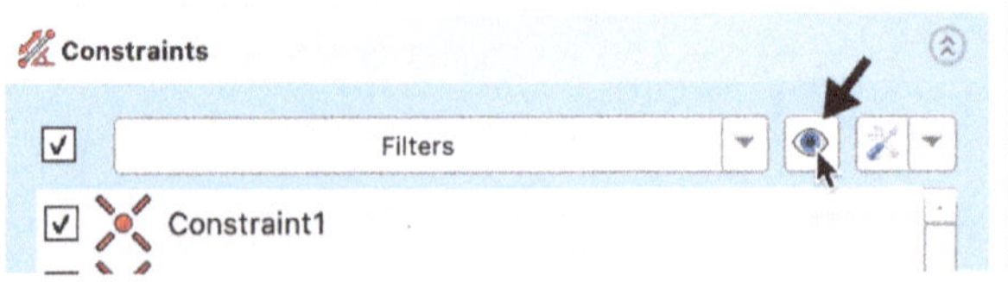

43. Click the **Trim/Extend** drop-down >**Trim Edge** icon on the **Sketcher tools** toolbar.
44. Click on the edges to trim, as shown.

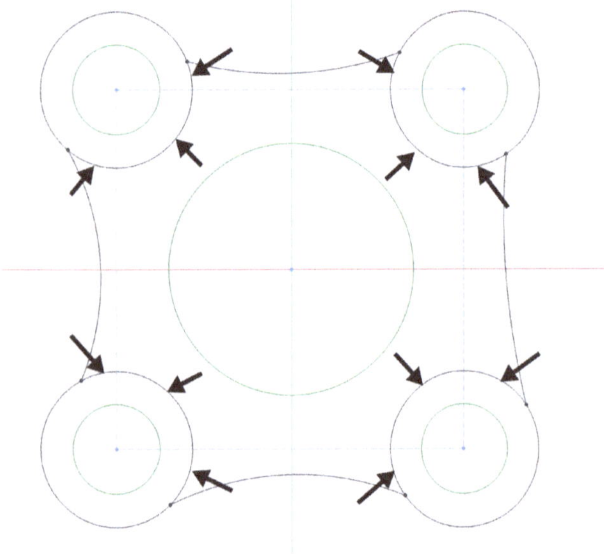

45. Click the **Constrain tangent** icon on the **Sketcher constraints** toolbar.
46. Create the tangent constraints between the entities, as shown.

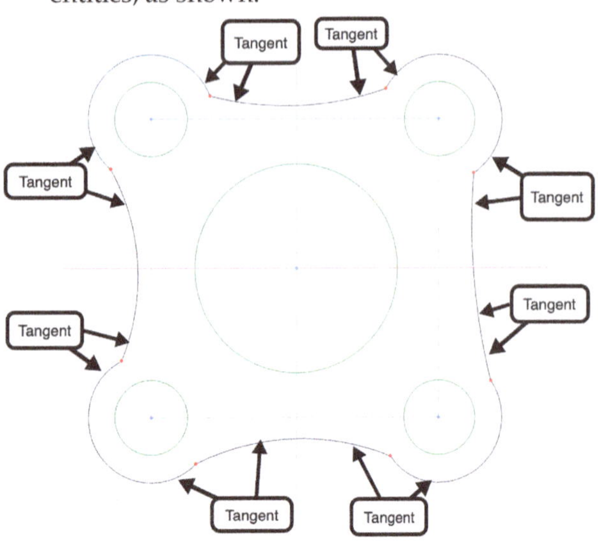

47. Click the **Constrain equal** icon on the **Sketcher constraints** toolbar.
48. Make the arcs equal, as shown.

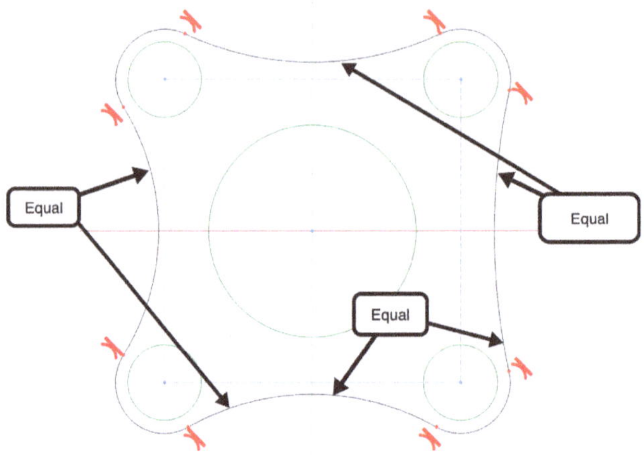

49. Click the **Dimension** drop-down. > **Constrain radius** icon on the **Sketcher constraints** toolbar.
50. Select any one of the arcs concentric to the circles.
51. Type **25** in the **Radius** box and click **OK**.
52. Select any one of the tangent arcs.
53. Type **60** in the **Radius** box and click **OK**.

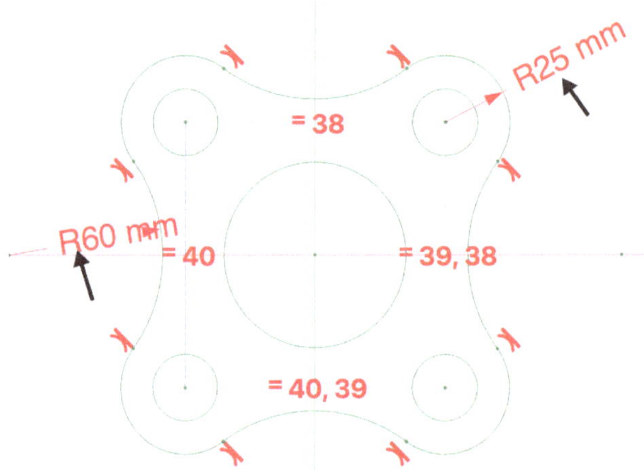

54. Click the **Show/hide all constraints** button on the Constraints section of the **Tasks** panel.
55. Click **Leave Sketch** on the **Sketcher** toolbar.
56. Save and close the file.

Chapter 5: Additional Modeling Tools

In this chapter, you create models using additional modeling tools. You learn to:

- Create slots
- Create circular patterns
- Create holes
- Create chamfers
- Create shells
- Create coils
- Create a loft feature
- Create a sweep feature

TUTORIAL 1

In this tutorial, you create the model shown in the figure:

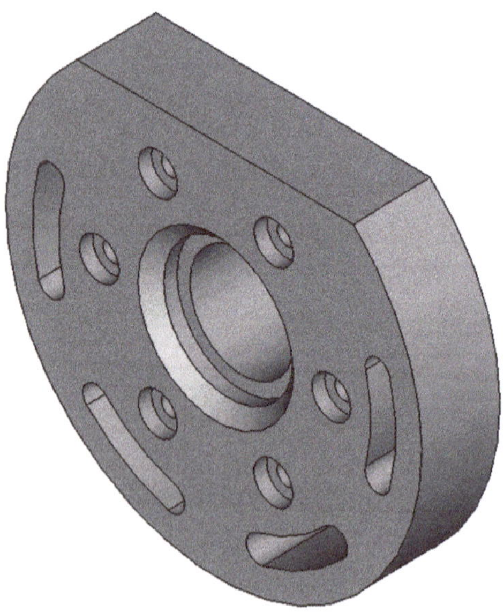

Creating the First Feature

1. Open the FreeCAD application.
2. Click **File > New** on the Menu bar.
3. Select the **Part Design** option from the **Workbenches** drop-down.
4. Click **Edit > Preferences** on the Menu bar.

   The **Preferences** dialog box appears. If you are working on MacOS, then click **FreeCAD > Preferences** on the title bar.
5. Click the **General** > **General** on the left-side of the **Preferences** dialog.
6. Select **Default unit system > Imperial decimal**.
7. Type **3** in the **Number of decimals** box.
8. Check the **Ignore project unit system and use default** option.
9. Click **OK**.
10. Click the **Create sketch** icon on the **Part Design Helper** toolbar, and then select the XZ Plane.
11. Deactivate the **Toggle Construction geometry** icon on the **Sketcher geometries** toolbar.
12. Click the **Create Circle** icon on the **Sketcher geometries** toolbar.
13. Select the origin point of the sketch.
14. Move the pointer outward and click to create a circle.

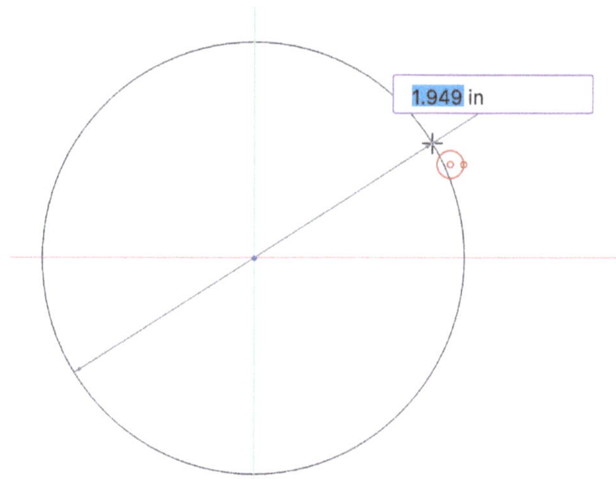

15. Click the **Create Line** icon on the **Sketcher geometries** toolbar.
16. Specify a point at the location outside the circle, as shown.

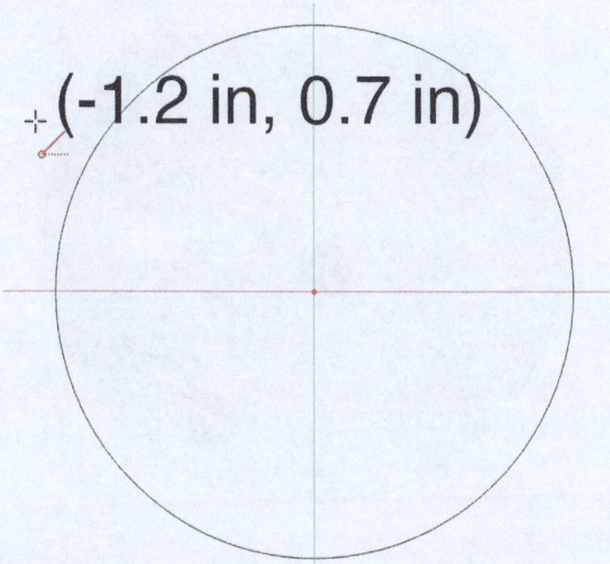

17. Move the pointer horizontally and notice the Horizontal constraint symbol.
18. Click outside the circle – Press Esc to deactivate the **Create Line** tool.

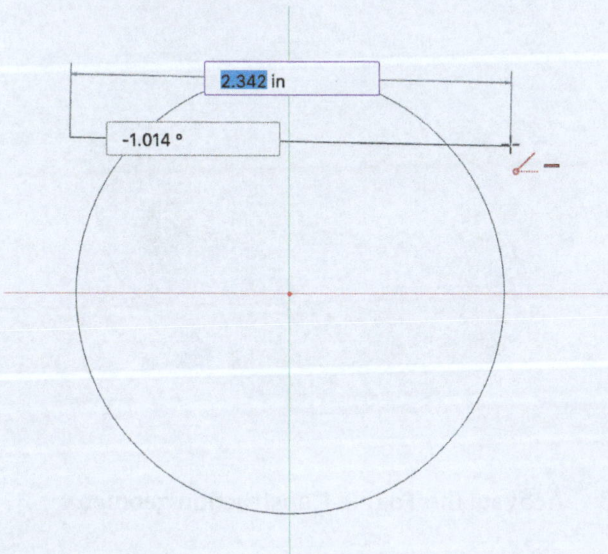

19. Click the **Trim/Extend** drop-down > **Trim Edge** icon on the **Sketcher tools** toolbar.
20. Click on the portions of the sketch to be trimmed, as shown below.

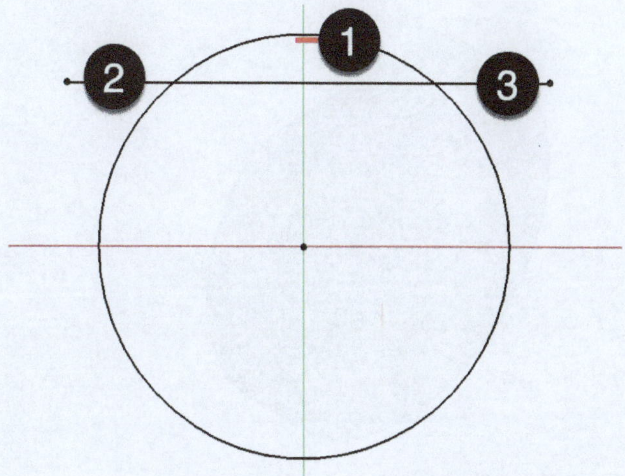

21. Add the **Radius** and **Horizontal Distance** constraints to the sketch.

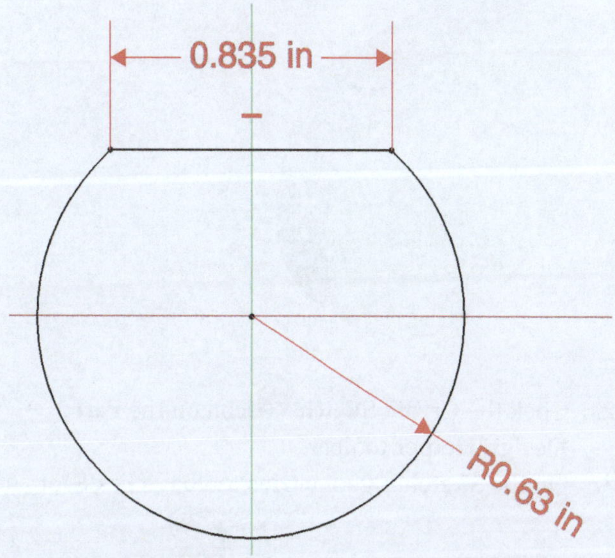

22. Click the **Close** button on the **Tasks** panel.
23. Click the **Pad** icon on the **Part Design Modeling** toolbar.
24. Type **0.236** inches in the **Length** box and click **OK**.

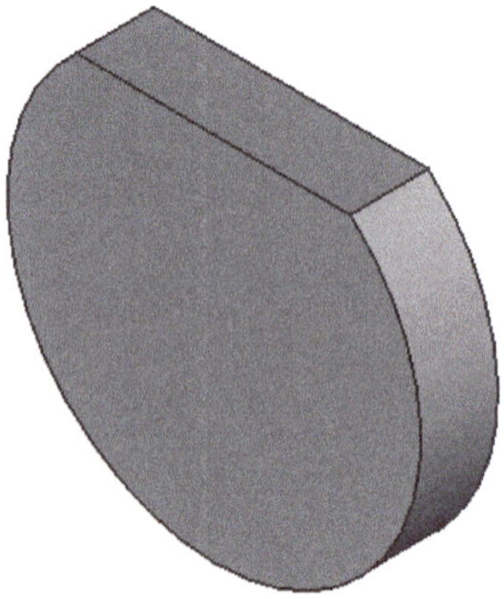

Creating the Pocket feature

1. Click on the front face of the model.

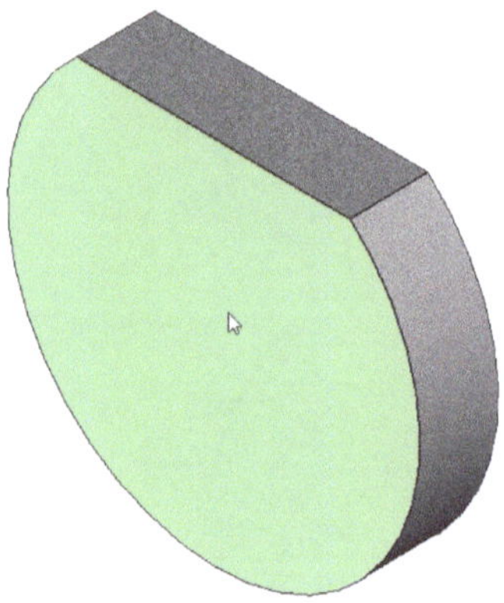

2. Click the **Create Sketch** icon on the **Part Design Helper** toolbar.
3. On the **Sketcher geometries** toolbar, click **Slot drop-down > Create arc slot** .
4. Select the origin as the center point.
5. Move the cursor outside and click in the first quadrant of the circle to specify the start point of the arc slot.
6. Move the cursor and click in the fourth quadrant of the circle to specify the endpoint of the arc slot.

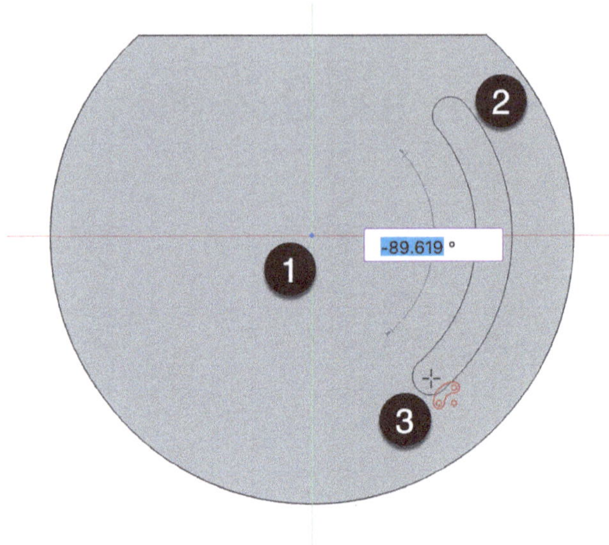

7. Move the pointer and click to specify the slot width.

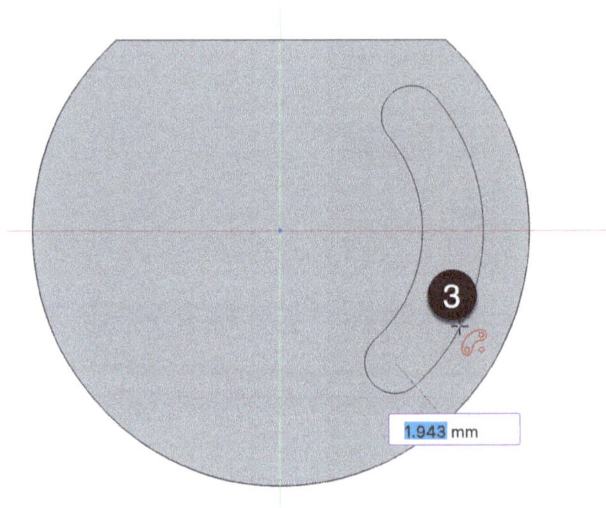

8. Activate the **Toggle Construction geometry** icon on the **Sketcher geometries** toolbar; This will turn on construction mode and switch the color of the icons to blue. Any new geometry you make will be in construction mode.
9. Click the **Create Line** icon on the **Sketcher geometries** toolbar.
10. Select the origin point of the sketch.
11. Select the centerpoint of the small arc.

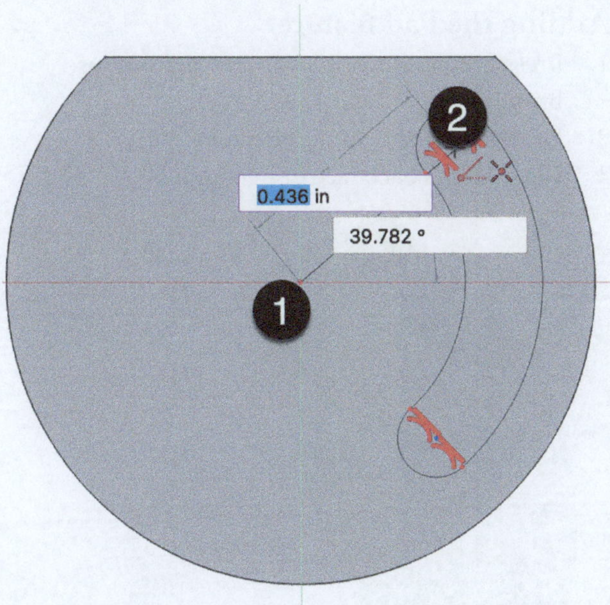

12. Likewise, create a line by selecting the origin and center point of another small arc.

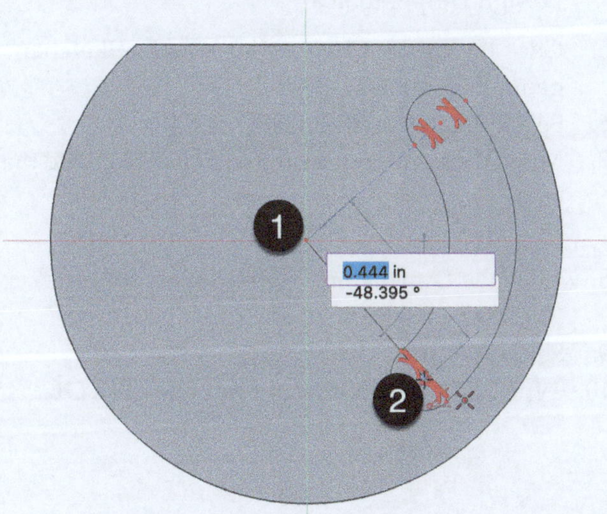

13. Use the **Constrain Coincident** tool and connect the endpoint of the line and the center point of the small arc, if not correctly connected.
14. Click the **Toggle construction geometry** 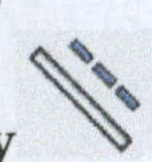 icon on the **Sketcher geometries** toolbar; the construction mode is turned OFF.
15. Click the **Dimension** icon on the **Sketcher constraints** toolbar.
16. Select any one of the lines.
17. Type 0.512 in the **Length** box and click **OK**.

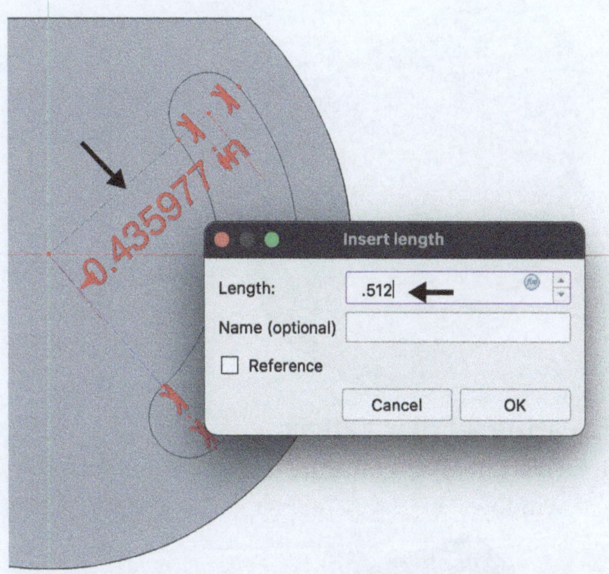

18. Select any one of the small arcs.
19. Type 0.039 in the **Radius** box, and then click **OK**.
20. Select the two construction lines.
21. Type **30** in the **Angle** box, and then click **OK**.
22. Select the horizontal axis of the sketch and anyone of the lines.
23. Type **15** in the **Angle** box, and then click **OK**.

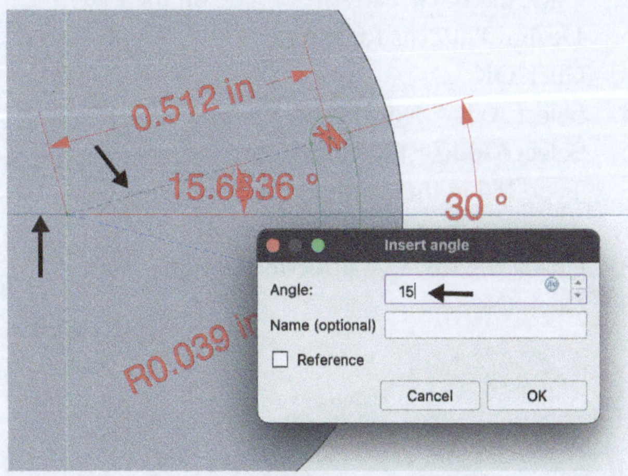

24. Click **Close** on the **Tasks** panel.
25. Click the **Pocket**  icon on the **Part Design Modeling** toolbar.
26. Select **Type > Through All** from the **Pocket Parameters** dialog.
27. Click **OK**.

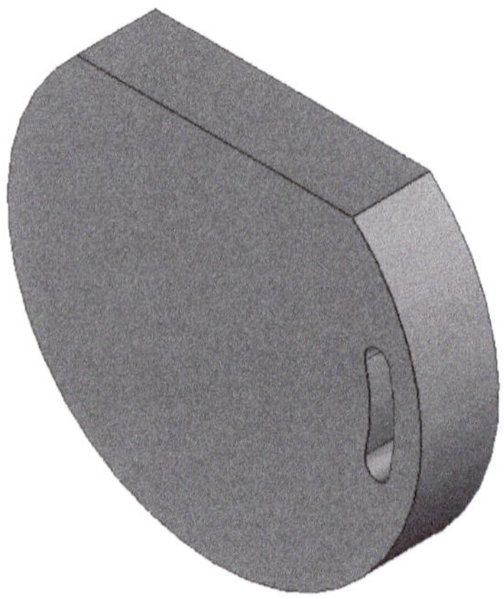

Creating a Polar Pattern

1. Select the Pocket feature from the graphics window.

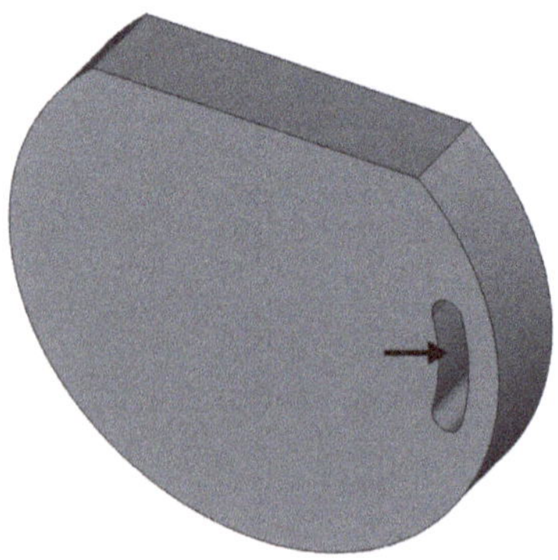

2. Click the **Polar Pattern** icon on the **Part Design Patterns** toolbar.
3. Click **OK**.
4. Select **Axis > Normal sketch axis**.
5. Select **Mode > Overall Angle**.
6. Type **180** in the **Angle** box.
7. Type **4** in the **Occurrences** box.
8. Check the **Reverse direction** option.
9. Click **OK**.

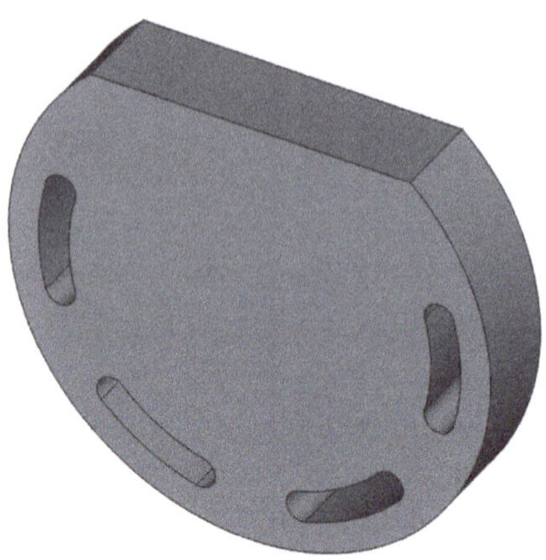

Adding the Pad feature

1. Press and hold the middle and right mouse button.
2. Drag the pointer to rotate the model.
3. Click on the back face of the model.

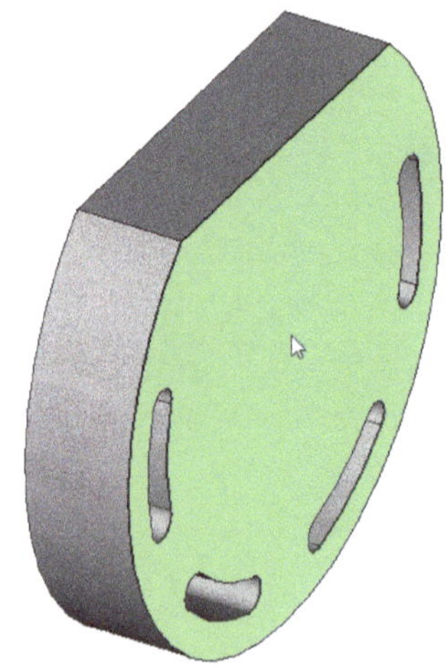

4. Click the **Create Sketch** icon on the **Part Design Helper** toolbar.
5. Click the **Create Circle** icon on the **Sketcher geometries** toolbar.
6. Select the sketch origin.
7. Move the pointer outward and click to create the circle.
8. Click the **Dimension** icon on the **Sketcher constraints** toolbar.
9. Select the circle.
10. Type **0.472** in the **Diameter** box and click **OK**.

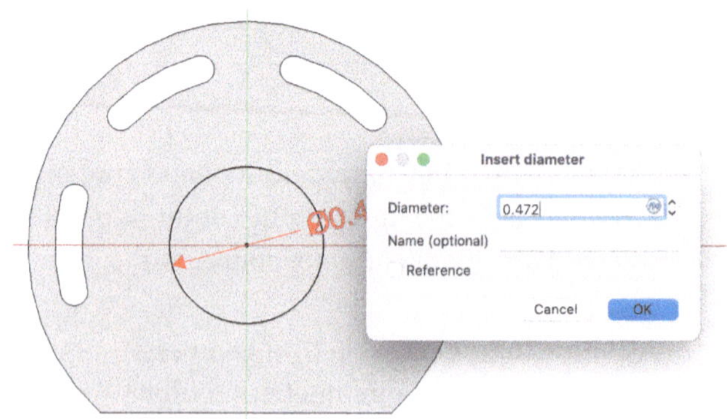

11. Click **Close** on the **Tasks** panel.
12. Click the **Pad** icon on the **Part Design Modeling** toolbar.

13. Type **0.078** in the **Length** box.
14. Click **OK**.

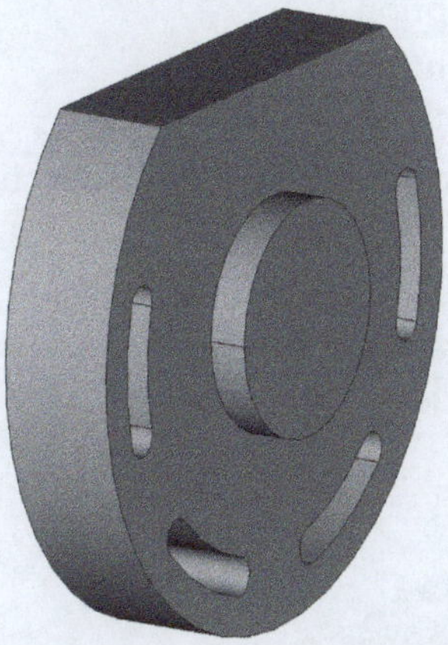

Creating a Counterbore Hole

In this section, you create a counterbore hole concentric to the circular face.

1. Click the small cube located next to the Navigation cube, and then select the **Isometric** option.

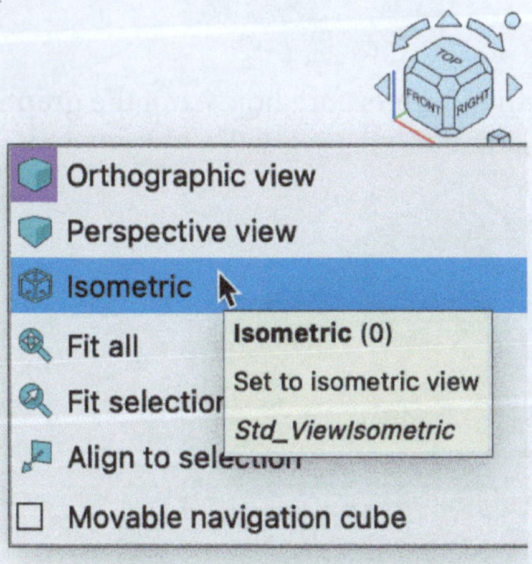

2. Select the front face of the model.

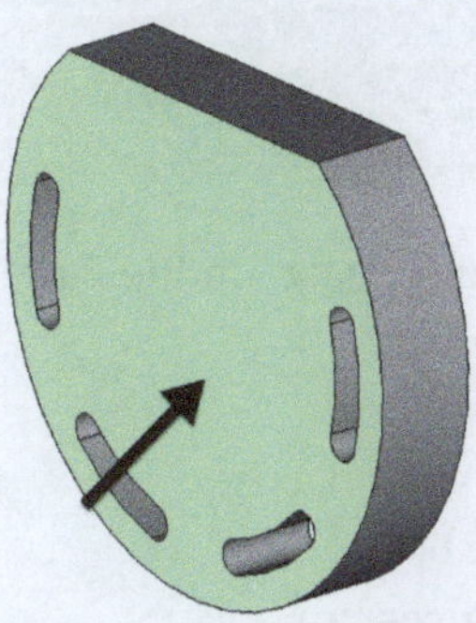

3. Click the **Create Sketch** icon on the **Part Design Helper** toolbar.
4. Click the **Create Circle** icon on the **Sketcher geometries** toolbar.
5. Select the origin point of the sketch.
6. Move the pointer outward and click to create a circle.

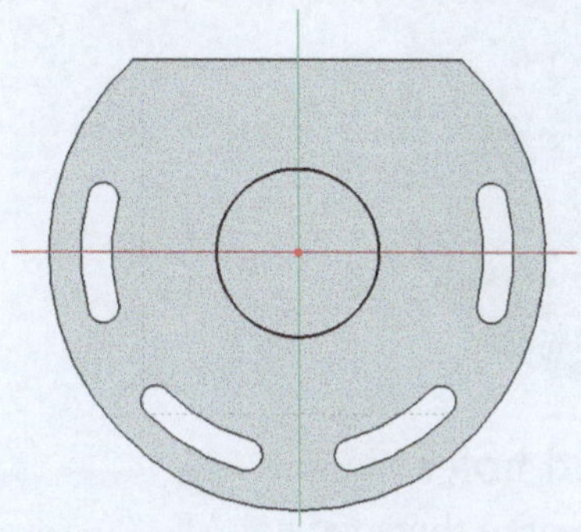

7. Click **Close** on the **Tasks** panel.
8. Click the **Hole** icon on the **Part Design Modeling** toolbar.
9. Type **0.314** in the **Diameter** box.
10. Select **Depth > Through All.**
11. On the **Hole Parameters** section, select **Hole cut Type > Counterbore.**
12. Type **0.394** in the **Diameter** box.
13. Type **0.078** in the **Depth** box.

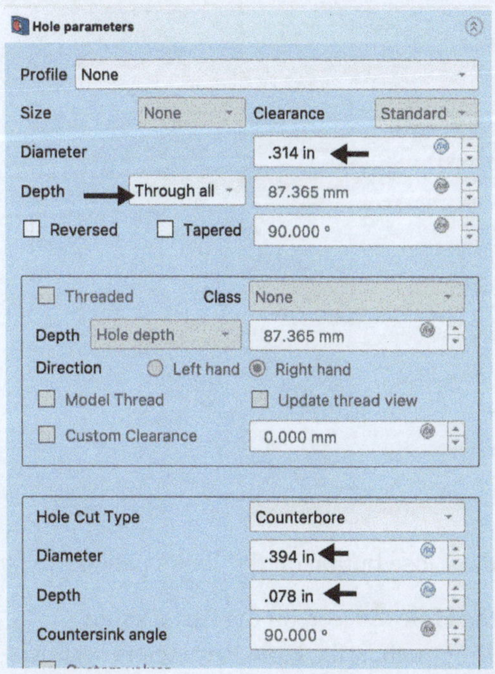

14. Click **OK** on the **Tasks** panel; the counterbore hole is created.

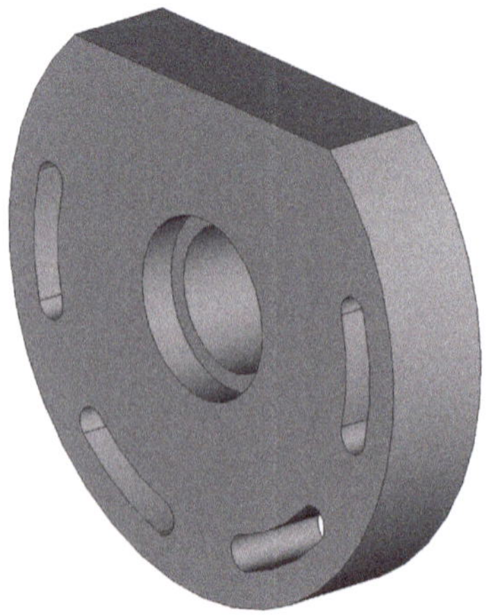

Creating Threaded holes

In this section, you create a threaded hole.

1. Click on the front face of the model.
2. Click the **Create Sketch** icon.
3. Click the **Create Circle** icon on the **Sketcher geometries** toolbar.
4. Click on the horizontal axis on the right side.
5. Move the pointer outward and click to create the circle.
6. Add the horizontal distance constraint between the centerpoint of the circle and the origin point.

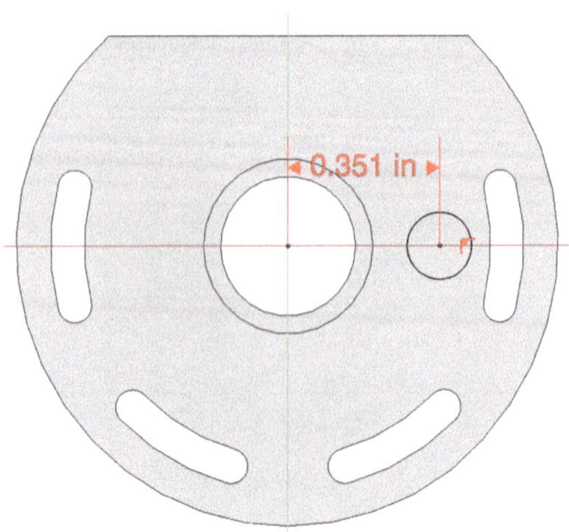

7. Click the **Close** button on the **Tasks** panel.
8. Click the **Hole** icon on the **Part Design Modeling** toolbar; the **Hole Parameters** section appears.
9. Select **Profile > UTS coarse profile**.
10. Select **Size > #1**.
11. Select **Depth > Through all**.
12. Check the **Threaded** option.
13. Select **Direction > Right hand**.
14. Select **Class > 2B**.
15. Select the **Counterbore** option from the **Hole cut Type** drop-down.
16. Set the Counterbore **Diameter** to 0.118.
17. Set the Counterbore **Depth** to 0.039.
18. Click **OK** to create the hole.

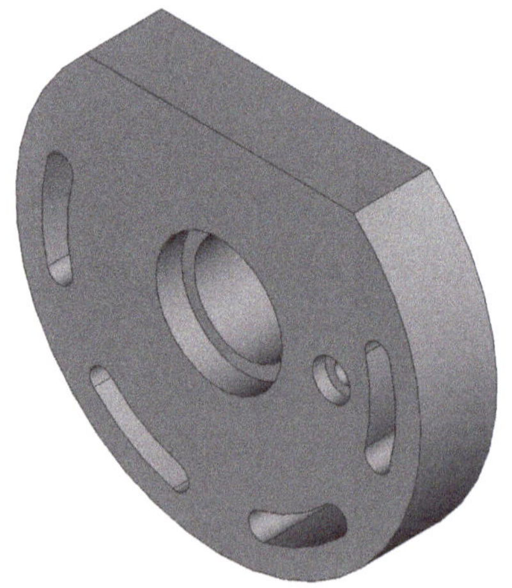

19. Select the Counterbore hole from the graphics window.

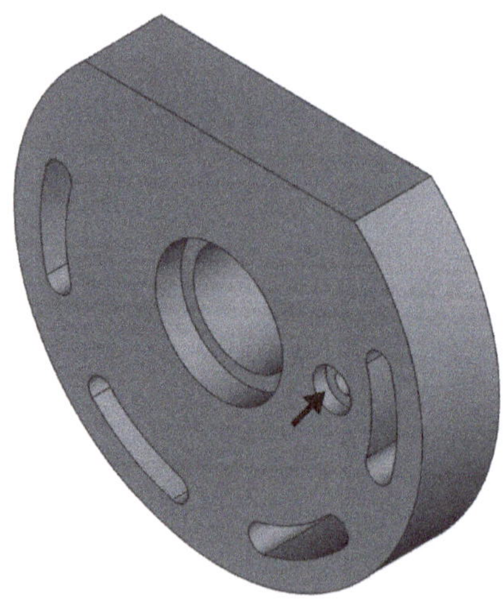

20. Click the **Polar Pattern** icon on the **Part Design Modeling** toolbar.
21. Click **OK**.
22. Select **Axis > Normal sketch axis**.
23. Type **360** in the **Angle** box.
24. Type **6** in the **Occurrences** box.
25. Click **OK**.

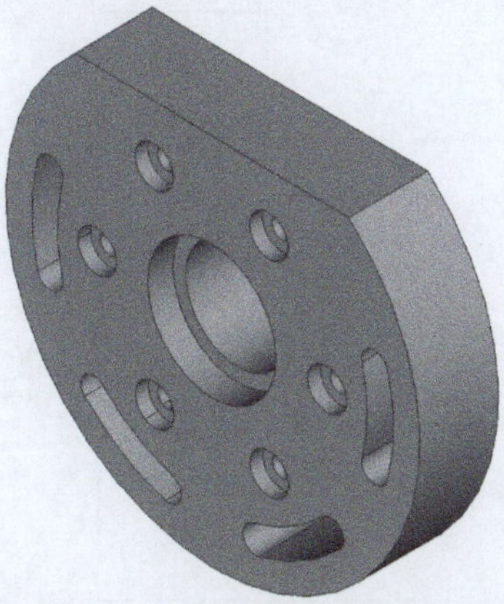

Creating Chamfers

1. Select the circular edge of the counterbore hole.

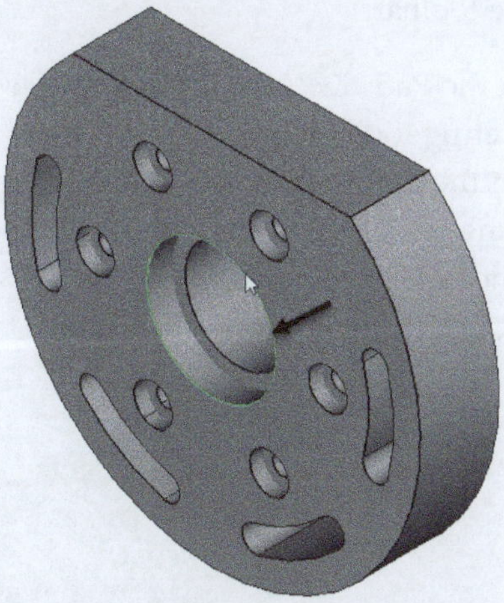

2. Click the **Chamfer** icon on the **Part Design Dressup** toolbar.
3. Enter 0.039 in the **Size** box.

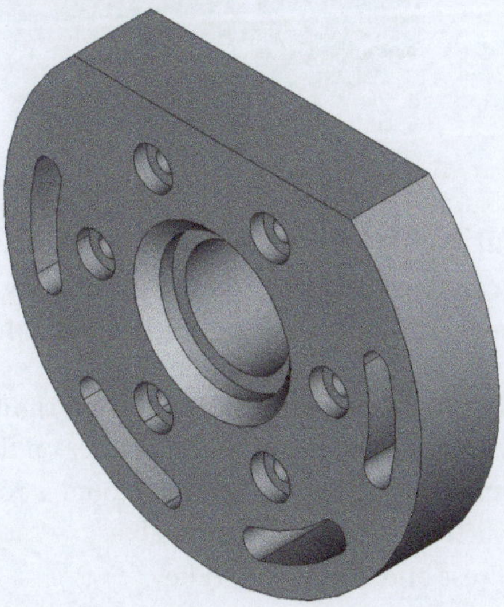

4. Click **OK** to create the chamfer.
5. Save the model and close it.

TUTORIAL 2

In this tutorial, you create the model shown in the figure.

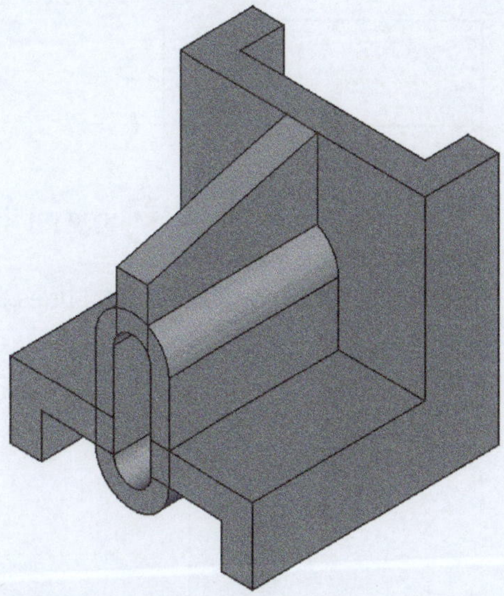

Creating the first feature

1. Open a new FreeCAD file.
2. Select the **Part Design** from the **Workbenches** drop-down.
3. Click the **Create sketch** icon on the **Part Design Helper** toolbar, and then Select the YZ-Plane from the **Tasks** panel and click **OK.**
4. On the **Tasks** panel, click the drop-down in the **Constraints** section, and then select the **Auto remove redundants** option.

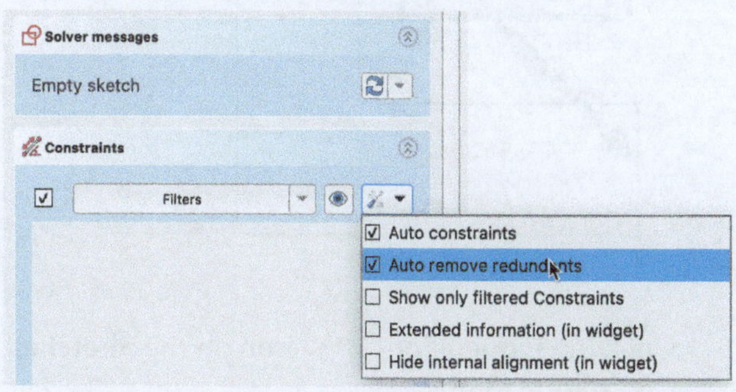

5. Draw the sketch using the **Polyline** tool, as shown.

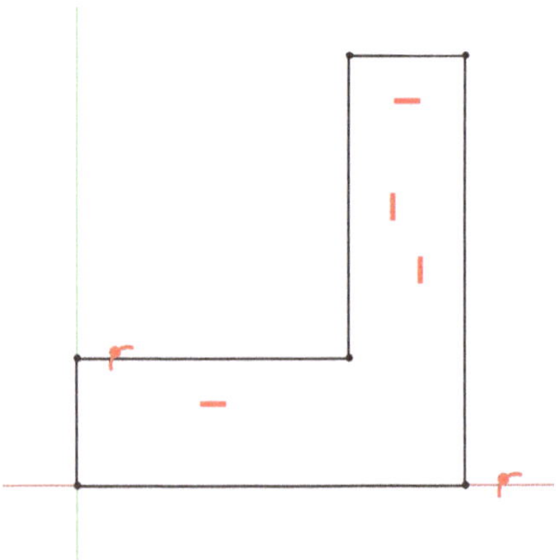

6. Click the **Constrain Equal** icon on the **Sketcher constraints** toolbar.
7. Select the vertical and horizontal lines, as shown.

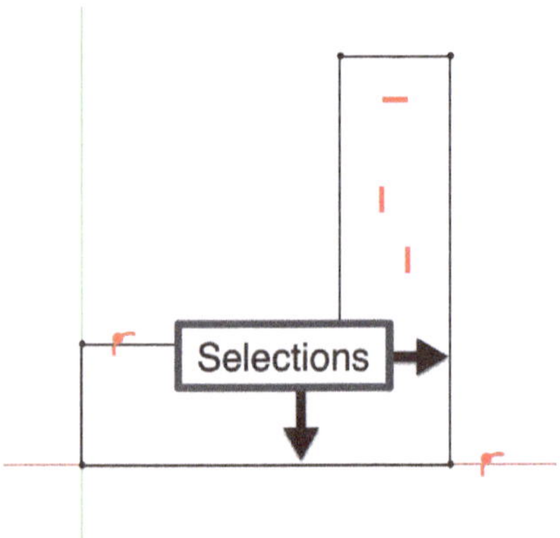

8. Select the two lines to make them equal in length.

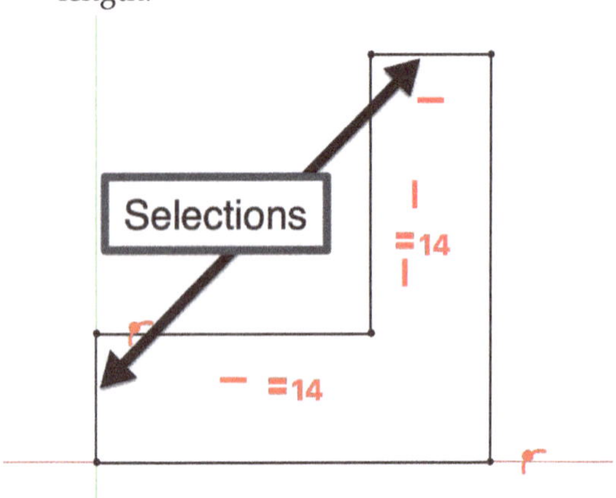

9. Click the **Dimension** icon on the **Sketcher constraints** toolbar.
10. Add the constraints to the vertical lines, as shown.

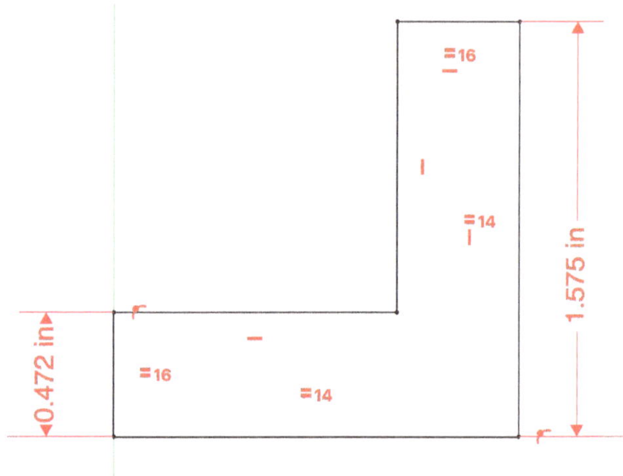

11. Click **Leave Sketch** on the **Sketcher edit mode** toolbar.
12. Click the **Pad** icon on the **Part Design Modeling** toolbar.
13. Select the **Symmetric plane** option from the **Pad parameters** section.
14. Set the **Length** to 1.575.
15. Click **OK** to create the first feature.

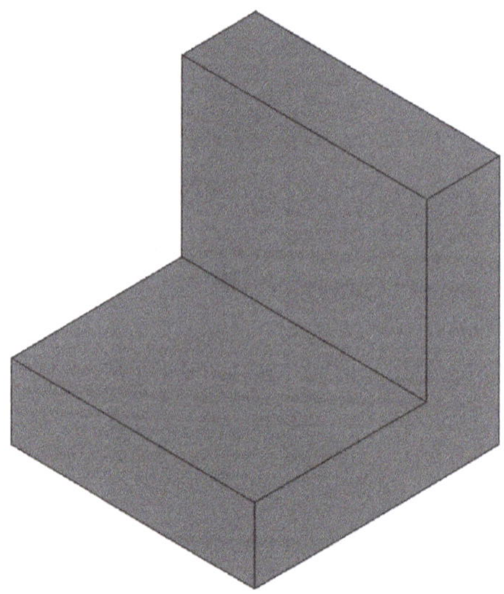

Creating the Shell feature

You can create a shell feature by removing the face of the model and applying thickness to other faces.

1. Press and how2ld the middle and right mouse button. Next, position the pointer on the model and drag it toward left; the model is rotated such that it back face is visible.
2. Press and hold the Ctrl key.
3. Select the top face and the back face of the

model.

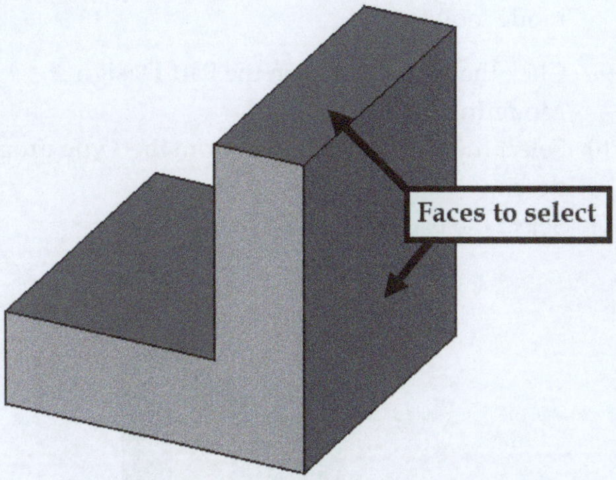

4. Click the **Thickness** icon on the **Part Design Modeling** toolbar.
5. Set **Thickness** to 0.197.
6. Select **Join type > Intersection.**
7. Check the **Make thickness inward** option.

Now, you need to select more faces.

8. Click the **Select** button.
9. Select the front face and the bottom face of the model.

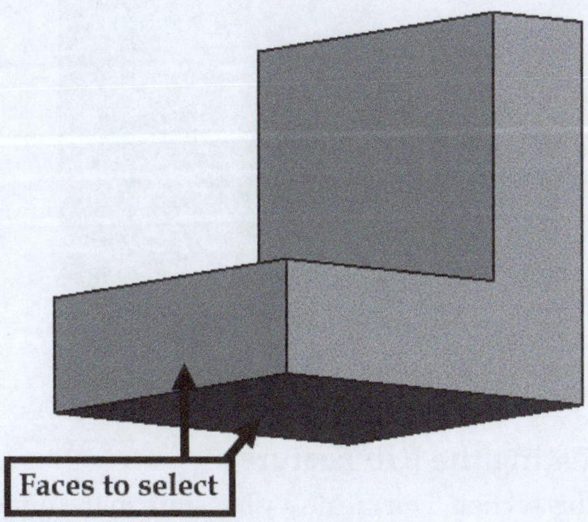

10. Click **OK** to shell the model.

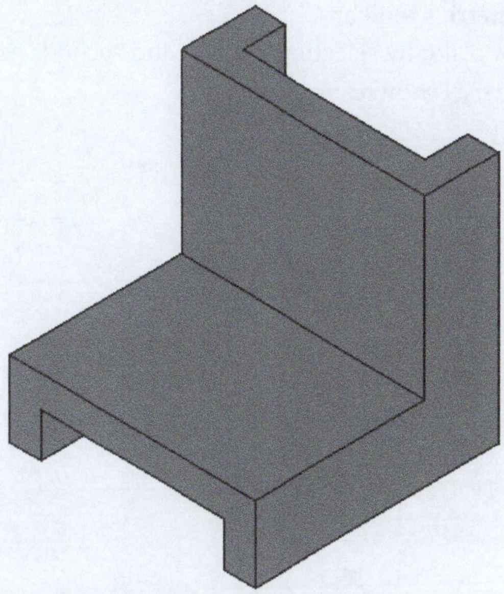

Creating the Third feature

1. Select the front face of the model.

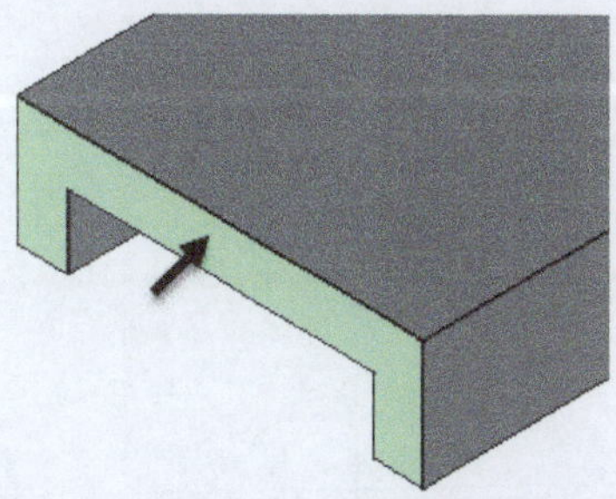

2. Click the **Create Sketch** icon on the **Part Design Helper** toolbar.
3. Click the **Create external geometry** icon on the **Sketcher tools** toolbar.
4. Select the edges of the model, as shown.

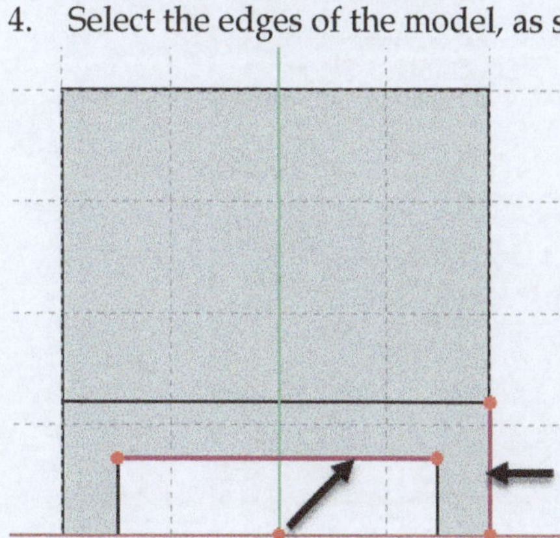

5. Click **Create Slot** on the **Sketcher**

geometries toolbar.

6. Draw a slot by selecting the first and second points, as shown.

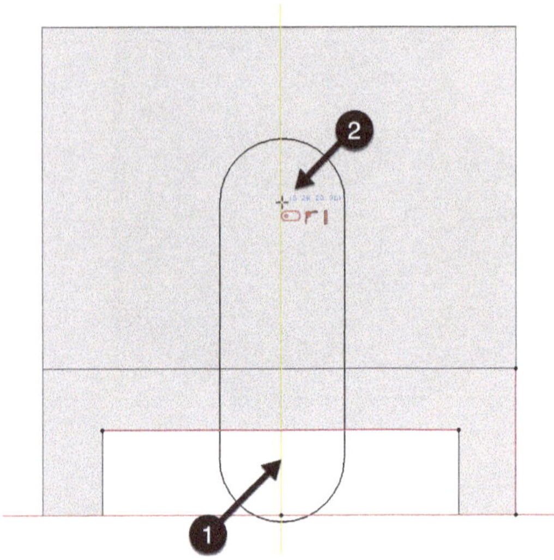

7. Add constraints to the slot.

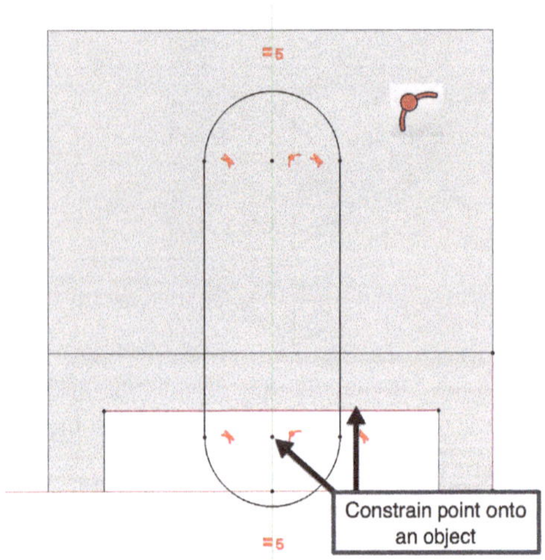

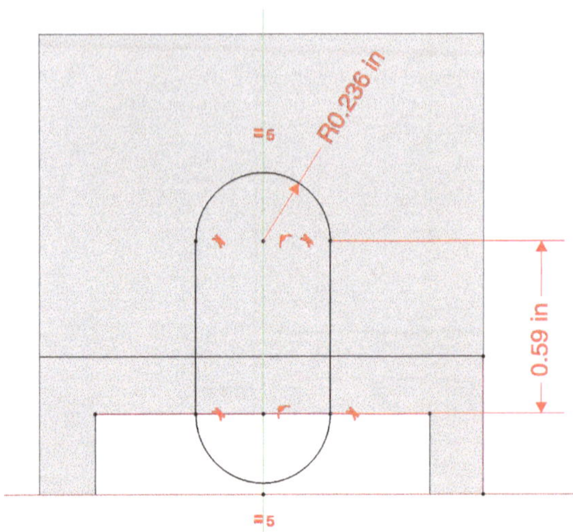

8. Click **Leave Sketch** on the **Sketcher edit mode** toolbar.
9. Click the **Pad** icon on the **Part Design Modeling** toolbar.
10. Select the **Up to face** option from the **Type** drop-down.
11. Select the back face of the model.

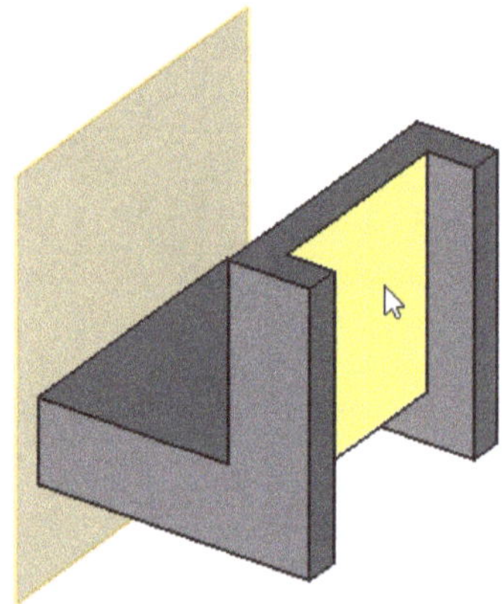

12. Click **OK** to create the feature.

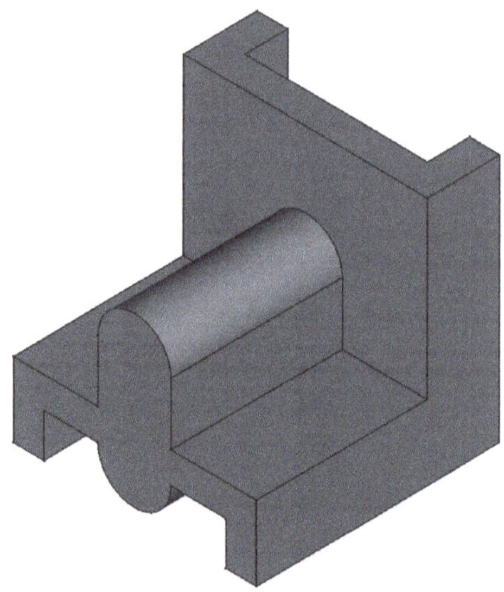

Creating the Rib Feature

In this section, you create a rib feature in the middle of the model. To do this, you must create an offset plane.

1. Select the right face of the model.
2. To create an offset plane, click the **Create a datum plane** icon on the **Part Design Helper** toolbar.

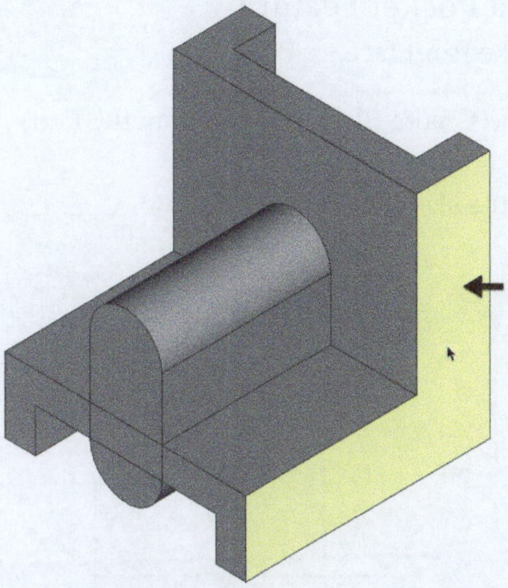

3. Type **0.7875** in the **Z** box available in the **Attachment** section.
4. Check the **Flip sides** option.

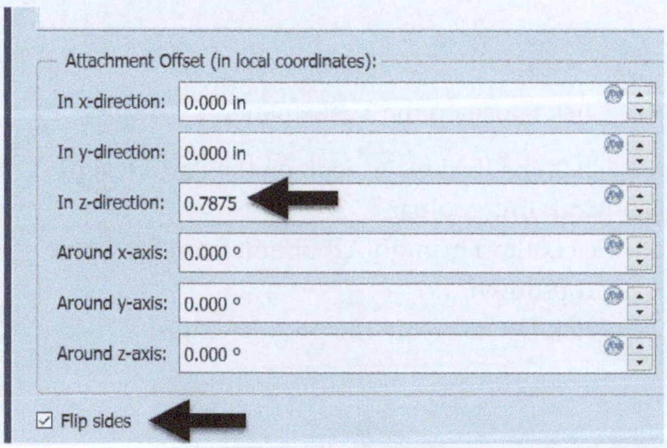

5. Click **OK** to create the plane.

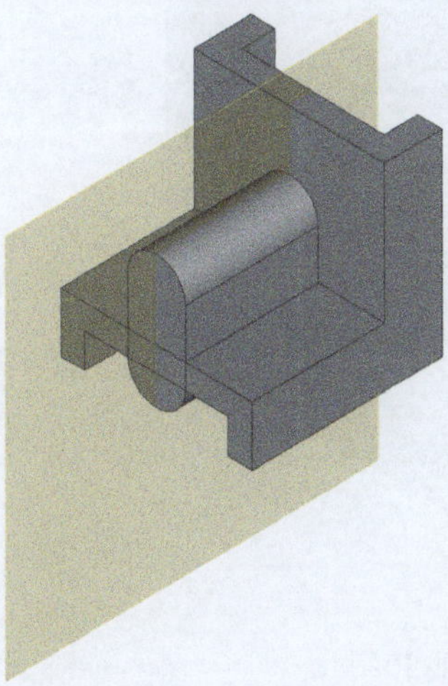

6. Click the **Create Sketch** icon on the **Part Design Helper** toolbar.
7. Select the newly created plane.
8. On the **View** toolbar, set the **Draw Style** to **Wireframe**.
9. Click the **Create external geometry** icon on the **Sketcher tools** toolbar.
10. Select the model edges, as shown.

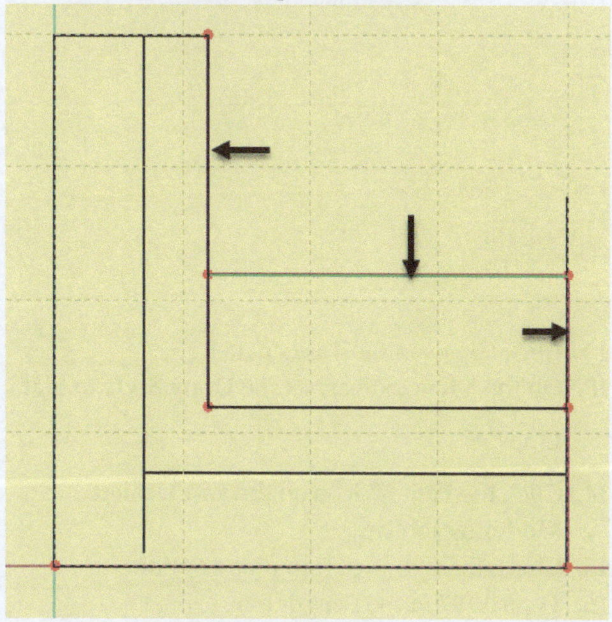

11. Draw the sketch, as shown below.

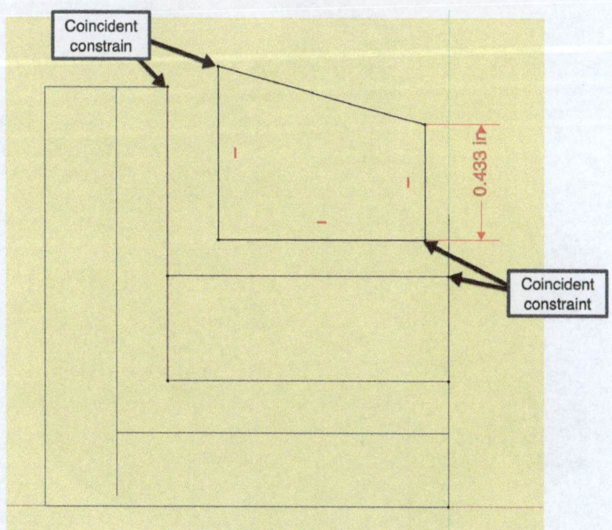

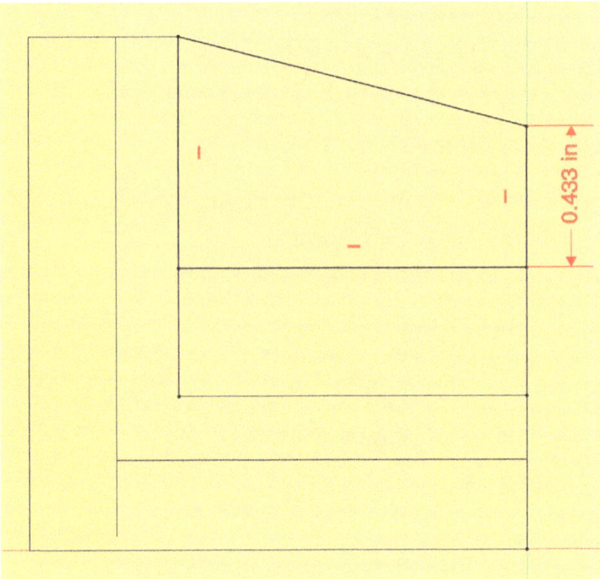

12. Click **Close** on the **Tasks** panel.
13. On the **View** toolbar, set the **Draw Style** to **Flat Lines**.
14. Click the **Pad** icon on the **Part Design Modeling** toolbar.
15. Check the **Symmetric to plane** option.
16. Type **0.197** in the **Length** box.
17. Click **OK** to create the rib feature.

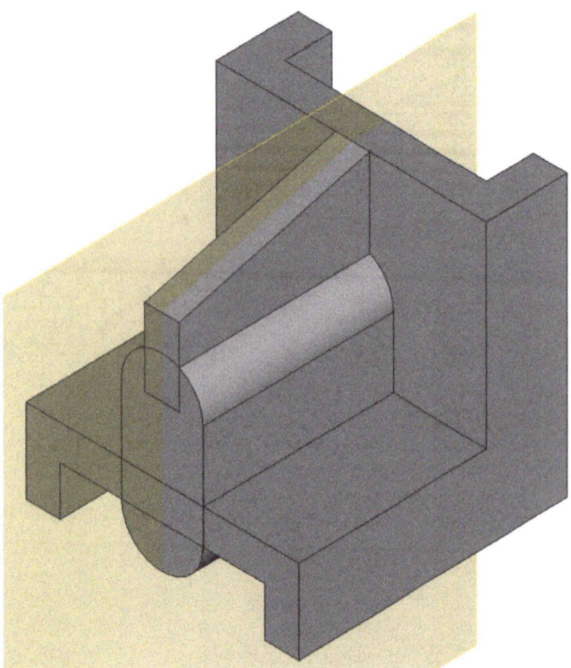

Creating a Pocket Feature

1. Select the front face.
2. Click the **Create Sketch** icon on the **Part Design Helper** toolbar.
3. Create the sketch, as shown below.

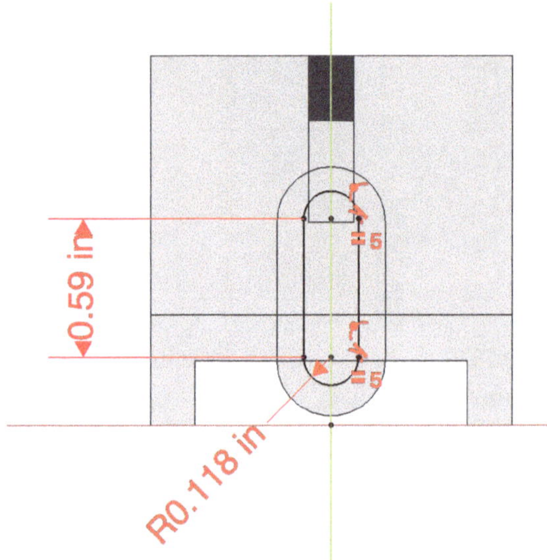

4. Click **Close** on the **Tasks** panel.
5. Click the **Pocket** icon on the **Part Design Modeling** toolbar.
6. Select the **Through All** option from the **Type** drop-down.
7. Click **OK** to create the pocket feature.

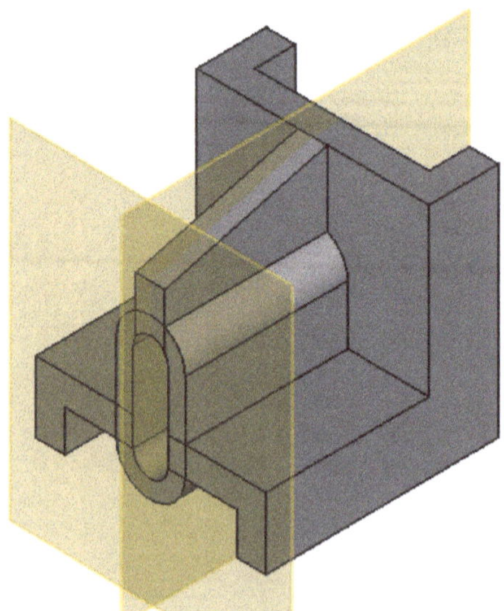

18. Save the model and close it.

TUTORIAL 3

In this tutorial, you create a helical spring.

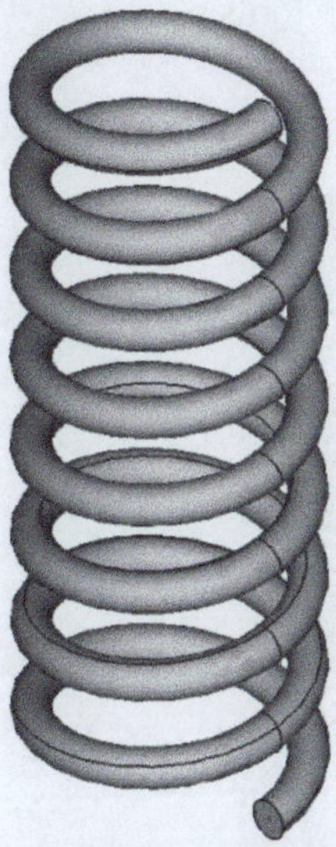

Creating the Profile

1. Open a new FreeCAD file.
2. Select **Part Design** from the **Workbenches** drop-down.
3. Click the **Create Sketch**  icon on the **Part Design Helper** toolbar.
4. Select the XZ-Plane from the **Tasks** panel.
5. Create a circle, as shown.

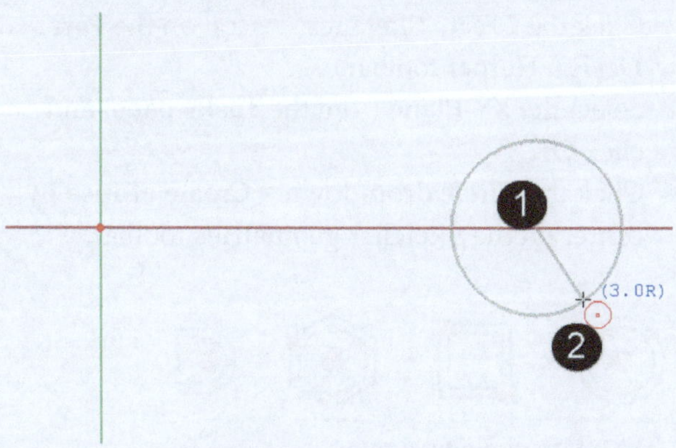

6. Add constraints to it, as shown.

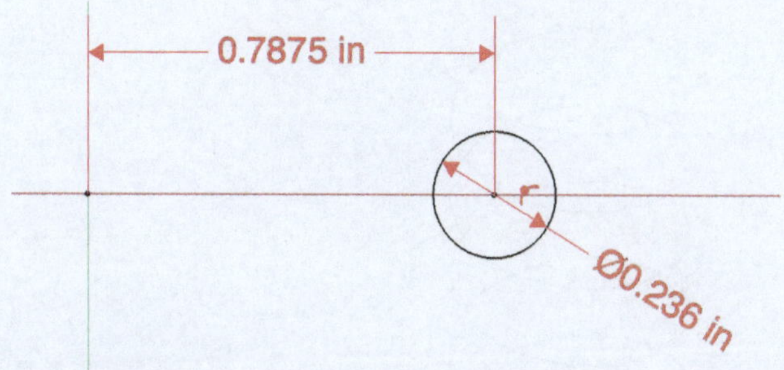

7. Click **Close** on the **Tasks** panel.

Creating the Helix

1. Select **Part** from the **Workbenches** drop-down.
2. Click the **Create primitives**  icon on the **Solids** toolbar.
3. In the **Geometric Primitives** dialog, select **Helix** from the drop-down.
4. Type **0.59** in the **Pitch** box.
5. Type **4.72** in the **Height** box.
6. Type **0.7875** in the **Radius** box.
7. Select **Right-handed** from the **Coordinate system** drop-down.

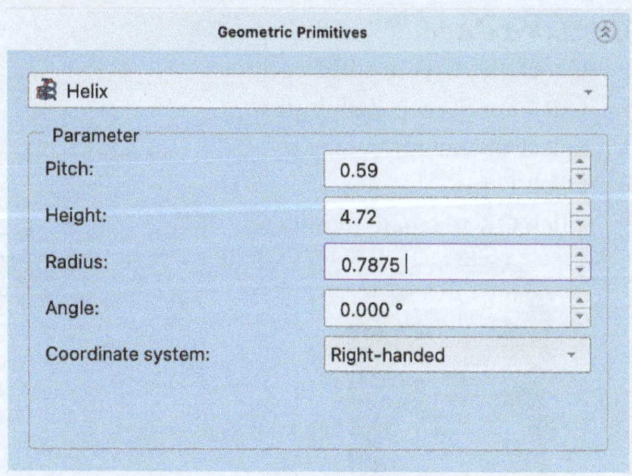

8. Expand the **Location** section.
9. Type **0** in the **X**, **Y**, and **Z** boxes.
10. Click the **Create** button.
11. On the **View** toolbar, click the **Isometric**  icon.

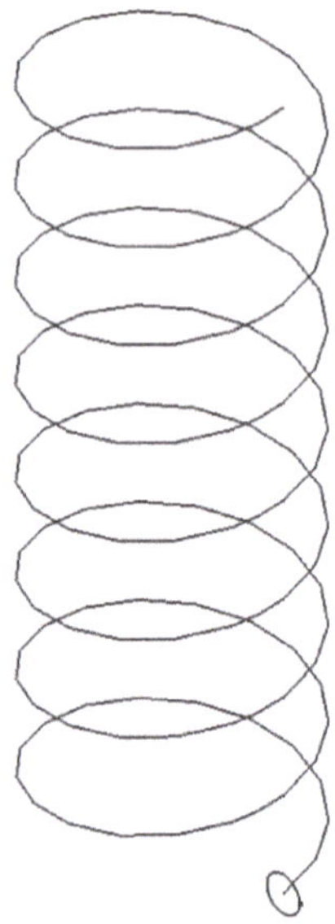

12. Click the **Close** button.

Creating the Sweep

1. Click the **Sweep** icon on the **Part tools** toolbar.
2. Select the **Sketch** from the **Available profiles** section.
3. Click the **Add** button.
4. Check the **Create solid** option.
5. Click the **Sweep Path** button.
6. Select the helix.
7. Click **Done**.
8. Click **OK** to create the sweep.

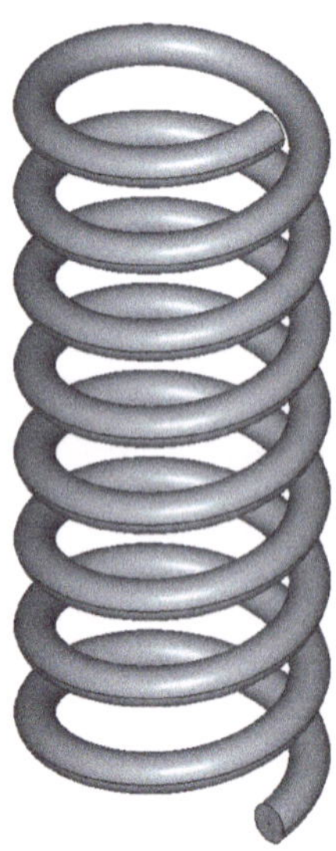

9. Save the model and close the file.

TUTORIAL 4

In this tutorial, you create a shampoo bottle using the **Loft**, **Pad**, and **Sweep** tools.

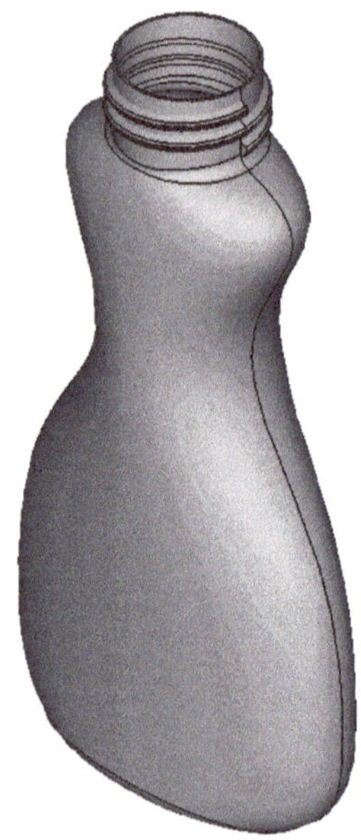

Creating the Loft feature

To create a loft feature, you need to create sections.

1. Start a new FreeCAD file.
2. Select the **Part Design** option from the **Workbenches** drop-down.
3. Click the **Create Sketches** icon on the **Part Design Helper** toolbar.
4. Select the **XY-Plane** from the **Tasks** panel and click **OK**.
5. Click the **Circle** drop-down > **Create ellipse by center** on the **Sketcher geometries** toolbar.

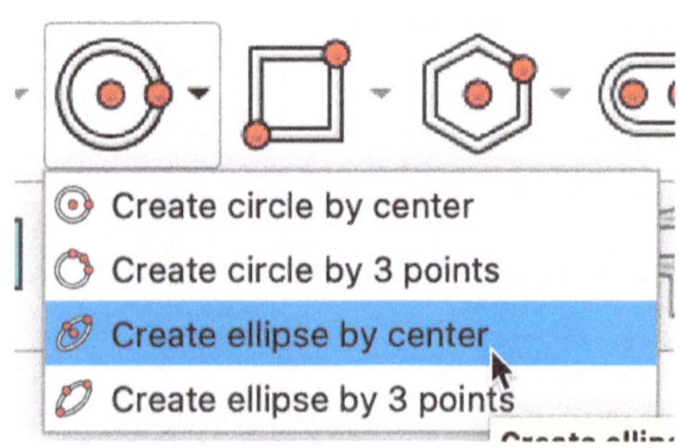

6. Draw the ellipse by selecting the points, as shown.

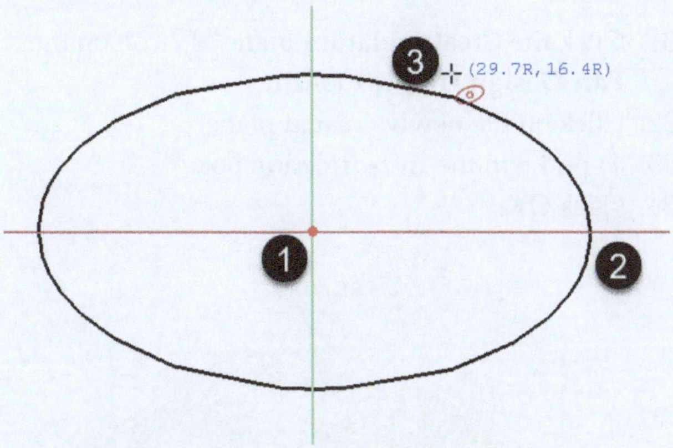

7. On the **Sketcher constraints** toolbar, click the **Dimension** icon.
8. Select the horizontal axis of the ellipse.
9. Type **3.50** in the **Length** box of the **Insert Length** dialog.
10. Click **OK**.
11. Select the vertical axis of the ellipse.
12. Type **1.968** in the **Length** box of the **Insert Length** dialog.
13. Click **OK**.

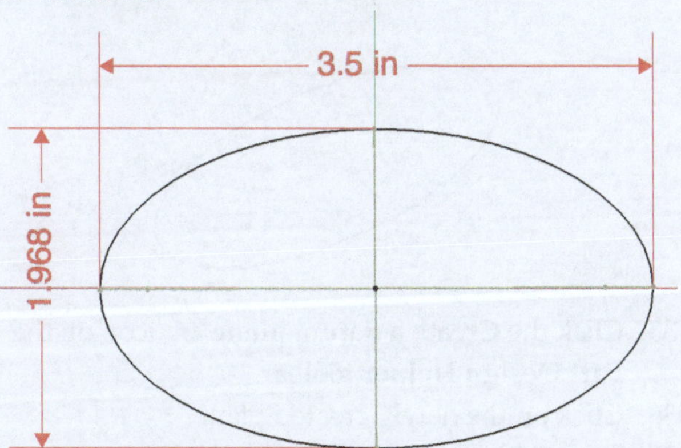

14. Click the **Close** button on the **Tasks** panel.
15. Click the **Create a datum plane** icon on the **Part Design Helper** toolbar.
16. Click on the ellipse, if not already selected.
17. Type **1.5** in the **In z-direction** box.
18. Click **OK**.

19. Click the **Create a datum plane** icon on the **Part Design Helper** toolbar.
20. Click on the newly created plane.
21. Type **1.5** in the **In z-direction** box.
22. Click **OK**.

23. Click the **Create a datum plane** icon on the **Part Design Helper** toolbar.
24. Click on the newly created plane.
25. Type **1.2** in the **In z-direction** box.
26. Click **OK**.

27. Click the **Create a datum plane** icon on the **Part Design Helper** toolbar.
28. Click on the newly created plane.
29. Type **1.2** in the **In z-direction** box.
30. Click **OK.**

31. Click the **Create a datum plane** icon on the **Part Design Helper** toolbar.
32. Click on the newly created plane.
33. Type **1.5** in the **In z-direction** box.
34. Click **OK.**

35. Click the **Create a datum plane** icon on the **Part Design Helper** toolbar.
36. Click on the newly created plane.
37. Type **1.2** in the **In z-direction** box.
38. Click **OK**

39. Click the **Create Sketch** icon on the **Part Design Modeling** toolbar.
40. Select the first datum plane.

41. Click the **View Section** icon on the **Sketcher edit mode** toolbar.
42. Create an ellipse, as shown.

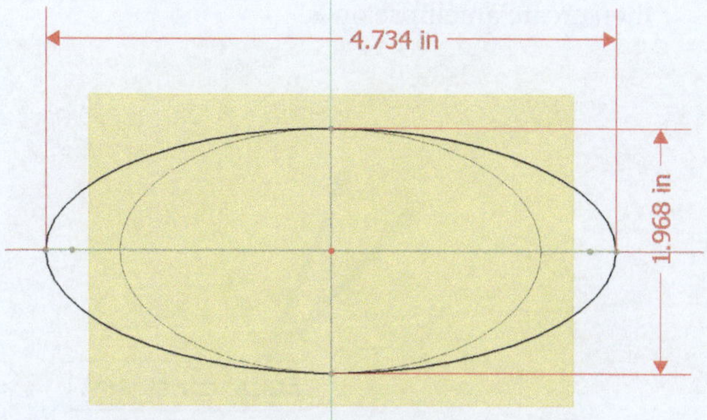

43. Click the **Close** button on the **Tasks** panel.
44. Click the **Create Sketch** icon on the **Part Design Helper** toolbar.
45. Select the second datum plane.
46. On the Menu bar, click **Sketch > View section** .
47. Create an ellipse, as shown.

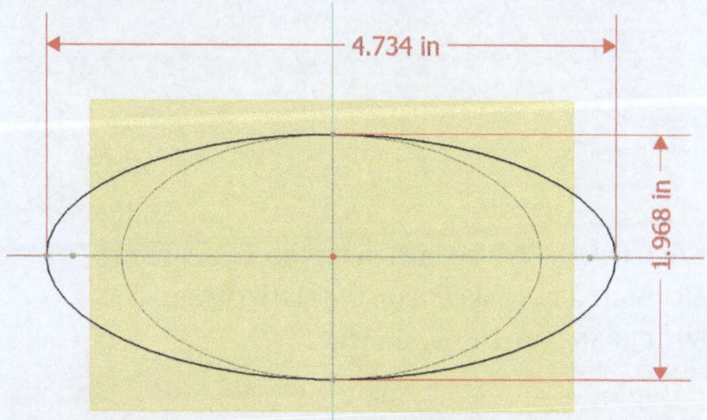

48. Click the **Close** button on the **Tasks** panel.
49. Start a sketch on the third datum plane.
50. Click the **View Section** icon on the **Sketcher edit mode** toolbar.
51. Create an ellipse, as shown.

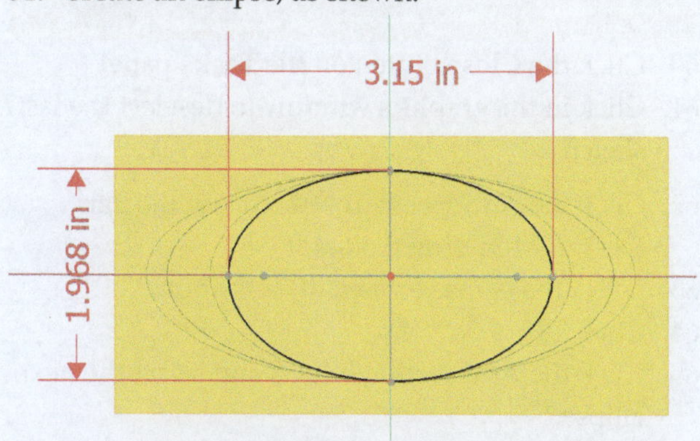

52. Click the **Close** button on the **Tasks** panel.
53. Start a sketch on the fourth datum plane, and

then create an ellipse on it.

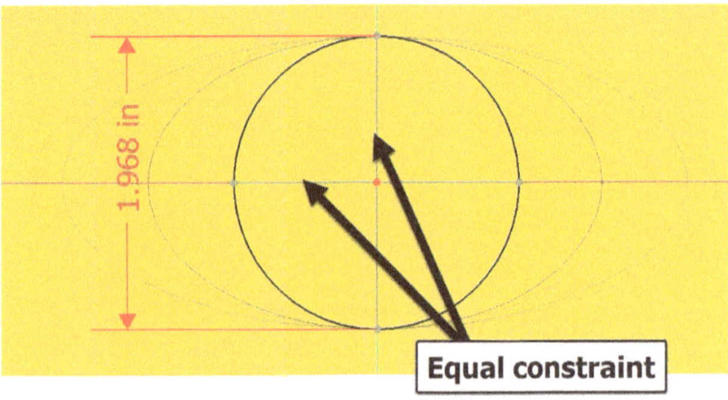

54. Click the **Close** button on the **Tasks** panel.
55. Start a new sketch on the fifth plane.
56. Create an ellipse, as shown.

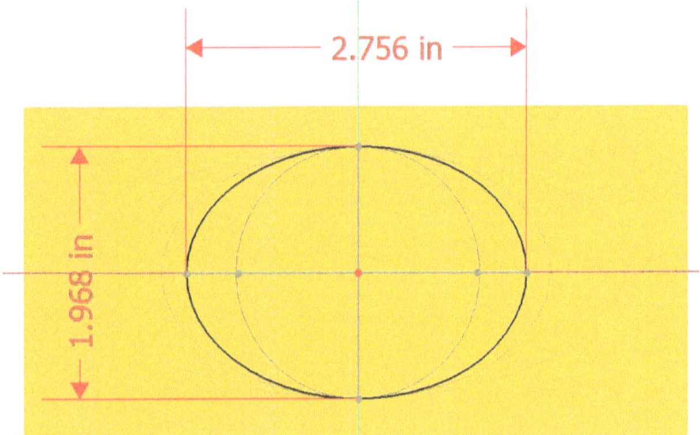

57. Click the **Close** button on the **Tasks** panel.
58. Start a new sketch on the sixth plane.
59. Create a circle, as shown.

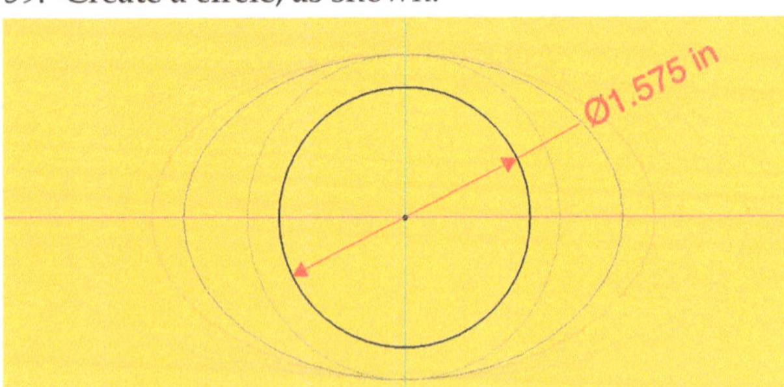

60. Click the **Close** button on the **Tasks** panel.
61. Click in the graphics window to deselect the last sketch.
62. Click the **Additive Loft**  icon on the **Part Design Modeling** toolbar.
63. Select the ellipse located at the bottom.
64. Click **OK**.
65. Click the **Add section** button and select the next ellipse.

66. Likewise, select the remaining sketches in the order, as shown.

67. Click **OK** to create the loft feature.

Creating the Extruded feature

1. Click the **Pad** icon on the **Part Design Modeling** toolbar.
2. Check the **Allow used features** option from the **Select Features** dialog.
3. Select the last sketch from the sketch list.

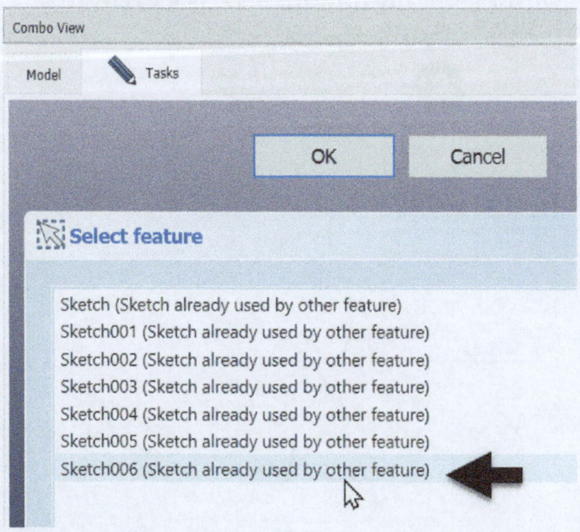

4. Click **OK**.
5. Type **1** in the **Length** box and click **OK**.

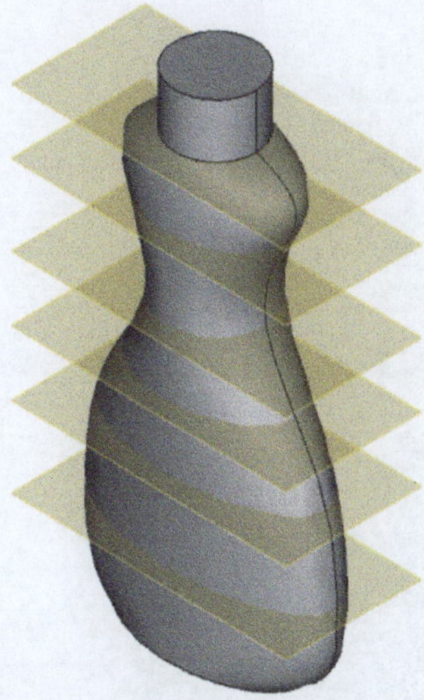

Creating Fillets

1. Press and hold the Ctrl key.
2. Click on the bottom and top edges of the swept feature.

3. Click the **Fillet** icon on the **Part Design Dressup** toolbar.
4. Set **Radius** to 0.2.

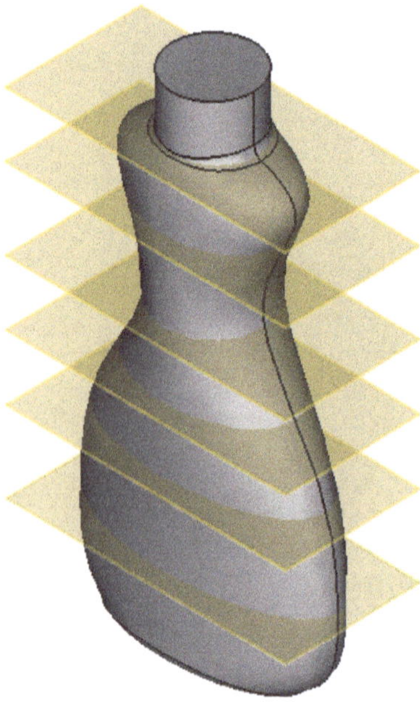

5. Click **OK**.

Shelling the Model

1. Select the top face of the cylindrical feature.

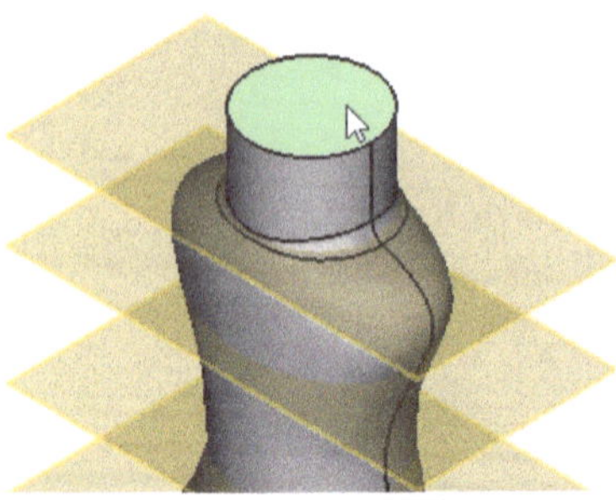

2. Click the **Thickness** icon on the **Part Design Modeling** toolbar.
3. Set **Thickness** to 0.03.
4. Click **OK** to create the shell.

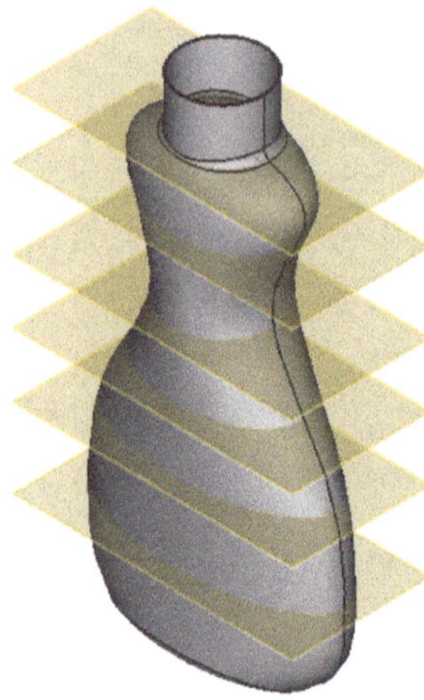

Adding Threads

1. Click the **Create Sketch** icon on the **Part Design Helper** toolbar.
2. Select the XZ Plane from the Tasks panel and click **OK**.
3. Click **Draw Style > Wireframe** on the **View** toolbar.
4. Click the **Toggle Construction geometry** icon on the **Sketcher geometries** toolbar.
5. Click the **Create Line** icon on the **Sketcher geometries** toolbar.
6. Select the origin point of the sketch, move the cursor vertically upward and click to create a vertical construction line.

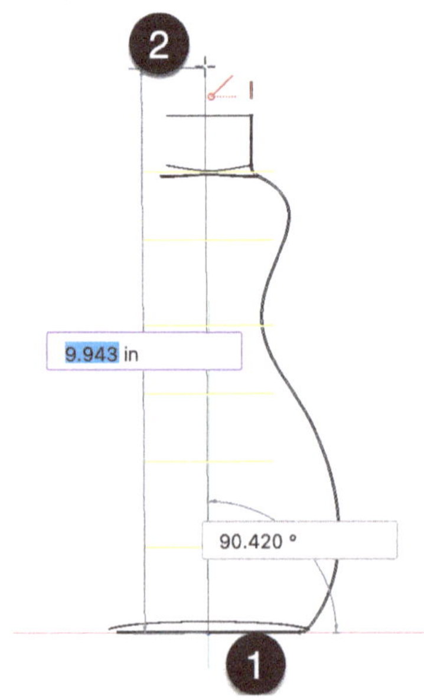

7. Create a horizontal construction line, as shown.

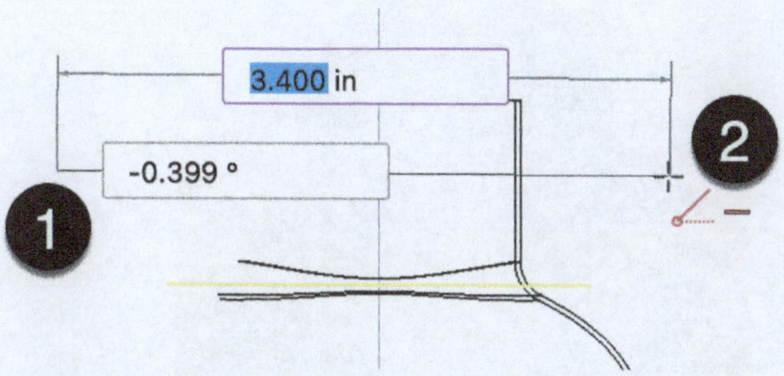

8. Click the **Toggle construction geometry** icon on the **Sketcher geometries** toolbar.
9. Click the **Create Polyline** icon on the **Sketcher geometries** toolbar.
10. Create a closed profile, as shown.

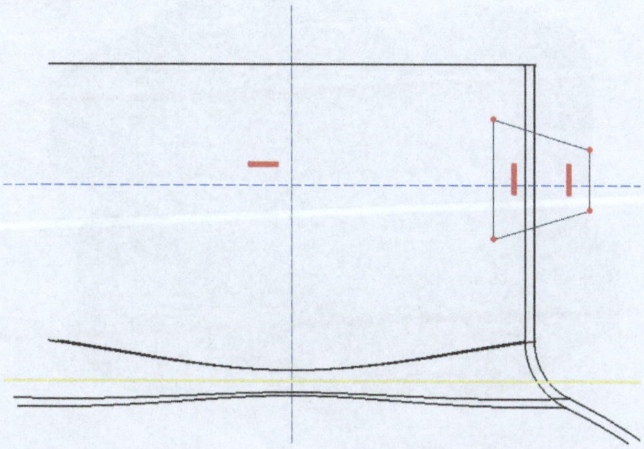

11. Press Esc to deactivate the **Create Polyline** tool.
12. Add fillets, constraints, and dimensions to the profile.

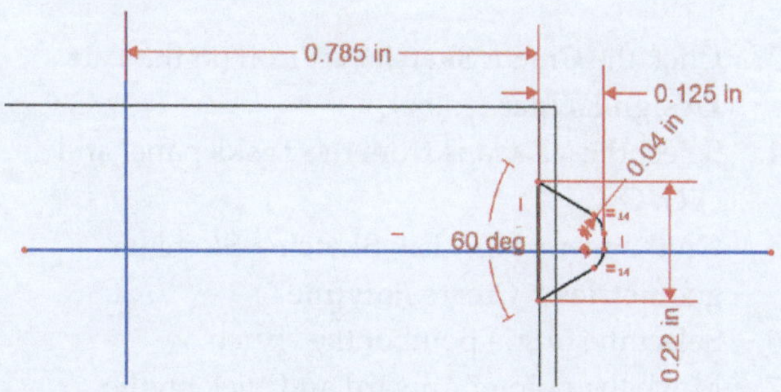

13. Click the **Constrain symmetrical** icon on the **Sketcher constraints** toolbar.
14. Select the centerpoints of the arcs.
15. Select the right endpoint of the construction line.

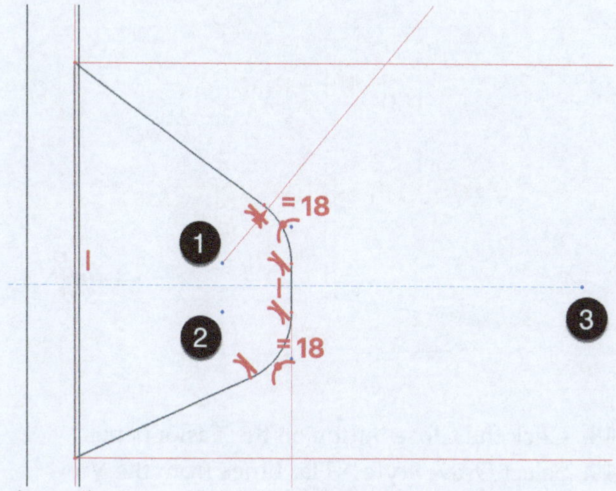

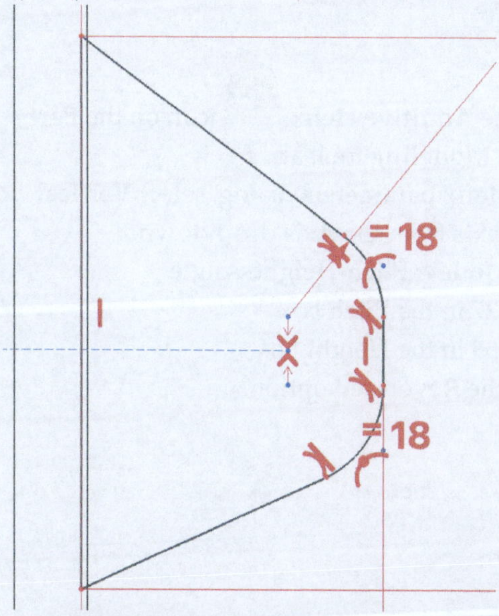

16. Add angular dimension between the inclined line and the horizontal construction line, as shown.

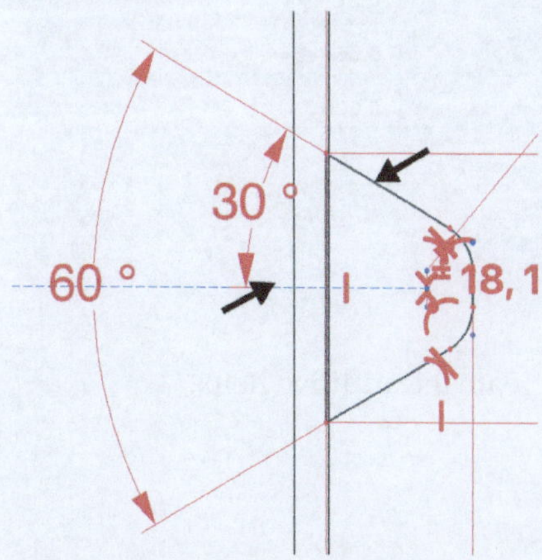

17. Create a **Vertical distance** constraint, as shown.

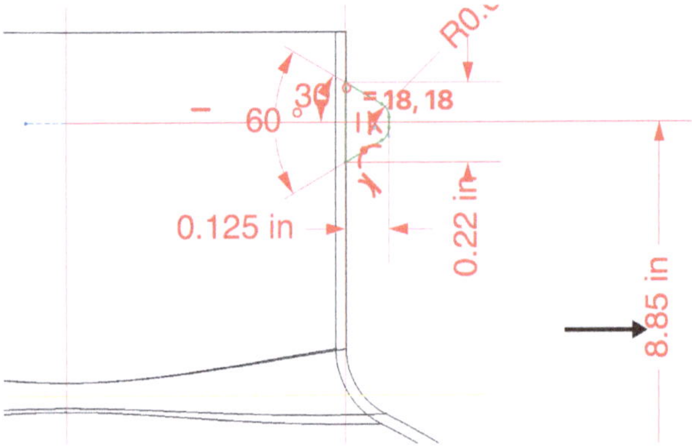

18. Click the **Close** button on the **Tasks** panel.
19. Select **Draw Style > Flat Lines** from the **View** toolbar.
20. Click the **Additive Helix**  icon on the **Part Design Modeling** toolbar.
21. In the **Helix parameters** dialog, select **Vertical sketch axis** from the **Axis** drop-down.
22. Select **Mode > Pitch-Height-Angle**.
23. Type **0.27** in the **Pitch** box.
24. Type **0.55** in the **Height** box.
25. Check the **Reveresed** option.

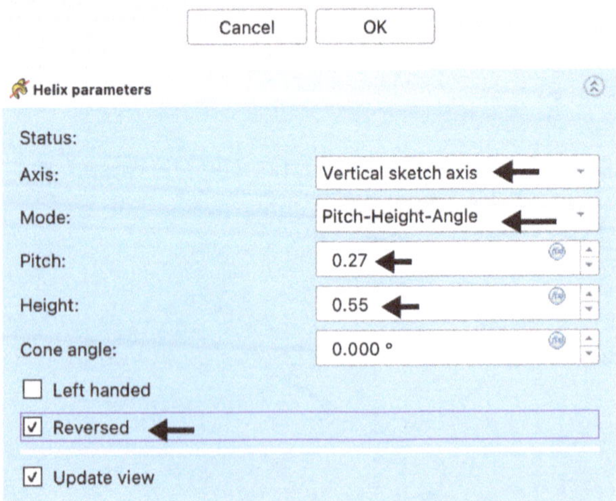

26. Click **OK** to create the additive helix.

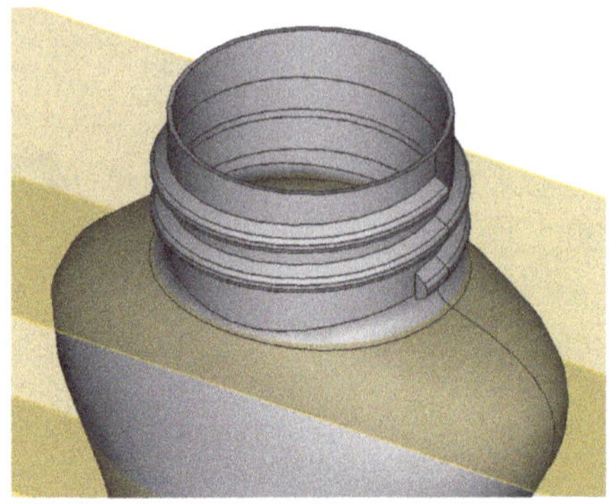

27. Save the model.

TUTORIAL 5

In this tutorial, you create the model, as shown.

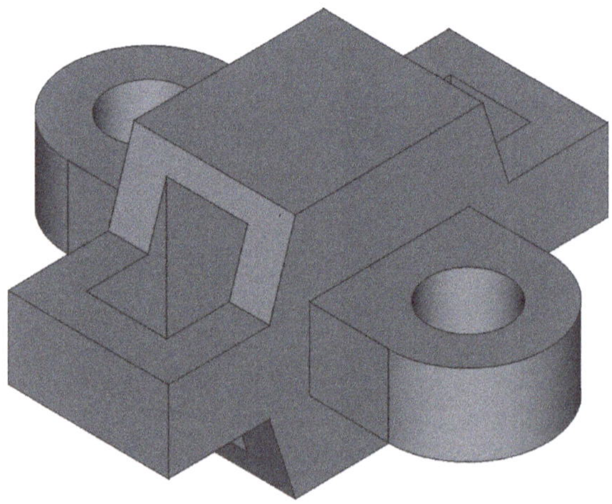

Creating the First feature

1. Open a new FreeCAD file.
2. Select **Part Design** from the **Workbenches** drop-down.
3. Click the **Create Sketch**  icon on the **Part Design Helper** toolbar.
4. Select the YZ Plane from the **Tasks** panel and click **OK**.
5. On the menu bar, click **Sketch > Sketcher geometries > Create Polyline**.
6. Select the origin point of the sketch.
7. Move the pointer upward and click on the vertical axis of the sketch.
8. Move the pointer horizontally toward left.
9. Move the pointer toward bottom-left corner upto a small distance and click to create the inclined line.

10. Move the pointer horizontally toward left.
11. Move pointer vertically downward and click on the horizontal axis.
12. Move the pointer toward right and select the sketch origin to close the sketch.
13. Add dimensions to the sketch, as shown.

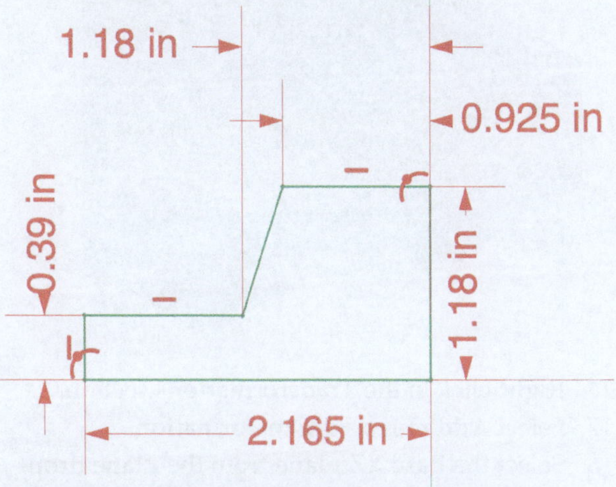

14. Click the **Close** button on the **Tasks** panel.
15. Click the **Pad** icon on the **Part Design Modeling** toolbar.
16. Type **1.575** in the **Length** box.
17. Check the **Symmetric to plane** option.
18. Click **OK**.

Creating the Pocket Feature

1. Click the **Create Sketch** icon on the **Part Design Helper** toolbar.
2. Select the XY Plane from the **Tasks** panel and click **OK**.
3. Click the **View section** icon on the **Sketcher edit mode** toolbar.
4. Create a rectangle and add constraints to it, as shown.

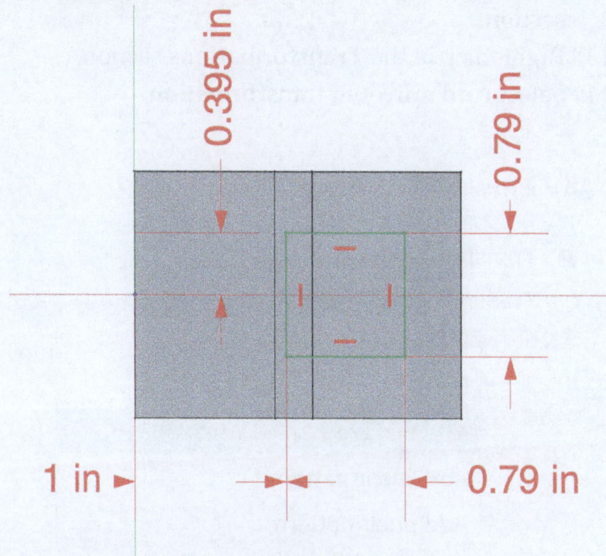

5. Click **Close** on the **Tasks** panel.
6. Click the **Pocket** icon on the **Part Design Modeling** toolbar.
7. Select **Type > Through All**.
8. Check the **Symmetric to plane** option.
9. Click **OK**.
10. Select **Draw Style > Flat Lines** from the **View** toolbar.

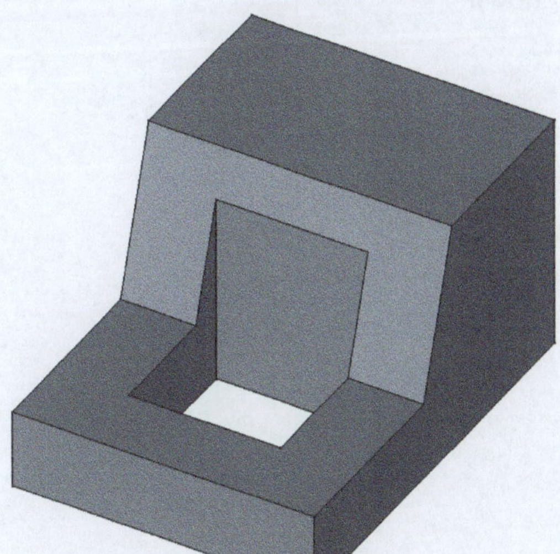

11. Click the **Create MultiTransform**  icon on the **Part Design Patterns** toolbar.
12. Make sure that the Transform Body option is selected in the MultTransform parameters section.
13. Right-click in the **Transformations** section.
14. Select **Add mirrored transformation**.

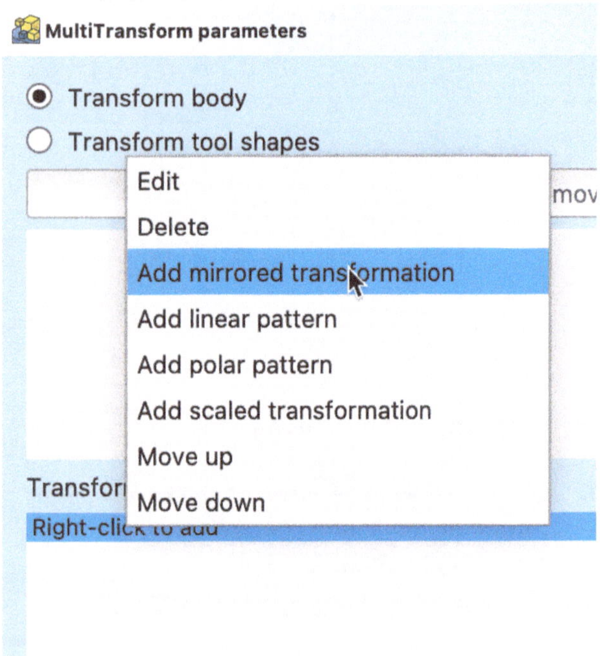

15. Select the **Base XY plane** from the **Plane** drop-down.

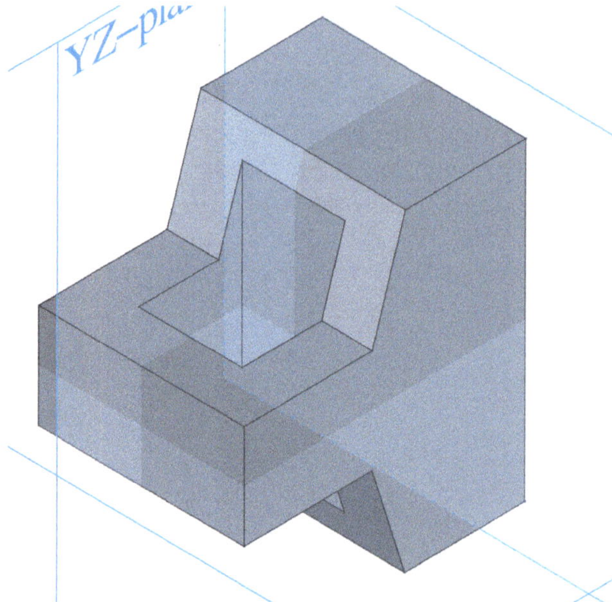

16. Right-click in the **Transformations** section.
17. Select **Add mirrored transformation**.
18. Select the **Base XZ plane** from the **Plane** drop-down.
19. Click **OK** at the bottom of the **Tasks** panel
20. **Click OK** at the top of the **Tasks** panel to mirror the pocket feature.

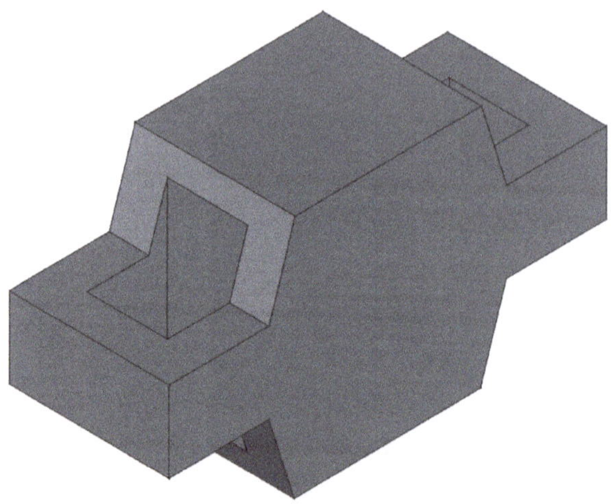

Creating the Second feature

1. Click the **Create Sketch** icon on the **Part Design Helper** toolbar.
2. Select the XY Plane from the **Tasks** panel and click **OK**.
3. Click the **View section**  icon on the **Sketcher edit mode** toolbar.

4. Click the **Create Slot** icon on the **Sketcher geometries** toolbar.
5. Click on the horizontal axis on the left side.
6. Move the pointer toward right and click on the horizontal axis.
7. Move the pointer outward and click to specify the slot width.
8. On the menu bar, click **Sketch > Sketcher geometries > Create circle.**
9. Select the centerpoint of the left arc of the slot.
10. Move the pointer outward and click.
11. Likewise, create a circle concentric to the right arc of the slot.
12. Add dimensions to the sketch, as shown.

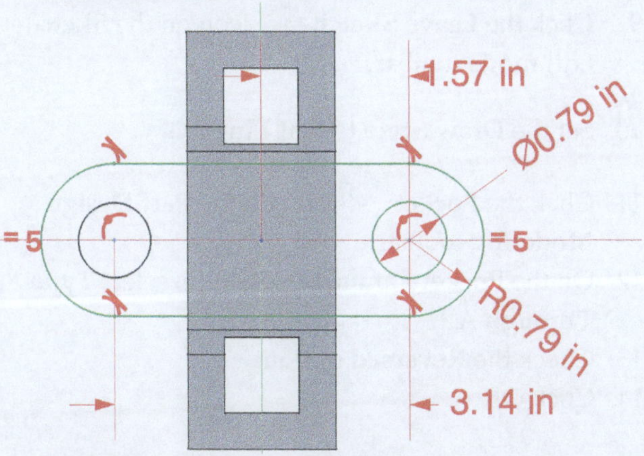

13. Click **Close** on the **Tasks** panel.
14. Click the **Pad** icon on the **Part Design Modeling** toolbar.
15. Type **0.78** in the **Length** box.
16. Check the **Symmetric to plane** option.
17. Click **OK.**

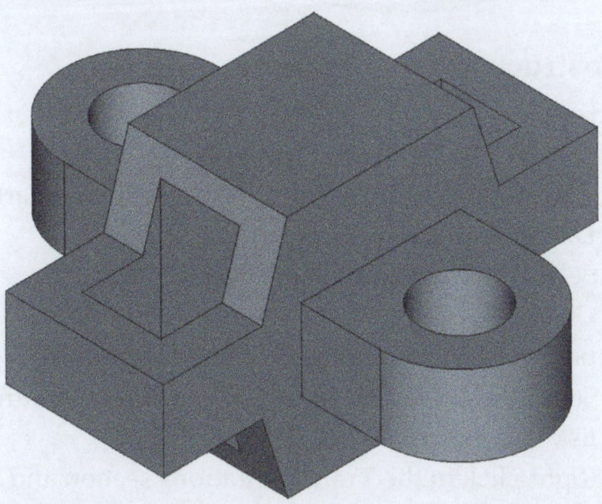

21. Save and close the file.

TUTORIAL 6

In this tutorial, you construct a patterned cylindrical shell.

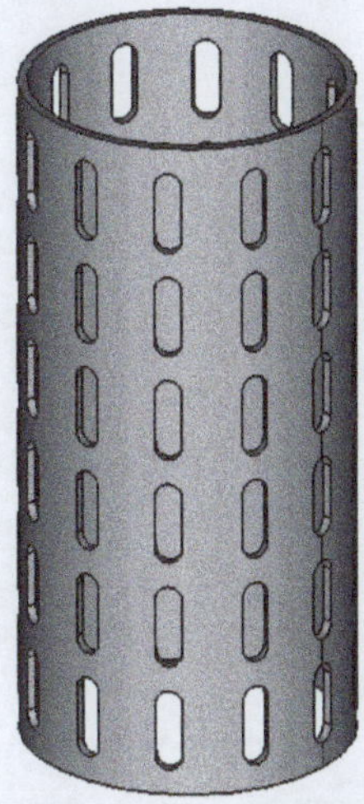

Constructing a cylindrical shell

1. Start a new FreeCAD file.
2. Select **Part Design** from the **Workbenches** drop-down.
3. Create a sketch on the XY plane (add Diameter constraints to the circles).

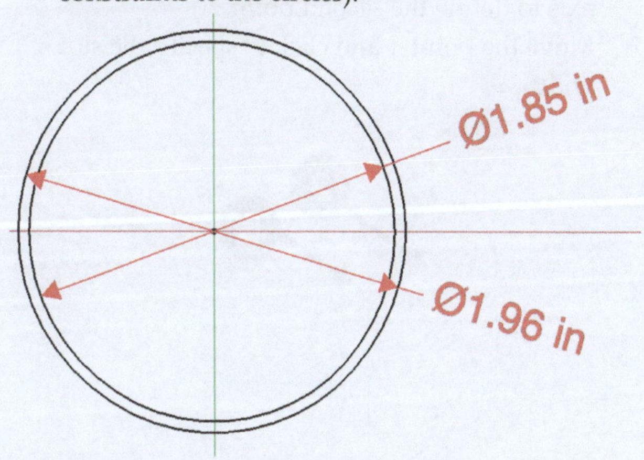

4. Extrude the sketch up to 3.93 depth.

Adding a Slot

1. Activate the **Create Sketch** tool.
2. Select the **XZ Plane** from the graphics window.
3. Set the **Draw Style** to **Wireframe**.
4. Click the **Create Slot**  icon on the **Sketcher geometries** toolbar.
5. Click on the vertical axis of the sketch to define the first point of the slot.
6. Move the pointer up and click on the vertical axis to define the second point.
7. Move the pointer and click to specify the slot width.

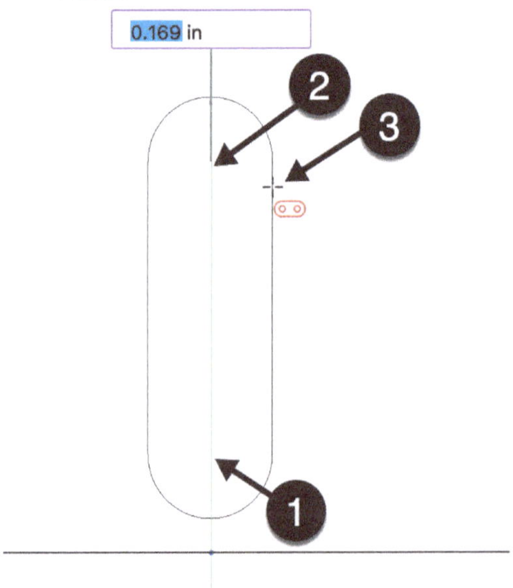

8. Add constraints to the slot.

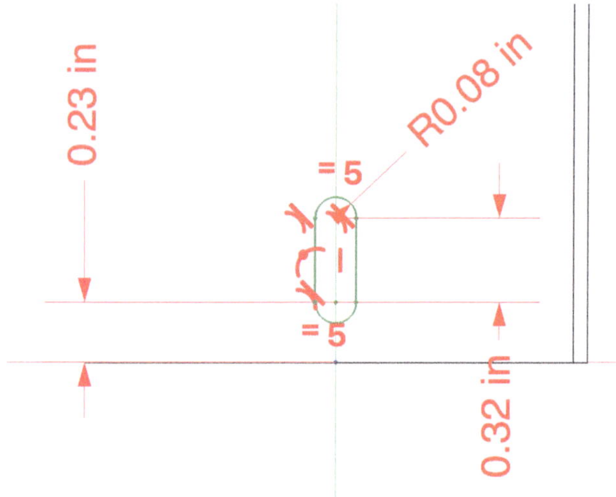

9. Click the **Leave Sketch**  icon on the **Sketcher edit mode** toolbar.
10. Set the **Draw Style** to **Flat Lines** .
11. Click the **Pocket**  icon on the **Part Design Modeling** toolbar.
12. On the **Pocket Parameters** section, select **Type > Through All**.
13. Check the **Reversed** option.
14. Click **OK**.

Constructing the Linear and Circular patterns using the MultiTransform tool

1. Click the **MultiTransform**  icon on the **Part Design Patterns** toolbar.
2. Select the **Transform tool shapes** option.
3. Click the **Add feature** button and select the pocket feature from the graphics window.
4. Select the **Pocket** feature from the **Select feature** list, and then click **OK**.
5. Right-click in the **Transformations** section and select **Add linear pattern**.
6. Select **Direction > Base Z axis**.

7. Type **3.145** in the **Length** box.
8. Type **6** in the **Occurrences** box.
9. Right-click in the **Transformations** section and select **Add polar pattern.**
10. Select the **Base Z axis** from the **Axis** drop-down.
11. Select **Mode > Overall Angle**.
12. Type **360** in the **Angle** box.
13. Type-in **12** in the **Occurrences** box.
14. Click **OK** to create the circular pattern.

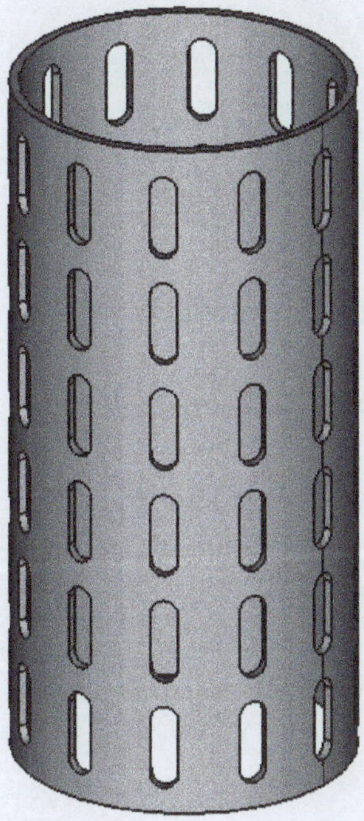

11. Save and close the model.

TUTORIAL 7

In this tutorial, you construct a pulley wheel using the **Revolution** and **Groove** tools.

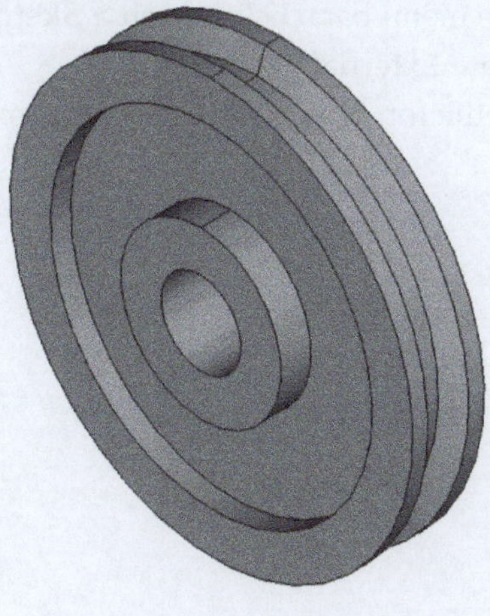

1. Open a new FreeCAD file.
2. Select **Part Design** from the **Workbenches** drop-down.
3. Click the **Create Sketch** icon on the **Part Design Helper** toolbar.
4. Select the YZ Plane from the **Tasks** panel and click **OK**.
5. Click the **Create Polyline** icon on the **Sketcher geometries** toolbar.
6. Create a closed sketch, as shown.

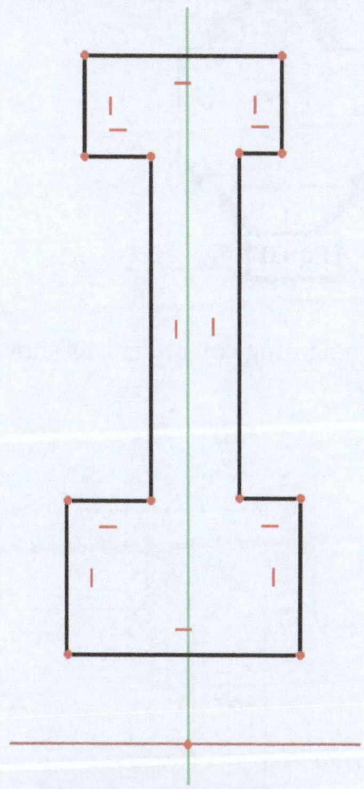

7. Click the **Constrain Equal**  icon on the **Sketcher constraints** toolbar.
8. Make the entities of the sketch equal in length, as shown.

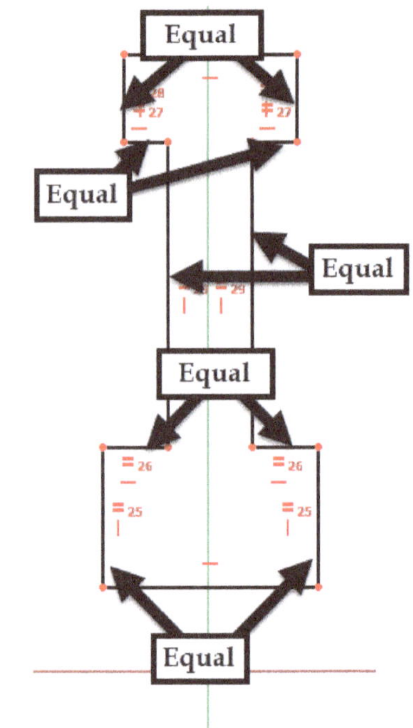

9. Create remaining constraints, as shown.

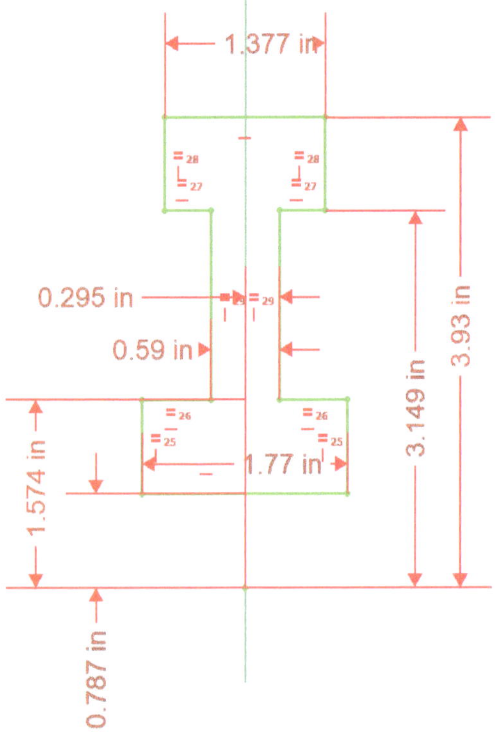

10. Click the **Close** button on the **Tasks** panel.
11. Click the **Revolution** icon on the **Part Design Modeling** toolbar; the sketch is selected automatically.
12. Select **Axis > Base Yaxis** from the **Revolution parameters** section of the **Model** panel.
13. Type **360** in the **Angle** box.
14. Click **OK** to construct the revolved feature.

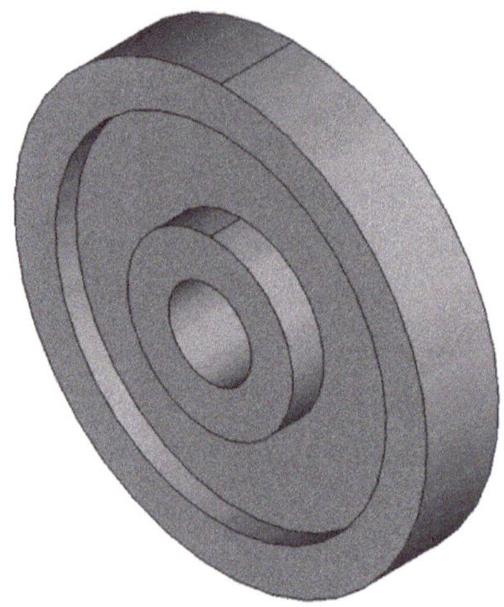

Constructing the Groove feature

1. Click the **Create Sketch** icon on the **Part Design Helper** toolbar.
2. Select the YZ Plane.
3. Set the **Draw Style** to **Wireframe**.
4. Create the sketch, as shown.

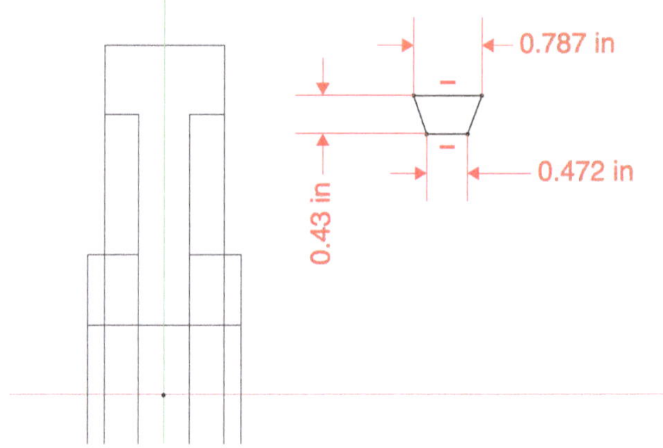

5. On the menu bar, click **Sketch > Sketcher tools > Create External geometry**.
6. Select the top horizontal edge of the model, as shown.

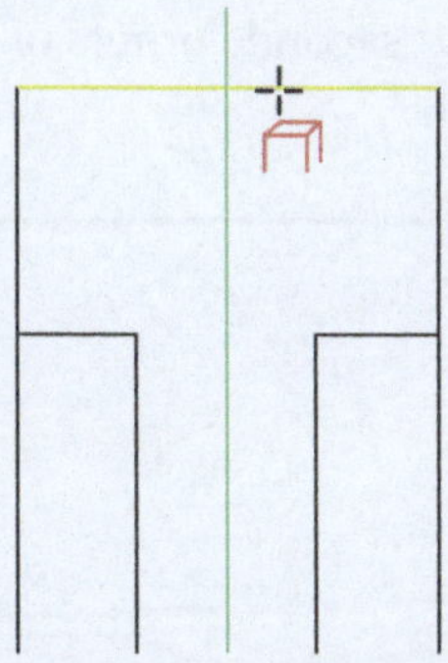

7. On the menu bar, click **Sketch > Sketcher constraints > Constrain Coincident**.
8. Select the endpoint of the sketch and the external geometry, as shown.

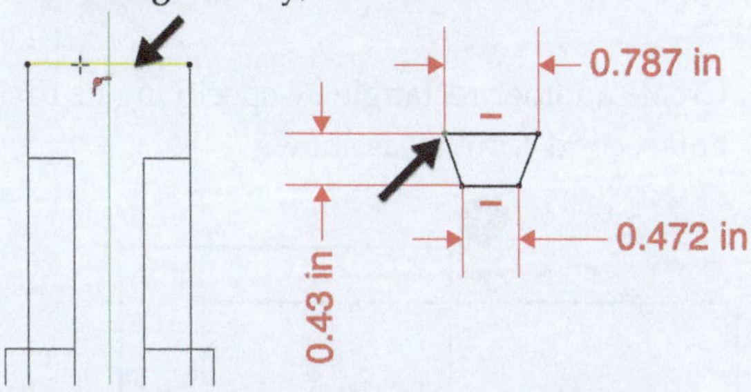

9. On the menu bar, click **Sketch > Sketcher geometries > Create line.**
10. Select the sketch origin, move the pointer vertically upward and click on the external geometry.

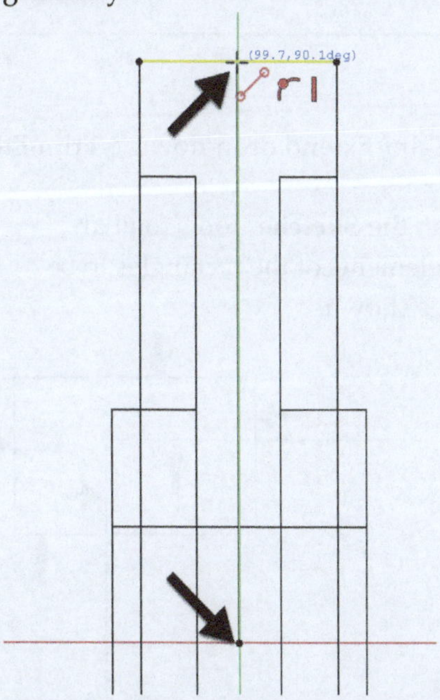

11. Select the newly created vertical line.
12. Click the **Toggle Construction geometry** icon on the **Sketcher geometries** toolbar.
13. Add the Angle constraint between the left inclined line and the bottom horizontal line, as shown.

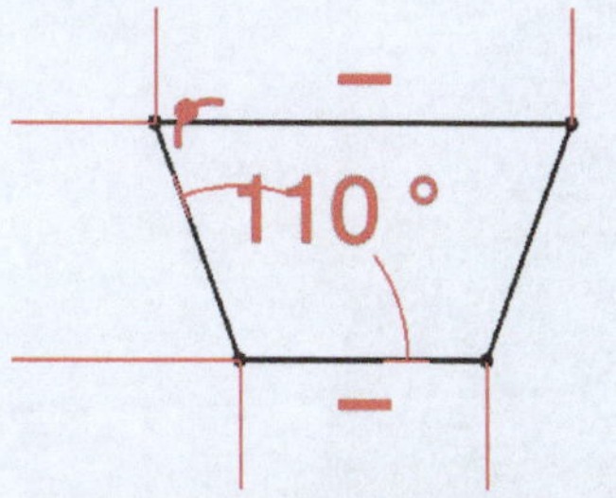

14. Click the **Constraint Symmetrical** icon on the **Sketcher constraints** toolbar.
15. Select the endpoints of the top horizontal line of the sketch.
16. Select the top endpoint of the vertical line.

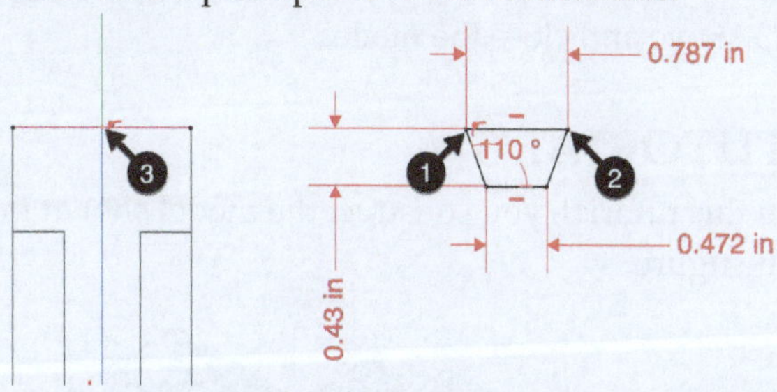

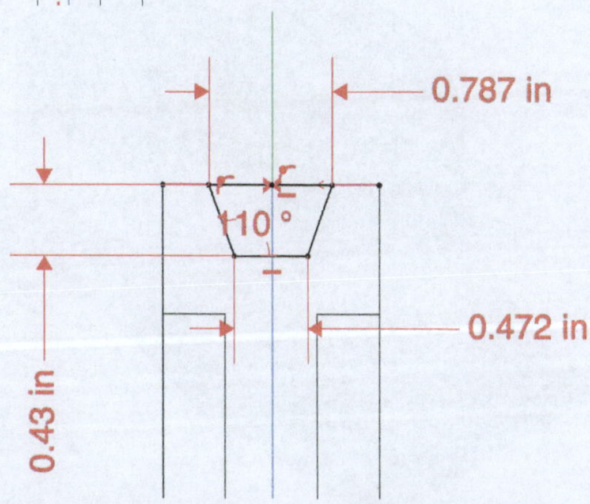

17. Click the **Close** button on the **Tasks** panel.
18. Set the **Draw Style** to **Flat Lines.**
19. Click the **Groove** icon on the **Part Design geometries** toolbar.
20. Select **Axis > Base Yaxis** from the **Revolution parameters** section of the **Model** panel.
21. Type 360 in the **Angle** box.
22. Click **OK.**

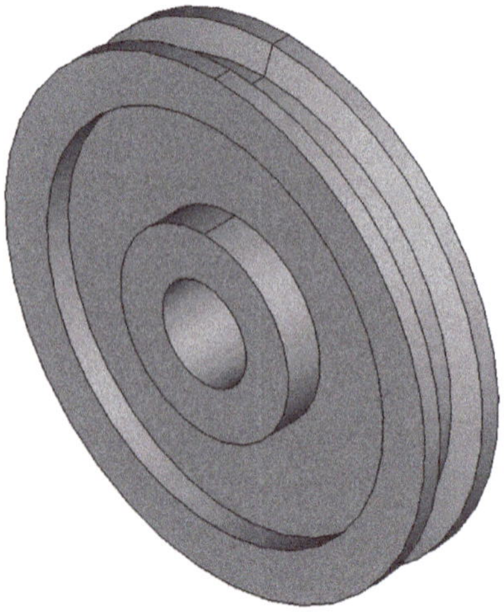

23. Save and close the model.

TUTORIAL 8

In this tutorial, you construct the model shown in the figure.

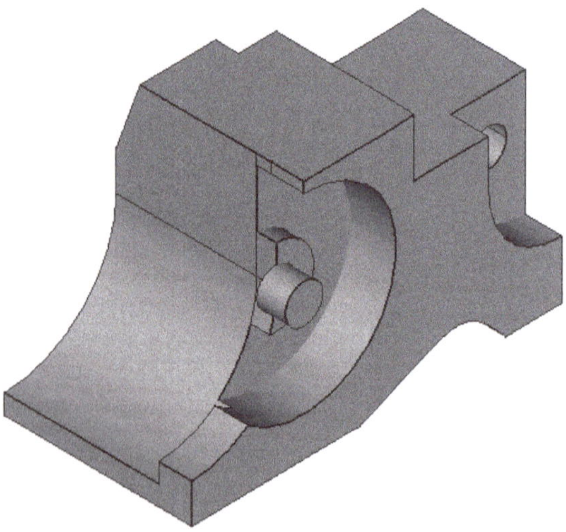

Creating the Base Feature

1. Open a new FreeCAD file.
2. Select **Part Design** from the **Workbenches** drop-down.
3. Click the **Create Sketch** icon on the **Part Design Helper** toolbar.
4. Select the YZ Plane from the Tasks panel and click OK.
5. Click the **Rectangle** drop-down > **Create Rectangle** 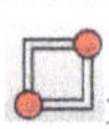 icon on the **Sketcher geometries** toolbar.
6. Specify the first and second corners of the rectangle, as shown.

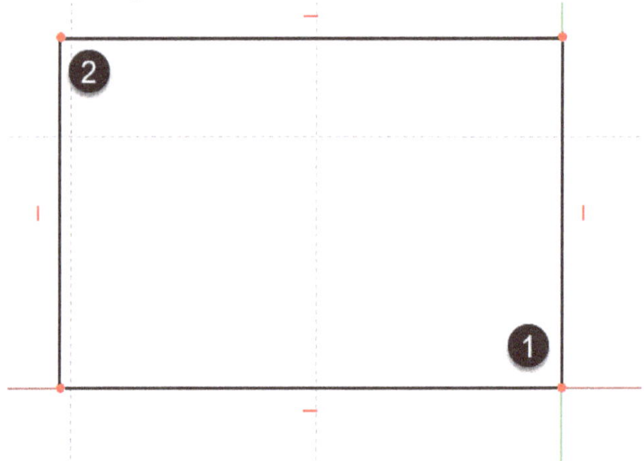

7. Create another rectangle by specifying its first and second corners, as shown.

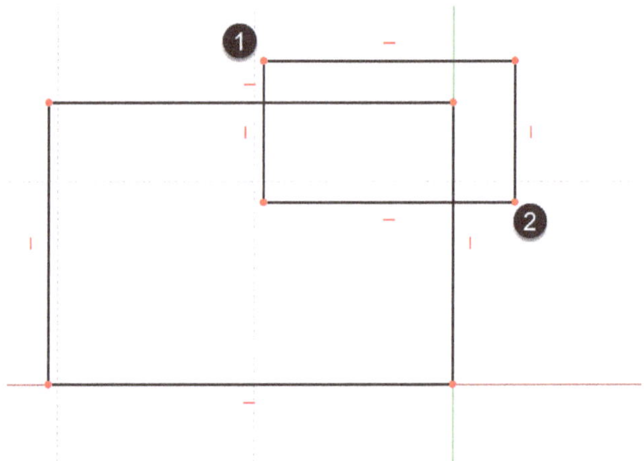

8. Click the **Trim/Extend** drop-down > **Trim Edge** 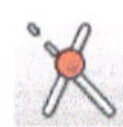 icon on the **Sketcher tools** toolbar.
9. Select the elements of the rectangles to be trimmed, as shown.

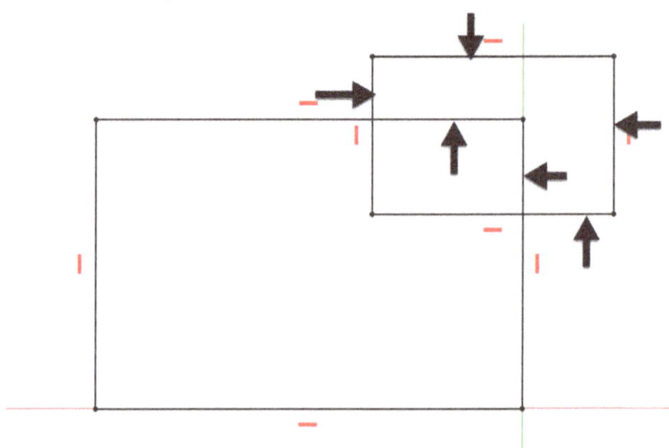

10. Add vertical and horizontal distance constraints to the sketch, as shown.

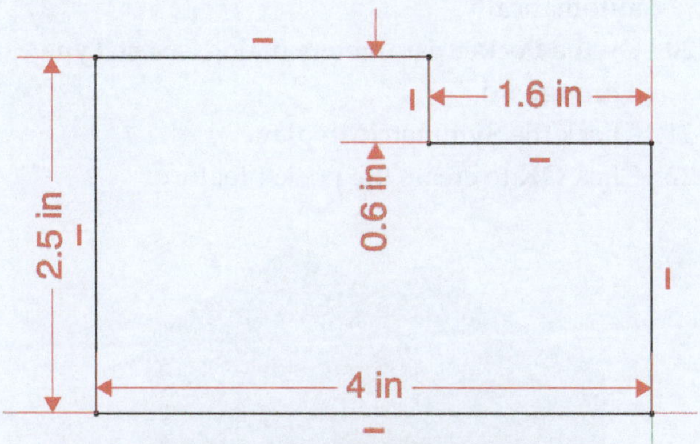

11. Click **Close** on the **Tasks** panel.
12. Click the **Pad** icon on the **Part Design Modeling** toolbar; the sketch is selected automatically.
13. Type 2 in the **Length** box.
14. Check the **Symmetric to Plane** option.
15. Click **OK**.

Creating the Pocket Features

1. Click the **Create Sketch** icon on the **Part Design Helper** toolbar.
2. Select the YZ Plane from the **Tasks** panel and click **OK**.
3. On the menu bar, click **Sketch > View Section**.
4. Click the **Create Polyline** icon on the **Sketcher geometries** toolbar.
5. Specify the endpoints of the polyline, as shown.

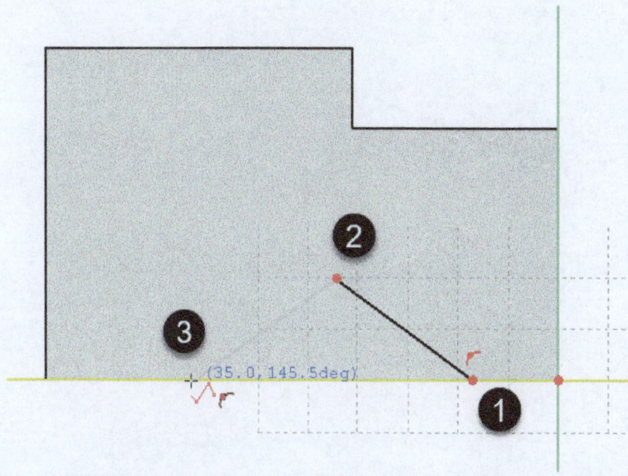

6. Right-click.
7. Click the **Create Fillet** icon on the **Sketcher tools** toolbar.
8. Select the corner point of the sketch, as shown.

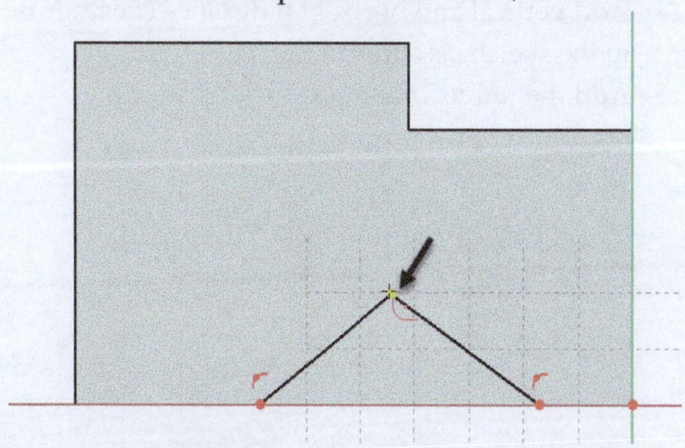

9. Click the Dimension drop-down > **Constrain Angle** icon on the **Sketcher constraints** toolbar.
10. Select the inclined line and the horizontal axis of the sketch.

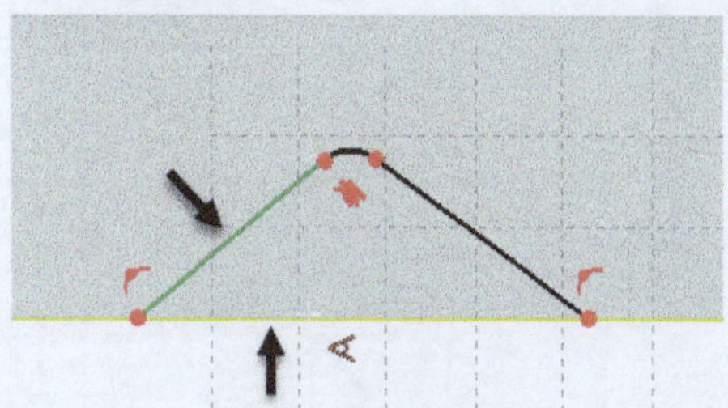

11. Type **20** in the **Angle** box and click **OK**.
12. Select the other inclined line and the horizontal axis of the sketch, as shown.

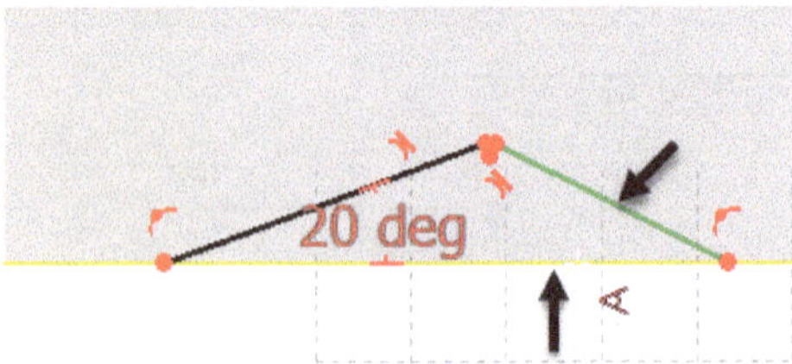

13. Type **135** in the **Angle** box and click **OK**.

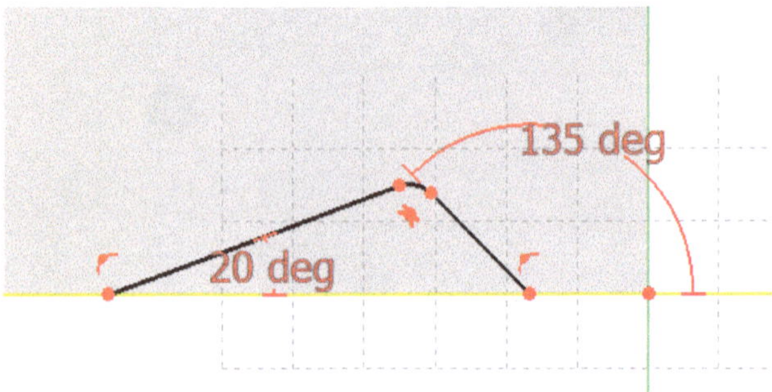

14. Add vertical and horizontal distance constraints to the sketch, as shown.
15. Add the radius constraint to the fillet.

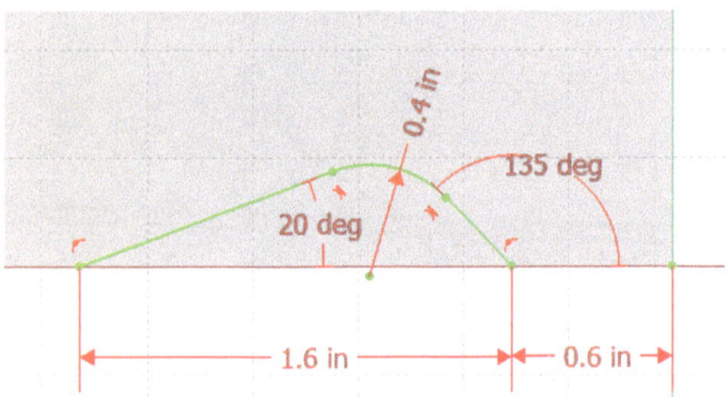

16. Click the **Create line** icon on the **Sketcher geometries** toolbar.
17. Select the endpoints of the sketch, as shown.

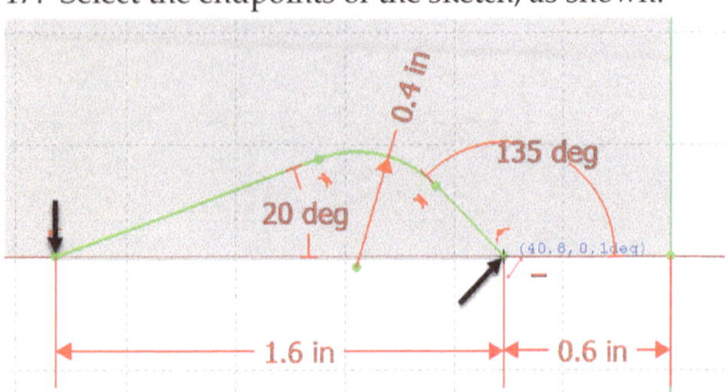

18. Click **Close** on the **Tasks** panel.
19. Click the **Pocket** icon on the **Part Design Modeling** toolbar; the sketch is selected automatically.
20. On the **Pocket parameters** dialog, select **Type > Through all**.
21. Check the **Symmetric to plane**.
22. Click **OK** to create the pocket feature.

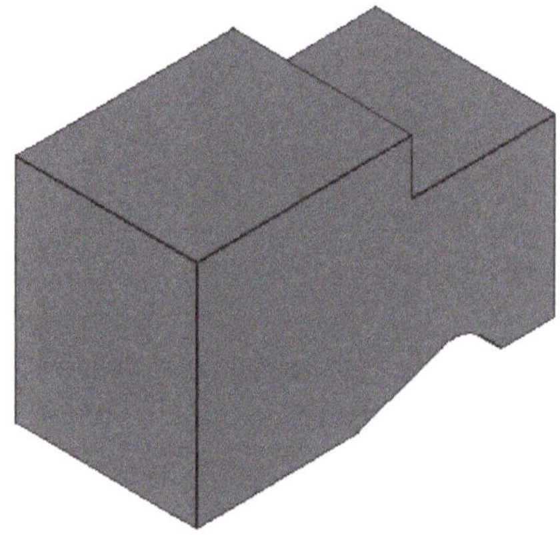

23. Click on the right side face of the model.

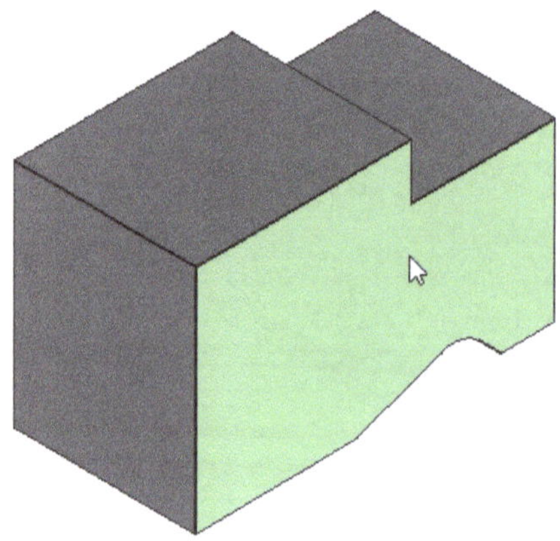

24. Click the **Create Sketch** icon on the **Part Design Helper** toolbar.
25. Click the **Create Polyline** icon on the **Sketcher geometries** toolbar.
26. Click on the vertical axis of the sketch to define the start point.

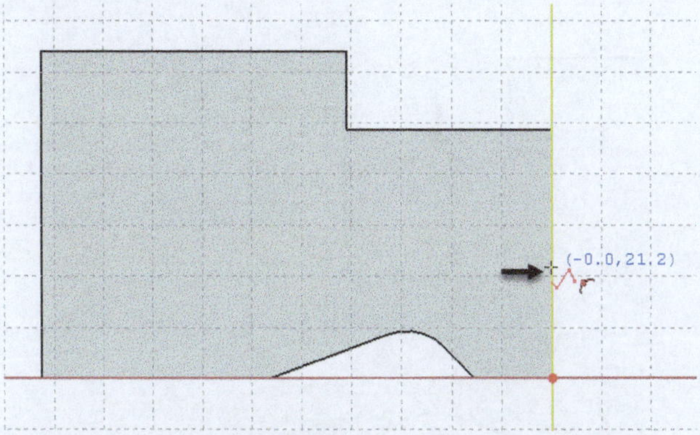

27. Move the pointer vertically upward, and then click to create the vertical line.

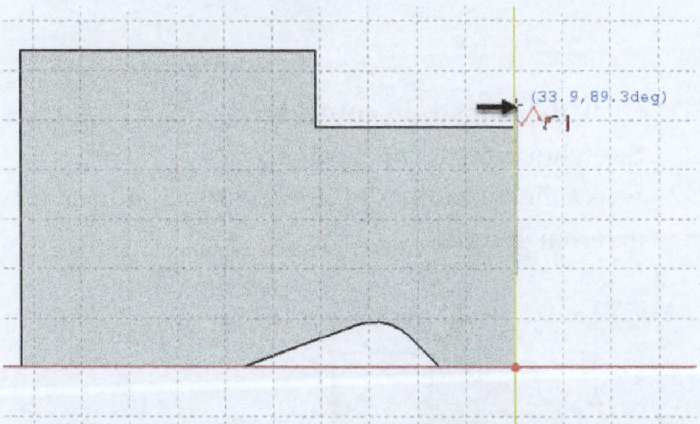

28. Move the pointer horizontally toward left, and then click.

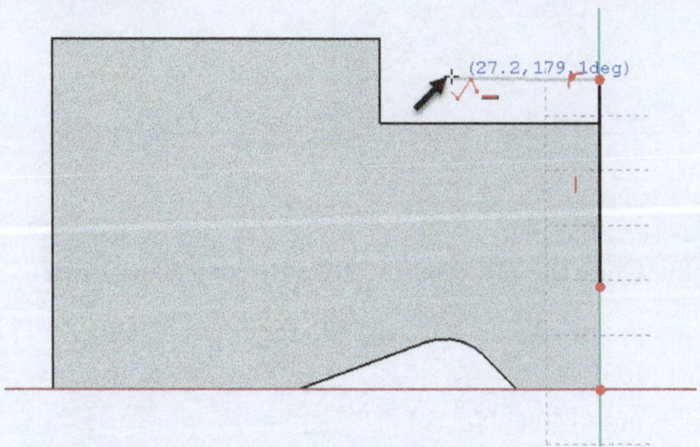

29. Move the vertically downward and click.

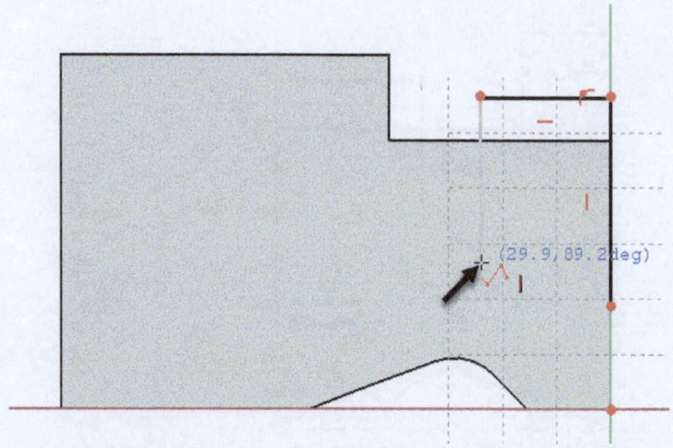

30. Right-click.
31. Click the **Arc** drop-down > **Create arc by 3 points** on the **Sketcher geometries** toolbar.
32. Select the endpoints of the two vertical lines.

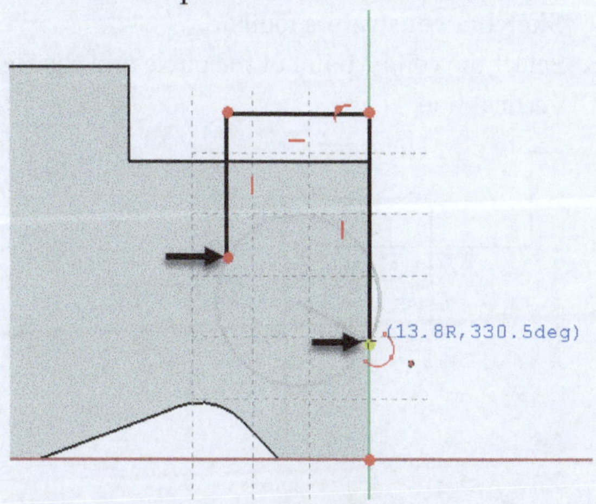

33. Move the pointer outward and click to create the arc.

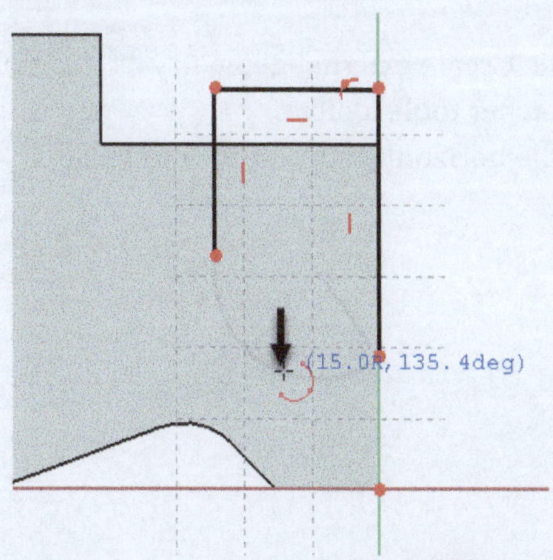

34. Click the **Constrain Tangent** icon on the **Sketcher constraints** toolbar.
35. Select the left vertical line and the arc.

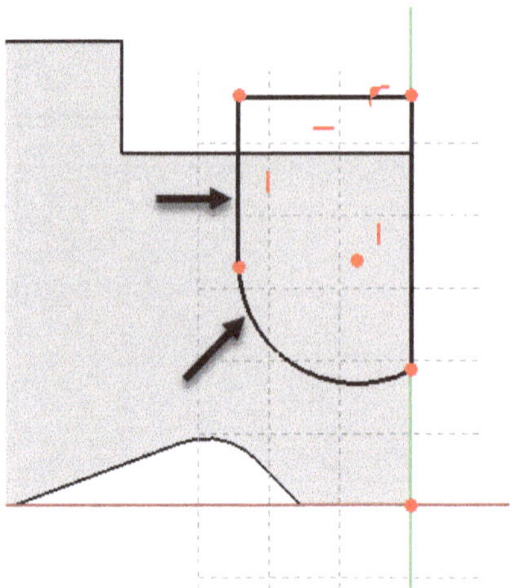

36. Click **OK** on the **Sketcher Constrain Substitution** message box.
37. Click the **Constrain Coincident** icon on the **Sketcher constraints** toolbar.
38. Select the center point of the circle and the right vertical line.

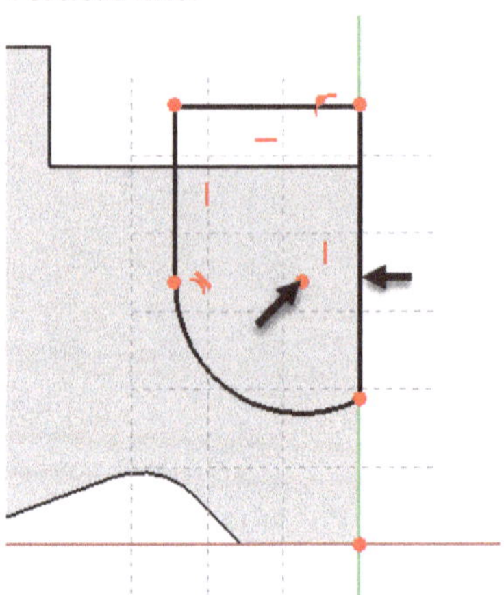

39. Click the **Create external geometry** icon on the **Sketcher tools** toolbar.
40. Select the horizontal edge of the model, as shown.

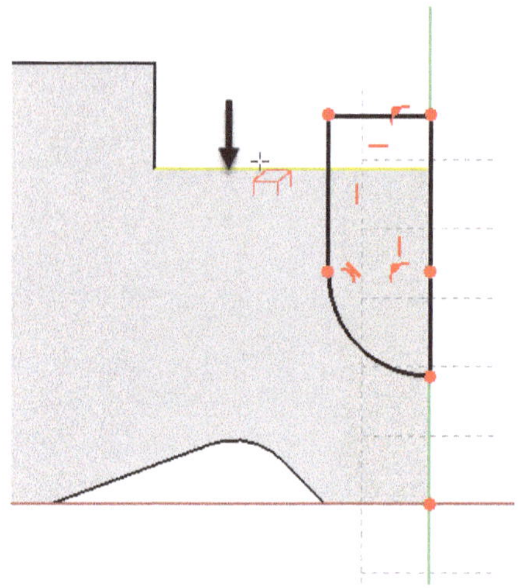

41. Click the **Constrain coincident** icon on the **Sketcher constraints** toolbar.
42. Select the endpoint of the horizontal line and the external geometry.

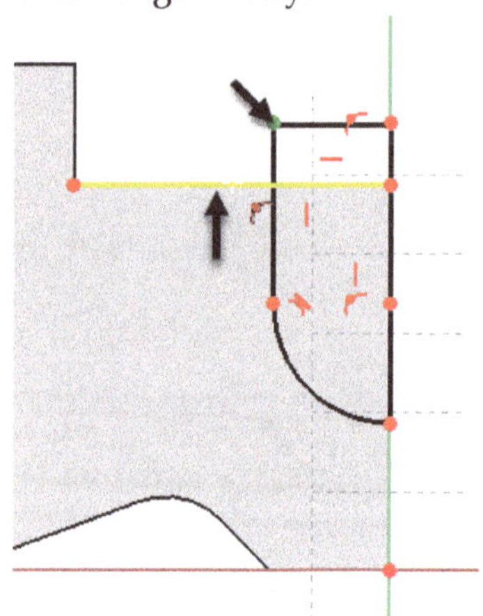

43. Click the **Dimension** drop-down > **Constrain arc or circle** on the **Sketcher constraints** toolbar.
44. Select the arc.
45. Type **0.8** and click **OK**.
46. Click the **Constrain vertical distance** icon on the **Sketcher constraints** toolbar.
47. Select the centerpoint of the arc and the sketch origin.
48. Type 1.4 in the **Length** box and click **OK**.

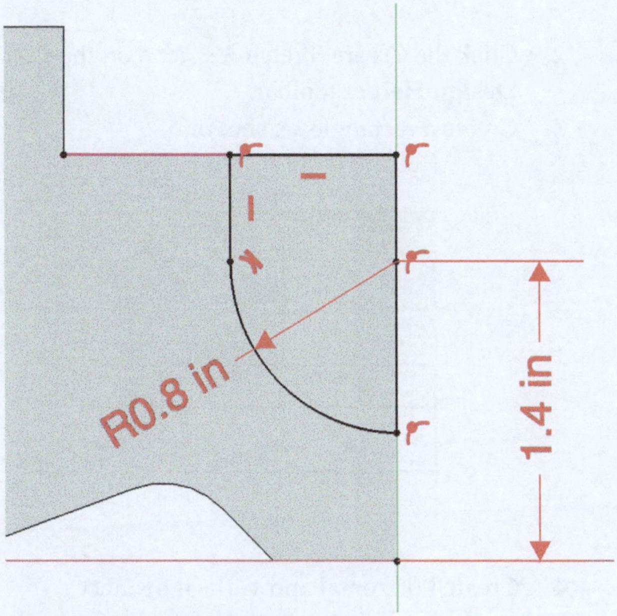

49. Click **Close** on the **Tasks** panel.
50. Click the **Pocket** icon on the **Part Design Modeling** toolbar; the sketch is selected automatically.
51. On the **Pocket parameters** dialog, select **Type > Dimension.**
52. Type **0.4** in the **Length** box.
53. Click **OK.**

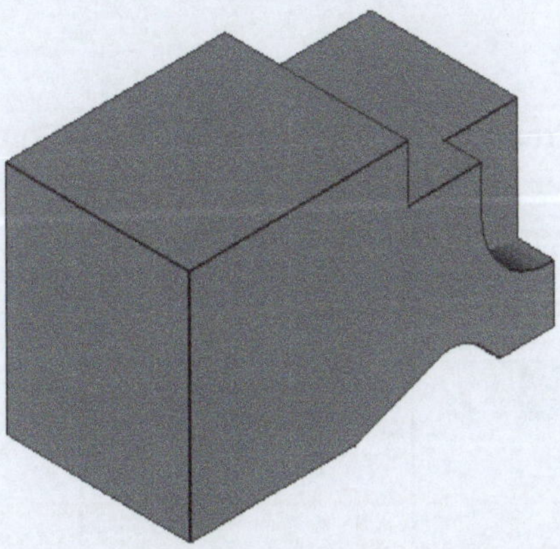

54. Select the flat face of the pocket feature.
55. Click the **Create Sketch** icon on the **Part Design Helper** toolbar.
56. Create a circle.
57. Click the **Create external geometry** icon on the **Sketcher tools** toolbar.
58. Select the curved edge of the model, as shown.

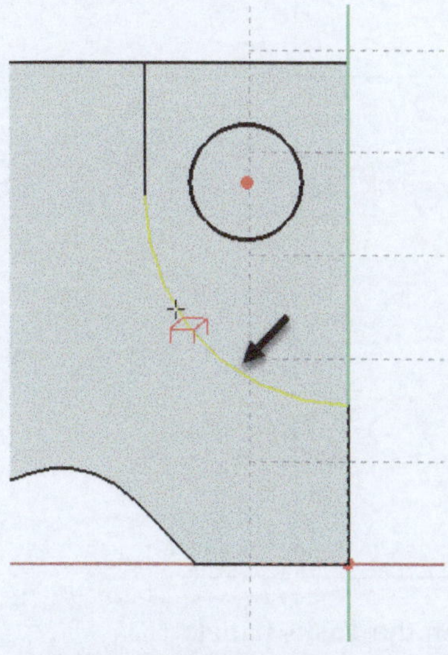

59. Click the **Constrain symmetrical** icon on the **Sketcher constraints** toolbar.
60. Select the centerpoint of the curved edge.
61. Select the endpoint of the curved edge.
62. Select the centerpoint of the circle.

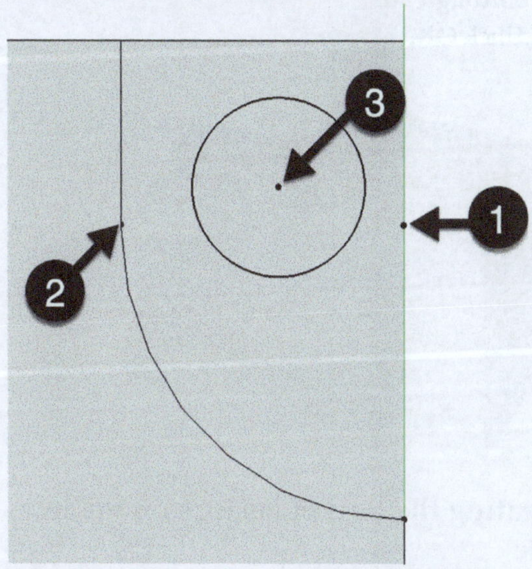

63. Add the diameter constraint to the circle.

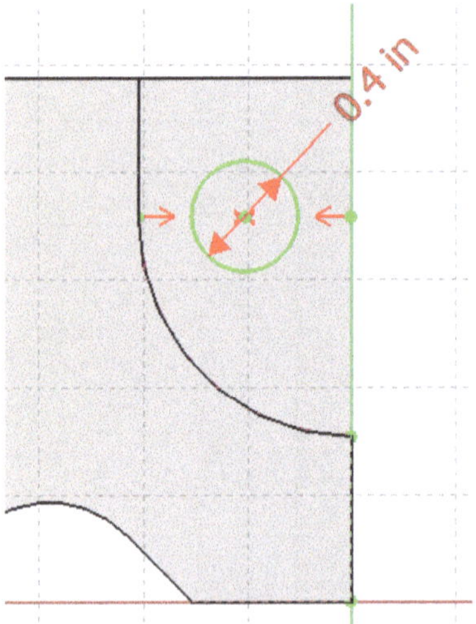

64. Click **Close** on the **Tasks** panel.
65. Click the **Pocket** icon on the **Part Design Modeling** toolbar; the sketch is selected automatically.
66. On the **Pocket parameters** dialog, select **Type > Through all**.
67. Click **OK**.

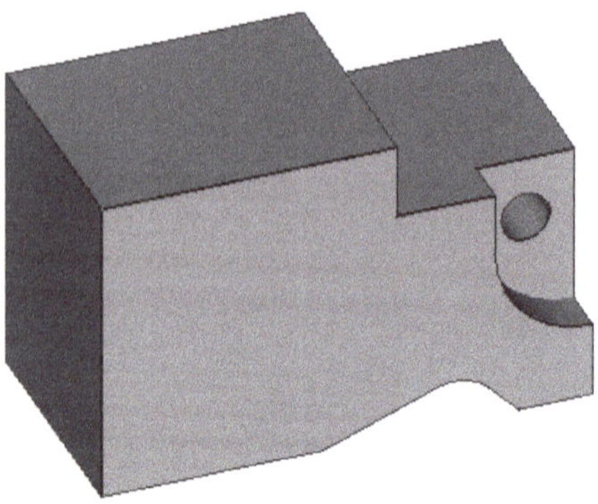

Creating the Pocket Feature on the left side

1. Click on the top face of the model.

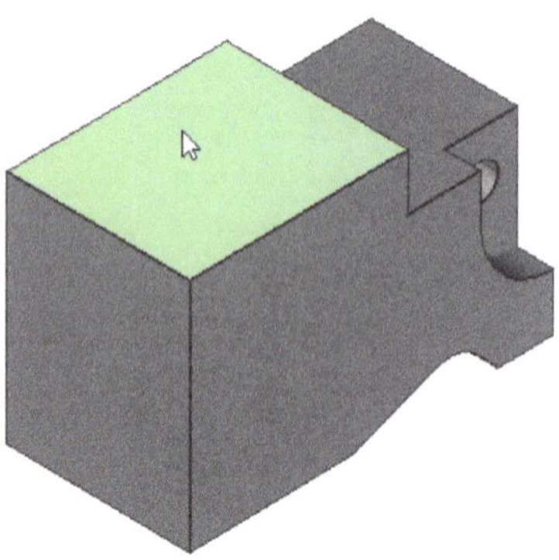

2. Click the **Create Sketch** icon on the **Part Design Helper** toolbar.
3. Create a rectangle, as shown.

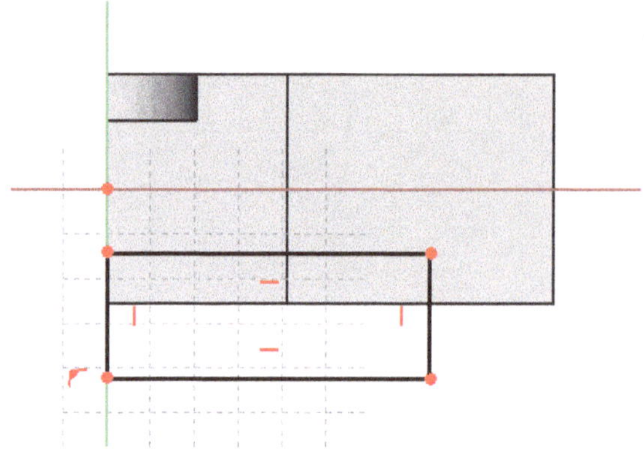

4. Create horizontal and vertical distance constraints, as shown.

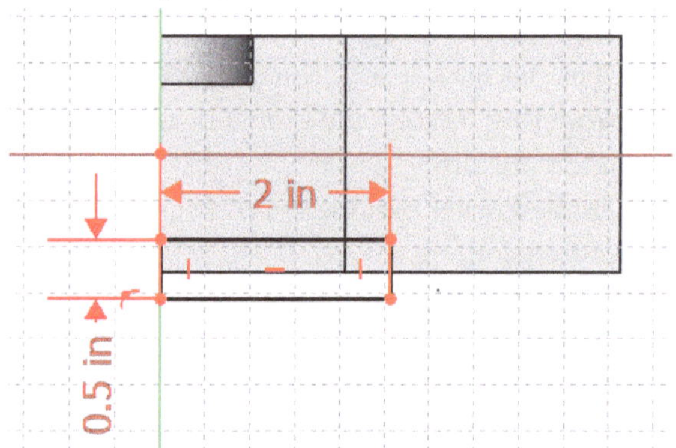

5. Click the **Create external geometry** icon on the **Sketcher tools** toolbar.
6. Select the horizontal edge of the model, as shown.

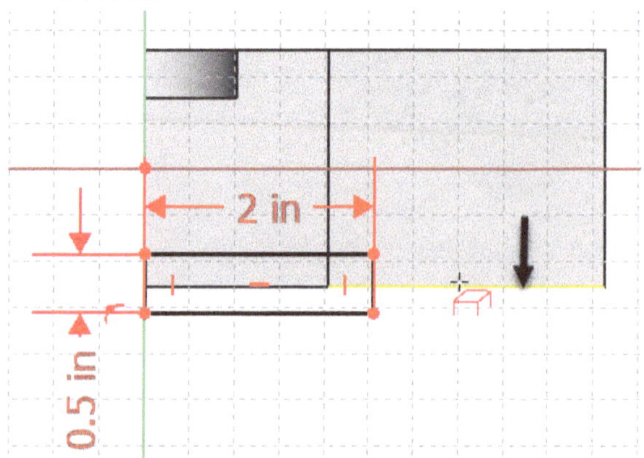

7. Click the **Constrain Coincident** icon on the **Sketcher constraints** toolbar.
8. Select the endpoint of the horizontal line and the

external geometry.

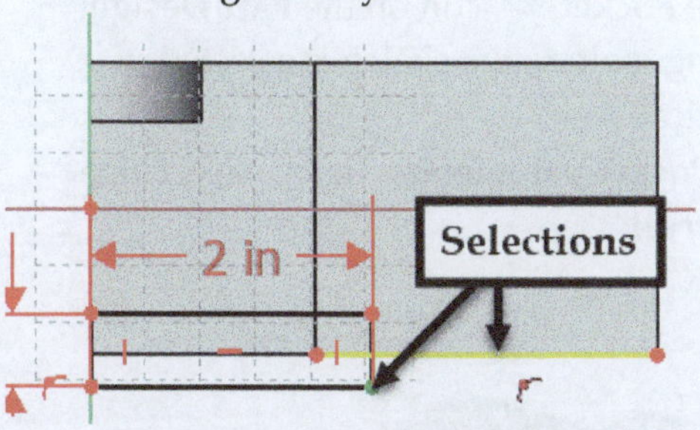

68. Click **Close** on the **Tasks** panel.
69. Click the **Pocket** icon on the **Part Design Modeling** toolbar; the sketch is selected automatically.
70. On the **Pocket parameters** dialog, select **Type > Through all.**
71. Click **OK.**

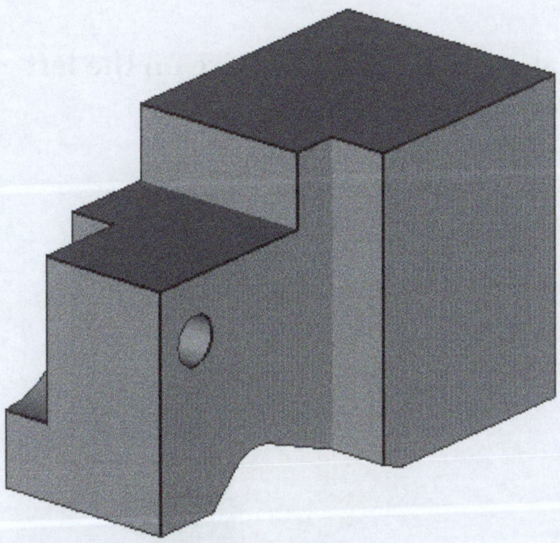

Creating the Angled Cut

1. Click on the front face of the model.

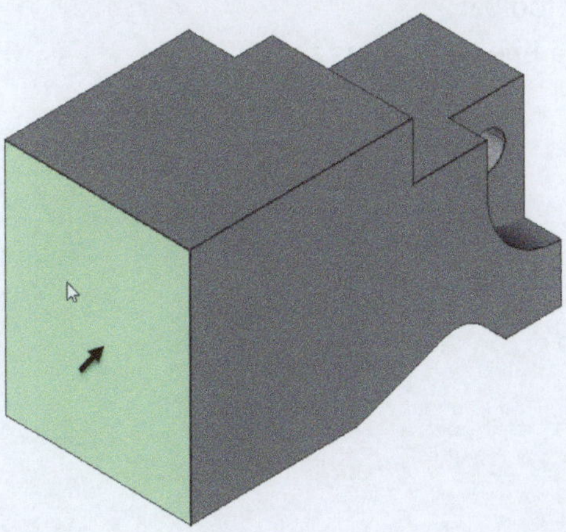

2. Click the **Create Sketch** icon on the **Part Design Helper** toolbar.
3. Create a line, as shown.

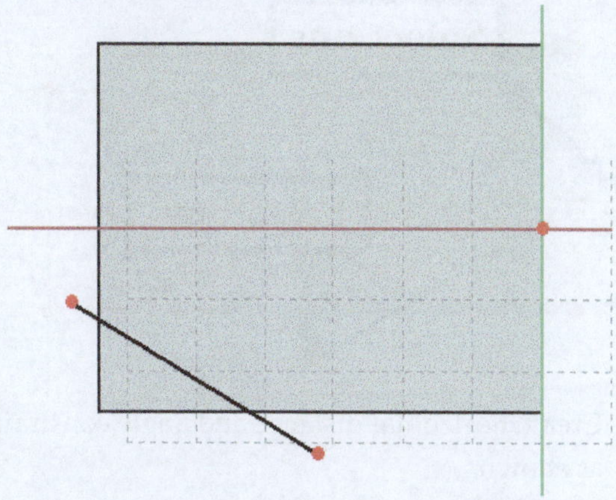

4. Click the **Create external geometry** icon on the **Sketcher tools** toolbar.
5. Select the horizontal and vertical edges of the model, as shown.

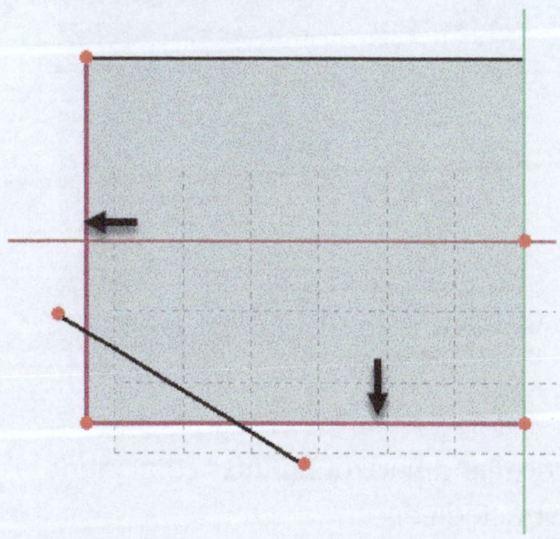

6. Click the **Constraint coincident** icon on the **Sketcher constraints** toolbar.
7. Select the endpoint of the line and the vertical edge.
8. Select the endpoint of the line and the horizontal edge.

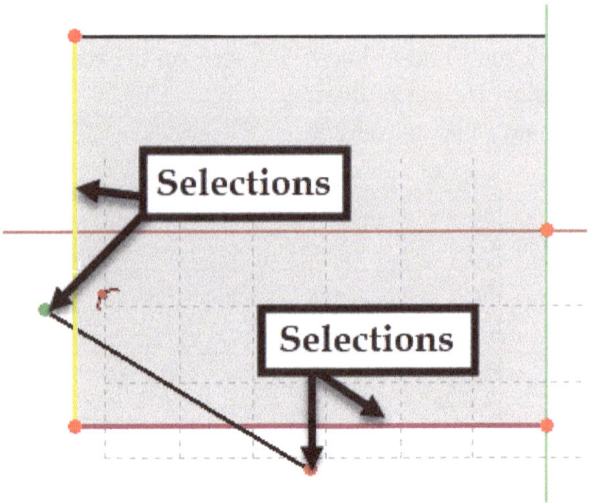

9. Create horizontal distance and angle constraints, as shown.

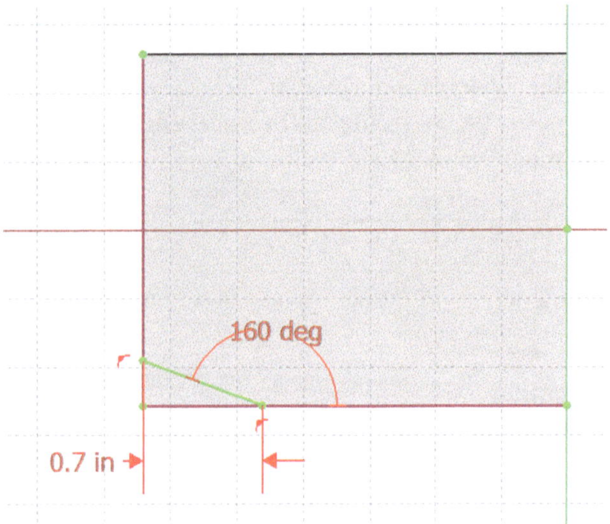

10. Create vertical and horizontal lines coincident with the extracted edges.

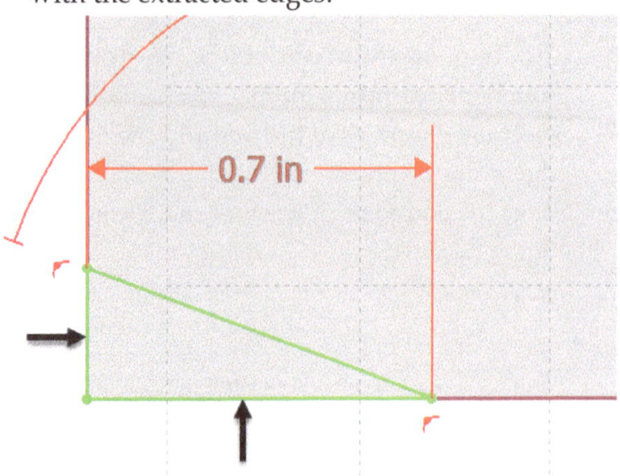

11. Click **Close** on the **Tasks** panel.

12. Click the **Pocket** icon on the **Part Design Modeling** toolbar; the sketch is selected automatically.
13. On the **Pocket parameters** dialog, select **Type > Through all**.
14. Click **OK**.

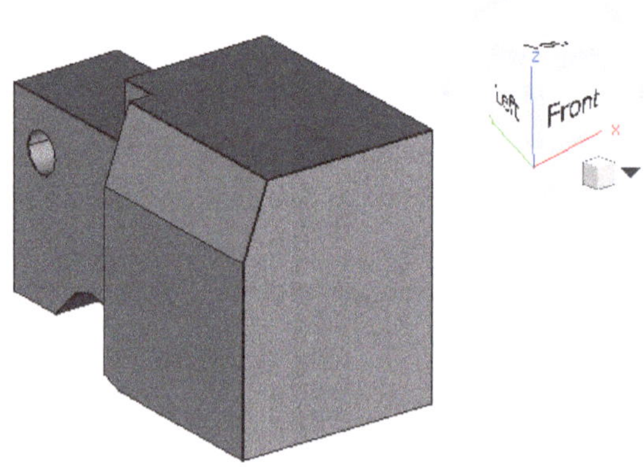

Creating the Pocket feature on the left

1. Click on the left face of the model.

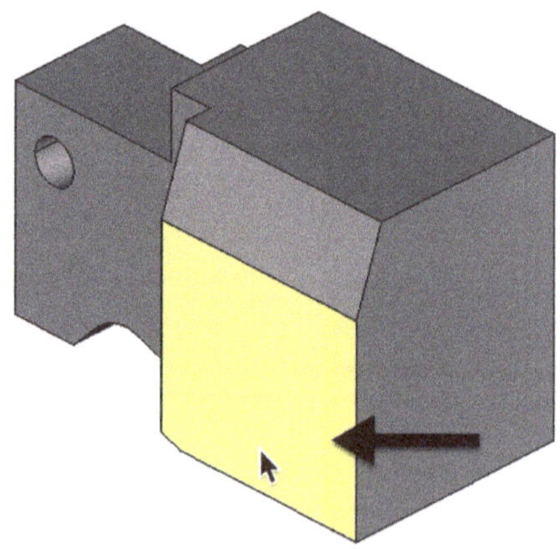

2. Click the **Create Sketch** icon on the **Part Design Helper** toolbar.
3. Create a line and arc, as shown.

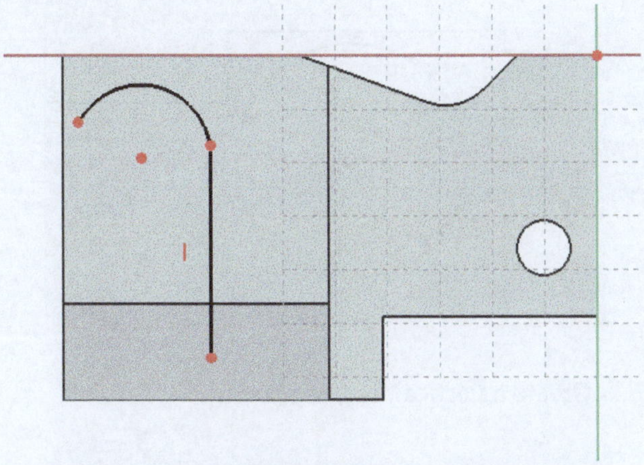

4. Click the **Create external geometry** icon on the **Sketcher tools** toolbar.
5. Select the horizontal and vertical edges of the model, as shown.

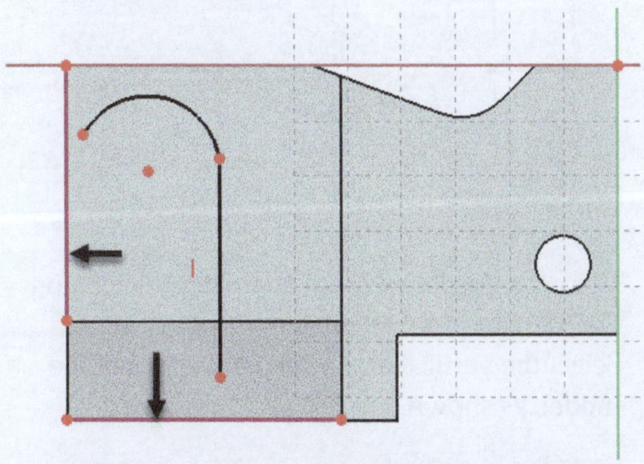

6. Click the **Constrain Coincident** icon on the **Sketcher constraints** toolbar.
7. Select the endpoint of the arc and the vertical edge.
8. Select the endpoint of the line and the horizontal edge.

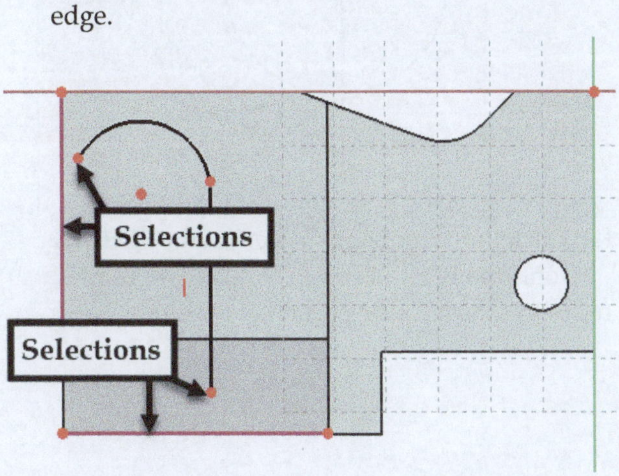

9. Click the **Constrain Tangent** icon on the **Sketcher constraints** toolbar.
10. Select the vertical line and the arc.
11. Create vertical and horizontal lines, as shown.

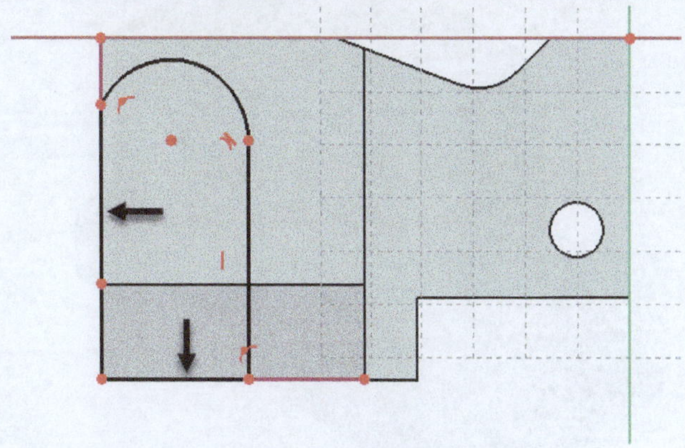

12. Click the **Constrain Coincident** icon on the **Sketcher constraints** toolbar.
13. Select the centerpoint of the arc and the vertical edge.

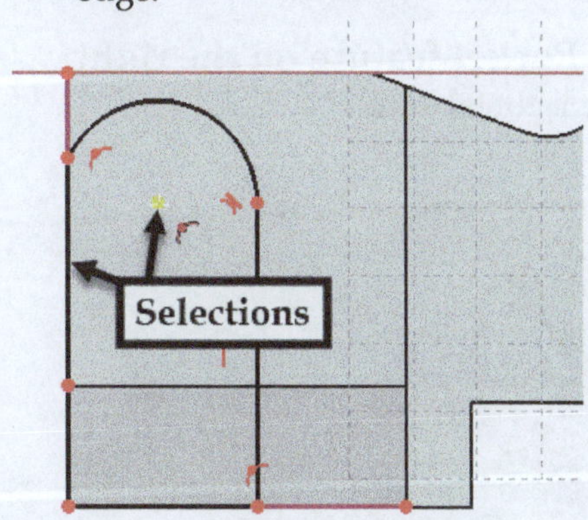

14. Create the radius and vertical distance constraints, as shown.

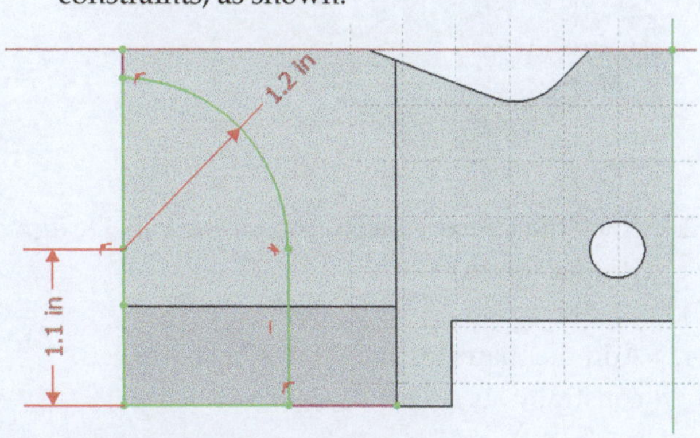

15. Click **Close** on the **Tasks** panel.
16. Click the **Pocket** icon on the **Part Design Modeling** toolbar; the sketch is selected automatically.

17. On the **Pocket parameters** dialog, select **Type > Dimension**.
18. Type **1.65** in the **Length** box.

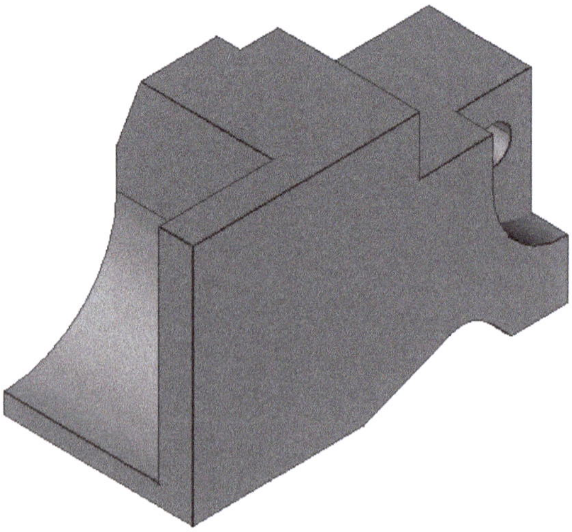

19. Click **OK**.

Creating the Pocket feature on the right

1. Click on the right face of the model.

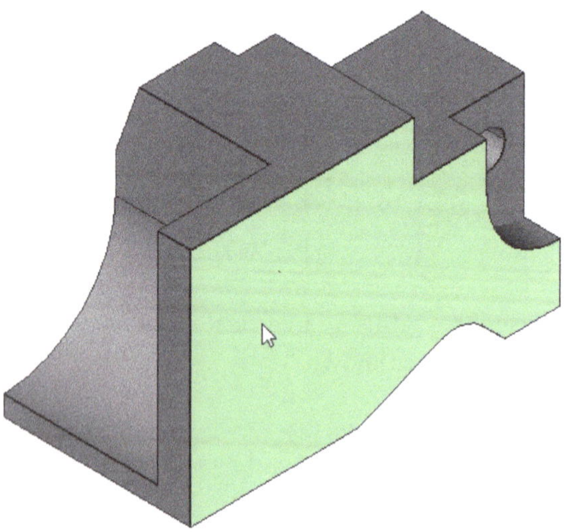

2. Click the **Create Sketch** icon on the **Part Design Helper** toolbar.
3. Create a circle.
4. Add the diameter and vertical distance constraint, as shown.

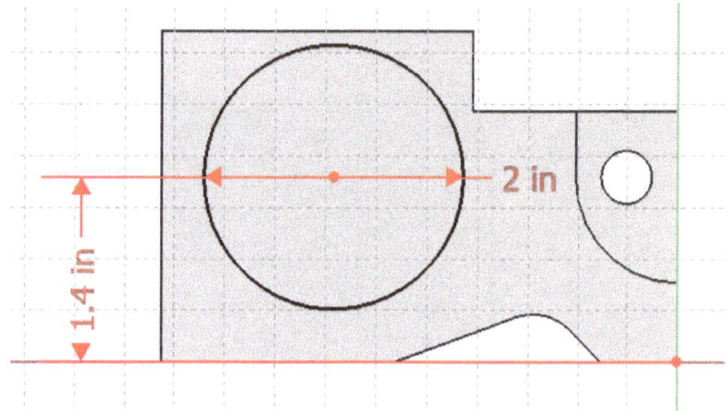

5. Create a vertical line, as shown.

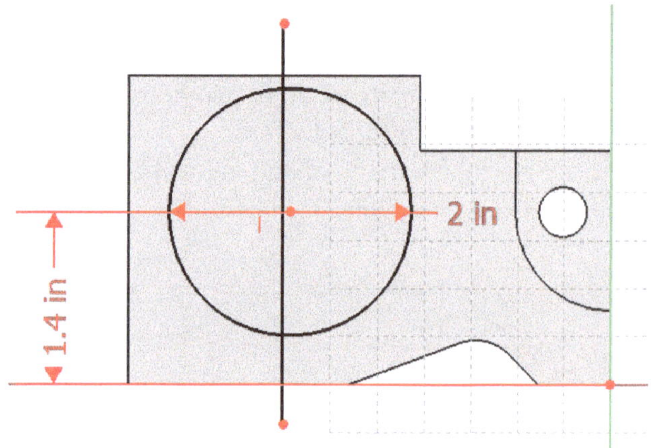

6. Click the **Create external geometry** icon on the **Sketcher tools** toolbar.
7. Select the vertical and horizontal edges of the model, as shown.

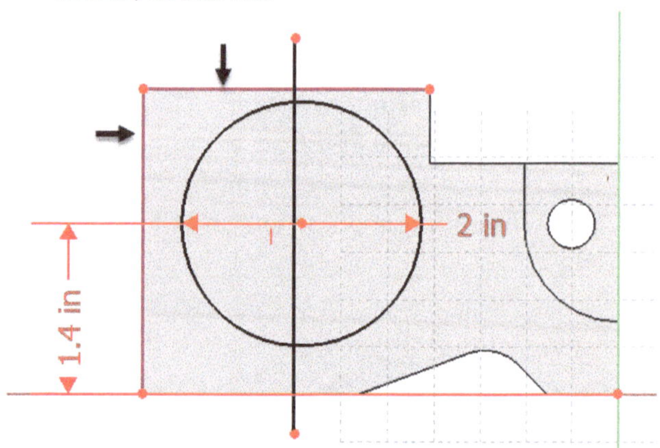

15. Click the **Trim Edge** icon on the **Sketcher tools** toolbar.
16. Select the left side portion of the circle.

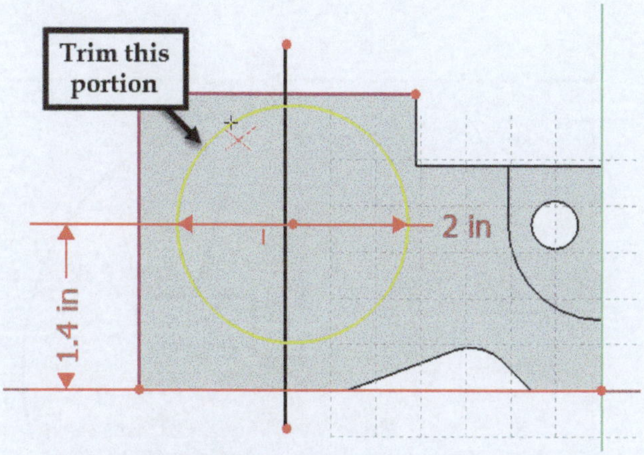

17. Click the **Constrain Coincident** icon on the **Sketcher constraints** toolbar.
18. Select endpoint the vertical line and the horizontal edge.

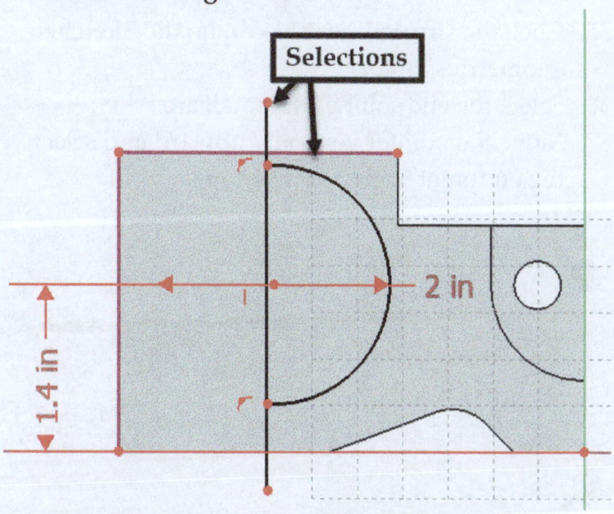

19. Trim the bottom and middle portions of the vertical line.

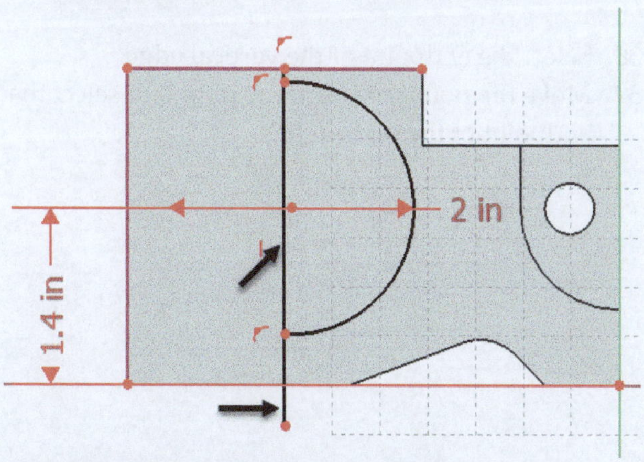

20. Click the **Arc** drop-down > **Create arc by 3 points** on the **Sketcher geometries** toolbar.
21. Select the endpoint of the arc.
22. Move the pointer toward the left and click on the extracted edge.

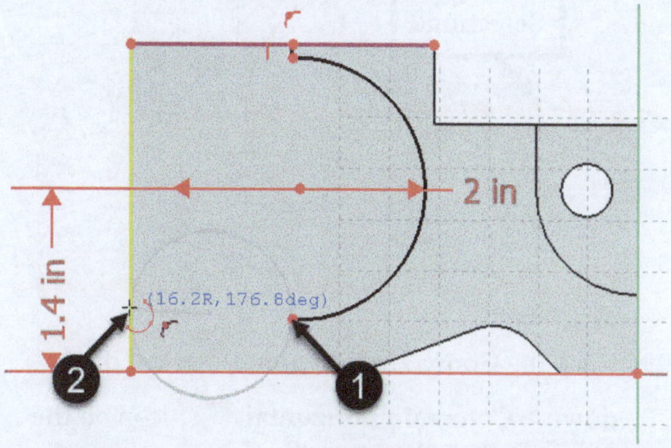

23. Move the pointer downward and click to create the arc.

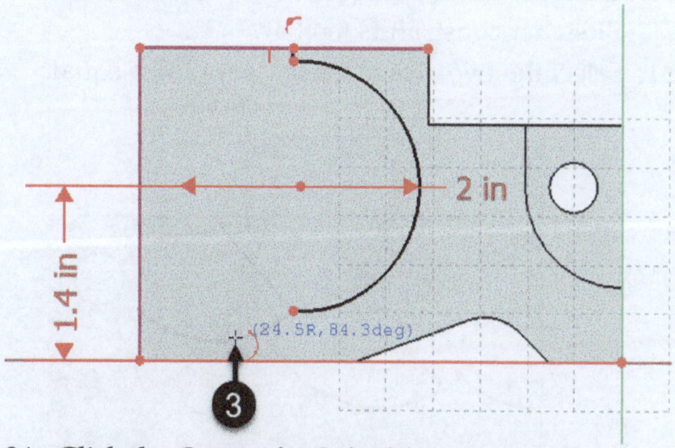

24. Click the **Constrain Coincident** icon on the **Sketcher constraints** toolbar.
25. Select the centerpoint of the new arc.
26. Select the extracted vertical edge.

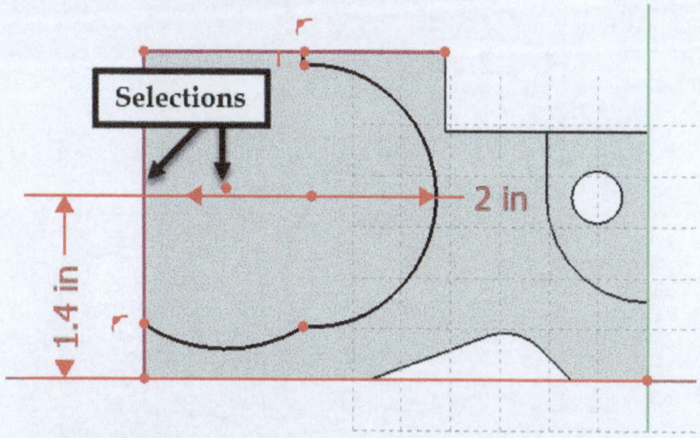

27. Right-click.
28. Select the centerpoints of the two arcs.

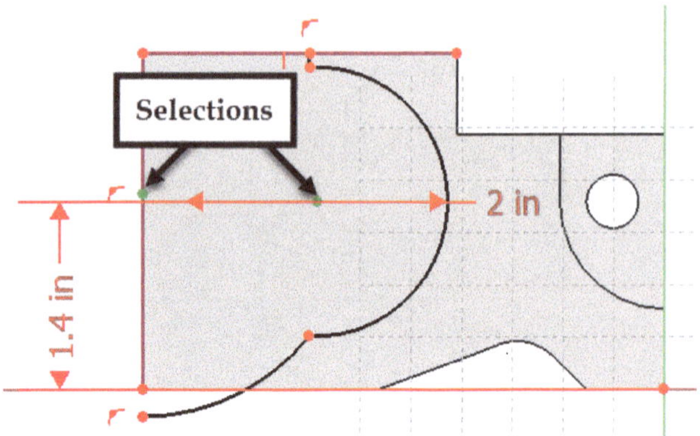

29. Click the **Constrain horizontal/vertical** drop-down > **Constrain horizontal** icon on the **Sketcher constraints** toolbar.
30. Click the **Constrain equal** icon on the **Sketcher constraints** toolbar.
31. Select the two arcs to make their radius equal.

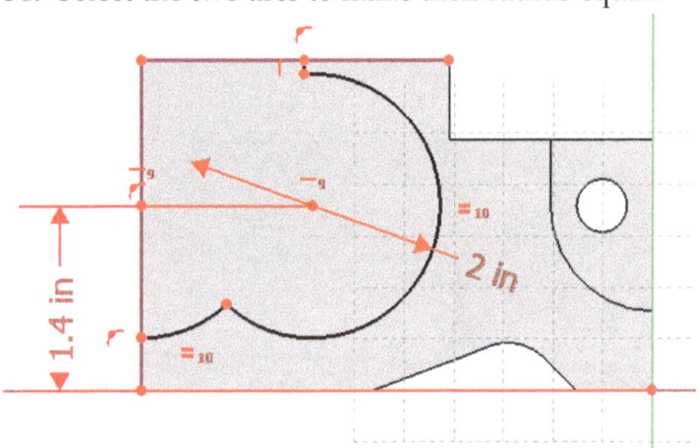

32. Create a horizontal distance constraint, as shown.

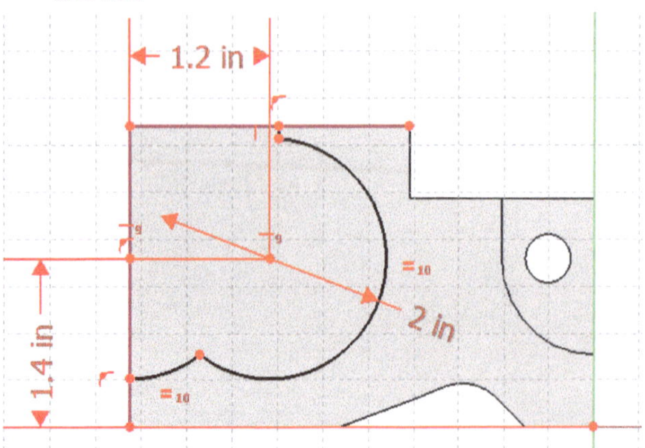

33. Select the center point and endpoint of the arc, as shown.

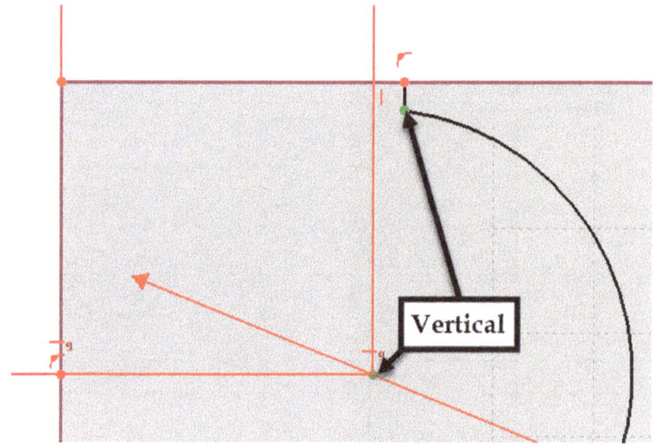

34. Click the **Constrain horizontal/vertical** drop-down > **Constrain vertical** icon on the **Sketcher constraints** toolbar.
35. Click the **Create line** icon on the **Sketcher geometries** toolbar.
36. Select the endpoint of the small arc.
37. Move the pointer vertically upward and select the endpoint of the vertical edge.

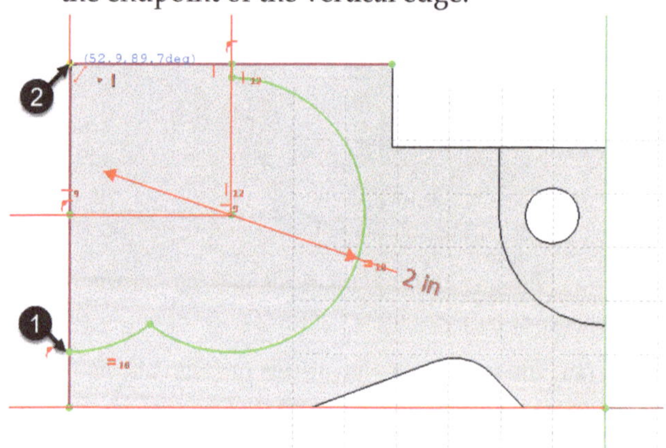

38. Select the endpoint of the vertical edge.
39. Move the pointer toward the right and select the endpoint of the vertical line.

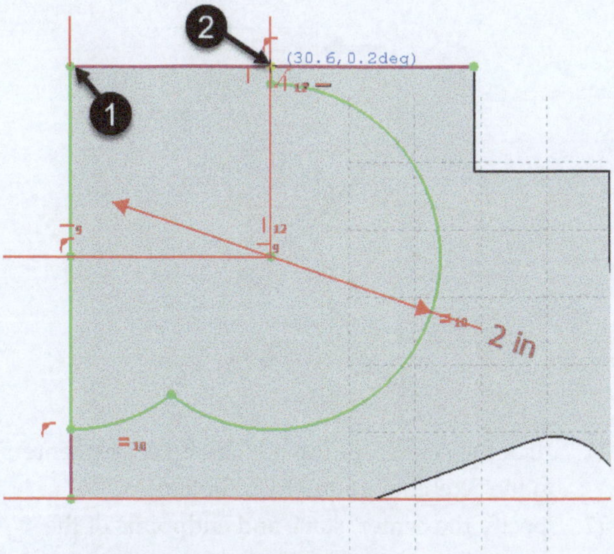

40. Click **Close** on the **Tasks** panel.
41. Click the **Pocket** icon on the **Part Design Modeling** toolbar; the sketch is selected automatically.
42. On the **Pocket parameters** dialog, select **Type > Dimension**.x
43. Type **0.5** in the **Length** box.
44. Click **OK**.

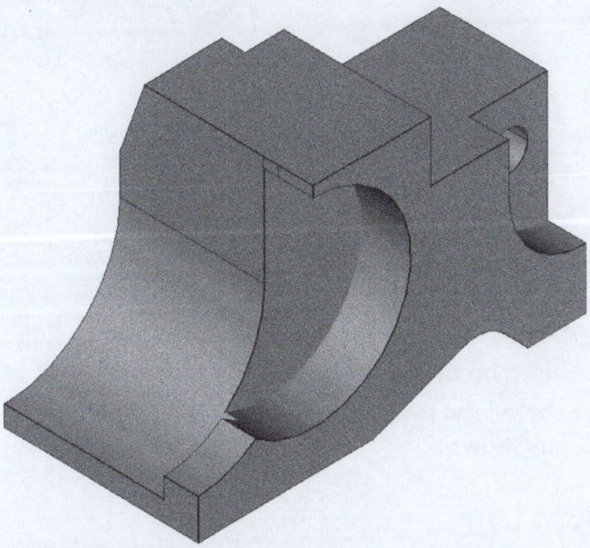

Adding the Pad Features

1. Click on the flat face of the pocket feature.

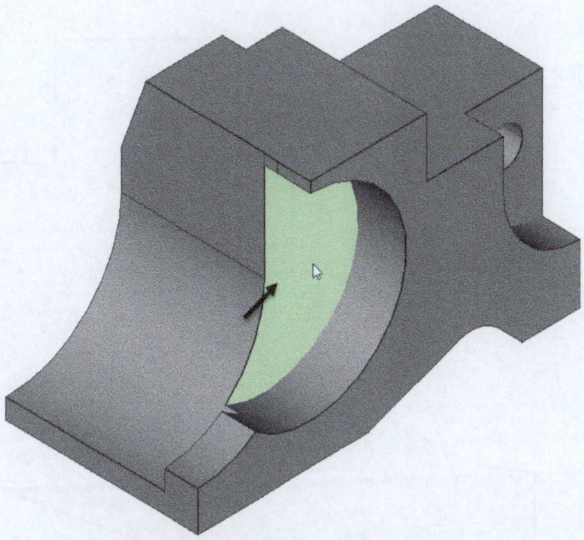

2. Click the **Create Sketch** icon on the **Part Design Helper** toolbar.
3. Create a circle and add the diameter constraint to it.

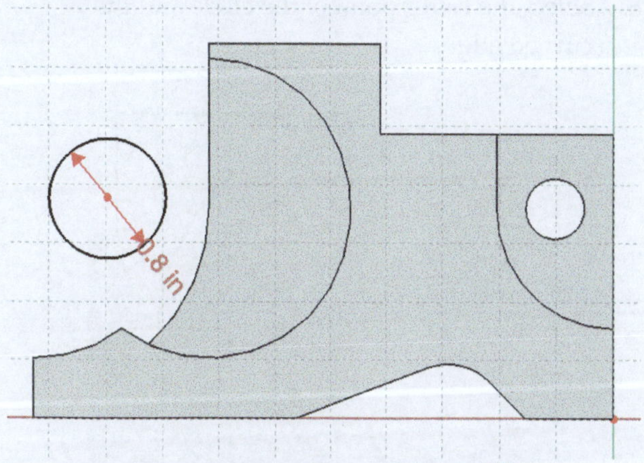

4. Click the **Create external geometry** icon on the **Sketcher tools** toolbar.
5. Select the circular edge of the model.
6. Select the vertical and circular edge, as shown.

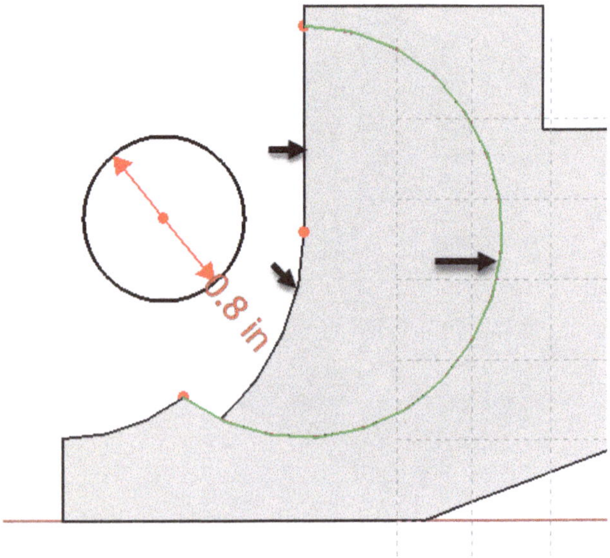

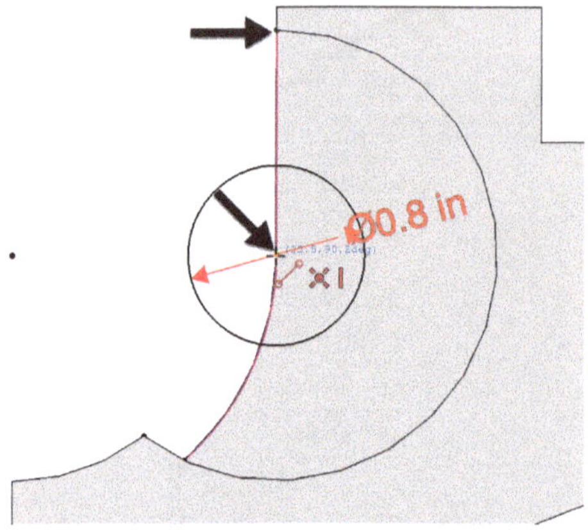

7. Click the **Constrain coincident** icon on the **Sketcher constraints** toolbar.
8. Select the centerpoint of the circle and the curved edge.

11. Click the **Arc** drop-down > **Create arc by center** on the **Sketcher geometries** toolbar.
12. Specify the center, start, and endpoints of the arc, as shown.

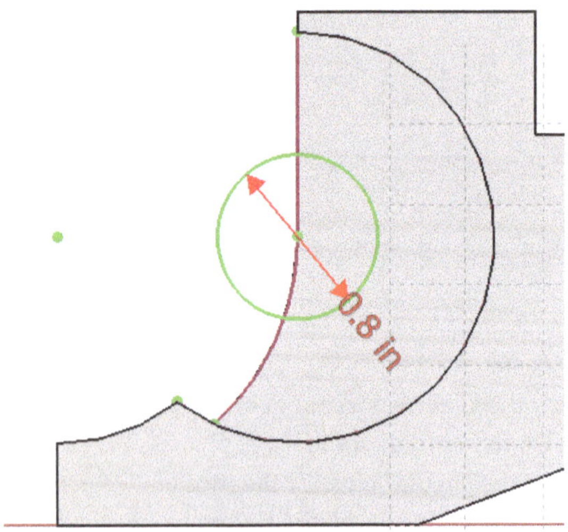

9. Click the **Create Line** icon on the **Sketcher geometries** toolbar.
10. Specify the start and endpoint of the line, as shown.

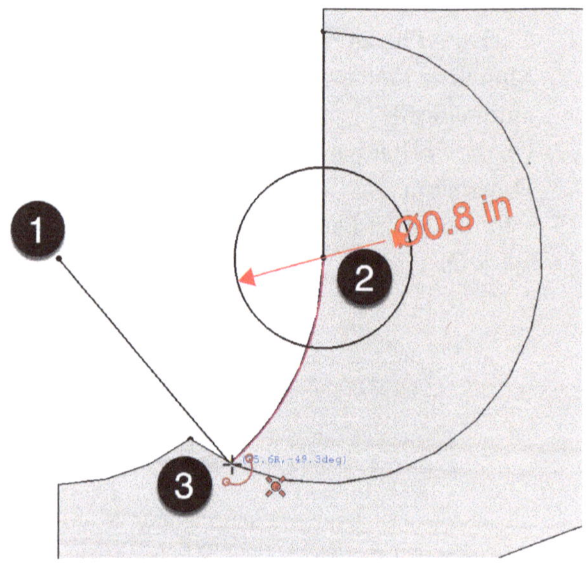

13. Click the **Trim/Extend** drop-down > **Trim Edge** icon on the **Sketcher tools** toolbar.
14. Select the portions of the sketch to be trimmed, as shown.

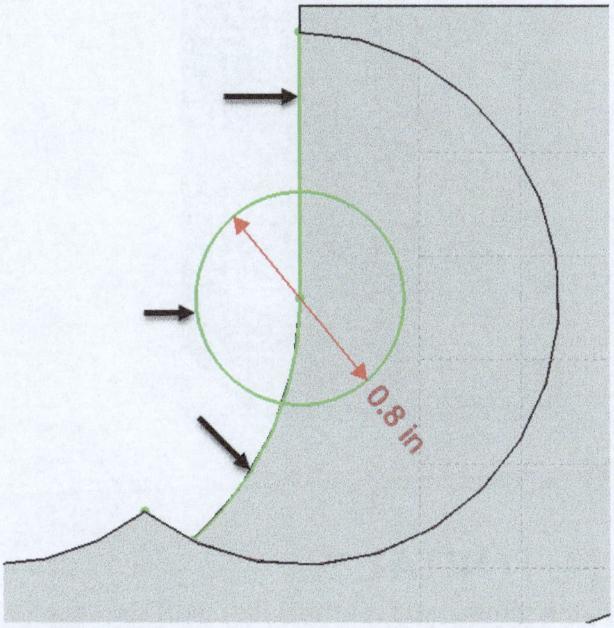

15. Click the **Constrain horizontal/vertical** drop-down > **Constrain vertical** icon on the **Sketcher constraints** toolbar.
16. Select the line, as shown.

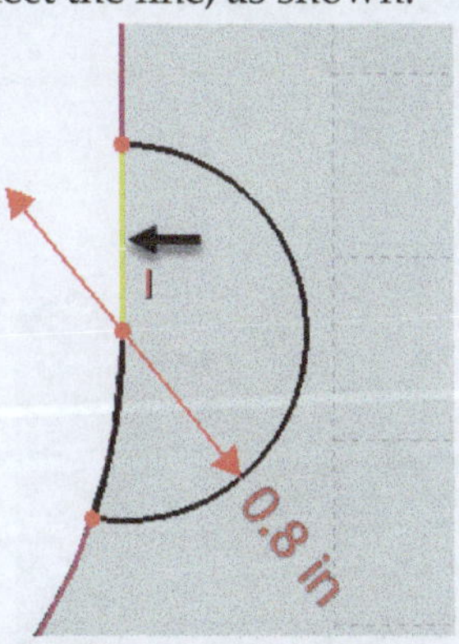

17. Click **Close** on the **Tasks** panel.
18. Click the **Pad** icon on the **Part Design Modeling** toolbar; the sketch is selected automatically.
19. Type **0.2** in the **Length** box.
20. Click **OK**.

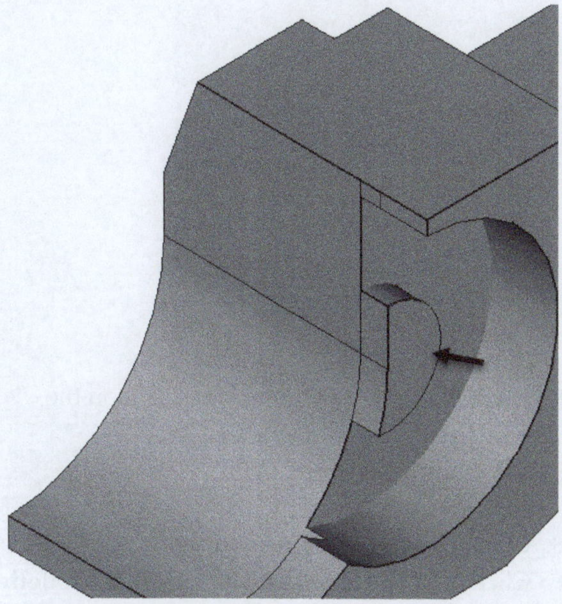

21. Click on the face of the pad feature, as shown.

22. Click the **Create Sketch** icon on the **Part Design Helper** toolbar.
23. Create a circle and add the diameter constraint to it.
24. Click the **Create external geometry** icon on the **Sketcher tools** toolbar.
25. Select the circular edge of the model, as shown.

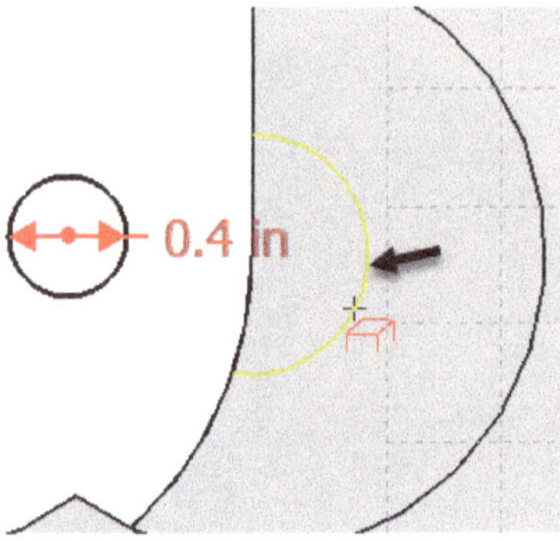

26. Click the **Constrain coincident** icon on the **Sketcher constraints** toolbar.
27. Select the centerpoint of the circle and the curved edge.
28. Click **Close** on the **Tasks** panel.
29. Click the **Pad** icon on the **Part Design Modeling** toolbar; the sketch is selected automatically.
30. On the **Pad parameters** dialog, select **Type > Up To face**.
31. Select the right face of the model, as shown.

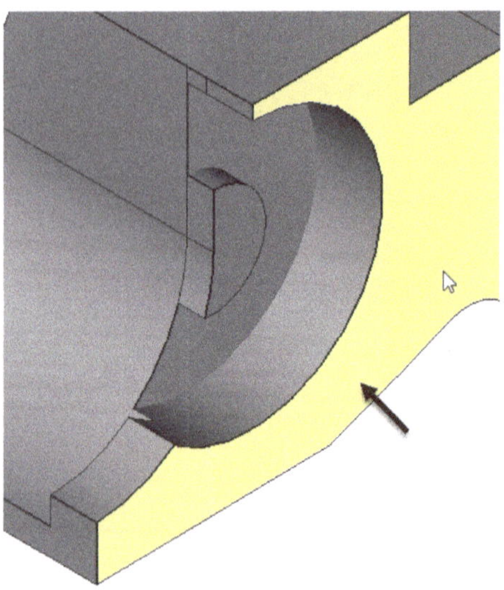

32. Click **OK**.

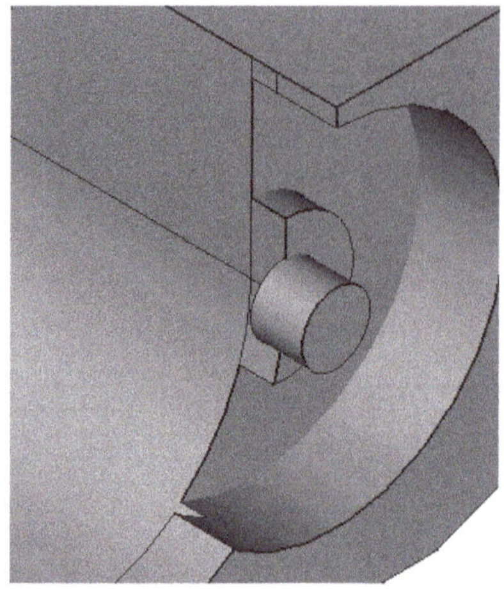

33. Save and close the model.

TUTORIAL 9

In this tutorial, you construct the model shown in the figure.

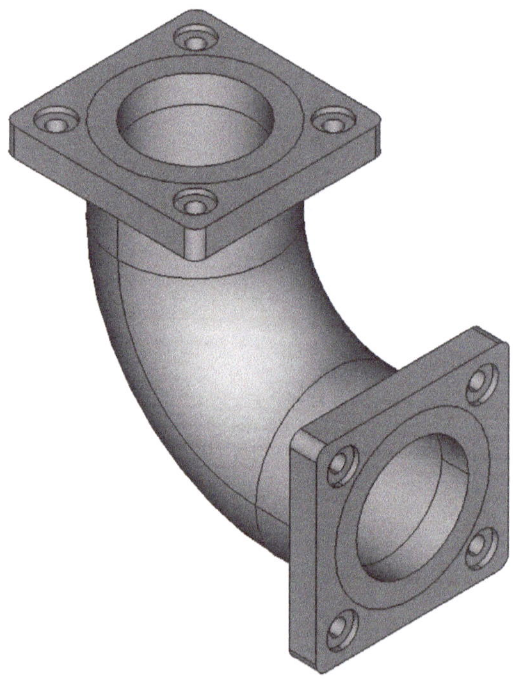

Creating the first feature

1. Open the FreeCAD application.
2. Click **File > New** on the Menu bar.
3. Select the **Part Design** option from the **Workbenches** drop-down.
4. Click the **Create sketch**  icon on the **Part Design Helper** toolbar, and then select the XZ Plane.

5. Click **OK** to start the sketch.
6. Click the **Polyline** icon on the **Sketcher geometries** toolbar.
7. Create a vertical and horizontal lines connected to each other, as shown.

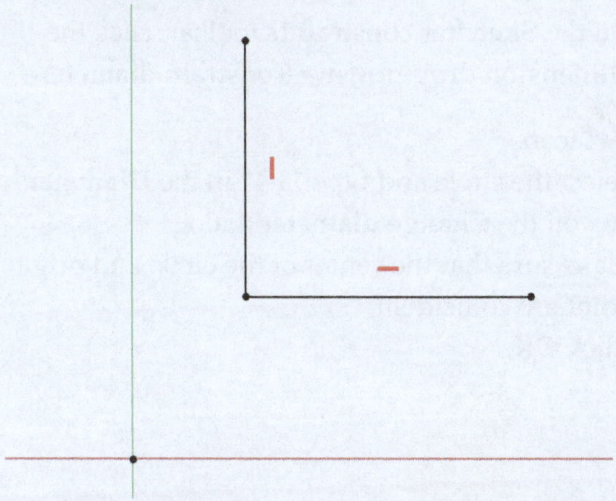

8. Click the **Fillet** drop-down > **Sketch Fillet** on the **Sketcher tools** toolbar.
9. Select the vertical and horizontal lines; a fillet created at the intersection of the two lines.

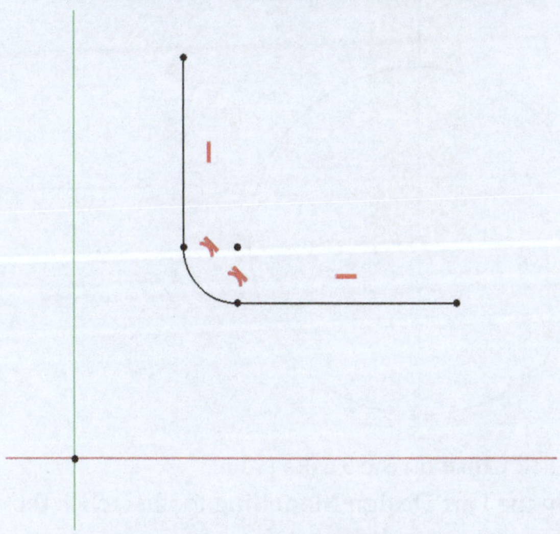

10. Click **Sketcher constraints** toolbar > **Constrain vertical distance** (or) click **Sketch > Sketcher constraints > Constrain vertical distance** on the menu bar.
11. Select the vertical line.
12. Enter **5.9** in the **Length** box of the **Insert Length** dialog and click **OK**.

1. On the **Sketcher constraints** toolbar, click **Dimension** drop-down > **Constrain radius** icon.
2. Select the circle and type **10.24** in the **Radius** box of the **Change Radius** dialog.
3. Click **OK**.
4. Click **Sketcher constraints** toolbar > **Dimension** drop-down > **Constrain horizontal distance** (or) click **Sketch > Sketcher constraints > Constrain horizontal distance** on the menu bar.
5. Select the horizontal line.
6. Enter **5.9** in the **Length** box of the **Insert Length** dialog and click the **OK** button.
7. Click the **Constrain Coincident** icon on the **Sketcher constraints** toolbar.
8. Select the origin point of the sketch
9. Select the center point of the fillet.

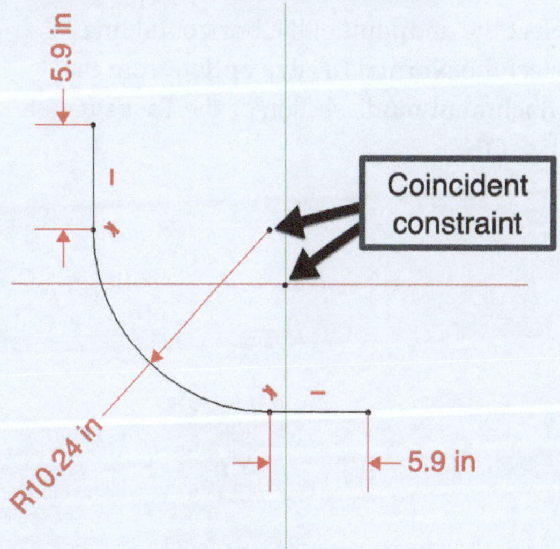

10. Click **Close** on the **Tasks** panel.

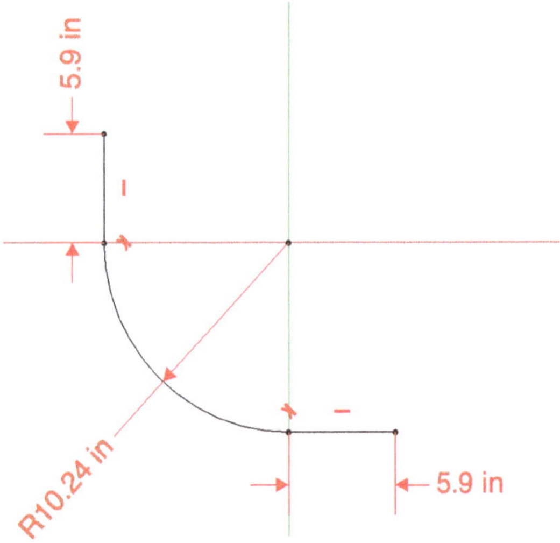

11. On the **Part Design Helper** toolbar, click the **Create a new datum plane** icon.
12. Select the horizontal line of the sketch.
13. Select the endpoint of the horizontal line.
14. Select the **Normal to edge** option from the **Attachment mode** section of the **Tasks** panel.
15. Click **OK**.

16. Click the **Create Sketch** icon the **Part Design Helper** toolbar.
17. Select the newly created datum Plane on the **Model** panel.
18. Click the **Create Circle** on the **Sketcher geometries** toolbar.
19. Click on the origin.
20. Move the pointer outward and click to create a circle.
21. On the **Sketcher constraints** toolbar, click the **Dimension** drop-down > **Constrain diameter** icon.
22. Select the circle and type **11.41** in the **Diameter** box on the **Change diameter** dialog.
23. Make sure that the center of the circle and origin point are coincident.
24. Click **OK**.

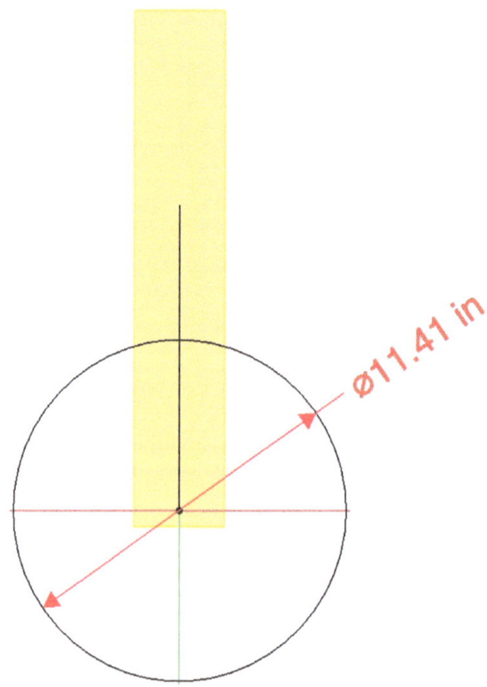

25. Click **Close** on the **Tasks** panel.
26. On the **Part Design Modelling** toolbar, click the **Additive pipe** icon.
27. Select Sketch001 from the **Select feature** and click **OK** on the **Tasks** panel.
28. Click on the **Object** button under the **Path to sweep along** section and select the first sketch.
29. Click **OK** on the **Tasks** panel.

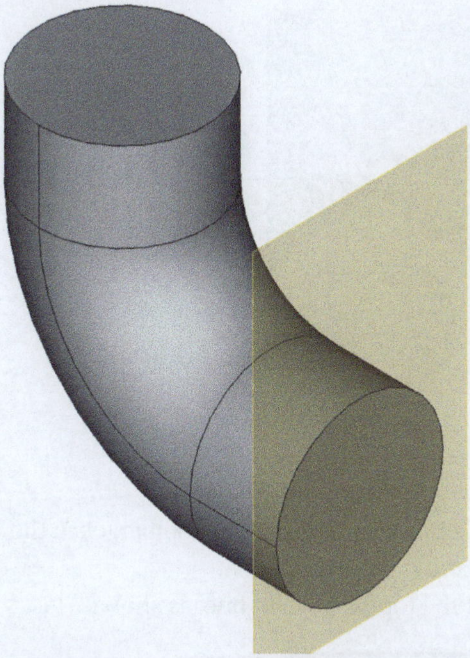

30. Select the datum plane from the graphics window.
31. Click the **Model** panel.
32. Click the View tab at the bottom.
33. Set the **Visibility** value to **false**.

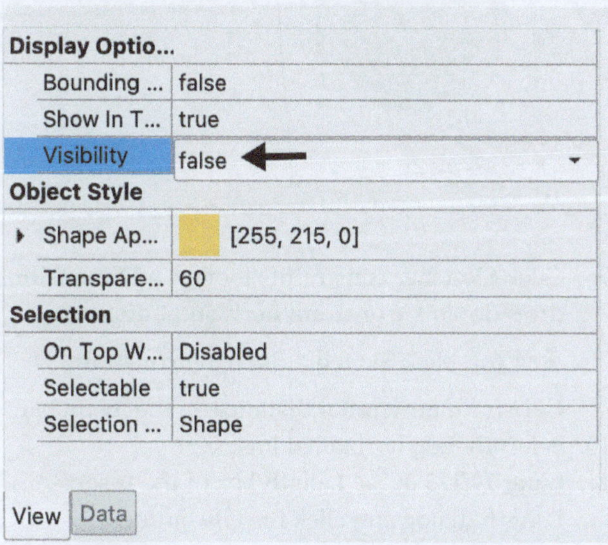

34. Click in the graphics window to deselect the datum plane.

Creating the Shell feature

1. Press **Ctrl** and select the faces, as shown.

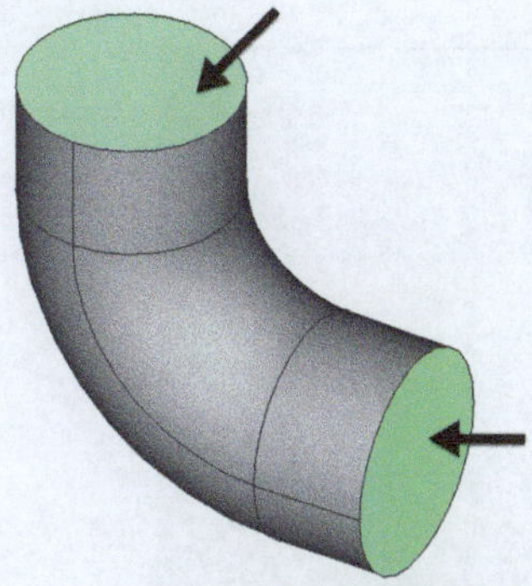

2. Click the **Thickness**  tool on the **Part Design Dressup** toolbar.
3. Enter **1.575** in the **Thickness** box under the **Thickness Parameter** section.
4. Check **Make thickness inwards** option.
5. Click **OK** on the **Tasks** panel.
6. Select the flat face of the AdditivePipe, as shown.

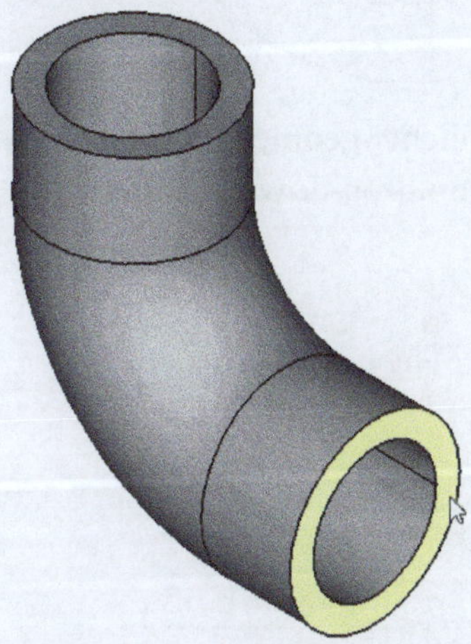

Creating the Flanges

1. Click **Create new Sketch**  icon on the **Part Design Helper toolbar**.
2. Click the **Create external geometry**  icon on the **Sketcher tools** toolbar.
3. Select the inner circular edge of the model, as shown.

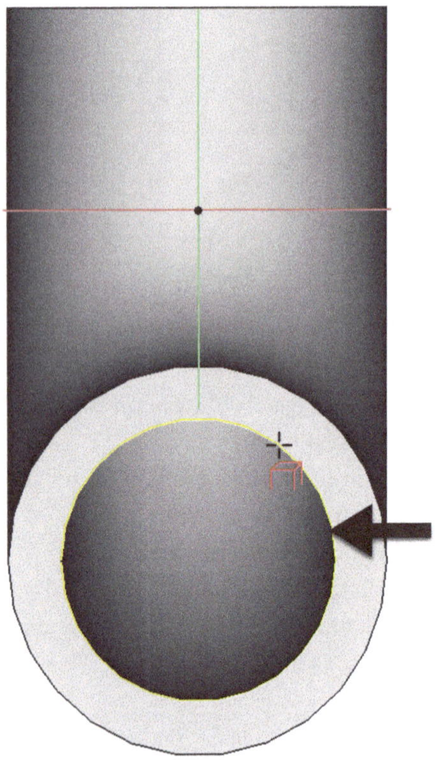

4. Expand the **Sketcher geometries** toolbar and click the **Polygon** drop-down > **Square**.

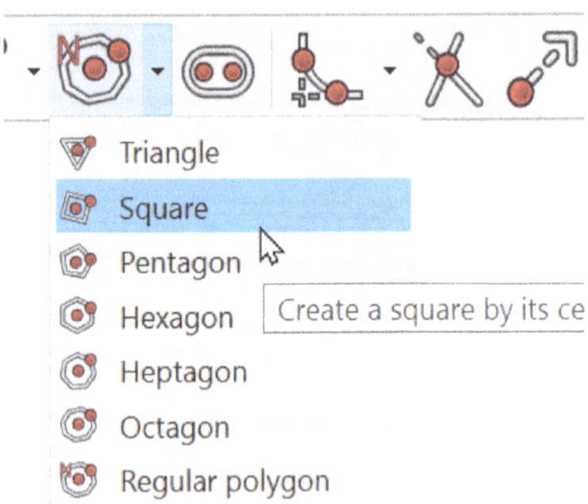

5. Select the centerpoint of the circular edge.
6. Move the pointer outward and click to create a square. Next, Press **Esc**.

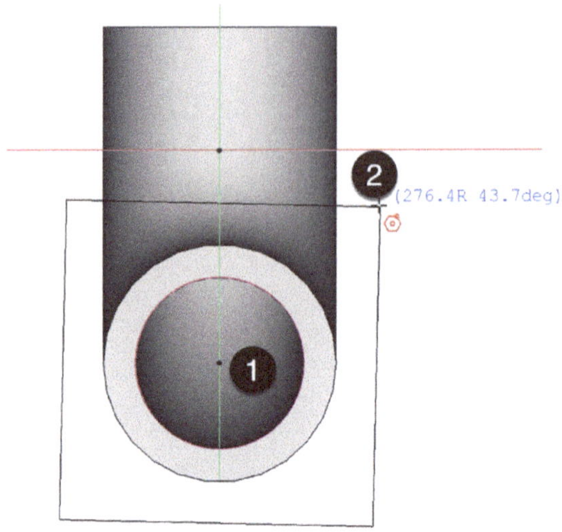

7. On the **Sketcher constraints** toolbar, click the **Horizontal constraint** icon.
8. Select the top horizontal line, as shown.

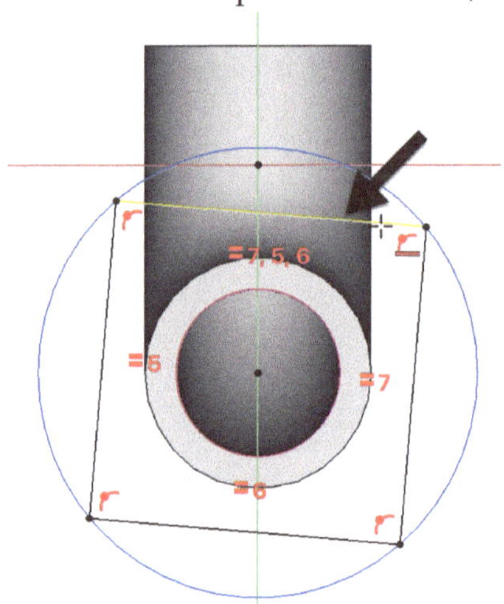

9. Click **Sketcher constraints** toolbar > **Dimension** drop-down > **Constrain horizontal distance** (or) click **Sketch > Sketcher constraints > Constrain horizontal distance** on the menu bar.
10. Select the top horizontal line.
11. Enter **14.173** in the **Length** box of the **Insert Length** dialog and click the **OK** button.

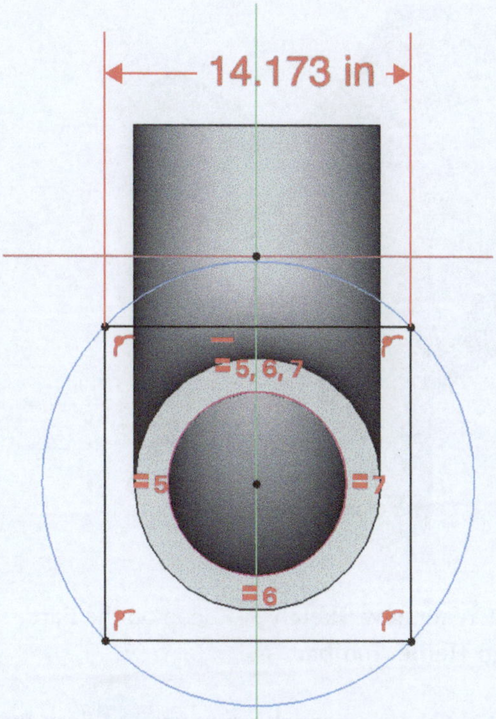

12. Click the **Create Circle**  on the **Sketcher geometries** toolbar.
13. Select the centerpoint of the circular edge.
14. Move the pointer outward and click on the inner circular edge.

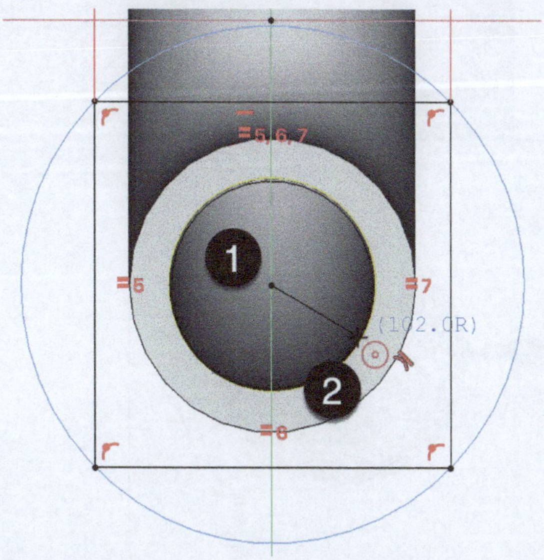

15. Click **Close** on the **Tasks** panel.
16. On the **Part Design Modeling** toolbar, click the **Pad**  icon.
17. Type **1.969** in the **Length** box of the **Pad Parameters** dialog.
18. Check the **Reversed** option and click **OK**.

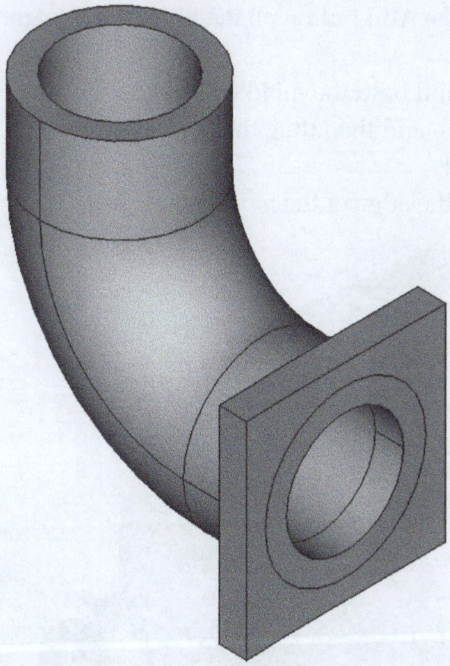

19. Press and hold the Ctrl key and select the edges of the model, as shown.

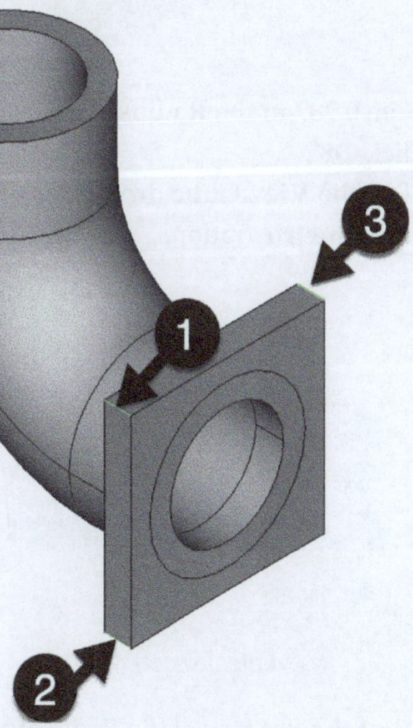

20. On the **Part Design Dressup** toolbar, click the **Fillet**  icon.
21. Click the **Add** button on the **Fillet Parameters** dialog.
22. Press and hold the middle and right mouse buttons, and then drag the pointer; the model is rotated.
23. Select the edge of the model, as shown.

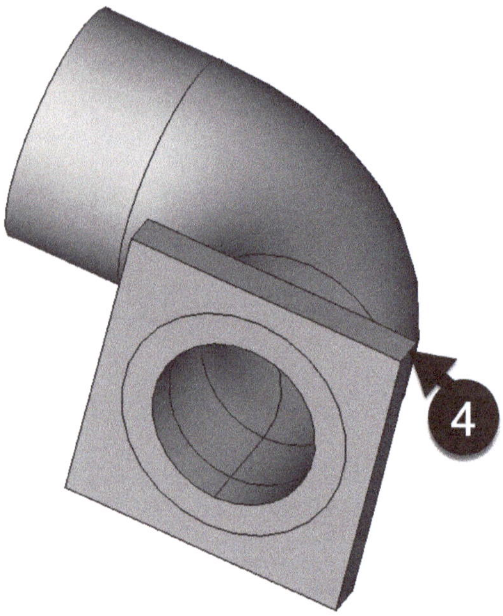

24. Type **0.787** in the **Radius** box.
25. Click **OK**.
26. Click the **ViewCube** drop-down, and then select the **Isometric** option.

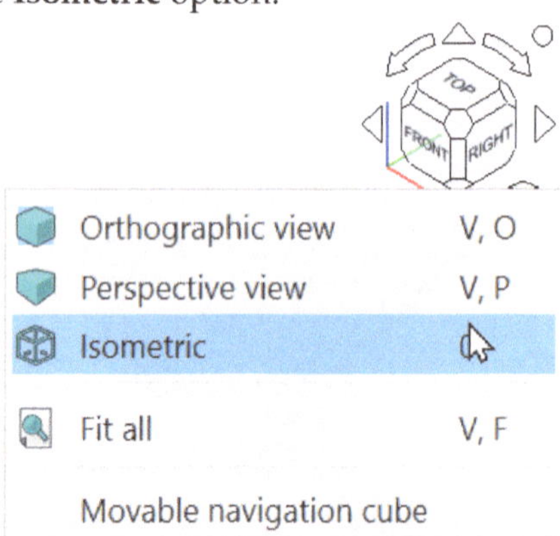

27. Select the flat face of the **Pad** feature, as shown.

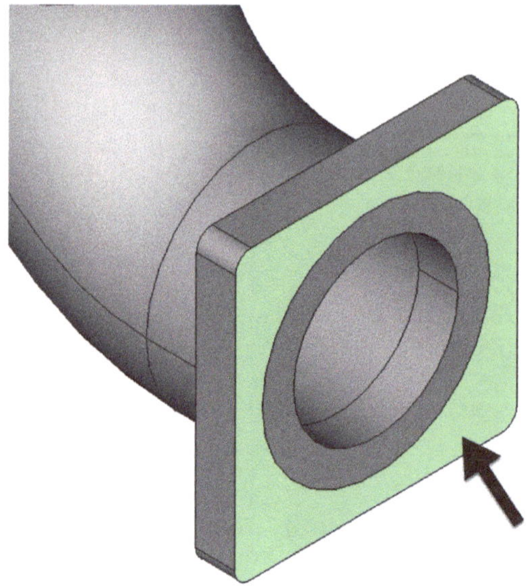

28. Click **Create new Sketch**  icon on the **Part Design Helper toolbar**.
29. Click the **Create external geometry**  icon on the **Sketcher tools** toolbar.
30. Select the horizontal and vertical edges, as shown.

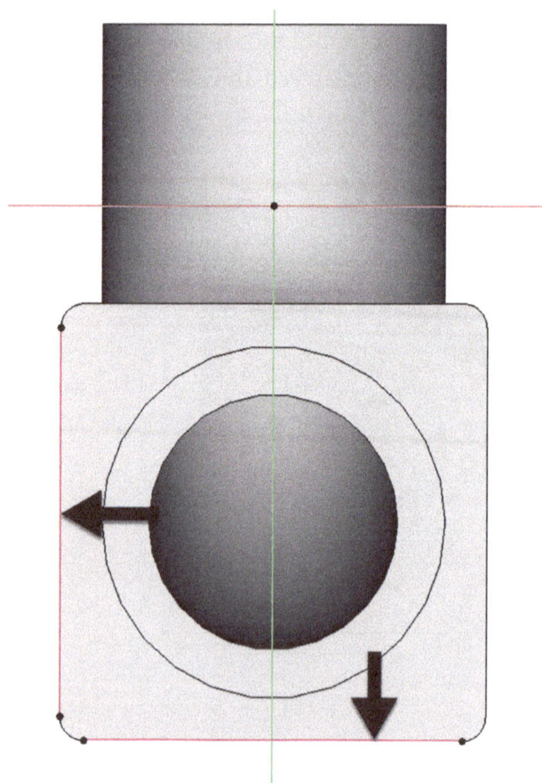

31. Click the **Create Circle**  on the **Sketcher**

geometries toolbar.

32. Create a circle, as shown.

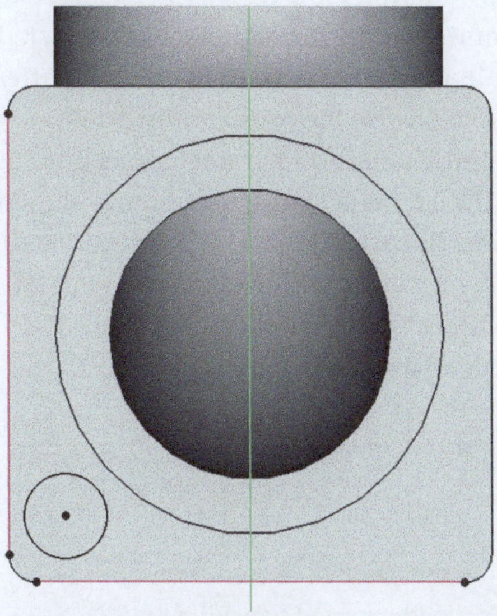

33. Click **Sketcher constraints** toolbar **> Constrain vertical distance** (or) click **Sketch > Sketcher constraints > Constrain vertical distance** on the menu bar.
34. Select the centerpoint of the circle.
35. Select the left endpoint of the horizontal edge, as shown.

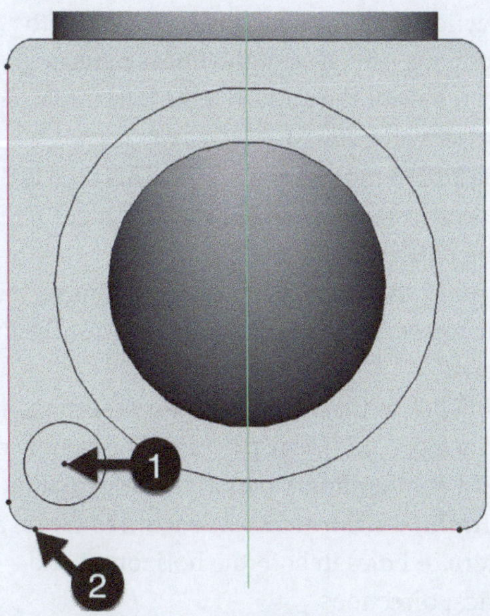

36. Enter **1.969** in the **Length** box of the **Insert Length** dialog and click **OK**.
37. Click **Sketcher constraints** toolbar > **Dimension** drop-down > **Constrain horizontal distance** (or) click **Sketch > Sketcher constraints > Constrain horizontal distance** on the menu bar.
38. Select the centerpoint of the circle.
39. Select the lower endpoint of the vertical edge, as shown.
40. Enter **1.969** in the **Length** box of the **Insert Length** dialog and click the **OK** button.

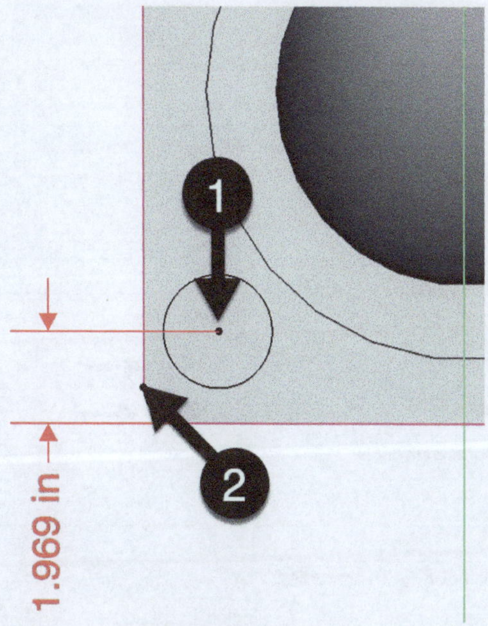

41. Click **Close** on the **Tasks** panel.
42. Click the **Hole** icon on the **Part Design Modeling** toolbar.
43. Type **1.181 in** in the **Diameter** box. This sets the diameter of the initial hole.
44. Select **Depth > Dimension**. This sets the depth of the hole to be a specific dimension rather than a blind hole.
45. Type 1.969 in the **Depth** box located next to the **Depth** drop-down. This sets the depth of the hole.
46. Select **Hole cut Type > Counterbore**. This changes the hole type to a counterbore hole, which has a larger diameter at the top.
47. Type **2.362** in the **Diameter** box. This sets the diameter of the counterbore hole.
48. Type **0.394** in the **Depth** box. This sets the depth of the counterbore hole.
49. Under **Drill point**, select **Type > Flat**. This sets the drill point to be flat rather than pointed.

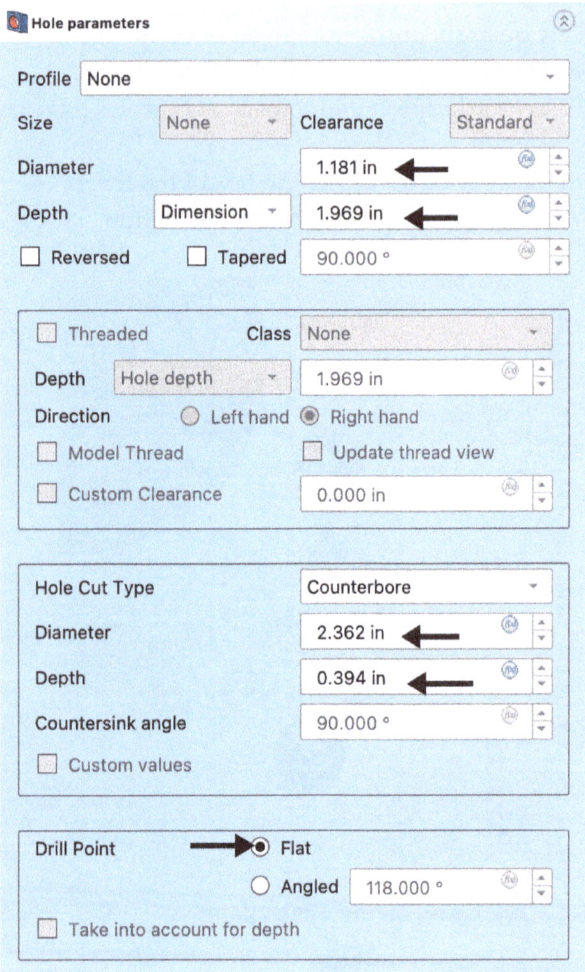

50. Click **OK** on the **Tasks** panel; the counterbore hole is created.

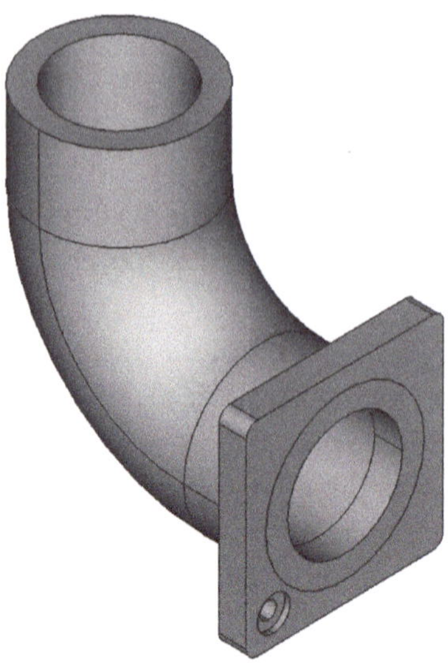

51. Select the **Hole** feature from the **Model** panel.

52. Click the **MultiTransform**  tool on the **Part Design Modeling** toolbar. This step is done to apply multiple transformations to the selected feature. In this case, we want to create a pattern of holes, so we use the **MultiTransform** tool.
53. In the **MultiTransform parameters** section, right click in the **Transformations** section, and then select **Add linear pattern**. This step is done to add a linear pattern transformation to model. A linear pattern is a series of equally spaced objects along a straight line.

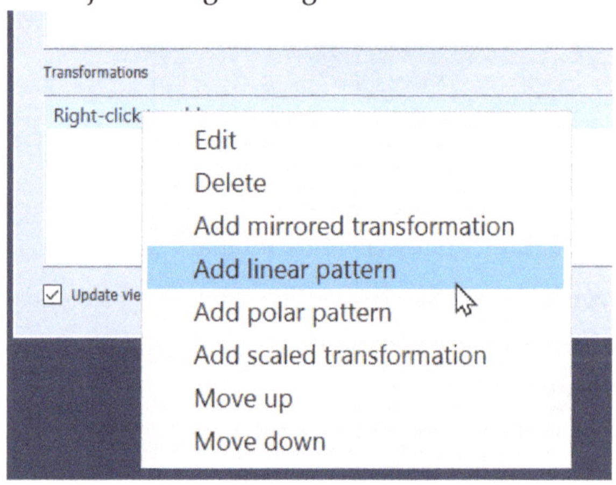

54. Select the **Horizontal sketch axis** from the **Direction** drop-down. This step is done to specify the direction of the linear pattern. In this case, we want the pattern to be horizontal, so we select the Horizontal sketch axis.
55. Type **10.235** in the **Length** box. This step is done to specify the distance between each occurrence of the pattern.
56. Type-in **2** in the **Occurrences** box. This step is done to specify the number of occurrences in the pattern.
57. Right click in the **Transformations** section, and then select **Add linear pattern**. This step is done to add another linear pattern transformation to the MultiTransform tool. We want to create a pattern of holes in both the horizontal and vertical directions.
58. Select the **Vertical sketch axis** from the **Direction** drop-down. This step is done to specify the direction of the second linear pattern. In this case, we want the pattern to be vertical,

so we select the Vertical sketch axis.

59. Type **10.235** in the **Length** box. This step is done to specify the distance between each occurrence of the second pattern.
60. Type-in **2** in the **Occurrences** box. This step is done to specify the number of occurrences in the second pattern.
61. Click **OK** to create the multi transformation pattern. After clicking **OK**, you should see the pattern of holes created according to the specified parameters.

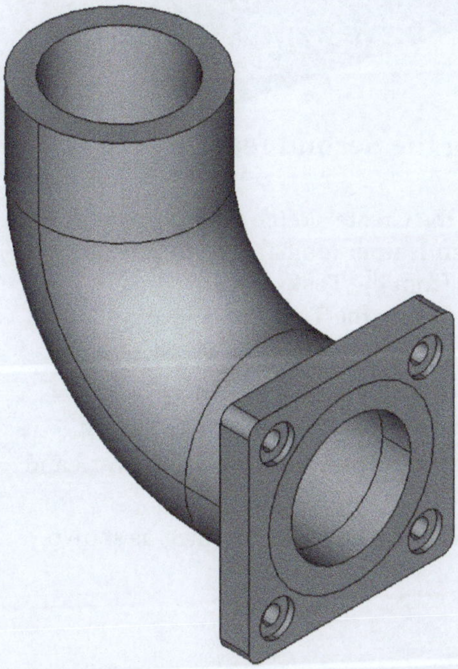

62. Likewise, create another flange on the other end of the AdditivePipe, as shown.

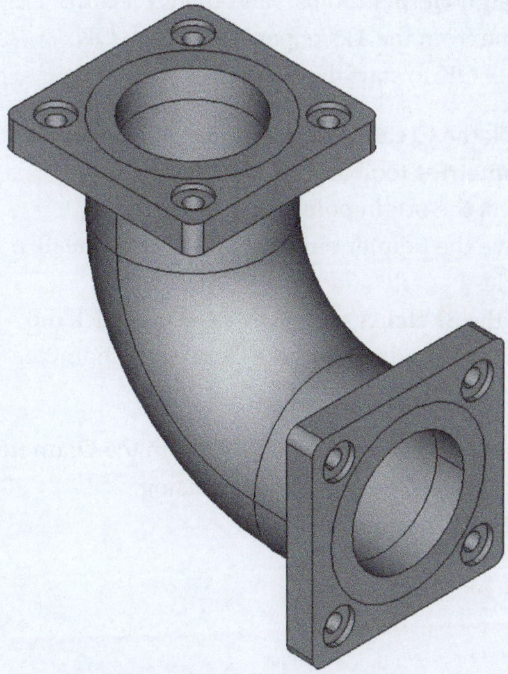

TUTORIAL 10

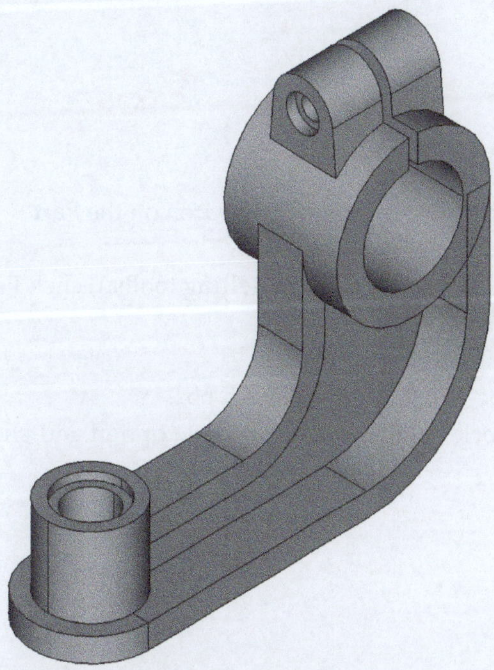

Creating the first feature

1. Open the FreeCAD application.
2. Click **File > New** on the Menu bar.
3. Select the **Part Design** option from the **Workbenches** drop-down.
4. Click the **Create sketch** icon on the **Part**

Design Helper toolbar, and then Select the YZ Plane from the **Tasks** panel and click **OK**.

5. Click **OK** to start the sketch.
6. Click the **Create circle** icon on the **Sketcher geometries** toolbar.
7. Select the origin point of the sketch.
8. Move the pointer outward and click to create a circle.
9. On the **Sketcher constraints** toolbar, click the **Dimension** drop-down > **Constrain Diameter** Ø.
10. Select the circle and type in **3.937** in the **Diameter** box on the **Change diameter** dialog.
11. Click **OK**.

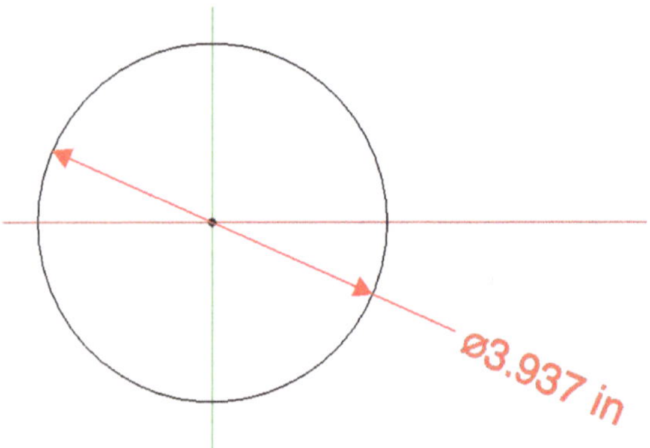

12. Click the **Leave Sketch** icon on the **Part Design Helper** toolbar.
13. On the **Part Design Modelling** toolbar, click **Pad** icon.
14. Type-in **2.953** in the **Length** box.
15. Check the **Symmetric to plane** option and click **OK**.

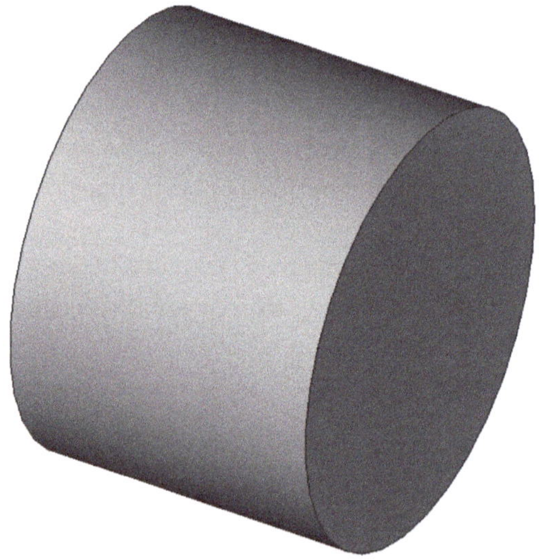

Creating the Second feature

1. Click the **Create sketch** icon on the **Part Design Helper** toolbar, and then Select the YZ Plane from the **Tasks** panel.
2. Click **OK** on the **Tasks** panel.
3. Click the **Polyline** tool on the **Sketcher geometries** toolbar, and then click on the horizontal axis of the sketch, as shown.
4. Move the pointer vertically downward and click.
5. Likewise, create the other lines, as shown.

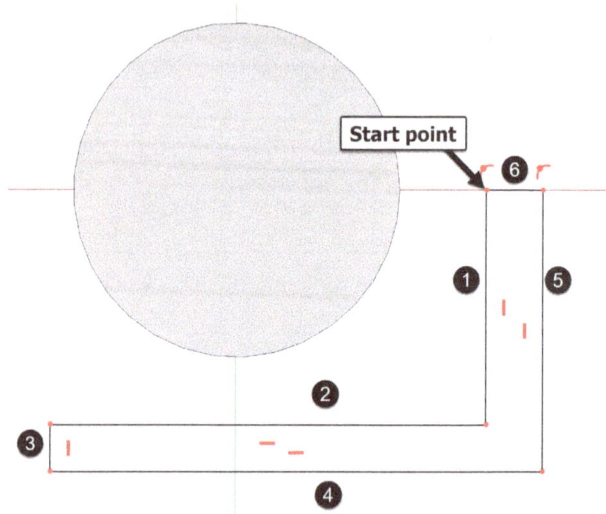

6. Click the **Sketch Fillet** icon on the **Sketcher tools** toolbar and select the corner points of the sketch, as shown.

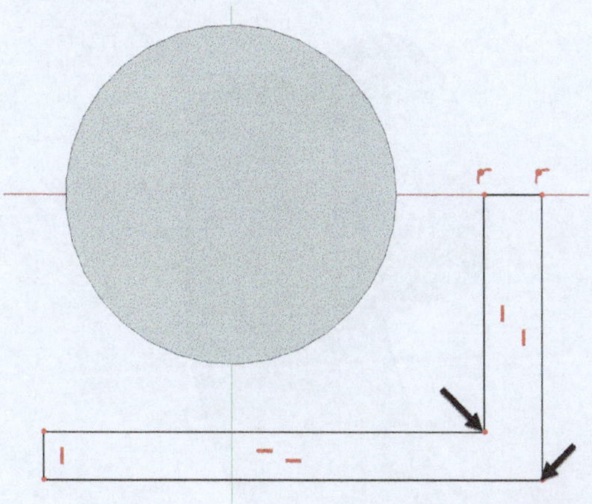

7. Click the **Coincident Constraint**  icon on the **Sketcher Constraints** toolbar and select the centerpoints of the fillets. The Coincident Constraint is used to affix a point onto (coincident with) one or more other points. In this case, it is used to connect the centerpoints of the fillets. This constraint acts as a concentric constraint if two or more circles are selected. The result of this step is that the centerpoints of the fillets are connected, ensuring that they remain equidistant from each other and that the fillets maintain their shape.

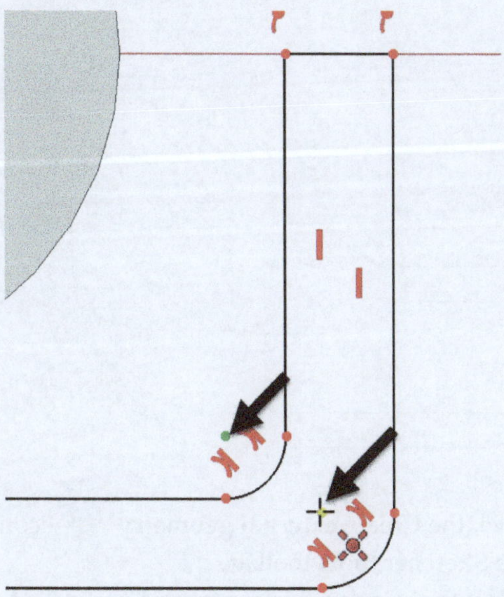

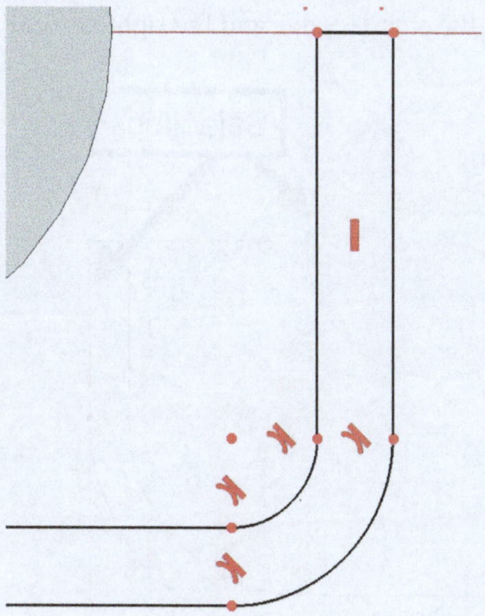

8. Add dimensions to the sketch, as shown.

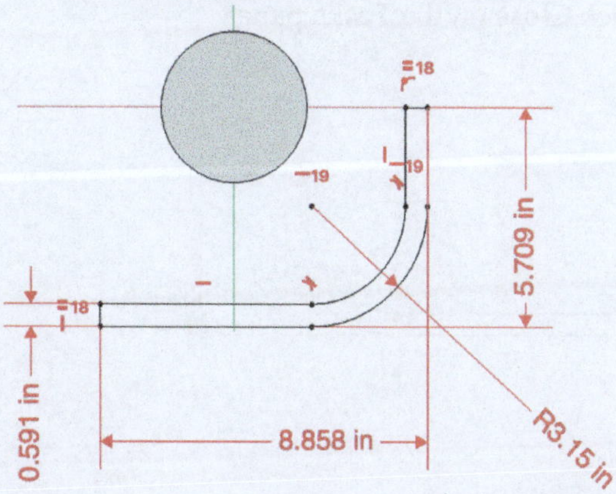

9. Click the **Create external geometry**  icon on the **Sketcher tools** toolbar.
10. Select the circular edge of the model, as shown.

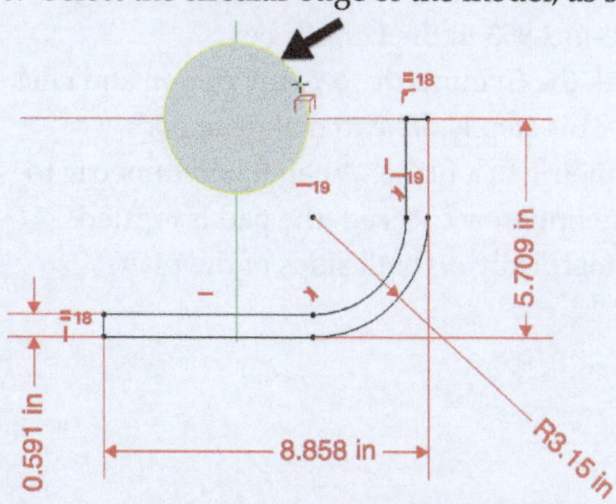

11. On the **Sketcher constraints** toolbar, click the **Tangent Constraint**  icon.

12. Select the circular edge and the right vertical line.

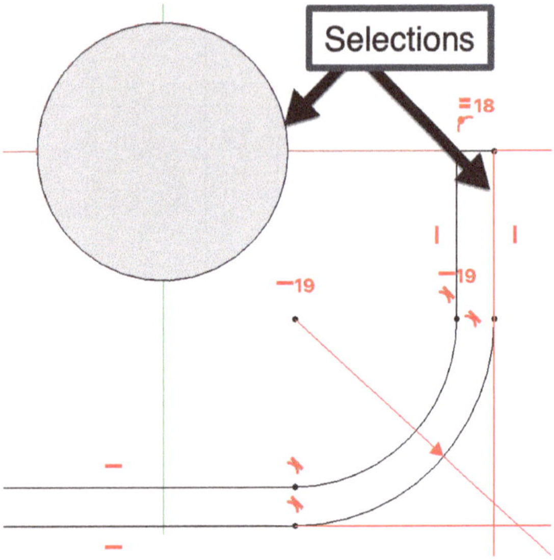

13. Click **Close** on the **Tasks** panel.

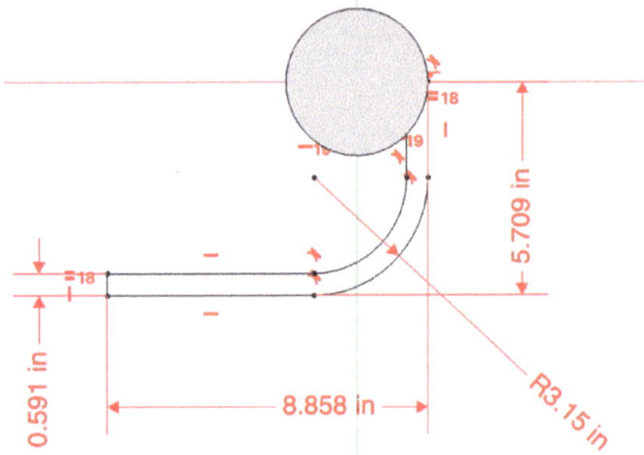

14. Click **Model** panel.
15. On the **Part Design Modelling** toolbar, click **Pad**  icon.
16. Type-in **2.953** in the **Length** box.
17. Check the **Symmetric to plane** option and click **OK**. This step is done to make the pad symmetric to a plane. When the **Symmetric to plane** option is checked, the pad is created symmetrically on both sides of the plane.

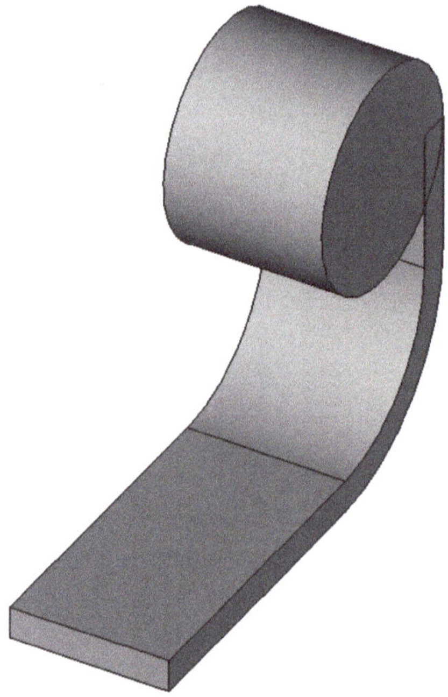

18. Click the **Create sketch**  icon on the **Part Design Helper** toolbar, and then select the YZ Plane.
19. Click **OK** on the **Tasks** panel.
20. Create a sketch using the **Polyline** and **Fillet** tools, as shown.

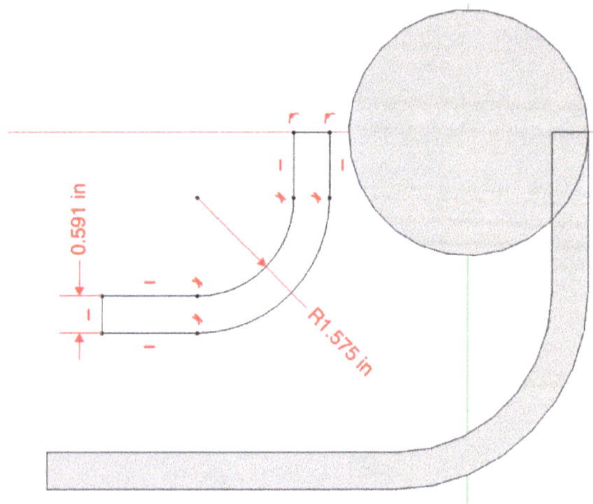

21. Click the **Create external geometry**  icon on the **Sketcher tools** toolbar.
22. Select the circular, horizontal and vertical edges of the model, as shown.

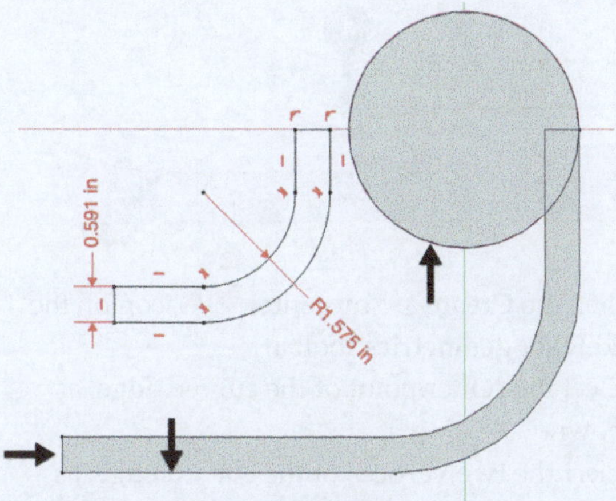

23. On the **Sketcher constraints** toolbar, click the **Tangent Constraint** icon.
24. Select the circular edge and the left vertical line.

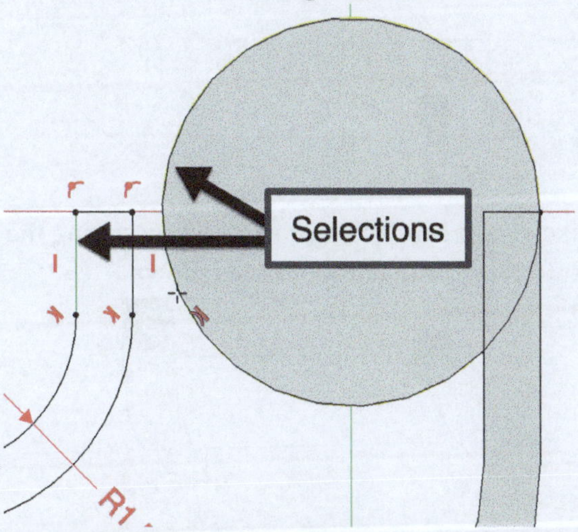

25. On the **Sketcher constraints** toolbar, click the **Vertical Constraint** icon.
26. Select the lower end point of the vertical line, as shown.
27. Select anyone of the vertices of the vertical edge, as shown.

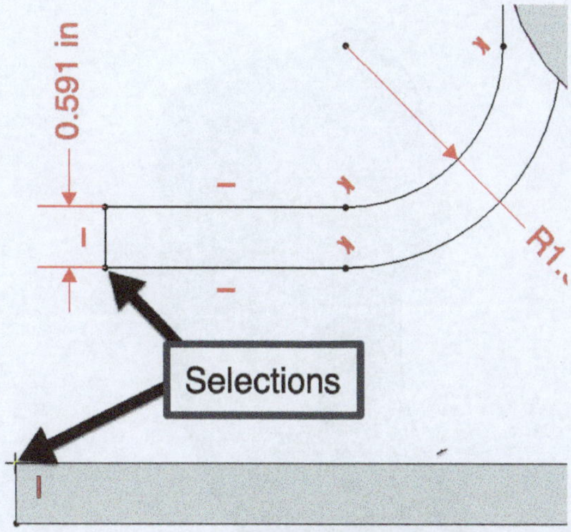

28. Click **Sketcher constraints** toolbar **Dimension drop-down > Constrain vertical distance** (or) click **Sketch > Sketcher constraints > Constrain vertical distance** on the menu bar.
29. Select the top endpoint of the vertical line, as shown
30. Select the left endpoint of the horizontal edge, as shown.

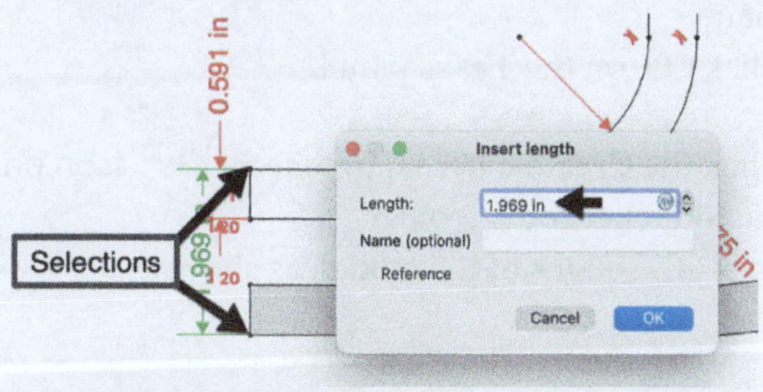

31. Type **1.969** in the **Length** box and click **OK**.
32. Click **Close** on the **Tasks** panel.
33. On the **Part Design Modeling** toolbar, click the **Pad** icon.
34. Type **1.181** in the **Length** box of the **Pad Parameters** dialog.
35. Check the **Symmetric to plane** option and click **OK**.

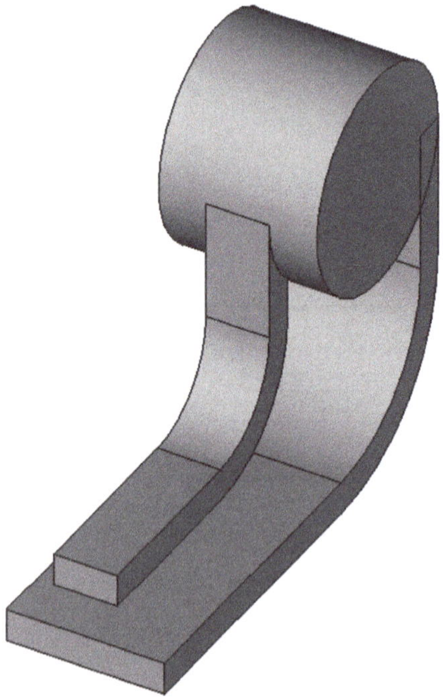

36. Click the **Create sketch** icon on the **Part Design Helper** toolbar, and then select the YZ Plane.
37. Click **OK** on the **Tasks** panel.
38. Click the **Create external geometry** icon on the **Sketcher tools** toolbar.
39. Select the edges of the model, as shown.

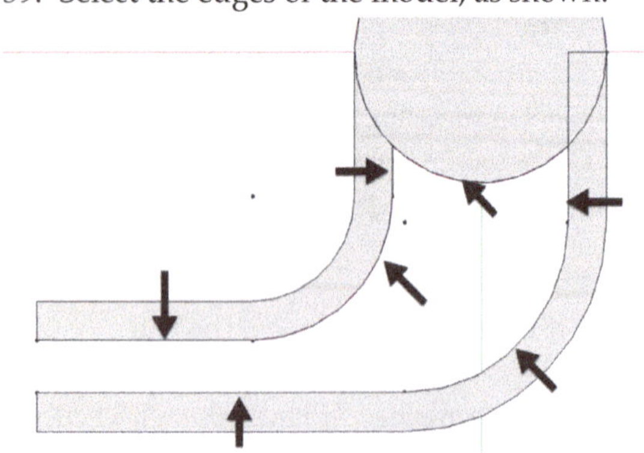

40. Click the **View section** icon on the **Part Design Helper** toolbar.
41. Click the **Create Polyline** icon on the **Sketcher geometries** toolbar.
42. Select the vertices of the external geometry in the sequence shown in figure.

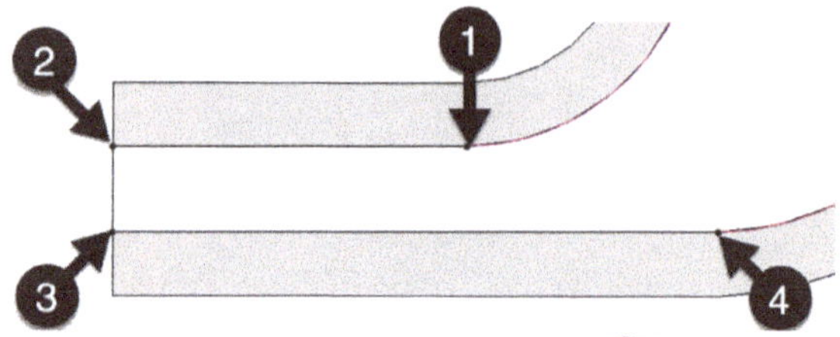

43. Click the **Create arc by center** icon on the **Sketcher geometries** toolbar.
44. Select the center point of the curved edge, as shown.
45. Select the two vertices of the curved edge, as shown.

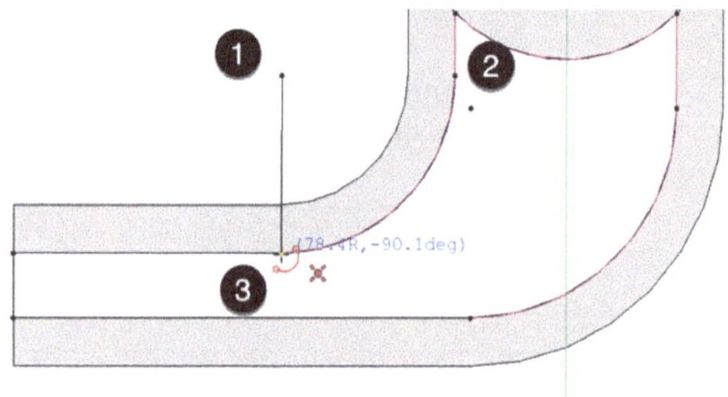

46. Likewise, create two more arcs by specifying the center, start, and end points, as shown.

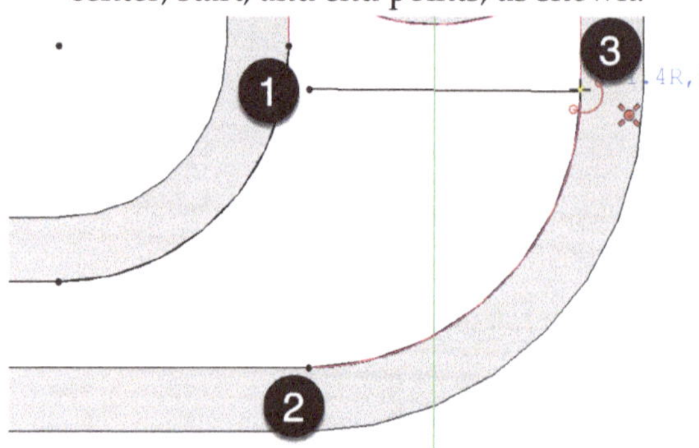

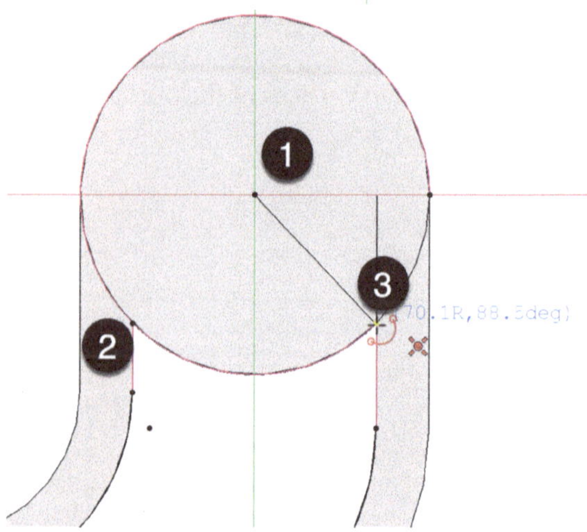

47. Click the **Create line**  icon on the **Sketcher geometries** toolbar.
48. Select the vertices of the vertical edges, as shown.

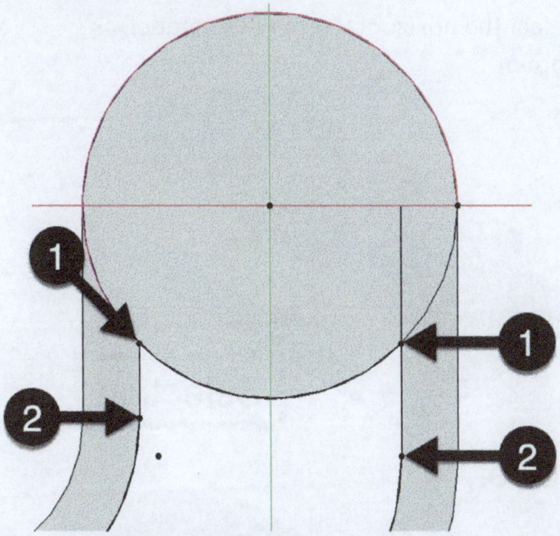

49. Click **Close** on the **Tasks** panel.
50. On the **Part Design Modeling** toolbar, click the **Pad**  icon.
51. Type **0.787** in the **Length** box of the **Pad Parameters** dialog.
52. Check the **Symmetric to plane** option and click **OK**.

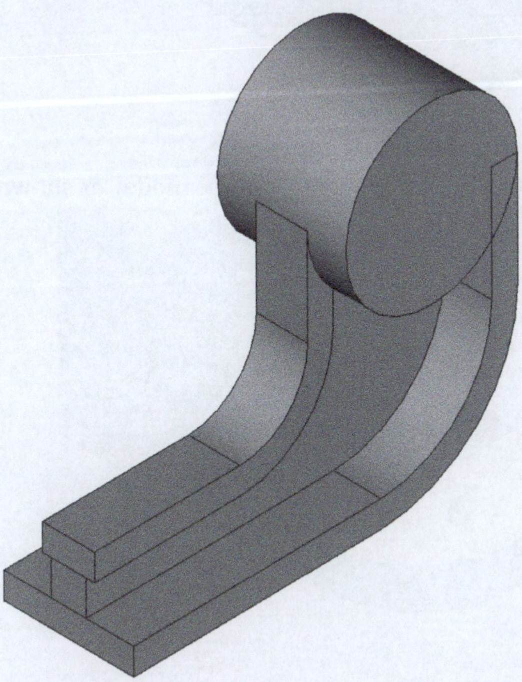

53. Press and hold the right and middle mouse button and drag the pointer upward.
54. Select the bottom flat face.

55. Click **Create new Sketch**  icon on the **Part Design Helper toolbar**.
56. Click the **Create external geometry**  icon on the **Sketcher tools** toolbar.
57. Select the edge of the model, as shown.

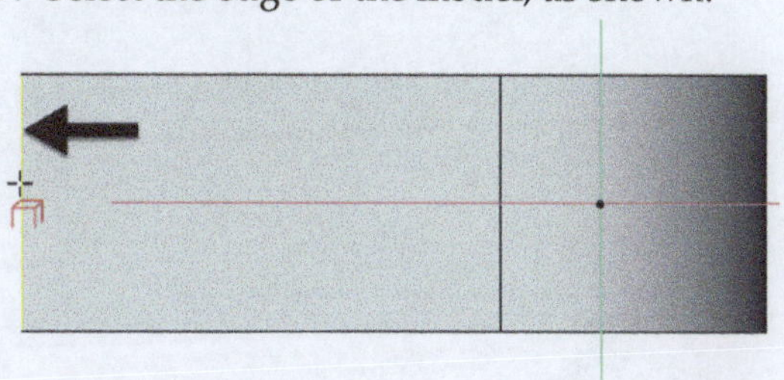

58. Click the **Create arc by three points** 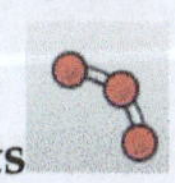 icon on the **Sketcher geometries** toolbar.
59. Select the two vertices of the edge, as shown.
60. Move the pointer towards left and click.

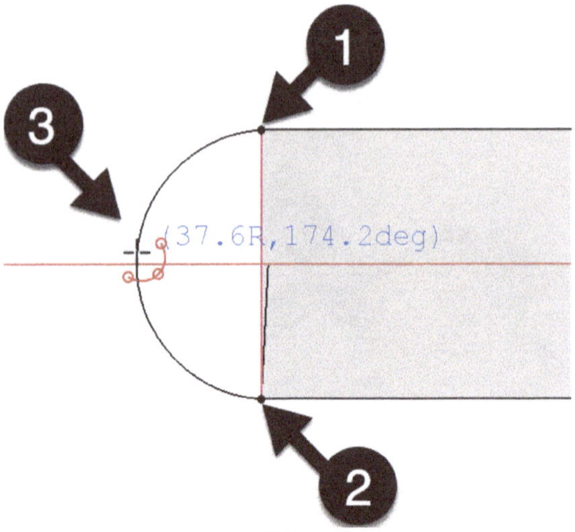

61. Click the **Create line** icon on the **Sketcher geometries** toolbar.
62. Select the vertices of the vertical edge, as shown.

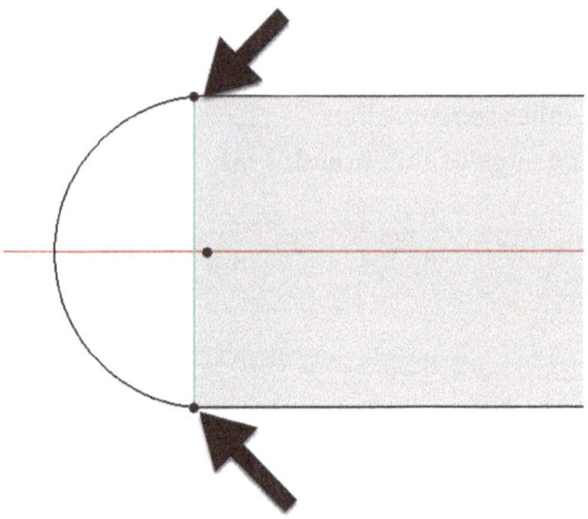

63. On the **Sketcher constraints** toolbar, click the **Constrain Coincident** icon.
64. Select the centerpoint of the arc and the vertical line, as shown.

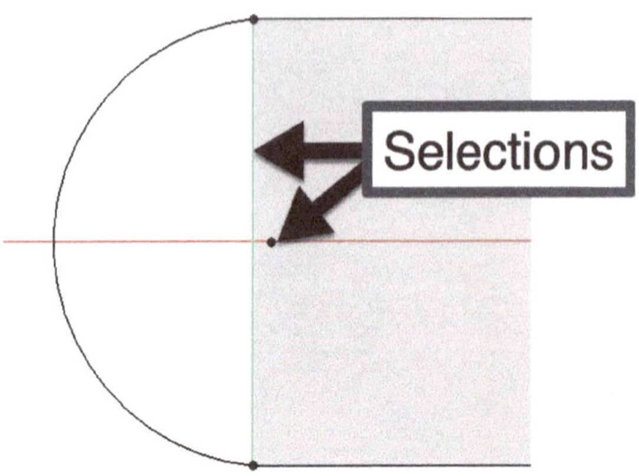

65. Click **Close** on the **Tasks** panel.
66. On the **Part Design Modeling** toolbar, click the **Pad** icon.
67. Select **Type > Up to face** on the Pad parameters dialog.
68. Select the horizontal face of the model, as shown.

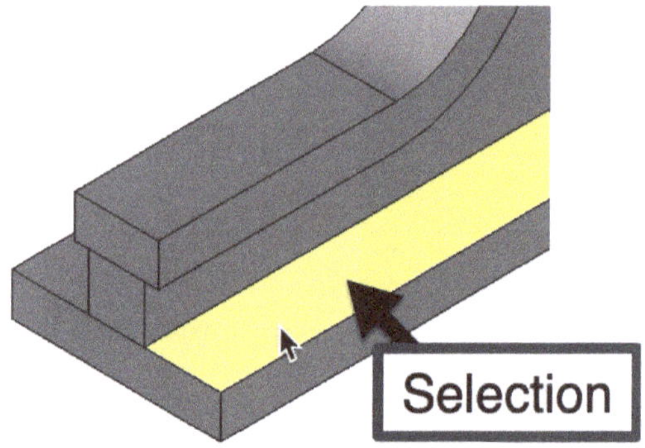

69. Click **OK**.

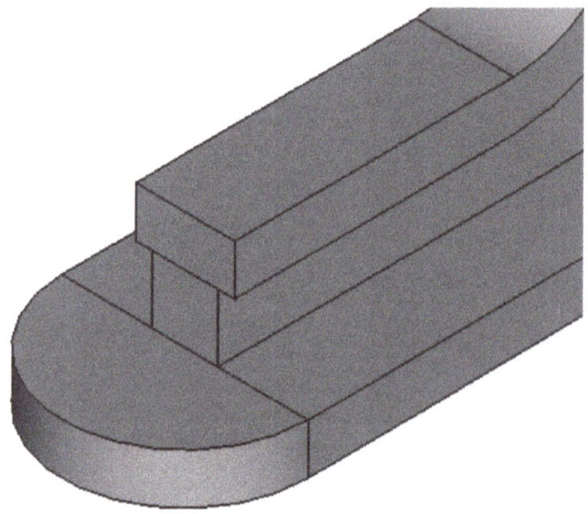

Creating the third feature

1. Select the horizontal face of the model, as shown.

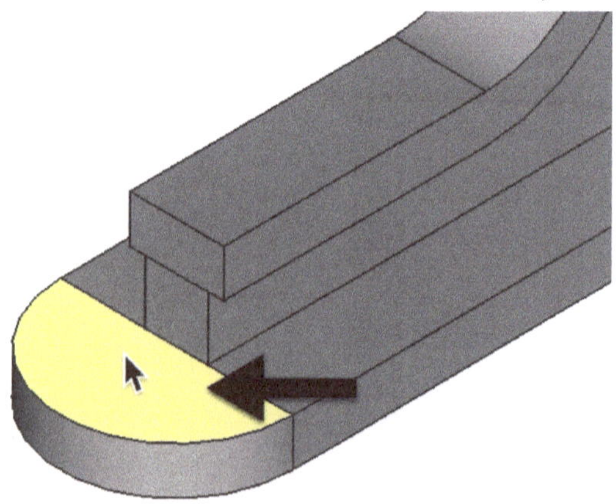

2. Click **Create new Sketch** icon on the **Part**

Design Helper toolbar.

3. Click the **Create external geometry** icon on the **Sketcher tools** toolbar.
4. Select the circular edge of the model, as shown.

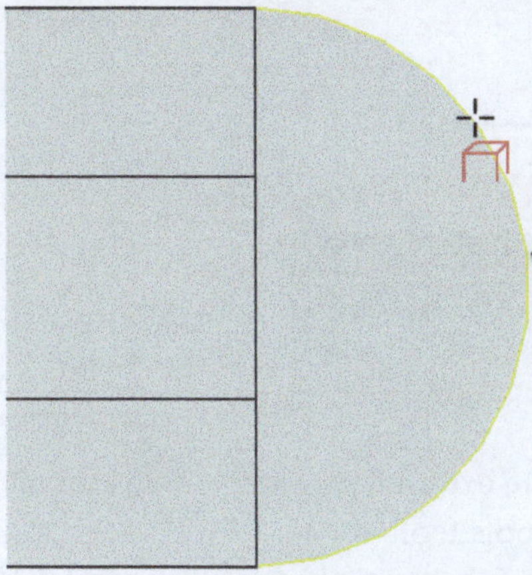

5. Click the **Create circle** icon on the **Sketcher geometry** toolbar.
6. Click on the centerpoint of the curved edge.
7. Move the pointer outward and click to create the circle.

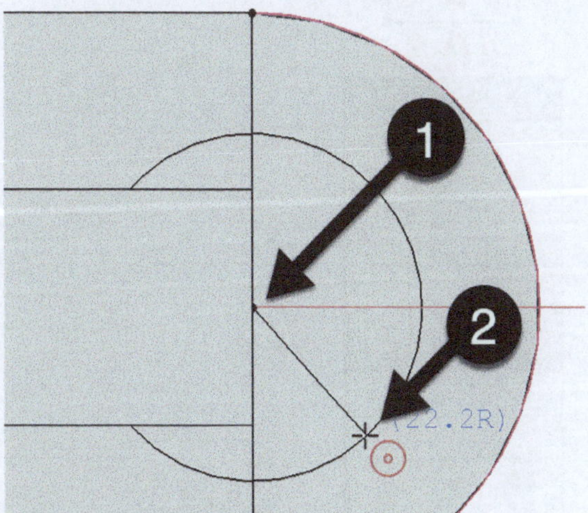

8. On the **Sketcher constraints** toolbar, click the **Dimension** drop-down and select **Constrain diameter** .
9. Select the circle and type-in **2.165** in the **Diameter** box on the **Change Diameter** dialog.
10. Click **OK**.

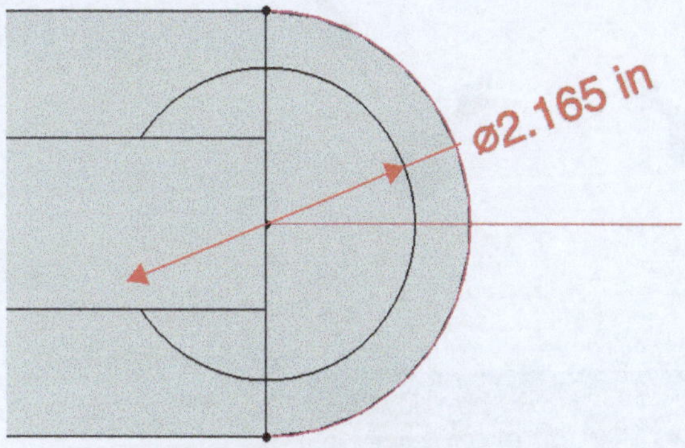

11. Click **Close** on the **Tasks** panel.
12. On the **Part Design Modeling** toolbar, click the **Pad** icon.
13. Type **1.969** in the **Length** box of the **Pad Parameters** dialog.

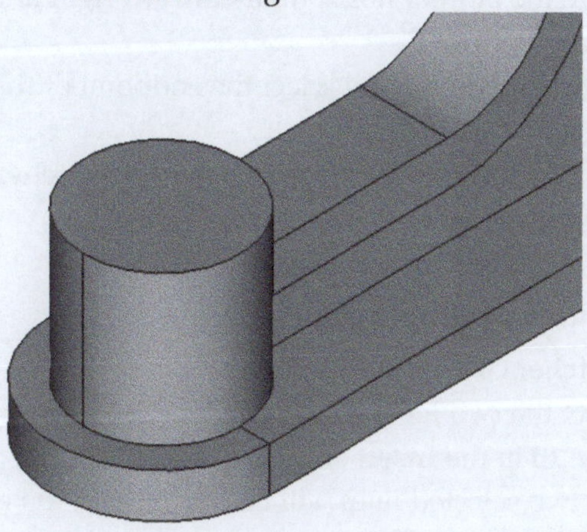

Creating the fourth feature

1. Click the **Create sketch** icon on the **Part Design Helper** toolbar, and then select the XZ Plane from the **Tasks** panel.
2. Click **OK** to start the sketch.
3. Click the **Center and end points** icon on the **Sketcher geometries** toolbar.
4. Click on the vertical axis of the sketch.
5. Move the pointer outward and click to specify the first point of the arc.
6. Specify the second point of the arc.

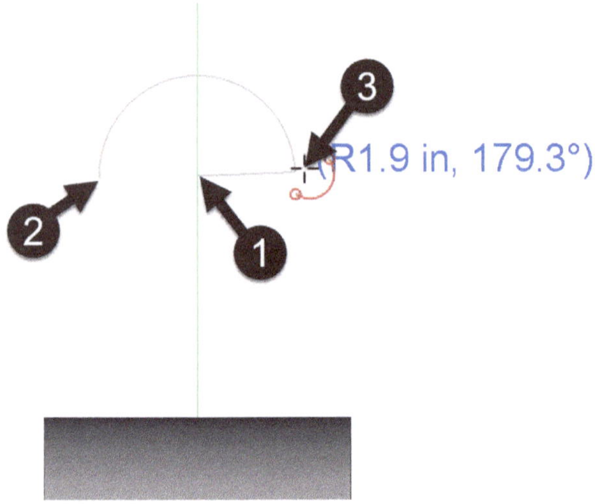

7. Click the **Create polyline** tool on the **Sketcher geometries** toolbar.
8. Select the startpoint of the arc.
9. Move the pointer downward at the inclined angle and click.
10. Move the pointer horizontally toward right and click.
11. Move the pointer and select the endpoint of the arc.
12. Click the **Constrain equal** icon on the **Sketcher constraints** toolbar.
13. Select the two inclined lines.
14. Click the **Constrain angle** icon on the **Sketcher constraints** toolbar.
15. Select the two inclined lines.
16. Type **10** in the **Insert angle** box and click **OK**. The two selected lines will be constrained to be equal in length and have a specific angle between them.
17. Click the **Constrain Tangent** icon on the **Sketcher constraints** toolbar and apply the tangent constraint between the lines and the arc.
18. Click the **Dimension** drop-down > **Constrain radius** icon on the **Sketcher constraints** toolbar.
19. Select the arc, type **0.787** in the **Radius** box and click **OK**.

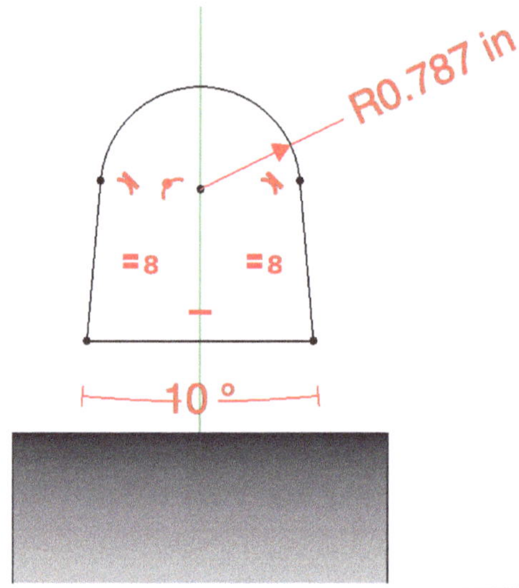

20. Click the **Create external geometry** icon on the **Sketcher tools** toolbar.
21. Select the bottom horizontal edge of the model, as shown.

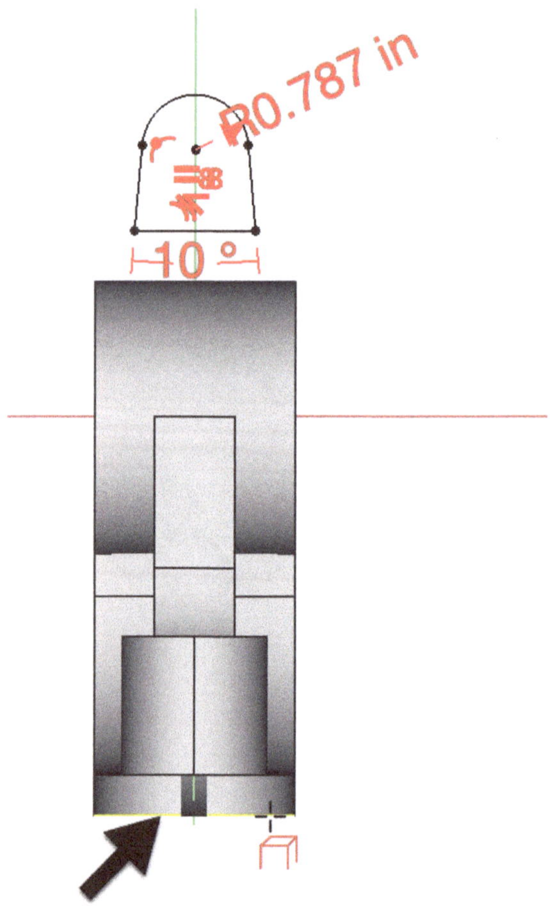

22. Select the horizontal edge of the model, as shown.

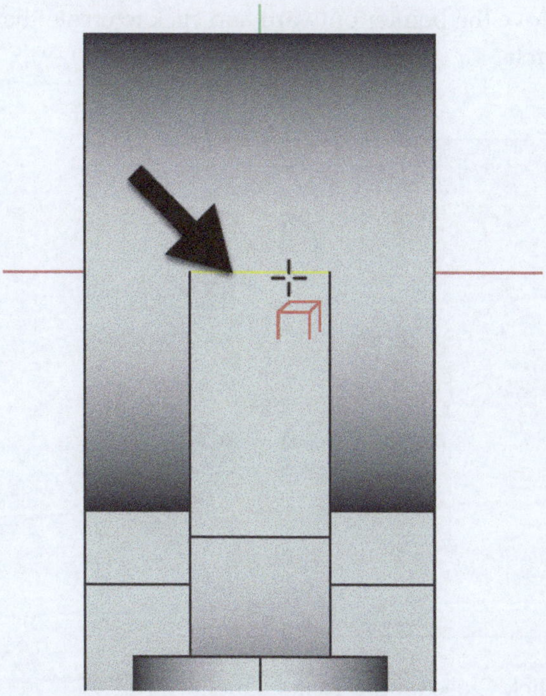

23. Click the **View section** icon on the **Part Design Helper** toolbar.
24. On the **Sketcher constraints** toolbar, click the **Constrain Coincident** icon.
25. Select the endpoint of the horizontal line, as shown.
26. Select the external geometry, as shown.

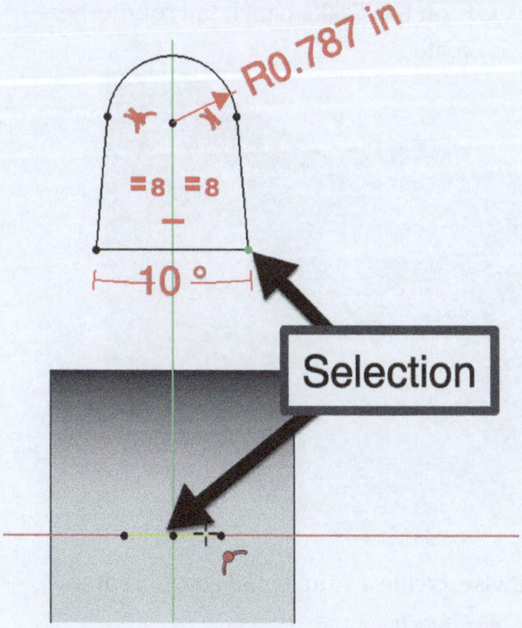

27. Click **Sketcher constraints** toolbar **> Constrain vertical distance** (or) click **Sketch > Sketcher constraints > Constrain vertical distance** on the menu bar.
28. Select the centerpoint of the arc.
29. Select the endpoint of the bottom external geometry.

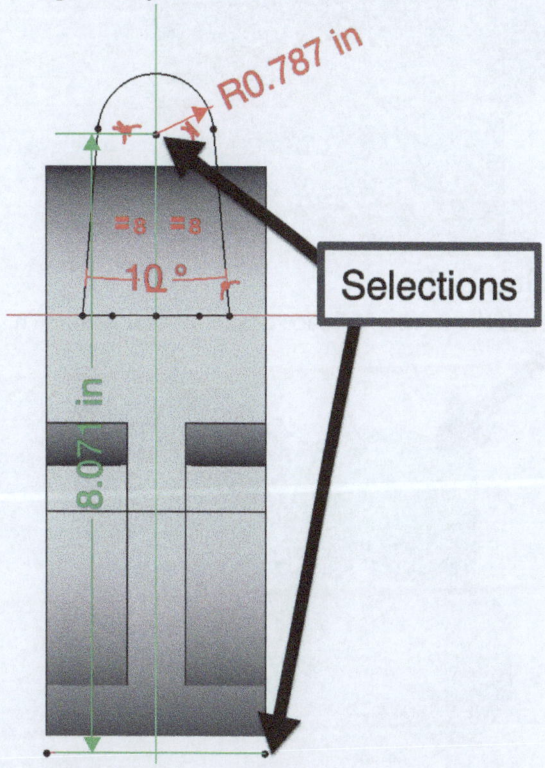

30. Enter **8.071** in the **Length** box of the **Insert Length** dialog and click **OK**.
31. Click **Close** on the **Tasks** panel.
32. On the **Part Design Modeling** toolbar, click the **Pad** icon.
33. Type **2.756** in the **Length** box of the **Pad Parameters** dialog.
34. Check the **Symmetric to plane** option and click **OK**.

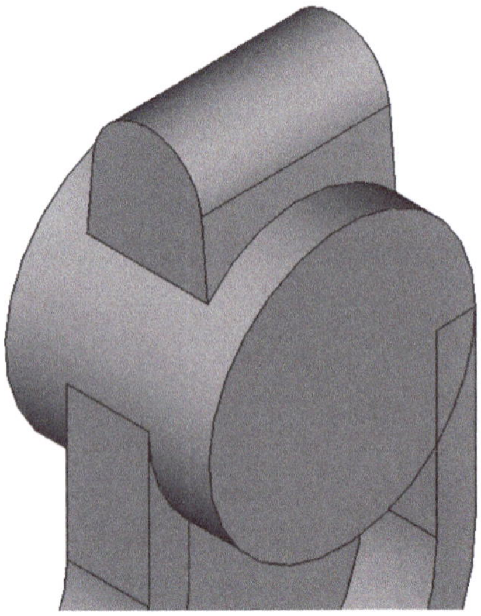

Creating Holes

1. Select the horizontal face of the model, as shown.

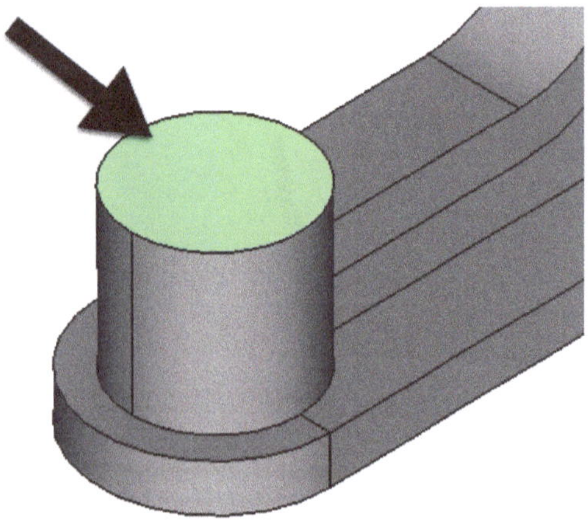

2. Click **Create new Sketch** icon on the **Part Design Helper toolbar**.
3. Click the **Create external geometry** icon on the **Sketcher tools** toolbar.
4. Select the circular edge of the model, as shown.

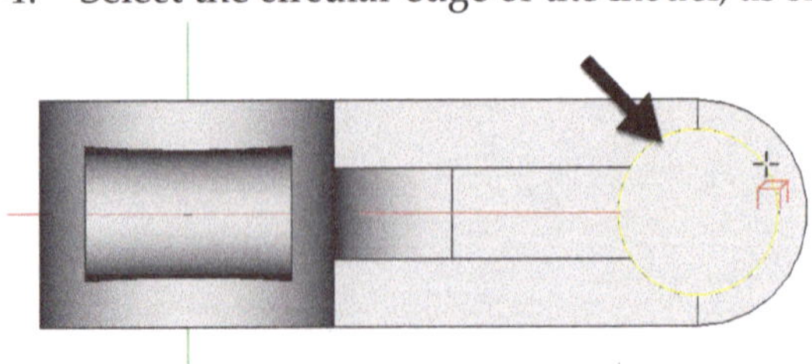

5. Click the **Create circle** icon on the **Sketcher geometry** toolbar.
6. Click on the centerpoint of the curved edge.
7. Move the pointer outward and click to create the circle.

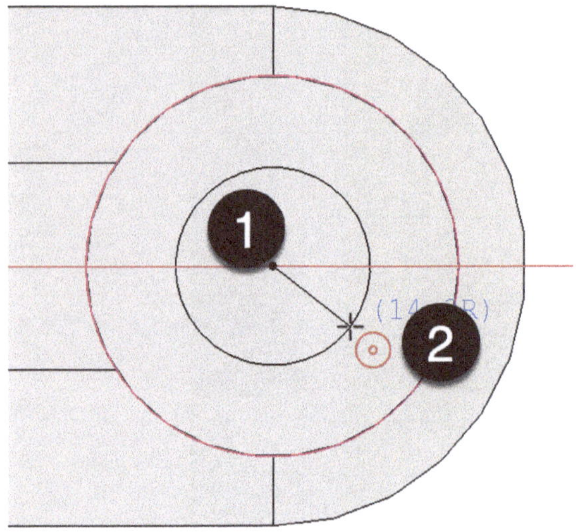

8. Click **Close** on the **Tasks** panel.
9. Click the **Hole** icon on the **Part Design Modeling** toolbar.
10. Type **1.181** in the **Diameter** box.
11. Select **Depth > Through All**.
12. On the **Hole Parameters** section, under **Hole cut**, select **Type > Counterbore**.
13. Type **1.575** in the **Diameter** box.
14. Type **0.197** in the **Depth** box.
15. Click **OK** on the **Tasks** panel; the counterbore hole is created.

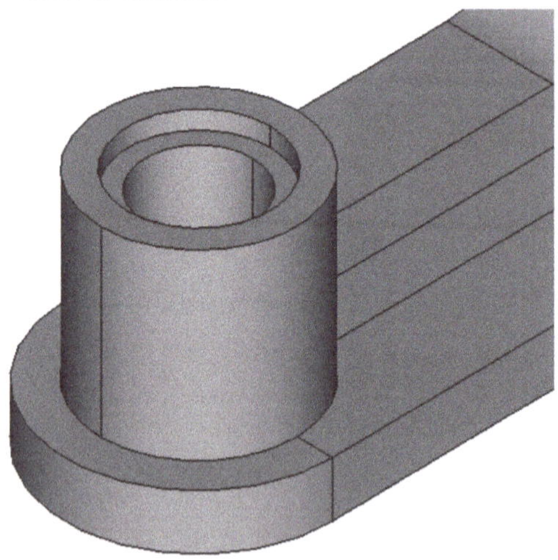

16. Likewise, create a simple and counterbored hole, as shown.

Hole diameter: 2.559 in
Depth: Through all

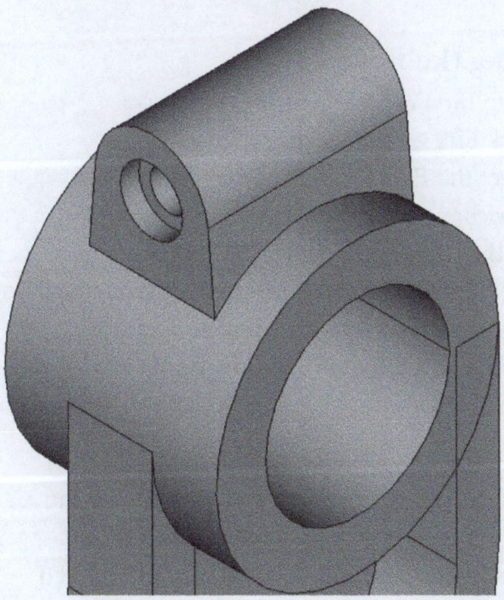

Diameter: 0.551 in
Depth: Through all
Type: Counterbore
Counterbore Diameter: 0.866 in
Depth: 0.260 in

Creating the Pocket feature

1. Select the flat face of the model, as shown.

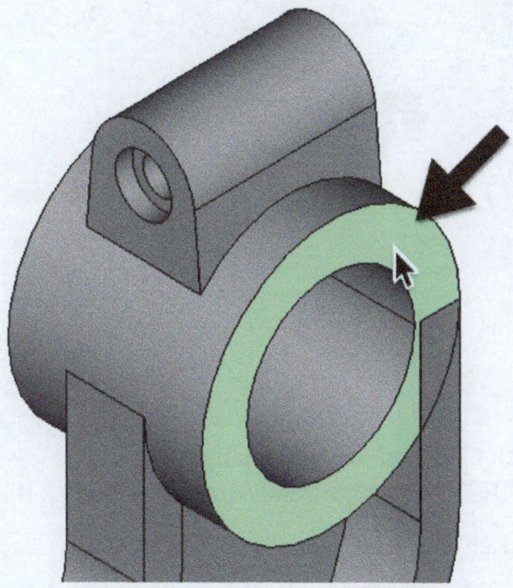

2. Click **Create new Sketch** icon on the **Part Design Helper toolbar**.
3. Create a rectangle and dimensions to it, as shown.

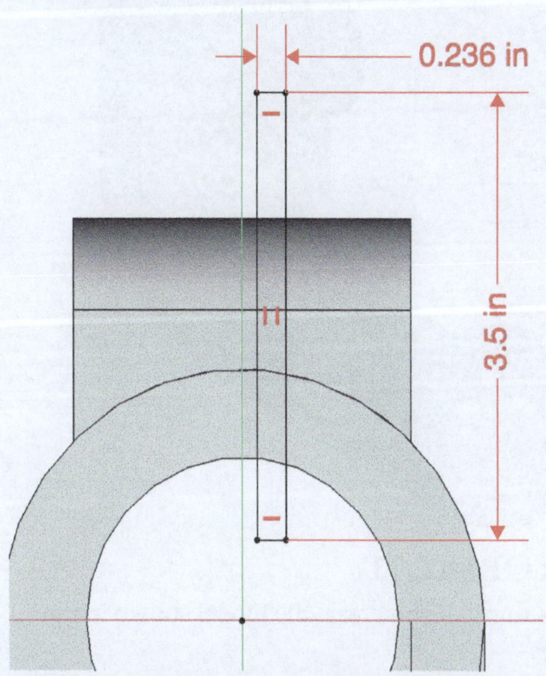

4. On the **Sketcher constraints** toolbar, click the **Constrain symmetrical** icon.
5. Select the endpoints of the horizontal line, as shown.
6. Select the sketch origin.

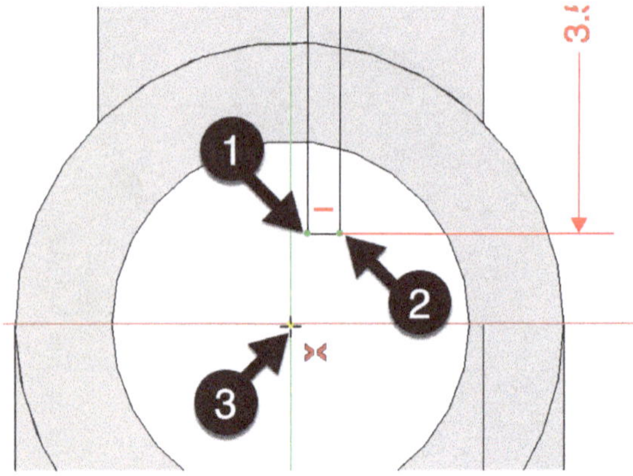

7. Click **Close** on the **Tasks** panel.
8. On the **Part Design Modeling** toolbar, click the **Pocket** icon.
9. Select **Type > Through all**, and then click **OK**.

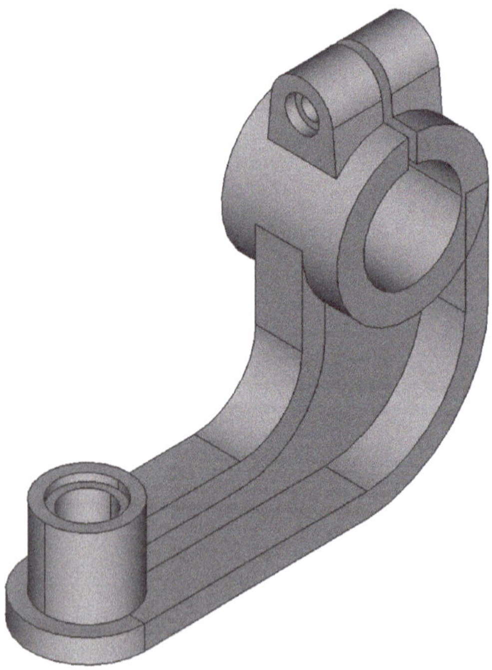

TUTORIAL 11

In this tutorial, you create the model shown in the figure:

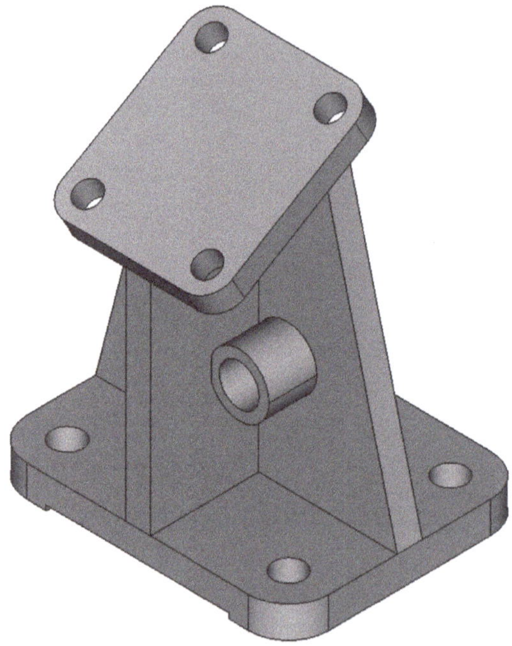

Creating the Base

1. Open the FreeCAD application.
2. Click **File > New** on the Menu bar.
3. Select the **Part Design** option from the **Workbenches** drop-down.
4. On the Menu bar, click **Edit > Preferences**.
5. Click the **General tab** on the **Preferences** dialog.
6. Select **User system > Imperial decimal**.
7. Type **3** in the **Number of decimals** box.
8. Click **OK**.
9. Click the **Create sketch** icon on the **Part Design Helper** toolbar, and then Select the XY Plane from the **Tasks** panel and click **OK**.
10. Click the **Rectangle** drop-down > **Centered Rectangle** on the **Sketcher geometries** toolbar.
11. Select the sketch origin, move the pointer outward and click. Next, add dimensions to the sketch.

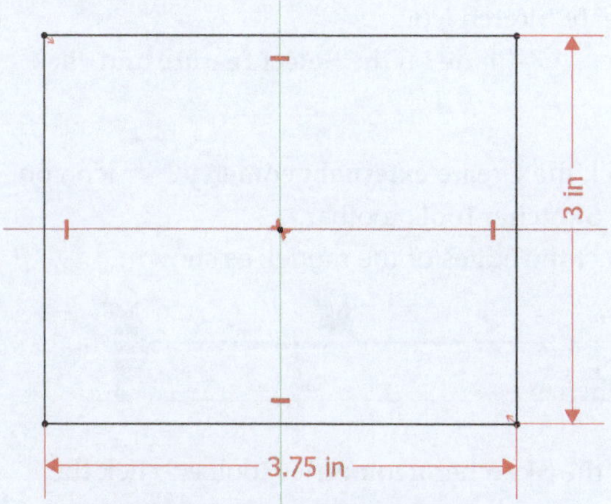

12. Click **Close** on the **Tasks** panel.
13. Click the **Pad** icon on the **Part Design Modelling** toolbar.
14. Select **Type > Dimension** on the **Pad parameters** section.
15. Type-in **0.38** in in the **Length** box.
16. Click **OK** on the **Tasks** panel.

17. Select the front right edge, as shown.

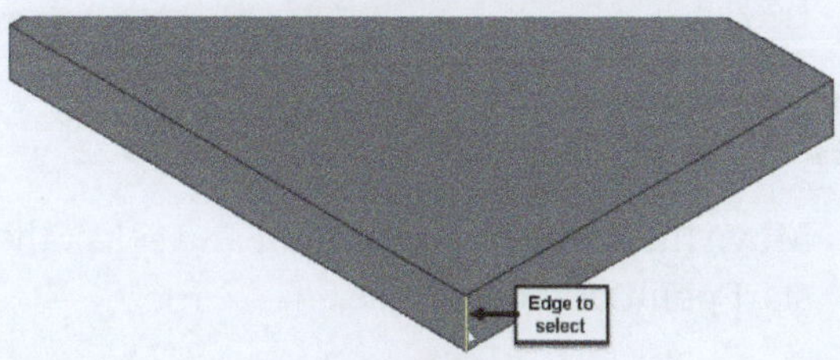

18. Click the **Create fillet**  icon on the **Part Design Modeling** toolbar.
19. Click the **Select** button on the **Fillet parameters** section.
20. Select the front left edge.
21. Likewise, select the back vertical edges of the pad features.
22. Type-in **0.50** in in the **Radius** box.
23. Click **OK** on the **Tasks** panel.

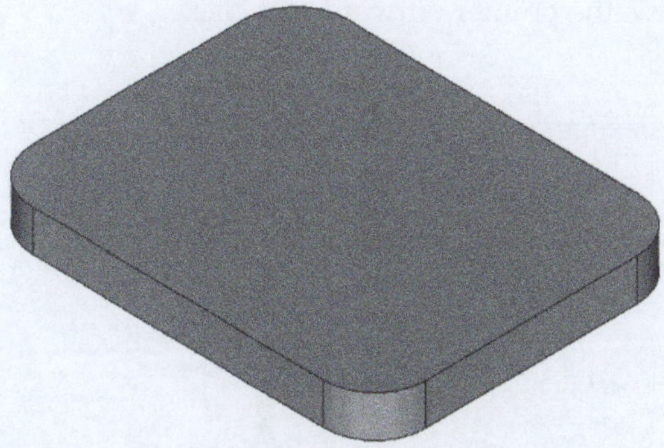

24. Click on the top face of the **Pad** feature and click **Create Sketch** on the **Part Design Helper toolbar**.

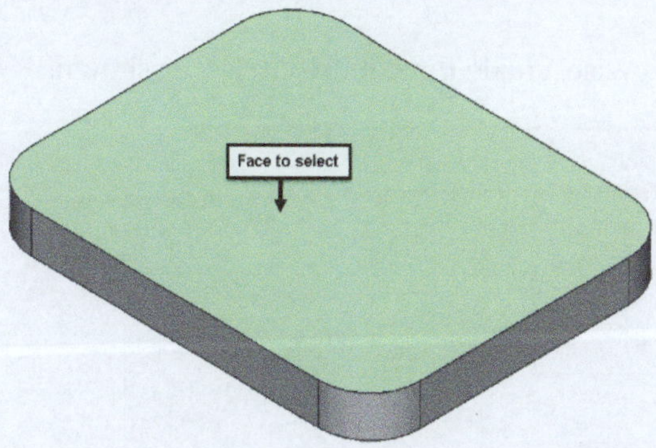

25. Click the **Create external geometry**  icon on the **Sketcher tools** toolbar.
26. Select the top right arc of the Pad feature, as shown.
27. Likewise, select the remaining arcs of the pad feature, as shown.

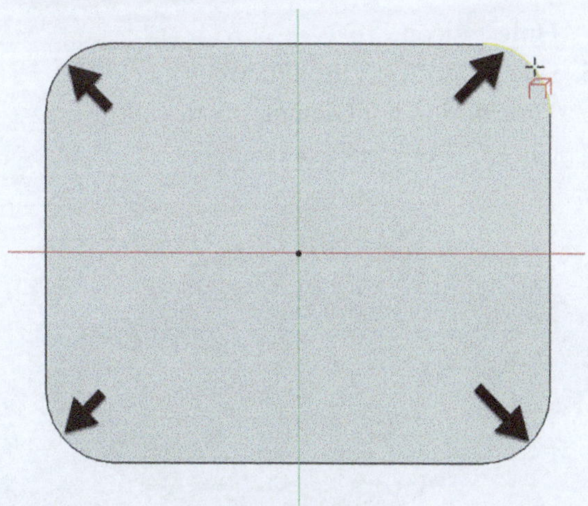

28. Press **Esc** to deactivate the tool.
29. On the **Sketcher geometries** toolbar, click the **Create circle** icon.
30. Select the centerpoint of the circular edge.

31. Move the pointer outward and click.

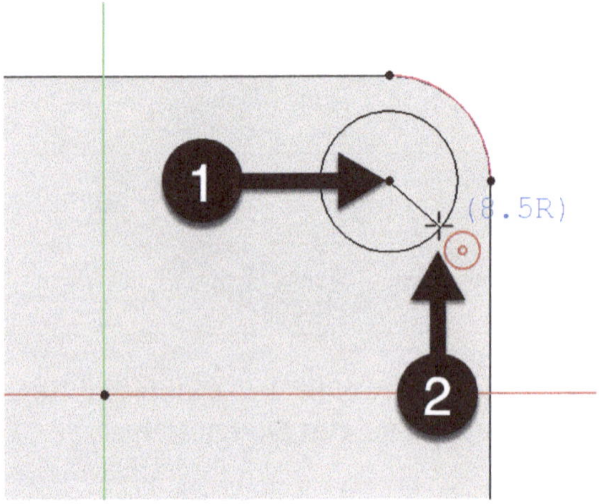

32. Likewise, create three more circles, as shown.

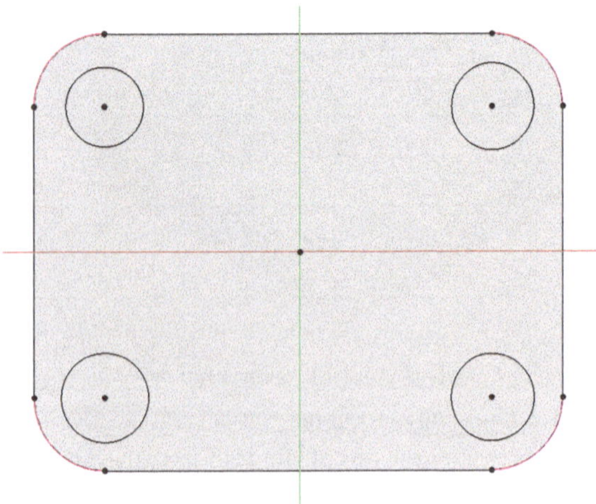

33. Click **Close** on the **Tasks** panel.
34. On the **Part Design Modelling** toolbar, click the **Hole** icon.
35. Select **Depth > Through all.**
36. Type **0.38** in the **Diameter** box.
37. Click **OK** on the **Tasks** panel.

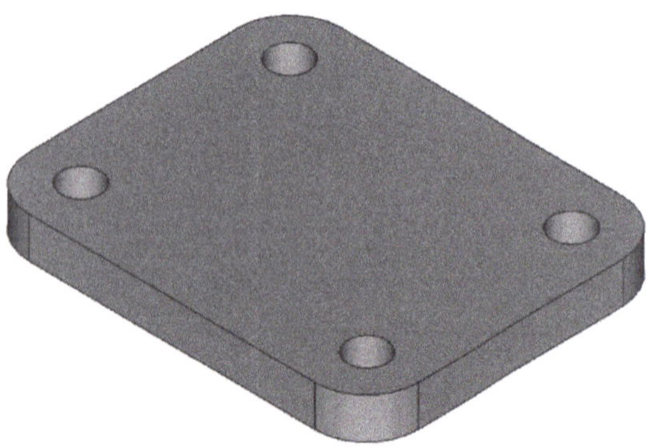

Creating the Rib

1. On the **Part Design Helper** toolbar, click the **Create Sketch** icon.
2. Select **XZ-Plane** on the **Select feature** and click **OK**.
3. Click the **Create external geometry** icon on the **Sketcher tools** toolbar.
4. Select the edges of the model, as shown.

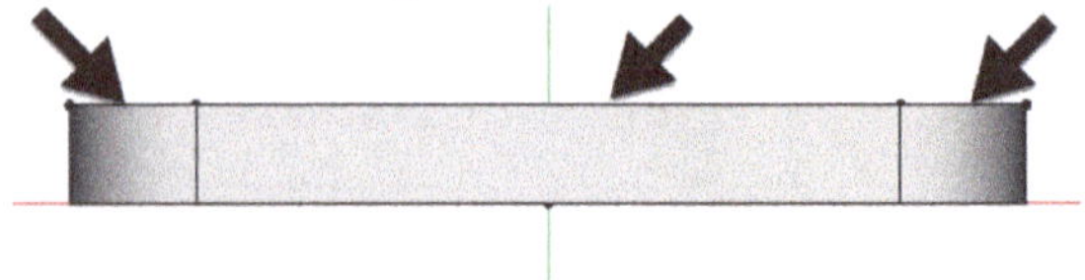

5. On the **Sketcher geometries** toolbar, click the **Create Polyline** icon.
6. Select the right endpoint of the external geometry, as shown.

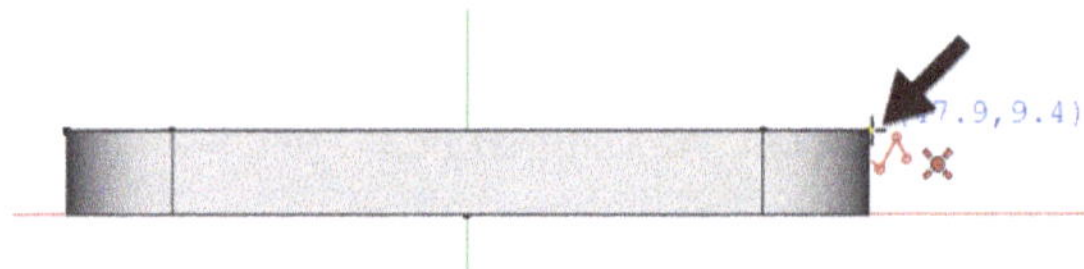

7. Specify the second and third points of the polyline, as shown.
8. Select the left point of the external geometry, as shown.

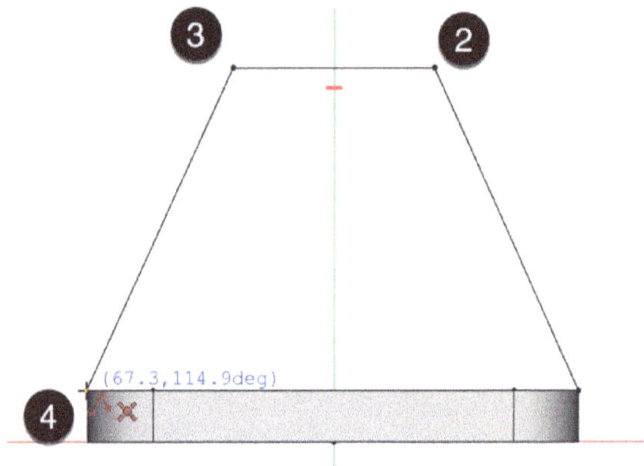

9. Move the pointer toward right and select the start point of the polyline.

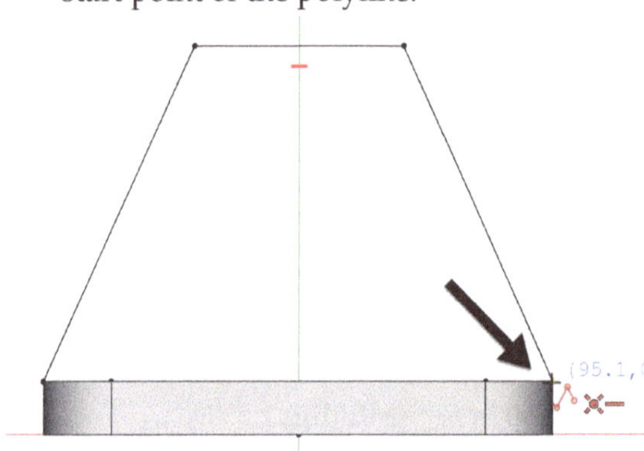

10. Add dimensional constraints to the sketch, and then click **Leave Sketch**.

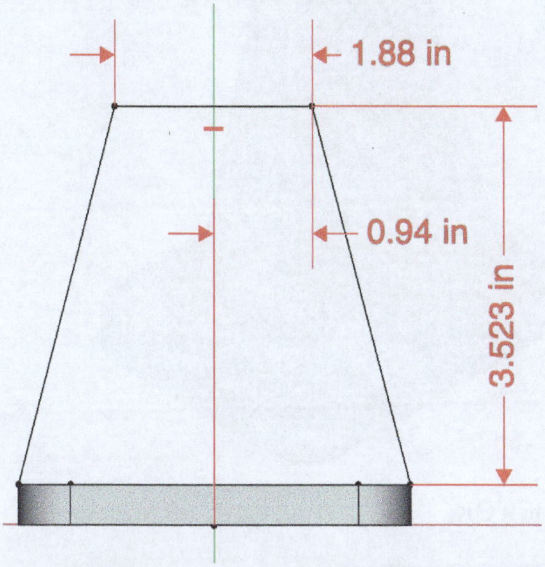

11. On the **Part Design Modeling** toolbar, click the **Pad** icon.
12. Type **0.31** in the **Length** box of the **Pad Parameters** dialog.
13. Check the **Symmetric to plane** option and click **OK**.

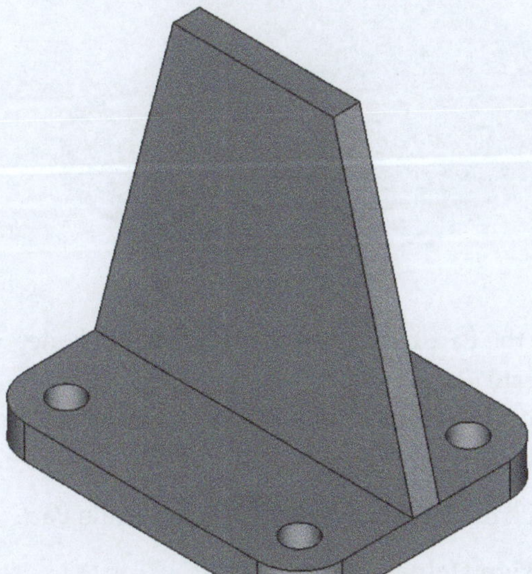

14. Click on the horizontal face of the model, as shown.

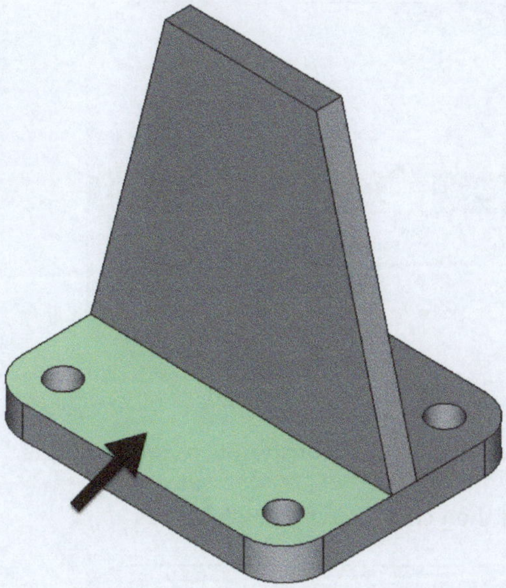

15. Click **Create Sketch** on the **Part Design Helper** toolbar.
16. Click the **Create external geometry** icon on the **Sketcher tools** toolbar.
17. Select the horizontal edges of the model, as shown.

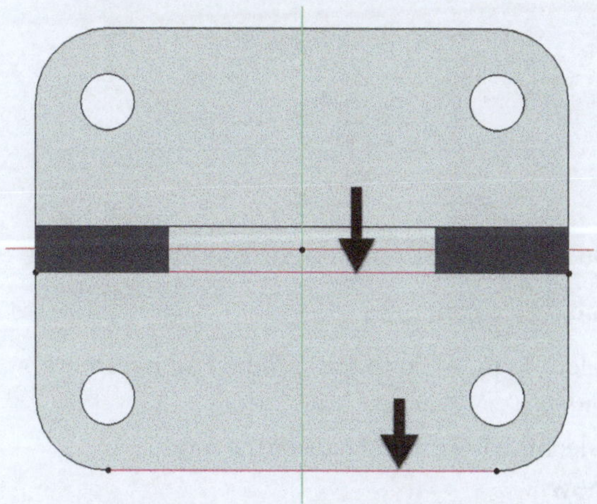

18. Specify the first and second corners of the rectangle of the two external geometries, as shown.

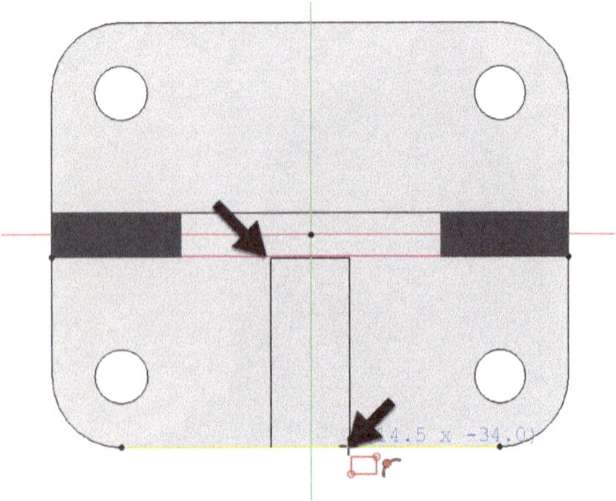

19. Add dimensional constraints to the rectangle, and then click **Leave Sketch** .

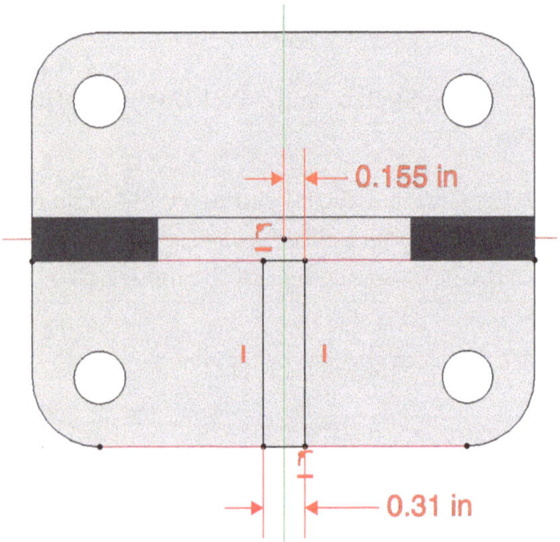

20. On the **Part Design Modeling** toolbar, click the **Pad**  icon.
21. Select **Type > Up to face** on the **Pad parameters** dialog.
22. Select the horizontal face of the model, as shown.

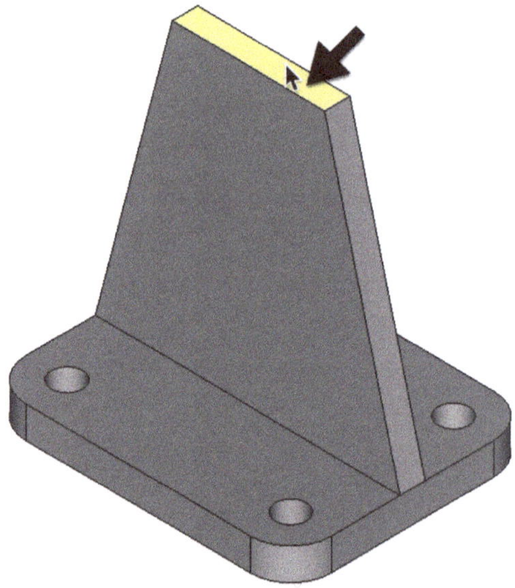

23. Click **OK**.

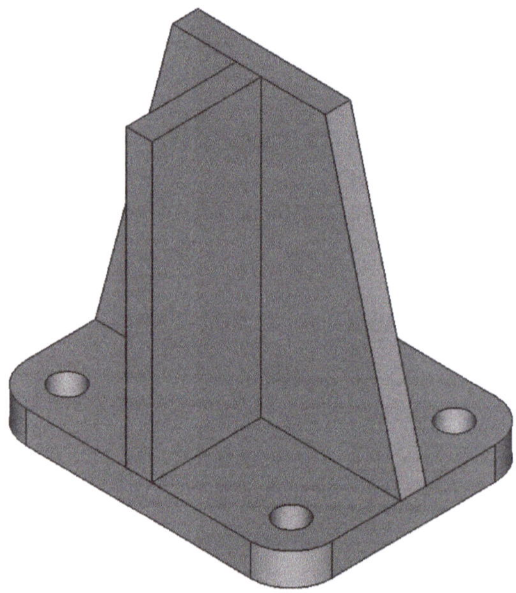

24. On the **Part Design Helper** toolbar, click the **Create Sketch** icon.
25. Select **YZ-Plane** on the **Select feature** and click **OK**.
26. Click the **View section**  icon on the **Part Design Helper** toolbar.
27. On the **Sketcher geometries** toolbar, click the **Create Polyline** icon.
28. Create a closed sketch, as shown.

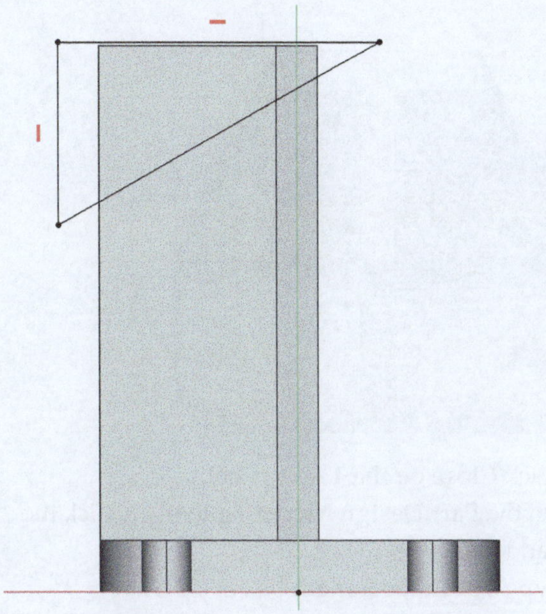

29. Add dimensions to the sketch, as shown.

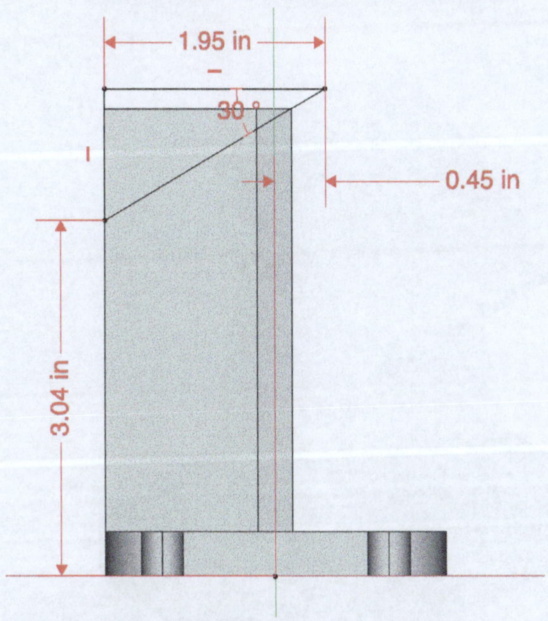

30. Click **Close** on the **Tasks** panel.
31. On the **Part Design Modelling** toolbar, click the **Pocket** icon.
32. Select **Type > Through all** under the **Pad parameters** section.
33. Check the **Symmetric to plane** option.
34. Click **OK** on the **Tasks** panel.

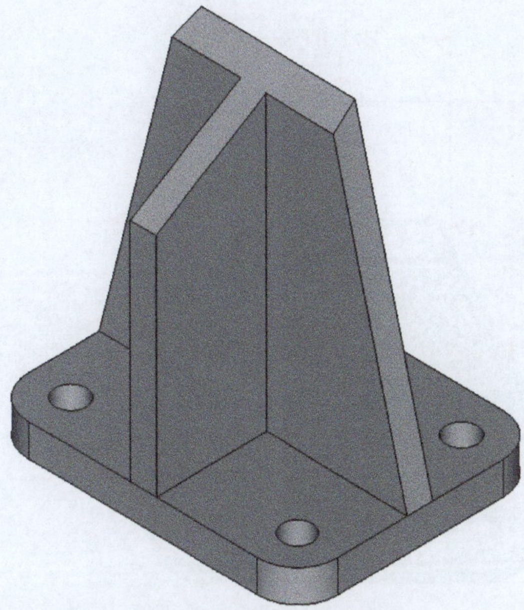

Creating the Third feature

1. Click on the inclined face of the model, as shown.

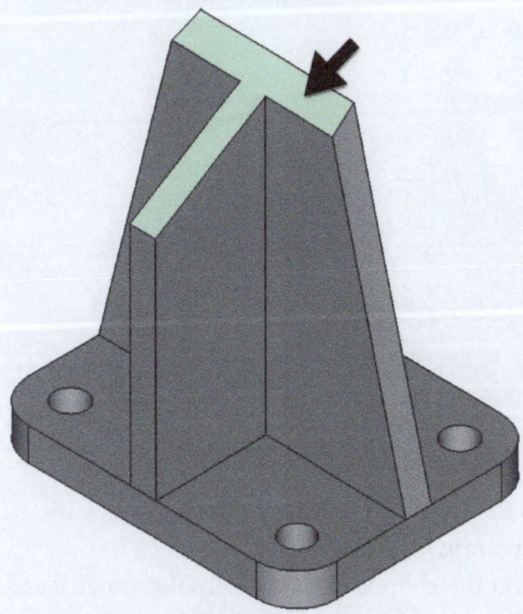

2. On the **Part Design Helper** toolbar, click the **Create Sketch** icon.
3. Create the rectangle and add dimensions to it, as shown.

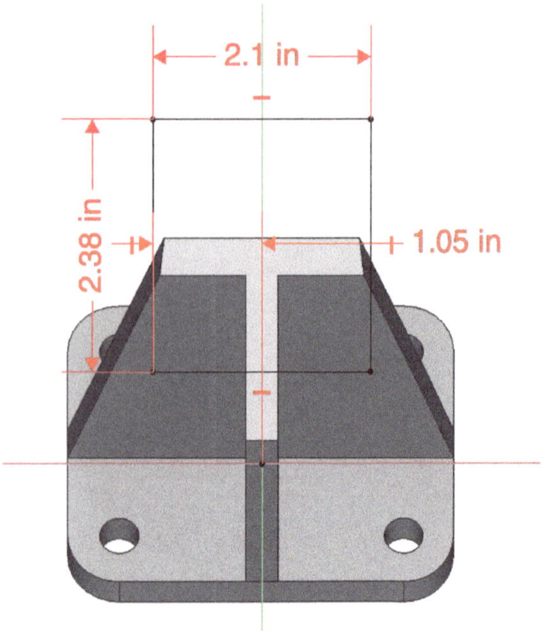

4. Click the **Create external geometry**  icon on the **Sketcher tools** toolbar.
5. Select the horizontal edges of the model, as shown.

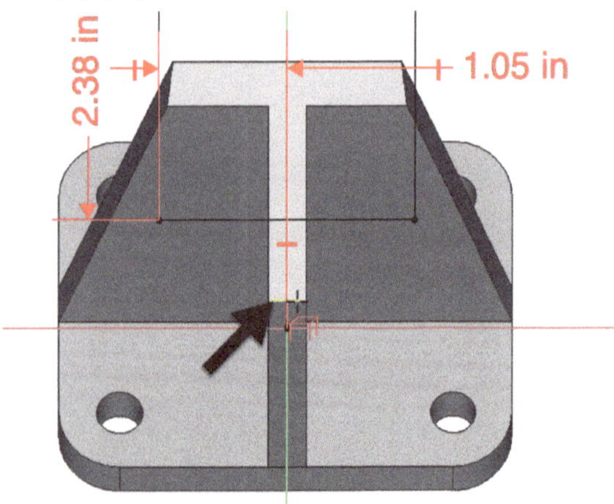

6. On the **Sketcher constraints** toolbar, click the **Constrain Coincident** icon.
7. Select the endpoint of the external geometry and the horizontal line, as shown.

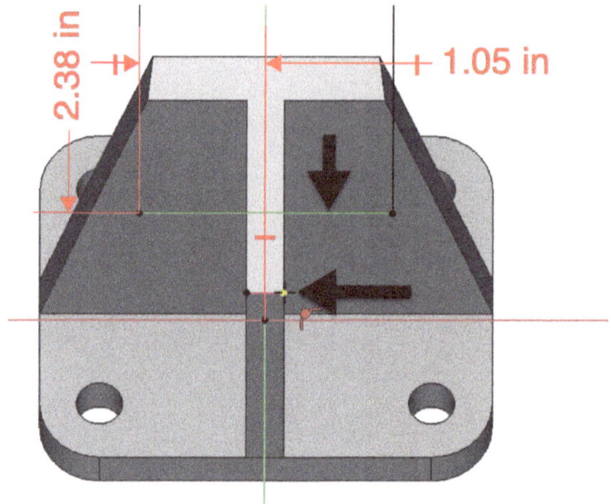

8. Click **Close** on the **Tasks** panel.
9. On the **Part Design Modeling** toolbar, click the **Pad** icon.
10. Type **0.31** in the **Length** box of the **Pad Parameters** dialog.
11. Click **OK**.

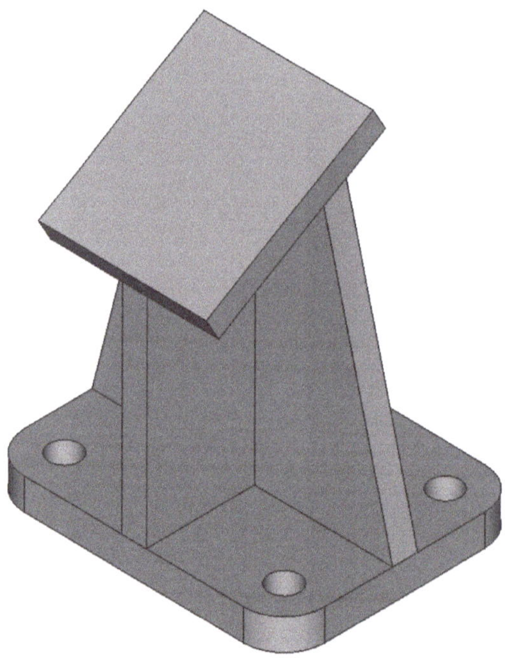

12. Add fillets of 0.31 in radius, as shown.

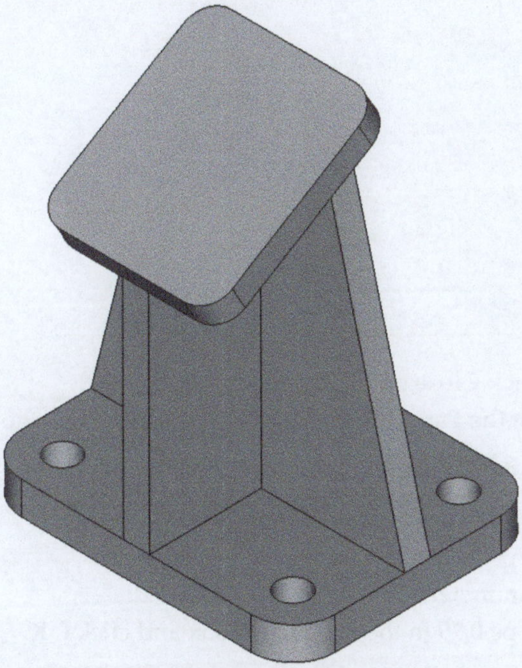

13. Click on the inclined face, as shown.

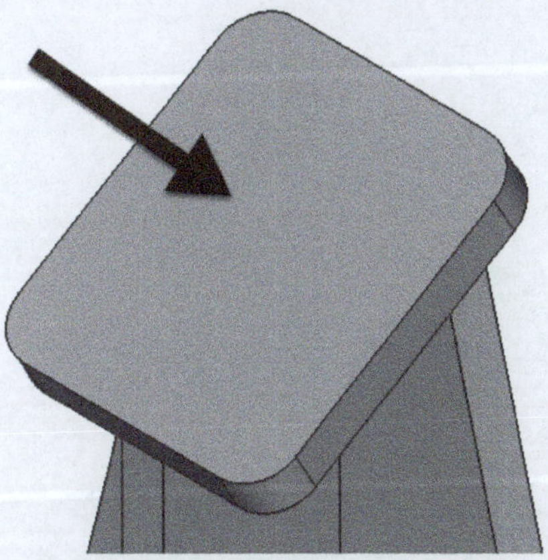

14. On the **Part Design Helper** toolbar, click the **Create Sketch** icon.
15. Click the **Create external geometry**  icon on the **Sketcher tools** toolbar.
16. Select the curved edges of the model, as shown.

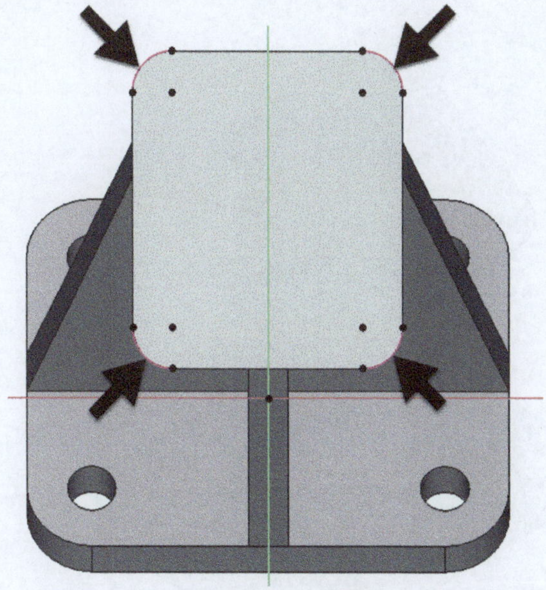

17. Click the **Create Circle**  on the **Sketcher geometries** toolbar.
18. Create circles, as shown.

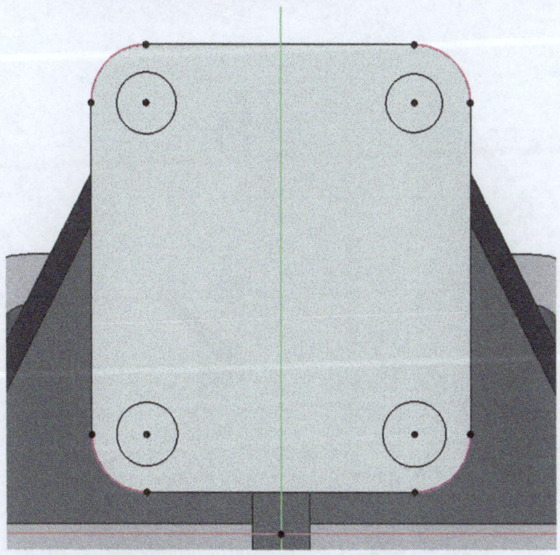

19. Click **Close** on the **Tasks** panel.
20. Click the **Hole** icon on the **Part Design Modeling** toolbar.
21. Type **0.31** in the **Diameter** box.
22. Select **Depth > Dimension.**
23. Type **0.31** in the **Depth** box.
24. Click **OK** on the **Tasks** panel; the holes are created.

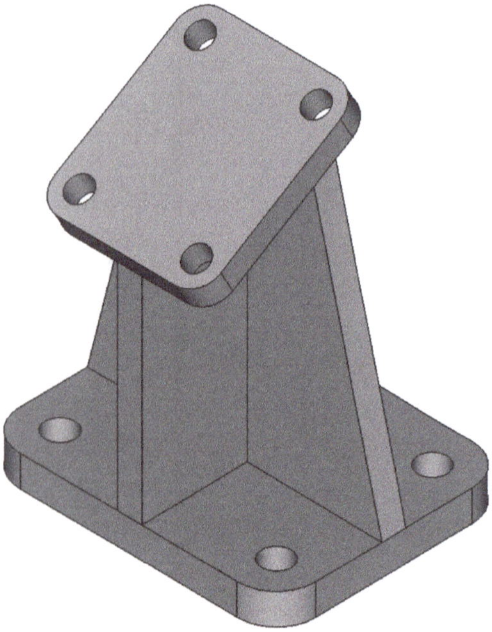

25. Click on the vertical face, as shown.

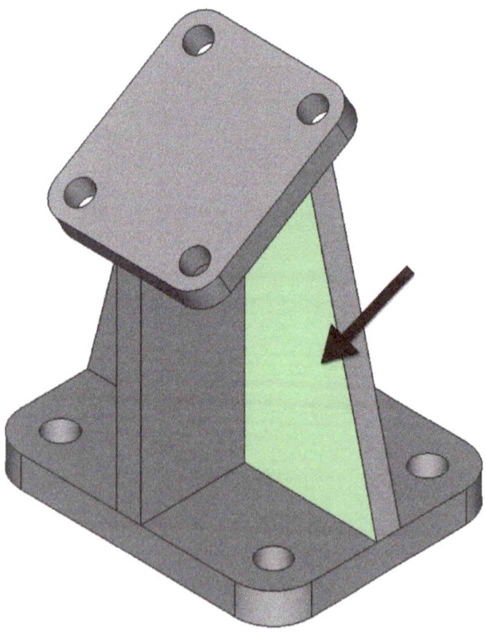

26. On the **Part Design Helper** toolbar, click the **Create Sketch** icon.
27. Create two circles and add dimensions to it, as shown.

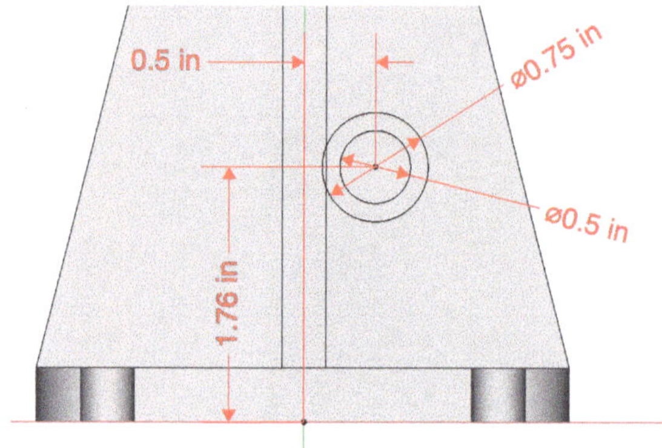

28. Click **Close** on the **Tasks** panel.
29. On the **Part Design Modeling** toolbar, click the **Pad**  icon.
30. Select **Type > Two dimensions**.
31. Type **0.59** in the **Length** box of the **Pad Parameters** dialog.
32. Type **0.79** in the **2nd Length** box and click **OK**.

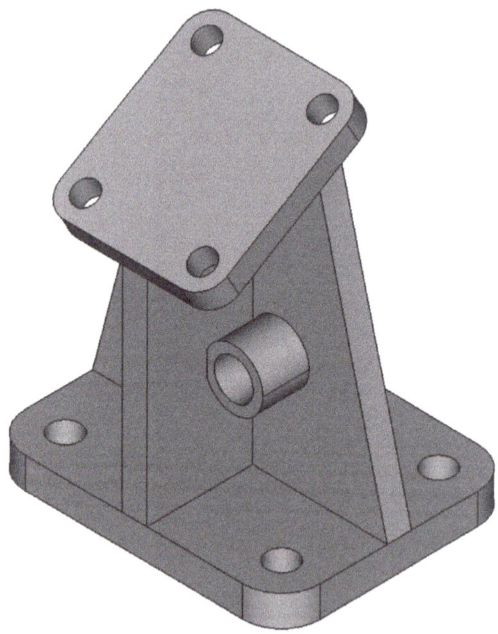

Creating the Pocket Feature

1. Click on the vertical face, as shown.

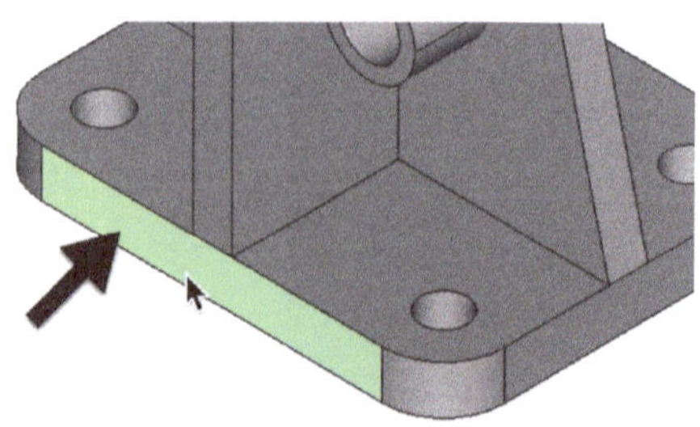

2. On the **Part Design Helper** toolbar, click the **Create Sketch** icon.
3. Create a rectangle and add dimensions to it.

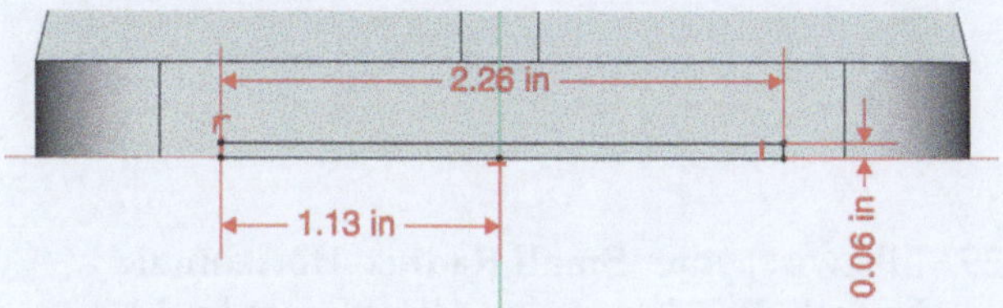

4. Click **Close** on the **Tasks** panel.
5. On the **Part Design Modeling** toolbar, click the **Pocket** icon.
6. Select **Type > Through all.**
7. Click **OK.**

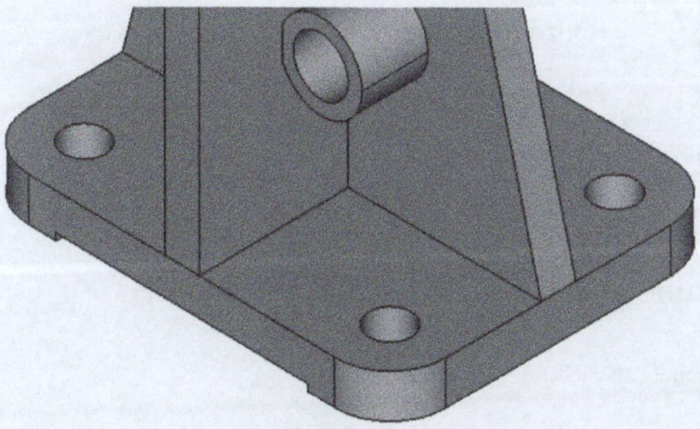

8. Save and close the file.

TUTORIAL 12

In this tutorial, you will create a spreadsheet and use the data in the spreadsheet to control the model.

1. Start a new file and select the **Part Design** option from the **Workbenches** drop-down.
2. On the Menu bar, click **Edit > Preferences.**
3. Click the **General** tab on the **Preferences** dialog.
4. Select **User system > Standard (mm, kg, s degree).**
5. Type **2** in the **Number of decimals** box.
6. Click **OK.**
7. Activate the **Create Sketch** command and select the XY plane. Next, click **OK.**
8. Create the sketch, as shown.

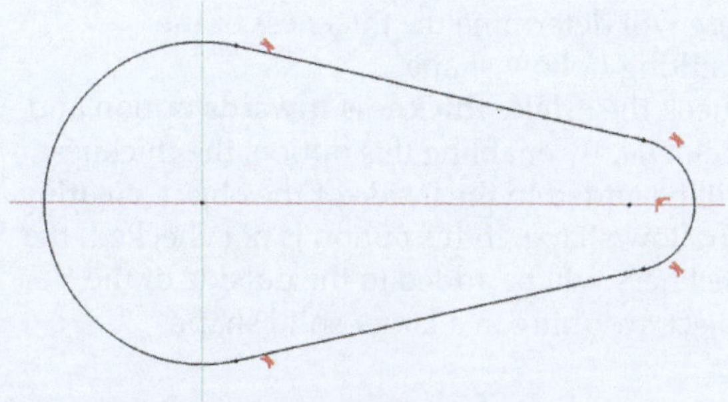

9. Click **Sketch > Sketcher Constraints > Constrain radius** on the menu bar.
10. Select the large arc.
11. On the **Rapid Dimension** dialog, check the **Expression** on the **Driving** section.
12. Type **30** and press ENTER.
13. Select the small arc.
14. Type **15** and press ENTER.
15. Click the **Constrain horizontal distance** icon on the **Sketcher constraints** toolbar.
16. Select the sketch origin and the center point of the small arc.
17. Type **60** and press ENTER.

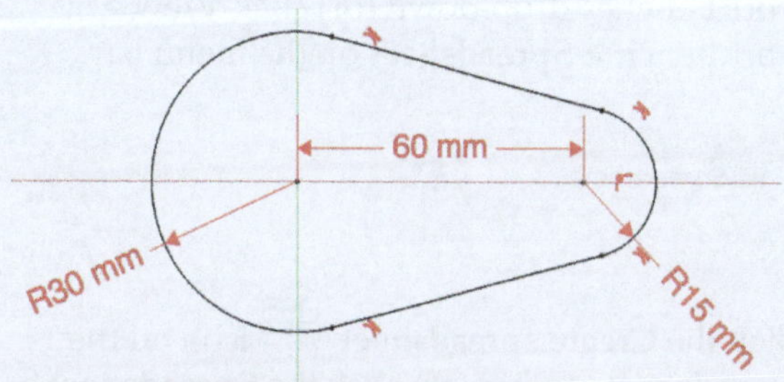

18. Click **Close** on the **Tasks** panel.
19. On the menu bar, click **Part Design > Create an additive feature > Pad.**
20. On the **Pad Parameters** section, type **15** in the **Length** box, and then click **OK.**

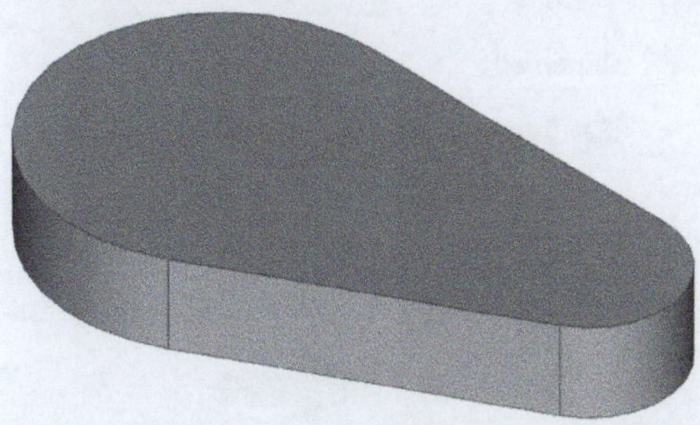

21. Press and hold the CTRL key and select the top and bottom faces of the model.
22. Click the **Thickness** icon on the **Part Design Dressup** toolbar.
23. Type **5** in the **Thickness** box. The value entered

here will determine the thickness of the resulting hollow shape.

24. Check the **Make thickness inwards** option and click **OK**. By enabling this option, the thickness will be added to the inside of the object, creating a hollow shape. If this option is not checked, the thickness will be added to the outside of the object, resulting in a larger solid shape.

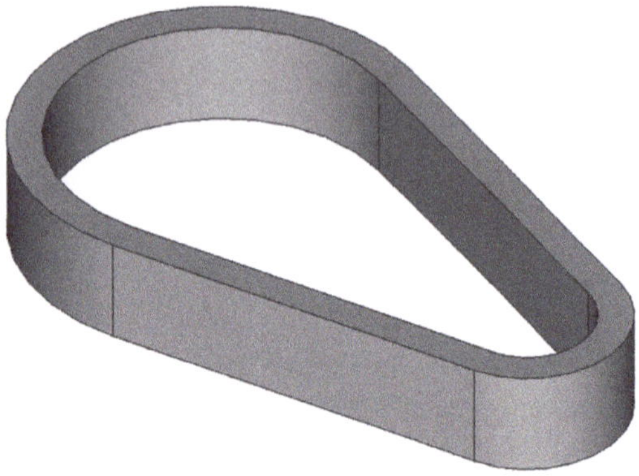

25. Select the **Spreadsheet** option from the **Workbenches** drop-down (or) click **View > Workbench > Spreadsheet** on the menu bar.

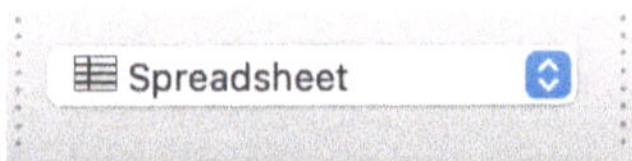

26. Click the **Create spreadsheet** icon on the **Spreadsheet** toolbar (or) click the **Spreadsheet > Create Spreadsheet** on the menu bar.
27. Click the **Model** panel and double-click on the newly created spreadsheet.

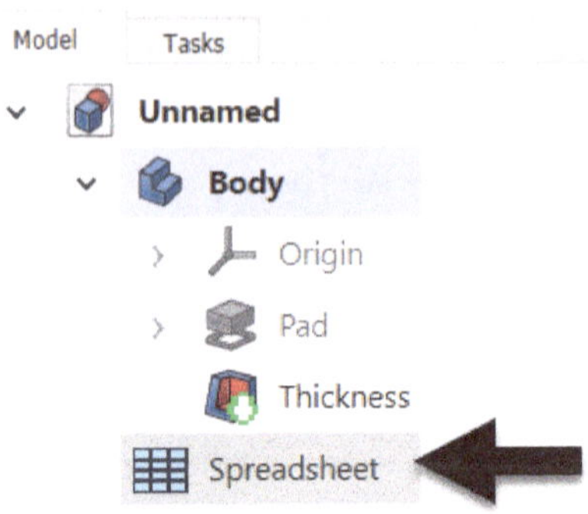

A spreadsheet is displayed in the window.

28. Double-click in the **A1** cell of the spreadsheet and type **Large Radius**.

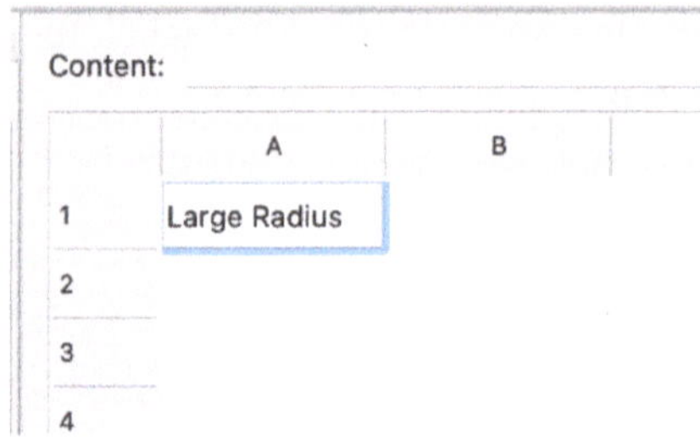

29. Likewise, enter **Small Radius**, **Horizontal Length**, **Pad Length**, and **Thickness** in the **A2**, **A3**, **A4**, and **A5** cells, respectively.

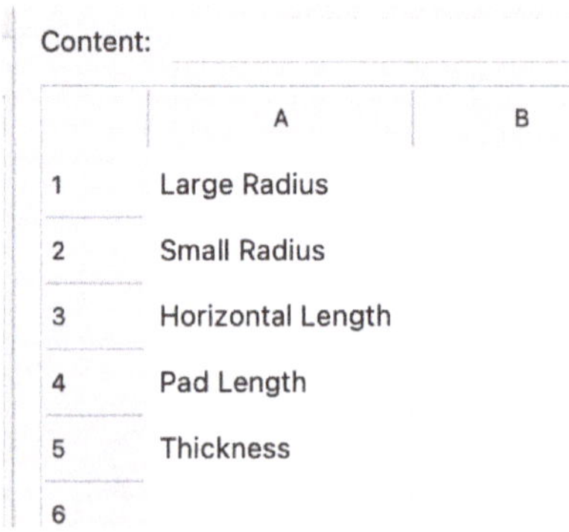

30. Double-click in the **B1** cell and type **30**.

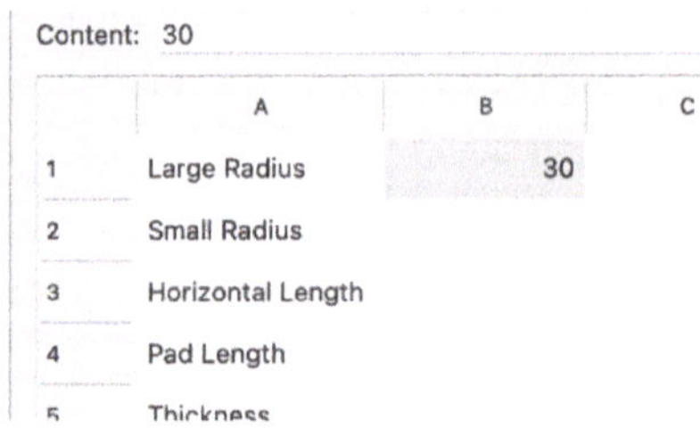

31. Click in the **Alias** box displayed at the top right corner of the spreadsheet and type **Large_radius**. Next, press ENTER.

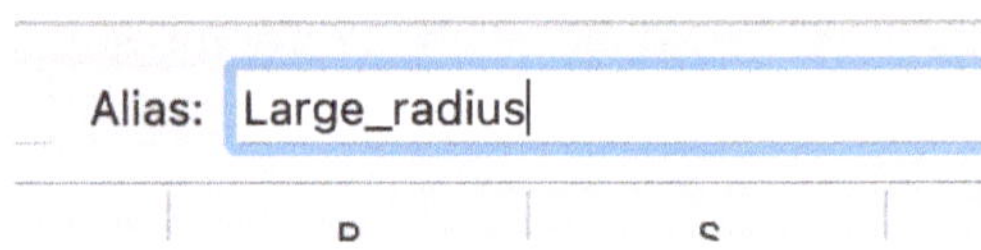

32. Likewise, enter 15, 60, 15, and 5 in the B2, B3, B4, and B5 cells respectively.

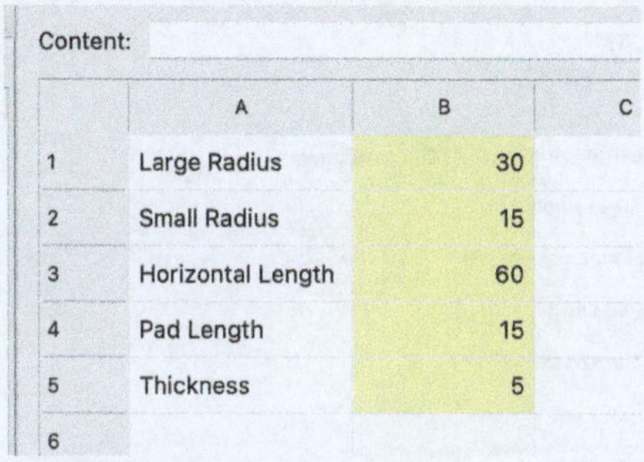

33. Enter **Small_radius**, **Horizontal_length**, **Pad_length**, and **Thickness** as the **Aliases** of **B2**, **B3**, **B4**, and **B5** cells respectively.
34. Click the **Model** panel and expand the **Pad** feature.
35. Right-click on the **Sketch**, and then select **Edit Sketch**.

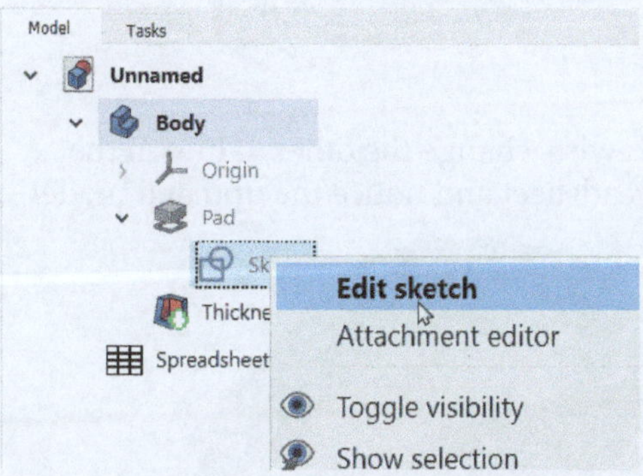

36. Double-click on the 30 mm radius dimension.
37. Click the **Enter an expression** icon located in the **Radius** box on the **Insert Radius** dialog.

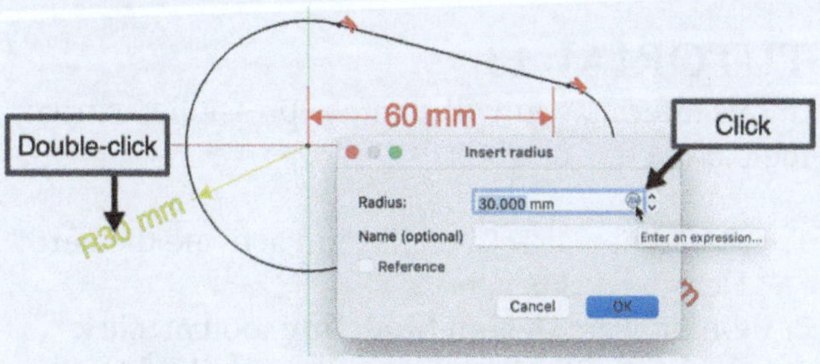

38. On the **Formula editor** dialog, type Spreadsheet, and then select the **Spreadsheet** option.

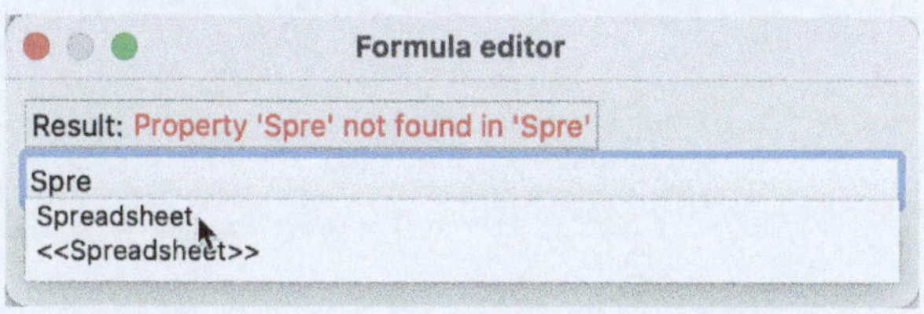

39. Click next to the Spreadsheet. value and type La. Next, select the **Large_radius** value from the listed value.

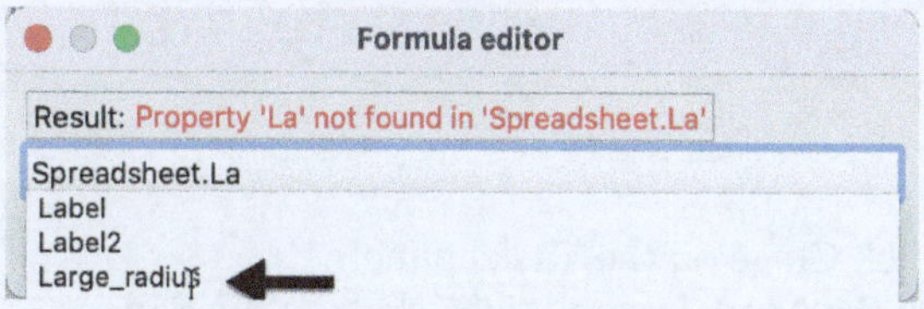

40. Click **OK** on the **Formula editor** dialog.

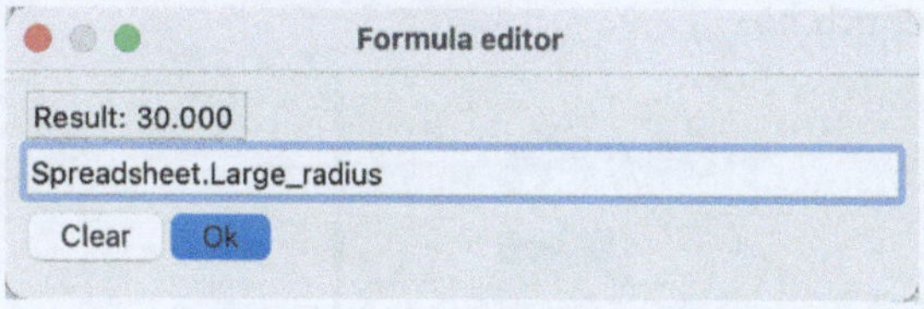

41. Click **OK** on the **Insert radius** dialog.
42. Double-click on the 15 mm radius value, and then click the **Enter an expression** button in the **Radius** box.

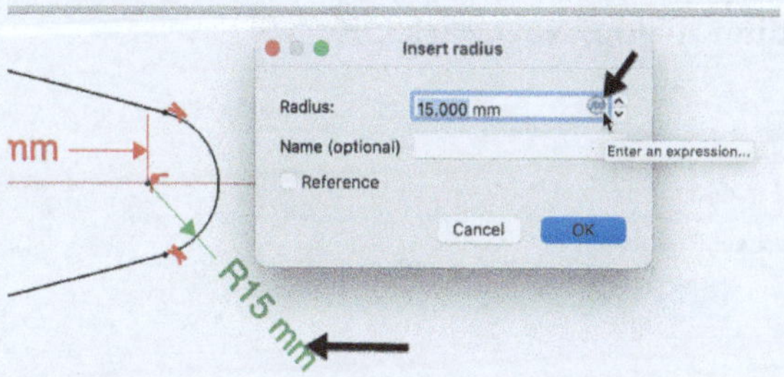

43. Type **Spreadsheet.Small_radius** in the **Formula editor** dialog. Next, click **OK** twice.

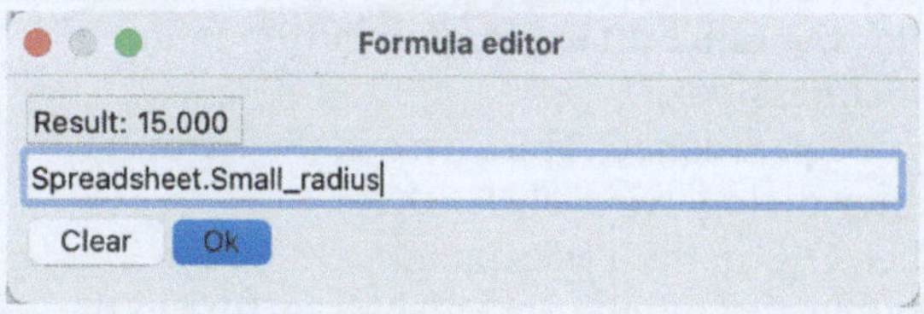

44. Likewise, change the 60 mm dimension value to **Spreadsheet.Horizontal_length** formula using the **Formula editor** dialog.

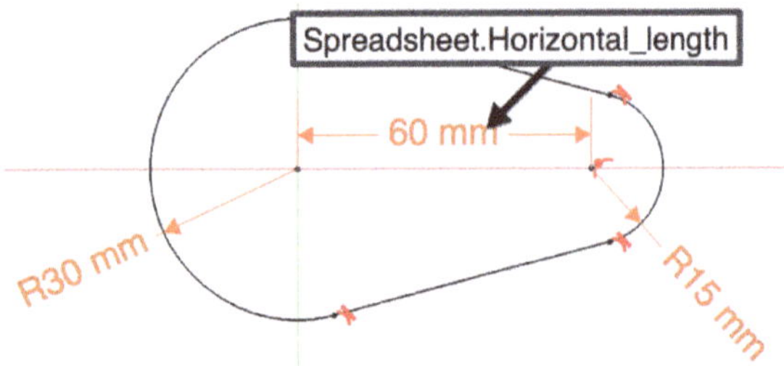

45. Click **Close** on the **Tasks** panel.
46. On the **Model** panel, right-click on the **Pad** feature, and then select **Edit Pad**.
47. Click the **Enter an expression** button in the **Length** box.

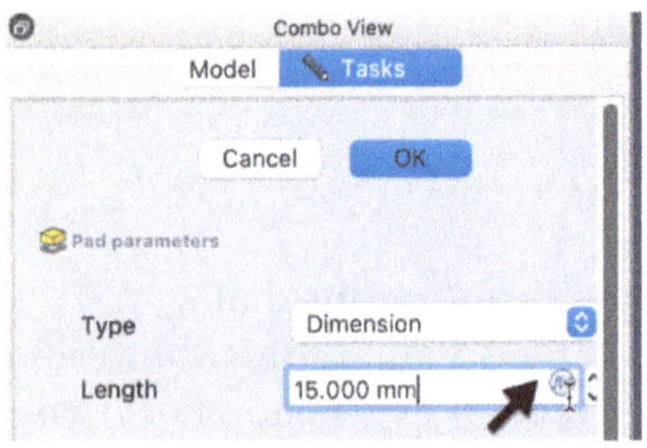

48. Type **Spreadsheet.Pad_length** in the **Formula editor** dialog. Next, click **OK**.

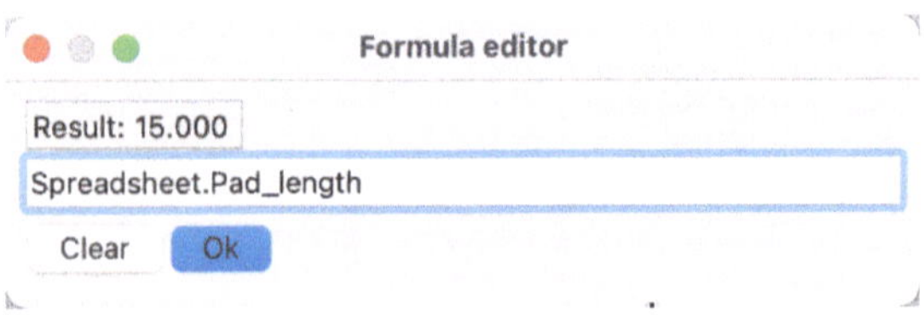

49. Click **OK** on the **Tasks** panel.
50. On the **Model** panel, right-click on the **Thickness** feature, and then select **Edit thickness**.
51. Click the **Enter an expression** button in the **Thickness** box.
52. Type **Spreadsheet.Thickness** in the **Formula editor** dialog. Next, click **OK**.
53. Click **OK** on the **Tasks** panel.
54. Double-click on the Spreadsheet feature in the **Model** panel to open the spreadsheet.
55. Click in the B1 cell and change the value to 40.

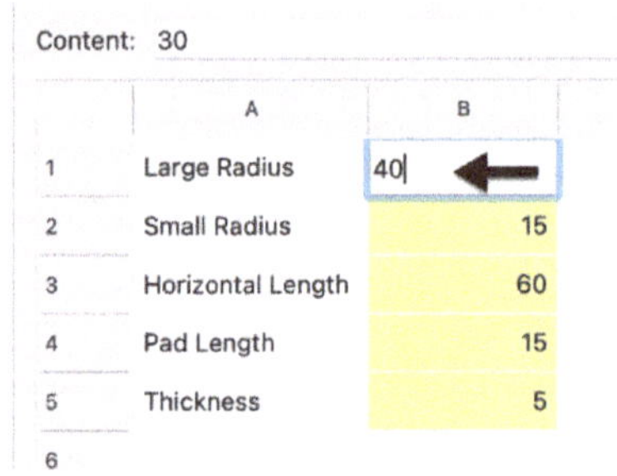

56. Switch to the model window and notice that the model is updated, as shown.

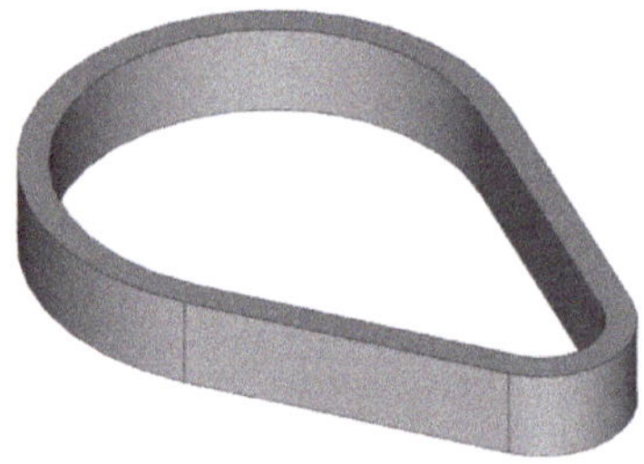

57. Likewise, change the other values in the spreadsheet and notice the updated model.

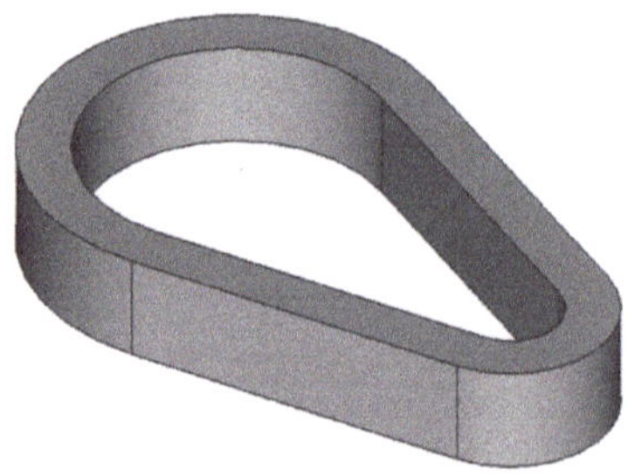

58. Save and close the part file.

TUTORIAL 13

In this tutorial, you will create expressions to drive the parameters of a bolt.

1. Start a new FreeCAD file and activate the Part Design workbench.
2. On the **Part Design Modeling** toolbar, click **Additive Primitives** drop-down > **Additive Cylinder**.

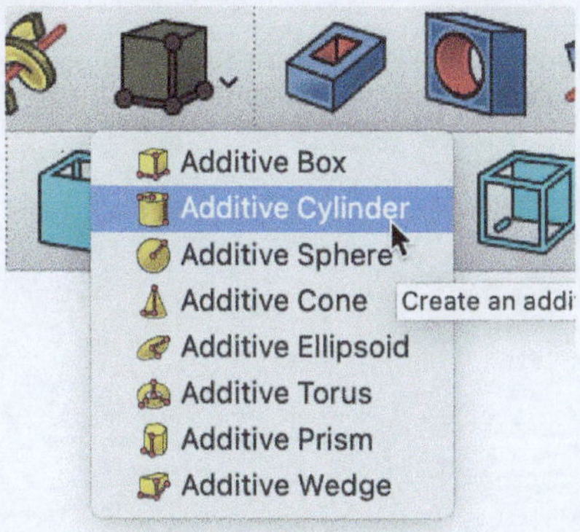

3. Select the YZ_Plane from the graphics window.

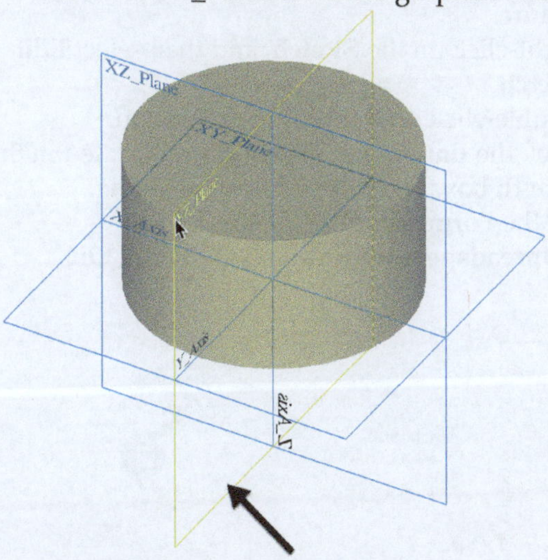

4. Type **10** and **80** in the **Radius** and **Height** boxes, respectively.

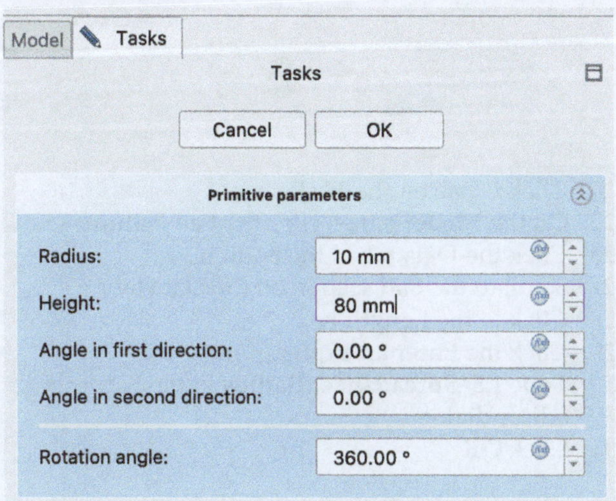

5. Click **OK** to create a cylinder.

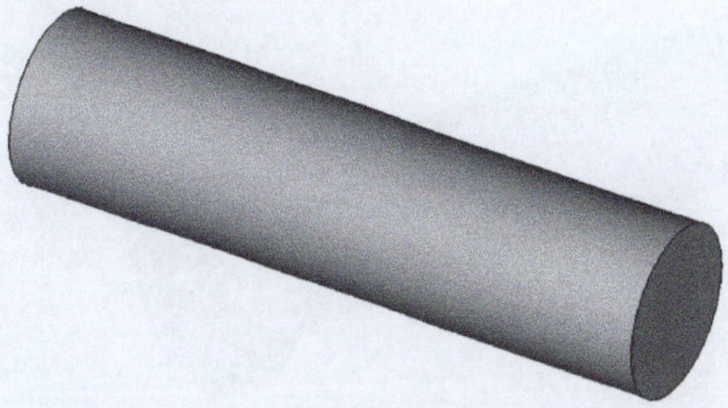

6. Select the right end face of the cylinder.
7. Click the **Create Sketch** icon on the **Part Design Helper** toolbar.

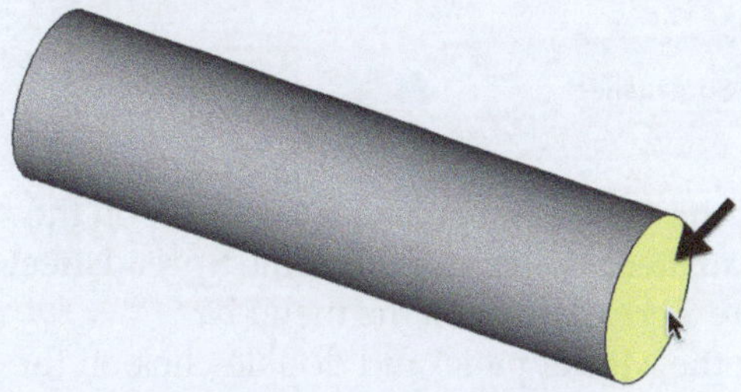

8. Create a hexagon, as shown.
9. Create a dimension between the sketch origin and the right vertex of the hexagon by selecting them.

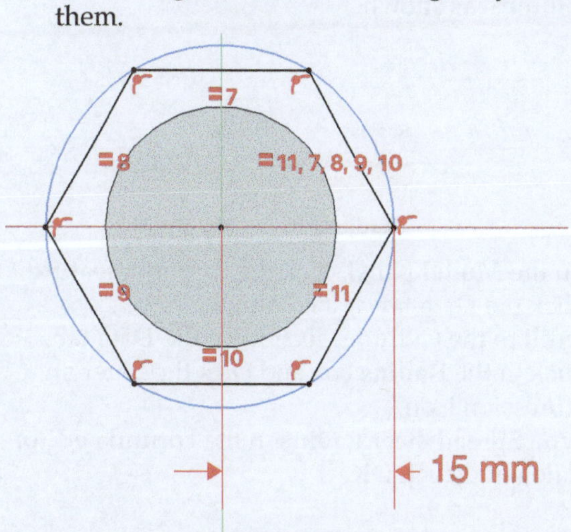

10. Click **Close** on the **Tasks** panel.
11. Click the **Pad** icon on the **Part Design Modeling** toolbar.
12. Type **10** in the **Length** box and click **OK**.

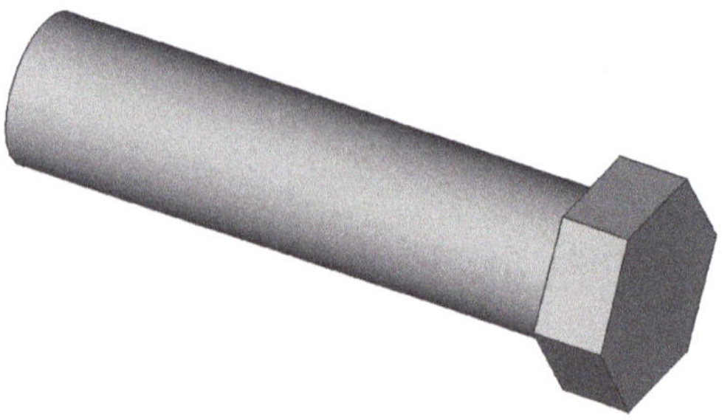

Creating the Spreadsheet

1. Select the **Spreadsheet** option from the **Workbenches** drop-down (or) click **View > Workbench > Spreadsheet** on the menu bar.

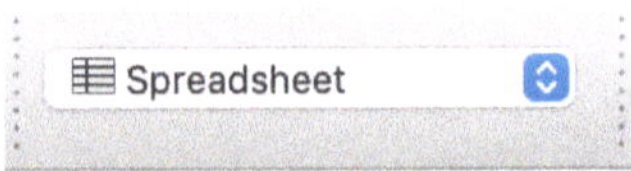

2. Click the **Create spreadsheet** icon on the **Spreadsheet** toolbar (or) click the **Spreadsheet > Create Spreadsheet** on the menu bar.
3. Click the **Model** panel and double-click on the newly created spreadsheet.
4. Type-in the values in the **B** and **C** columns in the spreadsheet.
5. Specify the **Aliases** for the values in the **B** and **C** columns, as shown.

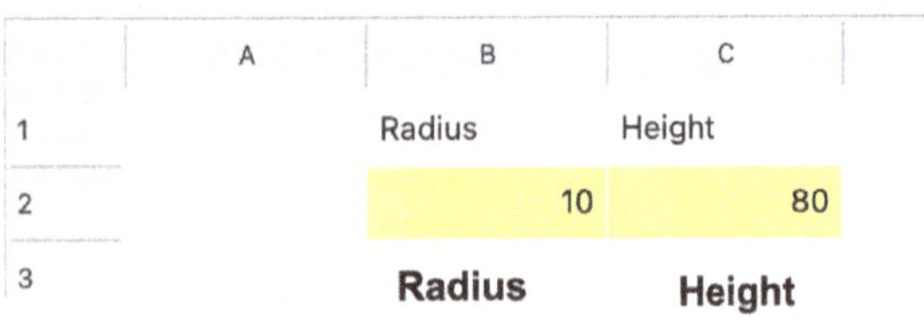

13. On the **Model** panel, click the **Cylinder** feature.
14. Click the **Data** tab at the bottom.
15. Scroll to the **Cylinder** section on the **Data** tab.
16. Click in the **Radius** box and click the Enter an expression icon.
17. Type **Spreadsheet.Radius** in the **Formula editor** dialog and click **OK**.

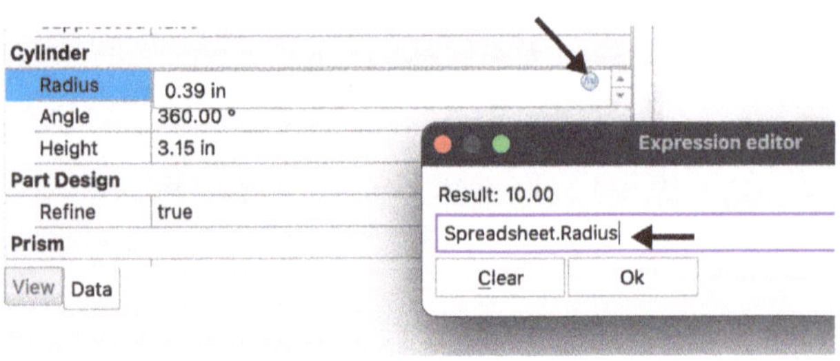

18. Likewise, change the **Height** value to **Spreadsheet.Height**.

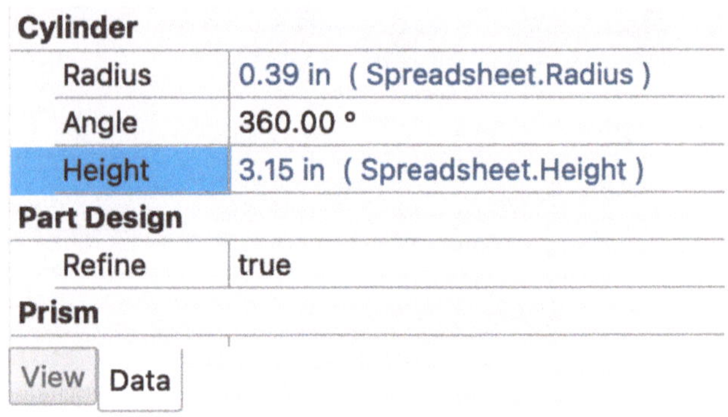

19. Click the **Model** panel and expand the **Pad** feature.
20. Right-click on the **Sketch**, and then select **Edit Sketch**.
21. Double-click on the 15 mm dimension.
22. Click the **Enter an expression** icon located in the **Length** box on the **Insert Radius** dialog.
23. On the **Formula editor** dialog, type **2*Spreadsheet.Radius**, and then click **OK**.

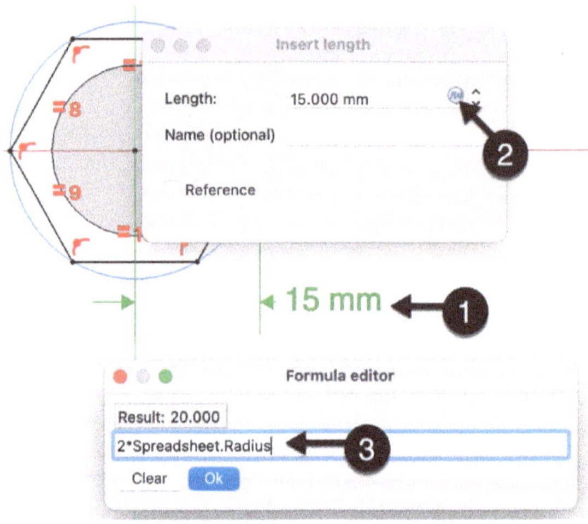

24. Click **Close** on the **Tasks** panel.
25. On the **Model** panel, click the **Pad** feature.
26. Click the **Data** tab at the bottom.
27. Scroll to the **Pad** section on the **Data** tab.
28. Click in the **Length** box.
29. Click the **Enter an expression**.
30. Type **1.5*Spreadsheet.Radius** in the **Formula editor** dialog.
31. Click **OK**.

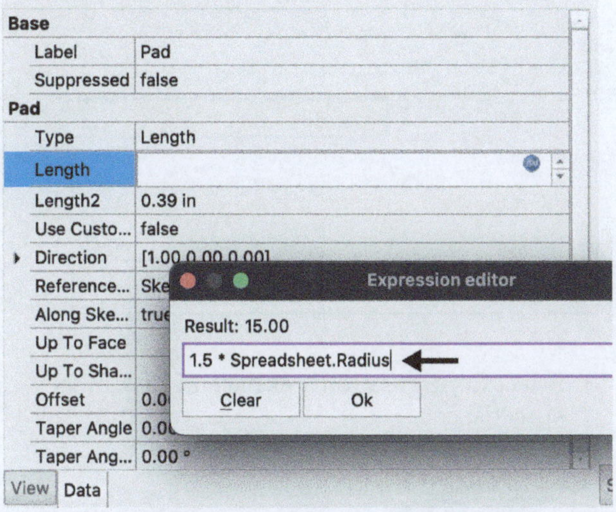

32. Switch to the model window and notice that the model is updated.

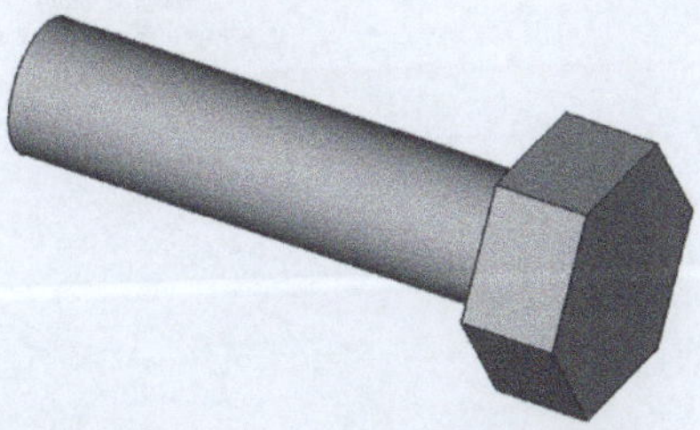

Creating Configuration Table

1. Double-click on the **Spreadsheet** in the **Model** panel.

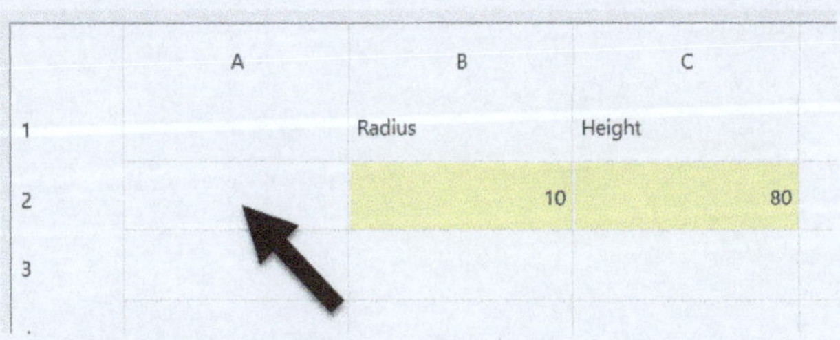

2. Enter **10x80**, **20x60** and **6x20** in the **A3**, **A4**, and **A5** cells.
3. Enter **10**, **20** and **6** in the **B3**, **B4**, and **B5** cells, respectively.
4. Enter **80, 60** and **20** in the **C3, C4**, and **C5** cells, respectively.

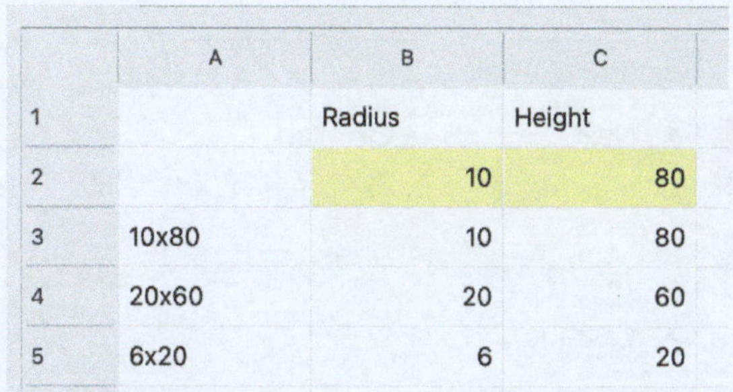

5. Click the right-mouse button in the **A2** cell and select **Configuration Table** from the shortcut menu.

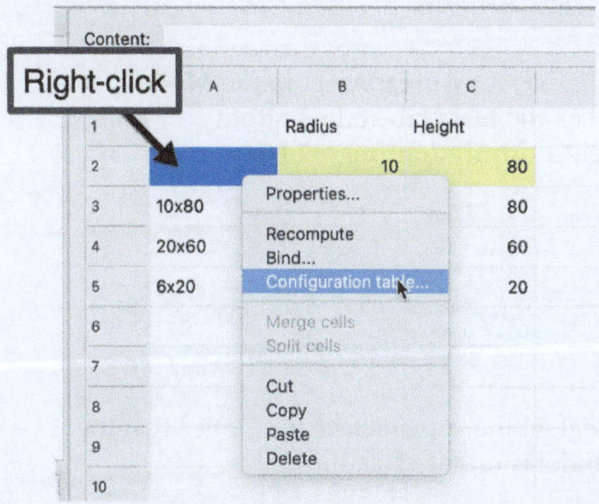

6. On the **Setup Configuration Table** dialog, type **Configuration** (or any name) in the **Property** box.
7. Type **Parameters** (or any name) in the **Group** box and click **OK**.

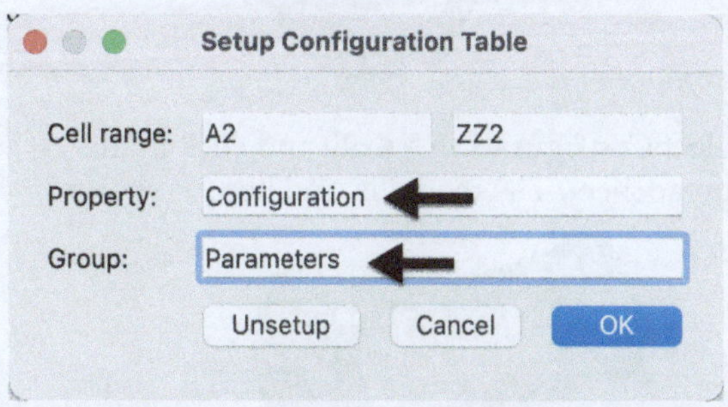

8. On the menu bar, click **Windows > Tile**.

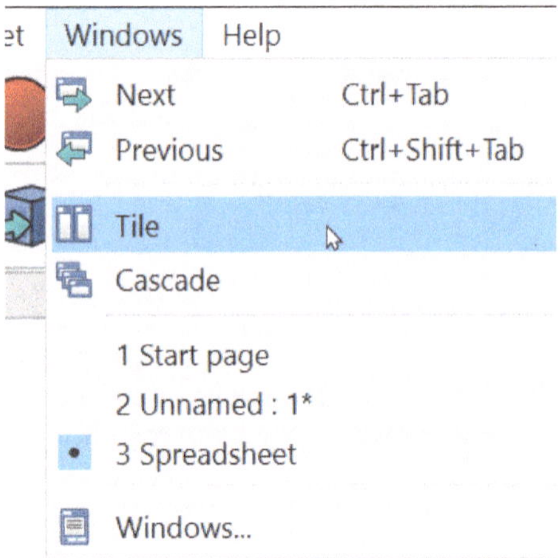

9. Click on the **Spreadsheet** in the **Model** panel.
10. Click the **Data** tab at the bottom.
11. Select **Configurations > 20x60.**

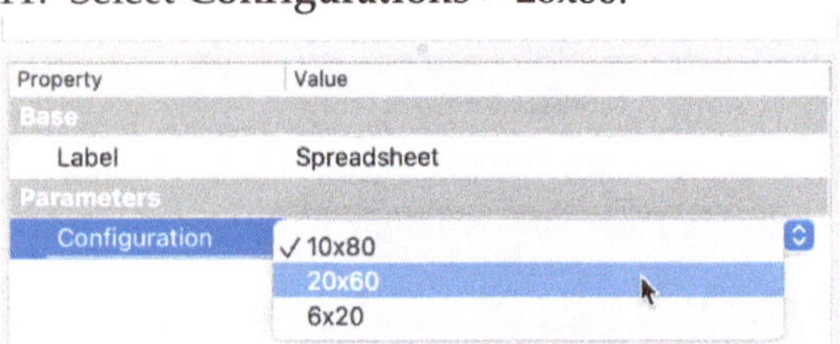

12. Click in the spreadsheet and notice that the model is updated, as shown.

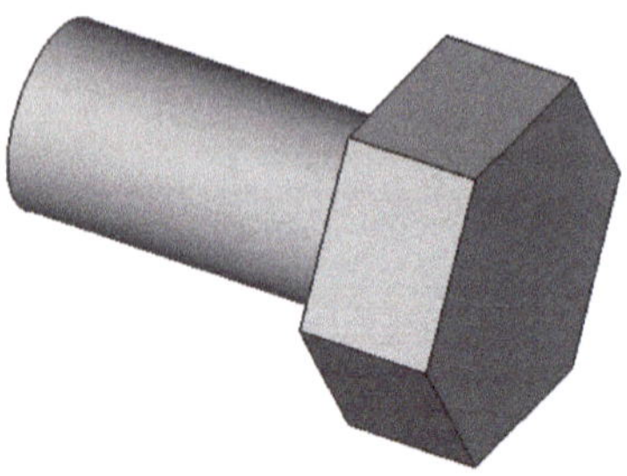

13. Select **Configuration > 6x20** and click in the spreadsheet. The model is updated, as shown.

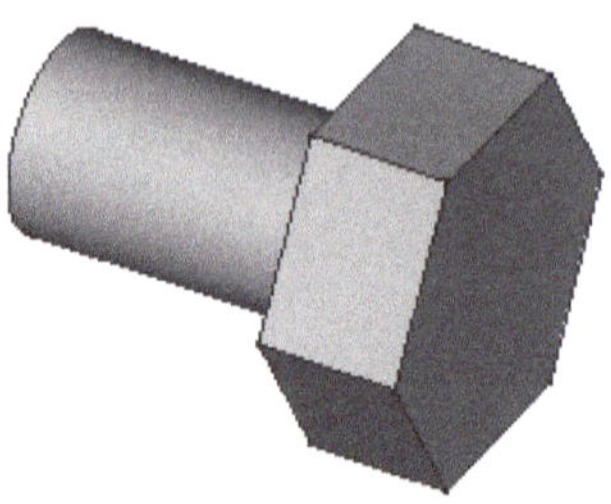

14. Add one more configuration to the table, as shown.

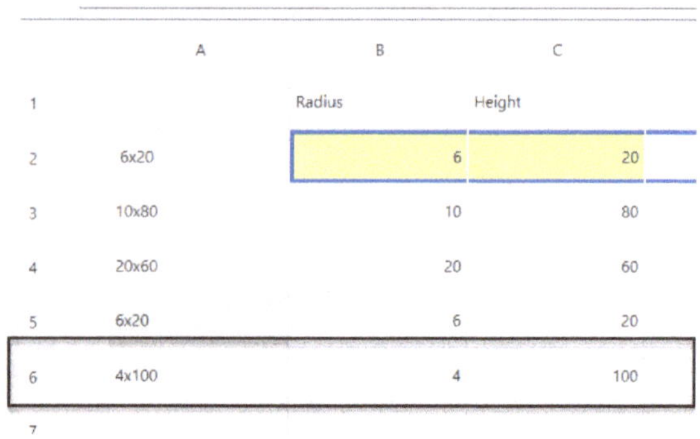

	A	B	C
1		Radius	Height
2	6x20	6	20
3	10x80	10	80
4	20x60	20	60
5	6x20	6	20
6	4x100	4	100
7			

15. Select **Configuration > 4x100** and click in the spreadsheet.

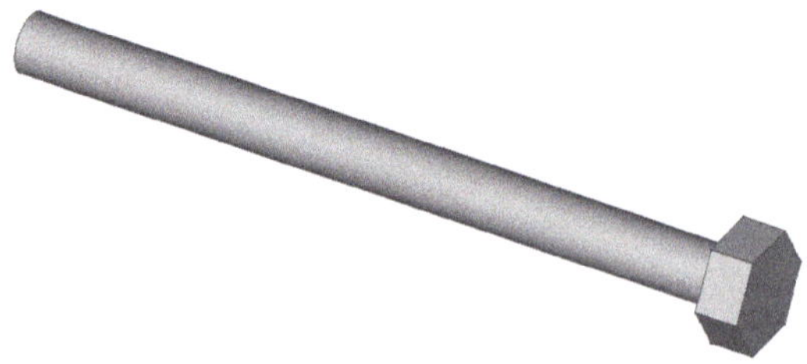

16. Save and close the part file.

Chapter 6: Creating Drawings

In this chapter, you generate 2D drawings of the parts. You learn to:

- Insert standard views of a part model
- Add dimensions

TUTORIAL 1

In this tutorial, you create the drawing of the Tutorial 7 file created in the fourth chapter.

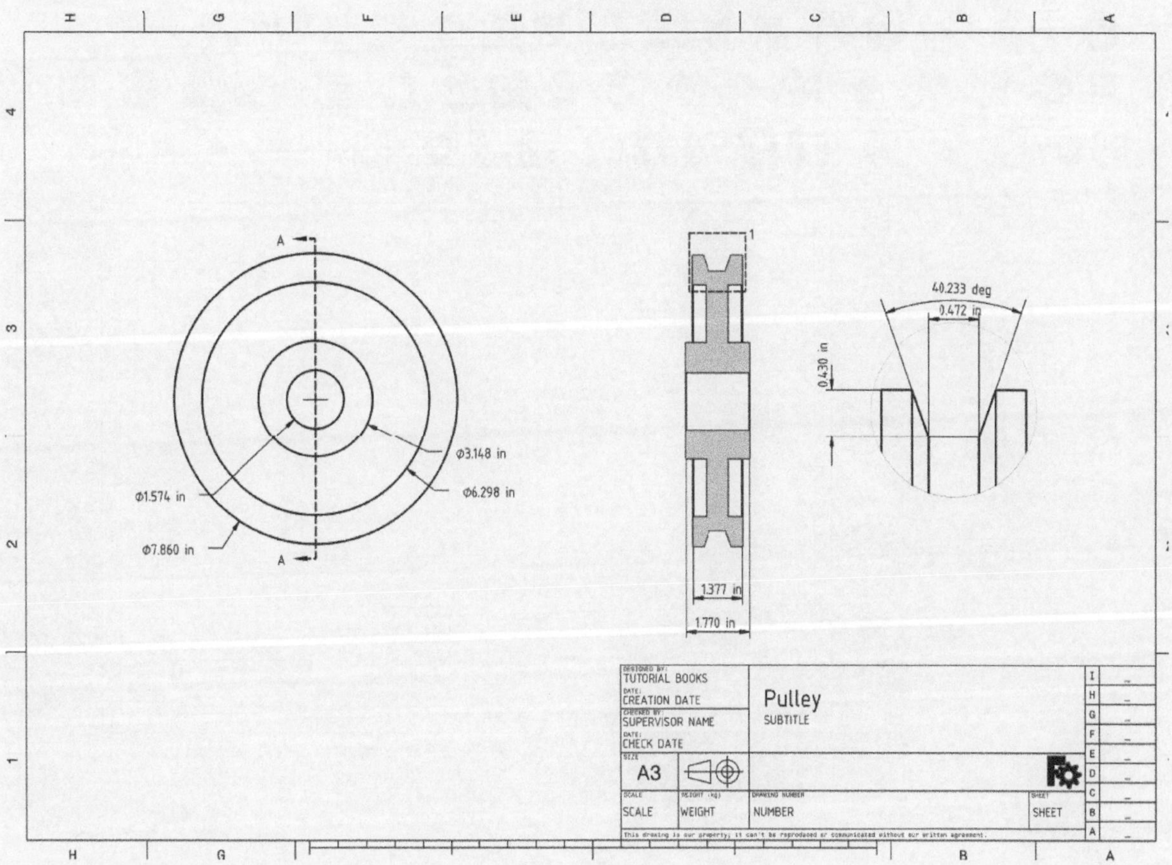

Starting a New Drawing File

1. Click **File > Open** on the Menu bar.
2. Go to the location of the Tutorial 7 file of Chapter 5.
3. Select the Tutorial 7 file and click the **Open** button.
4. Click **Edit > Preferences** on the Menu bar.

   The **Preferences** dialog box appears. If you are working on MacOS, then click **FreeCAD > Preferences** on the title bar.
5. On the **Preferences** dialog box, click the **TechDraw > Dimensions** at the left side.
6. Select **Standard and Style > ASME Referencing**
7. Click **OK**.

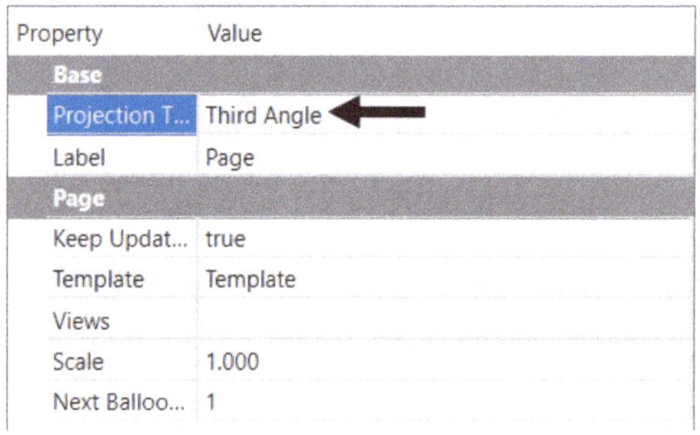

8. Select **TechDraw** from the **Workbenches** drop-down.

9. Click the **Insert page using template**  icon on the **TechDraw Pages** toolbar.
10. Select the **A3_LandscapeTD** template.
11. Click **Open**.
12. In the **Model** panel, select the **Page**.
13. Click the **Data** tab on the bottom.
14. In the **Properties** section of the **Model** panel, select **Projection Type > Third Angle**.

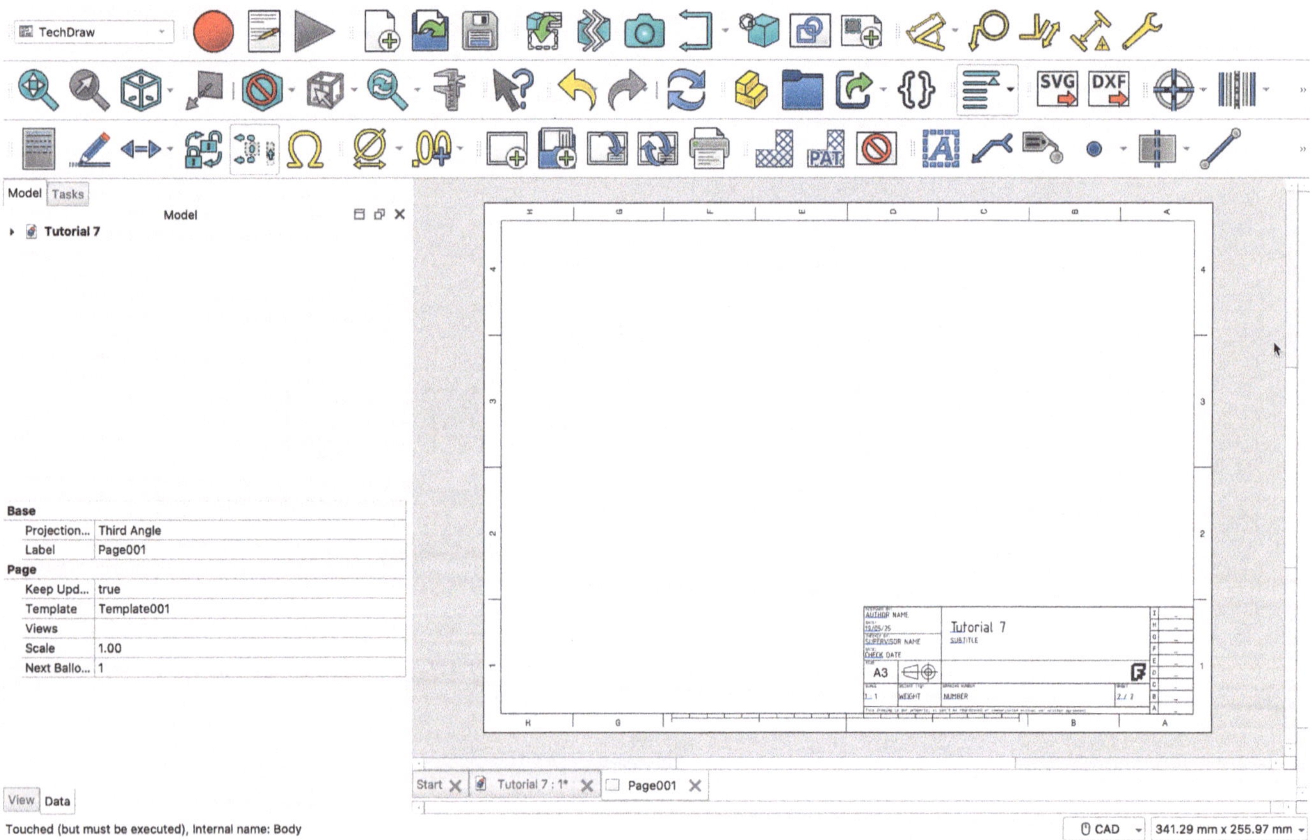

Generating the Base View

1. Click the **Tutorial 7** tab on the bottom of the window.

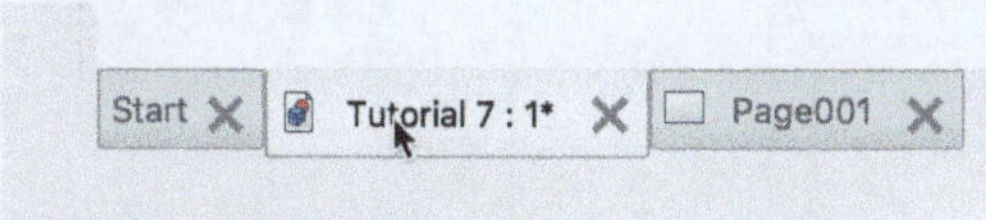

2. Select the front face of the model.

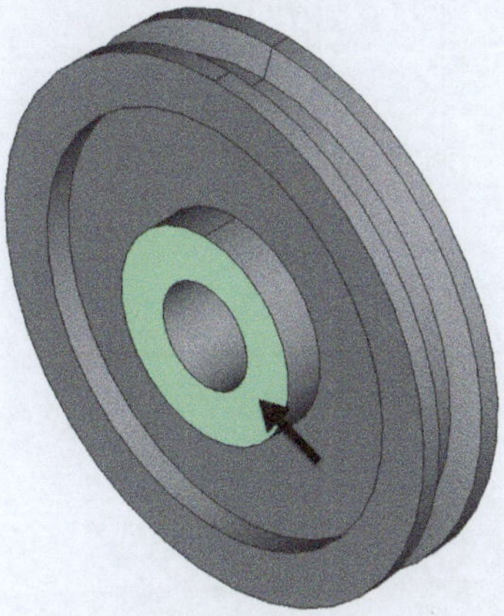

3. Click the **Page** tab on the bottom of the window.

4. To generate the base view, click the **Insert View**  icon on the **TechDraw Views** toolbar.
5. On the **Projection Group** section, select **Scale > Custom**.
6. Type **1** and **2** in the **Scale Numerator** and **Scale Denominator** boxes located next to **Custom Scale**.
7. Click **OK** on the **Tasks** panel.
8. Click on the dotted borderline of the view.
9. Press and hold the left mouse and drag the view to left.

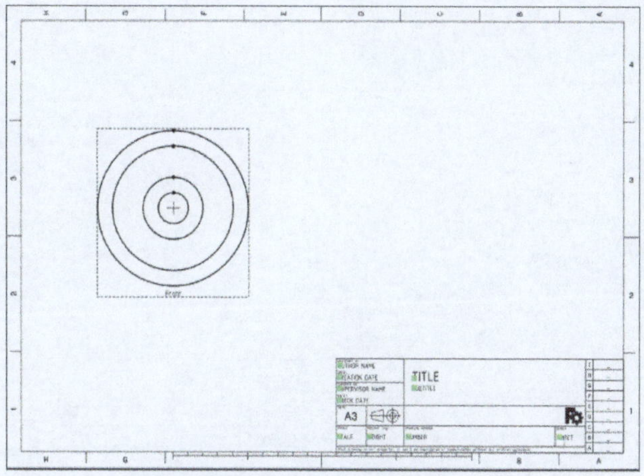

Generating the Section View

1. Select the base view.
2. Click the **Section view** drop-down **> Section View** on the **TechDraw Views** toolbar.

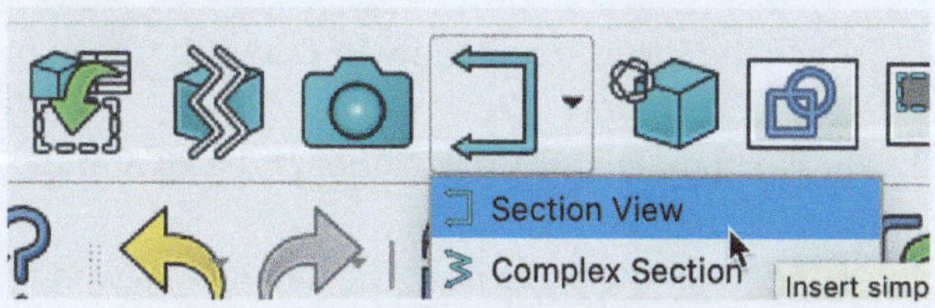

3. Click the **Preset view direction looking left** 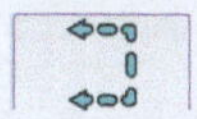 icon on the **Set View Direction** section.
4. Type **0** in the **X**, **Y**, and **Z** boxes, respectively. These values define the location of the section plane.
5. Type **A** in the **Identifier** box.
6. Click **OK** to create the section view.
7. Select the section view from the drawing page.
8. Click the **Position Section View**  icon on the **TechDraw Attributes** toolbar. The section view is horizontally in-line with the base view.

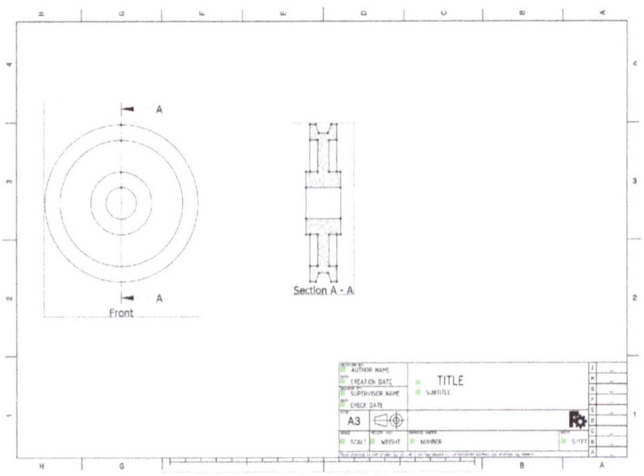

Creating the Detailed View

Now, you have to create the detailed view of the groove, which is displayed, in the section view.

1. Select the section view.
2. Click the **Insert detail view in drawing** icon on the **TechDraw Views** toolbar.
3. In the **New Detail View** section, type **20** mm in the **Radius** box.
4. Type **1.5** in the **Scale** box. The detailed view is generated.
5. Drag the detailed view to the right side on the drawing sheet.

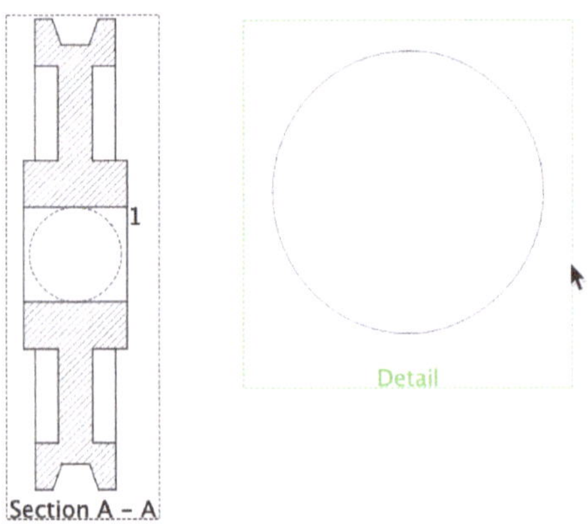

Now, you need to specify the portion of the section view to be displayed in the detailed view.

6. Click the **Drag Highlight** button on the **Tasks** panel.
7. Click on the drag text displayed next to the boundary of the detail view.
8. Drag it upward and place at the location, as shown.

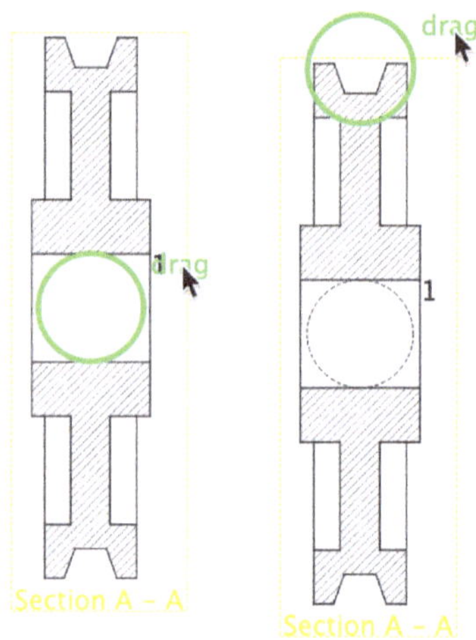

9. Click **OK**.

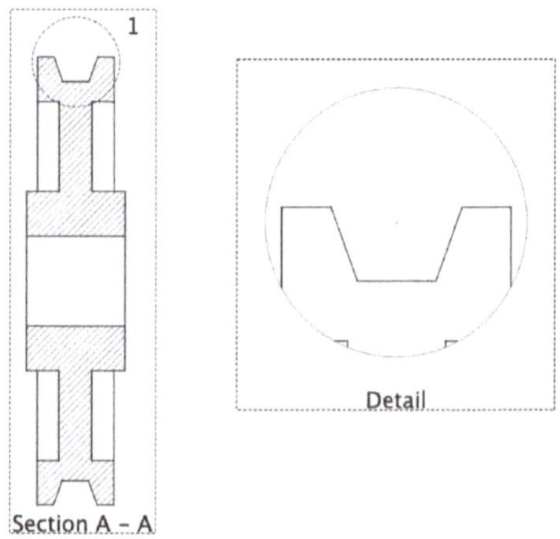

Adding Dimensions

Now, you add dimensions to the drawing.

1. Select the outer circular edge of the base view.
2. Click the **Dimension** drop-down > **Diameter dimension** icon on the **TechDraw Dimensions** toolbar.
3. Click and drag the dimension outside the view.

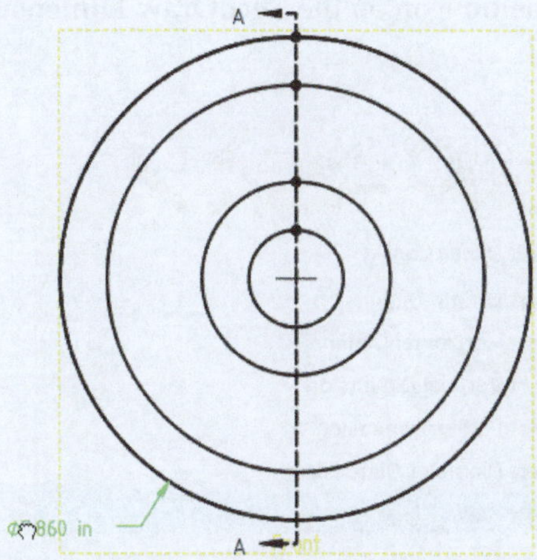

4. Likewise, add remaining dimensions to the base view, as shown.

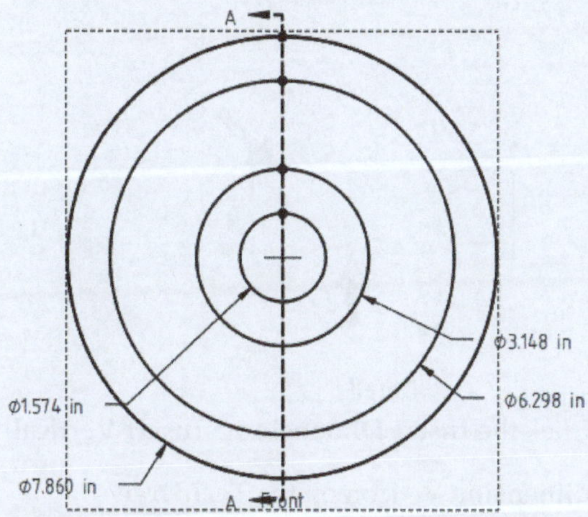

5. Press and hold the Ctrl key and select the vertical edges of the section view, as shown.

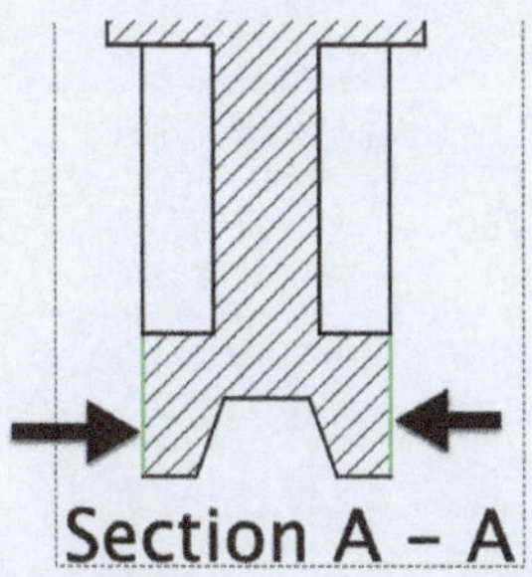

6. Click the **Insert Dimension > Insert Horizontal Dimension** icon on the **TechDraw Dimensions** toolbar.
7. Click in the drawing page to deselect the selected edges.
8. Press and hold the Ctrl key and select the vertical edges of the section view, as shown.

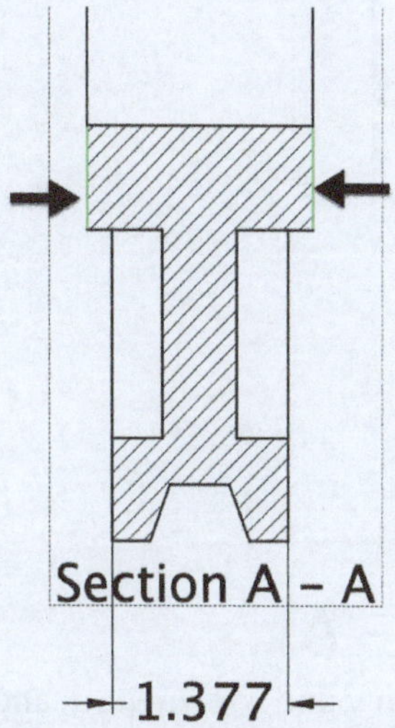

9. Click the **Insert Dimension > Insert Horizontal-dimension** icon on the **TechDraw Dimensions** toolbar.
10. Press and hold the CTRL key and select the two newly created dimensions.

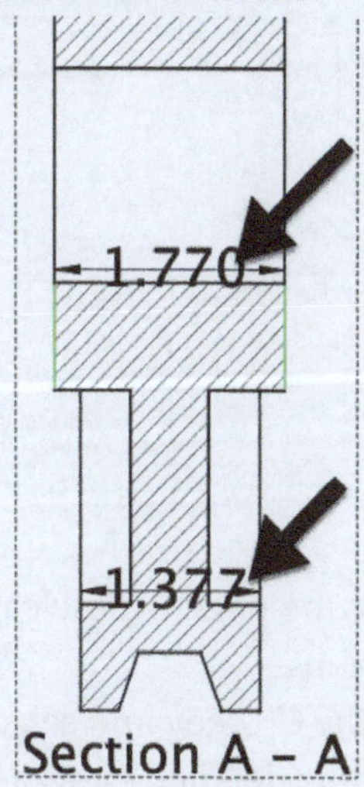

11. On the menu bar, click **TechDraw > Extensions: Attributes/Modifications > Cascade Horizontal Dimensions**. The selected dimensions are arranged.

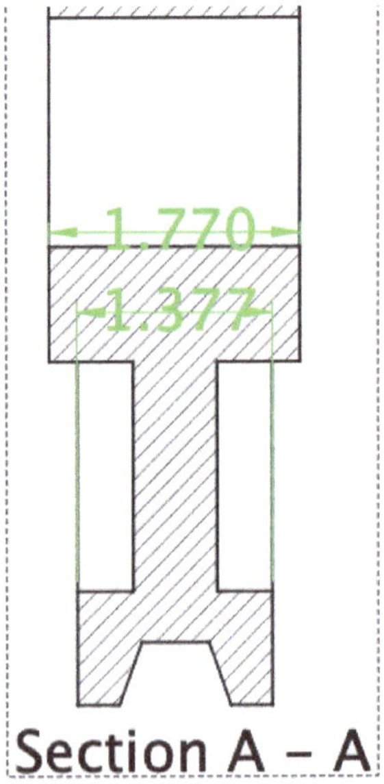

12. Drag the dimension values downward, and then toward right, as shown.

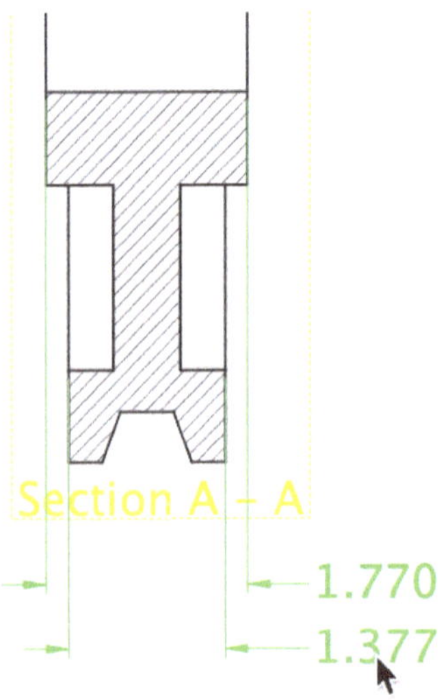

13. Click in the drawing page to deselect the selected dimensions.
14. Press and hold the Ctrl key and select the two inclined lines in the detailed view, as shown.

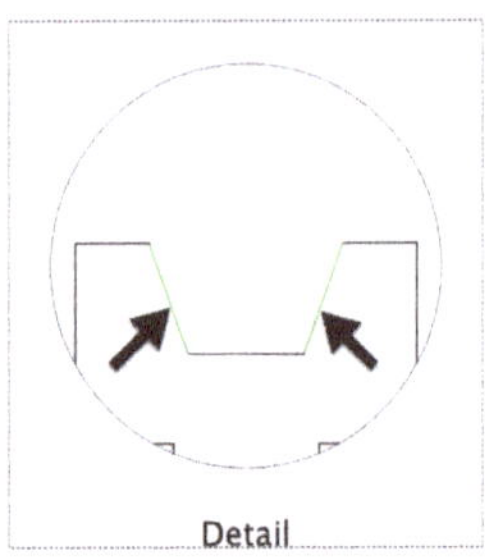

15. Click **Insert Dimension > Insert Angle Dimension** icon on the **TechDraw Dimensions** toolbar.

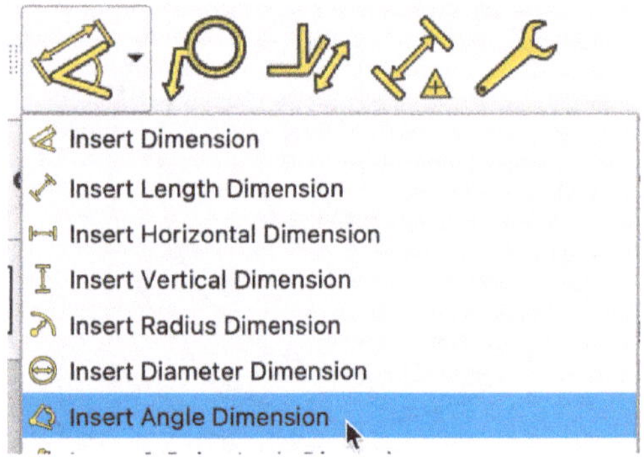

16. Press and hold the Ctrl key and select the horizontal edges of the detailed view, as shown.

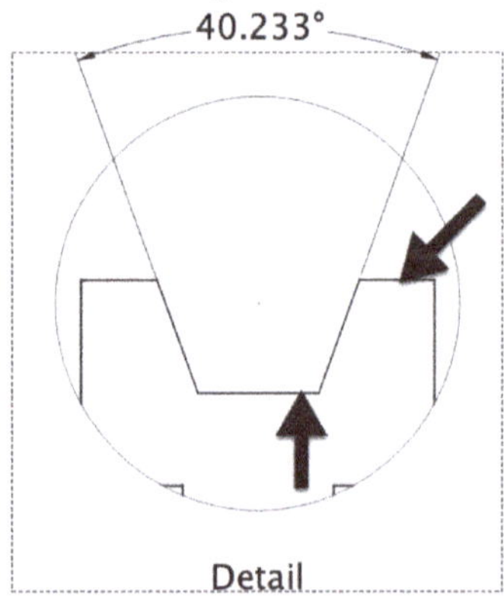

17. Click the **Insert Dimension > Insert Vertical dimension** icon on the **TechDraw Dimensions** toolbar.

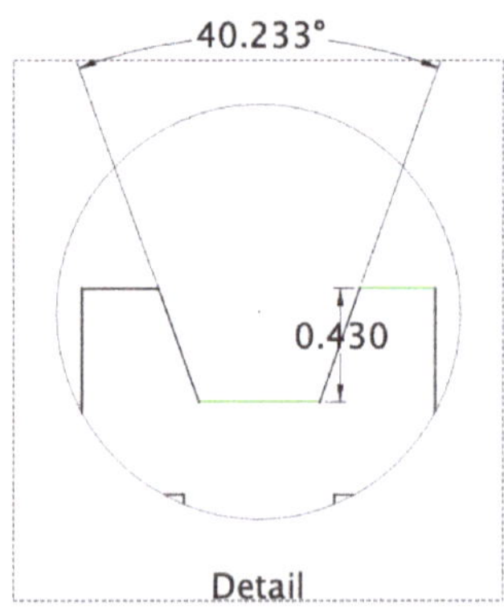

18. Create the remaining dimension, as shown.

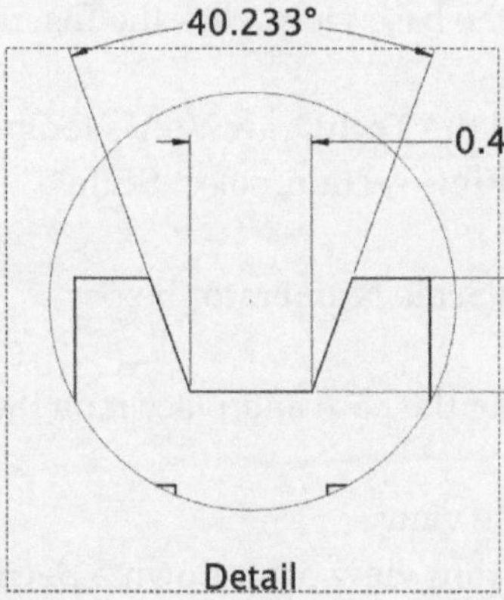

19. Save and close the file.

TUTORIAL 2

In this tutorial, you create the drawing shown below.

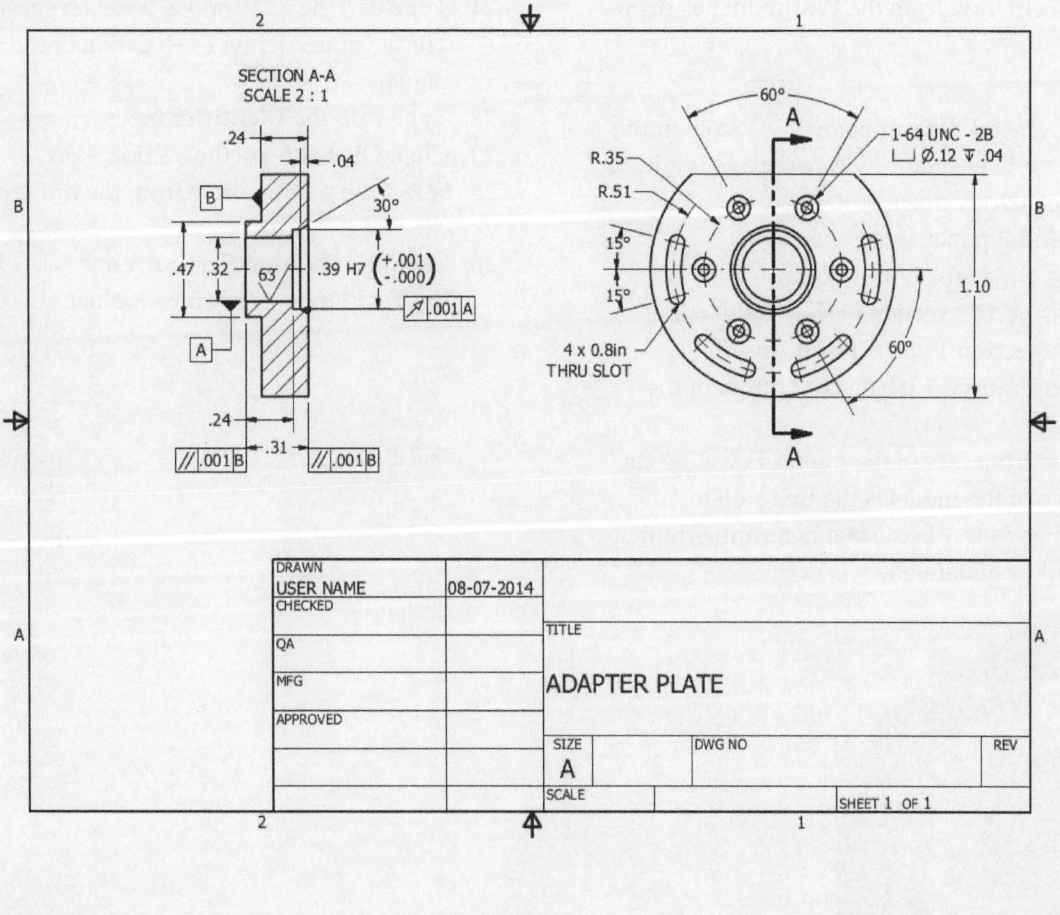

1. Click **File > Open** on the Menu bar.
2. Go to the location of the Tutorial 1 file of Chapter 5.
3. Select the Tutorial 1 file and click the **Open** button.
4. Click **Edit > Preferences** on the Menu bar. The **Preferences** dialog box appears. If you are working on MacOS, then click **FreeCAD > Preferences** on the title bar.
5. On the **Preferences** dialog box, click the **TechDraw > Dimensions** at the left side .
6. Select **Standard ans Style > ASME Referencing**.
7. Uncheck the **Use Global Decimals** option.
8. Type **3** in the **Alternate Decimals** box.
9. Click **OK**.
10. Select **TechDraw** from the **Workbenches** drop-down.
11. Click the **Insert default page** icon on the **TechDraw Pages** toolbar. A new page is added to the TechDraw document.
12. In the **Model** panel, select the **Page**.
13. Click the **Data** tab on the bottom.
14. In the **Properties** section of the **Model** panel, select **Projection Type > Third Angle**.

10. Click the **Tutorial 1** tab on the bottom of the window.
11. Select the front face of the model. Selecting the front face of the model is the first step to generating a view because it determines which view will be generated.

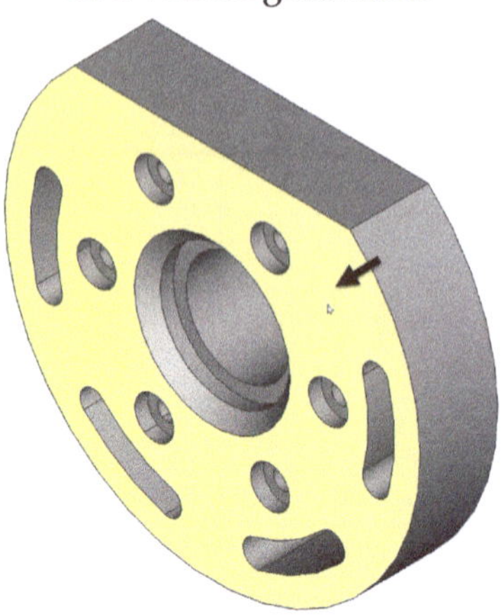

12. Click the **Page** tab on the bottom of the window.
13. To generate the base view, click the **Insert View** icon on the **TechDraw Views** toolbar.
14. On the **Part View** section, select **Scale > Custom**.
15. Type **2** in the **Scale Numerator** box.
16. Click **OK**.
17. Click and drag the base and place it on the right side.
18. Select the base view.
19. Click the **Section view** drop-down **> Section View** on the **TechDraw Views** toolbar.
20. Click the **Looking Right** icon on the **Quick Set View Direction** section.
21. Type **0** in the **X**, **Y**, and **Z** boxes, respectively. These values define the location of the section plane.
22. Type **A** in the **Identifier** box.
23. Click **OK** to create the section view.
24. Select the section view from the drawing page.
25. Click the **Position Section View** icon on the **TechDraw Attributes** toolbar.

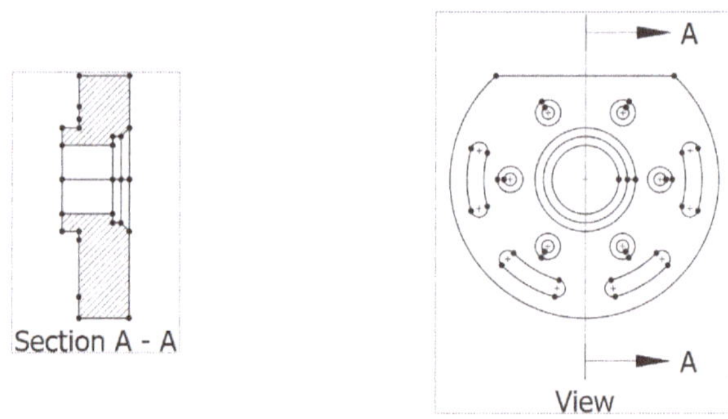

Creating Centerlines and Bolt Circle Centerlines

1. Press and hold the CTRL key and select the parallel lines on the section view, as shown below.

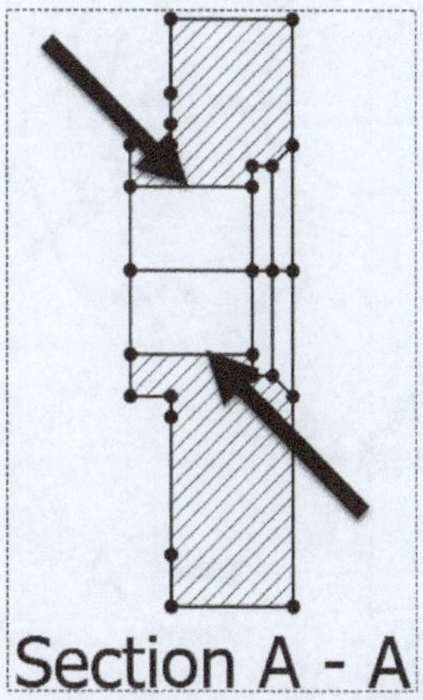

2. Click the **Centerline** drop-down > **Add Centerline between 2 Lines** on the **TechDraw Annotation** toolbar. This step is done to add a centerline between the two selected parallel lines.

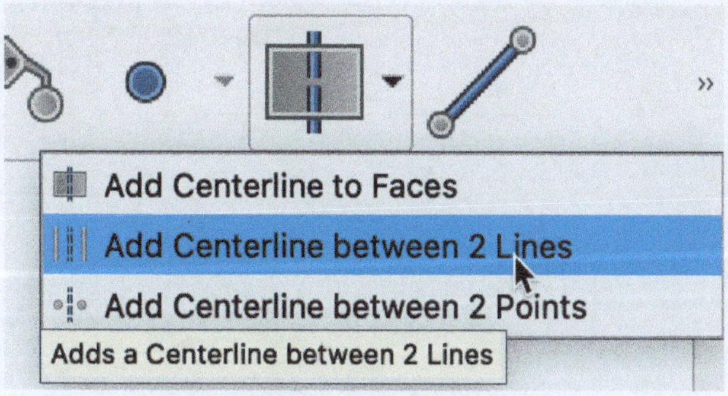

3. On the **Create Center line** section of the **Tasks** panel, select **Style > Center**. This step is done to change the style of the centerline to DashDot.
4. Type **0.3** in the **Extend By** box. This step is done to extend the centerline by a certain distance.

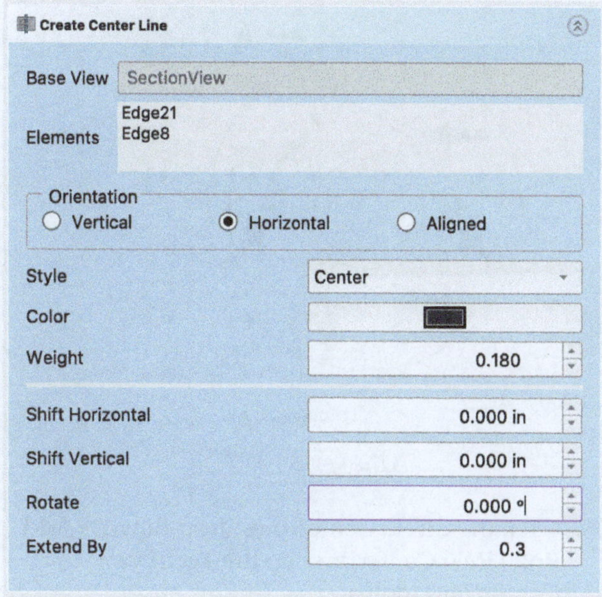

5. Click **OK**. This step is done to finalize the creation of the centerline with the specified style and extension.

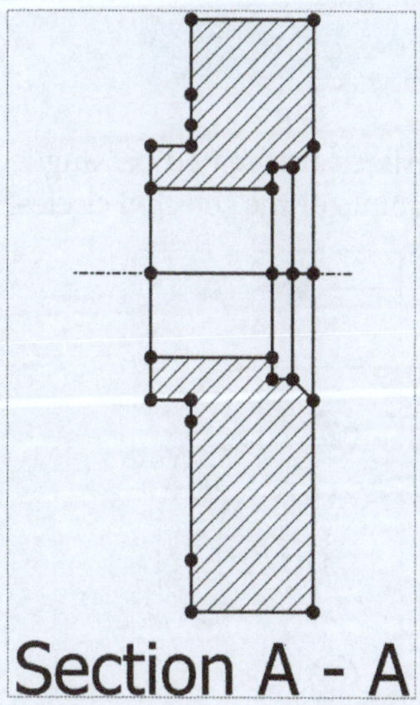

22. Press and hold CTRL key and select the counterbore circles, as shown.

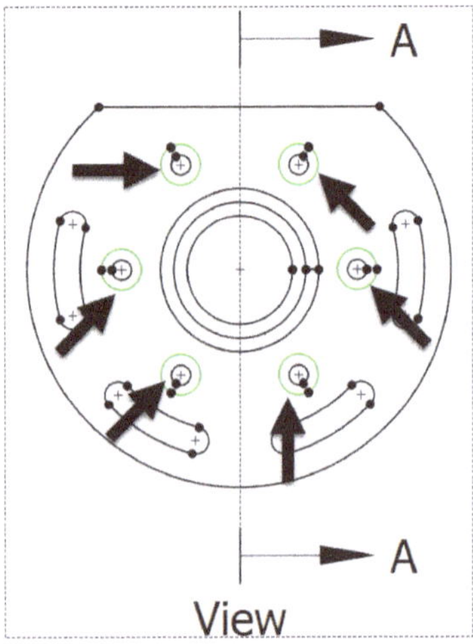

23. Click the **Circle Centerlines drop-down > Add Bolt circle Centerlines** on the **TechDraw Centerlines** toolbar.

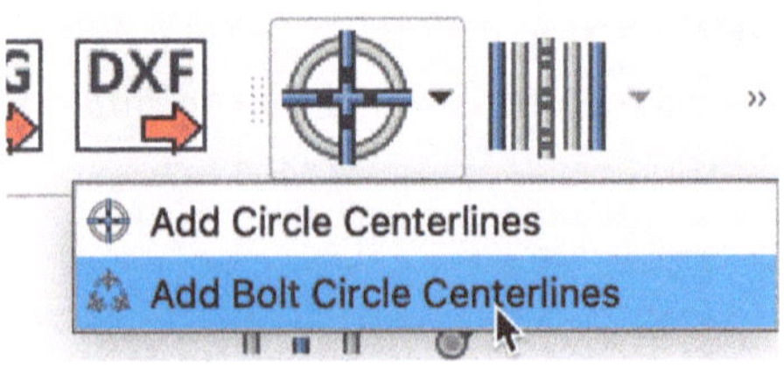

The bolt circle centerlines are created passing through the center points of the selected circles.

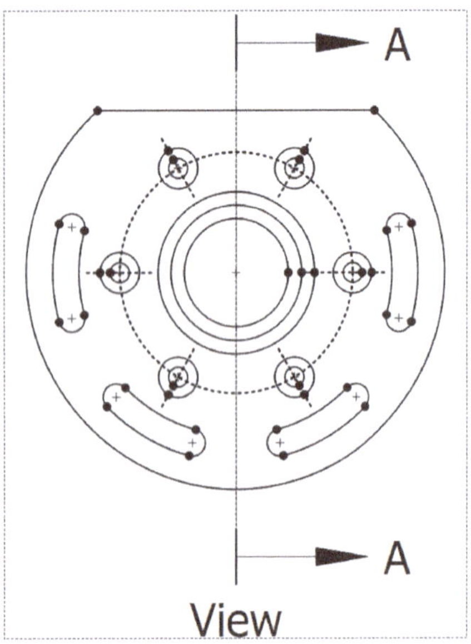

24. Press and hold the CTRL key and select the arcs, as shown.

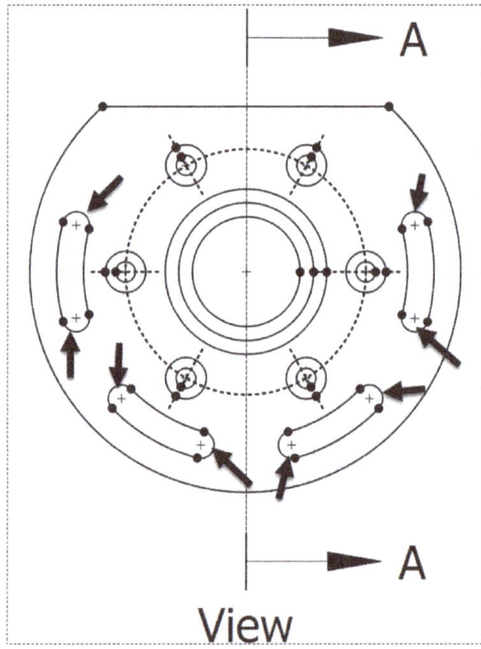

25. Click the **Circle Centerlines drop-down > Add Bolt circle Centerlines**  on the **TechDraw Centerlines** toolbar.

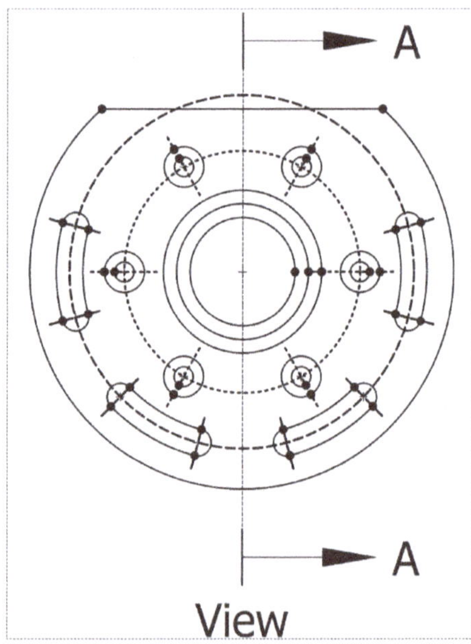

26. Select the circle located at the center.

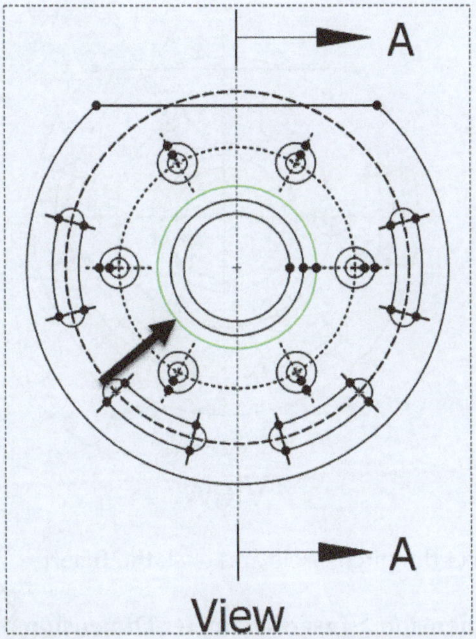

27. Click the **Circle Centerlines** drop-down > **Add Circle Centerlines** on the **TechDraw Centerlines** toolbar. Centerlines are added to the selected circle.

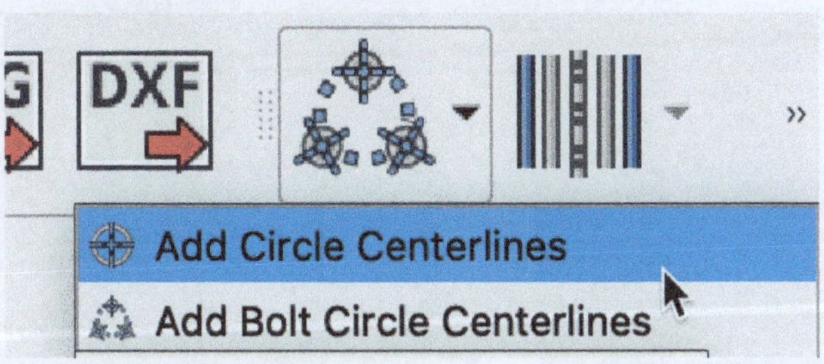

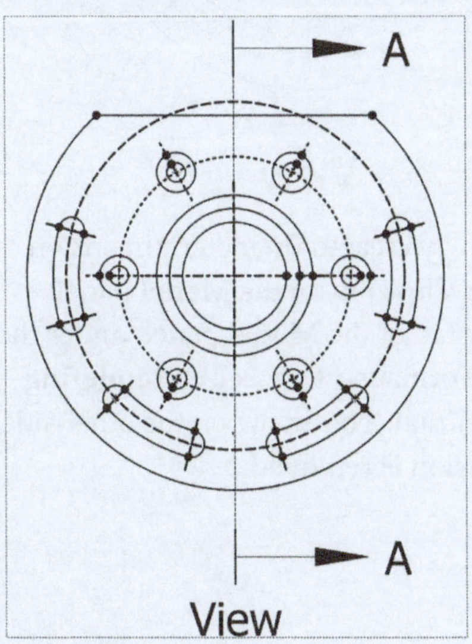

Applying Dimensions

1. Click **Edit > Preferences** on the Menu bar.
2. The Preferences dialog box appears. If you are working on MacOS, then click **FreeCAD > Preferences** on the title bar.
3. On the **Preferences** dialog box, click the **TechDraw > Dimensions** at the left side.
4. Select **Standard and Style > ASME Referencing**.
5. Type **0.1** in the **Font Size** box.
6. Type **0.1** in the **Arrow Size** box.
7. Click **OK**.
8. Press and hold the CTRL key and select the centerline on the slot located on the left.
9. Select the centerline of the counterbore hole located at the left.

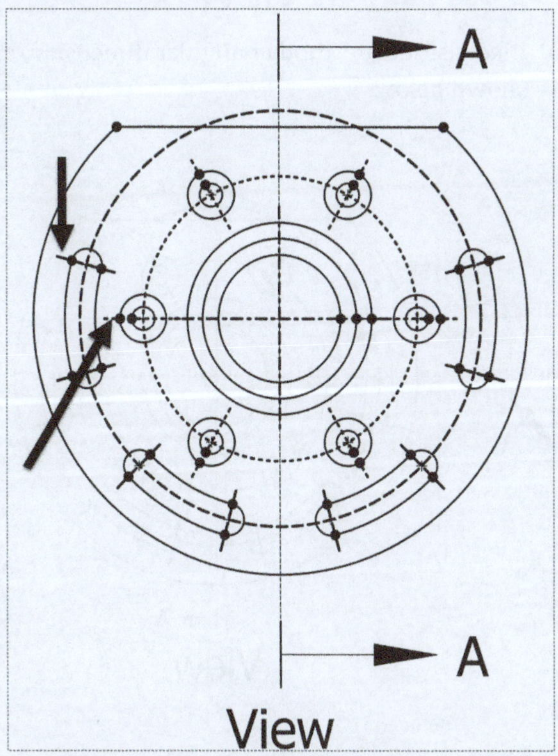

10. Click the Insert Dimensions > Insert **Angle Dimension**  icon on the **TechDraw Dimensions** toolbar.
11. Left-click and hold on the angle dimension.
12. Drag the cursor to the left, then release it.

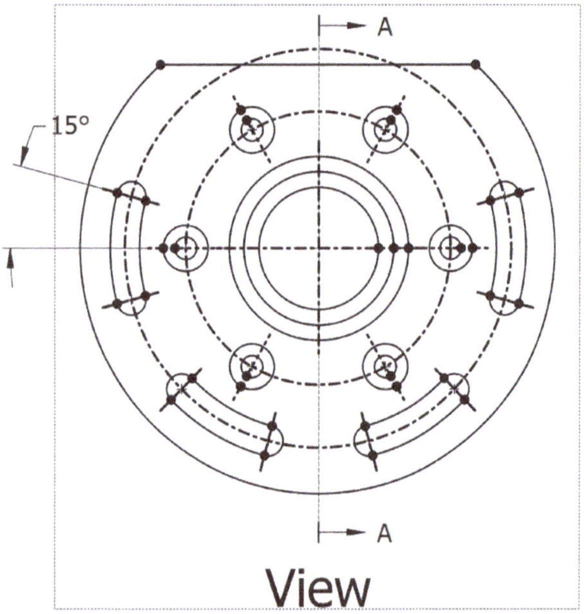

13. Likewise, create another angular dimension, as shown below.

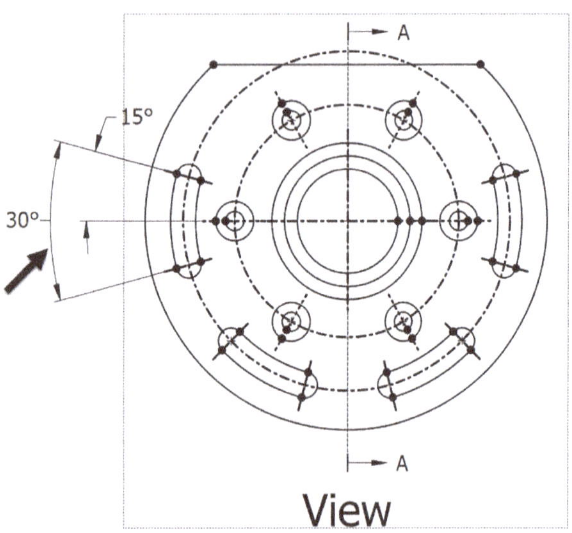

14. Create angular dimensions between the holes, and then between slots. To create the angular dimension between the slot, you need to create the angular dimension between the bolt circles.

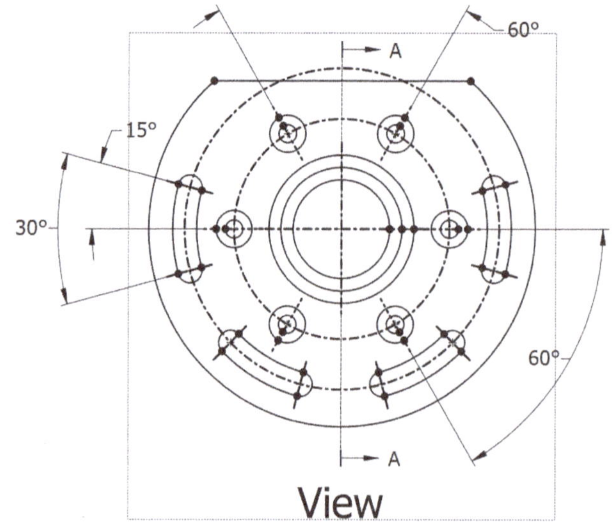

15. Select the pitch circle and click the **Insert Dimension > Insert Diameter Dimension** icon on the **TechDraw Dimensions** toolbar.
16. Left-click and hold on the diameter dimension.
17. Drag the cursor to the left, then release it.

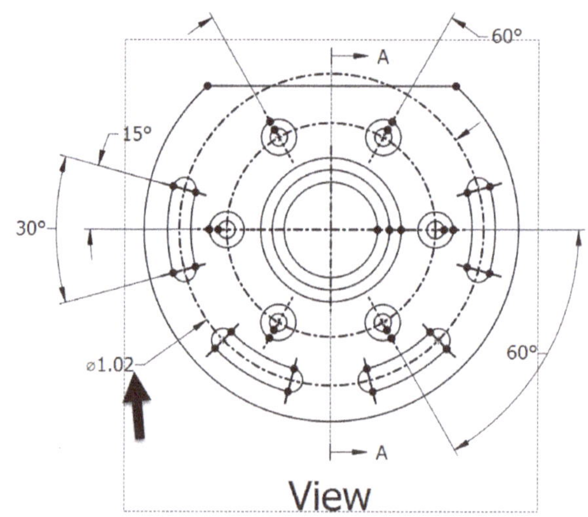

18. Select the newly created diameter dimension and click the **View** tab on the **Model** panel.
19. On the **View** tab of the **Model** panel, under the **Dimension Format** section, select **Rendering Extent > Minimal**. The arrow on the other side of the dimension is removed.

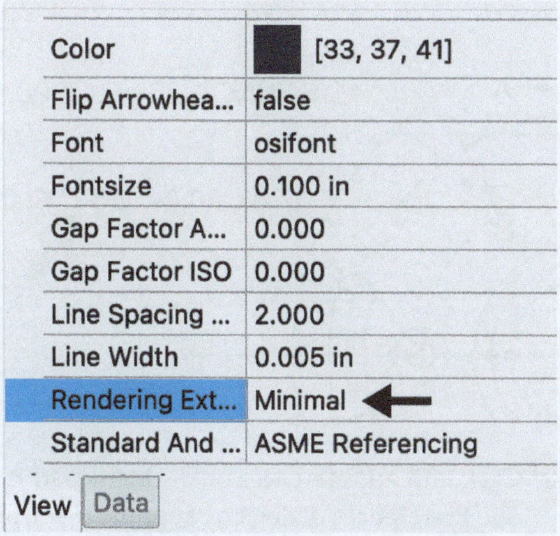

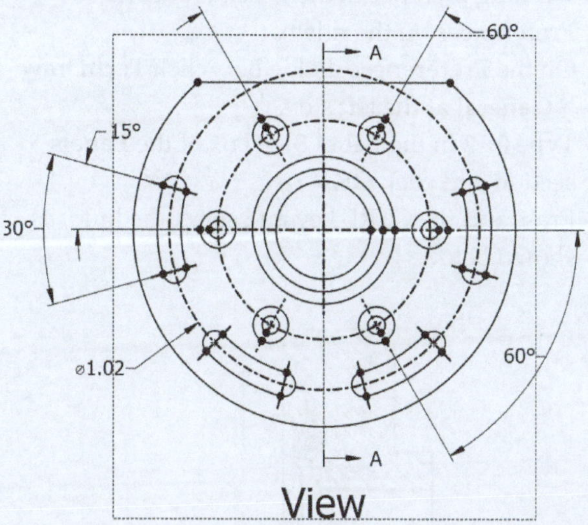

20. Select the counterbore hole and click the **Insert Dimension > Insert Diameter Dimension** icon on the **TechDraw Dimensions** toolbar.
21. Left-click and hold on the diameter dimension.
22. Drag the cursor to the right, then release it.

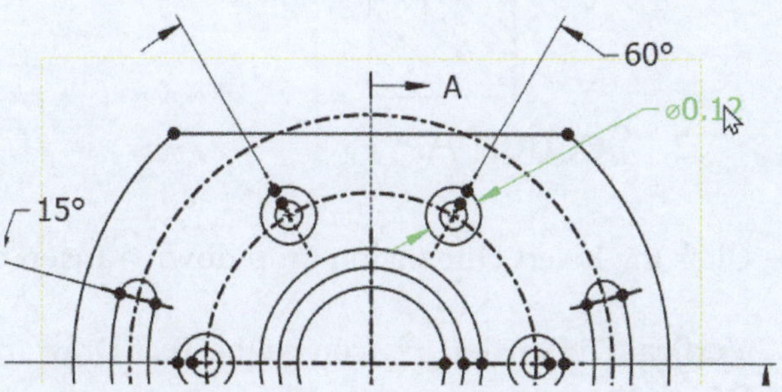

23. Select the diameter dimension of the small hole.

    Next, click the **Customize Format Label** icon on the **TechDraw Attributes** toolbar.
24. In the **Format** box, click before the diameter value.
25. Type **1-64 UNC - 2B**. Next, press the SPACEBAR.
26. Click next to **ø%.2w** and press the SPACEBAR.
27. Click the **Downward arrow** button in the **Other** section.

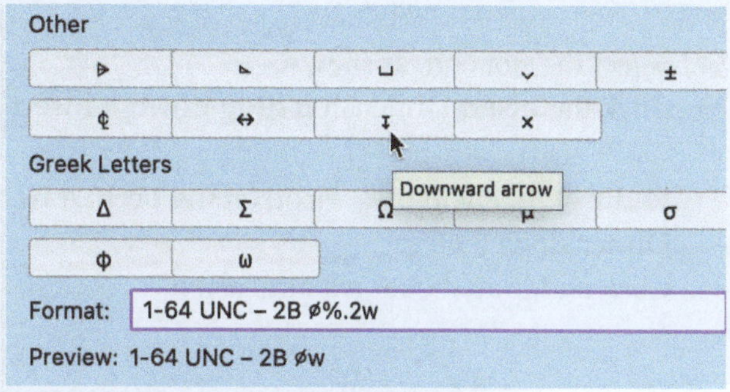

28. Press the SPACEBAR and type 0.4.
29. Click **OK**.
30. On the **View** tab of the **Model** panel, under the **Dimension Format** section, select **Rendering Extent > Minimal**. The arrow on the other side of the dimension is removed.

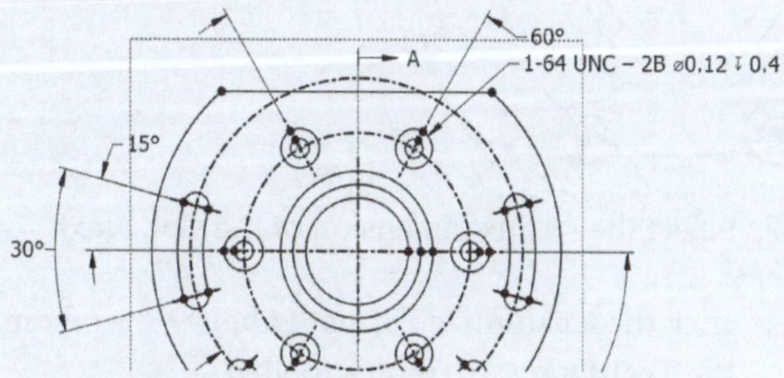

31. Add the pitch circle diameter to counterbore holes.
32. Click the circular edge of the model, click the **Insert Dimension** drop-down > **Insert Radius Dimension** icon on the **TechDraw Dimensions** toolbar.
33. Click and drag the radius dimension.

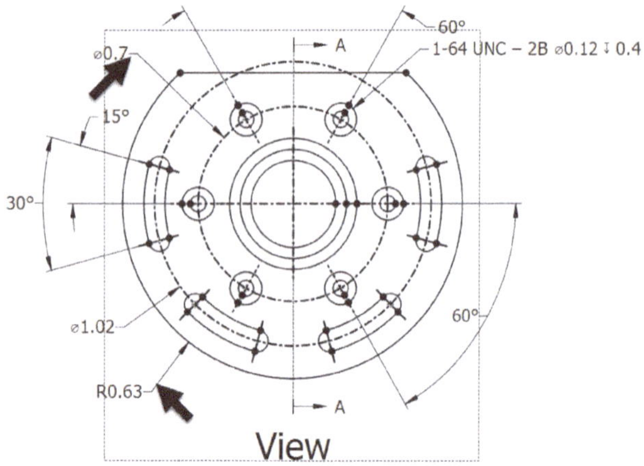

34. Select the slot end, as shown.
35. Click the **Insert Dimension** drop-down > **Insert Radius Dimension**  icon on the **TechDraw Dimensions** toolbar.
36. Click and drag the radius dimension.

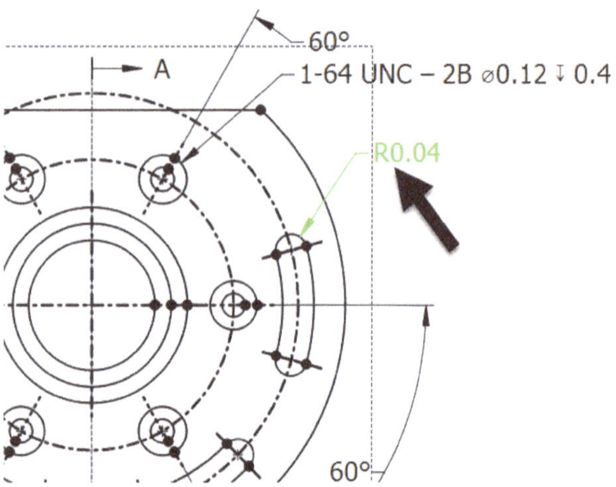

37. Select the radius dimension of the slot. Next, click the **Customize Format Label**  icon on the **TechDraw Attributes** toolbar.
38. In the **Format** box, click next to the radius value.
39. Type **4X**. Next, press the SPACEBAR.
40. Click next to **ø%.2w** and press the SPACEBAR.
41. Type THRU SLOT and click **OK**.

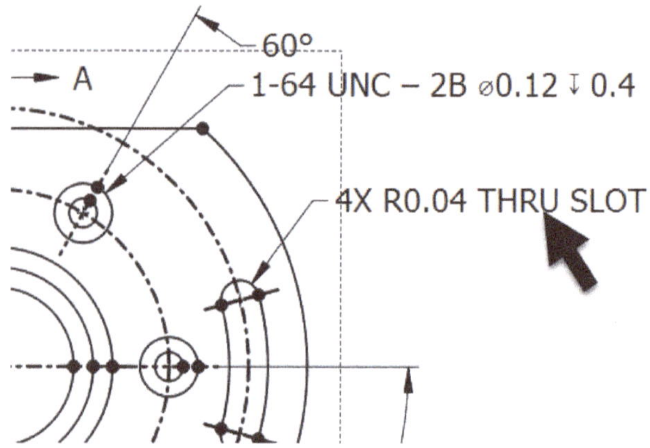

42. Click **Edit > Preferences** on the Menu bar. The **Preferences** dialog box appears. If you are working on MacOS, then click **FreeCAD > Preferences** on the title bar.
43. On the **Preferences** dialog box, click **TechDraw > General** at the left side.
44. Type **0.12** in the **Label Size** box of the **Labels** section and click **OK**.
45. Press and the CTRL key and select the lines, as shown below.

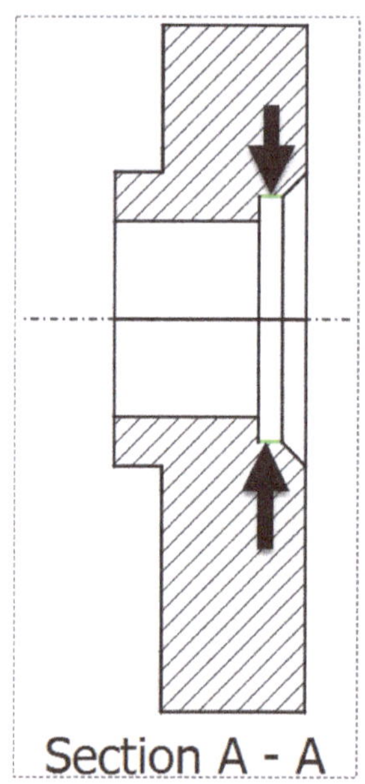

46. Click the **Insert Dimension** drop-down > **Insert Vertical Dimension**  icon on the **TechDraw Dimensions** toolbar.
47. Left-click and hold on the dimension Move the

pointer toward the right and click to place the dimension.

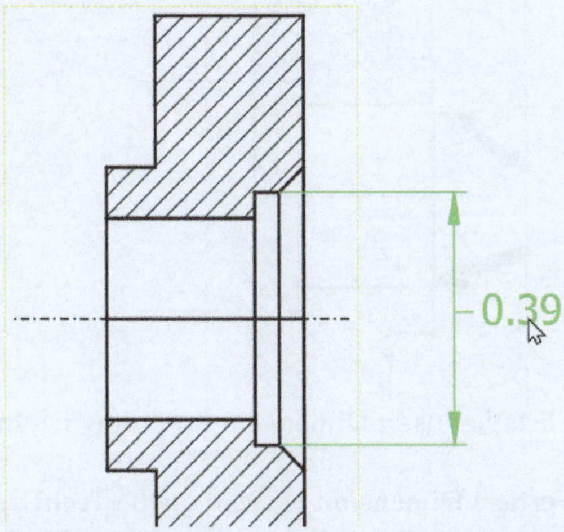

48. Double-click on the newly created dimension.
49. On the **Dimension** section of the **Tasks** panel, uncheck the the **Equal Tolerance** option.
50. Type 0.001 in the **Overtolerance** and **Undertolerance** boxes, respectively.
51. Type %+.3w in the **OverTolerance Format Specifier** and **UnderTolerance Format Specifier boxes**, respectively.

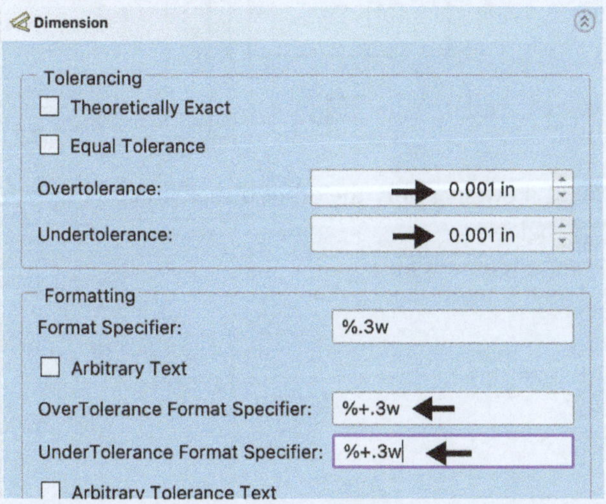

52. Select the newly created dimension and click **Increase decimal Places**  icon on the **TechDraw Attributes** toolbar.
53. Select the newly created dimension and click the **View** tab on the **Model** panel.
54. Select the **Standard and Style > ASME Inlined** under the **Dimension Format** section.

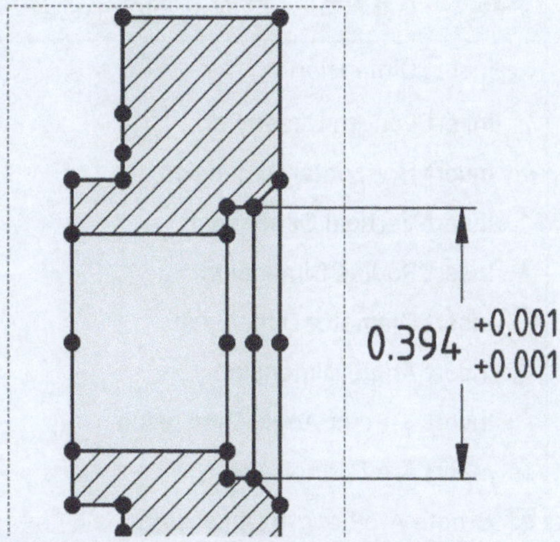

55. Press and hold the CTRL key and select the vertices of the section view, as shown.

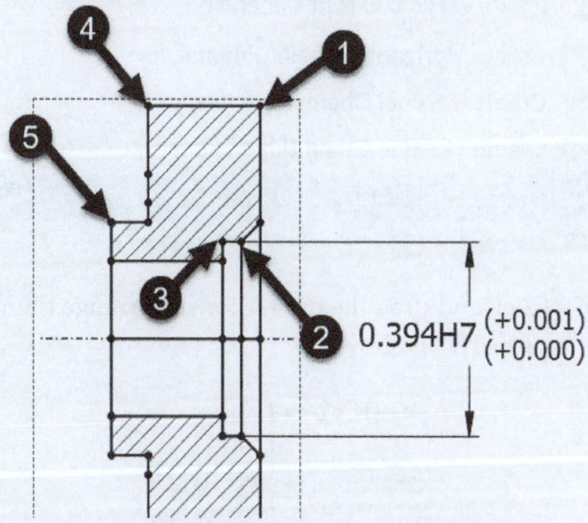

56. Click **Insert Dimension** drop-down **> Create Horizontal Coordinate Dimensions** on the **TechDraw Dimensions** toolbar.

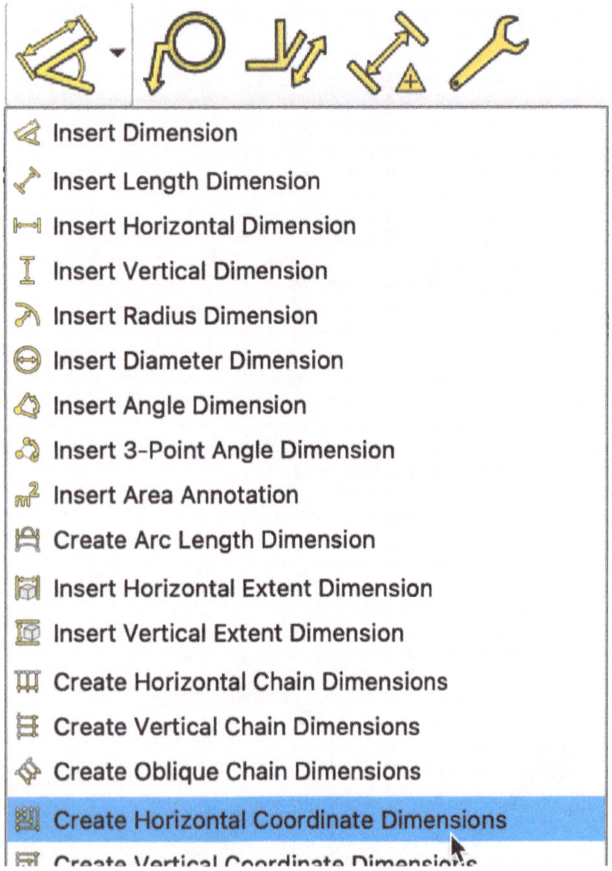

57. Click and drag the dimensions to arrange them properly, as shown.

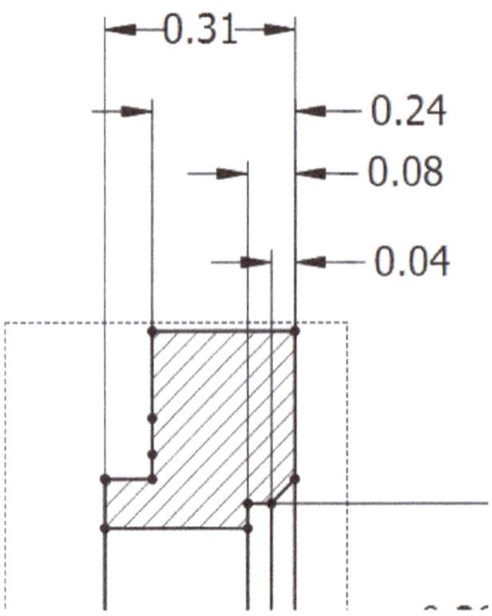

58. Press and hold the CTRL key and select the vertices of the section view, as shown.

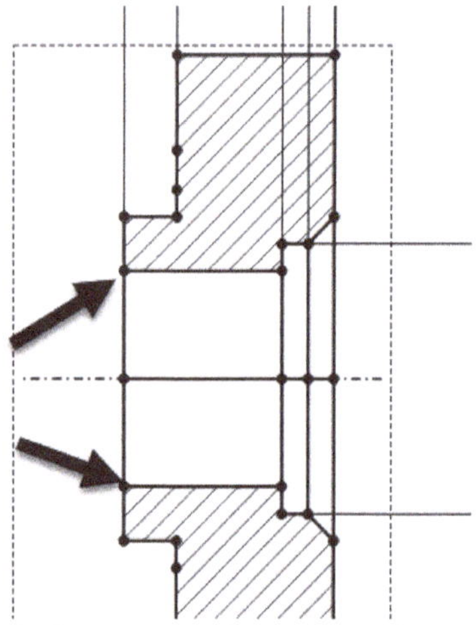

59. Click the **Insert Dimension** drop-down > **Insert Vertical Dimension** icon on the **TechDraw Dimensions** toolbar.

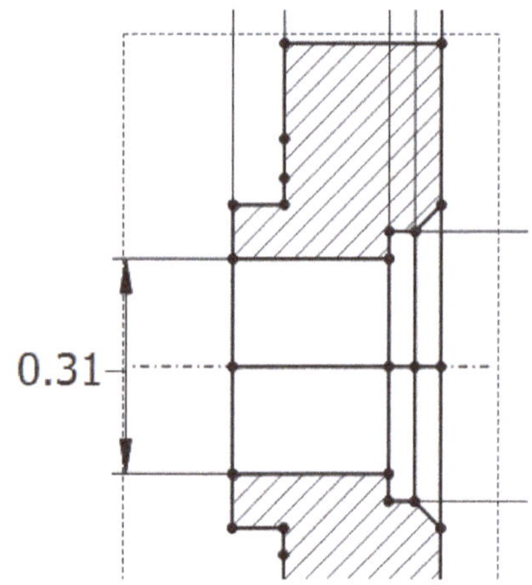

60. Likewise, apply the other dimensions, as shown below.

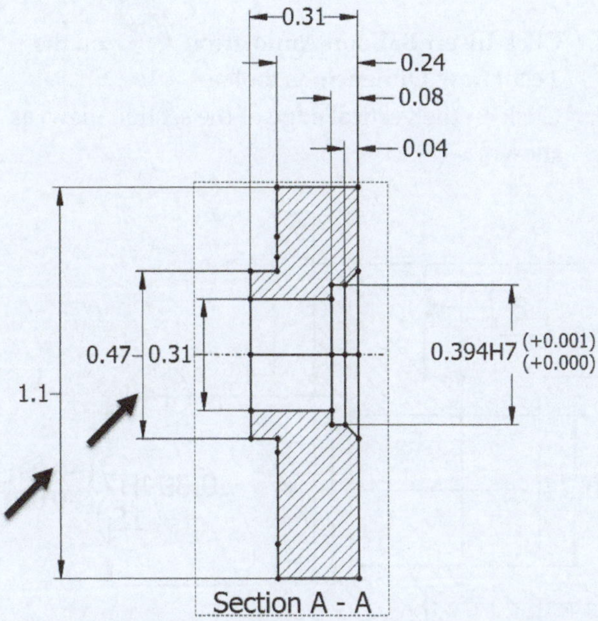

61. Press and hold CTRL key and select the newly created dimensions and click the **View** tab on the **Model** panel.
62. Select the **Standard and Style > ASME Inlined** under the **Dimension Format** section.

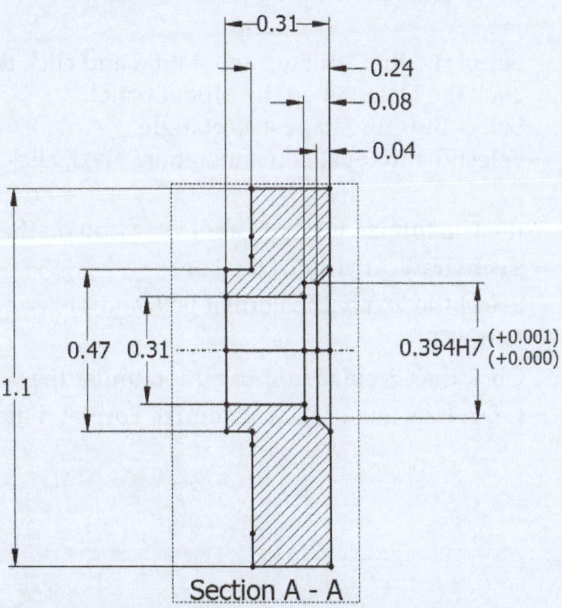

Placing the Balloon Annotation

1. Click on the inner horizontal edge of the section view, as shown.

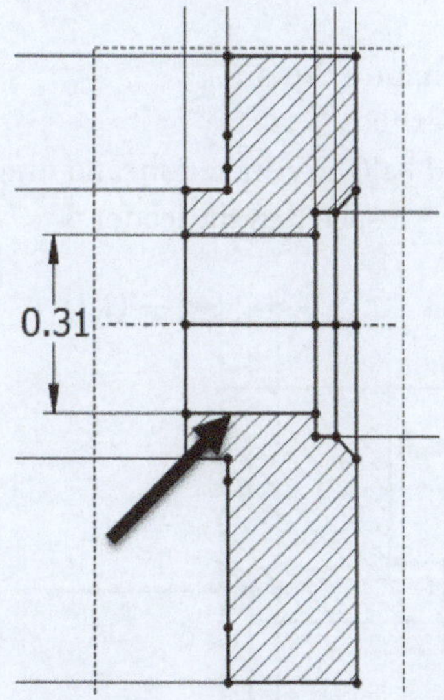

2. Click **Insert Balloon Annotation** on the **TechDraw Dimensions** toolbar.

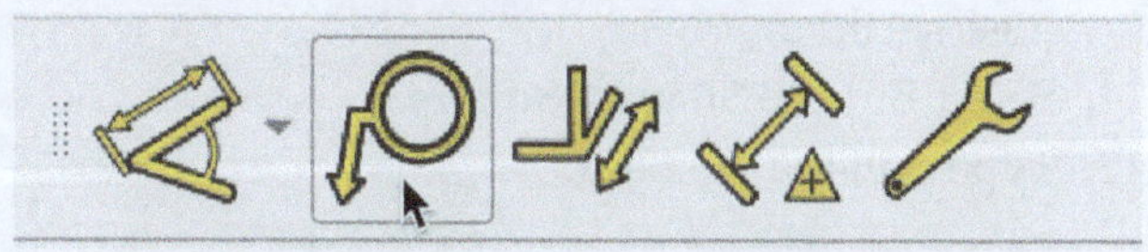

3. Select the vertical edge of the section view, as shown.

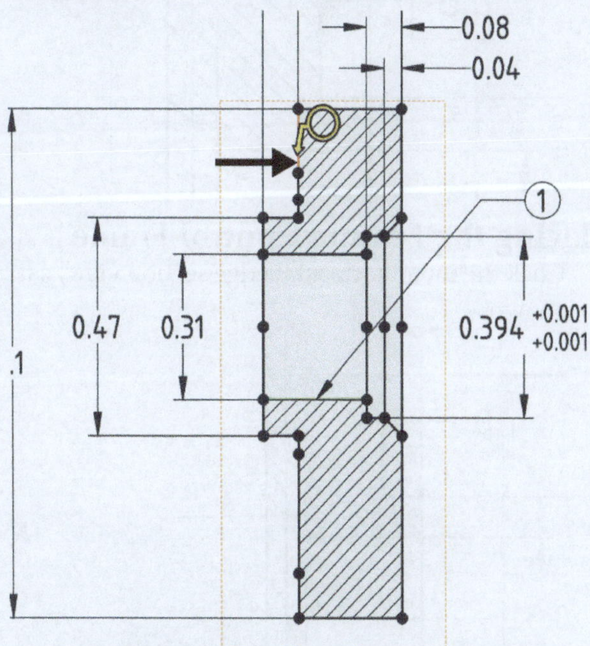

4. Left-click and hold on the balloon annotation. Move the pointer toward the bottom left and click to place the balloon.
5. Select the first balloon annotation and click the **Data** tab on the **Model** panel.

6. Select the **End Type > Filled Arrow** under the **Base** section.
7. Select **Bubble Shape > Square**.
8. Type **A** in the **Text** box.
9. Select the second balloon annotation, and drag it toward left. Place it such that the leader is horizontal.

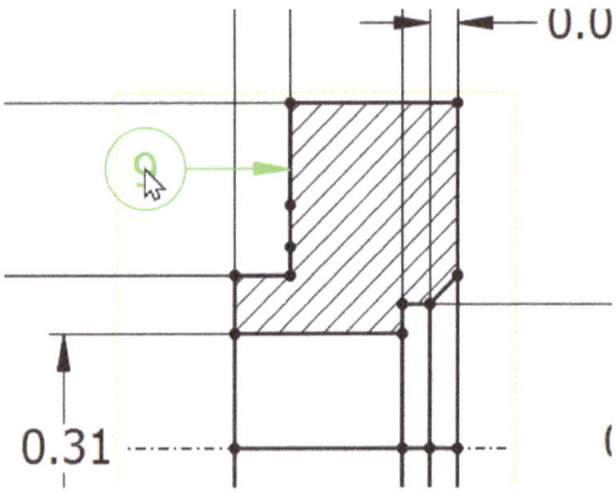

10. Select the **End Type > Filled Triangle** under the **Base** section.
11. Select **Bubble Shape > Square**.
12. Type **B** in the **Text** box.

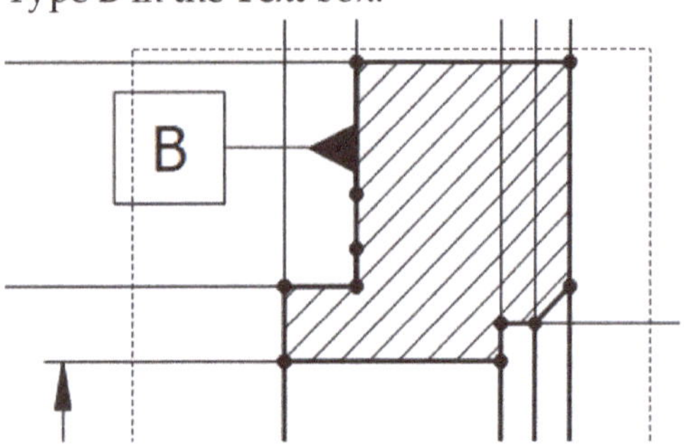

Placing the Feature Control Frame

1. Click the inner horizontal edge section view, as shown.

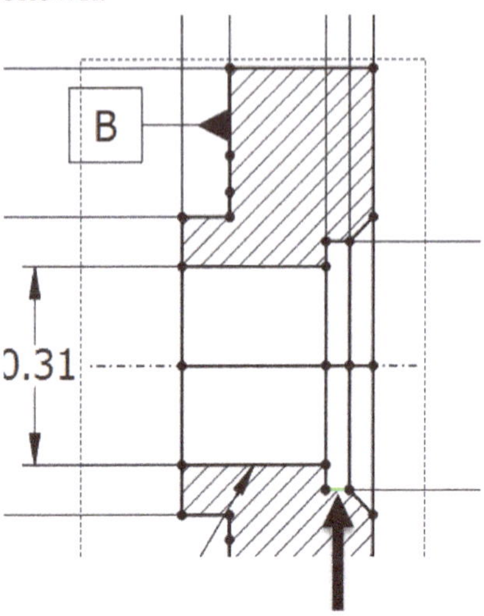

2. Click **Insert Balloon Annotation** on the **TechDraw Dimensions** toolbar.
3. Click on the vertical edge of the section view, as shown.

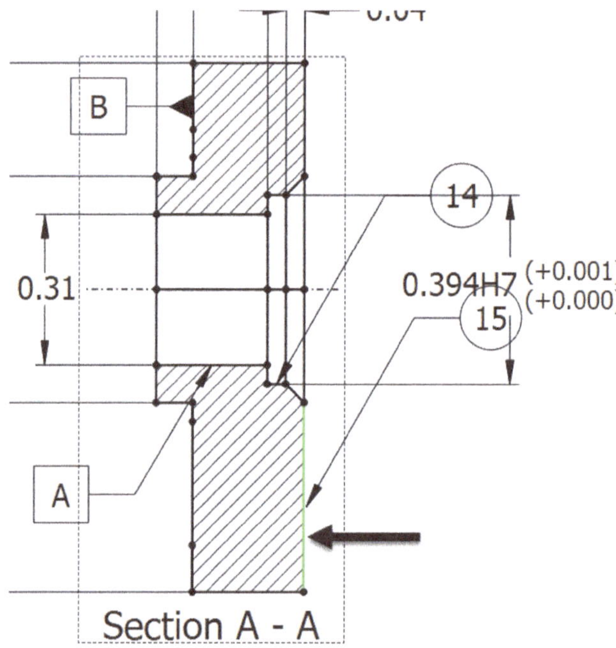

4. Select the first balloon annotation and click the click the **Data** tab on the **Model** panel.
5. Select **Bubble Shape > Rectangle**.
6. Select the first balloon annotation. Next, click the **Customize Format Label** icon on the **TechDraw Attributes** toolbar.
7. Select the text in the **Format** box, and press DELETE.
8. Click the **Circular runout** button under the **GD&T** section of the **Customize Format** dialog.

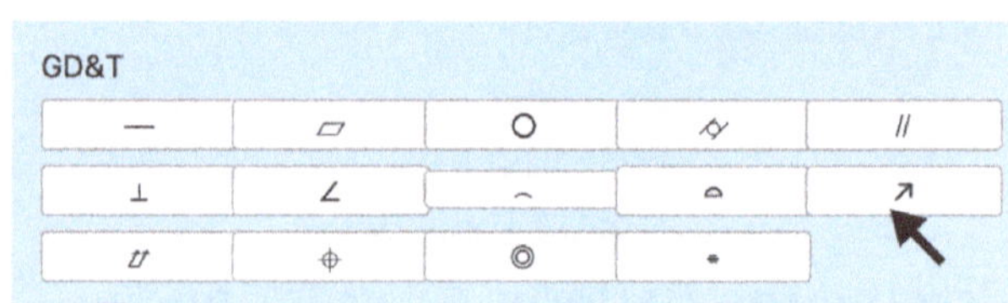

9. Type " | " on your keyoboard in the **Format** box. A new indicator field is initiated
10. Type **.001**.
11. Type " | " on your keyoboard in the **Format** box. A new indicator field is initiated

12. Type **A** and click **OK**.
13. Click and drag the balloon annotation to the location, as shown.

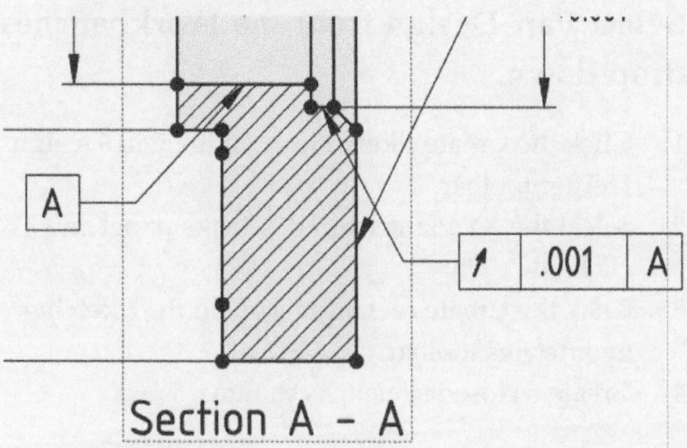

14. Likewise, modify the second balloon annotation and adjust its location, as shown.

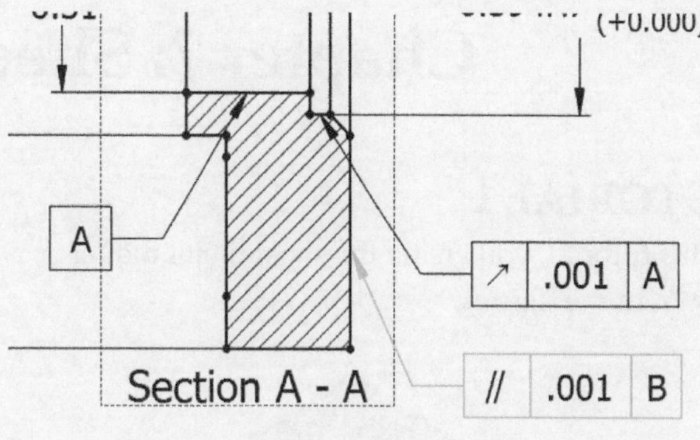

15. Click **Save**.
16. Close the file.

Chapter 7: Sheet Metal Modeling

TUTORIAL 1

In this tutorial, you create the sheet metal model shown in the figure.

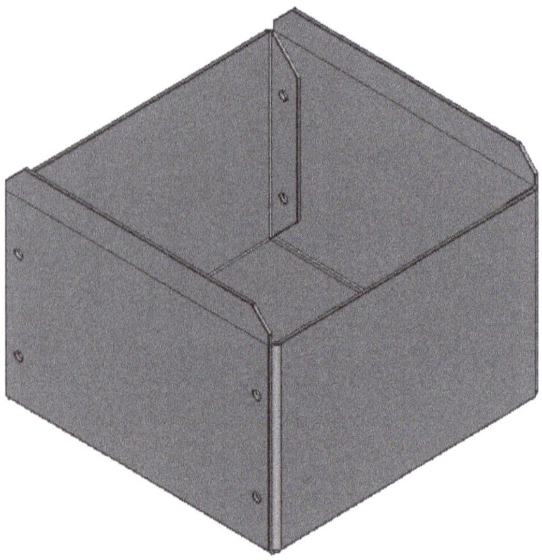

Creating the Base Feature

1. Open a new FreeCAD file.
2. Click **Tools > Addon Manager** on the Menu bar.
3. On the **Addon Manager** dialog, type Sheetmetal in the Search bar and press ENTER.
4. Select **Sheetmetal Workbench** from the list.
5. Click **Install.**
6. Click **Close** twice.
7. Close the FreeCAD application, and then restart it.
8. Click **Edit > Preferences** on the Menu bar.
   The **Preferences** dialog box appears. If you are working on MacOS, then click **FreeCAD > Preferences** on the title bar.
9. Click the **General** > **General** on the left-side of the **Preferences** dialog.
10. Select **Default unit system > Standard.**
11. Type **2** in the **Number of decimals** box.
12. Check the **Ignore Project unit system and use default** option.
13. Click the **Apply** button located at the bottom.
14. Click **OK.**

Select Part Design from the Workbenches drop-down.

1. Click the **Create Sketch** icon on the **Part Design Helper** toolbar.
2. Select the XY Plane from the **Tasks** panel and click **OK.**
3. Click the **Create rectangle** icon on the **Sketcher geometries** toolbar.
4. Create a closed sketch, as shown.

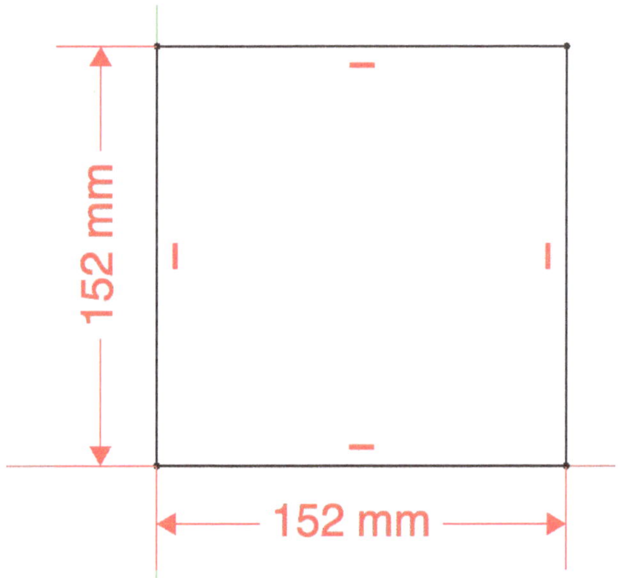

5. Click the **Close** button on the **Tasks** panel.
6. Select **Sheet Metal** from the **Workbenches** drop-down. The user interface changes to the Sheet Metal workbench
7. Select the sketch, if not already selected.
8. Click the **Make Base Wall**  icon on the **Sheetmetal** toolbar.
9. Select the **BaseBend** feature from the **Model** panel. A base wall is created.

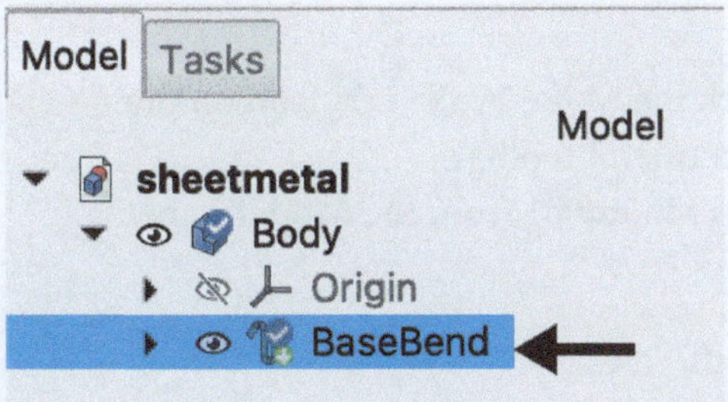

10. Click the **Data** tab at the bottom of the **Model** panel. The BaseBend feature is highlighted.
11. Type **1.5** in the **thickness** box. The thickness of the base wall is changed.

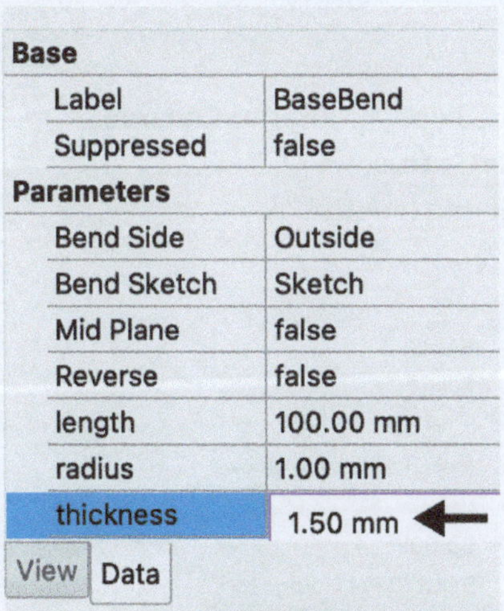

Creating the flange

1. Press and hold the CTRL key and select the edges on the top face, as shown.

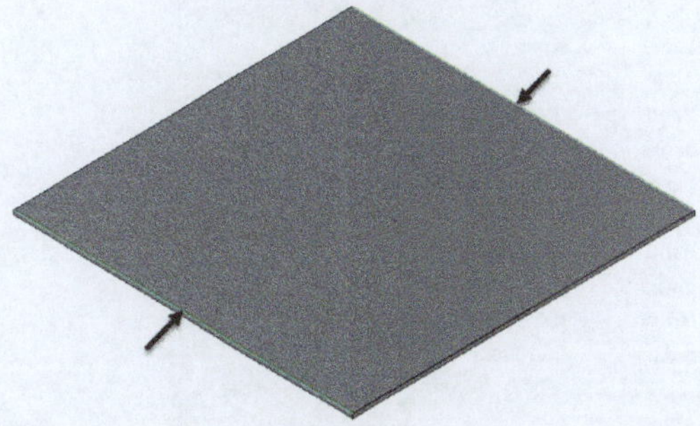

2. Click the **Make Wall** icon on the **Sheet Metal** toolbar.
3. Click the **Model** panel.
4. Select **Bend** from the model tree. The Bend feature is highlighted.

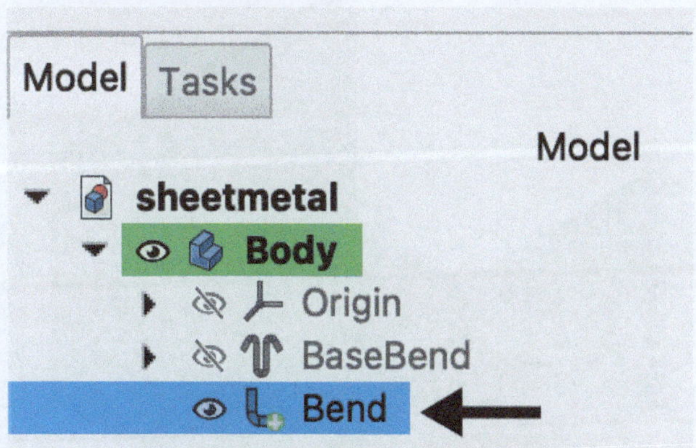

5. On the **Properties** panel, enter **100** and **1** in the **length** and **radius** boxes, respectively. The length and radius of the bend are changed.
6. Select **Bend Type > Offset**.
7. Enter **1.75** in the **offset** box.
8. Select **invert > true**. The direction of the bend is inverted.

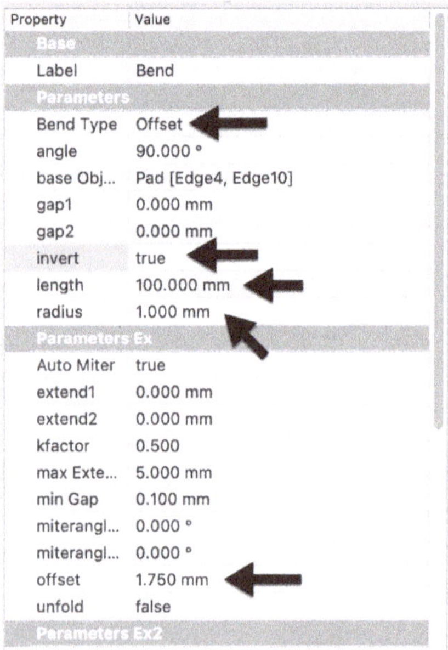

9. Press and hold the CTRL key and select the edges on the top face, as shown.

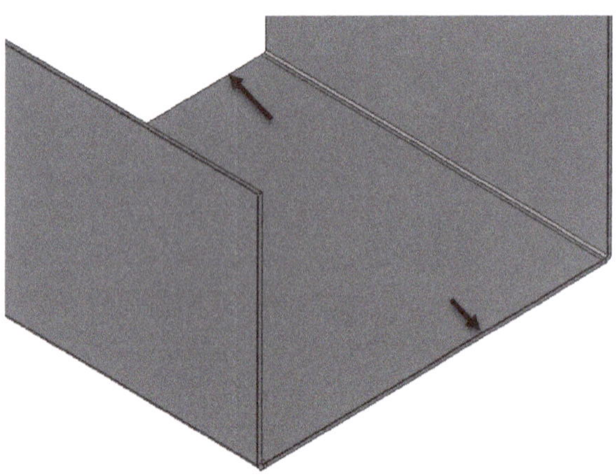

10. Click the **Make Wall** icon on the **Sheetmetal** toolbar.
11. Select **Bend001** from the **Model** panel.

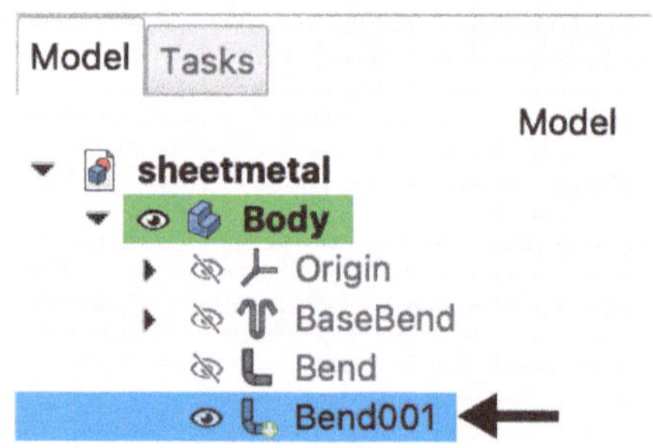

12. Select **Bend Type > Material Outside**.
13. Select **invert > true**.
14. Type **100** in the **length** box.

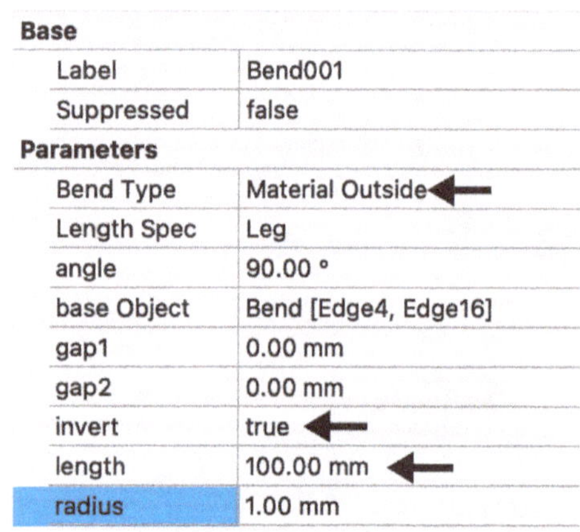

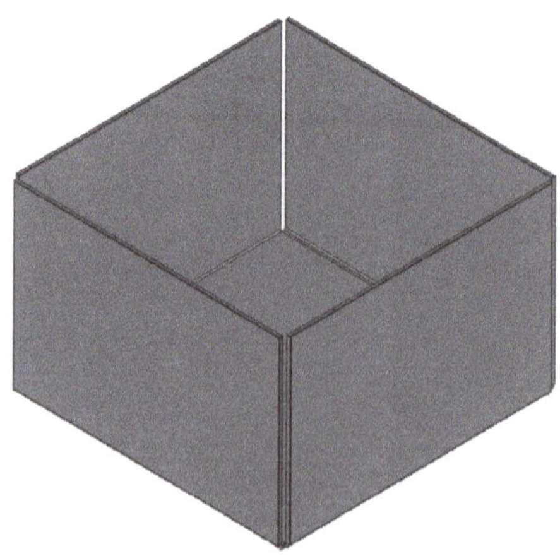

15. Select the inner edge of the flange, as shown.

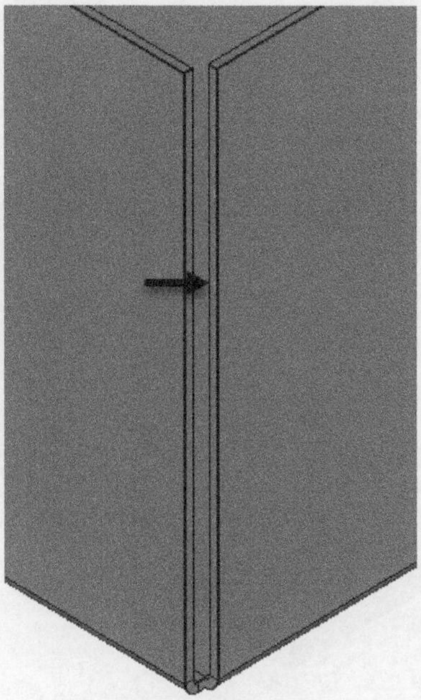

16. Click the **Make Wall** icon on the **Sheetmetal** toolbar.
17. Select **Bend002** from the **Model** panel.
18. Select **Bend Type > Material Inside.**
19. Type **15** in the **length** box.
20. Select **invert > true.**
21. In the **Parameters Ex** section, select **Auto Miter > false.**

Parameters	
Bend Type	Material Inside
Length Spec	Leg
angle	90.00 °
base Object	Bend001 [Edge34]
gap1	0.00 mm
gap2	0.00 mm
invert	true
length	15.00 mm
radius	1.00 mm
Parameters Ex	
Auto Miter	false
extend1	0.00 mm
extend2	0.00 mm

View Data

22. Type **45** in the **miterangle1** and **miterangle2** boxes, respectively.

Parameters Miterangl	
miterangle1	45.00 °
miterangle2	45.00 °

23. Press and hold the middle mouse button and the right mouse button.
24. Drag the pointer toward left such that the other end of the flange is displayed.

The flange is displayed.

25. Likewise, create three more miter flanges, as shown.

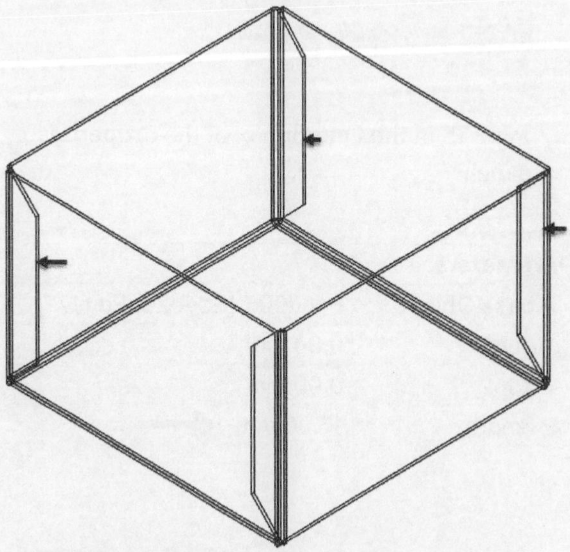

Extending a face

1. Press and hold the CTRL key and select the outer edges of the flanges, as shown.

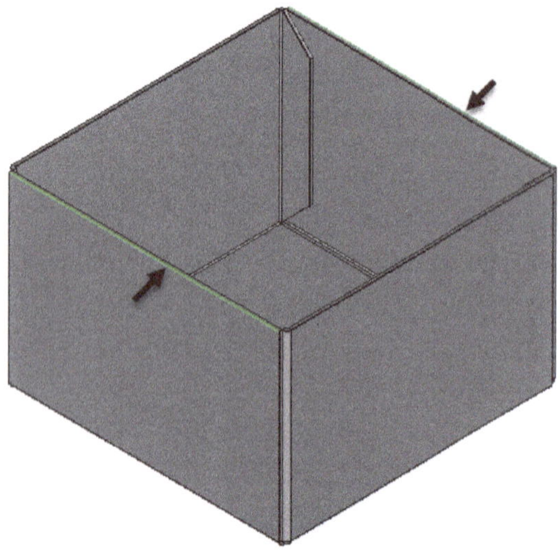

2. Click the **Extend face** icon on the **Sheetmetal** toolbar.
3. Select **Extend** from the **Model** panel.

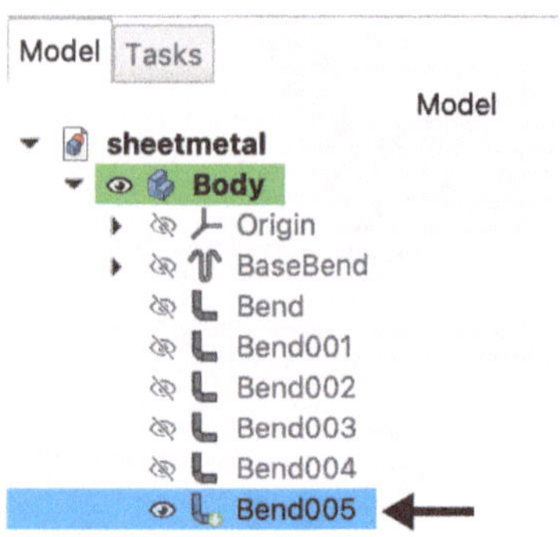

4. Type **15** in the **Length** box of the **Properties** panel.

Parameters	
base Object	Bend005 [Edge26, Edge71]
gap1	0.00 mm
gap2	0.00 mm
length	15.00 mm

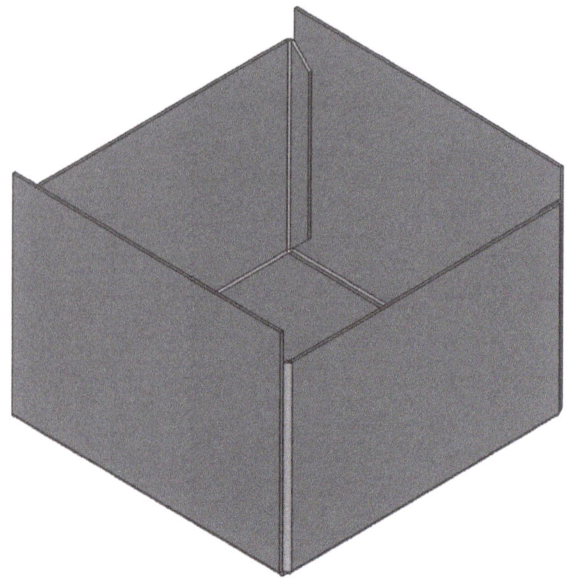

5. Select **Part Design** from the **Workbenches** drop-down.
6. Select the edge of the extended face, as shown.

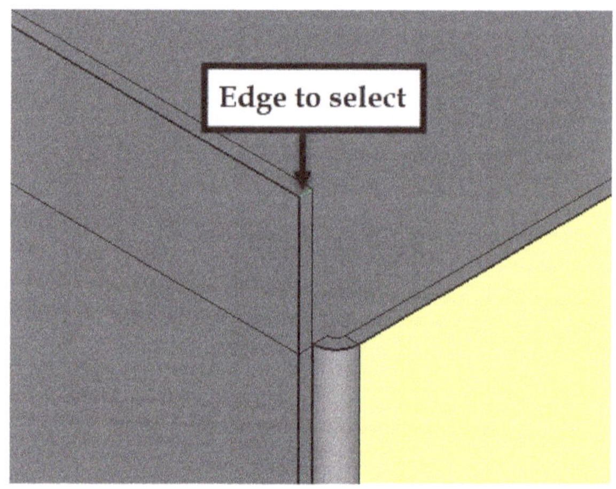

7. On the **Part Design Dressup** toolbar, click the **Chamfer** icon.
8. On the **Chamfer parameters** dialog, click the **Select** button.
9. Select the corner edge of the extended face, as shown.

10. Select the corner edges of another extended face.

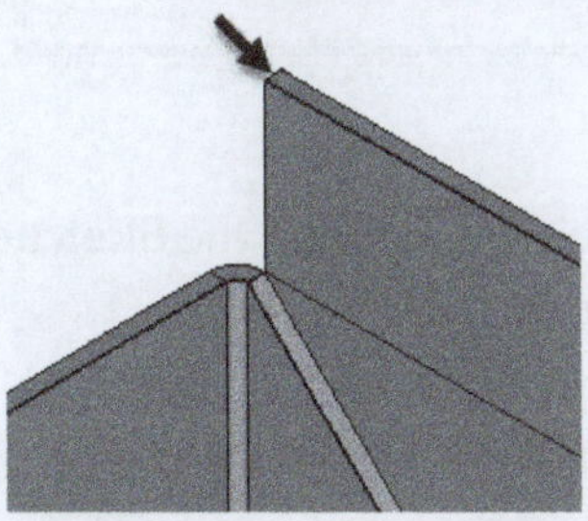

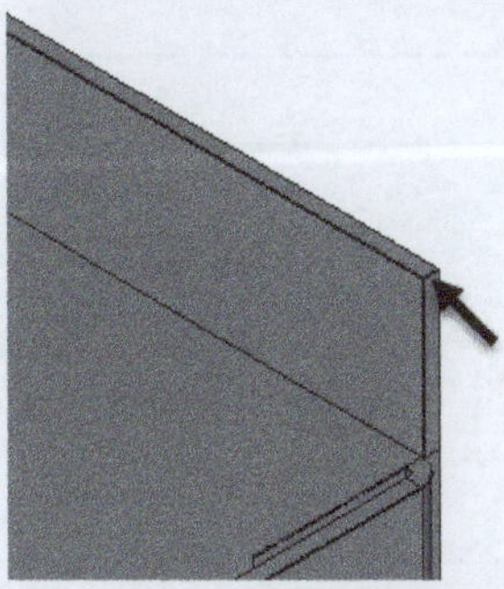

11. Type **10** in the **Size** box and click **OK**.

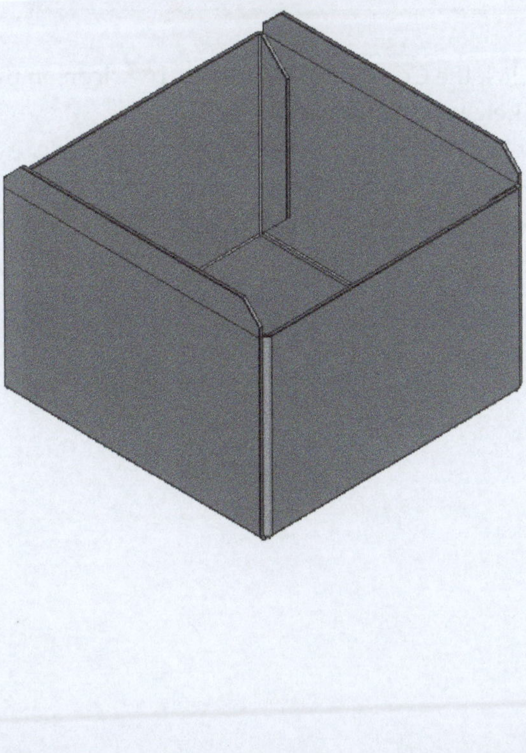

Creating the Pockets

1. Select the flat face of the flange.

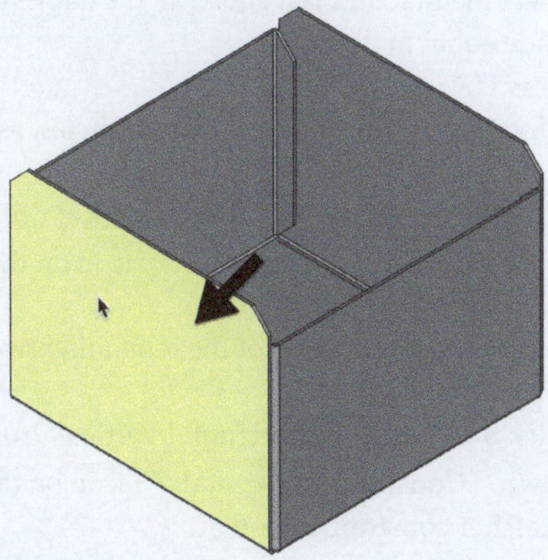

2. Click the **Create Sketch** icon on the **Part Design Helper** toolbar.
3. On the **View** toolbar, click **Draw Style** drop-down > **Wireframe.**

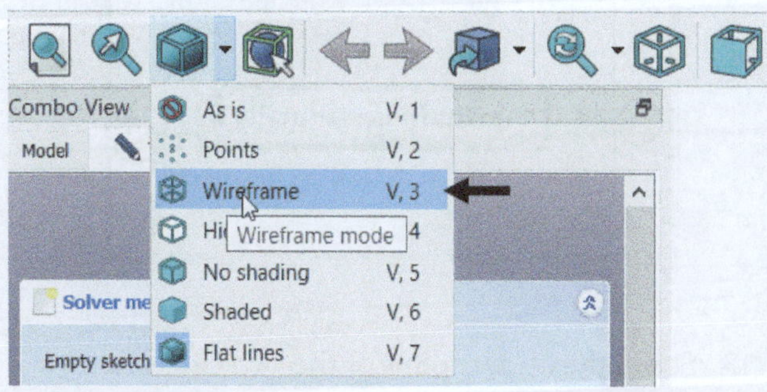

4. Create four circles, as shown.

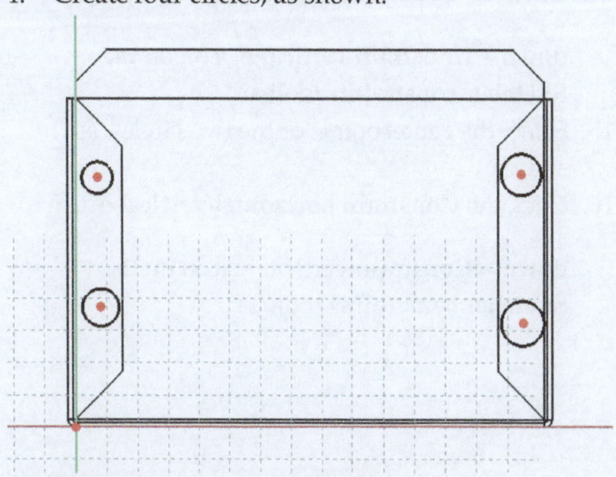

5. Click the **Constrain equal** icon on the **Sketcher constraints** toolbar.

6. Select all the circles one-by-one in the clockwise direction.
7. Select the first and last circle; all the circles are made equal in diameter.
8. Press ESC.
9. Select the center points of the two circles, as shown.
10. Click the **Constrain horizontal/vertical** drop-down >**Constrain horizontal** icon on the **Sketcher constraints** toolbar.
11. Select the center points of the remaining two circles.
12. Click the **Constrain horizontal/vertical** drop-down > **Constrain horizontal** icon on the **Sketcher constraints** toolbar.

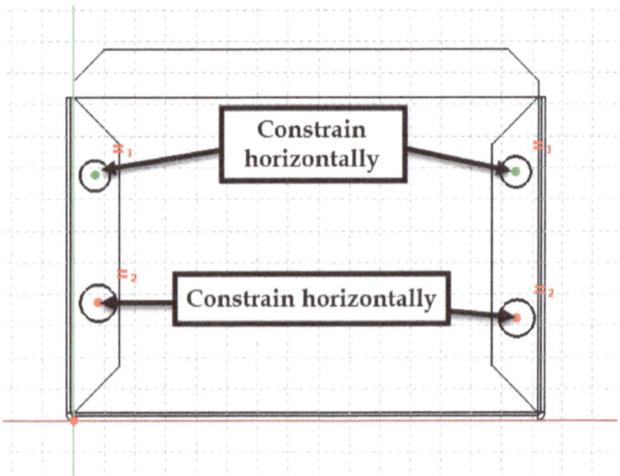

13. Select the centerpoints of the two circles, as shown.
14. Click the **Constrain horizontal/vertical** drop-down > **Constrain vertical** icon on the **Sketcher constraints** toolbar.
15. Select the centerpoints of the two circles, as shown.
16. Click the **Constrain horizontal/vertical** drop-down > **Constrain vertical** icon on the **Sketcher constraints** toolbar.

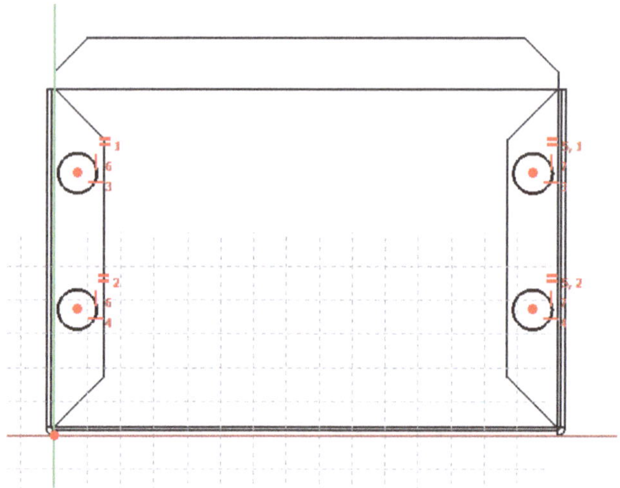

17. Click the **Create point** icon on the **Sketcher geometries** toolbar.
18. Click in the center of the model.
19. Add vertical and horizontal dimensions to the point, as shown.

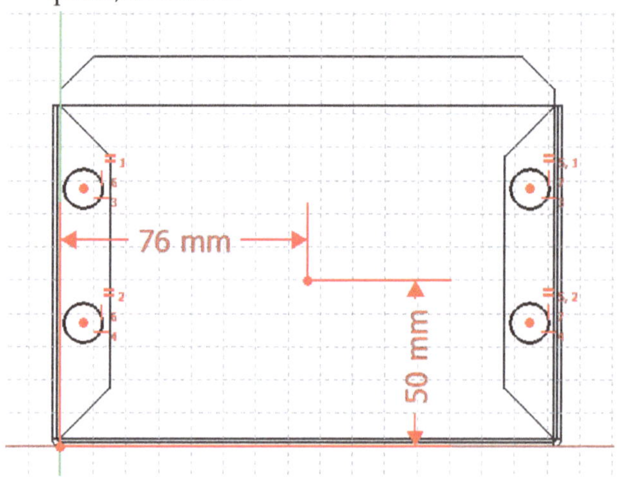

20. Click the **Constrain symmetrical** icon on the **Sketcher constraints** toolbar.
21. Select the center point of the top-right circle.
22. Select the center point of the bottom-left circle.
23. Select the newly created point.

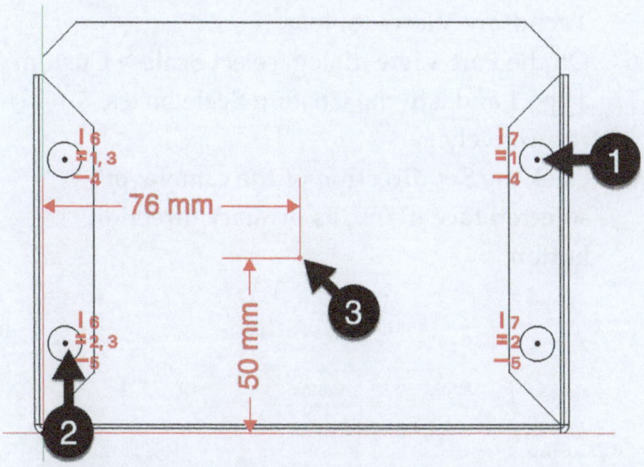

24. Create horizontal and vertical distance constraints, as shown.
25. Create the diameter constraint, as shown.

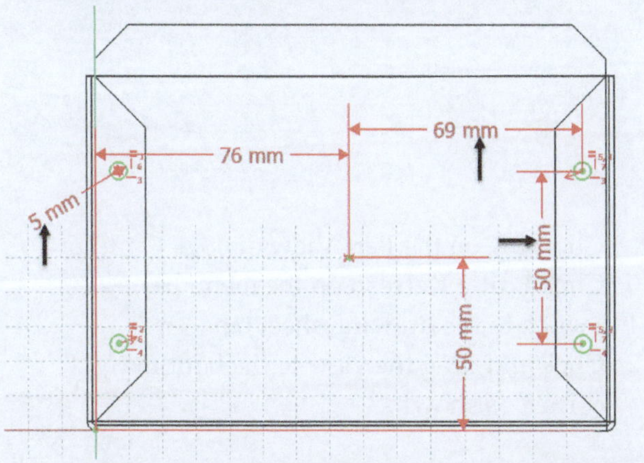

26. Click **Leave Sketch** on the **Sketcher edit mode** toolbar.
27. On the **Part Design Modeling** toolbar, click the **Pocket** icon.
28. On the **Pocket Parameters** dialog, select **Type > Through All.**
29. Click **OK.**
30. On the **View** toolbar, click **Draw Style** drop-down > **Flat Lines.**

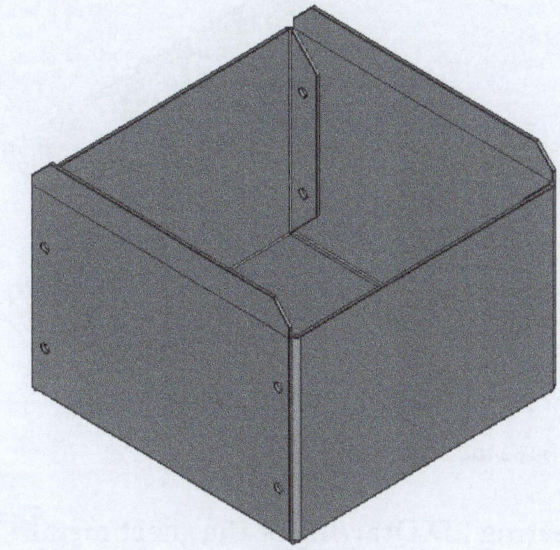

Creating the Flat Pattern

1. Select **Sheet Metal** from the **Workbenches** drop-down.
2. Click on the flat face of the sheet metal model.

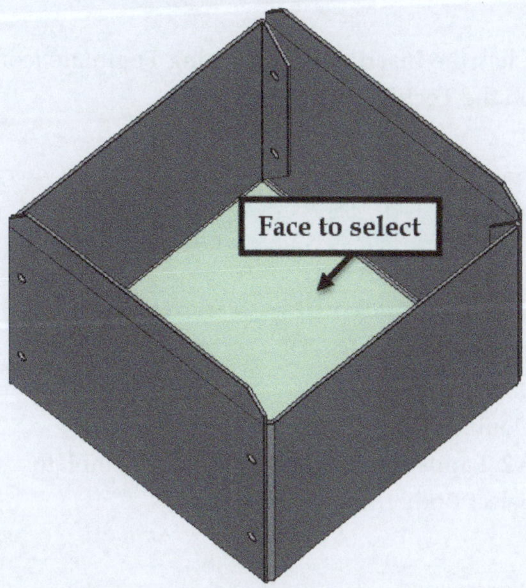

3. Click the **Unfold** icon on the **Sheetmetal** toolbar.
4. Select the **ANSI** option.
5. Click **OK.**

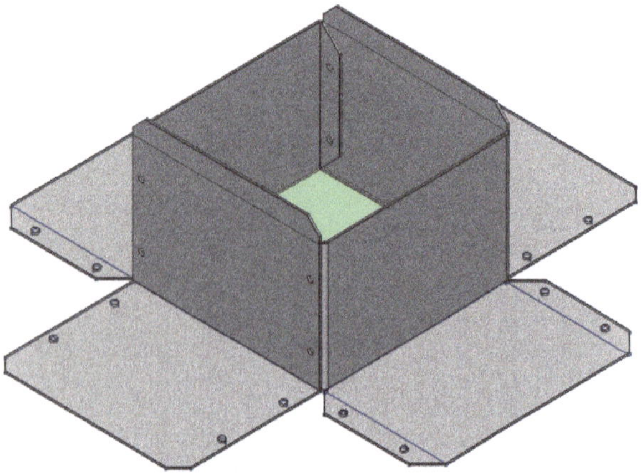

6. Save the sheet metal part.

Creating 2D Drawing of the sheet metal part

1. Select **TechDraw** from the **Workbenches** drop-down.

2. Click the **Insert new Page using Template** icon on the **TechDraw pages** toolbar.

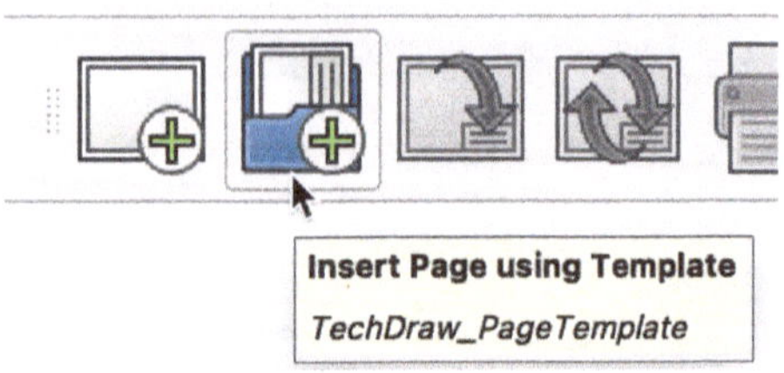

3. Double-click on the **A2_Landscape_ISO5457_minimal** template.
4. Select **Body** from the **Model** tab.

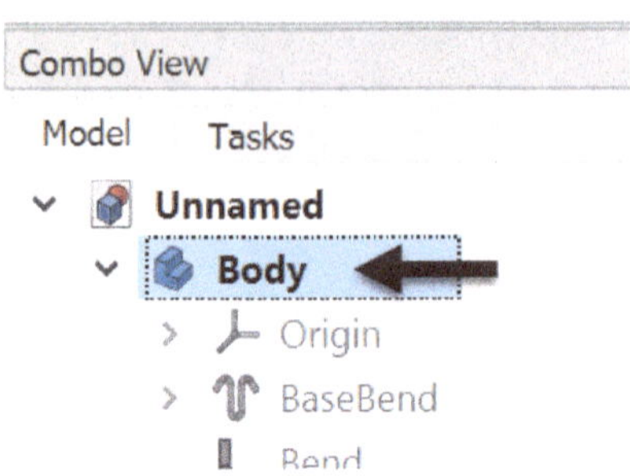

5. Click the **Insert View**  icon on the **Techdraw Views** toolbar.
6. On the **Part View** dialog, select **Scale > Custom**.
7. Type **1** and **2** in the **Custom Scale** boxes, respectively.
8. Click the **Set direction of the camera, or selected face if any, as primary direction** button.

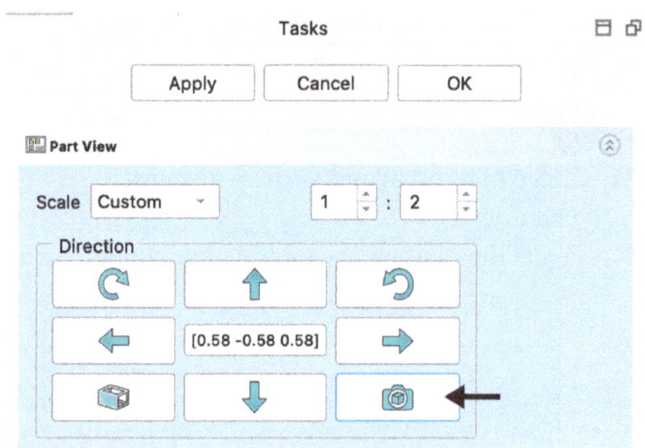

9. Click **OK** on the **Part View** dialog.
10. Click **Edit** > **Refresh** on the menu bar.
11. Switch to the drawing sheet tab.
12. Click and drag the view to the bottom right corner, as shown.

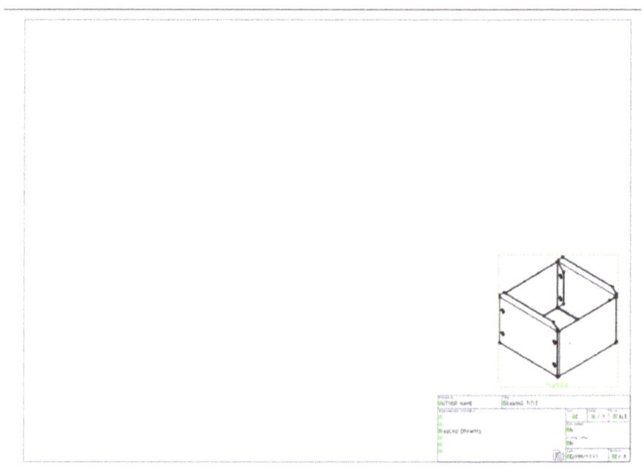

13. Switch to the sheet metal model file.
14. On the **View** toolbar, click the **View orientation** drop-down > **Top**.

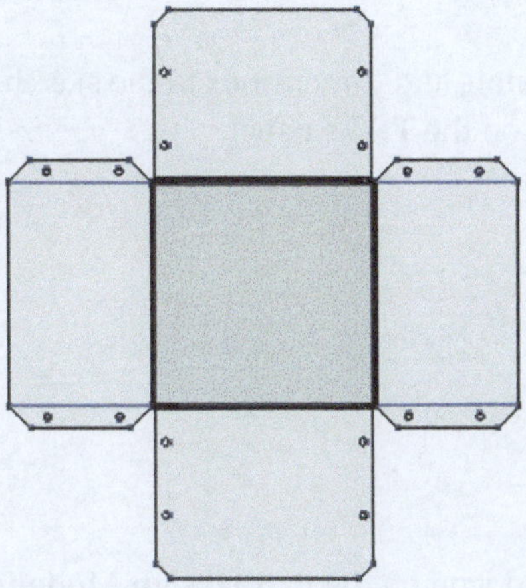

15. Select **Unfold_Sketch** from the **Model** tab.

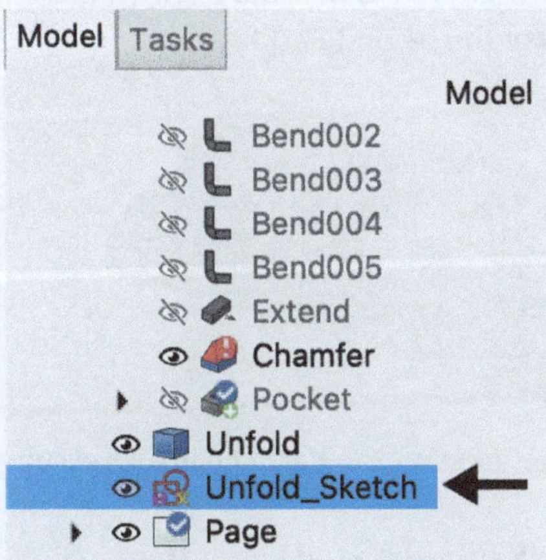

16. Switch to the drawing view.
17. Click the **Insert View**  icon on the **Techdraw Views** toolbar.
18. On the **Part View** dialog, select **Scale > Custom**.
19. Type **3** and **4** in the **Custom Scale** boxes, respectively.
20. Click the **Rotate up** button on the **Tasks** panel.
21. Click **OK** on the **Part View** dialog.

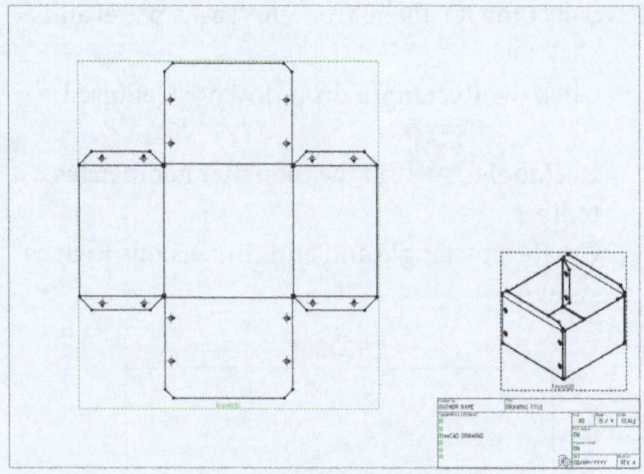

22. Add dimensions to the unfolded view.

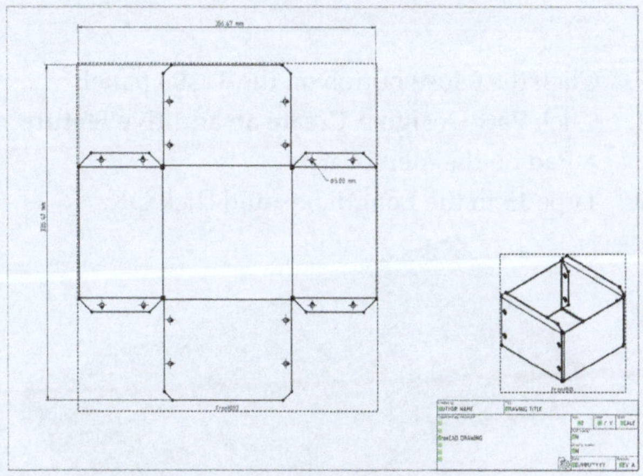

23. Save and close the sheet metal files.

TUTORIAL 2

In this tutorial, you create the model shown in the figure.

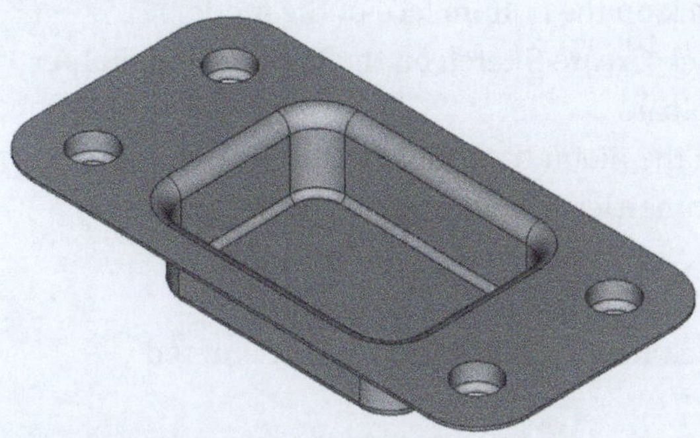

Creating the Base Feature

1. Open a new FreeCAD file.
2. Select **Part Design** from the **Workbenches** drop-down.
3. Click the **Create Sketch** icon on the **Part Design Helper** toolbar.

4. Select the XY Plane from the Tasks panel and click OK.
5. Click the **Rectangle** drop-down > **Centered Rectangle**  on the **Sketcher geometries** toolbar.
6. Create a rectangle and add dimensions to it, as shown.

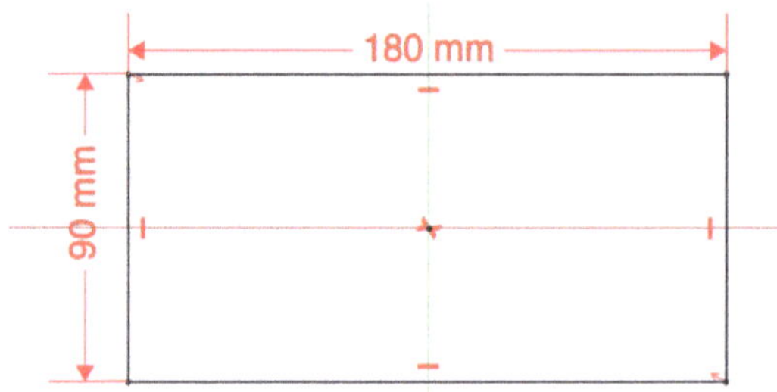

7. Click the **Close** button on the **Tasks** panel.
8. Click **Part Design > Create an additive feature > Pad** on the menu bar.
9. Type **15** in the **Length** box and click **OK**.

10. Press and hold the middle and right mouse buttons. Next, drag the pointer to rotate the model.
11. Click on the bottom face of the model.
12. Click **Create Sketch** on the **Part Design Helper** toolbar.
13. On the menu bar, click **Sketch > Sketcher geometries > Toggle construction geometry** .
14. Click **Rectangle** drop-down > **Centered rectangle** 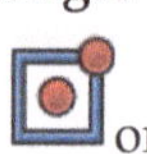 on the **Sketcher geometries** toolbar.
15. Select the sketch origin, move the pointer outward and click.
16. Click the **Toggle construction geometry** icon on the **Sketcher geometries** toolbar.
17. Create four circles on the vertices of the rectangle.
18. Add constraints and dimensions to the sketch.
19. Click **Close** on the **Tasks** panel.

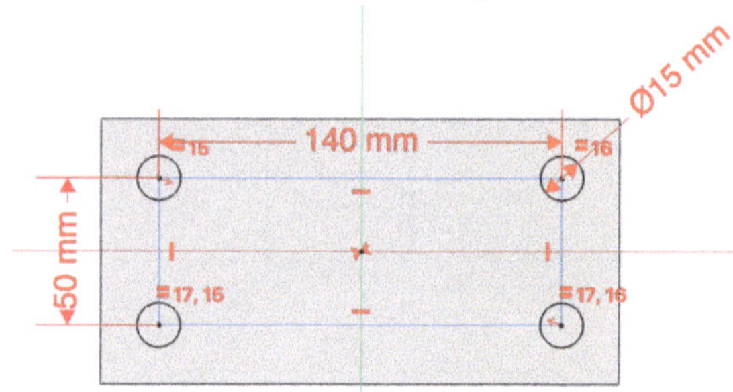

20. Click the **Pad** icon on the **Part Design Modeling** toolbar.
21. Type **8** in the **Length** box and click **OK**.
22. Press and hold the CTRL key and click on the bottom faces of the second Pad feature.

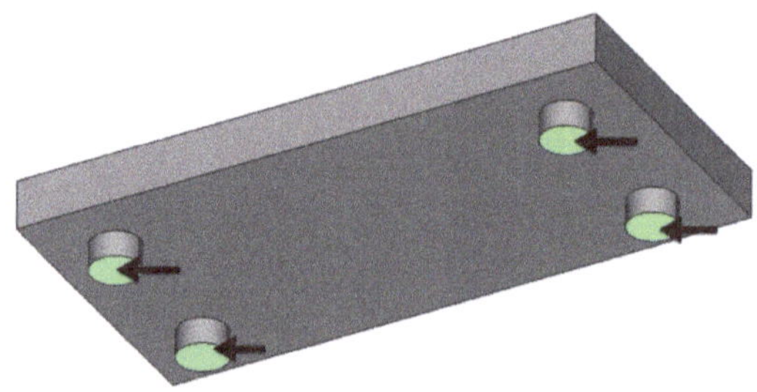

23. Click the **Fillet** icon on the **Part Design Dressup** toolbar.
24. Type 2 in the **Radius** box and click **OK**.

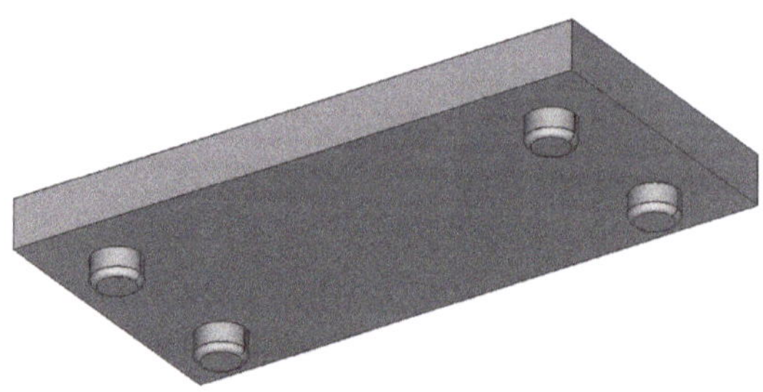

25. Click on the bottom face of the first Pad feature.
26. Click the **Create Sketch** icon on the **Part Design Helper** toolbar.
27. Create a centered rectangle and add dimensions to it, as shown.

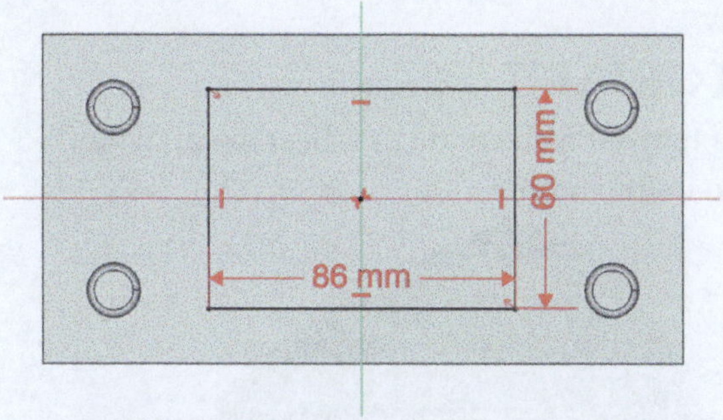

28. Click the **Close** button on the **Tasks** panel.
29. Click **Part Design > Create an additive feature > Pad** on the menu bar.
30. Type **25** in the **Length** box and click **OK**.

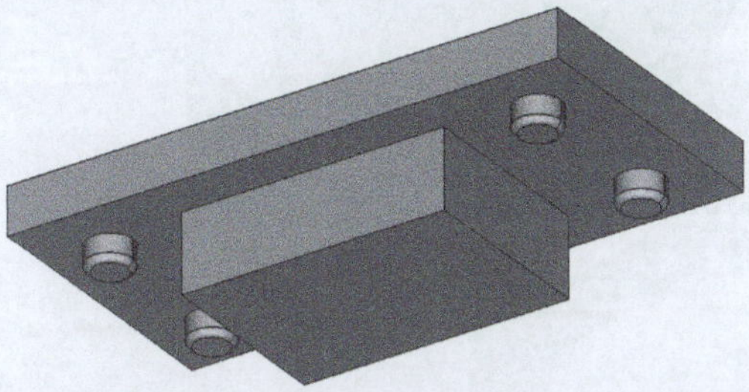

31. Press and hold the CTRL key and select the vertical edges of the newly created Pad feature.
32. Click the **Fillet** icon on the **Part Design Dressup** toolbar.
33. Type **10** in the **Radius** box and click **OK**.

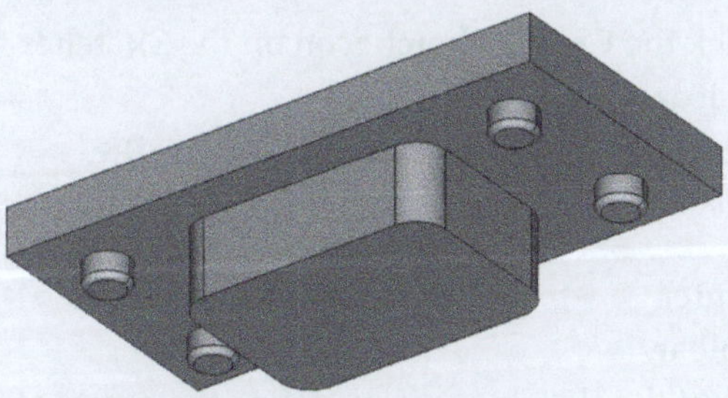

34. Click on the bottom face of the newly created Pad feature.

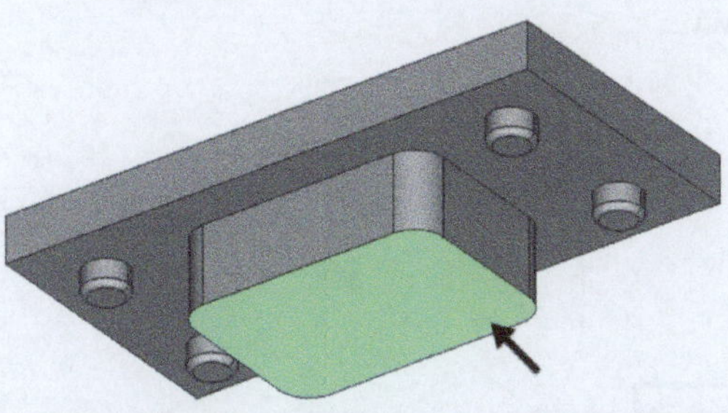

35. Type **2** in the **Radius** box and click **OK**.
36. Click on the edge of the model, as shown.

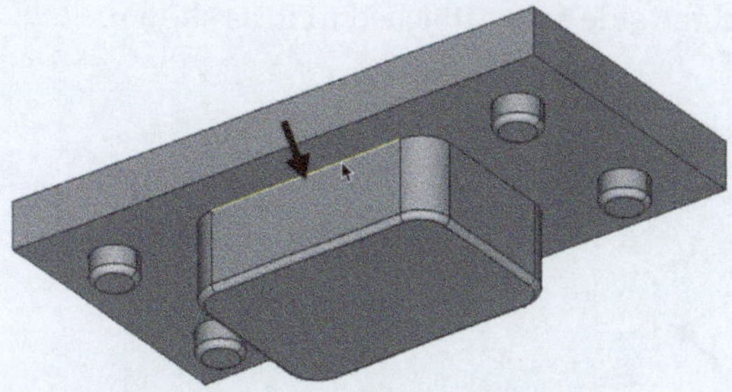

37. Click the **Fillet** icon on the **Part Design Dressup** toolbar.
38. Type **5** in the **Radius** box and click **OK**.

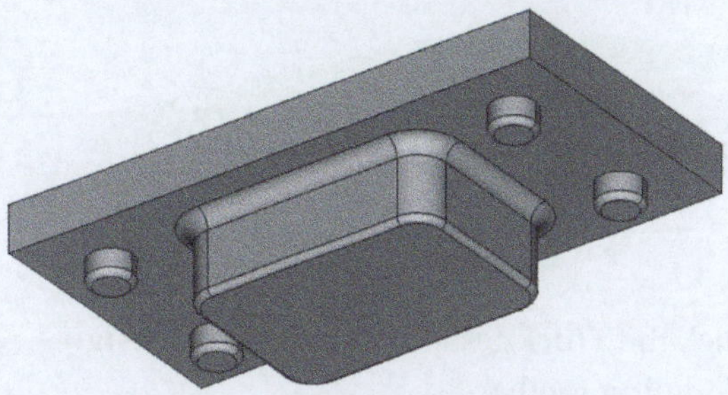

39. Press and hold the CTRL key and click on the vertical edges of the model, as shown.

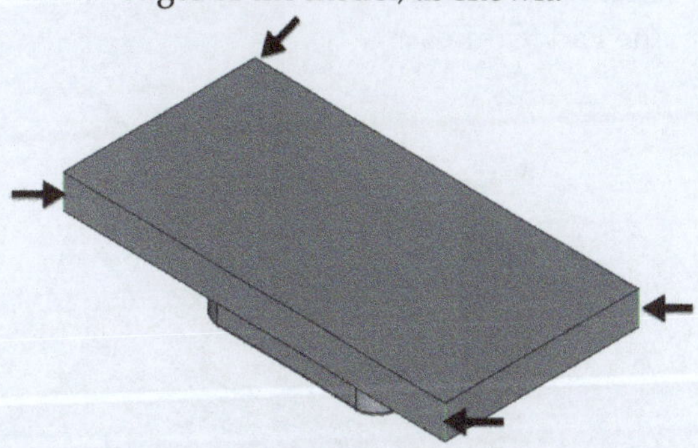

40. Click the **Fillet** icon on the **Part Design Dressup** toolbar.
41. Type **18** in the **Radius** box and click **OK**.

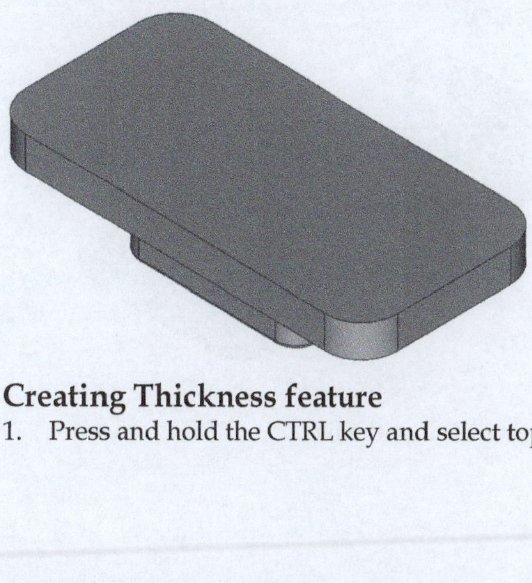

Creating Thickness feature

1. Press and hold the CTRL key and select top face

and the side faces attached to it, as shown.

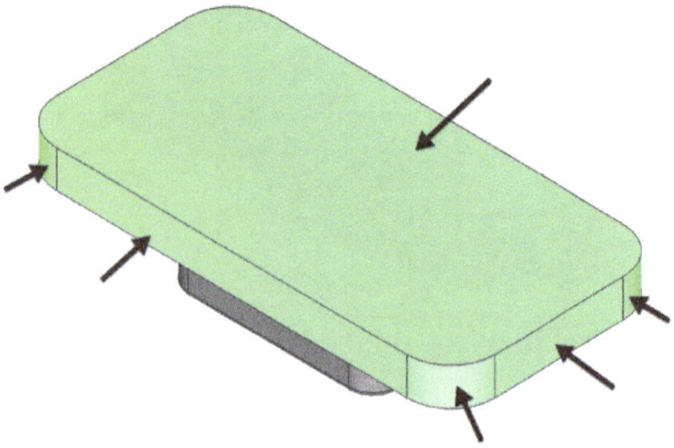

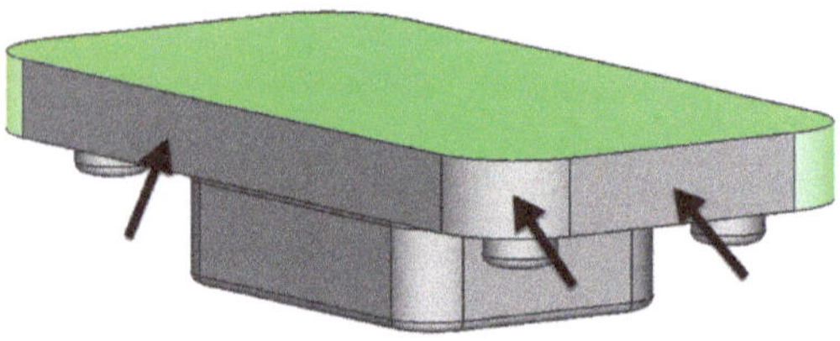

2. Click the **Thickness** icon on the **Part Design Modeling** toolbar.
3. Click the **Select** button on the **Tasks** panel.
4. Rotate the model and select the bottom faces of the Pad features.

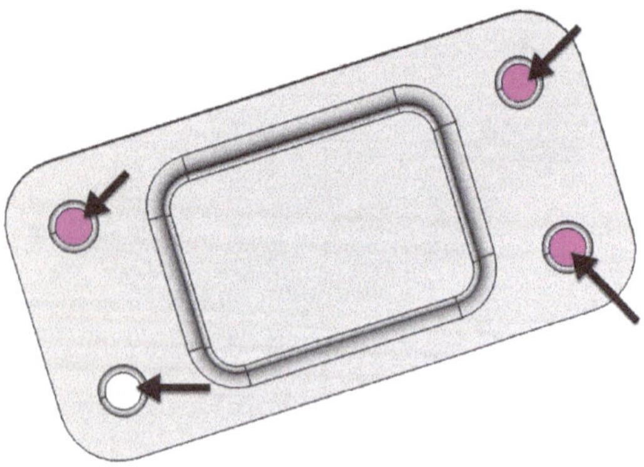

5. Type **1** in the **Thickness** box.
6. Click **OK**.

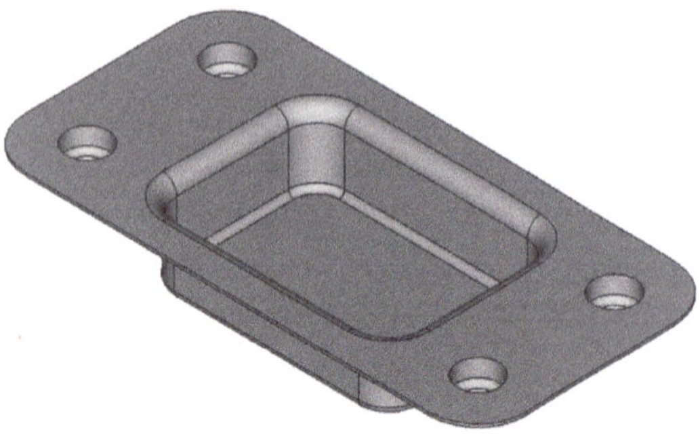

7. Save and close the file.

TUTORIAL 3

In this tutorial, you create the sheet metal model shown in the figure.

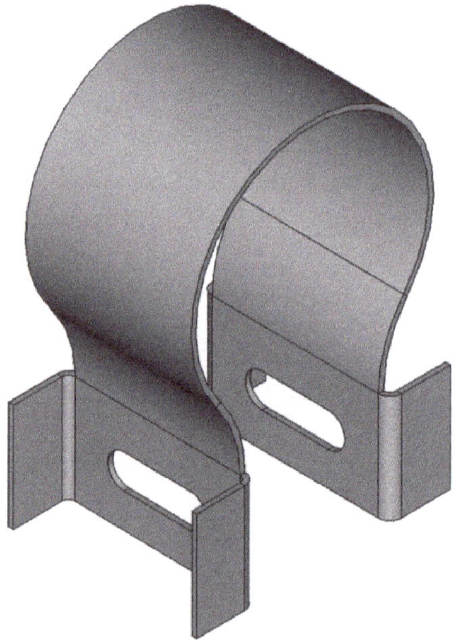

Creating the Base Feature

1. Open a new FreeCAD file.
2. Select **Part Design** from the **Workbenches** drop-down.
3. Click the **Create Sketch** icon on the **Sketcher** toolbar.
4. Select the **YZ-Plane** option and click **OK**.
5. Select the **Arc** drop-down > **Create arc by Center**  from the **Sketcher geometries** toolbar.
6. Select the sketch origin to define the center of the arc.
7. Specify the start and end points of the arc, as shown.

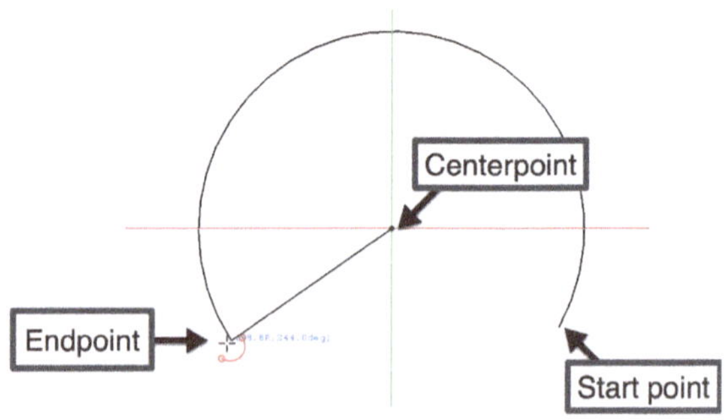

8. Select the **Arc** drop-down > **Create arc by 3 points** from the **Sketcher geometries** toolbar.

9. Select the endpoint of the arc.
10. Move the pointer downward and click.
11. Move the pointer toward right and click to create the arc.

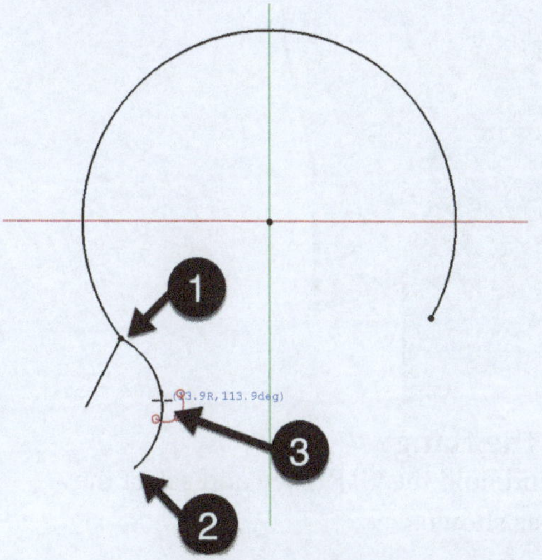

12. Likewise, create another arc, as shown.

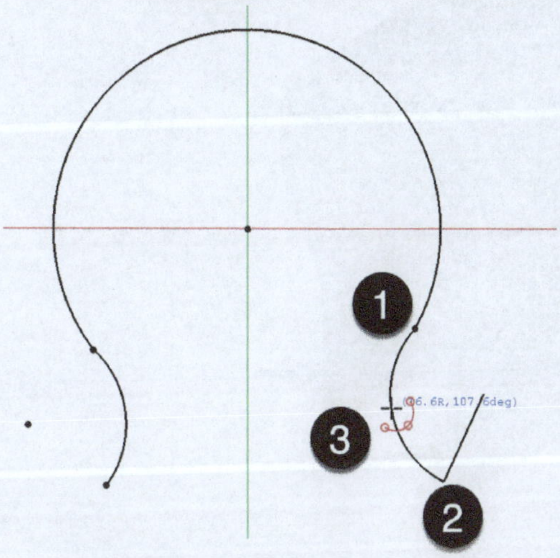

13. Create two vertical lines from the endpoints of the arcs, as shown.

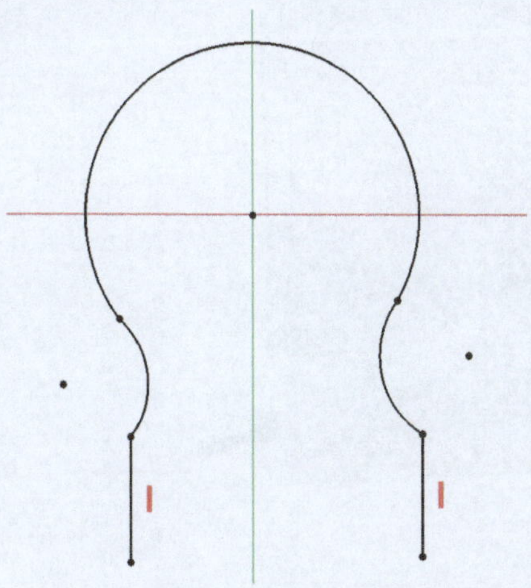

14. Add dimensions to the sketch, as shown.

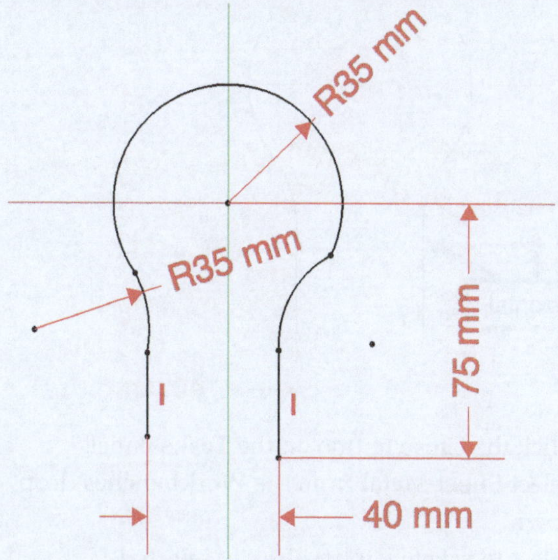

15. Add constraints to the sketch, as shown.

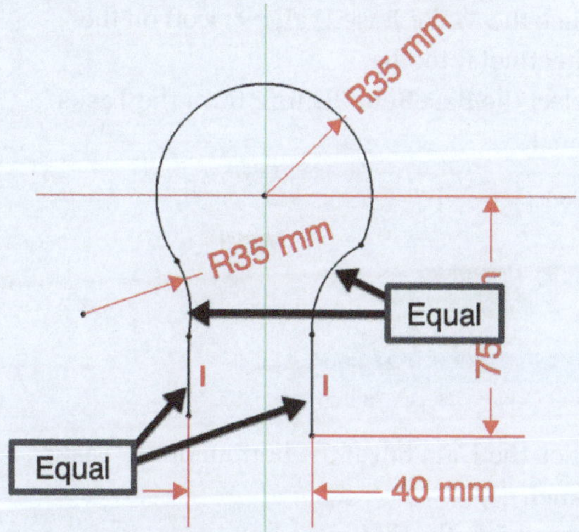

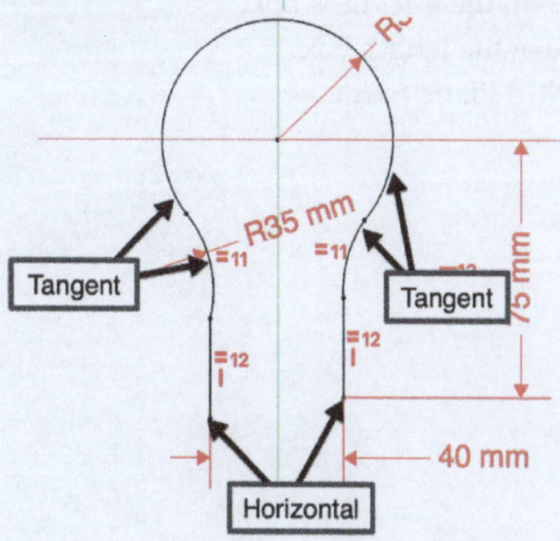

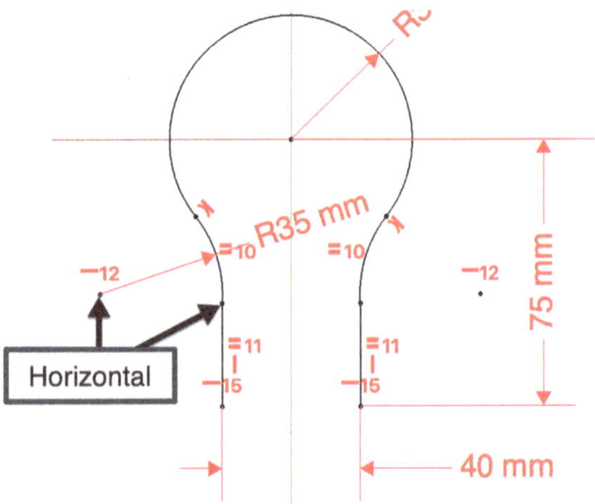

16. Click the **Close** button on the **Tasks** panel.
17. Select **Sheet Metal** from the **Workbenches** drop-down.
18. Select the sketch, if not already selected.
19. Click the **Make Base Wall** icon on the **Sheetmetal** toolbar.
20. Select the **BaseBend** feature from the **Tasks** panel.

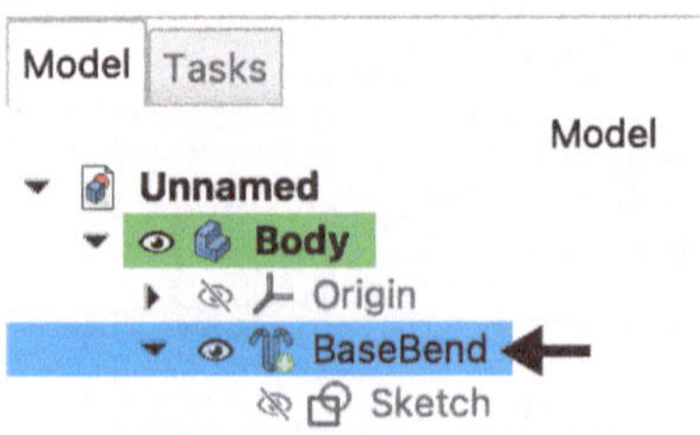

21. Click the **Data** tab at the bottom of the **Tasks** panel.
22. Type **1.5** in the **thickness** box.
23. Type **50** in the **length** box.
24. Select **Mid Plane > true**.

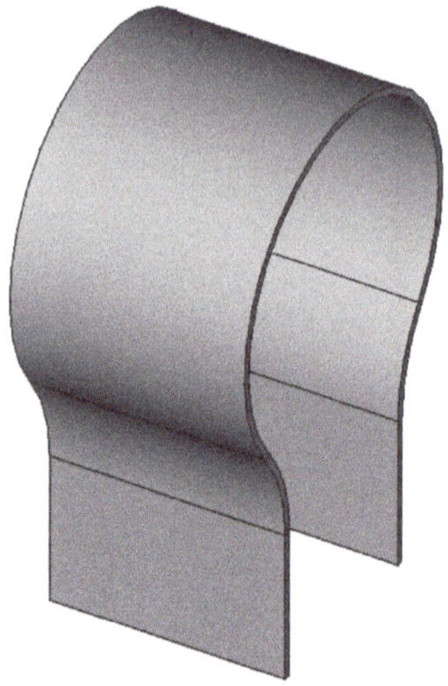

Creating the flange

1. Press and hold the CTRL key and select the edges, as shown.

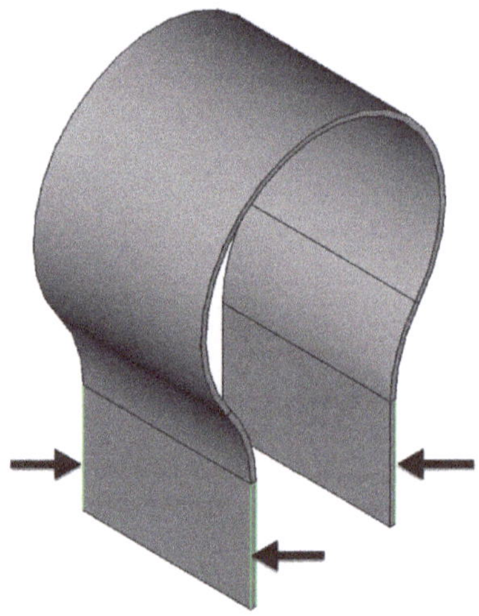

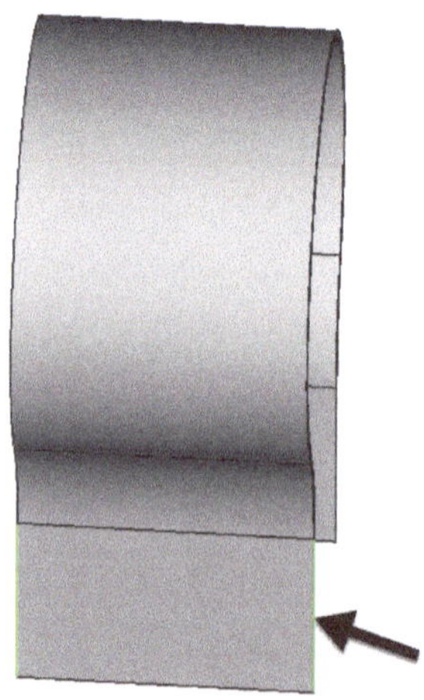

2. Click the **Make Wall**  icon on the **Sheetmetal** toolbar.
3. Click the **Model** panel.
4. Select **Bend** from the model tree.

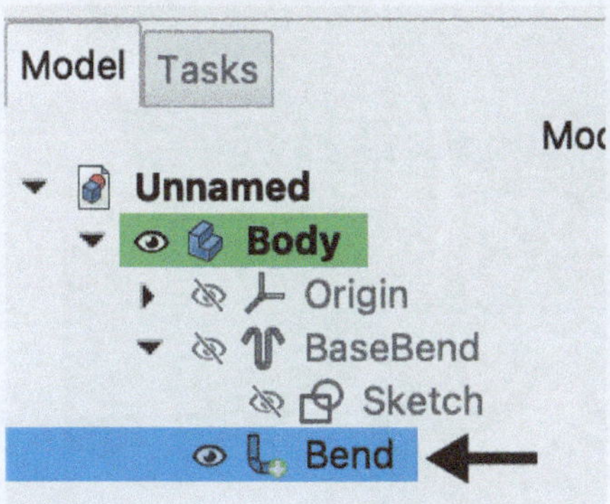

5. On the **Properties** panel, select **invert > true**.
6. Enter **18** and **2** in the **length** and **radius** boxes, respectively.
7. Select **Length Spec > Outer Sharp**.
8. Select **Bend Type > Material Outside**.
9. Select **invert > true**.

Property	Value
Label	Bend
Parameters	
Bend Type	Material Outside
Length Spec	Outer Sharp
angle	90.000 °
base Object	BaseBend [Edge14, Edge...
gap1	0.000 mm
gap2	0.000 mm
invert	true
length	18.000 mm
radius	2.000 mm

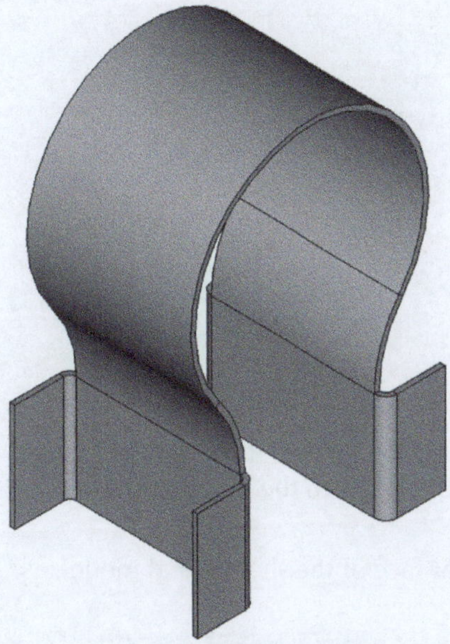

Creating Extruded Cuts

1. Select **Part Design** from the **Workbenches** drop-down.
2. Click on the flat face of the flange, as shown.

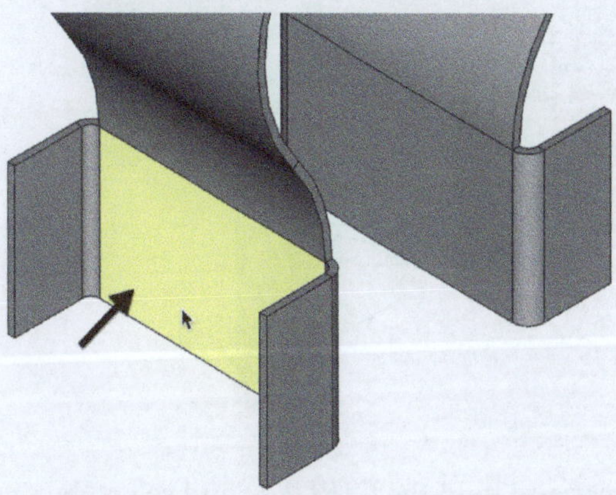

3. Click the **Create Sketch** icon on the **Sketcher** toolbar.
4. Select the **Create slot** icon from the **Sketcher geometries** toolbar.
5. Create a slot and add dimensions to it, as shown.

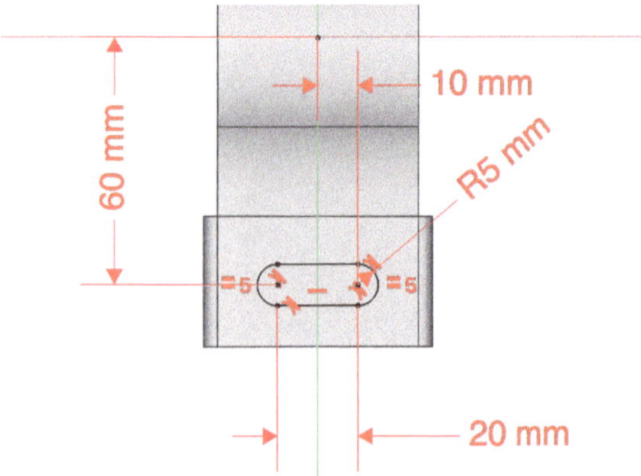

6. Click **Close** on the **Tasks** panel.
7. Select **Sheetmetal** from the **Workbenches** drop-down.
8. Select the flat face of the sheet metal model, as shown.

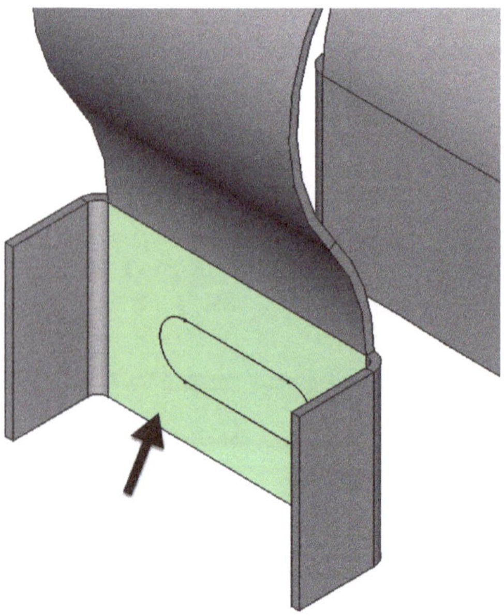

9. Press and hold the CTRL key and select the newly created sketch from the **Model** panel.

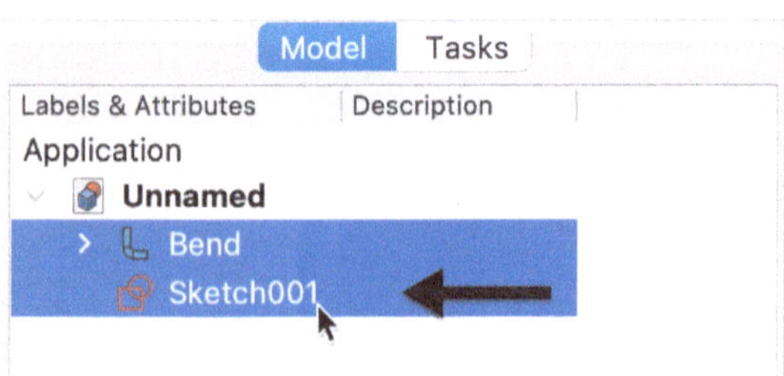

10. Click the **Sketch on Sheet Metal** icon on the **Sheetmetal** toolbar. An extruded cut is created on the flat face using the sketch.

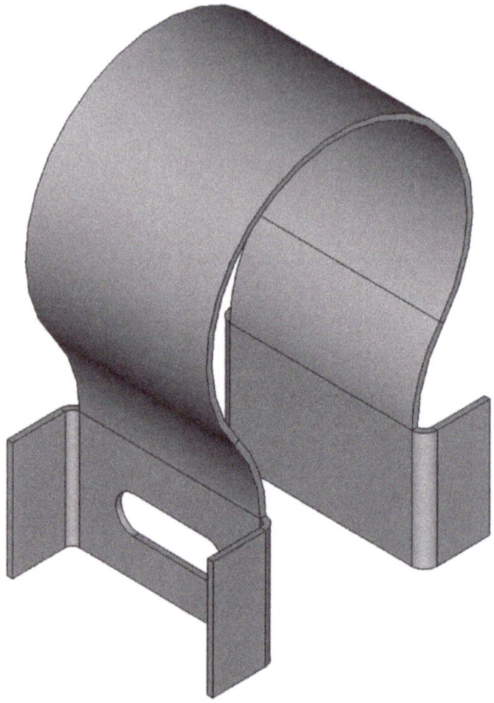

11. Likewise, create another extruded cut on the right vertical face of the sheet metal body.

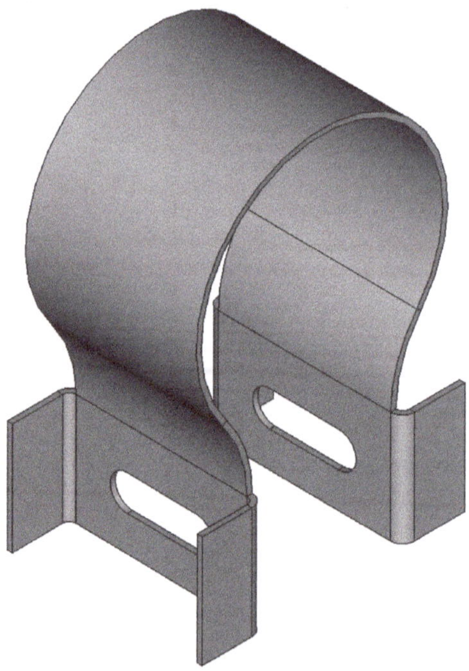

12. Save and close the sheet metal file.

TUTORIAL 4

In this tutorial, you create the sheet metal model shown in the figure.

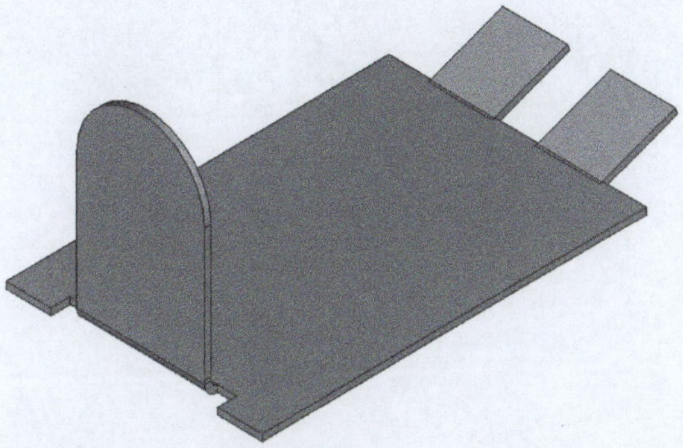

Adding Corner Reliefs

1. Start a new FreeCAD file.
2. Select **Part Design** from the **Workbenches** drop-down.
3. Click the **Create Sketch** icon on the **Sketcher** toolbar.
4. Select the XY Plane.
5. Create the sketch, as shown. Next, click **Close** on the **Tasks** panel.

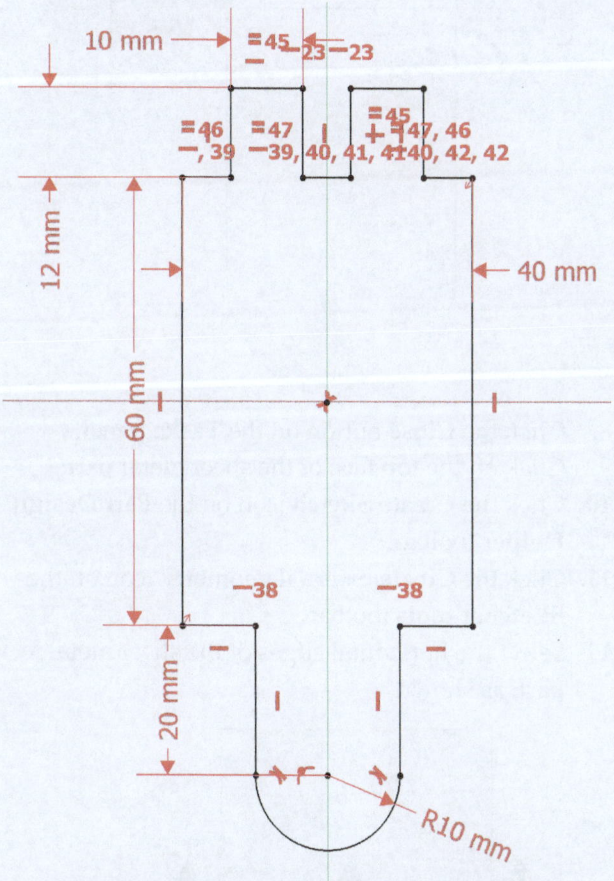

6. Select **Sheet Metal** from the **Workbenches** drop-down.
7. Click the **Make Base Wall**  icon on the **Sheetmetal** toolbar.

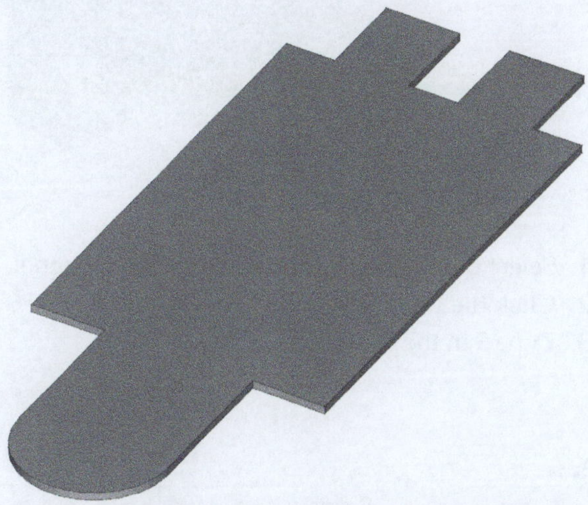

8. Click on the lower endpoint of the vertical edge, as shown.

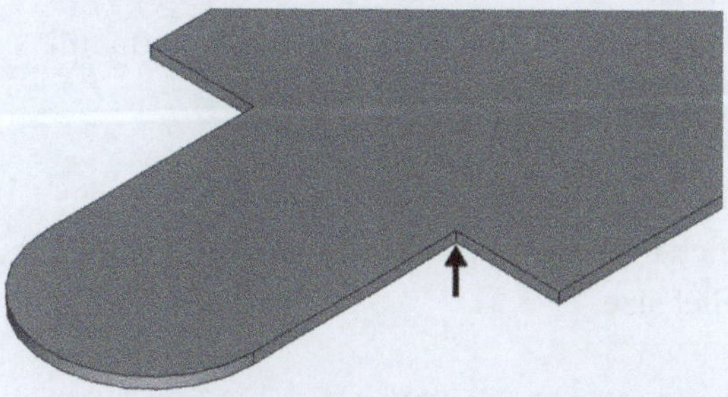

9. Press and hold the CTRL key and select the upper endpoint of the vertical edge, as shown.

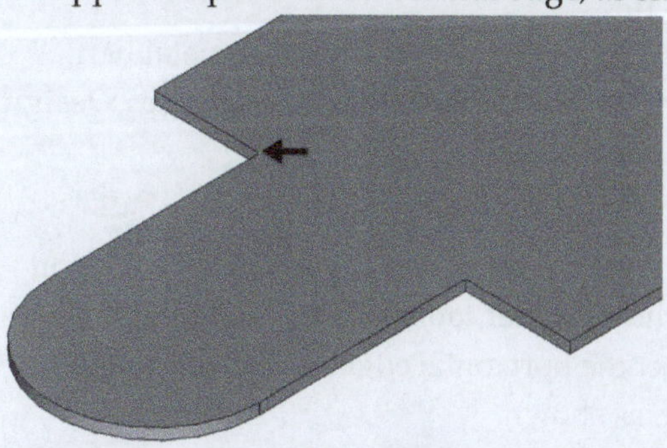

10. Click the **Make Relief** 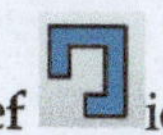 icon on the **Sheet Metal** toolbar. Reliefs are added at the selected corners.

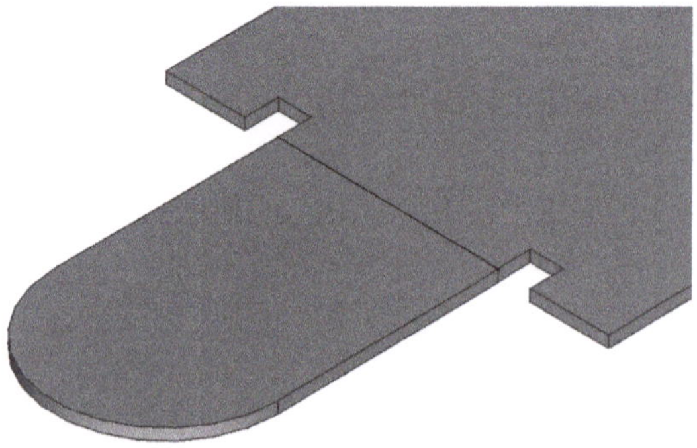

11. Select the **Relief** feature from the **Model** panel.
12. Click the **Data** tab on the **Model** panel.
13. Type **3** in the **relief** box.

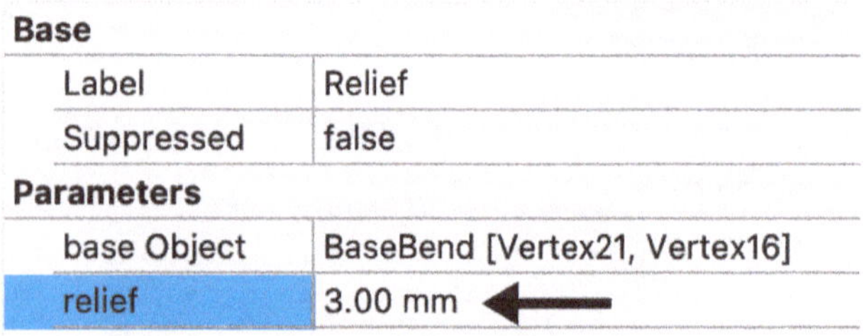

Base	
Label	Relief
Suppressed	false
Parameters	
base Object	BaseBend [Vertex21, Vertex16]
relief	3.00 mm

14. Click in the graphics window to update the relief size.

Fold a wall using a Sketch

1. Select **Part Design** from the **Workbenches** drop-down.
2. Click on the top face of the sheet metal part.
3. Click the **Create Sketch** icon on the **Part Design Helper** toolbar.
4. Click the **Create external geometry**  icon on the **Sketcher tools** toolbar.
5. Select the horizontal edges of the sheet metal part, as shown.

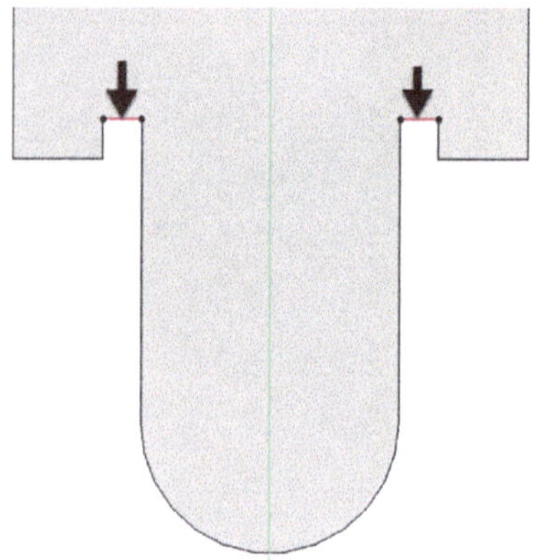

6. Click the **Create Line**  icon on the **Sketcher geometries** toolbar.
7. Select the inner endpoint of the external geometry, as shown.

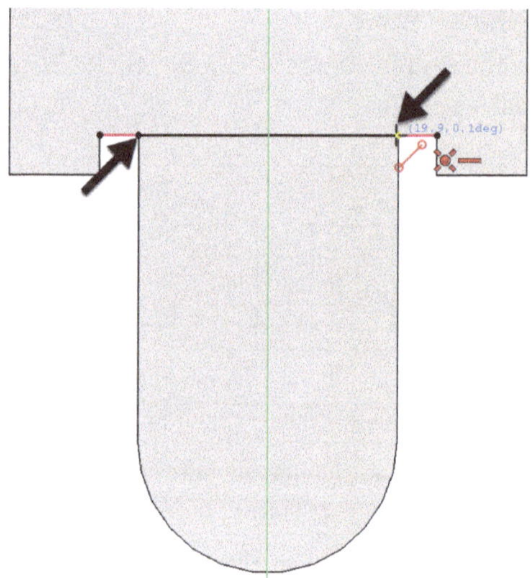

8. Click the **Close** button on the **Tasks** panel.
9. Click on the top face of the sheet metal part.
10. Click the **Create Sketch** icon on the **Part Design Helper** toolbar.
11. Click the **Create external geometry** icon on the **Sketcher tools** toolbar.
12. Select the horizontal edges of the sheet metal part, as shown.

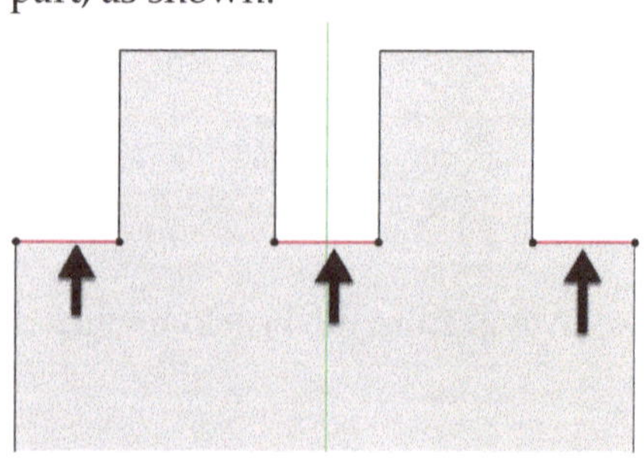

13. Click the **Create Line** icon on the **Sketcher geometries** toolbar.
14. Select the endpoints of the external geometry, as shown.

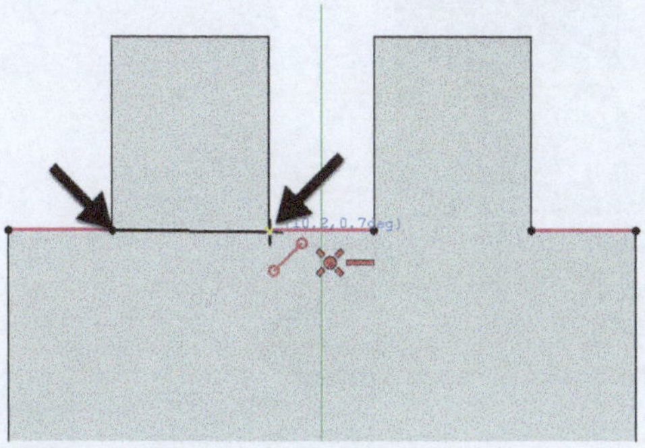

15. Likewise, create another horizontal line, as shown.

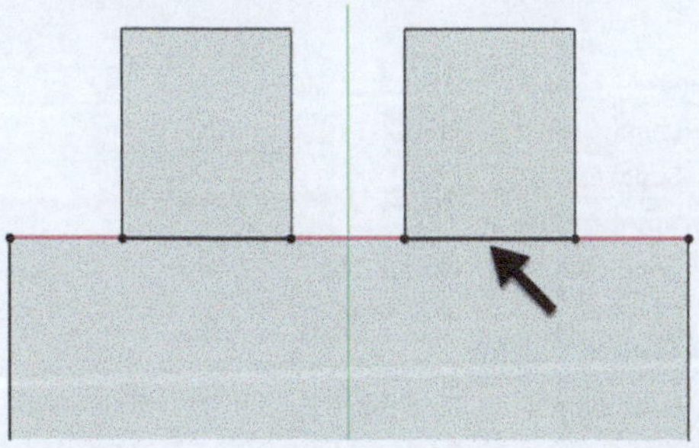

16. Select **Sheet Metal** from the **Workbenches** drop-down.
17. Press and hold the CTRL key and select the top face of the sheetmetal part and the line, as shown.

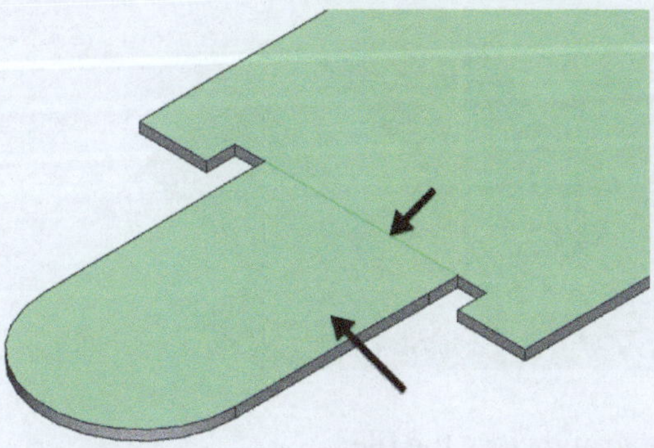

18. Click the **Fold a Wall**  icon on the **Sheet Metal** toolbar. The wall is folded, as shown.

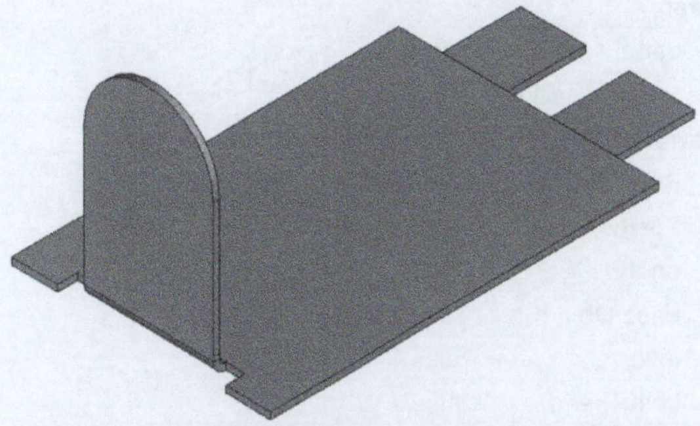

19. Press and hold the CTRL key and select the top face of the sheetmetal part and the lines, as shown.

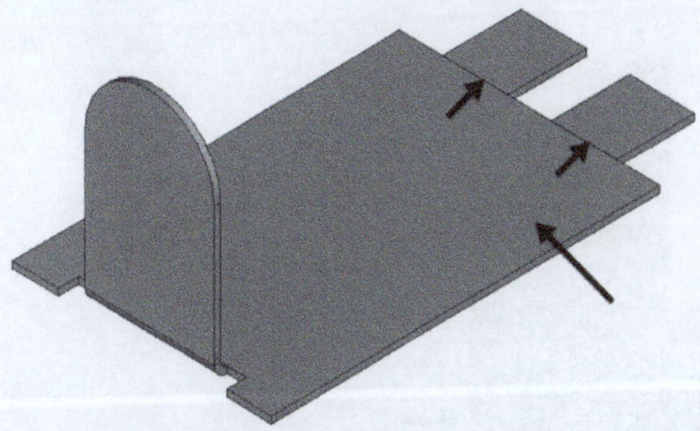

The wall is folded, as shown.

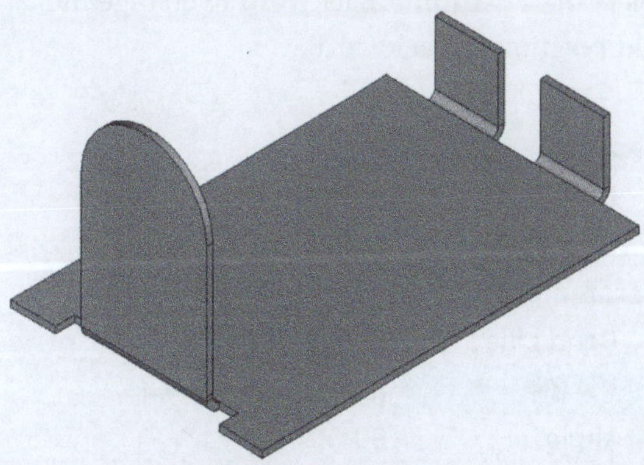

20. On the **Model** panel, select the Fold001 feature.
21. Click the **Data** tab on the bottom of the **Model** panel.
22. Select **Position > Middle**. The position of the fold is changed to middle.

Property	Value
Base	
Label	Fold001
Suppressed	false
Parameters	
Bend Line	Sketch002
Position	middle
angle	90.00 °
base Object	Fold [Face2]
invert	false
invertbend	false
kfactor	0.50
radius	1.00 mm
unfold	false

View | Data

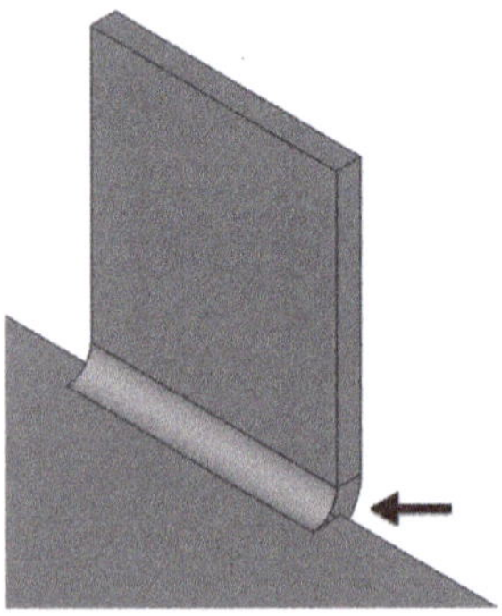

23. Select the **Position > Backward** to change the fold position to backward.

Property	Value
Base	
Label	Fold001
Suppressed	false
Parameters	
Bend Line	Sketch002
Position	backward
angle	90.00 °
base Object	Fold [Face2]
invert	false
invertbend	false
kfactor	0.50
radius	1.00 mm
unfold	false

View | Data

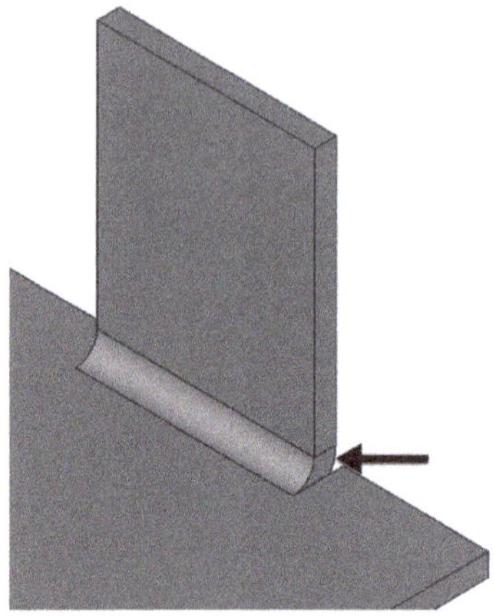

24. Type **20** in the **angle** box, and then click in the graphics window.

Property	Value
Base	
Label	Fold001
Suppressed	false
Parameters	
Bend Line	Sketch002
Position	backward
angle	20.00 °
base Object	Fold [Face2]
invert	false
invertbend	false
kfactor	0.50
radius	1.00 mm
unfold	false

View | Data

13. Save and close the file.

TUTORIAL 5

In this tutorial, you create the sheet metal model shown in the figure.

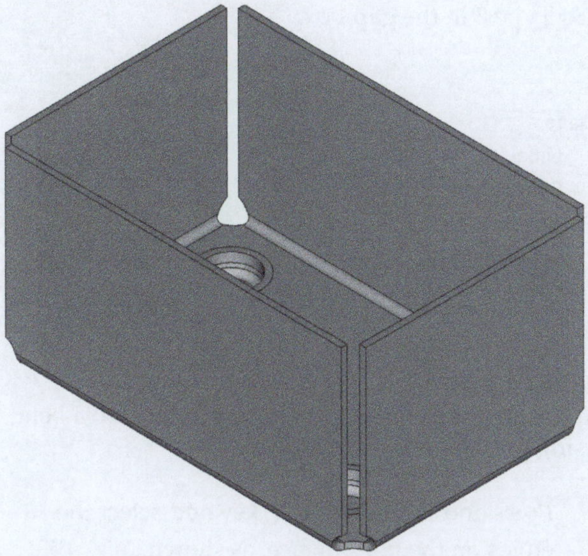

Ripping the Edges of the Model

1. Close the FreeCAD application, and then restart it.
2. Open a new FreeCAD file.
3. Select **Part Design** from the **Workbenches** drop-down.
4. Click the **Create Sketch** icon on the **Part Design Helper** toolbar.
5. Select the XY Plane from the **Tasks** panel and click **OK**.
6. Click the **Rectangle** drop-down > **Centered Rectangle** on the **Sketcher geometries** toolbar.
7. Create a closed sketch, as shown.

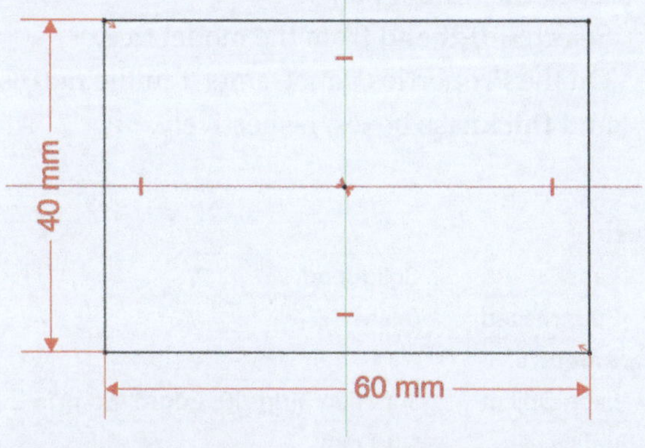

8. Click the **Close** button on the **Tasks** panel.
9. Click the **Pad**  icon on the **Part Design Modeling** toolbar.
10. Type **30** in the **Length** box.
11. Click **OK**.

12. Select the top face of the model.
13. Click the **Thickness** icon on the **Part Design Dressup** toolbar.
14. Type **1** in the **Thickness** box.
15. Select **Joint Type > Intersection**.
16. Check the **Make thickness inwards** option.
17. Click **OK**.

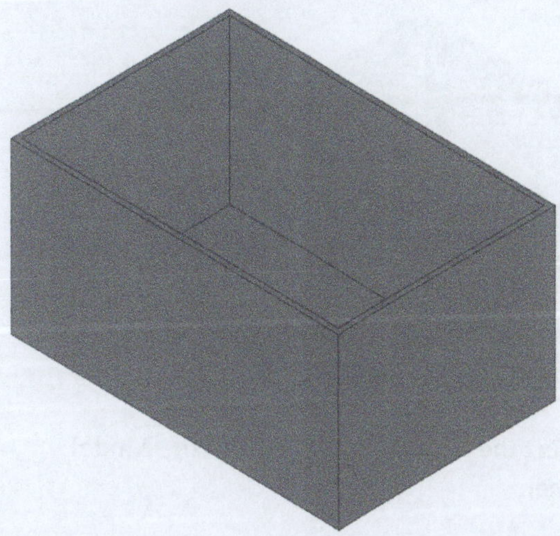

18. Select **Sheet Metal** from the **Workbenches** drop-down.
19. Press and hold the CTRL key and select the vertical edges of the model, as shown.

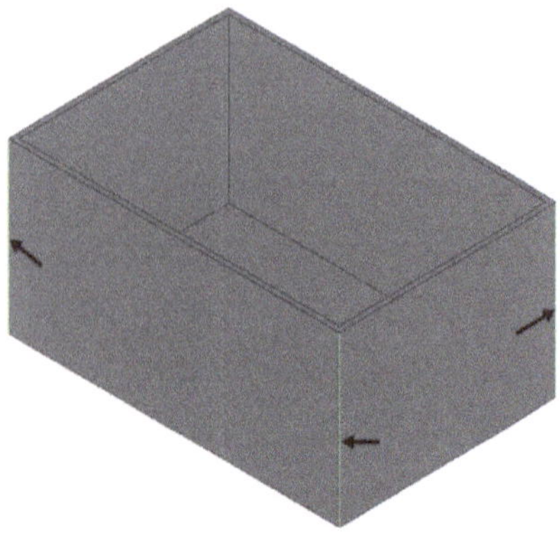

20. Click the **Make Junction** icon on the **Sheetmetal** toolbar. The selected edges are ripped opened.

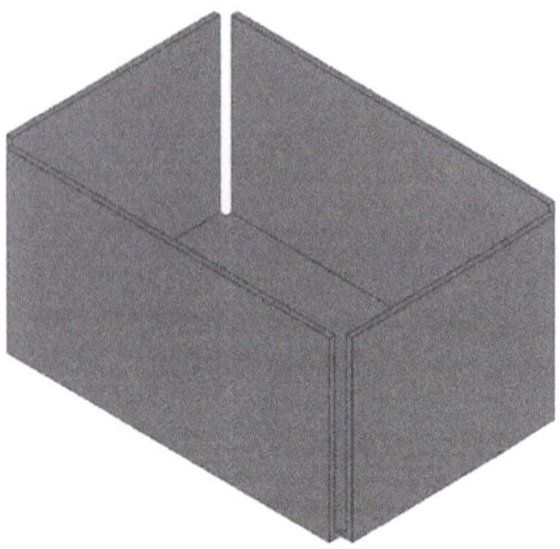

21. Select the **Junction** feature from the **Model** panel.

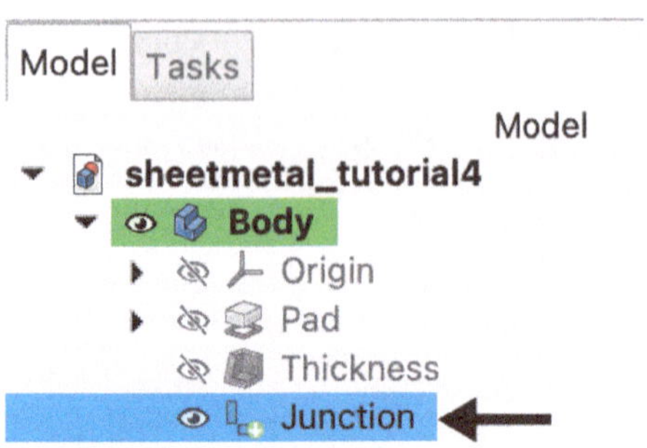

22. Click the **Data** tab at the bottom of the **Model** panel.

23. Type **2** in the **gap** box.

Base	
Label	Junction
Suppressed	false
Parameters	
base Object	Thickness [Edge5, Edge8, Edge18 ...]
gap	2.00 mm

Making Bends

In this section, you will convert an edge into a bend using the **Make Bend** command.

1. Press and hold the CTRL key and select the edges on the bottom face, as shown.

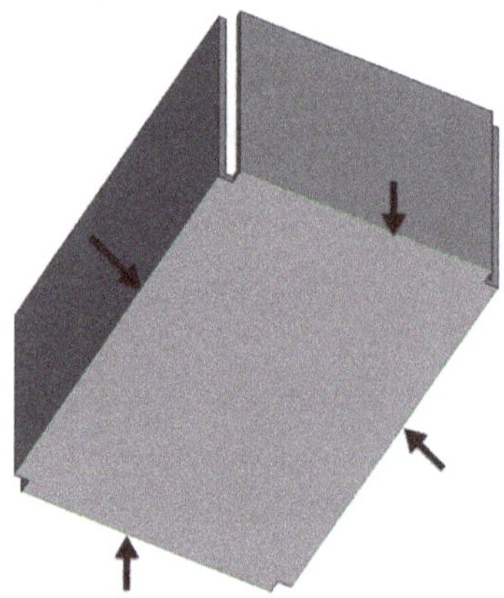

2. Click the **Make Bend** icon on the **Sheetmetal** toolbar.
3. Click the **Model** panel.
4. Select **Solidbend** from the model tree.
5. On the **Properties** panel, enter **1** in the **radius** and **thickness** boxes, respectively.

Base	
Label	SolidBend
Suppressed	false
Parameters	
base Object	Junction [Edge10, Edge1, Edge15 ...]
radius	1.00 mm
thickness	1.00 mm

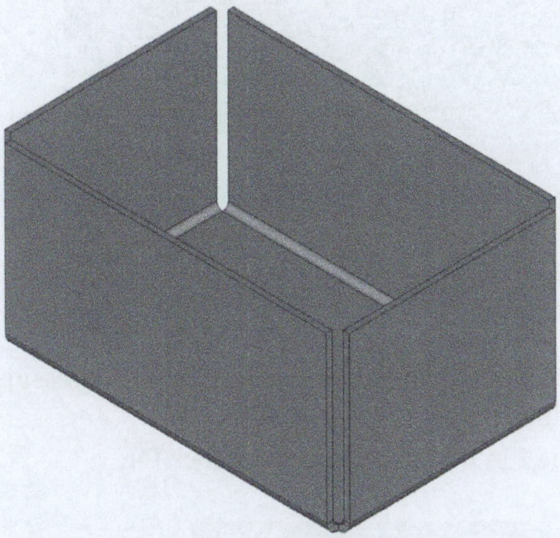

Adding Corner Relief

In this section, you will add corner reliefs to the bends. You add corner reliefs to the model to prevent deformation when the sheetmetal model is folded or unfolded.

1. Press and hold the CTRL key and select the intersecting edges of the bends, as shown.

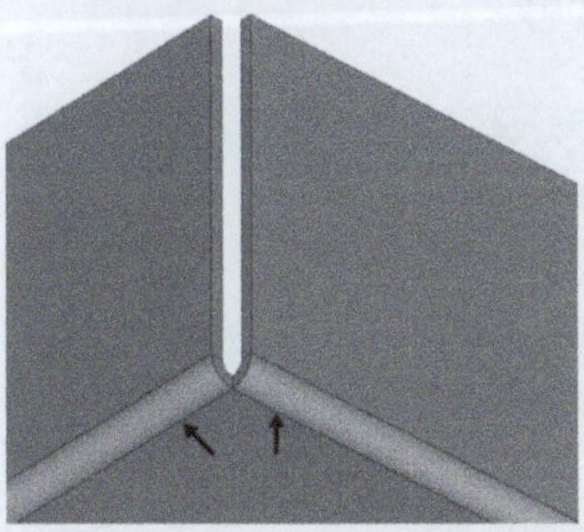

2. Click the **Add Corner relief** icon on the **Sheetmetal** toolbar.
3. Select **CornerRelief** from the **Model** panel.

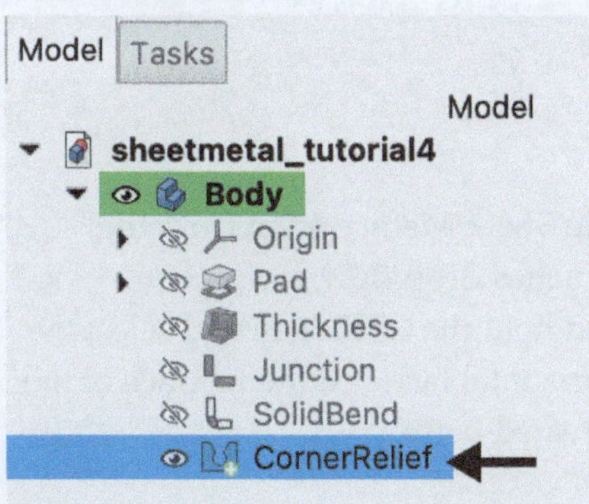

4. Select **Relief Sketch > Circle.**

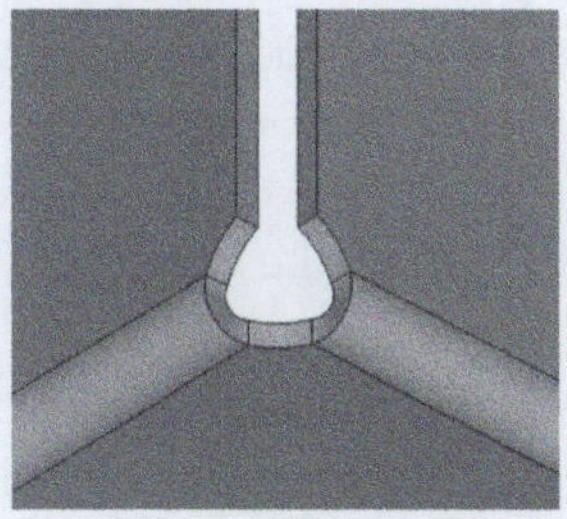

You can also select the **Circle-Scaled**, **Square**, **Square-Scaled**, or **Sketch** from the **Relief Sketch** drop-down.

Circle-Scaled

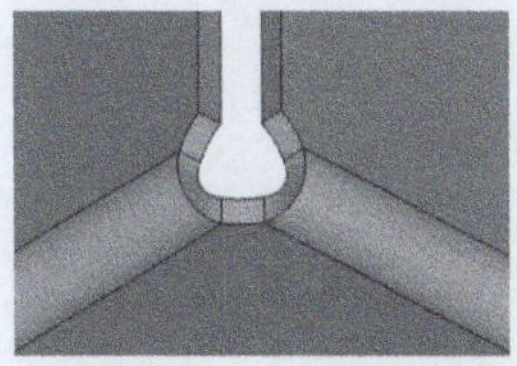

Square

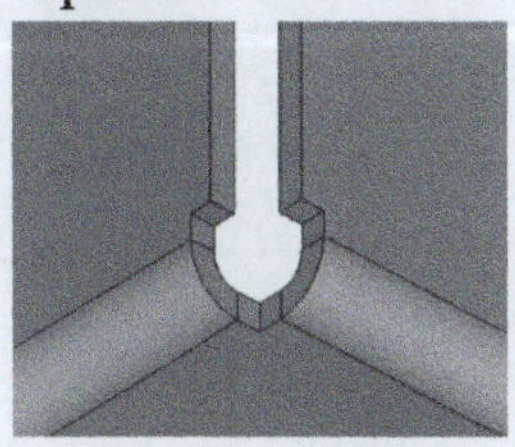

Square-Scaled

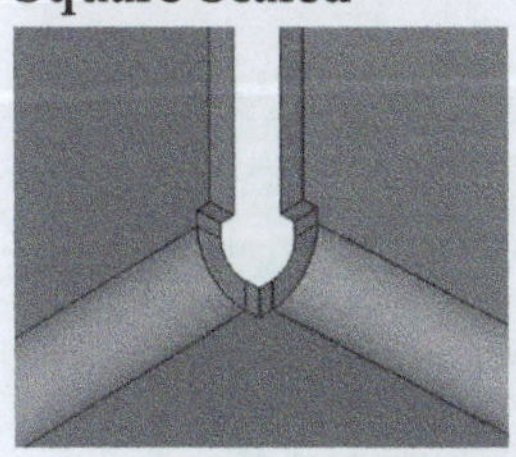

5. Likewise, add reliefs to other corners, as shown.

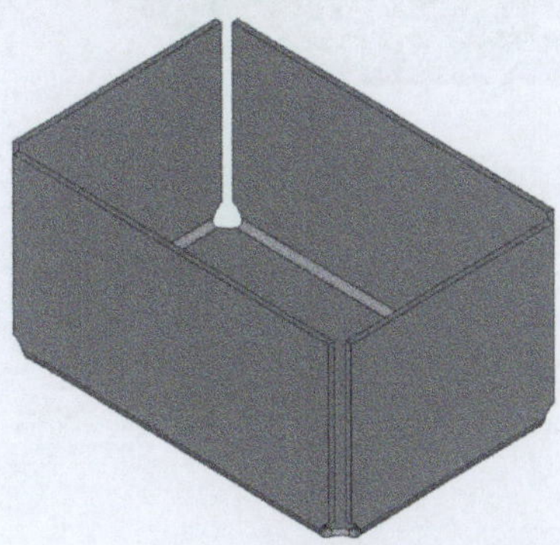

Making a Forming in Wall

1. Select the **Part Design** option from the **Workbenches** drop-down.
2. Click the **Create Body**  icon on the **Part Design Helper** toolbar.
3. Click the **Create Sketch** icon on the **Part Design Helper** toolbar.
4. Select the **XY_Plane** and click **OK**.
5. Click **Sketch > View Section** on the menu bar.
6. Create a sketch, as shown.

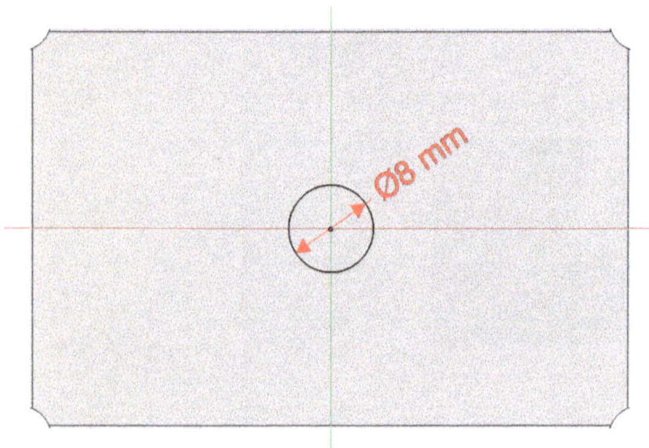

7. Click **Close** on the **Tasks** panel.
8. Click the **Pad** icon on the **Part Design Modeling** toolbar.
9. Select **Type > Two dimensions**.
10. Type **1.5** and **8** in the **Length** and **Taper angle** boxes, respectively.
11. Type **1.5** in the 2nd **Length** box and click **OK**.

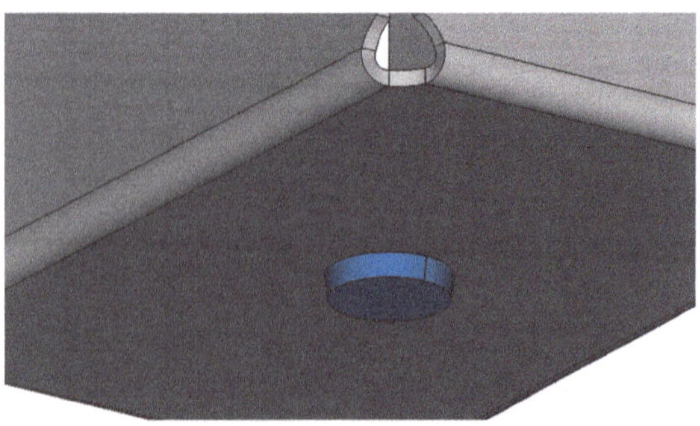

12. Click on the circular edge of the pad feature, as shown.

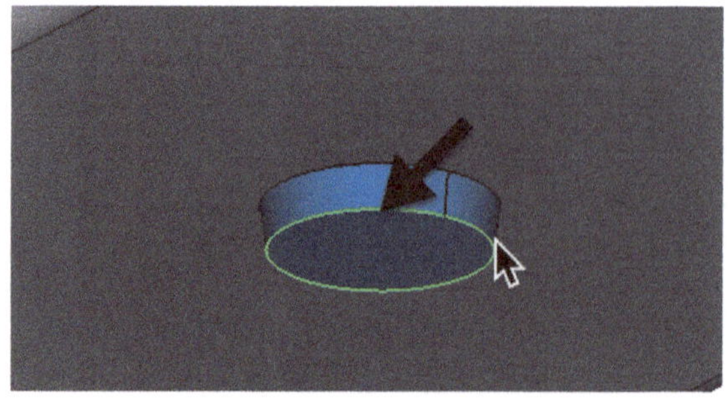

13. Click the **Fillet** icon on the **Part Design Dressup** toolbar.
14. Type **1** in the **Radius** box and click **OK**.

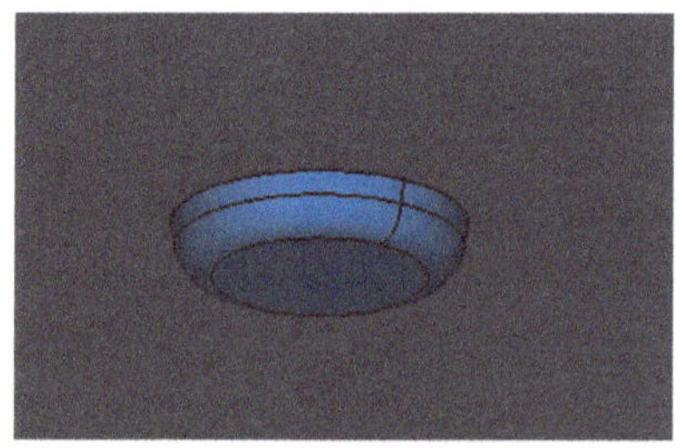

15. In the **Model** panel, right-click on the first **Body** and select **Active body**.

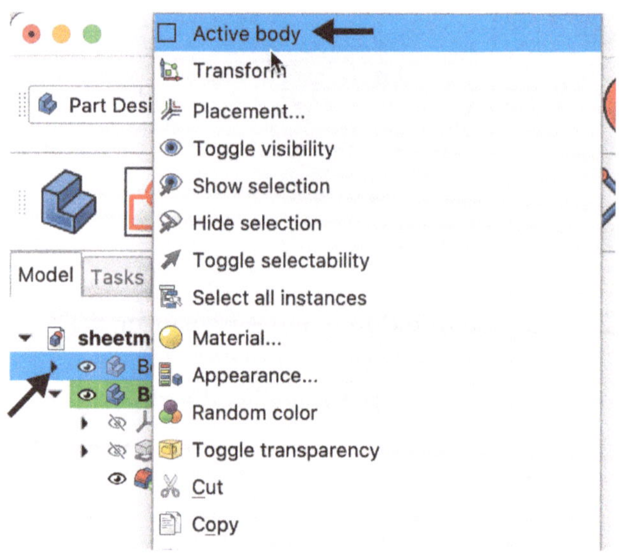

16. Select the **Sheet Metal** option from the **Workbenches** drop-down.
17. Press and hold the CTRL key and select the inner horizontal face and the top face of the newly created body.

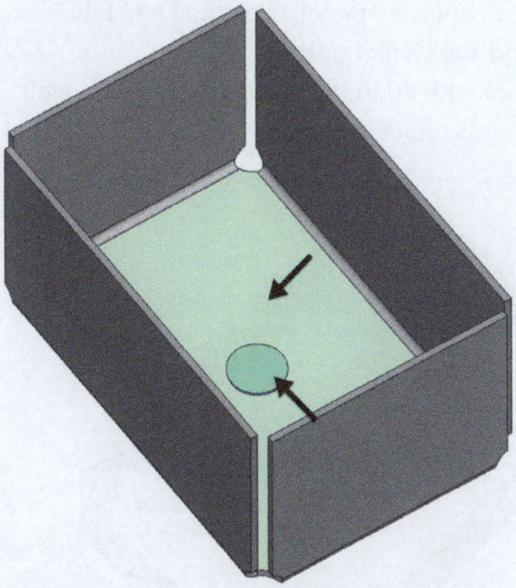

18. Click the **Make Forming in Wall** icon on the **Sheet Metal** toolbar. The forming is created in the wall.

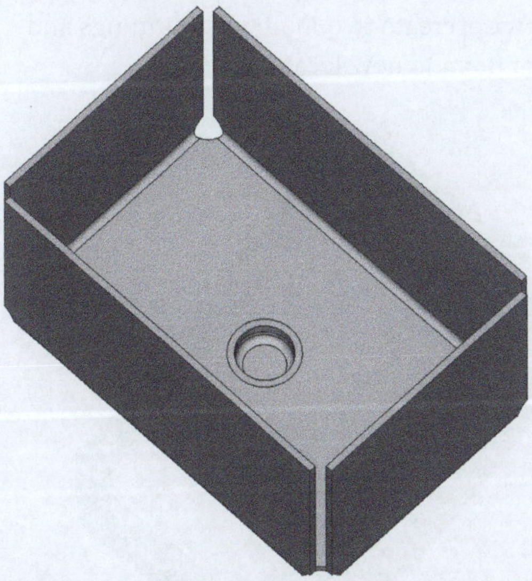

19. In the **Model** panel, select the **WallForming** feature.
20. In the **Properties** panel, expand the **Offset** option.

Property	Value
Base	
Label	WallForming
Parameters	
Suppress Feat...	false
angle	0.000 °
base Object	CornerRelief003 [Face21]
offset	[0.000 mm 0.000 mm 0.000...
thickness	1.000 mm
tool Object	Fillet [Face5]
Parameters1	

21. Type **20** and **10** in the **x** and **y** boxes.

Property	Value
Base	
Label	WallForming
Parameters	
Suppress Feat...	false
angle	0.000 °
base Object	CornerRelief003 [Face21]
offset	[20.000 mm 10.000 mm 0.0...
x	20.000 mm
y	10.000 mm
z	0.000 mm
thickness	1.000 mm
tool Object	Fillet [Face5]
Parameters1	
Sketch	

The wallforming feature is offset along the x and y coordinates, as shown.

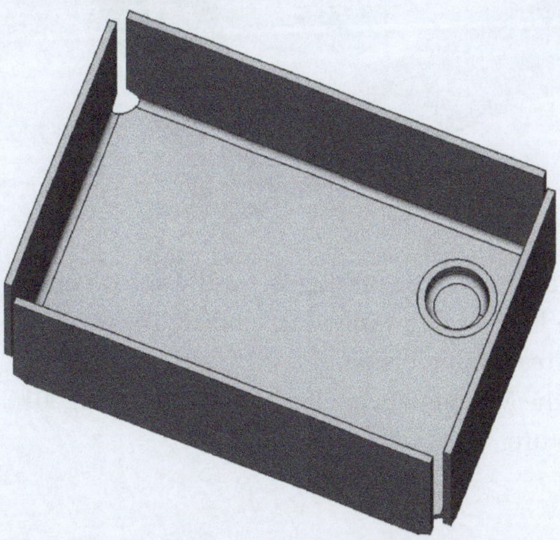

22. In the **Model** panel, expand the **Body001** node, and then select the **Fillet** feature.

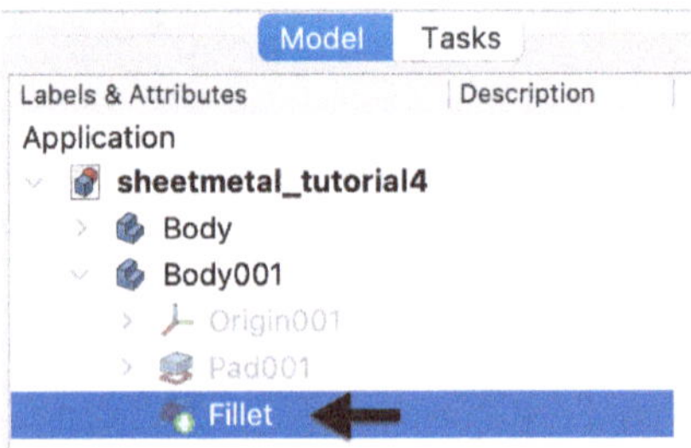

23. Click the **View** tab and select **Visibility > true**.

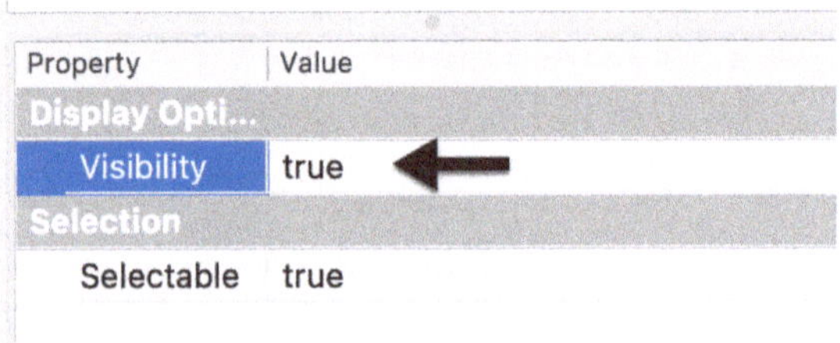

24. In the **Model** panel, right-click on the first **Body** and select **Toggle active body**.
25. Select the **Sheet Metal** option from the **Workbenches** drop-down.
26. Press and hold the CTRL key and select the inner horizontal face and the top face of **Body001**.

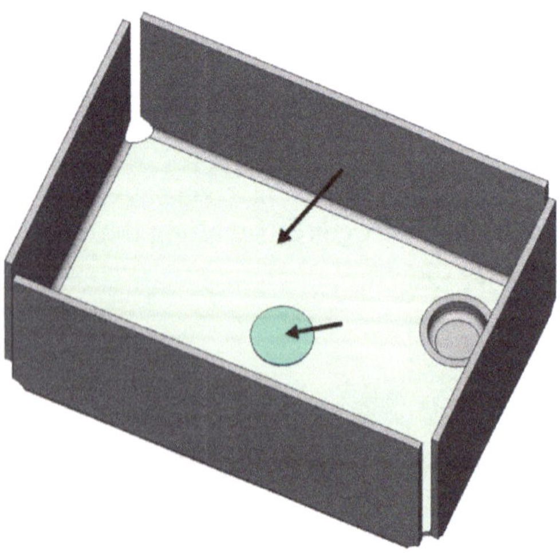

27. Click the **Make Forming in Wall**  icon on the **Part Design Modeling** toolbar. The forming is created in the wall.
28. In the **Model** panel, select the **WallForming001** feature.
29. In the **Properties** panel, click the **Data** tab.
30. Expand the **Offset** option.
31. Type **20** and **-10** in the **x** and **y** boxes. The wall forming is offset to the new location.

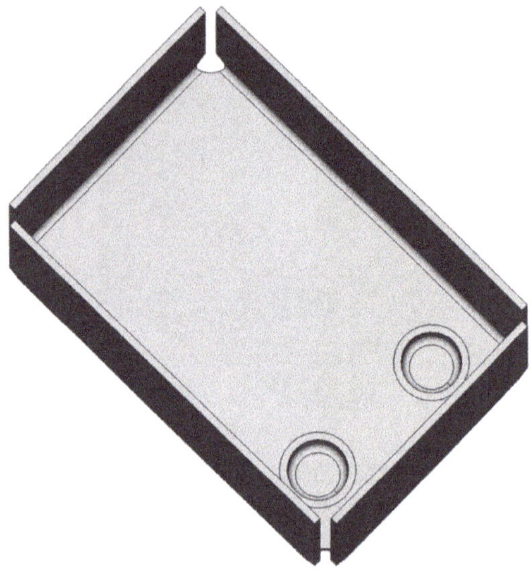

32. Likewise, create two more wall formings and offset them to new locations.

14. Save and close the file.

Chapter 8: CAM Overview

TUTORIAL 1

In this tutorial, you generate paths for the machining operations of the part shown in the figure below.

1. Start the FreeCAD 1.0 application.
2. Download the Tutorial 1-part file of Chapter 12, and open it.
3. Select **CAM** from the **Workbenches** drop-down.

4. Click **Edit > Preferences** on the menu bar. If you are working on MacOS, then click **FreeCAD > Preferences** on the title bar. This will open the **Preferences** dialog box, where you can customize various settings for your FreeCAD workspace.
5. Click the **General** > **General** on the left side of the **Preferences** dialog.
6. Select **Default Unit system > Metric small parts and CNC (mm, mm/min)**.
7. Check the **Ignore project unit system and use default** option.
8. Click **OK**.

Creating the Job

1. Click the **Job** icon on the **Project Setup** toolbar.

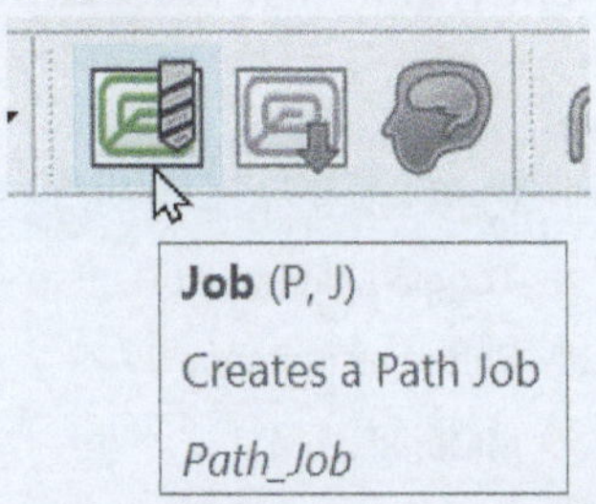

2. On the **Create Job** dialog, select the checkbox next to the Body.

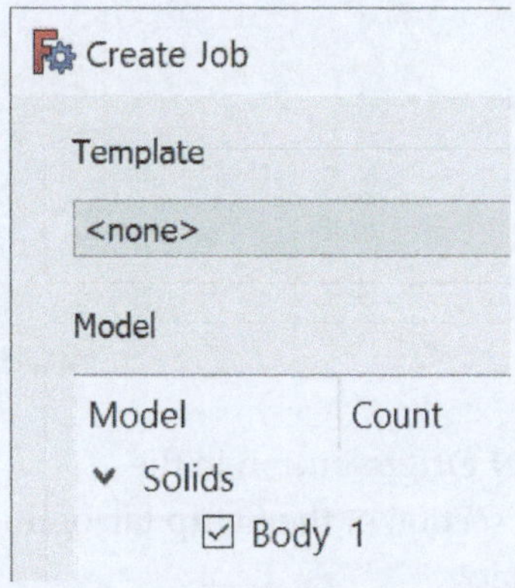

3. Click **OK**.
4. On the **Job Edit** dialog, click the **Setup** tab.
5. Select **Extend Model's Bound Box** from the drop-down located at the top.
6. Type **5** in the **Ext. X** and **Ext. Y** boxes.
7. Type **50** and **2** in the first and second **Ext. Z** boxes, respectively.

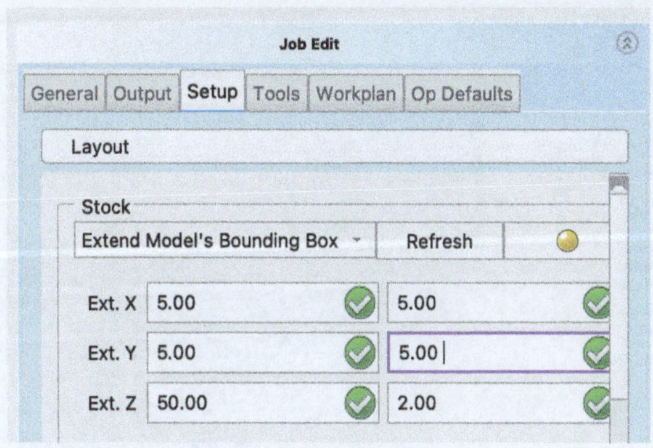

8. Click on the top-left corner of the bounding box.

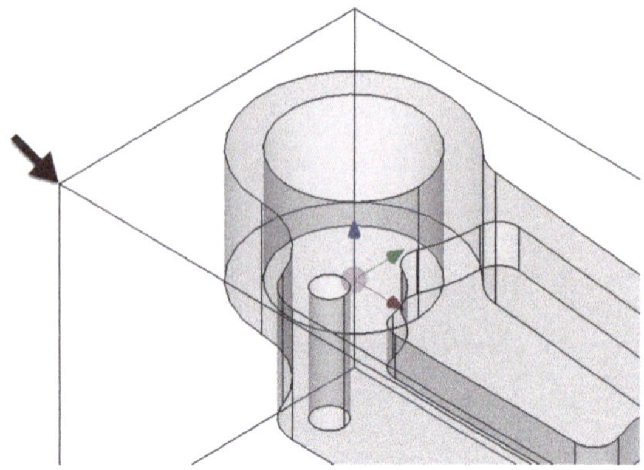

9. Click the **Set Origin** button in the **Alignment** section of the **Setup** tab of the **Job Edit** dialog.

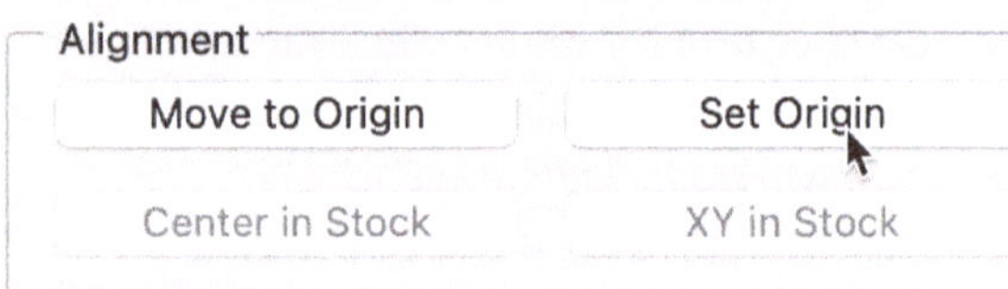

The origin is moved to the selected location, as shown.

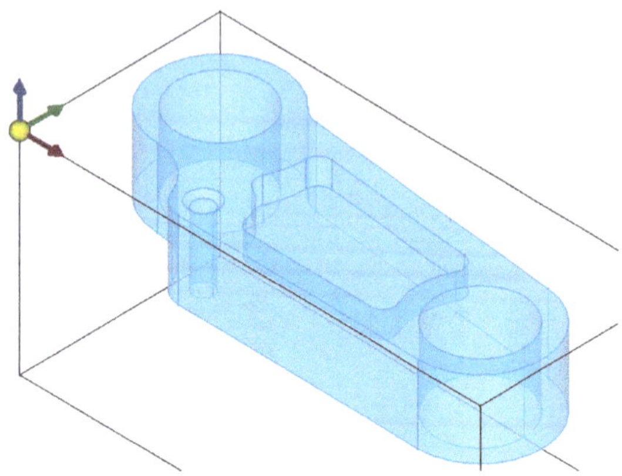

10. Click the **Output** tab on the **Job Edit** dialog.
11. Select **linuxcnc** from the **Processor** drop-down.
12. Type **Tutorial1.ngc** in the **Output file** box.
13. Click **OK**.

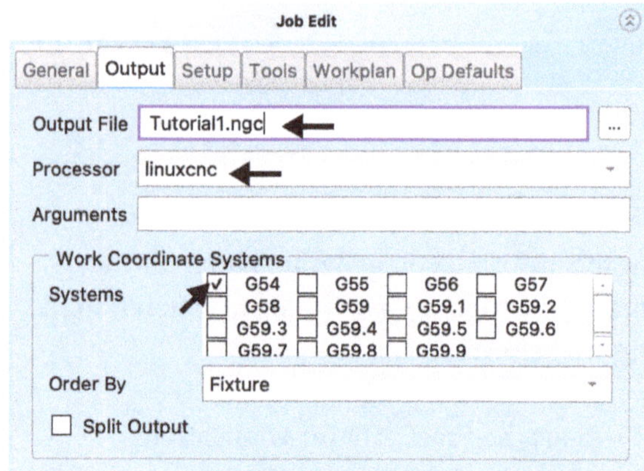

14. In the **Model** panel, go to **Job > Model**.
15. Press and hold the Ctrl key and select **Stock** and **Model-Body**.
16. Right-click and select **Show selection**.

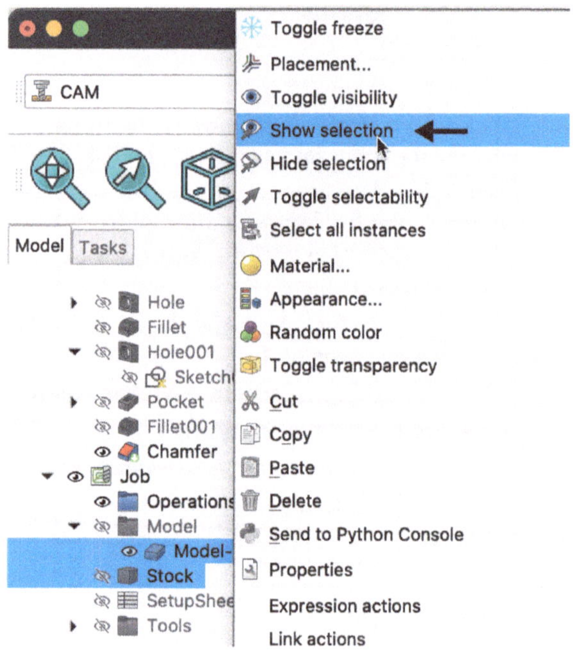

17. Right click on **Body**, and then select **Hide selection**.

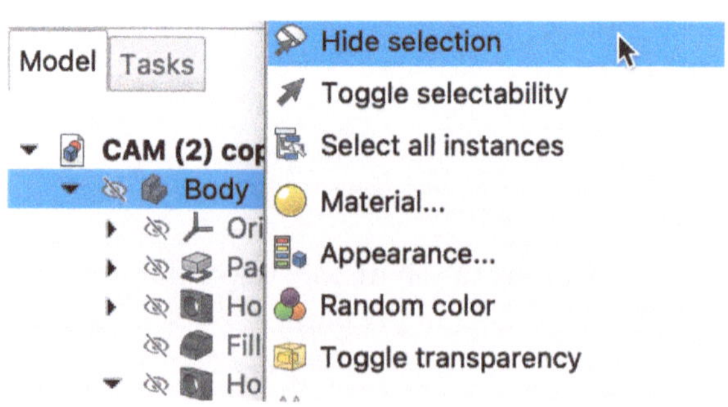

Adding Tools to the Job

Follow the steps given next to add tools in Windows version of FreeCAD 1.0.

1. Click the **ToolBit Dock** icon on the **Tool Commands** toolbar.

2. Click **Yes** on the message box showing **"Toolbit working directory is not set up. Do that now?"**.
3. Browse to the desired location click **Select Folder** button.
4. Click the **Library editor** button on the Tool Selector.

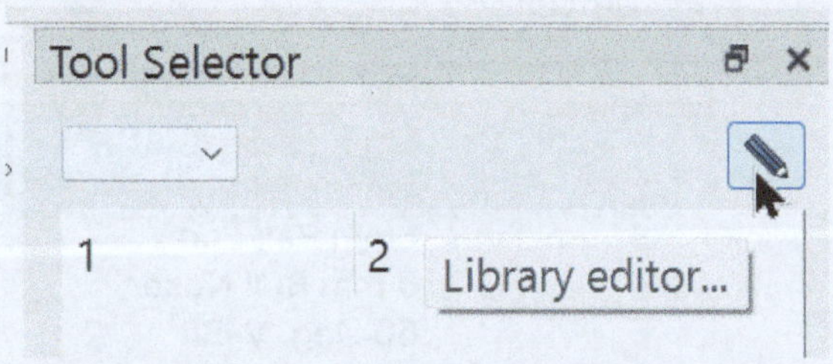

5. Click **Create Toolbit** on the **Library editor** dialog.
6. Click the **Endmill** button on the **Select a Tool Shape** dialog.
7. Click **Open**.
8. On the **Tool** dialog, type **End Mill 5 mm** in the **Name** box.
9. Click **Save**.
10. Double-click on the **End Mill 5 mm** tool available on the tool table on the **Library editor** dialog.
11. Click the **Attributes** tab.
12. Select **Material > Carbide**.
13. Type **4** in the **Flutes** box.

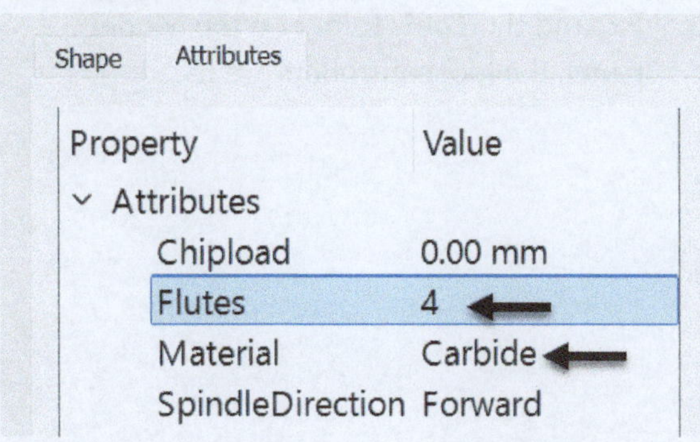

14. Click the **Shape** tab.
15. Type **5** and **30** in the **Diameter** and **Cutting Edge Height** boxes, respectively.
16. Type **6** in the **Shank diameter** box.
17. Type **55** in the **Length** box.
18. Click **OK**.

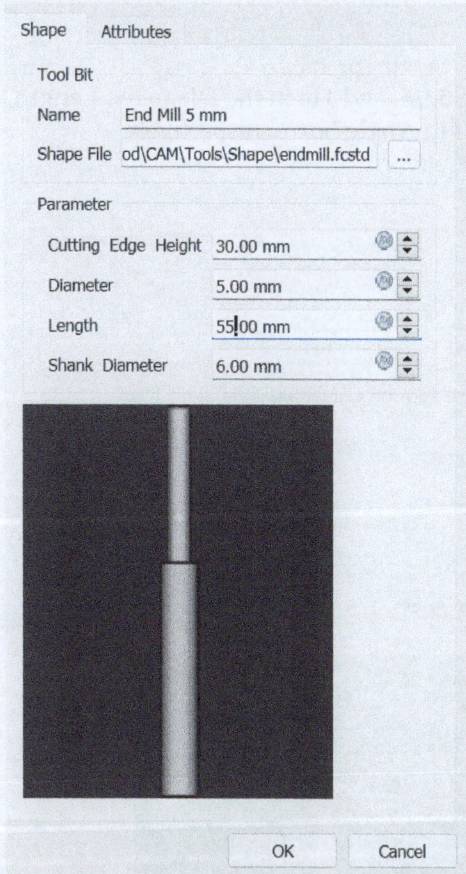

19. Click **Create Toolbit** on the **Library editor** dialog.
20. Click the **Drill** button on the **Select a Tool Shape** dialog.
21. Click **Open**.
22. On the **Tool** dialog, type **Drill 5 mm** in the **Name** box.
23. Click **Save**.
24. Double-click on the **Drill 5 mm** tool available on the tool table on the **Library editor** dialog.
25. Click the **Attributes** tab.
26. Select the **Material > Carbide**.
27. Type **2** in the **Flutes** box.

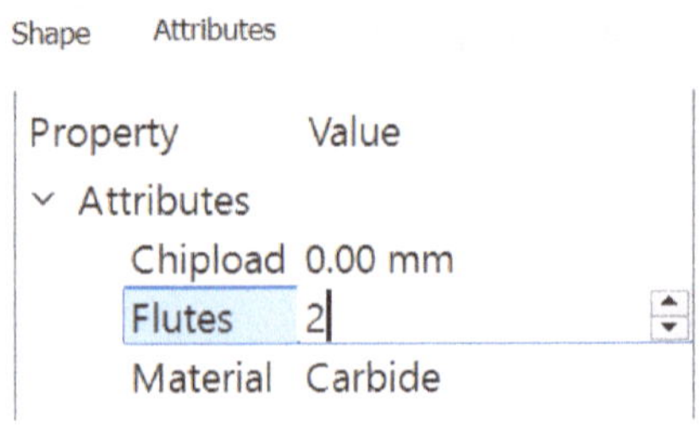

28. Click the **Shape** tab.
29. Type **5**, **15**, and **118** in the **Diameter**, **Length**, and **Tip Angle** boxes, respectively.
30. Click **OK**.

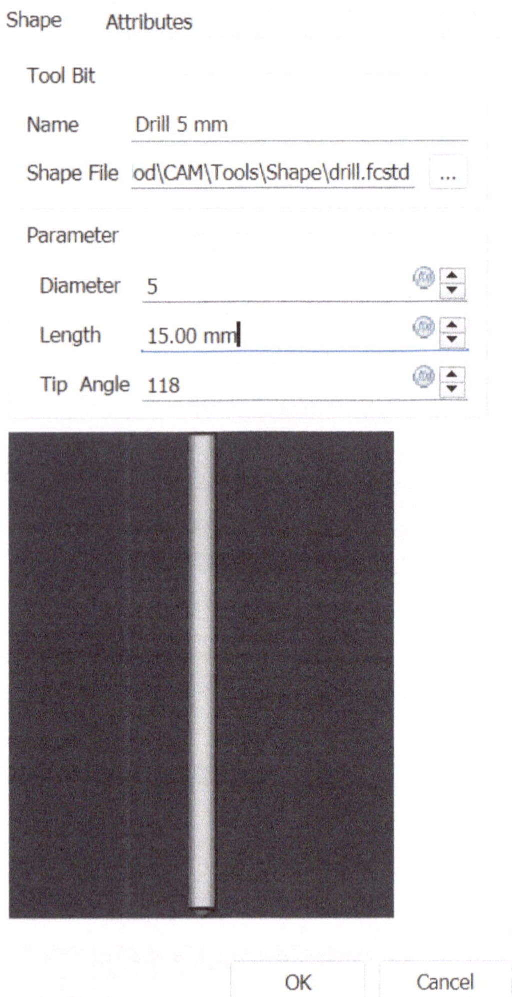

31. Click the **Save**  button on the **Library Editor** dialog.
32. Type **Tutorial Library** in the **File name** box.
33. Click **Close**.
34. On the **Tool Select** panel, select the **Tutorial Library** table from the drop-down.
35. Select the two newly created tools and click the **Add to Job** button to add the tools to the job.

Follow the steps given next to add tools to the Job in the Mac version of the FreeCAD 1.0.1.

1. Click the **ToolBit Dock**  icon on the **Tool Commands** toolbar.
2. Select **Default** from the drop-down located on the **Tool Selector**.
3. Press and hold the CTRL key and select the End Mill 5 mm and 5 mm Drill tools from the Tool Selector.

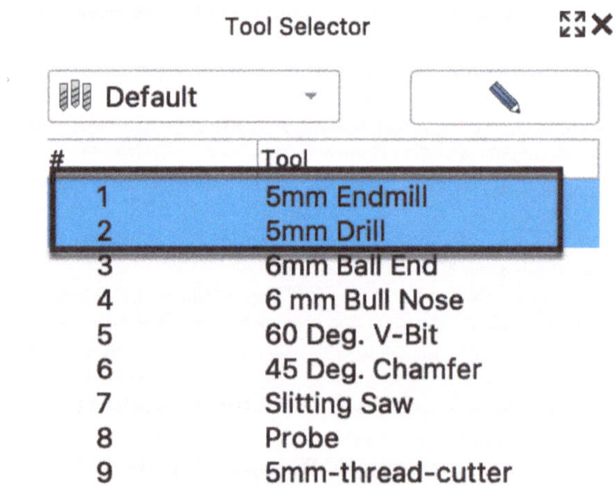

4. Click the **Add to Job** button located at the bottom of the Tool Selector.

5. Expand the **Tools** folder on the **Model** panel; the tool controllers are listed.

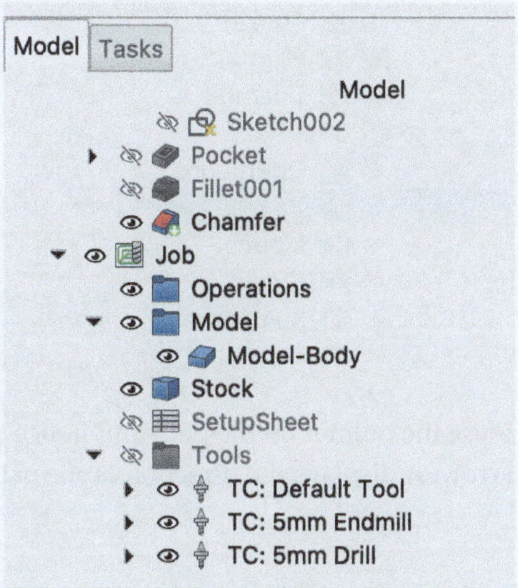

Creating the Facing Operation

1. Click the **Face** icon on the **New Operations** toolbar.

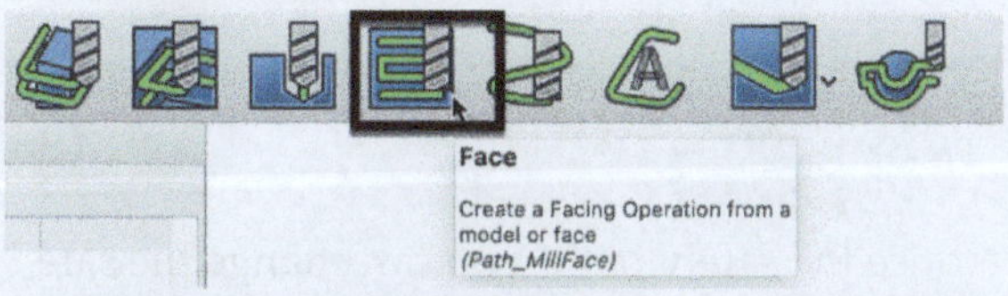

2. Select the **Endmill 5mm** tool controller from the **Tool controller** drop-down. Click **OK**.

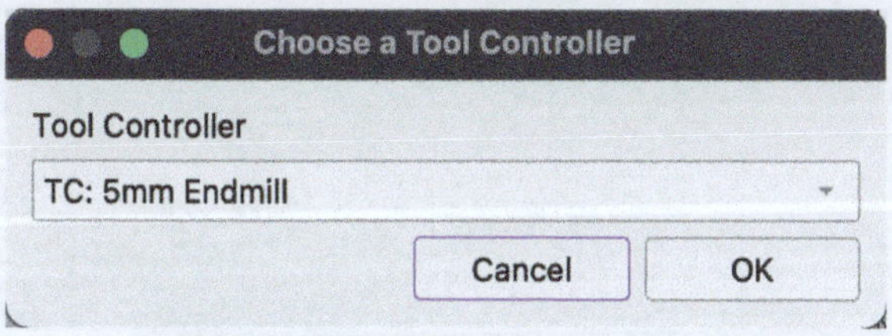

3. Expand the **Base Geometry** section on the **MillFace** dialog.
4. Select the top face of the model.

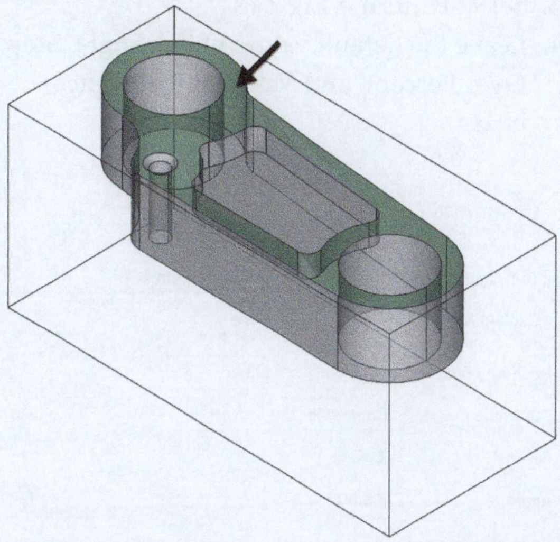

5. Click the **Add** button in the **Base Geometry** section.
6. Expand the **Depths** section on the **MillFace** dialog. Notice that the **Final Depth** value is calculated automatically.
7. Click the **Formula** icon next to the **Step Down** box.

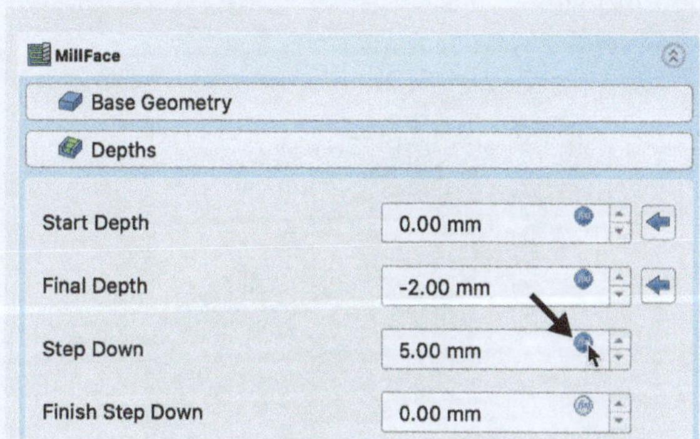

8. Type **1** in the **Expression editor** dialog.

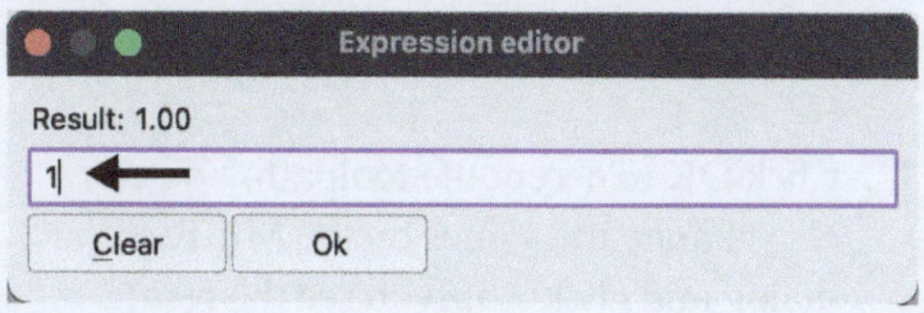

9. Click **OK**.
10. Expand the **Operation** section on the **MillFace** dialog.
11. Select **Boundary Shape > Stock**.
12. Select **Cut Mode > Conventional**.

13. Select **Pattern > Zig Zag**.
14. Leave the default values in the **Angle**, **Step Over Percent**, and **Material Allowance** boxes.

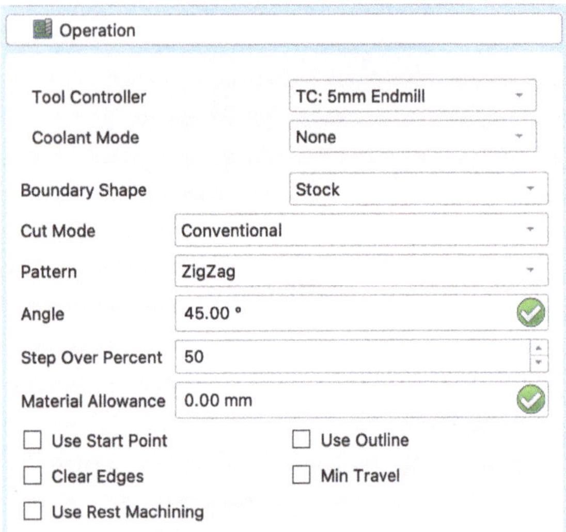

15. Click the **Apply** button located at the top of the **Tasks** tab; the preview of the toolpath appears.

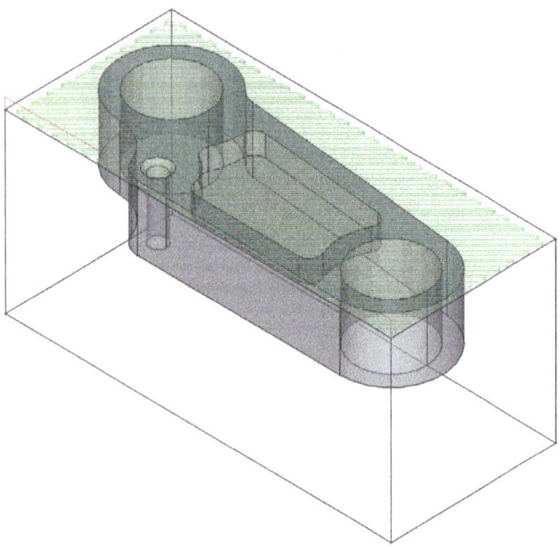

16. Click **OK** to accept the toolpath. You can also change the values on the **MillFace** dialog and click **Apply** to see the result.
17. Expand the **Operations** node in the **Model** tab of the **Model** panel; the **MillFace** operation is listed.

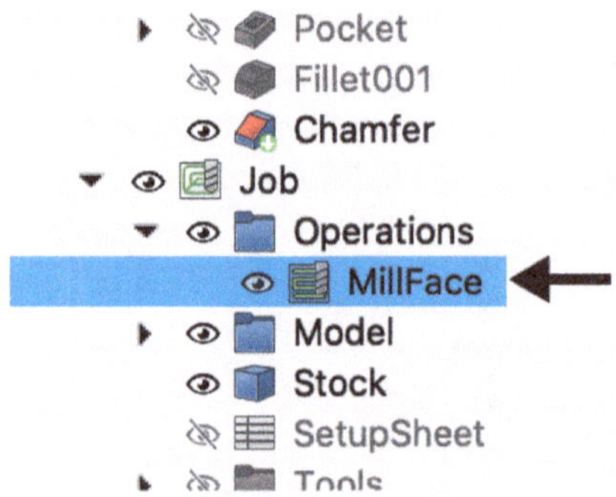

18. Place the pointer on the path and notice that arrow. It displays the direction of the path.

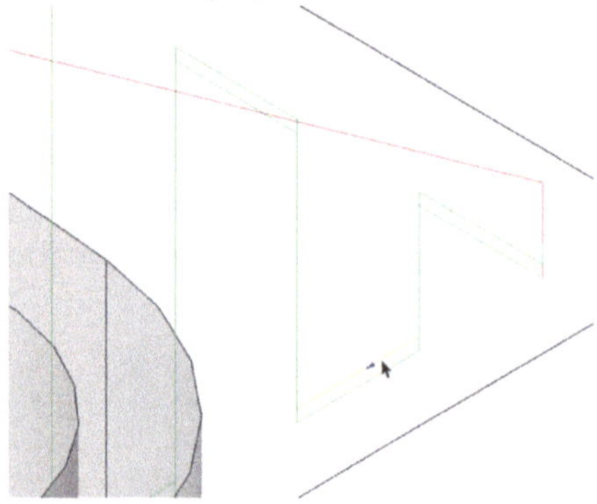

Notice the safety path. You can change the safe height and clearance using the **SetupSheet**.

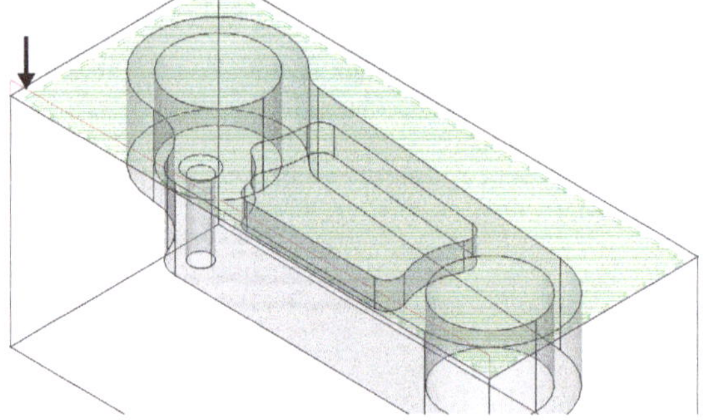

19. Select **SetupSheet** under the Job node in the **Model** tab.

You can change the **Clearance Height Offset** and **Safe Height Offset** values in the **Properties** panel.

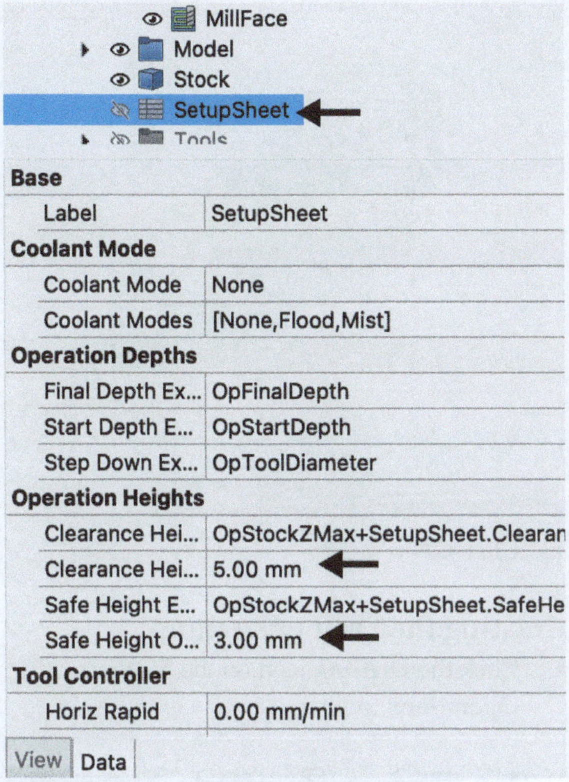

You can also define the feed of the tool.

20. Double-click on **Endmill 5mm** tool controller under the **Job** node.

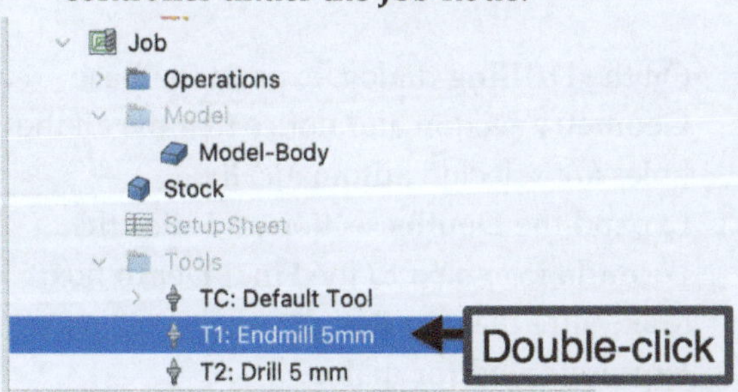

21. Type **200**, **60**, and **10000** in the **Horiz. Feed**, **Vert. Feed** and **Spindle** boxes, respectively.

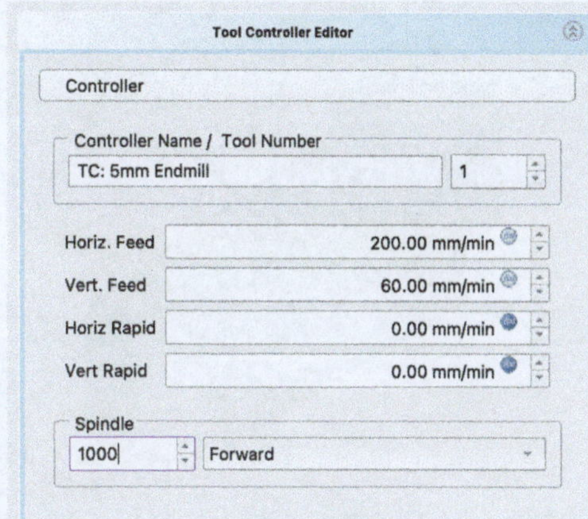

22. Click **OK**.
23. Select the **MillFace** operation from the **Model** tab.

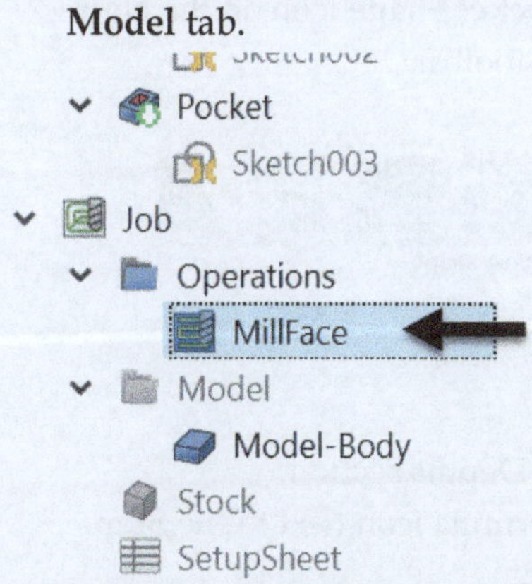

24. Click the **Toggle the Active State of the Operation** icon on the **Tool Commands** toolbar.

The MillFace path is hidden.

Creating the Pocket Operation

1. Select the flat face of the pocket, as shown.

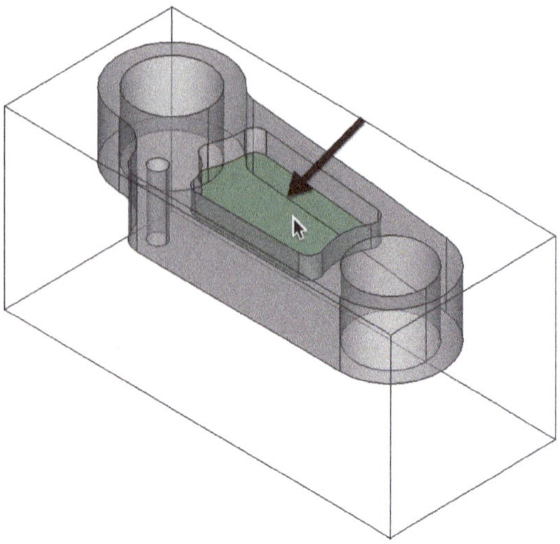

2. Click the **Pocket Shape** icon on the **New Operations** toolbar.

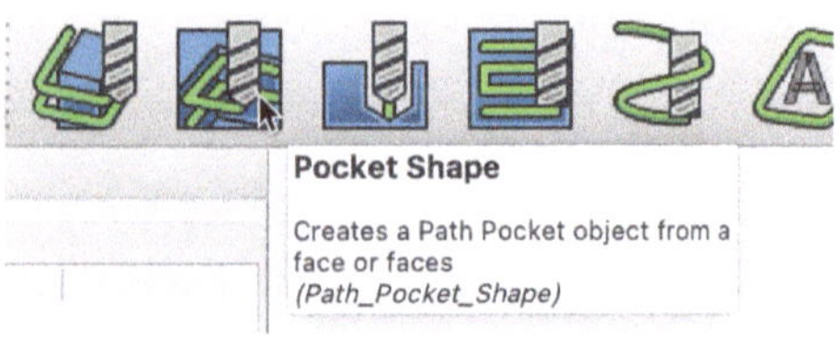

3. Expand the **Depths** section.
4. Click the **Formula** icon next to the **Step Down** box.
5. Type **1** in the **Expression editor** dialog, and then click **OK**.
6. Expand the **Operation** section.
7. Select **5mm Endmill** from the **Tool Controller** drop-down.
8. Select **Cut Mode > Conventional**.
9. Select **Pattern > ZigZagOffset**.
10. Click **Apply** to view the path.

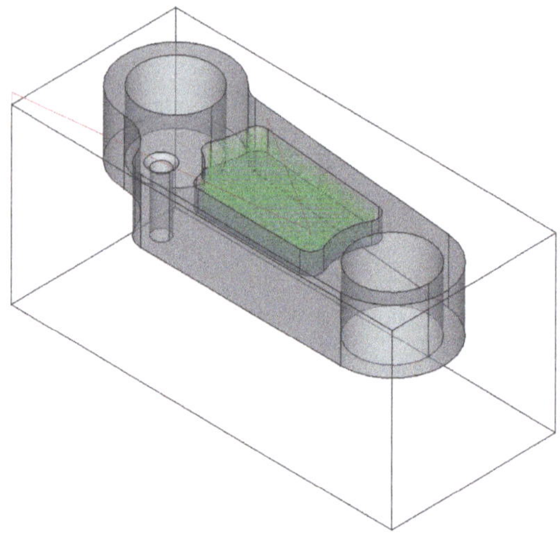

11. Click **OK**.

Creating the Drill Operation

1. Click the **Drilling** icon on the **New Operations** toolbar.

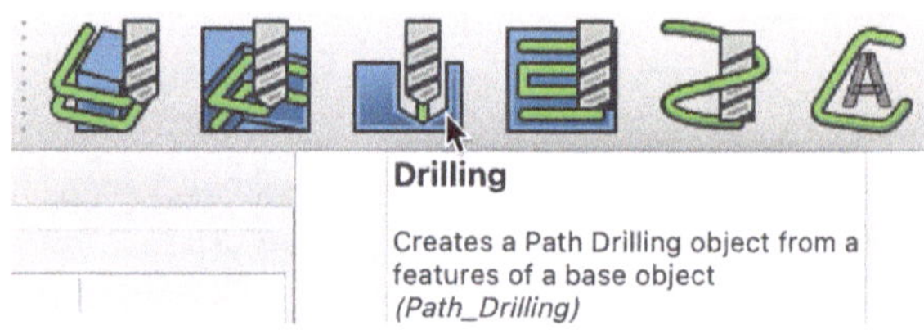

2. On the **Drilling** dialog, expand the **Base Geometry** section and notice that the all the holes are selected automatically.
3. Expand the **Depths** section and click the **Formula** icon next to the **Final Depth** box.
4. Make sure that the **Result** value is -32 on the **Expression editor** dialog.
5. Click **OK**.

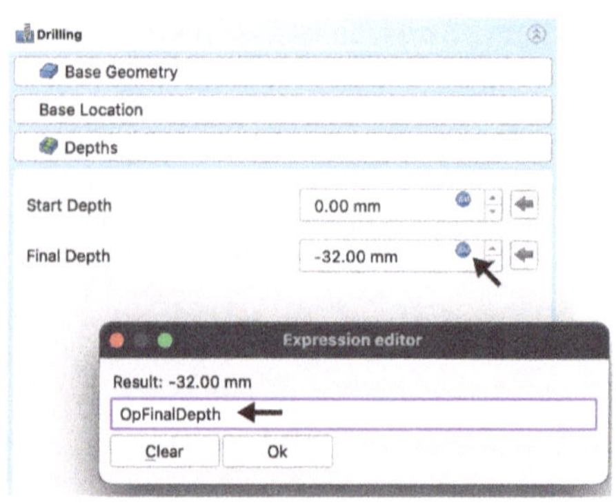

6. Expand the **Operation** section and select **5mm Drill** from the **Tool Controller** drop-down.
7. Click **Apply** and **OK**. The drill operation is created on three holes, as shown.

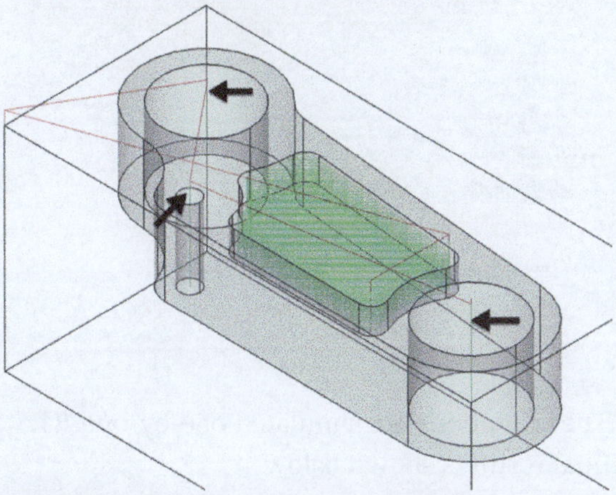

Drilling Holes using the Helix Operation

1. Click the **Helix** icon on the **New Operations** toolbar.

2. Select **5mm Endmill** from the **Tool Controller** drop-down in the **Operations** section.
3. Expand the **Base Geometry** section and click the **Reset** button; all the holes available on the model are selected.
4. Expand the **Depths** section and click the **Formula** icon next to the **Step Down** box.
5. Type **2** in the **Formula editor** dialog.

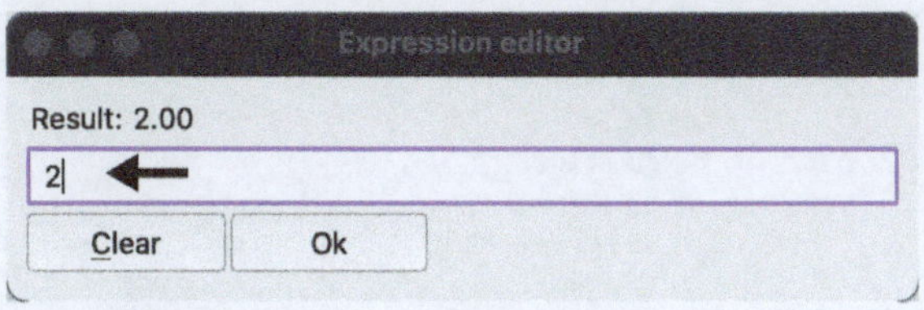

6. Click **OK**.
7. Click **Apply** and **OK**.

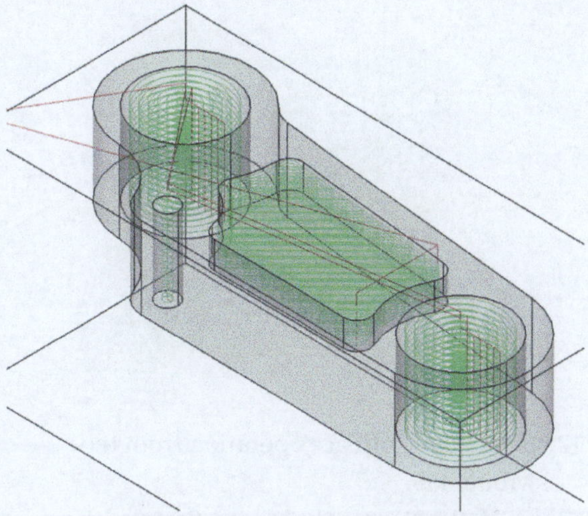

Creating the Contour Operation

1. Click the **Profile** icon on the **New Operations** toolbar.

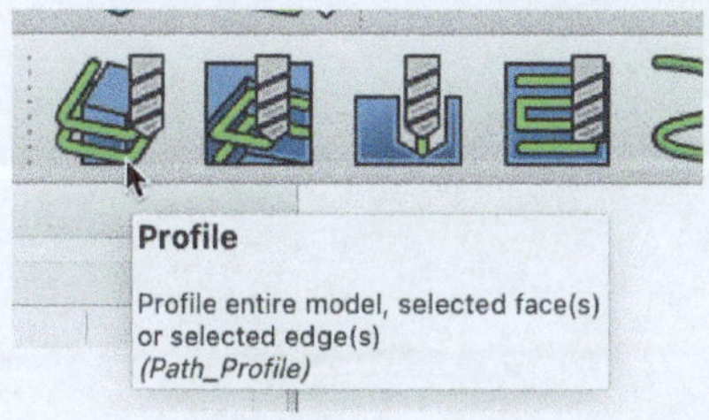

2. Select **5mm Endmill** from the **Tool Controller** drop-down in the **Operations** section.
3. Check the **Use Compensation** option.
4. Expand the **Depths** section.
5. Click the **Formula** icon next to the **Step Down** box.
6. Type **2** in the **Expression editor** dialog.
7. Click **OK**.
8. Click the **Formula** icon next to the **Final Depth** box.
9. Type **-32** in the **Expression editor** dialog.
10. Click **OK**.
11. Click **Apply** and **OK**.

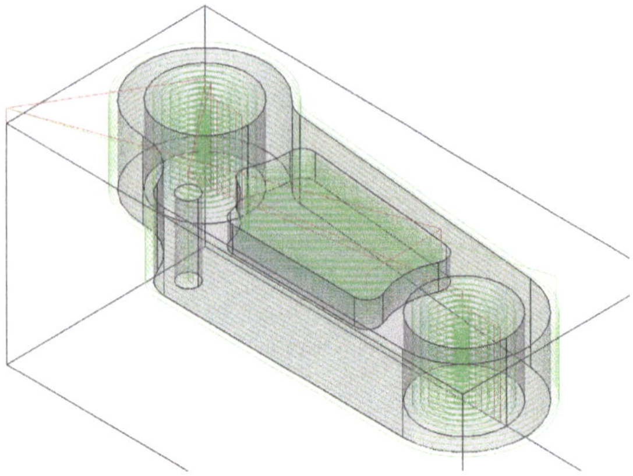

12. Select the **MillFace** operation from the **Model** tab.
13. Click the **Toggle the Active State of the Operation** icon on the **Tool Commands** toolbar.

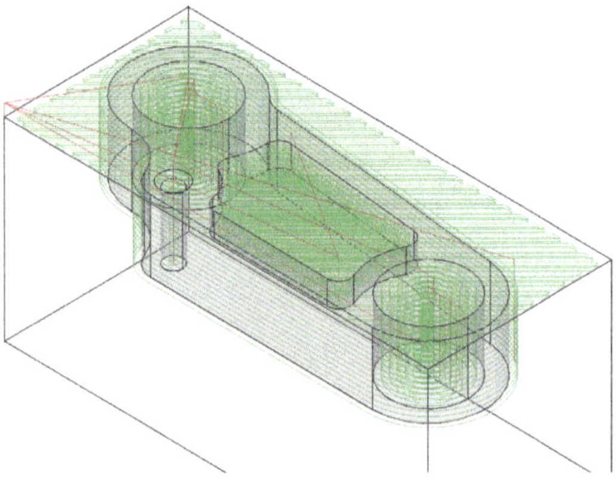

Simulating the Operations

1. Click the **CAM Simulator** icon on the **Tool Commands** toolbar.

2. Make sure that all the operations are selected on the **Path Simulator** dialog.
3. Click the **Activate/resume simulation** icon.

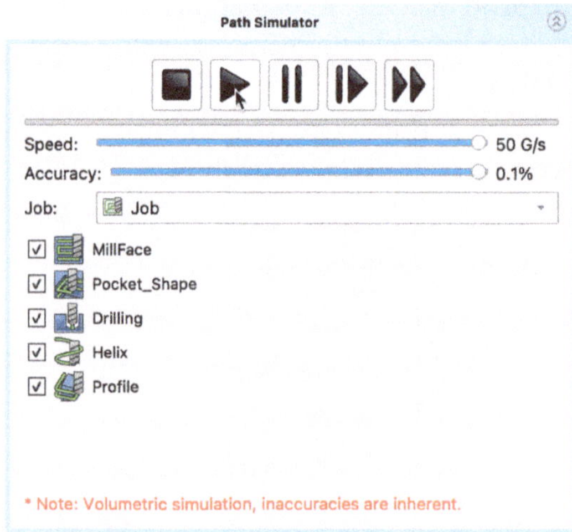

The operations are simulated one-by-one. The final result is shown below.

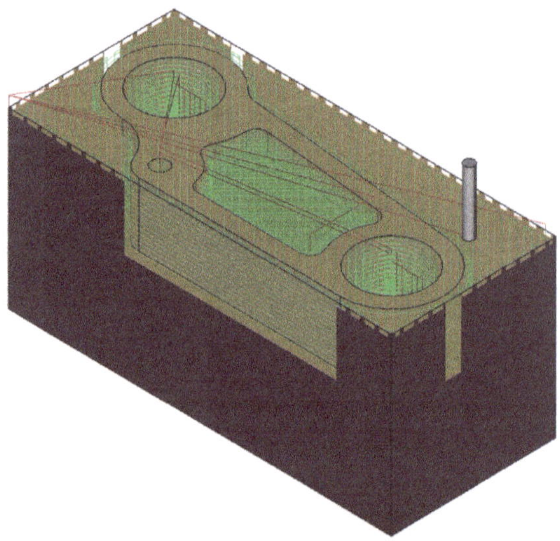

4. Click **OK**; the CutMaterial is displayed in the Model tab, as shown.

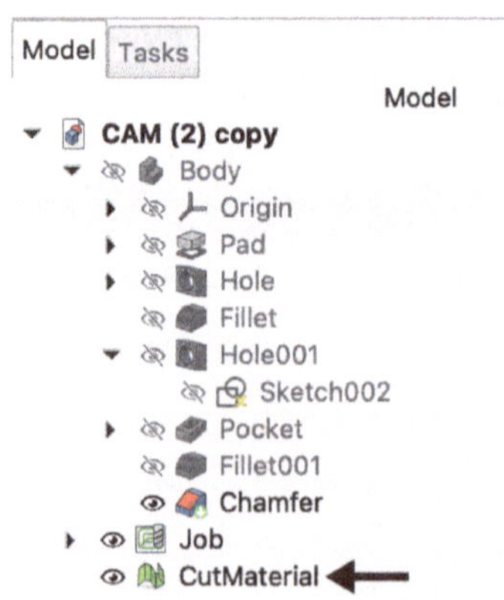

Post Processing

1. On the **Model** panel, expand the **Job > Operations** node.
2. Select the **MillFace** operation.

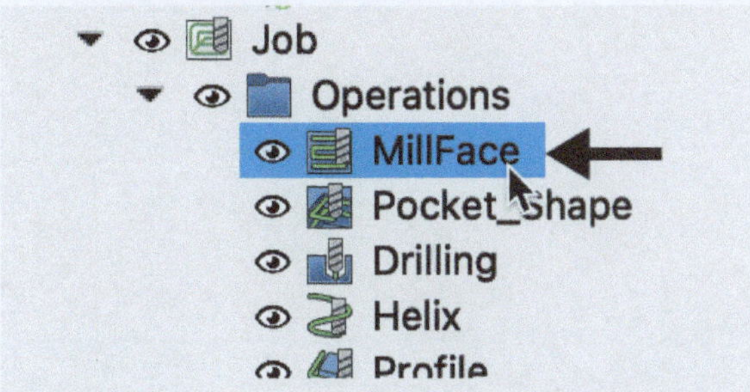

3. Click the **Inspect Path Commands** icon on the **Tool Commands** toolbar.

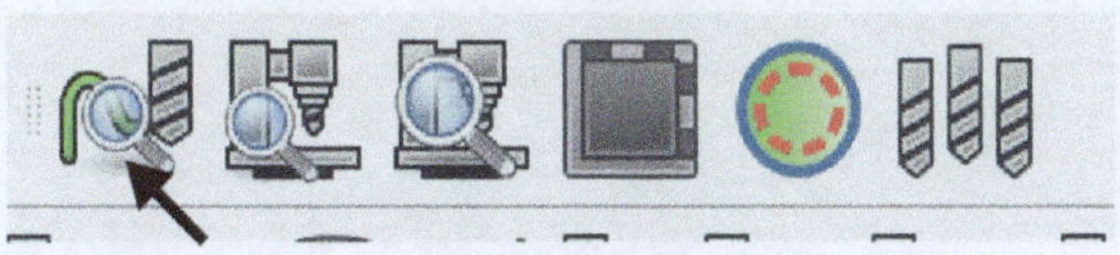

The G-Code is displayed on the FreeCAD dialog. If you want to learn about the G-code, please visit:

https://linuxcnc.org/docs/html/gcode/g-code.html

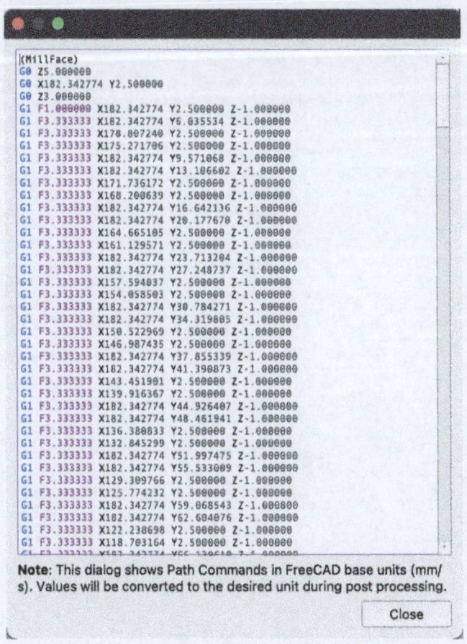

4. Inspect the G-Code and click **Close**.
5. Likewise, inspect the G-Code of other operations.
6. Select the **Job** node from the **Model** tab.
7. Click the **Post Process** icon on the **Project Setup** toolbar.

8. Click **OK** on the **FreeCAD** dialog.

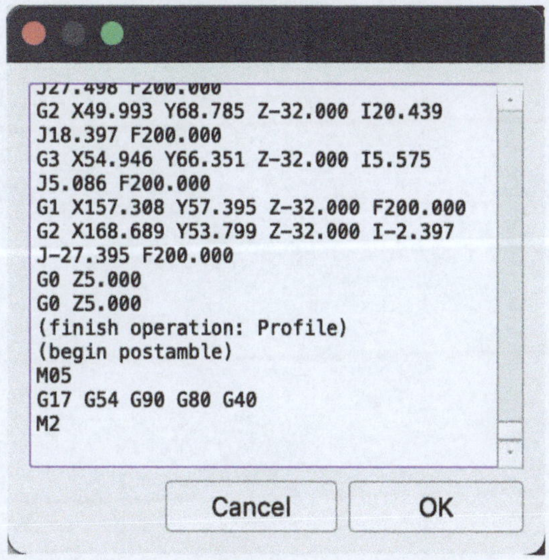

9. Specify the location of the post-processor file and click **Save**.
10. Save and close the FreeCAD file.

Index

Printed at Repro India Ltd.